HERSHMAN & McFARLANE CHILDREN ACT HANDBOOK

Editors

David Hershman QC

Andrew McFarlane QC

Family Law

Published by
Jordan Publishing Limited
21 St Thomas Street
Bristol BS1 6JS

© Jordan Publishing Limited 2003

British Library Cataloguing-in-Publication Data
A catalogue record for this book is available from the British Library.

ISBN   0 85308 901 9

Printed in Great Britain by Hobbs The Printers Limited, Southampton

HERSHMAN & McFARLANE
CHILDREN ACT HANDBOOK

Preface to the First Edition

In the ten years since the publication of *Children Law and Practice*, one drawback of the layout of the text has been that, in order to have both the commentary and the statutory material at court, it has been necessary for users to carry both volumes of the work with them. This modestly sized handbook is being published in order to ease the physical burden on users by providing core statutory material in a portable supplement.

We hope that this handbook will be a useful addition to the family law library and that the selection that we have made is sufficient to meet both the need for portability and the need to provide essential core material. Any suggestions for additional material are welcome.

The *Children Act Handbook* will be updated each year and issued as part of the subscription package to all *Children Law and Practice* subscribers. In addition, the *Handbook* will be available for sale separately to non-subscribers.

David Hershman and
Andrew McFarlane

August 2001

Contents

PART I

Children Act 1989

PART I

Children Act 1989

Children Act 1989
(1989 c 41)

PART I

ARRANGEMENT OF SECTIONS

PART I
INTRODUCTORY

PART II
ORDERS WITH RESPECT TO CHILDREN IN FAMILY AND OTHER PROCEEDINGS

General

Financial relief

Family assistance orders

PART III
LOCAL AUTHORITY SUPPORT FOR CHILDREN AND FAMILIES

Provision of services for children and their families

Provision of accommodation for children

PART V
PROTECTION OF CHILDREN

PART VI
COMMUNITY HOMES

PART VII
VOLUNTARY HOMES AND VOLUNTARY ORGANISATIONS

PART VIII
REGISTERED CHILDREN'S HOMES

PART IX
PRIVATE ARRANGEMENTS FOR FOSTERING CHILDREN

PART I

PART XII
MISCELLANEOUS AND GENERAL

Notification of children accommodated in certain establishments

Adoption

Criminal care and supervision orders

Effect and duration of orders etc

Jurisdiction and procedure etc

Search warrants

General

An Act to reform the law relating to children; to provide for local authority services for children in need and others; to amend the law with respect to children's homes, community homes, voluntary homes and voluntary organisations; to make provision with respect to fostering, child minding and day care for young children and adoption; and for connected purposes. [16 November 1989]

PART I
INTRODUCTORY

1 Welfare of the child

(1) When a court determines any question with respect to –

(a) the upbringing of a child; or

(b) the administration of a child's property or the application of any income arising from it,

the child's welfare shall be the court's paramount consideration.

(2) In any proceedings in which any question with respect to the upbringing of a child arises, the court shall have regard to the general principle that any delay in determining the question is likely to prejudice the welfare of the child.

(3) In the circumstances mentioned in subsection (4), a court shall have regard in particular to –

(a) the ascertainable wishes and feelings of the child concerned (considered in the light of his age and understanding);

(b) his physical, emotional and educational needs;

(c) the likely effect on him of any change in his circumstances;

(d) his age, sex, background and any characteristics of his which the court considers relevant;

(e) any harm which he has suffered or is at risk of suffering;

(f) how capable each of his parents, and any other person in relation to whom the court considers the question to be relevant, is of meeting his needs;

(g) the range of powers available to the court under this Act in the proceedings in question.

(4) The circumstances are that –

(a) the court is considering whether to make, vary or discharge a section 8 order, and the making, variation or discharge of the order is opposed by any party to the proceedings; or

(b) the court is considering whether to make, vary or discharge an order under Part IV.

(5) Where a court is considering whether or not to make one or more orders under this Act with respect to a child, it shall not make the order or any of the orders unless it considers that doing so would be better for the child than making no order at all.

NOTES

Definitions. 'A section 8 order': s 8(2); 'child': s 105(1); 'harm': ss 31(9), 105(1); 'the court': s 92(7); 'upbringing': s 105(1).

2 Parental responsibility for children

(1) Where a child's father and mother were married to each other at the time of his birth, they shall each have parental responsibility for the child.

(2) Where a child's father and mother were not married to each other at the time of his birth –

(a) the mother shall have parental responsibility for the child;

(b) the father shall not have parental responsibility for the child, unless he acquires it in accordance with the provisions of this Act.

(3) References in this Act to a child whose father and mother were, or (as the case may be) were not, married to each other at the time of his birth must be read with section 1 of the Family Law Reform Act 1987 (which extends their meaning).

(4) The rule of law that a father is the natural guardian of his legitimate child is abolished.

(5) More than one person may have parental responsibility for the same child at the same time.

(6) A person who has parental responsibility for a child at any time shall not cease to have that responsibility solely because some other person subsequently acquires parental responsibility for the child.

(7) Where more than one person has parental responsibility for a child, each of them may act alone and without the other (or others) in meeting that responsibility; but nothing in this Part shall be taken to affect the operation of any enactment which requires the consent of more than one person in a matter affecting the child.

(8) The fact that a person has parental responsibility for a child shall not entitle him to act in any way which would be incompatible with any order made with respect to the child under this Act.

---

(9) A person who has parental responsibility for a child may not surrender or transfer any part of that responsibility to another but may arrange for some or all of it to be met by one or more persons acting on his behalf.

(10) The person with whom any such arrangement is made may himself be a person who already has parental responsibility for the child concerned.

(11) The making of any such arrangement shall not affect any liability of the person making it which may arise from any failure to meet any part of his parental responsibility for the child concerned.

NOTES

Definitions. 'Child': s 105(1); 'married ... at the time of his birth': s 2(3); 'parental responsibility': s 3.

3 Meaning of 'parental responsibility'

(1) In this Act 'parental responsibility' means all the rights, duties, powers, responsibilities and authority which by law a parent of a child has in relation to the child and his property.

(2) It also includes the rights, powers and duties which a guardian of the child's estate (appointed, before the commencement of section 5, to act generally) would have had in relation to the child and his property.

(3) The rights referred to in subsection (2) include, in particular, the right of the guardian to receive or recover in his own name, for the benefit of the child, property of whatever description and wherever situated which the child is entitled to receive or recover.

(4) The fact that a person has, or does not have, parental responsibility for a child shall not affect –

    (a) any obligation which he may have in relation to the child (such as a statutory duty to maintain the child); or

    (b) any rights which, in the event of the child's death, he (or any other person) may have in relation to the child's property.

(5) A person who –

    (a) does not have parental responsibility for a particular child; but

    (b) has care of the child,

may (subject to the provisions of this Act) do what is reasonable in all the circumstances of the case for the purpose of safeguarding or promoting the child's welfare.

NOTES

Definitions. 'Child': s 105(1); 'parental responsibility': s 3.

4 Acquisition of parental responsibility by father

(1) Where a child's father and mother were not married to each other at the time of his birth –

    (a) the court may, on the application of the father, order that he shall have parental responsibility for the child; or

(b) the father and mother may by agreement ('a parental responsibility agreement') provide for the father to have parental responsibility for the child.

(2) No parental responsibility agreement shall have effect for the purposes of this Act unless –

(a) it is made in the form prescribed by regulations made by the Lord Chancellor; and

(b) where regulations are made by the Lord Chancellor prescribing the manner in which such agreements must be recorded, it is recorded in the prescribed manner.

(3) Subject to section 12(4), an order under subsection (1)(a), or a parental responsibility agreement, may only be brought to an end by an order of the court made on the application –

(a) of any person who has parental responsibility for the child, or

(b) with leave of the court, of the child himself.

(4) The court may only grant leave under subsection (3)(b) if it is satisfied that the child has sufficient understanding to make the proposed application.

NOTES

Definitions. 'Child': s 105(1); 'parental responsibility': s 3; 'parental responsibility agreement': s 4(1)(b); 'prescribed': s 105(1); 'the court': s 92(7).

5 Appointment of guardians

(1) Where an application with respect to a child is made to the court by any individual, the court may by order appoint that individual to be the child's guardian if –

(a) the child has no parent with parental responsibility for him; or

(b) a residence order has been made with respect to the child in favour of a parent or guardian of his who has died while the order was in force.

(2) The power conferred by subsection (1) may also be exercised in any family proceedings if the court considers that the order should be made even though no application has been made for it.

(3) A parent who has parental responsibility for his child may appoint another individual to be the child's guardian in the event of his death.

(4) A guardian of a child may appoint another individual to take his place as the child's guardian in the event of his death.

(5) An appointment under subsection (3) or (4) shall not have effect unless it is made in writing, is dated and is signed by the person making the appointment or –

(a) in the case of an appointment made by a will which is not signed by the testator, is signed at the direction of the testator in accordance with the requirements of section 9 of the Wills Act 1837; or

(b) in any other case, is signed at the direction of the person making the appointment, in his presence and in the presence of two witnesses who each attest the signature.

(6) A person appointed as a child's guardian under this section shall have parental responsibility for the child concerned.

(7) Where –

    (a) on the death of any person making an appointment under subsection (3) or (4), the child concerned has no parent with parental responsibility for him; or

    (b) immediately before the death of any person making such an appointment, a residence order in his favour was in force with respect to the child,

the appointment shall take effect on the death of that person.

(8) Where, on the death of any person making an appointment under subsection (3) or (4) –

    (a) the child concerned has a parent with parental responsibility for him; and

    (b) subsection (7)(b) does not apply,

the appointment shall take effect when the child no longer has a parent who has parental responsibility for him.

(9) Subsections (1) and (7) do not apply if the residence order referred to in paragraph (b) of those subsections was also made in favour of a surviving parent of the child.

(10) Nothing in this section shall be taken to prevent an appointment under subsection (3) or (4) being made by two or more persons acting jointly.

(11) Subject to any provision made by rules of court, no court shall exercise the High Court's inherent jurisdiction to appoint a guardian of the estate of any child.

(12) Where the rules of court are made under subsection (11) they may prescribe the circumstances in which, and conditions subject to which, an appointment of such a guardian may be made.

(13) A guardian of a child may only be appointed in accordance with the provisions of this section.

NOTES

    Commencement. Sub-ss (11) and (12): 1 Feb 1992: SI 1991/1990, amending SI 1991/828.

    Definitions. 'Child': s 105(1); 'family proceedings': s 8(3); 'guardian of a child': s 105(1); 'parental responsibility': s 3; 'residence order': s 8(1); 'signed': s 105(1); 'the court': s 92(7).

6 Guardians: revocation and disclaimer

(1) An appointment under section 5(3) or (4) revokes an earlier such appointment (including one made in an unrevoked will or codicil) made by the same person in respect of the same child, unless it is clear (whether as the result of an express provision in the later appointment or by any necessary implication) that the purpose of the later appointment is to appoint an additional guardian.

(2) An appointment under section 5(3) or (4) (including one made in an unrevoked will or codicil) is revoked if the person who made the appointment revokes it by a written and dated instrument which is signed –

    (a) by him; or

    (b) at his direction, in his presence and in the presence of two witnesses who each attest the signature.

(3) An appointment under section 5(3) or (4) (other than one made in a will or codicil) is revoked if, with the intention of revoking the appointment, the person who made it –

(a) destroys the instrument by which it was made; or

(b) has some other person destroy that instrument in his presence.

[(3A) An appointment under section 5(3) or (4) (including one made in an unrevoked will or codicil) is revoked if the person appointed is the spouse of the person who made the appointment and either –

(a) a decree of a court of civil jurisdiction in England and Wales dissolves or annuls the marriage, or

(b) the marriage is dissolved or annulled and the divorce or annulment is entitled to recognition in England and Wales by virtue of Part II of the Family Law Act 1986,

unless a contrary intention appears by the appointment.][1]

(4) For the avoidance of doubt, an appointment under section 5(3) or (4) made in a will or codicil is revoked if the will or codicil is revoked.

(5) A person who is appointed as a guardian under section 5(3) or (4) may disclaim his appointment by an instrument in writing signed by him and made within a reasonable time of his first knowing that the appointment has taken effect.

(6) Where regulations are made by the Lord Chancellor prescribing the manner in which such disclaimers must be recorded, no such disclaimer shall have effect unless it is recorded in the prescribed manner.

(7) Any appointment of a guardian under section 5 may be brought to an end at any time by order of the court –

(a) on the application of any person who has parental responsibility for the child;

(b) on the application of the child concerned, with leave of the court; or

(c) in any family proceedings, if the court considers that it should be brought to an end even though no application has been made.

NOTES

Amendments. [1] Subsection inserted: Law Reform (Succession) Act 1995, s 4(1).

Definitions. 'Child': s 105(1); 'family proceedings': s 8(3); 'parental responsibility': s 3; 'signed': s 105(1); 'the court': s 92(7).

7 Welfare reports

(1) A court considering any question with respect to a child under this Act may –

(a) ask [an officer of the Service][1]; or

(b) ask a local authority to arrange for –

    (i) an officer of the authority; or

    (ii) such other person (other than a probation officer) as the authority considers appropriate,

to report to the court on such matters relating to the welfare of that child as are required to be dealt with in the report.

(2) The Lord Chancellor may make regulations specifying matters which, unless the court orders otherwise, must be dealt with in any report under this section.

(3) The report may be made in writing, or orally, as the court requires.

(4) Regardless of any enactment or rule of law which would otherwise prevent it from doing so, the court may take account of –

(a) any statement contained in the report; and

(b) any evidence given in respect of the matters referred to in the report,

in so far as the statement or evidence is, in the opinion of the court, relevant to the question which it is considering.

(5) It shall be the duty of the authority or [an officer of the Service][1] to comply with any request for a report under this section.

NOTES

Amendments. [1] Words substituted: Criminal Justice and Court Services Act 2000, s 74, Sch 7, paras 87, 88.

Definitions. 'Child': s 105(1); 'local authority': s 105(1); 'the court': s 92(7).

PART II
ORDERS WITH RESPECT TO CHILDREN IN FAMILY AND OTHER PROCEEDINGS

General

8 Residence, contact and other orders with respect to children

(1) In this Act –

'a contact order' means an order requiring the person with whom a child lives, or is to live, to allow the child to visit or stay with the person named in the order, or for that person and the child otherwise to have contact with each other;

'a prohibited steps order' means an order that no step which could be taken by a parent in meeting his parental responsibility for a child, and which is of a kind specified in the order, shall be taken by any person without the consent of the court;

'a residence order' means an order settling the arrangements to be made as to the person with whom a child is to live; and

'a specific issue order' means an order giving directions for the purpose of determining a specific question which has arisen, or which may arise, in connection with any aspect of parental responsibility for a child.

(2) In this Act 'a section 8 order' means any of the orders mentioned in subsection (1) and any order varying or discharging such an order.

(3) For the purposes of this Act 'family proceedings' means any proceedings –

(a) under the inherent jurisdiction of the High Court in relation to children; and

(b) under the enactments mentioned in subsection (4),

but does not include proceedings on an application for leave under section 100(3).

(4) The enactments are –

(a) Parts I, II and IV of this Act;

(b) the Matrimonial Causes Act 1973;

(c) ...[1]

(d) the Adoption Act 1976;

(e) the Domestic Proceedings and Magistrates' Courts Act 1978;

(f) ...[1]

(g) Part III of the Matrimonial and Family Proceedings Act 1984;

[(h) the Family Law Act 1996]¹;
[(i) sections 11 and 12 of the Crime and Disorder Act 1998.]²

NOTES

Amendments. ¹ Paragraphs inserted or repealed: Family Law Act 1996, s 66(1), Sch 8, Pt III, para 60. ² Subparagraph inserted: Crime and Disorder Act 1998, s 119, Sch 8, para 68.

Definitions. 'A section 8 order': s 8(2); 'child': s 105(1); 'contact order': s 8(1); 'family proceedings': s 8(3); 'parental responsibility': s 3; 'prohibited steps order': s 8(1); 'residence order': s 8(1); 'specific issue order': s 8(1).

9 Restrictions on making section 8 orders

(1) No court shall make any section 8 order, other than a residence order, with respect to a child who is in the care of a local authority.

(2) No application may be made by a local authority for a residence order or contact order and no court shall make such an order in favour of a local authority.

(3) A person who is, or was at any time within the last six months, a local authority foster parent of a child may not apply for leave to apply for a section 8 order with respect to the child unless –

(a) he has the consent of the authority;
(b) he is relative of the child; or
(c) the child has lived with him for at least three years preceding the application.

(4) The period of three years mentioned in subsection (3)(c) need not be continuous but must have begun not more than five years before the making of the application.

(5) No court shall exercise its powers to make a specific issue order or prohibited steps order –

(a) with a view to achieving a result which could be achieved by making a residence or contact order; or
(b) in any way which is denied to the High Court (by section 100(2)) in the exercise of its inherent jurisdiction with respect to children.

(6) No court shall make any section 8 order which is to have effect for a period which will end after the child has reached the age of sixteen unless it is satisfied that the circumstances of the case are exceptional.

(7) No court shall make any section 8 order, other than one varying or discharging such an order, with respect to a child who has reached the age of sixteen unless it is satisfied that the circumstances of the case are exceptional.

NOTES

Definitions. 'A section 8 order': s 8(2); 'child': s 105(1); 'contact order': s 8(1); 'local authority': s 105(1); 'local authority foster parent': s 23(3); 'prohibited steps order': s 8(1); 'relative': s 105(1); 'residence order': s 8(1); 'specific issue order': s 8(1); 'the court': s 92(7).

10 Power of court to make section 8 orders

(1) In any family proceedings in which a question arises with respect to the welfare of any child, the court may make a section 8 order with respect to the child if –

(a) an application for the order has been made by a person who –

PART I

> (i) is entitled to apply for a section 8 order with respect to the child; or
>
> (ii) has obtained the leave of the court to make the application; or

(b) the court considers that the order should be made even though no such application has been made.

(2) The court may also make a section 8 order with respect to any child on the application of a person who –

(a) is entitled to apply for a section 8 order with respect to the child; or

(b) has obtained the leave of the court to make the application.

(3) This section is subject to the restrictions imposed by section 9.

(4) The following persons are entitled to apply to the court for any section 8 order with respect to a child –

(a) any parent or guardian of the child;

(b) any person in whose favour a residence order is in force with respect to the child.

(5) The following persons are entitled to apply for a residence or contact order with respect to a child –

(a) any party to a marriage (whether or not subsisting) in relation to whom the child is a child of the family;

(b) any person with whom the child has lived for a period of at least three years;

(c) any person who –

> (i) in any case where a residence order is in force with respect to the child, has the consent of each of the persons in whose favour the order was made;
>
> (ii) in any case where the child is in the care of a local authority, has the consent of that authority; or
>
> (iii) in any other case, has the consent of each of those (if any) who have parental responsibility for the child.

(6) A person who would not otherwise be entitled (under the previous provisions of this section) to apply for the variation or discharge of a section 8 order shall be entitled to do so if –

(a) the order was made on his application; or

(b) in the case of a contact order, he is named in the order.

(7) Any person who falls within a category of person prescribed by rules of court is entitled to apply for any such section 8 order as may be prescribed in relation to that category of person.

(8) Where the person applying for leave to make an application for a section 8 order is the child concerned, the court may only grant leave if it is satisfied that he has sufficient understanding to make the proposed application for the section 8 order.

(9) Where the person applying for leave to make an application for a section 8 order is not the child concerned, the court shall, in deciding whether or not to grant leave, have particular regard to –

(a) the nature of the proposed application for the section 8 order;

(b) the applicant's connection with the child;

(c) any risk there might be of that proposed application disrupting the child's life to such an extent that he would be harmed by it; and

(d) where the child is being looked after by a local authority –

PART I

(i) the authority's plans for the child's future; and

(ii) the wishes and feelings of the child's parents.

(10) The period of three years mentioned in subsection (5)(b) need not be continuous but must not have begun more than five years before, or ended more than three months before, the making of the application.

NOTES

Definitions. 'A section 8 order': s 8(2); 'child': s 105(1); 'child who is looked after by a local authority': s 22(1); 'child of the family': s 105(1); 'contact order': s 8(1); 'family proceedings': s 8(3); 'guardian of a child': s 105(1); 'harm': ss 31(a), 105(1); 'local authority': s 105(1); 'parental responsibility': s 3; 'residence order': s 8(1); 'the court': s 92(7).

11 General principles and supplementary provisions

(1) In proceedings in which any question of making a section 8 order, or any other question with respect to such an order, arises, the court shall (in the light of any rules made by virtue of subsection (2)) –

(a) draw up a timetable with a view to determining the question without delay; and

(b) give such directions as it considers appropriate for the purpose of ensuring, so far as is reasonably practicable, that that timetable is adhered to.

(2) Rules of court may –

(a) specify periods within which specified steps must be taken in relation to proceedings in which such questions arise; and

(b) make other provision with respect to such proceedings for the purpose of ensuring, so far as is reasonably practicable, that such questions are determined without delay.

(3) Where a court has power to make a section 8 order, it may do so at any time during the course of the proceedings in question even though it is not in a position to dispose finally of those proceedings.

(4) Where a residence order is made in favour of two or more persons who do not themselves all live together, the order may specify the periods during which the child is to live in the different households concerned.

(5) Where –

(a) a residence order has been made with respect to a child; and

(b) as a result of the order the child lives, or is to live, with one of two parents who each have parental responsibility for him,

the residence order shall cease to have effect if the parents live together for a continuous period of more than six months.

(6) A contact order which requires the parent with whom a child lives to allow the child to visit, or otherwise have contact with, his other parent shall cease to have effect if the parents live together for a continuous period of more than six months.

(7) A section 8 order may –

(a) contain directions about how it is to be carried into effect;

(b) impose conditions which must be complied with by any person –

(i) in whose favour the order is made;

(ii) who is a parent of the child concerned;

      (iii) who is not a parent of his but who has parental responsibility for him; or

      (iv) with whom the child is living,

and to whom the conditions are expressed to apply;

  (c) be made to have effect for a specified period, or contain provisions which are to have effect for a specified period;

  (d) make such incidental, supplemental or consequential provision as the court thinks fit.

NOTES

Definitions. 'A section 8 order': s 8(2); 'child': s 105(1); 'contact order': s 8(1); 'parental responsibility': s 3; 'residence order': s 8(1); 'the court': s 92(7).

12 Residence orders and parental responsibility

(1) Where the court makes a residence order in favour of the father of a child it shall, if the father would not otherwise have parental responsibility for the child, also make an order under section 4 giving him that responsibility.

(2) Where the court makes a residence order in favour of any person who is not the parent or guardian of the child concerned that person shall have parental responsibility for the child while the residence order remains in force.

(3) Where a person has parental responsibility for a child as a result of subsection (2), he shall not have the right –

  (a) to consent, or refuse to consent, to the making of an application with respect to the child under section 18 of the Adoption Act 1976;

  (b) to agree, or refuse to agree, to the making of an adoption order, or an order under section 55 of the Act of 1976, with respect to the child; or

  (c) to appoint a guardian for the child.

(4) Where subsection (1) requires the court to make an order under section 4 in respect of the father of a child, the court shall not bring that order to an end at any time while the residence order concerned remains in force.

NOTES

Definitions. 'Child': s 105(1); 'guardian of a child': s 105(1); 'parental responsibility': s 3; 'residence order': s 8(1); 'the court': s 92(7).

13 Change of child's name or removal from jurisdiction

(1) Where a residence order is in force with respect to a child, no person may –

  (a) cause the child to be known by a new surname; or

  (b) remove him from the United Kingdom;

without either the written consent of every person who has parental responsibility for the child or the leave of the court.

(2) Subsection (1)(b) does not prevent the removal of a child, for a period of less than one month, by the person in whose favour the residence order is made.

(3) In making a residence order with respect to a child the court may grant the leave required by subsection (1)(b), either generally or for specified purposes.

NOTES

Definitions. 'Child': s 105(1); 'parental responsibility': s 3; 'residence order': s 8(1); 'the court': s 92(7).

14 Enforcement of residence orders

(1) Where –

    (a) a residence order is in force with respect to a child in favour of any person; and

    (b) any other person (including one in whose favour the order is also in force) is in breach of the arrangements settled by that order,

the person mentioned in paragraph (a) may, as soon as the requirement in subsection (2) is complied with, enforce the order under section 63(3) of the Magistrates' Courts Act 1980 as if it were an order requiring the other person to produce the child to him.

(2) The requirement is that a copy of the residence order has been served on the other person.

(3) Subsection (1) is without prejudice to any other remedy open to the person in whose favour the residence order is in force.

NOTES

Definitions. 'Child': s 105(1); 'residence order': s 8(1).

Financial relief

15 Orders for financial relief with respect to children

(1) Schedule 1 (which consists primarily of the re-enactment, with consequential amendments and minor modifications, of provisions of [section 6 of the Family Law Reform Act 1969][1], the Guardianship of Minors Acts 1971 and 1973, the Children Act 1975 and of sections 15 and 16 of the Family Law Reform Act 1987) makes provision in relation to financial relief for children.

(2) The powers of a magistrates' court under section 60 of the Magistrates' Courts Act 1980 to revoke, revive or vary an order for the periodical payment of money [and the power of a clerk of a magistrates' court to vary such an order][2] shall not apply in relation to an order made under Schedule 1.

NOTES

Amendments. [1] Words inserted: Courts and Legal Services Act 1990, s 116, Sch 16, para 10(1). [2] Words inserted: Maintenance Enforcement Act 1991, s 11(1), Sch 2, para 10.

Family assistance orders

16 Family assistance orders

(1) Where, in any family proceedings, the court has power to make an order under this Part with respect to any child, it may (whether or not it makes such an order) make an order requiring –

    (a) [an officer of the Service][1] to be made available; or

    (b) a local authority to make an officer of the authority available, to advise, assist and (where appropriate) befriend any person named in the order.

(2) The persons who may be named in an order under this section ('a family assistance order') are –

  (a) any parent or guardian of the child;
  (b) any person with whom the child is living or in whose favour a contact order is in force with respect to the child;
  (c) the child himself.

(3) No court may make a family assistance order unless –

  (a) it is satisfied that the circumstances of the case are exceptional; and
  (b) it has obtained the consent of every person to be named in the order other than the child.

(4) A family assistance order may direct –

  (a) the person named in the order; or
  (b) such of the persons named in the order as may be specified in the order,

to take such steps as may be so specified with a view to enabling the officer concerned to be kept informed of the address of any person named in the order and to be allowed to visit any such person.

(5) Unless it specifies a shorter period, a family assistance order shall have effect for a period of six months beginning with the day on which it is made.

(6) Where –

  (a) a family assistance order is in force with respect to a child; and
  (b) a section 8 order is also in force with respect to the child,

the officer concerned may refer to the court the question whether the section 8 order should be varied or discharged.

(7) A family assistance order shall not be made so as to require a local authority to make an officer of theirs available unless –

  (a) the authority agree; or
  (b) the child concerned lives or will live within their area.

(8), (9) ...[1]

NOTES

Amendments. [1] Words substituted or omitted: Criminal Justice and Court Services Act 2000, s 74, Sch 7, paras 87, 89, Sch 8.

Definitions. 'A section 8 order': s 8(2); 'child': s 105(1); 'contact order': s 8(1); 'family assistance order': s 16(2); 'family proceedings': s 8(3); 'guardian of a child': s 105(1); 'local authority': s 105(1); 'the court': s 92(7).

PART III
LOCAL AUTHORITY SUPPORT FOR CHILDREN AND FAMILIES

Provision of services for children and their families

17 Provision of services for children in need, their families and others

(1) It shall be the general duty of every local authority (in addition to the other duties imposed on them by this Part) –

(a) to safeguard and promote the welfare of children within their area who are in need; and

(b) so far as is consistent with that duty, to promote the upbringing of such children by their families,

by providing a range and level of services appropriate to those children's needs.

(2) For the purpose principally of facilitating the discharge of their general duty under this section, every local authority shall have the specific duties and powers set out in Part 1 of Schedule 2.

(3) Any service provided by an authority in the exercise of functions conferred on them by this section may be provided for the family of a particular child in need or for any member of his family, if it is provided with a view to safeguarding or promoting the child's welfare.

(4) The Secretary of State may by order amend any provision of Part I of Schedule 2 or add any further duty or power to those for the time being mentioned there.

(5) Every local authority –

(a) shall facilitate the provision by others (including in particular voluntary organisations) of services which the authority have power to provide by virtue of this section, or section 18, 20, [23, 23B to 23D, 24A or 24B][4]; and

(b) may make such arrangements as they see fit for any person to act on their behalf in the provision of any such service.

(6) The services provided by a local authority in the exercise of functions conferred on them by this section may include [providing accommodation and][5] giving assistance in kind or, in exceptional circumstances, in cash.

(7) Assistance may be unconditional or subject to conditions as to the repayment of the assistance or of its value (in whole or in part).

(8) Before giving any assistance or imposing any conditions, a local authority shall have regard to the means of the child concerned and of each of his parents.

(9) No person shall be liable to make any repayment of assistance or of its value at any time when he is in receipt of income support, [working families' tax credit or disabled person's tax credit][3] under [Part VII of the Social Security Contributions and Benefits Act 1992][1] [or of an income-based jobseeker's allowance][2].

(10) For the purposes of this Part a child shall be taken to be in need if –

(a) he is unlikely to achieve or maintain, or to have the opportunity of achieving or maintaining, a reasonable standard of health or development without the provision for him of services by a local authority under this Part;

(b) his health or development is likely to be significantly impaired, or further impaired, without the provision for him of such services; or

(c) he is disabled,

and 'family', in relation to such a child, includes any person who has parental responsibility for the child and any other person with whom he has been living.

(11) For the purposes of this Part, a child is disabled if he is blind, deaf or dumb or suffers from mental disorder of any kind or is substantially and permanently handicapped by illness, injury or congenital deformity or such other disability as may be prescribed; and in this Part –

'development' means physical, intellectual, emotional, social or behavioural development; and

'health' means physical or mental health.

NOTES

Amendments. [1] Words substituted: Disability Living Allowance and Disability Working Allowance Act 1991, s 7(2), Sch 3, Pt II, para 13. [2] Words substituted: Social Security (Consequential Provisions) Act 1992, s 4, Sch 2, para 108. [3] Words (as previously substituted by Disability Living Allowance and Disability Working Allowance Act 1991) substituted: Tax Credits Act 1999, s 1(2), Sch 1, paras 1, 6(d)(i). [4] Words substituted: Children (Leaving Care) Act 2000, s 7(1), (2). [5] Words inserted: Adoption and Children Act 2002, s 116(1).

Definitions. 'Child': s 105(1); 'child in need': s 17(10); 'development': s 17(11); 'disabled': s 17(11); 'family': s 17(10); 'functions': s 105(1); 'health': s 17(11); 'local authority': s 105(1); 'parental responsibility': s 3; 'prescribed': s 105(1); 'service': s 105(1); 'upbringing': s 105(1); 'voluntary organisation': s 105(1).

[17A Direct payments

(1) The Secretary of State may by regulations make provision for and in connection with requiring or authorising the responsible authority in the case of a person of a prescribed description who falls within subsection (2) to make, with that person's consent, such payments to him as they may determine in accordance with the regulations in respect of his securing the provision of the service mentioned in that subsection.

(2) A person falls within this subsection if he is –

(a) a person with parental responsibility for a disabled child,

(b) a disabled person with parental responsibility for a child, or

(c) a disabled child aged 16 or 17,

and a local authority ('the responsible authority') have decided for the purposes of section 17 that the child's needs (or, if he is such a disabled child, his needs) call for the provision by them of a service in exercise of functions conferred on them under that section.

(3) Subsections (3) to (5) and (7) of section 57 of the 2001 Act shall apply, with any necessary modifications, in relation to regulations under this section as they apply in relation to regulations under that section.

(4) Regulations under this section shall provide that, where payments are made under the regulations to a person falling within subsection (5) –

(a) the payments shall be made at the rate mentioned in subsection (4)(a) of section 57 of the 2001 Act (as applied by subsection (3)); and

(b) subsection (4)(b) of that section shall not apply.

(5) A person falls within this subsection if he is –

(a) a person falling within subsection (2)(a) or (b) and the child in question is aged 16 or 17, or

(b) a person who is in receipt of income support, working families' tax credit or disabled person's tax credit under Part 7 of the Social Security Contributions and Benefits Act 1992 or of an income-based jobseeker's allowance.

(6) In this section –

'the 2001 Act' means the Health and Social Care Act 2001;

'disabled' in relation to an adult has the same meaning as that given by section 17(11) in relation to a child;

'prescribed' means specified in or determined in accordance with regulations under this section (and has the same meaning in the provisions of the 2001 Act mentioned in subsection (3) as they apply by virtue of that subsection).][1]

NOTES

Amendments. [1] Section inserted: Carers and Disabled Children Act 2000, s 7(1); and subsequently substituted: Health and Social Care Act 2001, s 58 (applies to England only).

18 Day care for pre-school and other children

(1) Every local authority shall provide such day care for children in need within their area who are –

(a) aged five or under; and

(b) not yet attending schools,

as is appropriate.

(2) A local authority may provide day care for children within their area who satisfy the conditions mentioned in subsection (1)(a) and (b) even though they are not in need.

(3) A local authority may provide facilities (including training, advice, guidance and counselling) for those –

(a) caring for children in day care; or

(b) who at any time accompany such children while they are in day care.

(4) In this section 'day care' means any form of care or supervised activity provided for children during the day (whether or not it is provided on a regular basis).

(5) Every local authority shall provide for children in need within their area who are attending any school such care or supervised activities as is appropriate –

(a) outside school hours; or

(b) during school holidays.

(6) A local authority may provide such care or supervised activities for children within their area who are attending any school even though those children are not in need.

(7) In this section 'supervised activity' means an activity supervised by a responsible person.

Definitions. 'Child': s 105(1); 'child in need': s 17(10); 'day care': s 18(4); 'local authority': s 105(1); 'school': s 105(1); 'supervised activity': s 18(7).

19 Review of provision for day care, child minding etc

(1), (2) ...[4]

(3) Every local authority in Scotland shall, at least once in every review period, review –

  (a) the provision for day care within their area made for children under the age of eight by the local authority and by persons required to register under section 71(1)(b); and
  (b) the extent to which the services of child minders are available within their area with respect to children under the age of eight.

(4) In conducting any such review, ...[4] the authority shall have regard to the provision made with respect to children under the age of eight in relevant establishments within their area.

(5) In this section –

  ['relevant establishment' means –
      (a) in relation to Scotland, any establishment which is mentioned in paragraphs 3 and 4 of Schedule 9 (establishments exempt from the registration requirements which apply in relation to the provision of day care in Scotland); and
      (b) in relation to England and Wales, any establishment which is mentioned in paragraphs 1 and 2 of Schedule 9A (establishments exempt from the registration requirements which apply in relation to the provision of day care in England and Wales);][3]
  'review period' means the period of one year beginning with the commencement of this section and each subsequent period of three years beginning with an anniversary of that commencement.

(6) Where a local authority have conducted a review under this section they shall publish the result of the review –

  (a) as soon as is reasonably practicable;
  (b) in such form as they consider appropriate; and
  (c) together with any proposals they may have with respect to the matters reviewed.

(7) The authorities conducting any review under this section shall have regard to –

  (a) any representations made to any one of them by any relevant [Health Authority, Special Health Authority][1] [, Primary Care Trust][2] or health board; and
  (b) any other representations which they consider to be relevant.

(8) In the application of this section to Scotland, 'day care' has the same meaning as in section 79 and 'health board' has the same meaning as in the National Health Service (Scotland) Act 1978.

Amendments. [1] Words substituted: Health Authorities Act 1995, s 2(1), Sch I, Part III, para 118(1), (2). [2] Words inserted: Health Act 1999 (Supplementary, Consequential etc Provisions)

Order 2000, SI 2000/90. [3] Words and definition substituted: Care Standards Act 2000, s 116, Sch 4, para 14(1), (2). [4] Subsections repealed and words omitted (except in relation to Wales): Education Act 2002, ss 149(2), 215(2), Sch 22, Pt 3.

Definitions. 'Child': s 105(1); 'childminder': s 71(2); 'day care': s 18(4); 'health authority': s 105(1); 'local authority': s 105(1); 'local education authority': s 105(1); 'relevant establishment': s 19(5); 'review period': s 19(5).

Provision of accommodation for children

20 Provision of accommodation for children: general

(1) Every local authority shall provide accommodation for any child in need within their area who appears to them to require accommodation as a result of –

    (a) there being no person who has parental responsibility for him;

    (b) his being lost or having been abandoned; or

    (c) the person who has been caring for him being prevented (whether or not permanently, and for whatever reason) from providing him with suitable accommodation or care.

(2) Where a local authority provide accommodation under subsection (1) for a child who is ordinarily resident in the area of another local authority, that other local authority may take over the provision of accommodation for the child within –

    (a) three months of being notified in writing that the child is being provided with accommodation; or

    (b) such other longer period as may be prescribed.

(3) Every local authority shall provide accommodation for any child in need within their area who has reached the age of sixteen and whose welfare the authority consider is likely to be seriously prejudiced if they do not provide him with accommodation.

(4) A local authority may provide accommodation for any child within their area (even though a person who has parental responsibility for him is able to provide him with accommodation) if they consider that to do so would safeguard or promote the child's welfare.

(5) A local authority may provide accommodation for any person who has reached the age of sixteen but is under twenty-one in any community home which takes children who have reached the age of sixteen if they consider that to do so would safeguard or promote his welfare.

(6) Before providing accommodation under this section, a local authority shall, so far as is reasonably practicable and consistent with the child's welfare –

    (a) ascertain the child's wishes regarding the provision of accommodation; and

    (b) give due consideration (having regard to his age and understanding) to such wishes of the child as they have been able to ascertain.

(7) A local authority may not provide accommodation under this section for any child if any person who –

    (a) has parental responsibility for him; and

    (b) is willing and able to –

        (i) provide accommodation for him; or

        (ii) arrange for accommodation to be provided for him,

objects.

(8) Any person who has parental responsibility for a child may at any time remove the child from accommodation provided by or on behalf of the local authority under this section.

(9) Subsections (7) and (8) do not apply while any person –

   (a) in whose favour a residence order is in force with respect to the child; or
   (b) who has care of the child by virtue of an order made in the exercise of the High Court's inherent jurisdiction with respect to children,

agrees to the child being looked after in accommodation provided by or on behalf of the local authority.

(10) Where there is more than one such person as is mentioned in subsection (9), all of them must agree.

(11) Subsections (7) and (8) do not apply where a child who has reached the age of sixteen agrees to being provided with accommodation under this section.

NOTES

Definitions. 'Child': s 105(1); 'child in need': s 17(10); 'community home': s 53(1); 'local authority': s 105(1); 'ordinary residence': s 105(6); 'parental responsibility': s 3; 'prescribed': s 105(1); 'residence order': s 8(1).

21 Provision of accommodation for children in police protection or detention or on remand, etc

(1) Every local authority shall make provision for the reception and accommodation of children who are removed or kept away from home under Part V.

(2) Every local authority shall receive, and provide accommodation for, children –

   (a) in police protection whom they are requested to receive under section 46(3)(f);
   (b) whom they are requested to receive under section 38(6) of the Police and Criminal Evidence Act 1984;
   (c) who are –
      (i) on remand under [paragraph 7(5) of Schedule 7 to the Powers of Criminal Courts (Sentencing) Act 2000 or section][4] 23(1) of the Children and Young Persons Act 1969; or
      (ii) the subject of a supervision order imposing a [local authority residence requirement under paragraph 5 of Schedule 6 to that Act of 2000][4],
   and with respect to whom they are the designated authority.

(3) Where a child has been –

   (a) removed under Part V; or
   (b) detained under section 38 of the Police and Criminal Evidence Act 1984,

and he is not being provided with accommodation by a local authority or in a hospital vested in the Secretary of State [or a Primary Care Trust][3] [or otherwise made available pursuant to arrangements made by a [Health Authority][2]][1] [or a Primary Care Trust][3], any reasonable expenses of accommodating him shall be recoverable from the local authority in whose area he is ordinarily resident.

NOTES

Amendments. [1] Words inserted: National Health Service and Community Care Act 1990, s 66(1), Sch 36, para 1. [2] Words substituted: Health Authorities Act 1995, s 2(1), Sch 1, Pt III, para 118(1), (3). [3] Words inserted: Health Act 1999 (Supplementary, Consequential etc Provisions) Order 2000, SI 2000/90. [4] Words substituted: Powers of Criminal Courts (Sentencing) Act 2000, s 165(1), Sch 9, para 126.

Definitions. 'Child': s 105(1); 'hospital': s 105(1); 'local authority': s 105(1); 'police protection': s 46(2); 'supervision order': s 31(11).

Duties of local authorities in relation to children looked after by them

22 General duty of local authority in relation to children looked after by them

(1) In this Act, any reference to a child who is looked after by a local authority is a reference to a child who is –

    (a) in their care; or

    (b) provided with accommodation by the authority in the exercise of any functions (in particular those under this Act) which [are social services functions within the meaning of][1] the Local Authority Social Services Act 1970 [, apart from functions under sections [17][3] 23B and 24B][2].

(2) In subsection (1) 'accommodation' means accommodation which is provided for a continuous period of more than 24 hours.

(3) It shall be the duty of a local authority looking after any child –

    (a) to safeguard and promote his welfare; and

    (b) to make such use of services available for children cared for by their own parents as appears to the authority reasonable in his case.

(4) Before making any decision with respect to a child whom they are looking after, or proposing to look after, a local authority shall, so far as is reasonably practicable, ascertain the wishes and feelings of –

    (a) the child;

    (b) his parents;

    (c) any person who is not a parent of his but who has parental responsibility for him; and

    (d) any other person whose wishes and feelings the authority consider to be relevant,

regarding the matter to be decided.

(5) In making any such decision a local authority shall give due consideration –

    (a) having regard to his age and understanding, to such wishes and feelings of the child as they have been able to ascertain;

    (b) to such wishes and feelings of any person mentioned in subsection (4)(b) to (d) as they have been able to ascertain; and

    (c) to the child's religious persuasion, racial origin and cultural and linguistic background.

(6) If it appears to a local authority that it is necessary, for the purposes of protecting members of the public from serious injury, to exercise their powers with respect to a child whom they are looking after in a manner which may not be consistent with their duties under this section, they may do so.

(7) If the Secretary of State considers it necessary, for the purpose of protecting members of the public from serious injury, to give directions to a local authority with respect to the exercise of their powers with respect to a child whom they are looking after, he may give such directions to the authority.

(8) Where any such directions are given to an authority they shall comply with them even though doing so is inconsistent with their duties under this section.

NOTES

Amendments. [1] Words substituted: Local Government Act 2000, s 107, Sch 5, para 19. [2] Words inserted: Children (Leaving Care) Act 2000, s 2(2). [3] Reference inserted: Adoption and Children Act 2002, s 116(2).

Definitions. 'Accommodation': s 22(2); 'child': s 105(1); 'child who is looked after by a local authority': s 22(1); 'functions': s 105(1); 'local authority': s 105(1); 'parental responsibility': s 3; 'service': s 105(1).

23 Provision of accommodation and maintenance by local authority for children whom they are looking after

(1) It shall be the duty of any local authority looking after a child –

  (a) when he is in their care, to provide accommodation for him; and
  (b) to maintain him in other respects apart from providing accommodation for him.

(2) A local authority shall provide accommodation and maintenance for any child whom they are looking after by –

  (a) placing him (subject to subsection (5) and any regulations made by the Secretary of State) with –
       (i) a family;
       (ii) a relative of his; or
       (iii) any other suitable person,
       on such terms as to payment by the authority and otherwise as the authority may determine;
  [(aa) maintaining him in an appropriate children's home;
  (b)–(e) ...][2]
  (f) making such other arrangements as –
       (i) seem appropriate to them; and
       (ii) comply with any regulations made by the Secretary of State.

[(2A) Where under subsection (2)(aa) a local authority maintains a child in a home provided, equipped and maintained by the Secretary of State under section 82(5), it shall do so on such terms as the Secretary of State may from time to time determine.][2]

(3) Any person with whom a child has been placed under subsection (2)(a) is referred to in this Act as a local authority foster parent unless he falls within subsection (4).

(4) A person falls within this subsection if he is –

  (a) a parent of the child;
  (b) a person who is not a parent of the child but who has parental responsibility for him; or
  (c) where the child is in care and there was a residence order in force with respect to him immediately before the care order was made, a person in whose favour the residence order was made.

PART I

(5) Where a child is in the care of a local authority, the authority may only allow him to live with a person who falls within subsection (4) in accordance with regulations made by the Secretary of State.

[(5A) For the purposes of subsection (5) a child shall be regarded living with a person if he stays with that person for a continuous period of more than 24 hours.] [1]

(6) Subject to any regulations made by the Secretary of State for the purposes of this subsection, any local authority looking after a child shall make arrangements to enable him to live with –

 (a) a person falling within subsection (4); or
 (b) a relative, friend or other person connected with him,

unless that would not be reasonably practicable or consistent with his welfare.

(7) Where a local authority provide accommodation for a child whom they are looking after, they shall, subject to the provisions of this Part and so far as is reasonably practicable and consistent with his welfare, secure that –

 (a) the accommodation is near his home; and
 (b) where the authority are also providing accommodation for a sibling of his, they are accommodated together.

(8) Where a local authority provide accommodation for a child whom they are looking after and who is disabled, they shall, so far as is reasonably practicable, secure that the accommodation is not unsuitable to his particular needs.

(9) Part II of Schedule 2 shall have effect for the purposes of making further provision as to children looked after by local authorities and in particular as to the regulations that may be made under subsections (2)(a) and (f) and (5).

[(10) In this Act –

 'appropriate children's home' means a children's home in respect of which a person is registered under Part II of the Care Standards Act 2000; and
 'children's home' has the same meaning as in that Act.] [2]

NOTES
 Amendments. [1] Subsection inserted: Courts and Legal Services Act 1990, s 116, Sch 16, para 12(2). [2] Paragraph (aa) substituted for paras (b)–(e) and subsections inserted: Care Standards Act 2000, s 116, Sch 4, para 14(3).
 Definitions. 'Care order': s 8(1); 'child': s 105(1); 'child who is looked after by a local authority': s 22(1); 'community home': s 53(1); 'disabled': s 17(11); 'family': s 17(10); 'local authority': s 105(1); 'local authority foster parent': s 23(3); 'parental responsibility': s 3; 'registered children's home': s 63(8); 'relative': s 105(1); 'residence order': s 8(1); 'voluntary home': s 60(3).

[23A The responsible authority and relevant children

(1) The responsible local authority shall have the functions set out in section 23B in respect of a relevant child.

(2) In subsection (1) 'relevant child' means (subject to subsection (3)) a child who –

 (a) is not being looked after by any local authority;
 (b) was, before last ceasing to be looked after, an eligible child for the purposes of paragraph 19B of Schedule 2; and
 (c) is aged sixteen or seventeen.

(3) The Secretary of State may prescribe –

    (a) additional categories of relevant children; and

    (b) categories of children who are not to be relevant children despite falling within subsection (2).

(4) In subsection (1) the 'responsible local authority' is the one which last looked after the child.

(5) If under subsection (3)(a) the Secretary of State prescribes a category of relevant children which includes children who do not fall within subsection (2)(b) (for example, because they were being looked after by a local authority in Scotland), he may in the regulations also provide for which local authority is to be the responsible local authority for those children.] [1]

NOTES

    Amendments. [1] Section inserted: Children (Leaving Care) Act 2000, s 2(4).

[23B Additional functions of the responsible authority in respect of relevant children

(1) It is the duty of each local authority to take reasonable steps to keep in touch with a relevant child for whom they are the responsible authority, whether he is within their area or not.

(2) It is the duty of each local authority to appoint a personal adviser for each relevant child (if they have not already done so under paragraph 19C of Schedule 2).

(3) It is the duty of each local authority, in relation to any relevant child who does not already have a pathway plan prepared for the purposes of paragraph 19B of Schedule 2 –

    (a) to carry out an assessment of his needs with a view to determining what advice, assistance and support it would be appropriate for them to provide him under this Part; and

    (b) to prepare a pathway plan for him.

(4) The local authority may carry out such an assessment at the same time as any assessment of his needs is made under any enactment referred to in sub-paragraphs (a) to (c) of paragraph 3 of Schedule 2, or under any other enactment.

(5) The Secretary of State may by regulations make provision as to assessments for the purposes of subsection (3).

(6) The regulations may in particular make provision about –

    (a) who is to be consulted in relation to an assessment;

    (b) the way in which an assessment is to be carried out, by whom and when;

    (c) the recording of the results of an assessment;

    (d) the considerations to which the local authority are to have regard in carrying out an assessment.

(7) The authority shall keep the pathway plan under regular review.

(8) The responsible local authority shall safeguard and promote the child's welfare and, unless they are satisfied that his welfare does not require it, support him by –

    (a) maintaining him;

    (b) providing him with or maintaining him in suitable accommodation; and

(c) providing support of such other descriptions as may be prescribed.

(9) Support under subsection (8) may be in cash.

(10) The Secretary of State may by regulations make provision about the meaning of 'suitable accommodation' and in particular about the suitability of landlords or other providers of accommodation.

(11) If the local authority have lost touch with a relevant child, despite taking reasonable steps to keep in touch, they must without delay –

(a) consider how to re-establish contact; and
(b) take reasonable steps to do so,

and while the child is still a relevant child must continue to take such steps until they succeed.

(12) Subsections (7) to (9) of section 17 apply in relation to support given under this section as they apply in relation to assistance given under that section.

(13) Subsections (4) and (5) of section 22 apply in relation to any decision by a local authority for the purposes of this section as they apply in relation to the decisions referred to in that section.] [1]

NOTES

Amendments. [1] Section inserted: Children (Leaving Care) Act 2000, s 2(4).

[23C Continuing functions in respect of former relevant children

(1) Each local authority shall have the duties provided for in this section towards –

(a) a person who has been a relevant child for the purposes of section 23A (and would be one if he were under eighteen), and in relation to whom they were the last responsible authority; and
(b) a person who was being looked after by them when he attained the age of eighteen, and immediately before ceasing to be looked after was an eligible child,

and in this section such a person is referred to as a 'former relevant child'.

(2) It is the duty of the local authority to take reasonable steps –

(a) to keep in touch with a former relevant child whether he is within their area or not; and
(b) if they lose touch with him, to re-establish contact.

(3) It is the duty of the local authority –

(a) to continue the appointment of a personal adviser for a former relevant child; and
(b) to continue to keep his pathway plan under regular review.

(4) It is the duty of the local authority to give a former relevant child –

(a) assistance of the kind referred to in section 24B(1), to the extent that his welfare requires it;
(b) assistance of the kind referred to in section 24B(2), to the extent that his welfare and his educational or training needs require it;
(c) other assistance, to the extent that his welfare requires it.

(5) The assistance given under subsection (4)(c) may be in kind or, in exceptional circumstances, in cash.

(6) Subject to subsection (7), the duties set out in subsections (2), (3) and (4) subsist until the former relevant child reaches the age of twenty-one.

(7) If the former relevant child's pathway plan sets out a programme of education or training which extends beyond his twenty-first birthday –

(a) the duty set out in subsection (4)(b) continues to subsist for so long as the former relevant child continues to pursue that programme; and

(b) the duties set out in subsections (2) and (3) continue to subsist concurrently with that duty.

(8) For the purposes of subsection (7)(a) there shall be disregarded any interruption in a former relevant child's pursuance of a programme of education or training if the local authority are satisfied that he will resume it as soon as is reasonably practicable.

(9) Section 24B(5) applies in relation to a person being given assistance under subsection (4)(b) as it applies in relation to a person to whom section 24B(3) applies.

(10) Subsections (7) to (9) of section 17 apply in relation to assistance given under this section as they apply in relation to assistance given under that section.] [1]

NOTES
  Amendments. [1] Section inserted: Children (Leaving Care) Act 2000, s 2(4).

[Personal advisers and pathway plans

23D Personal advisers

(1) The Secretary of State may by regulations require local authorities to appoint a personal adviser for children or young persons of a prescribed description who have reached the age of sixteen but not the age of twenty-one who are not –

(a) children who are relevant children for the purposes of section 23A;
(b) the young persons referred to in section 23C; or
(c) the children referred to in paragraph 19C of Schedule 2.

(2) Personal advisers appointed under or by virtue of this Part shall (in addition to any other functions) have such functions as the Secretary of State prescribes.] [1]

NOTES
  Amendments. [1] Cross-heading and section inserted: Children (Leaving Care) Act 2000, s 3.

[23E Pathway plans

(1) In this Part, a reference to a 'pathway plan' is to a plan setting out –

(a) in the case of a plan prepared under paragraph 19B of Schedule 2 –
    (i) the advice, assistance and support which the local authority intend to provide a child under this Part, both while they are looking after him and later; and
    (ii) when they might cease to look after him; and
(b) in the case of a plan prepared under section 23B, the advice, assistance and support which the local authority intend to provide under this Part,

and dealing with such other matters (if any) as may be prescribed.

(2) The Secretary of State may by regulations make provision about pathway plans and their review.]¹

NOTES
Amendments. ¹ Section inserted: Children (Leaving Care) Act 2000, s 3.

Advice and assistance for certain children [*and young persons*]¹

[24 Persons qualifying for advice and assistance

(1) In this Part 'a person qualifying for advice and assistance' means a person who –

    (a) is under twenty-one; and
    (b) at any time after reaching the age of sixteen but while still a child was, but is no longer, looked after, accommodated or fostered.

(2) In subsection (1)(b), 'looked after, accommodated or fostered' means –

    (a) looked after by a local authority;
    (b) accommodated by or on behalf of a voluntary organisation;
    (c) accommodated in a private children's home;
    (d) accommodated for a consecutive period of at least three months –
        (i) by any Health Authority, Special Health Authority, Primary Care Trust or local education authority, or
        (ii) in any care home or independent hospital or in any accommodation provided by a National Health Service trust; or
    (e) privately fostered.

(3) Subsection (2)(d) applies even if the period of three months mentioned there began before the child reached the age of sixteen.

(4) In the case of a person qualifying for advice and assistance by virtue of subsection (2)(a), it is the duty of the local authority which last looked after him to take such steps as they think appropriate to contact him at such times as they think appropriate with a view to discharging their functions under sections 24A and 24B.

(5) In each of sections 24A and 24B, the local authority under the duty or having the power mentioned there ('the relevant authority') is –

    (a) in the case of a person qualifying for advice and assistance by virtue of subsection (2)(a), the local authority which last looked after him; or
    (b) in the case of any other person qualifying for advice and assistance, the local authority within whose area the person is (if he has asked for help of a kind which can be given under section 24A or 24B).]¹

NOTES
Amendments. ¹ Section and words in cross-heading inserted: Children (Leaving Care) Act 2000, ss 2(3), 4(1).

[24A Advice and assistance

(1) The relevant authority shall consider whether the conditions in subsection (2) are satisfied in relation to a person qualifying for advice and assistance.

(2) The conditions are that –

(a) he needs help of a kind which they can give under this section or section 24B; and

(b) in the case of a person who was not being looked after by any local authority, they are satisfied that the person by whom he was being looked after does not have the necessary facilities for advising or befriending him.

(3) If the conditions are satisfied –

(a) they shall advise and befriend him if he was being looked after by a local authority or was accommodated by or on behalf of a voluntary organisation; and

(b) in any other case they may do so.

(4) Where as a result of this section a local authority are under a duty, or are empowered, to advise and befriend a person, they may also give him assistance.

(5) The assistance may be in kind [and, in exceptional circumstances, assistance may be given –

(a) by providing accommodation, if in the circumstances assistance may not be given in respect of the accommodation under section 24B, or

(b) in cash]².

(6) Subsections (7) to (9) of section 17 apply in relation to assistance given under this section or section 24B as they apply in relation to assistance given under that section.]¹

NOTES

Amendments. ¹ Section inserted: Children (Leaving Care) Act 2000, s 4(1). ² Words substituted: Adoption and Children Act 2002, s 116(3).

[24B Employment, education and training

(1) The relevant local authority may give assistance to any person who qualifies for advice and assistance by virtue of section 24(2)(a) by contributing to expenses incurred by him in living near the place where he is, or will be, employed or seeking employment.

(2) The relevant local authority may give assistance to a person to whom subsection (3) applies by –

(a) contributing to expenses incurred by the person in question in living near the place where he is, or will be, receiving education or training; or

(b) making a grant to enable him to meet expenses connected with his education or training.

(3) This subsection applies to any person who –

(a) is under twenty-four; and

(b) qualifies for advice and assistance by virtue of section 24(2)(a), or would have done so if he were under twenty-one.

(4) Where a local authority are assisting a person under subsection (2) they may disregard any interruption in his attendance on the course if he resumes it as soon as is reasonably practicable.

(5) Where the local authority are satisfied that a person to whom subsection (3) applies who is in full-time further or higher education needs accommodation during a vacation because his term-time accommodation is not available to him then, they shall give him assistance by –

(a) providing him with suitable accommodation during the vacation; or

(b) paying him enough to enable him to secure such accommodation himself.

(6) The Secretary of State may prescribe the meaning of 'full-time', 'further education', 'higher education' and 'vacation' for the purposes of subsection (5).] [1]

NOTES

Amendments. [1] Section inserted: Children (Leaving Care) Act 2000, s 4(1).

[24C Information

(1) Where it appears to a local authority that a person –

(a) with whom they are under a duty to keep in touch under section 23B, 23C or 24; or

(b) whom they have been advising and befriending under section 24A; or

(c) to whom they have been giving assistance under section 24B,

proposes to live, or is living, in the area of another local authority, they must inform that other authority.

(2) Where a child who is accommodated –

(*a*) by a voluntary organisation or in a private children's home;

(*b*) by any Health Authority, Special Health Authority, Primary Care Trust or local education authority; or

(*c*) in any care home or independent hospital or any accommodation provided by a National Health Service trust,

ceases to be so accommodated, after reaching the age of sixteen, the organisation, authority or (as the case may be) person carrying on the home shall inform the local authority within whose area the child proposes to live.

(3) Subsection (2) only applies, by virtue of paragraph (*b*) or (*c*), if the accommodation has been provided for a consecutive period of at least three months.][1]

NOTES

Amendments. [1] Section inserted: Children (Leaving Care) Act 2000, s 4(1).

[24D Representations: sections 23A to 24B

(1) Every local authority shall establish a procedure for considering representations (including complaints) made to them by –

(a) a relevant child for the purposes of section 23A or a young person falling within section 23C;

(b) a person qualifying for advice and assistance; or

(c) a person falling within section 24B(2),

about the discharge of their functions under this Part in relation to him.

(2) In considering representations under subsection (1), a local authority shall comply with regulations (if any) made by the Secretary of State for the purposes of this subsection.][1]

NOTES
  Amendments. [1] Section inserted: Children (Leaving Care) Act 2000, s 5.

Secure accommodation

25 Use of accommodation for restricting liberty

(1) Subject to the following provisions of this section, a child who is being looked after by a local authority may not be placed, and, if placed, may not be kept, in accommodation provided for the purpose of restricting liberty ('secure accommodation') unless it appears –

  (a) that –
    (i) he has a history of absconding and is likely to abscond from any other description of accommodation; and
    (ii) if he absconds, he is likely to suffer significant harm; or
  (b) that if he is kept in any other description of accommodation he is likely to injure himself or other persons.

(2) The Secretary of State may by regulations –

  (a) specify a maximum period –
    (i) beyond which a child may not be kept in secure accommodation without the authority of the court; and
    (ii) for which the court may authorise a child to be kept in secure accommodation;
  (b) empower the court from time to time to authorise a child to be kept in secure accommodation for such further period as the regulations may specify; and
  (c) provide that applications to the court under this section shall be made only by local authorities.

(3) It shall be the duty of a court hearing an application under this section to determine whether any relevant criteria for keeping a child in secure accommodation are satisfied in his case.

(4) If a court determines that any such criteria are satisfied, it shall make an order authorising the child to be kept in secure accommodation and specifying the maximum period for which he may be so kept.

(5) On any adjournment of the hearing of an application under this section, a court may make an interim order permitting the child to be kept during the period of the adjournment in secure accommodation.

(6) No court shall exercise the powers conferred by this section in respect of a child who is not legally represented in that court unless, having been informed of his right to apply for [representation funded by the Legal Services Commission as part of the Community Legal Service or Criminal Defence Service][1] and having had the opportunity to do so, he refused or failed to apply.

(7) The Secretary of State may by regulations provide that –

  (a) this section shall or shall not apply to any description of children specified in the regulations;
  (b) this section shall have effect in relation to children of a description specified in the regulations subject to such modifications as may be so specified;

(c) such other provisions as may be so specified shall have effect for the purpose of determining whether a child of a description specified in the regulations may be placed or kept in secure accommodation.

(8) The giving of an authorisation under this section shall not prejudice any power of any court in England and Wales or Scotland to give directions relating to the child to whom the authorisation relates.

(9) This section is subject to section 20(8).

NOTES

Amendments. [1] Words substituted: Access to Justice 1999, s 24, Sch 4, para 45.

Definitions. 'Child': s 105(1); 'child who is looked after by a local authority': s 22(1); 'harm': ss 31(9), 105(1); 'local authority': s 105(1); 'secure accommodation': s 25(1); 'significant harm': ss 31(9), (10), 105(1); 'the court': s 92(7).

Supplemental

26 Review of cases and inquiries into representations

(1) The Secretary of State may make regulations requiring the case of each child who is being looked after by a local authority to be reviewed in accordance with the provisions of the regulations.

(2) The regulations may, in particular, make provision –

    (a) as to the manner in which each case is to be reviewed;

    (b) as to the considerations to which the local authority are to have regard in reviewing each case;

    (c) as to the time when each case is first to be reviewed and the frequency of subsequent reviews;

    (d) requiring the authority, before conducting any review, to seek the views of –

        (i) the child;

        (ii) his parents;

        (iii) any person who is not a parent of his but who has parental responsibility for him; and

        (iv) any other person whose views the authority consider to be relevant, including, in particular, the views of those persons in relation to any particular matter which is to be considered in the course of the review;

    (e) requiring the authority to consider, in the case of a child who is in their care, whether an application should be made to discharge the care order;

    (f) requiring the authority to consider, in the case of a child in accommodation provided by the authority, whether the accommodation accords with the requirements of this Part;

    (g) requiring the authority to inform the child, so far as is reasonably practicable, of any steps he may take under this Act;

    (h) requiring the authority to make arrangements, including arrangements with such other bodies providing services as it considers appropriate, to implement any decision which they propose to make in the course, or as a result, of the review;

    (i) requiring the authority to notify details of the result of the review and of any decision taken by them in consequence of the review to –

        (i) the child;

        (ii) his parents;

PART I

      (iii) any person who is not a parent of his but who has had parental responsibility for him; and

      (iv) any other person whom they consider ought to be notified;

  (j) requiring the authority to monitor the arrangements which they have made with a view to ensuring that they comply with the regulations.

(3) Every local authority shall establish a procedure for considering any representations (including any complaint) made to them by –

  (a) any child who is being looked after by them or who is not being looked after by them but is in need;

  (b) a parent of his;

  (c) any person who is not a parent of his but who has parental responsibility for him;

  (d) any local authority foster parent;

  (e) such other person as the authority consider has a sufficient interest in the child's welfare to warrant his representations being considered by them,

about the discharge by the authority of any of their functions under this Part in relation to the child.

(4) The procedure shall ensure that at least one person who is not a member or officer of the authority takes part in –

  (a) the consideration; and

  (b) any discussions which are held by the authority about the action (if any) to be taken in relation to the child in the light of the consideration.

(5) In carrying out any consideration of representations under this section a local authority shall comply with any regulations made by the Secretary of State for the purpose of regulating the procedure to be followed.

(6) The Secretary of State may make regulations requiring local authorities to monitor the arrangements that they have made with a view to ensuring that they comply with any regulations made for the purposes of subsection (5).

(7) Where any representation has been considered under the procedure established by a local authority under this section, the authority shall –

  (a) have due regard to the findings of those considering the representation; and

  (b) take such steps as are reasonably practicable to notify (in writing) –

      (i) the person making the representation;

      (ii) the child (if the authority consider that he has sufficient understanding); and

      (iii) such other persons (if any) as appear to the authority to be likely to be affected,

    of the authority's decision in the matter and their reasons for taking that decision and of any action which they have taken, or propose to take.

(8) Every local authority shall give such publicity to their procedure for considering representations under this section as they consider appropriate.

NOTES

  Definitions. 'Accommodation': s 22(2); 'care order': s 31(11); 'child': s 105(1); 'child in need': s 17(10); 'child who is looked after by the local authority': s 22(1); 'functions': s 105(1); 'local authority': s 105(1); 'local authority foster parent': s 23(3); 'parental responsibility': s 3.

27 Co-operation between authorities

(1) Where it appears to a local authority that any authority ...[1] mentioned in subsection (3) could, by taking any specified action, help in the exercise of any of their functions under this Part, they may request the help of that other authority ...[1], specifying the action in question.

(2) An authority whose help is so requested shall comply with the request if it is compatible with their own statutory or other duties and obligations and does not unduly prejudice the discharge of any of their functions.

(3) The [authorities][2] are –

   (a) any local authority;
   (b) any local education authority;
   (c) any local housing authority;
   (d) any [Health Authority, Special Health Authority][4] [, Primary Care Trust][5] [or National Health Service trust][2]; and
   (e) any person authorised by the Secretary of State for the purposes of this section.

(4) ...[3]

NOTES

Amendments. [1] Words repealed: Courts and Legal Services Act 1990, ss 116, 125(7), Sch 16, para 14(a), Sch 20. [2] Words substituted or inserted: Courts and Legal Services Act 1990, s 116, Sch 16, para 14(b). [3] Subsection repealed: Education Act 1993, s 307, Sch 19, para 147. [4] Words substituted: Health Authorities Act 1995, s 2(1), Sch 1, Pt III, para 118(1), (5). [5] Words inserted: Health Act 1999 (Supplementary, Consequential etc Provisions) Order 2000, SI 2000/90.

Definitions. 'Child'; 'functions'; 'health authority'; 'local authority'; 'local education authority'; 'local housing authority'; 'Primary Care Trust'; 'special educational needs': s 105(1).

28 Consultation with local education authorities

(1) Where –

   (a) a child is being looked after by a local authority; and
   (b) the authority propose to provide accommodation for him in an establishment at which education is provided for children who are accommodated there,

they shall, so far as is reasonably practicable, consult the appropriate local education authority before doing so.

(2) Where any such proposal is carried out, the local authority shall, as soon as is reasonably practicable, inform the appropriate local education authority of the arrangements that have been made for the child's accommodation.

(3) Where the child ceases to be accommodated as mentioned in subsection (1)(b), the local authority shall inform the appropriate local education authority.

(4) In this section 'the appropriate local education authority' means –

   (a) the local education authority within whose area the local authority's area falls; or
   (b) where the child has special educational needs and a statement of his needs is maintained under [Part IV of the Education Act 1996][1], the local education authority who maintain the statement.

NOTES

Amendments. [1] Words substituted: Education Act 1996, s 582, Sch 37, Pt I, para 84.

Definitions. 'Appropriate local education authority': s 28(4); 'child': s 105(1); 'child who is looked after by a local authority': s 22(1); 'local authority': s 105(1); 'local education authority': s 105(1); 'special educational needs': s 105(1).

29 Recoupment of cost of providing services etc

(1) Where a local authority provide any service under section 17 or 18, other than advice, guidance or counselling, they may recover from a person specified in subsection (4) such charge for the service as they consider reasonable.

(2) Where the authority are satisfied that that person's means are insufficient for it to be reasonably practicable for him to pay the charge, they shall not require him to pay more than he can reasonably be expected to pay.

(3) No person shall be liable to pay any charge under subsection (1) [for a service provided under section 17 or section 18(1) or (5)][8] at any time when he is in receipt of income support [, working families' tax credit or disabled person's tax credit][6] under [Part VII of the Social Security Contributions and Benefits Act 1992][3] [or of an income-based jobseeker's allowance][5].

[(3A) No person shall be liable to pay any charge under subsection (1) for a service provided under section 18(2) or (6) at any time when he is in receipt of income support under Part VII of the Social Security and Benefits Act 1992 or of an income-based jobseeker's allowance.][8]

(4) The persons are –

(a) where the service is provided for a child under sixteen, each of his parents;
(b) where it is provided for a child who has reached the age of sixteen, the child himself; and
(c) where it is provided for a member of the child's family, that member.

(5) Any charge under subsection (1) may, without prejudice to any other method of recovery, be recovered summarily as a civil debt.

(6) Part III of Schedule 2 makes provision in connection with contributions towards the maintenance of children who are being looked after by local authorities and consists of the re-enactment with modifications of provisions in Part V of the Child Care Act 1980.

(7) Where a local authority provide any accommodation under section 20(1) for a child who was (immediately before they began to look after him) ordinarily resident within the area of another local authority, they may recover from that other authority any reasonable expenses incurred by them in providing the accommodation and maintaining him.

(8) Where a local authority provide accommodation under section 21(1) or (2)(a) or (b) for a child who is ordinarily resident within the area of another local authority and they are not maintaining him in –

(a) a community home provided by them;
(b) a controlled community home; or
(c) a hospital vested in the Secretary of State [or a Primary Care Trust][7], [or any other hospital made available pursuant to arrangements made by [a Strategic Health Authority,][10] a [Health Authority][4]][1] [or a Primary Care Trust][7],

they may recover from that other authority any reasonable expenses incurred by them in providing the accommodation and maintaining him.

(9) [Except where subsection (10) applies,]⁹ where a local authority comply with any request under section 27(2) in relation to a child or other person who is not ordinarily resident within their area, they may recover from the local authority in whose area the child or person is ordinarily resident any [reasonable expenses]² incurred by them in respect of that person.

[(10) Where a local authority ('authority A') comply with any request under section 27(2) from another local authority ('authority B') in relation to a child or other person –

(a) whose responsible authority is authority B for the purposes of section 23B or 23C; or

(b) whom authority B are advising or befriending or to whom they are giving assistance by virtue of section 24(5)(a),

authority A may recover from authority B any reasonable expenses incurred by them in respect of that person.]⁹

NOTES

Amendments. ¹ Words inserted: National Health Service and Community Care Act 1990, s 66(1), Sch 9, para 36(3); ² Words substituted: Courts and Legal Services Act 1990, s 116, Sch 16, para 15. ³ Words substituted: Social Security (Consequential Provisions) Act 1992, s 4, Sch 2, para 108. ⁴ Words substituted: Health Authorities Act 1995, s 2(1), Sch 1, Pt III, para 118(1), (6). ⁵ Words inserted: Jobseekers Act 1995, s 41(4), Sch 2, para 19. ⁶ Words (as previously substituted by Disability Living Allowance and Disability Working Allowance Act 1991) substituted: Tax Credits Act 1999, s 1(2), Sch 1, paras 1, 6(d)(ii). ⁷ Words inserted: Health Act 1999 (Supplementary, Consequential etc Provisions) Order 2000, SI 2000/90. ⁸ Words and subsection inserted: Local Government Act 2000, s 103. ⁹ Words and subsection inserted: Children (Leaving Care) Act 2000, s 7(3). ¹⁰ Words inserted: National Health Service Reform and Health Care Professions Act 2002 (Supplementary, Consequential etc Provisions) Regulations 2002, SI 2002/2469, reg 4, Sch 1, para 16(1), (2).

Definitions. 'Child': s 105(1); 'child who is looked after by a local authority': s 22(1); 'community home': s 53(1); 'controlled community home': s 53(4); 'hospital': s 105(1); 'local authority': s 105(1); 'ordinary residence': s 105(6); 'service': s 105(1).

30 Miscellaneous

(1) Nothing in this Part shall affect any duty imposed on a local authority by or under any other enactment.

(2) Any question arising under section 20(2), 21(3) or 29(7) to (9) as to the ordinary residence of a child shall be determined by agreement between the local authorities concerned or, in default of agreement, by the Secretary of State.

(3) Where the functions conferred on a local authority by this Part and the functions of a local education authority are concurrent, the Secretary of State may by regulations provide by which authority the functions are to be exercised.

(4) The Secretary of State may make regulations for determining, as respects any local education authority functions specified in the regulations, whether a child who is being looked after by a local authority is to be treated, for purposes so specified, as a child of parents of sufficient resources or as a child of parents without resources.

NOTES

Definitions. 'Child who is looked after by a local authority': s 22(1); 'functions': s 105(1); 'local authority': s 105(1); 'local education authority': s 105(1); 'ordinary residence': s 105(6).

PART IV
CARE AND SUPERVISION

General

31 Care and supervision orders

(1) On the application of any local authority or authorised person, the court may make an order –

    (a) placing the child with respect to whom the application is made in the care of a designated local authority; or

    (b) putting him under the supervision of a designated local authority ... [3].

(2) A court may only make a care order or supervision order if it is satisfied –

    (a) that the child concerned is suffering, or is likely to suffer, significant harm; and

    (b) that the harm, or likelihood of harm, is attributable to –

        (i) the care given to the child, or likely to be given to him if the order were not made, not being what it would be reasonable to expect a parent to give to him; or

        (ii) the child's being beyond parental control.

(3) No care order or supervision order may be made with respect to a child who has reached the age of seventeen (or sixteen, in the case of a child who is married).

(4) An application under this section may be made on its own or in any other family proceedings.

(5) The court may –

    (a) on an application for a care order, make a supervision order;

    (b) on an application for a supervision order, make a care order.

(6) Where an authorised person proposes to make an application under this section he shall –

    (a) if it is reasonably practicable to do so; and

    (b) before making the application,

consult the local authority appearing to him to be the authority in whose area the child concerned is ordinarily resident.

(7) An application made by an authorised person shall not be entertained by the court if, at the time when it is made, the child concerned is –

    (a) the subject of an earlier application for a care order, or supervision order, which has not been disposed of; or

    (b) subject to –

        (i) a care order or supervision order;

        (ii) an order under [section 63(1) of the Powers of Criminal Courts (Sentencing) Act 2000][2]; or

        (iii) a supervision requirement within the meaning of [Part II of the Children (Scotland) Act 1995][1].

(8) The local authority designated in a care order must be –

    (a) the authority within whose area the child is ordinarily resident; or

    (b) where the child does not reside in the area of a local authority, the authority within whose area any circumstances arose in consequence of which the order is being made.

(9) In this section –

'authorised person' means –

    (a) the National Society for the Prevention of Cruelty to Children and any of its officers; and

    (b) any person authorised by order of the Secretary of State to bring proceedings under this section and any officer of a body which is so authorised;

'harm' means ill-treatment or the impairment of health or development;

'development' means physical, intellectual, emotional, social or behavioural development;

'health' means physical or mental health; and

'ill-treatment' includes sexual abuse and forms of ill-treatment which are not physical.

(10) Where the question of whether harm suffered by a child is significant turns on the child's health or development, his health or development shall be compared with that which could reasonably be expected of a similar child.

(11) In this Act –

'a care order' means (subject to section 105(1)) an order under subsection (1)(a) and (except where express provision to the contrary is made) includes an interim care order made under section 38; and

'a supervision order' means an order under subsection (1)(b) and (except where express provision to the contrary is made) includes an interim supervision order made under section 38.

NOTES

Amendments. [1] Words substituted: Children (Scotland) Act 1995, s 105(4), Sch 4, para 48(1), (2). [2] Words substituted: Powers of Criminal Courts (Sentencing) Act 2000, s 165(1), Sch 9, para 129. [3] Words omitted: Criminal Justice and Court Services Act 2000, ss 74, 75, Sch 7, paras 87, 90, Sch 8.

Definitions. 'Authorised person': s 31(9); 'care order': ss 31(11), 105(1); 'child': s 105(1); 'designated local authority': s 31(8); 'development': s 31(9); 'family proceedings': s 8(3); 'harm': s 31(9); 'health': s 31(9); 'ill-treatment': s 31(9); 'local authority': s 105(1); 'ordinary residence': s 105(6); 'significant harm': s 31(10); 'supervision order': s 31(11); 'the court': s 92(7).

32 Period within which application for order under this Part must be disposed of

(1) A court hearing an application for an order under this Part shall (in the light of any rules made by virtue of subsection (2)) –

    (a) draw up a timetable with a view to disposing of the application without delay; and

    (b) give such directions as it considers appropriate for the purpose of ensuring, so far as is reasonably practicable, that that timetable is adhered to.

(2) Rules of court may –

(a) specify periods within which specified steps must be taken in relation to such proceedings; and

(b) make other provision with respect to such proceedings for the purpose of ensuring, so far as is reasonably practicable, that they are disposed of without delay.

NOTES

Definition. 'The court': s 92(7).

Care orders

33 Effect of care order

(1) Where a care order is made with respect to a child it shall be the duty of the local authority designated by the order to receive the child into their care and to keep him in their care while the order remains in force.

(2) Where –

(a) a care order has been made with respect to a child on the application of an authorised person; but

(b) the local authority designated by the order was not informed that that person proposed to make the application,

the child may be kept in the care of that person until received into the care of the authority.

(3) While a care order is in force with respect to a child, the local authority designated by the order shall –

(a) have parental responsibility for the child; and

(b) have the power (subject to the following provisions of this section) to determine the extent to which a parent or guardian of the child may meet his parental responsibility for him.

(4) The authority may not exercise the power in subsection (3)(b) unless they are satisfied that it is necessary to do so in order to safeguard or promote the child's welfare.

(5) Nothing in subsection (3)(b) shall prevent a parent or guardian of the child who has care of him from doing what is reasonable in all the circumstances of the case for the purpose of safeguarding or promoting his welfare.

(6) While a care order is in force with respect to a child, the local authority designated by the order shall not –

(a) cause the child to be brought up in any religious persuasion other than that in which he would have been brought up if the order had not been made; or

(b) have the right –

(i) to consent or refuse to consent to the making of an application with respect to the child under section 18 of the Adoption Act 1976;

(ii) to agree or refuse to agree to the making of an adoption order, or an order under section 55 of the Act of 1976, with respect to the child; or

(iii) to appoint a guardian for the child.

(7) While a care order is in force with respect to a child, no person may –

(a) cause the child to be known by a new surname; or

PART I

(b) remove him from the United Kingdom,

without either the written consent of every person who has parental responsibility for the child or the leave of the court.

(8) Subsection (7)(b) does not –

(a) prevent the removal of such a child, for a period of less than one month, by the authority in whose care he is; or
(b) apply to arrangements for such a child to live outside England and Wales (which are governed by paragraph 19 of Schedule 2).

(9) The power in subsection (3)(b) is subject (in addition to being subject to the provisions of this section) to any right, duty, power, responsibility or authority which a parent or guardian of the child has in relation to the child and his property by virtue of any other enactment.

NOTES

Definitions. 'Authorised person': s 31(9); 'care order': ss 31(11), 105(1); 'designated local authority': s 31(8); 'guardian of the child': s 105(1); 'local authority': s 105(1); 'parental responsibility': s 3; 'the court': s 92(7).

34 Parental contact etc with children in care

(1) Where a child is in the care of a local authority, the authority shall (subject to the provisions of this section) allow the child reasonable contact with –

(a) his parents;
(b) any guardian of his;
(c) where there was a residence order in force with respect to the child immediately before the care order was made, the person in whose favour the order was made; and
(d) where, immediately before the care order was made, a person had care of the child by virtue of an order made in the exercise of the High Court's inherent jurisdiction with respect to children, that person.

(2) On an application made by the authority or the child, the court may make such order as it considers appropriate with respect to the contact which is to be allowed between the child and any named person.

(3) On an application made by –

(a) any person mentioned in paragraphs (a) to (d) of subsection (1); or
(b) any person who has obtained the leave of the court to make the application,

the court may make such order as it considers appropriate with respect to the contact which is to be allowed between the child and that person.

(4) On an application made by the authority or the child, the court may make an order authorising the authority to refuse to allow contact between the child and any person who is mentioned in paragraphs (a) to (d) of subsection (1) and named in the order.

(5) When making a care order with respect to a child, or in any family proceedings in connection with a child who is in the care of a local authority, the court may make an order under this section, even though no application for such an order has been made with respect to the child, if it considers that the order should be made.

(6) An authority may refuse to allow the contact that would otherwise be required by virtue of subsection (1) or an order under this section if –

    (a) they are satisfied that it is necessary to do so in order to safeguard or promote the child's welfare; and

    (b) the refusal –

        (i) is decided upon as a matter of urgency; and

        (ii) does not last for more than seven days.

(7) An order under this section may impose such conditions as the court considers appropriate.

(8) The Secretary of State may by regulations make provision as to –

    (a) the steps to be taken by a local authority who have exercised their powers under subsection (6);

    (b) the circumstances in which, and conditions subject to which, the terms of any order under this section may be departed from by agreement between the local authority and the person in relation to whom the order is made;

    (c) notification by a local authority of any variation or suspension of arrangements made (otherwise than under an order under this section) with a view to affording any person contact with a child to whom this section applies.

(9) The court may vary or discharge any order made under this section on the application of the authority, the child concerned or the person named in the order.

(10) An order under this section may be made either at the same time as the care order itself or later.

(11) Before making a care order with respect to any child the court shall –

    (a) consider the arrangements which the authority have made, or propose to make, for affording any person contact with a child to whom this section applies; and

    (b) invite the parties to the proceedings to comment on those arrangements.

NOTES

Definitions. 'Care order': ss 31(11), 105(1); 'child': s 105(1); 'family proceedings': s 8(3); 'guardian of a child': s 105(1); 'local authority': s 105(1); 'residence order': s 8(1); 'the court': s 92(7).

Supervision orders

35 Supervision orders

(1) While a supervision order is in force it shall be the duty of the supervisor –

    (a) to advise, assist and befriend the supervised child;

    (b) to take such steps as are reasonably necessary to give effect to the order; and

    (c) where –

        (i) the order is not wholly complied with; or

        (ii) the supervisor considers that the order may no longer be necessary,

to consider whether or not to apply to the court for its variation or discharge.

(2) Parts I and II of Schedule 3 make further provision with respect to supervision orders.

NOTES

Definitions. 'Supervised child', 'supervisor': s 105(1); 'supervision order': s 31(11); 'the court': s 92(7).

36 Education supervision orders

(1) On the application of any local education authority, the court may make an order putting the child with respect to whom the application is made under the supervision of a designated local education authority.

(2) In this Act 'an education supervision order' means an order under subsection (1).

(3) A court may only make an education supervision order if it is satisfied that the child concerned is of compulsory school age and is not being properly educated.

(4) For the purposes of this section, a child is being properly educated only if he is receiving efficient full-time education suitable to his age, ability and aptitude and any special educational needs he may have.

(5) Where a child is –

  (a) the subject of a school attendance order which is in force under [section 437 of the Education Act 1996][2] and which has not been complied with; or

  (b) a registered pupil at a school which he is not attending regularly within the meaning of [section 444][2] of that Act,

then, unless it is proved that he is being properly educated, it shall be assumed that he is not.

(6) An education supervision order may not be made with respect to a child who is in the care of a local authority.

(7) The local education authority designated in an education supervision order must be –

  (a) the authority within whose area the child concerned is living or will live; or

  (b) where –

    (i) the child is a registered pupil at a school; and

    (ii) the authority mentioned in paragraph (a) and the authority within whose area the school is situated agree,

    the latter authority.

(8) Where a local education authority propose to make an application for an education supervision order they shall, before making the application, consult the …[1] appropriate local authority.

(9) The appropriate local authority is –

  (a) in the case of a child who is being provided with accommodation by, or on behalf of, a local authority, that authority; and

  (b) in any other case, the local authority within whose area the child concerned lives, or will live.

(10) Part III of Schedule 3 makes further provision with respect to education supervision orders.

NOTES

Amendments. [1] Words repealed: Education Act 1993, s 307, Sch 19, para 149. [2] Words substituted: Education Act 1996, s 582(1), Sch 37, Pt I, para 85.

Definitions. 'Appropriate local authority': s 36(9); 'child': s 105(1); 'education supervision order': s 36(2); 'local authority': s 105(1); 'local education authority': s 105(1); 'properly educated': s 36(4); 'registered pupil': s 105(1); 'school': s 105(1); 'special educational needs': s 105(1); 'the court': s 92(7).

Powers of court

37 Powers of court in certain family proceedings

(1) Where, in any family proceedings in which a question arises with respect to the welfare of any child, it appears to the court that it may be appropriate for a care or supervision order to be made with respect to him, the court may direct the appropriate authority to undertake an investigation of the child's circumstances.

(2) Where the court gives a direction under this section the local authority concerned shall, when undertaking the investigation, consider whether they should –

    (a) apply for a care order or for a supervision order with respect to the child;

    (b) provide services or assistance for the child or his family; or

    (c) take any other action with respect to the child.

(3) Where a local authority undertake an investigation under this section, and decide not to apply for a care order or supervision order with respect to the child concerned, they shall inform the court of –

    (a) their reasons for so deciding;

    (b) any service or assistance which they have provided, or intend to provide, for the child and his family; and

    (c) any other action which they have taken, or propose to take, with respect to the child.

(4) The information shall be given to the court before the end of the period of eight weeks beginning with the date of the direction, unless the court otherwise directs.

(5) The local authority named in a direction under subsection (1) must be –

    (a) the authority in whose area the child is ordinarily resident; or

    (b) where the child [is not ordinarily resident][1] in the area of a local authority, the authority within whose area any circumstances arose in consequence of which the direction is being given.

(6) If, on the conclusion of any investigation or review under this section, the authority decide not to apply for a care order or supervision order with respect to the child –

    (a) they shall consider whether it would be appropriate to review the case at a later date; and

    (b) if they decide that it would be, they shall determine the date on which that review is to begin.

NOTES

Amendments. [1] Words substituted: Courts and Legal Services Act 1990, s 116, Sch 16, para 16.

Definitions. 'Appropriate authority': s 37(5); 'care order': ss 31(11), 105(1); 'child': s 105(1); 'family proceedings': s 8(3); 'local authority': s 105(1); 'ordinary residence': s 105(6); 'supervision order': s 31(11); 'the court': s 92(7).

38 Interim orders

(1) Where –

(a) in any proceedings on an application for a care order or supervision order, the proceedings are adjourned; or
(b) the court gives a direction under section 37(1),

the court may make an interim care order or an interim supervision order with respect to the child concerned.

(2) A court shall not make an interim care order or interim supervision order under this section unless it is satisfied that there are reasonable grounds for believing that the circumstances with respect to the child are as mentioned in section 31(2).

(3) Where, in any proceedings on an application for a care order or supervision order, a court makes a residence order with respect to the child concerned, it shall also make an interim supervision order with respect to him unless satisfied that his welfare will be satisfactorily safeguarded without an interim order being made.

(4) An interim order made under or by virtue of this section shall have effect for such period as may be specified in the order, but shall in any event cease to have effect on whichever of the following events first occurs –

(a) the expiry of the period of eight weeks beginning with the date on which the order is made;
(b) if the order is the second or subsequent such order made with respect to the same child in the same proceedings, the expiry of the relevant period;
(c) in a case which falls within subsection (1)(a), the disposal of the application;
(d) in a case which falls within subsection (1)(b), the disposal of an application for a care order or supervision order made by the authority with respect to the child;
(e) in a case which falls within subsection (1)(b) and in which –
   (i) the court has given a direction under section 37(4), but
   (ii) no application for a care order or supervision order has been made with respect to the child,
   the expiry of the period fixed by that direction.

(5) In subsection (4)(b) 'the relevant period' means –

(a) the period of four weeks beginning with the date on which the order in question is made; or
(b) the period of eight weeks beginning with the date on which the first order was made if that period ends later than the period mentioned in paragraph (a).

(6) Where the court makes an interim care order, or interim supervision order, it may give such directions (if any) as it considers appropriate with regard to the medical or psychiatric examination or other assessment of the child; but if the child is of sufficient understanding to make an informed decision he may refuse to submit to the examination or other assessment.

(7) A direction under subsection (6) may be to the effect that there is to be –

(a) no such examination or assessment; or

(b) no such examination or assessment unless the court directs otherwise.

(8) A direction under subsection (6) may be –

(a) given when the interim order is made or at any time while it is in force; and

(b) varied at any time on the application of any person falling within any class of person prescribed by rules of court for the purposes of this subsection.

(9) Paragraphs 4 and 5 of Schedule 3 shall not apply in relation to an interim supervision order.

(10) Where a court makes an order under or by virtue of this section it shall, in determining the period for which the order is to be in force, consider whether any party who was, or might have been, opposed to the making of the order was in a position to argue his case against the order in full.

NOTES

Definitions. 'Care order': s 31(11); 'child': s 105(1); 'relevant period': s 38(5); 'residence order': s 8(1); 'supervision order': s 31(11); 'the court': s 92(7).

[38A Power to include exclusion requirement in interim care order

(1) Where –

(a) on being satisfied that there are reasonable grounds for believing that the circumstances with respect to a child are as mentioned in section 31(2)(a) and (b)(i), the court makes an interim care order with respect to a child, and

(b) the conditions mentioned in subsection (2) are satisfied,

the court may include an exclusion requirement in the interim care order.

(2) The conditions are –

(a) that there is reasonable cause to believe that, if a person ('the relevant person') is excluded from a dwelling-house in which the child lives, the child will cease to suffer, or cease to be likely to suffer, significant harm, and

(b) that another person living in the dwelling-house (whether a parent of the child or some other person) –

(i) is able and willing to give to the child the care which it would be reasonable to expect a parent to give him, and

(ii) consents to the inclusion of the exclusion requirement.

(3) For the purposes of this section an exclusion requirement is any one or more of the following –

(a) a provision requiring the relevant person to leave a dwelling-house in which he is living with the child,

(b) a provision prohibiting the relevant person from entering a dwelling-house in which the child lives, and

(c) a provision excluding the relevant person from a defined area in which a dwelling-house in which the child lives is situated.

(4) The court may provide that the exclusion requirement is to have effect for a shorter period than the other provisions of the interim care order.

(5) Where the court makes an interim care order containing an exclusion requirement, the court may attach a power of arrest to the exclusion requirement.

(6) Where the court attaches a power of arrest to an exclusion requirement of an interim care order, it may provide that the power of arrest is to have effect for a shorter period than the exclusion requirement.

(7) Any period specified for the purposes of subsection (4) or (6) may be extended by the court (on one or more occasions) on an application to vary or discharge the interim care order.

(8) Where a power of arrest is attached to an exclusion requirement of an interim care order by virtue of subsection (5), a constable may arrest without warrant any person whom he has reasonable cause to believe to be in breach of the requirement.

(9) Sections 47(7), (11) and (12) and 48 of, and Schedule 5 to, the Family Law Act 1996 shall have effect in relation to a person arrested under subsection (8) of this section as they have effect in relation to a person arrested under section 47(6) of that Act.

(10) If, while an interim care order containing an exclusion requirement is in force, the local authority have removed the child from the dwelling-house from which the relevant person is excluded to other accommodation for a continuous period of more than 24 hours, the interim care order shall cease to have effect in so far as it imposes the exclusion requirement.]¹

NOTES
Commencement. 1 Oct 1997: SI 1997/1892.
Amendments. ¹ Section inserted: Family Law Act 1996, s 52, Sch 6, para 1.

[38B Undertakings relating to interim care orders

(1) In any case where the court has power to include an exclusion requirement in an interim care order, the court may accept an undertaking from the relevant person.

(2) No power of arrest may be attached to any undertaking given under subsection (1).

(3) An undertaking given to a court under subsection (1) –

   (a) shall be enforceable as if it were an order of the court, and
   (b) shall cease to have effect if, while it is in force, the local authority have removed the child from the dwelling-house from which the relevant person is excluded to other accommodation for a continuous period of more than 24 hours.

(4) This section has effect without prejudice to the powers of the High Court and county court apart from this section.

(5) In this section 'exclusion requirement' and 'relevant person' have the same meaning as in section 38A.]¹

NOTES
Commencement. 1 Oct 1997: SI 1997/1892.
Amendments. ¹ Section inserted: Family Law Act 1996, s 52, Sch 6, para 1.

39 Discharge and variation etc of care orders and supervision orders

(1) A care order may be discharged by the court on the application of –

(a) any person who has parental responsibility for the child;
(b) the child himself; or
(c) the local authority designated by the order.

(2) A supervision order may be varied or discharged by the court on the application of –

(a) any person who has parental responsibility for the child;
(b) the child himself; or
(c) the supervisor.

(3) On the application of a person who is not entitled to apply for the order to be discharged, but who is a person with whom the child is living, a supervision order may be varied by the court in so far as it imposes a requirement which affects that person.

[(3A) On the application of a person who is not entitled to apply for the order to be discharged, but who is a person to whom an exclusion requirement contained in the order applies, an interim care order may be varied or discharged by the court in so far as it imposes the exclusion requirement.

(3B) Where a power of arrest has been attached to an exclusion requirement of an interim care order, the court may, on the application of any person entitled to apply for the discharge of the order so far as it imposes the exclusion requirement, vary or discharge the order in so far as it confers a power of arrest (whether or not any application has been made to vary or discharge any other provision of the order).][1]

(4) Where a care order is in force with respect to a child the court may, on the application of any person entitled to apply for the order to be discharged, substitute a supervision order for the care order.

(5) When a court is considering whether to substitute one order for another under subsection (4) any provision of this Act which would otherwise require section 31(2) to be satisfied at the time when the proposed order is substituted or made shall be disregarded.

NOTES

Amendments. [1] Subsections inserted: Family Law Act 1996, s 52, Sch 6, para 2.

Definitions. 'Care order': ss 31(11), 105(1); 'child': s 105(1); 'local authority': s 105(1); 'supervision order': s 31(11); 'supervisor': s 105(1); 'the court': s 92(7).

40 Orders pending appeals in cases about care or supervision orders

(1) Where –

(a) a court dismisses an application for a care order; and
(b) at the time when the court dismisses the application, the child concerned is the subject of an interim care order,

the court may make a care order with respect to the child to have effect subject to such directions (if any) as the court may see fit to include in the order.

(2) Where –

(a) a court dismisses an application for a care order, or an application for a supervision order; and

(b) at the time when the court dismisses the application, the child concerned is the subject of an interim supervision order,

the court may make a supervision order with respect to the child to have effect subject to such directions (if any) as the court may see fit to include in the order.

(3) Where a court grants an application to discharge a care order or supervision order, it may order that –

(a) its decision is not to have effect; or

(b) the care order, or supervision order, is to continue to have effect but subject to such directions as the court sees fit to include in the order.

(4) An order made under this section shall only have effect for such period, not exceeding the appeal period, as may be specified in the order.

(5) Where –

(a) an appeal is made against any decision of a court under this section; or

(b) any application is made to the appellate court in connection with a proposed appeal against that decision,

the appellate court may extend the period for which the order in question is to have effect, but not so as to extend it beyond the end of the appeal period.

(6) In this section 'the appeal period' means –

(a) where an appeal is made against the decision in question, the period between the making of that decision and the determination of the appeal; and

(b) otherwise, the period during which an appeal may be made against the decision.

NOTES

Definitions. 'Appeal period': s 40(6); 'care order': ss 31(11), 105(1); 'child': s 105(1); 'the court': s 92(7).

*[Representation of child]*²

41 Representation of child and of his interests in certain proceedings

(1) For the purpose of any specified proceedings, the court shall appoint [an officer of the Service]² for the child concerned unless satisfied that it is not necessary to do so in order to safeguard his interests.

(2) The [officer of the Service]² shall –

(a) be appointed in accordance with rules of court; and

(b) be under a duty to safeguard the interests of the child in the manner prescribed by such rules.

(3) Where –

(a) the child concerned is not represented by a solicitor; and

(b) any of the conditions mentioned in subsection (4) is satisfied,

the court may appoint a solicitor to represent him.

(4) The conditions are that –

    (a) no [officer of the Service]² has been appointed for the child;

    (b) the child has sufficient understanding to instruct a solicitor and wishes to do so;

    (c) it appears to the court that it would be in the child's best interests for him to be represented by a solicitor.

(5) Any solicitor appointed under or by virtue of this section shall be appointed, and shall represent the child, in accordance with rules of court.

(6) In this section 'specified proceedings' means any proceedings –

    (a) on an application for a care order or supervision order;

    (b) in which the court has given a direction under section 37(1) and has made, or is considering whether to make, an interim care order;

    (c) on an application for the discharge of a care order or the variation or discharge of a supervision order;

    (d) on an application under section 39(4);

    (e) in which the court is considering whether to make a residence order with respect to a child who is the subject of a care order;

    (f) with respect to contact between a child who is the subject of a care order and any other person;

    (g) under Part V;

    (h) on an appeal against –

        (i) the making of, or refusal to make, a care order, supervision order or any order under section 34;

        (ii) the making of, or refusal to make, a residence order with respect to a child who is the subject of a care order; or

        (iii) the variation or discharge, or refusal of an application to vary or discharge, an order of a kind mentioned in sub-paragraph (i) or (ii);

        (iv) the refusal of an application under section 39(4);

        (v) the making of, or refusal to make, an order under Part V; or

    (i) which are specified for the time being, for the purposes of this section, by rules of court.

(7)–(9) ...²

(10) Rules of court may make provision as to –

    (a) the assistance which any [officer of the Service]² may be required by the court to give to it;

    (b) the consideration to be given by any [officer of the Service]², where an order of a specified kind has been made in the proceedings in question, as to whether to apply for the variation or discharge of the order;

    (c) the participation of [officers of the Service]² in reviews, of a kind specified in the rules, which are conducted by the court.

(11) Regardless of any enactment or rule of law which would otherwise prevent it from doing so, the court may take account of –

    (a) any statement contained in a report made by [an officer of the Service]² who is appointed under this section for the purpose of the proceedings in question; and

    (b) any evidence given in respect of the matters referred to in the report,

in so far as the statement or evidence is, in the opinion of the court, relevant to the question which the court is considering.

[(12) ...²]¹

PART I

NOTES
  Amendments. ¹ Subsection inserted: Courts and Legal Services Act 1990, s 116, Sch 16, para 17. ² Words substituted or omitted: Criminal Justice and Court Services Act 2000, ss 74, 75, Sch 7, paras 87, 91, Sch 8.
  Definitions. 'Care order': ss 31(11), 105(1); 'child': s 105(1); 'local authority': s 105(1); 'residence order': s 8(1); 'specified proceedings': s 41(6); 'supervision order': s 31(11); 'the court': s 92(7).

42 [Right of officer of the Service to have access to local authority records]⁵

(1) Where [an officer of the Service]⁵ has been appointed [under section 41]⁵ he shall have the right at all reasonable times to examine and take copies of –

  (a) any records of, or held by, a local authority [or an authorised person]¹ which were compiled in connection with the making, or proposed making, by any person of any application under this Act with respect to the child concerned; …²
  (b) any …² records of, or held by, a local authority which were compiled in connection with any functions which [are social services functions within the meaning of]⁶ the Local Authority Social Services Act 1970, so far as those records relate to that child [; or
  (c) any records of, or held by, an authorised person which were compiled in connection with the activities of that person, so far as those records relate to that child.]³

(2) Where [an officer of the Service]⁵ takes a copy of any record which he is entitled to examine under this section, that copy or any part of it shall be admissible as evidence of any matter referred to in any –

  (a) report which he makes to the court in the proceedings in question; or
  (b) evidence which he gives in those proceedings.

(3) Subsection (2) has effect regardless of any enactment or rule of law which would otherwise prevent the record in question being admissible in evidence.

[(4) In this section 'authorised person' has the same meaning as in section 31 .]⁴

NOTES
  Amendments. ¹ Words inserted: Courts and Legal Services Act 1990, s 116, Sch 16, para 18(2). ² Words repealed: Courts and Legal Services Act 1990, s 125(7), Sch 20; ³ Words inserted: Courts and Legal Services Act 1990, s 116, Sch 16, para 18(3). ⁴ Words inserted: Courts and Legal Services Act 1990, s 116, Sch 16, para 18(4). ⁵ Words substituted: Criminal Justice and Court Services Act 2000, s 74, Sch 7, paras 87, 92. ⁶ Words substituted: Local Government Act 2000, s 107, Sch 5, para 20.
  Definitions. 'Child': s 105(1); 'functions': s 105(1); 'local authority': s 105(1).

PART V
PROTECTION OF CHILDREN

43 Child assessment orders

(1) On the application of a local authority or authorised person for an order to be made under this section with respect to a child, the court may make the order if, but only if, it is satisfied that –

(a) the applicant has reasonable cause to suspect that the child is suffering, or is likely to suffer, significant harm;

(b) an assessment of the state of the child's health or development, or of the way in which he has been treated, is required to enable the applicant to determine whether or not the child is suffering, or is likely to suffer, significant harm; and

(c) it is unlikely that such an assessment will be made, or be satisfactory, in the absence of an order under this section.

(2) In this Act 'a child assessment order' means an order under this section.

(3) A court may treat an application under this section as an application for an emergency protection order.

(4) No court shall make a child assessment order if it is satisfied –

(a) that there are grounds for making an emergency protection order with respect to the child; and

(b) that it ought to make such an order rather than a child assessment order.

(5) A child assessment order shall –

(a) specify the date by which the assessment is to begin; and

(b) have effect for such period, not exceeding 7 days beginning with that date, as may be specified in the order.

(6) Where a child assessment order is in force with respect to a child it shall be the duty of any person who is in a position to produce the child –

(a) to produce him to such person as may be named in the order; and

(b) to comply with such directions relating to the assessment of the child as the court thinks fit to specify in the order.

(7) A child assessment order authorises any person carrying out the assessment, or any part of the assessment, to do so in accordance with the terms of the order.

(8) Regardless of subsection (7), if the child is of sufficient understanding to make an informed decision he may refuse to submit to a medical or psychiatric examination or other assessment.

(9) The child may only be kept away from home –

(a) in accordance with directions specified in the order;

(b) if it is necessary for the purposes of the assessment; and

(c) for such period or periods as may be specified in the order.

(10) Where the child is to be kept away from home, the order shall contain such directions as the court thinks fit with regard to the contact that he must be allowed to have with other persons while away from home.

(11) Any person making an application for a child assessment order shall take such steps as are reasonably practicable to ensure that notice of the application is given to –

(a) the child's parents;

(b) any person who is not a parent of his but who has parental responsibility for him;

(c) any other person caring for the child;

(d) any person in whose favour a contact order is in force with respect to the child;

(e) any person who is allowed to have contact with the child by virtue of an order under section 34; and

PART I

(f) the child,

before the hearing of the application.

(12) Rules of court may make provision as to the circumstances in which –

(a) any of the persons mentioned in subsection (11); or

(b) such other person as may be specified in the rules,

may apply to the court for a child assessment order to be varied or discharged.

(13) In this section 'authorised person' means a person who is an authorised person for the purposes of section 31.

NOTES

Definitions. 'Authorised person': s 43(13); 'child': s 105(1); 'child assessment order': s 43(2); 'contact order': s 8(1); 'emergency protection order': s 44(4); 'harm': s 31(9); 'local authority': s 105(1); 'parental responsibility': s 3; 'significant harm': s 31(10); 'the court': s 92(7).

44 Orders for emergency protection of children

(1) Where any person ('the applicant') applies to the court for an order to be made under this section with respect to a child, the court may make the order if, but only if, it is satisfied that –

(a) there is reasonable cause to believe that the child is likely to suffer significant harm if –

(i) he is not removed to accommodation provided by or on behalf of the applicant; or

(ii) he does not remain in the place in which he is then being accommodated;

(b) in the case of an application made by a local authority –

(i) enquiries are being made with respect to the child under section 47(1)(b); and

(ii) those enquiries are being frustrated by access to the child being unreasonably refused to a person authorised to seek access and that the applicant has reasonable cause to believe that access to the child is required as a matter of urgency; or

(c) in the case of an application made by an authorised person –

(i) the applicant has reasonable cause to suspect that a child is suffering, or is likely to suffer, significant harm;

(ii) the applicant is making enquiries with respect to the child's welfare; and

(iii) those enquiries are being frustrated by access to the child being unreasonably refused to a person authorised to seek access and the applicant has reasonable cause to believe that access to the child is required as a matter of urgency.

(2) In this section –

(a) 'authorised person' means a person who is an authorised person for the purposes of section 31; and

(b) 'a person authorised to seek access' means –

(i) in the case of an application by a local authority, an officer of the local authority or a person authorised by the authority to act on their behalf in connection with the enquiries; or

(ii) in the case of an application by an authorised person, that person.

(3) Any person –

    (a) seeking access to a child in connection with enquiries of a kind mentioned in subsection (1); and

    (b) purporting to be a person authorised to do so,

shall, on being asked to do so, produce some duly authenticated document as evidence that he is such a person.

(4) While an order under this section ('an emergency protection order') is in force it –

    (a) operates as a direction to any person who is in a position to do so to comply with any request to produce the child to the applicant;

    (b) authorises –

        (i) the removal of the child at any time to accommodation provided by or on behalf of the applicant and his being kept there; or

        (ii) the prevention of the child's removal from any hospital, or other place, in which he was being accommodated immediately before the making of the order; and

    (c) gives the applicant parental responsibility for the child.

(5) Where an emergency protection order is in force with respect to a child, the applicant –

    (a) shall only exercise the power given by virtue of subsection (4)(b) in order to safeguard the welfare of the child;

    (b) shall take, and shall only take, such action in meeting his parental responsibility for the child as is reasonably required to safeguard or promote the welfare of the child (having regard in particular to the duration of the order); and

    (c) shall comply with the requirements of any regulations made by the Secretary of State for the purposes of this subsection.

(6) Where the court makes an emergency protection order, it may give such directions (if any) as it considers appropriate with respect to –

    (a) the contact which is, or is not, to be allowed between the child and any named person;

    (b) the medical or psychiatric examination or other assessment of the child.

(7) Where any direction is given under subsection (6)(b), the child may, if he is of sufficient understanding to make an informed decision, refuse to submit to the examination or other assessment.

(8) A direction under subsection (6)(a) may impose conditions and one under subsection (6)(b) may be to the effect that there is to be –

    (a) no such examination or assessment; or

    (b) no such examination or assessment unless the court directs otherwise.

(9) A direction under subsection (6) may be –

    (a) given when the emergency protection order is made or at any time while it is in force; and

    (b) varied at any time on the application of any person falling within any class of person prescribed by rules of court for the purposes of this subsection.

(10) Where an emergency protection order is in force with respect to a child and –

    (a) the applicant has exercised the power given by subsection (4)(b)(i) but it appears to him that it is safe for the child to be returned; or

PART I

(b) the applicant has exercised the power given by subsection (4)(b)(ii) but it appears to him that it is safe for the child to be allowed to be removed from the place in question,

he shall return the child or (as the case may be) allow him to be removed.

(11) Where he is required by subsection (10) to return the child the applicant shall –

(a) return him to the care of the person from whose care he was removed; or
(b) if that is not reasonably practicable, return him to the care of –
  (i) a parent of his;
  (ii) any person who is not a parent of his but who has parental responsibility for him; or
  (iii) such other person as the applicant (with the agreement of the court) considers appropriate.

(12) Where the applicant has been required by subsection (10) to return the child, or to allow him to be removed, he may again exercise his powers with respect to the child (at any time while the emergency protection order remains in force) if it appears to him that a change in the circumstances of the case makes it necessary for him to do so.

(13) Where an emergency protection order has been made with respect to a child, the applicant shall, subject to any direction given under subsection (6), allow the child reasonable contact with –

(a) his parents;
(b) any person who is not a parent of his but who has parental responsibility for him;
(c) any person with whom he was living immediately before the making of the order;
(d) any person in whose favour a contact order is in force with respect to him;
(e) any person who is allowed to have contact with the child by virtue of an order under section 34; and
(f) any person acting on behalf of any of those persons.

(14) Wherever it is reasonably practicable to do so, an emergency protection order shall name the child; and where it does not name him it shall describe him as clearly as possible.

(15) A person shall be guilty of an offence if he intentionally obstructs any person exercising the power under subsection (4)(b) to remove, or prevent the removal of, a child.

(16) A person guilty of an offence under subsection (15) shall be liable on summary conviction to a fine not exceeding level 3 on the standard scale.

NOTES

Definitions. 'Authorised person': s 44(2); 'child': s 105(1); 'contact order': s 8(1); 'emergency protection order': s 44(4); 'harm': s 31(9); 'hospital': s 105(1); 'local authority': s 105(1); 'parental responsibility': s 3; 'person authorised to seek access': s 44(2); 'significant harm': s 31(10); 'the applicant': s 44(1); 'the court': s 92(7).

[44A Power to include exclusion requirement in emergency protection order

(1) Where –

 (a) on being satisfied as mentioned in section 44(1)(a), (b) or (c), the court makes an emergency protection order with respect to a child, and
 (b) the conditions mentioned in subsection (2) are satisfied,

the court may include an exclusion requirement in the emergency protection order.

(2) The conditions are –

 (a) that there is reasonable cause to believe that, if a person ('the relevant person') is excluded from a dwelling-house in which the child lives, then –
  (i) in the case of an order made on the ground mentioned in section 44(1)(a), the child will not be likely to suffer significant harm, even though the child is not removed as mentioned in section 44(1)(a)(i) or does not remain as mentioned in section 44(1)(a)(ii), or
  (ii) in the case of an order made on the ground mentioned in paragraph (b) or (c) of section 44(1), the enquiries referred to in that paragraph will cease to be frustrated, and
 (b) that another person living in the dwelling-house (whether a parent of the child or some other person) –
  (i) is able and willing to give to the child the care which it would be reasonable to expect a parent to give him, and
  (ii) consents to the inclusion of the exclusion requirement.

(3) For the purposes of this section an exclusion requirement is any one or more of the following –

 (a) a provision requiring the relevant person to leave a dwelling-house in which he is living with the child,
 (b) a provision prohibiting the relevant person from entering a dwelling-house in which the child lives, and
 (c) a provision excluding the relevant person from a defined area in which a dwelling-house in which the child lives is situated.

(4) The court may provide that the exclusion requirement is to have effect for a shorter period than the other provisions of the order.

(5) Where the court makes an emergency protection order containing an exclusion requirement, the court may attach a power of arrest to the exclusion requirement.

(6) Where the court attaches a power of arrest to an exclusion requirement of an emergency protection order, it may provide that the power of arrest is to have effect for a shorter period than the exclusion requirement.

(7) Any period specified for the purposes of subsection (4) or (6) may be extended by the court (on one or more occasions) on an application to vary or discharge the emergency protection order.

(8) Where a power of arrest is attached to an exclusion requirement of an emergency protection order by virtue of subsection (5), a constable may arrest without warrant any person whom he has reasonable cause to believe to be in breach of the requirement.

(9) Sections 47(7), (11) and (12) and 48 of, and Schedule 5 to, the Family Law Act 1996 shall have effect in relation to a person arrested under subsection (8) of this section as they have effect in relation to a person arrested under section 47(6) of that Act.

(10) If, while an emergency protection order containing an exclusion requirement is in force, the applicant has removed the child from the dwelling-house from which the relevant person is excluded to other accommodation for a continuous period of more than 24 hours, the order shall cease to have effect in so far as it imposes the exclusion requirement.]¹

NOTES
Amendments. ¹ Section inserted: Family Law Act 1996, s 52, Sch 6, para 3.

[44B Undertakings relating to emergency protection orders

(1) In any case where the court has power to include an exclusion requirement in an emergency protection order, the court may accept an undertaking from the relevant person.

(2) No power of arrest may be attached to any undertaking given under subsection (1).

(3) An undertaking given to a court under subsection (1) –

    (a) shall be enforceable as if it were an order of the court, and
    (b) shall cease to have effect if, while it is in force, the applicant has removed the child from the dwelling-house from which the relevant person is excluded to other accommodation for a continuous period of more than 24 hours.

(4) This section has effect without prejudice to the powers of the High Court and county court apart from this section.

(5) In this section 'exclusion requirement' and 'relevant person' have the same meaning as in section 44A.]¹

NOTES
Amendments. ¹ Section inserted: Family Law Act 1996, s 52, Sch 6, para 3.

45 Duration of emergency protection orders and other supplemental provisions

(1) An emergency protection order shall have effect for such period, not exceeding eight days, as may be specified in the order.

(2) Where –

    (a) the court making an emergency protection order would, but for this subsection, specify a period of eight days as the period for which the order is to have effect; but
    (b) the last of those eight days is a public holiday (that is to say, Christmas Day, Good Friday, a bank holiday or a Sunday),

the court may specify a period which ends at noon on the first later day which is not such a holiday.

(3) Where an emergency protection order is made on an application under section 46(7), the period of eight days mentioned in subsection (1) shall begin with the first day on which the child was taken into police protection under section 46.

(4) Any person who –

(a) has parental responsibility for a child as the result of an emergency protection order; and

(b) is entitled to apply for a care order with respect to the child,

may apply to the court for the period during which the emergency protection order is to have effect to be extended.

(5) On an application under subsection (4) the court may extend the period during which the order is to have effect by such period, not exceeding seven days, as it thinks fit, but may do so only if it has reasonable cause to believe that the child concerned is likely to suffer significant harm if the order is not extended.

(6) An emergency protection order may only be extended once.

(7) Regardless of any enactment or rule of law which would otherwise prevent it from doing so, a court hearing an application for, or with respect to, an emergency protection order may take account of –

(a) any statement contained in any report made to the court in the course of, or in connection with, the hearing; or

(b) any evidence given during the hearing,

which is, in the opinion of the court, relevant to the application.

(8) Any of the following may apply to the court for an emergency protection order to be discharged –

(a) the child;

(b) a parent of his;

(c) any person who is not a parent of his but who has parental responsibility for him; or

(d) any person with whom he was living immediately before the making of the order.

[(8A) On the application of a person who is not entitled to apply for the order to be discharged, but who is a person to whom an exclusion requirement contained in the order applies, an emergency protection order may be varied or discharged by the court in so far as it imposes the exclusion requirement.

(8B) Where a power of arrest has been attached to an exclusion requirement of an emergency protection order, the court may, on the application of any person entitled to apply for the discharge of the order so far as it imposes the exclusion requirement, vary or discharge the order in so far as it confers a power of arrest (whether or not any application has been made to vary or discharge any other provision of the order).]²

(9) No application for the discharge of an emergency protection order shall be heard by the court before the expiry of the period of 72 hours beginning with the making of the order.

[(10) No appeal may be made against –

(a) the making of, or refusal to make, an emergency protection order;

(b) the extension of, or refusal to extend, the period during which such an order is to have effect;

(c) the discharge of, or refusal to discharge, such an order; or

(d) the giving of, or refusal to give, any direction in connection with such an order.]¹

(11) Subsection (8) does not apply –

(a) where the person who would otherwise be entitled to apply for the emergency protection order to be discharged –

    (i) was given notice (in accordance with rules of court) of the hearing at which the order was made; and

    (ii) was present at that hearing; or

(b) to any emergency protection order the effective period of which has been extended under subsection (5).

(12) A court making an emergency protection order may direct that the applicant may, in exercising any powers which he has by virtue of the order, be accompanied by a registered medical practitioner, registered nurse or registered health visitor, if he so chooses.

NOTES

Amendments. ¹ Words substituted: Courts and Legal Services Act 1990, s 116, Sch 16, para 19. ² Subsections inserted: Family Law Act 1996, s 52, Sch 6, para 4.

Definitions. 'Bank holiday': s 105(1); 'care order': ss 31(11), 105(1); 'child': s 105(1); 'emergency protection order': s 44(4); 'harm': s 31(9); 'parental responsibility': s 3; 'significant harm': s 31(10); 'the court': s 92(7).

46 Removal and accommodation of children by police in cases of emergency

(1) Where a constable has reasonable cause to believe that a child would otherwise be likely to suffer significant harm, he may –

(a) remove the child to suitable accommodation and keep him there; or

(b) take such steps as are reasonable to ensure that the child's removal from any hospital, or other place, in which he is then being accommodated is prevented.

(2) For the purposes of this Act, a child with respect to whom a constable has exercised his powers under this section is referred to as having been taken into police protection.

(3) As soon as is reasonably practicable after taking a child into police protection, the constable concerned shall –

(a) inform the local authority within whose area the child was found of the steps that have been, and are proposed to be, taken with respect to the child under this section and the reasons for taking them;

(b) give details to the authority within whose area the child is ordinarily resident ('the appropriate authority') of the place at which the child is being accommodated;

(c) inform the child (if he appears capable of understanding) –

    (i) of the steps that have been taken with respect to him under this section and of the reasons for taking them; and

    (ii) of the further steps that may be taken with respect to him under this section;

(d) take such steps as are reasonably practicable to discover the wishes and feelings of the child;

(e) secure that the case is inquired into by an officer designated for the purposes of this section by the chief officer of the police area concerned; and

(f) where the child was taken into police protection by being removed to accommodation which is not provided –

      (i) by or on behalf of a local authority; or
      (ii) as a refuge, in compliance with the requirements of section 51,
    secure that he is moved to accommodation which is so provided.

(4) As soon as is reasonably practicable after taking a child into police protection, the constable concerned shall take such steps as are reasonably practicable to inform –

    (a) the child's parents;
    (b) every person who is not a parent of his but who has parental responsibility for him; and
    (c) any other person with whom the child was living immediately before being taken into police protection,

of the steps that he has taken under this section with respect to the child, the reasons for taking them and the further steps that may be taken with respect to him under this section.

(5) On completing any inquiry under subsection (3)(e), the officer conducting it shall release the child from police protection unless he considers that there is still reasonable cause for believing that the child would be likely to suffer significant harm if released.

(6) No child may be kept in police protection for more than 72 hours.

(7) While a child is being kept in police protection, the designated officer may apply on behalf of the appropriate authority for an emergency protection order to be made under section 44 with respect to the child.

(8) An application may be made under subsection (7) whether or not the authority know of it or agree to its being made.

(9) While a child is being kept in police protection –

    (a) neither the constable concerned nor the designated officer shall have parental responsibility for him; but
    (b) the designated officer shall do what is reasonable in all the circumstances of the case for the purpose of safeguarding or promoting the child's welfare (having regard in particular to the length of the period during which the child will be so protected).

(10) Where a child has been taken into police protection, the designated officer shall allow –

    (a) the child's parents;
    (b) any person who is not a parent of the child but who has parental responsibility for him;
    (c) any person with whom the child was living immediately before he was taken into police protection;
    (d) any person in whose favour a contact order is in force with respect to the child;
    (e) any person who is allowed to have contact with the child by virtue of an order under section 34; and
    (f) any person acting on behalf of any of those persons,

to have such contact (if any) with the child as, in the opinion of the designated officer, is both reasonable and in the child's best interests.

(11) Where a child who has been taken into police protection is in accommodation provided by, or on behalf of, the appropriate authority, subsection (10) shall have effect as if it referred to the authority rather than to the designated officer.

PART I

NOTES

Definitions. 'Appropriate authority': s 46(3)(b); 'child': s 105(1); 'contact order': s 8(1); 'designated officer': s 46(3)(e); 'emergency protection order': s 44(4); 'harm': s 31(9); 'hospital': s 105(1); 'local authority': s 105(1); 'ordinary residence': s 105(6); 'police protection': s 46(2); 'significant harm': s 31(10).

47 Local authority's duty to investigate

(1) Where a local authority –

    (a) are informed that a child who lives, or is found, in their area –

        (i) is the subject of an emergency protection order; or

        (ii) is in police protection; or

        [(iii) has contravened a ban imposed by a curfew notice within the meaning of Chapter I of Part I of the Crime and Disorder Act 1998; or][3]

    (b) have reasonable cause to suspect that a child who lives, or is found, in their area is suffering, or is likely to suffer, significant harm,

the authority shall make, or cause to be made, such enquiries as they consider necessary to enable them to decide whether they should take any action to safeguard or promote the child's welfare.

[In the case of a child falling within paragraph (a)(iii) above, the enquiries shall be commenced as soon as practicable and, in any event, within 48 hours of the authority receiving the information.][3]

(2) Where a local authority have obtained an emergency protection order with respect to a child, they shall make, or cause to be made, such enquiries as they consider necessary to enable them to decide what action they should take to safeguard or promote the child's welfare.

(3) The enquiries shall, in particular, be directed towards establishing –

    (a) whether the authority should make any application to the court, or exercise any of their other powers under this Act [or section 11 of the Crime and Disorder Act 1998 (child safety orders)][3], with respect to the child;

    (b) whether, in the case of a child –

        (i) with respect to whom an emergency protection order has been made; and

        (ii) who is not in accommodation provided by or on behalf of the authority,

    it would be in the child's best interests (while an emergency protection order remains in force) for him to be in such accommodation; and

    (c) whether, in the case of a child who has been taken into police protection, it would be in the child's best interests for the authority to ask for an application to be made under section 46(7).

(4) Where enquiries are being made under subsection (1) with respect to a child, the local authority concerned shall (with a view to enabling them to determine what action, if any, to take with respect to him) take such steps as are reasonably practicable –

    (a) to obtain access to him; or

    (b) to ensure that access to him is obtained, on their behalf, by a person authorised by them for the purpose, unless they are satisfied that they already have sufficient information with respect to him.

(5) Where, as a result of any such enquiries, it appears to the authority that there are matters connected with the child's education which should be investigated, they shall consult the relevant local education authority.

(6) Where, in the course of enquiries made under this section –

(a) any officer of the local authority concerned; or
(b) any person authorised by the authority to act on their behalf in connection with those enquiries –
    (i) is refused access to the child concerned; or
    (ii) is denied information as to his whereabouts,

the authority shall apply for an emergency protection order, a child assessment order, a care order or a supervision order with respect to the child unless they are satisfied that his welfare can be satisfactorily safeguarded without their doing so.

(7) If, on the conclusion of any enquiries or review made under this section, the authority decide not to apply for an emergency protection order, a care order, a child assessment order or a supervision order they shall –

(a) consider whether it would be appropriate to review the case at a later date; and
(b) if they decide that it would be, determine the date on which that review is to begin.

(8) Where, as a result of complying with this section, a local authority conclude that they should take action to safeguard or promote the child's welfare they shall take that action (so far as it is both within their power and reasonably practicable for them to do so).

(9) Where a local authority are conducting enquiries under this section, it shall be the duty of any person mentioned in subsection (11) to assist them with those enquiries (in particular by providing relevant information and advice) if called upon by the authority to do so.

(10) Subsection (9) does not oblige any person to assist a local authority where doing so would be unreasonable in all the circumstances of the case.

(11) The persons are –

(a) any local authority;
(b) any local education authority;
(c) any local housing authority;
(d) any [Health Authority, Special Health Authority]²[, Primary Care Trust]⁴ [or National Health Service trust]¹; and
(e) any person authorised by the Secretary of State for the purposes of this section.

(12) Where a local authority are making enquiries under this section with respect to a child who appears to them to be ordinarily resident within the area of another authority, they shall consult that other authority, who may undertake the necessary enquiries in their place.

NOTES

Amendments. ¹ Words inserted: Courts and Legal Services Act 1990, s 116, Sch 16, para 20. ² Words substituted: Health Authorities Act 1995, s 2(1), Sch 1, Pt III, para 118(1), (7). ³ Words inserted: Crime and Disorder Act 1998, ss 15(4), 119, Sch 8, para 69. [4] Words inserted: Health Act 1999 (Supplementary, Consequential etc Provisions) Order 2000, SI 2000/90.

Definitions. 'Care order': s 31(11); 'child': s 105(1); 'child assessment order': s 43(2); 'emergency protection order': s 44(4); 'harm': s 31(9); 'health authority': s 105(1); 'local authority': s 105(1); 'local education authority': s 105(1); 'local housing authority': s 105(1); 'ordinary residence': s 105(6); 'police protection': s 46(2); 'significant harm': s 31(10); 'supervision order': s 31(11); 'the court': s 92(7).

48 Powers to assist in discovery of children who may be in need of emergency protection

(1) Where it appears to a court making an emergency protection order that adequate information as to the child's whereabouts –

    (a) is not available to the applicant for the order; but
    (b) is available to another person,

it may include in the order a provision requiring that other person to disclose, if asked to do so by the applicant, any information that he may have as to the child's whereabouts.

(2) No person shall be excused from complying with such a requirement on the ground that complying might incriminate him or his spouse of an offence; but a statement or admission made in complying shall not be admissible in evidence against either of them in proceedings for any offence other than perjury.

(3) An emergency protection order may authorise the applicant to enter premises specified by the order and search for the child with respect to whom the order is made.

(4) Where the court is satisfied that there is reasonable cause to believe that there may be another child on those premises with respect to whom an emergency protection order ought to be made, it may make an order authorising the applicant to search for that other child on those premises.

(5) Where –

    (a) an order has been made under subsection (4);
    (b) the child concerned has been found on the premises; and
    (c) the applicant is satisfied that the grounds for making an emergency protection order exist with respect to him,

the order shall have effect as if it were an emergency protection order.

(6) Where an order has been made under subsection (4), the applicant shall notify the court of its effect.

(7) A person shall be guilty of an offence if he intentionally obstructs any person exercising the power of entry and search under subsection (3) or (4).

(8) A person guilty of an offence under subsection (7) shall be liable on summary conviction to a fine not exceeding level 3 on the standard scale.

(9) Where, on an application made by any person for a warrant under this section, it appears to the court –

    (a) that a person attempting to exercise powers under an emergency protection order has been prevented from doing so by being refused entry to the premises concerned or access to the child concerned; or
    (b) that any such person is likely to be so prevented from exercising any such powers,

PART I

it may issue a warrant authorising any constable to assist the person mentioned in paragraph (a) or (b) in the exercise of those powers, using reasonable force if necessary.

(10) Every warrant issued under this section shall be addressed to, and executed by, a constable who shall be accompanied by the person applying for the warrant if –

    (a) that person so desires; and

    (b) the court by whom the warrant is issued does not direct otherwise.

(11) A court granting an application for a warrant under this section may direct that the constable concerned may, in executing the warrant, be accompanied by a registered medical practitioner, registered nurse or registered health visitor if he so chooses.

(12) An application for a warrant under this section shall be made in the manner and form prescribed by rules of court.

(13) Wherever it is reasonably practicable to do so, an order under subsection (4), an application for a warrant under this section and any such warrant shall name the child; and where it does not name him it shall describe him as clearly as possible.

NOTES

Definitions. 'Child': s 105(1); 'emergency protection order': s 44(4); 'the applicant': s 44(1); 'the court': s 92(7).

49 Abduction of children in care etc

(1) A person shall be guilty of an offence if, knowingly and without lawful authority or reasonable excuse, he –

    (a) takes a child to whom this section applies away from the responsible person;

    (b) keeps such a child away from the responsible person; or

    (c) induces, assists or incites such a child to run away or stay away from the responsible person.

(2) This section applies in relation to a child who is –

    (a) in care;

    (b) the subject of an emergency protection order; or

    (c) in police protection,

and in this section 'the responsible person' means any person who for the time being has care of him by virtue of the care order, the emergency protection order, or section 46, as the case may be.

(3) A person guilty of an offence under this section shall be liable on summary conviction to imprisonment for a term not exceeding six months, or to a fine not exceeding level 5 on the standard scale, or to both.

NOTES

Definitions. 'Care order': ss 31(11), 105(1); 'child': s 105(1); 'emergency protection order': s 44(4); 'police protection': s 46(2); 'responsible person': s 49(2).

50 Recovery of abducted children etc

(1) Where it appears to the court that there is reason to believe that a child to whom this section applies –

   (a) has been unlawfully taken away or is being unlawfully kept away from the responsible person;

   (b) has run away or is staying away from the responsible person; or

   (c) is missing,

the court may make an order under this section ('a recovery order').

(2) This section applies to the same children to whom section 49 applies and in this section 'the responsible person' has the same meaning as in section 49.

(3) A recovery order –

   (a) operates as a direction to any person who is in a position to do so to produce the child on request to any authorised person;

   (b) authorises the removal of the child by any authorised person;

   (c) requires any person who has information as to the child's whereabouts to disclose that information, if asked to do so, to a constable or an officer of the court;

   (d) authorises a constable to enter any premises specified in the order and search for the child, using reasonable force if necessary.

(4) The court may make a recovery order only on the application of –

   (a) any person who has parental responsibility for the child by virtue of a care order or emergency protection order; or

   (b) where the child is in police protection, the designated officer.

(5) A recovery order shall name the child and –

   (a) any person who has parental responsibility for the child by virtue of a care order or emergency protection order; or

   (b) where the child is in police protection, the designated officer.

(6) Premises may only be specified under subsection (3)(d) if it appears to the court that there are reasonable grounds for believing the child to be on them.

(7) In this section –

'an authorised person' means –

   (a) any person specified by the court;

   (b) any constable;

   (c) any person who is authorised –

      (i) after the recovery order is made; and

      (ii) by a person who has parental responsibility for the child by virtue of a care order or an emergency protection order,

   to exercise any power under a recovery order; and

'the designated officer' means the officer designated for the purposes of section 46.

(8) Where a person is authorised as mentioned in subsection (7)(c) –

   (a) the authorisation shall identify the recovery order; and

   (b) any person claiming to be so authorised shall, if asked to do so, produce some duly authenticated document showing that he is so authorised.

(9) A person shall be guilty of an offence if he intentionally obstructs an authorised person exercising the power under subsection (3)(b) to remove a child.

(10) A person guilty of an offence under this section shall be liable on summary conviction to a fine not exceeding level 3 on the standard scale.

(11) No person shall be excused from complying with any request made under subsection (3)(c) on the ground that complying with it might incriminate him or his spouse of an offence; but a statement or admission made in complying shall not be admissible in evidence against either of them in proceedings for an offence other than perjury.

(12) Where a child is made the subject of a recovery order whilst being looked after by a local authority, any reasonable expenses incurred by an authorised person in giving effect to the order shall be recoverable from the authority.

(13) A recovery order shall have effect in Scotland as if it had been made by the Court of Session and as if that court had had jurisdiction to make it.

(14) In this section 'the court', in relation to Northern Ireland, means a magistrates' court within the meaning of the Magistrates' Courts (Northern Ireland) Order 1981.

NOTES

Definitions. 'Authorised person': s 50(7); 'care order': s 31(11); 'child': s 105(1); 'child who is looked after by a local authority': s 22(1); 'emergency protection order': s 44(4); 'local authority': s 105(1); 'parental responsibility': s 3; 'police protection': s 46(2); 'recovery order': s 50(1); 'responsible person': s 49(2); 'the court': s 92(7); 'the designated officer': s 50(7).

51 Refuges for children at risk

(1) Where it is proposed to use a voluntary home or [private]² children's home to provide a refuge for children who appear to be at risk of harm, the Secretary of State may issue a certificate under this section with respect to that home.

(2) Where a local authority or voluntary organisation arrange for a foster parent to provide such a refuge, the Secretary of State may issue a certificate under this section with respect to that foster parent.

(3) In subsection (2) 'foster parent' means a person who is, or who from time to time is, a local authority foster parent or a foster parent with whom children are placed by a voluntary organisation.

(4) The Secretary of State may by regulations –

(a) make provision as to the manner in which certificates may be issued;
(b) impose requirements which must be complied with while any certificate is in force; and
(c) provide for the withdrawal of certificates in prescribed circumstances.

(5) Where a certificate is in force with respect to a home, none of the provisions mentioned in subsection (7) shall apply in relation to any person providing a refuge for any child in that home.

(6) Where a certificate is in force with respect to a foster parent, none of those provisions shall apply in relation to the provision by him of a refuge for any child in accordance with arrangements made by the local authority or voluntary organisation.

(7) The provisions are –

(a) section 49;

PART I

[(b) sections 82 (recovery of certain fugitive children) and 83 (harbouring) of the Children (Scotland) Act 1995, so far as they apply in relation to anything done in England and Wales;]¹
(c) section 32(3) of the Children and Young Persons Act 1969 (compelling, persuading, inciting or assisting any person to be absent from detention, etc), so far as it applies in relation to anything done in England and Wales;
(d) section 2 of the Child Abduction Act 1984.

NOTES
Amendments. ¹ Subsection substituted: Children (Scotland) Act 1995, s 105(4), Sch 4, para 48(1), (3). ² Word substituted: Care Standards Act 2000, s 116, Sch 4, para 14.
Definitions. 'Child': s 105(1); 'foster parent': s 51(3); 'harm': s 31(9); 'local authority': s 105(1); 'local authority foster parent': s 23(3); 'prescribed': s 105(1); 'registered children's home': s 63(8); 'voluntary home': s 60(3); 'voluntary organisation': s 105(1).

52 Rules and regulations

(1) Without prejudice to section 93 or any other power to make such rules, rules of court may be made with respect to the procedure to be followed in connection with proceedings under this Part.

(2) The rules may in particular make provision –

(a) as to the form in which any application is to be made or direction is to be given;
(b) prescribing the persons who are to be notified of –
   (i) the making, or extension, of an emergency protection order; or
   (ii) the making of an application under section 45(4) or (8) or 46(7); and
(c) as to the content of any such notification and the manner in which, and person by whom, it is to be given.

(3) The Secretary of State may by regulations provide that, where –

(a) an emergency protection order has been made with respect to a child;
(b) the applicant for the order was not the local authority within whose area the child is ordinarily resident; and
(c) that local authority are of the opinion that it would be in the child's best interests for the applicant's responsibilities under the order to be transferred to them,

that authority shall (subject to their having complied with any requirements imposed by the regulations) be treated, for the purposes of this Act, as though they and not the original applicant had applied for, and been granted, the order.

(4) Regulations made under subsection (3) may, in particular, make provision as to –

(a) the considerations to which the local authority shall have regard in forming an opinion as mentioned in subsection (3)(c); and
(b) the time at which responsibility under any emergency protection order is to be treated as having been transferred to a local authority.

NOTES
Definitions. 'Child': s 105(1); 'emergency protection order': s 44(4); 'local authority': s 105(1); 'ordinary residence': s 105(6).

PART VI
COMMUNITY HOMES

53 Provision of community homes by local authorities

(1) Every local authority shall make such arrangements as they consider appropriate for securing that homes ('community homes') are available –

    (a) for the care and accommodation of children looked after by them; and

    (b) for purposes connected with the welfare of children (whether or not looked after by them),

and may do so jointly with one or more other local authorities.

(2) In making such arrangements, a local authority shall have regard to the need for ensuring the availability of accommodation –

    (a) of different descriptions; and

    (b) which is suitable for different purposes and the requirements of different descriptions of children.

(3) A community home may be a home –

    (a) provided, [equipped, maintained and (subject to subsection (3A)) managed]¹ by a local authority; or

    (b) provided by a voluntary organisation but in respect of which a local authority and the organisation –

        (i) propose that, in accordance with an instrument of management, the [equipment, maintenance and (subject to subsection (3B)) management]¹ of the home shall be the responsibility of the local authority; or

        (ii) so propose that the management, equipment and maintenance of the home shall be the responsibility of the voluntary organisation.

[(3A) A local authority may make arrangements for the management by another person of accommodation provided by the local authority for the purpose of restricting the liberty of children.

(3B) Where a local authority are to be responsible for the management of a community home provided by a voluntary organisation, the local authority may, with the consent of the body of managers constituted by the instrument of management for the home, make arrangements for the management by another person of accommodation provided for the purpose of restricting the liberty of children.]¹

(4) Where a local authority are to be responsible for the management of a community home provided by a voluntary organisation, the authority shall designate the home as a controlled community home.

(5) Where a voluntary organisation are to be responsible for the management of a community home provided by the organisation, the local authority shall designate the home as an assisted community home.

(6) Schedule 4 shall have effect for the purpose of supplementing the provisions of this Part.

NOTES

    Amendments. ¹ Words or subsections inserted: Criminal Justice and Public Order Act 1994, s 22.

Definitions. 'Assisted community home': s 53(5); 'child': s 105(1); 'child who is looked after by the local authority': s 22(1); 'community home': s 53(1); 'controlled community home': s 53(4); 'local authority': s 105(1); 'voluntary organisation': s 105(1).

54 ...¹

NOTES

Amendments. ¹ Section repealed: Care Standards Act 2000, s 117, Sch 6.

55 Determination of disputes relating to controlled and assisted community homes

(1) Where any dispute relating to a controlled community home arises between the local authority specified in the home's instrument of management and –

(a) the voluntary organisation by which the home is provided; or
(b) any other local authority who have placed, or desire or are required to place, in the home a child who is looked after by them,

the dispute may be referred by either party to the Secretary of State for his determination.

(2) Where any dispute relating to an assisted community home arises between the voluntary organisation by which the home is provided and any local authority who have placed, or desire to place, in the home a child who is looked after by them, the dispute may be referred by either party to the Secretary of State for his determination.

(3) Where a dispute is referred to the Secretary of State under this section he may, in order to give effect to his determination of the dispute, give such directions as he thinks fit to the local authority or voluntary organisation concerned.

(4) This section applies even though the matter in dispute may be one which, under or by virtue of Part II of Schedule 4, is reserved for the decision, or is the responsibility, of –

(a) the local authority specified in the home's instrument of management; or
(b) (as the case may be) the voluntary organisation by which the home is provided.

(5) Where any trust deed relating to a controlled or assisted community home contains provision whereby a bishop or any other ecclesiastical or denominational authority has power to decide questions relating to religious instruction given in the home, no dispute which is capable of being dealt with in accordance with that provision shall be referred to the Secretary of State under this section.

(6) In this Part 'trust deed', in relation to a voluntary home, means any instrument (other than an instrument of management) regulating –

(a) the maintenance, management or conduct of the home; or
(b) the constitution of a body of managers or trustees of the home.

NOTES

Definitions. 'Assisted community home': s 53(5); 'child': s 105(1); 'child who is looked after by a local authority': s 22(1); 'community home': s 53(1); 'controlled community home': s 53(4); 'local authority': s 105(1); 'trust deed': s 55(6); 'voluntary home': s 60(3); 'voluntary organisation': s 105(1).

56 Discontinuance by voluntary organisation of controlled or assisted community home

(1) The voluntary organisation by which a controlled or assisted community home is provided shall not cease to provide the home except after giving to the Secretary of State and the local authority specified in the home's instrument of management not less than two years' notice in writing of their intention to do so.

(2) A notice under subsection (1) shall specify the date from which the voluntary organisation intend to cease to provide the home as a community home.

(3) Where such a notice is given and is not withdrawn before the date specified in it, the home's instrument of management shall cease to have effect on that date and the home shall then cease to be a controlled or assisted community home.

(4) Where a notice is given under subsection (1) and the home's managers give notice in writing to the Secretary of State that they are unable or unwilling to continue as its managers until the date specified in the subsection (1) notice, the Secretary of State may by order –

    (a) revoke the home's instrument of management; and
    (b) require the local authority who were specified in that instrument to conduct the home until –
        (i) the date specified in the subsection (1) notice; or
        (ii) such earlier date (if any) as may be specified for the purposes of this paragraph in the order,
    as if it were a community home provided by the local authority.

(5) Where the Secretary of State imposes a requirement under subsection (4)(b) –

    (a) nothing in the trust deed for the home shall affect the conduct of the home by the local authority;
    (b) the Secretary of State may by order direct that for the purposes of any provision specified in the direction and made by or under any enactment relating to community homes (other than this section) the home shall, until the date or earlier date specified as mentioned in subsection (4)(b), be treated as a controlled or assisted community home;
    (c) except in so far as the Secretary of State so directs, the home shall until that date be treated for the purposes of any such enactment as a community home provided by the local authority; and
    (d) on the date or earlier date specified as mentioned in subsection (4)(b) the home shall cease to be a community home.

NOTES
Definitions. 'Assisted community home': s 53(5); 'community home': s 53(1); 'controlled community home': s 53(4); 'local authority': s 105(1); 'trust deed': s 55(6); 'voluntary organisation': s 105(1).

57 Closure by local authority of controlled or assisted community home

(1) The local authority specified in the instrument of management for a controlled or assisted community home may give –

    (a) the Secretary of State; and
    (b) the voluntary organisation by which the home is provided,

not less than two years' notice in writing of their intention to withdraw their designation of the home as a controlled or assisted community home.

(2) A notice under subsection (1) shall specify the date ('the specified date') on which the designation is to be withdrawn.

(3) Where –

(a) a notice is given under subsection (1) in respect of a controlled or assisted community home;
(b) the home's managers give notice in writing to the Secretary of State that they are unable or unwilling to continue as managers until the specified date; and
(c) the managers' notice is not withdrawn,

the Secretary of State may by order revoke the home's instrument of management from such date earlier than the specified date as may be specified in the order.

(4) Before making an order under subsection (3), the Secretary of State shall consult the local authority and the voluntary organisation.

(5) Where a notice has been given under subsection (1) and is not withdrawn, the home's instrument of management shall cease to have effect on –

(a) the specified date; or
(b) where an earlier date has been specified under subsection (3), that earlier date,

and the home shall then cease to be a community home.

NOTES

Definitions. 'Assisted community home': s 53(5); 'controlled community home': s 53(4); 'community home': s 53(1); 'local authority': s 105(1); 'the specified date': s 57(2); 'voluntary organisation': s 105(1).

58 Financial provisions applicable on cessation of controlled or assisted community home or disposal etc of premises

(1) Where –

(a) the instrument of management for a controlled or assisted community home is revoked or otherwise ceases to have effect under section ...[3] 56(3) or (4)(a) or 57(3) or (5); or
(b) any premises used for the purposes of such a home are (at any time after 13th January 1987) disposed of, or put to use otherwise than for those purposes,

the proprietor shall become liable to pay compensation ('the appropriate compensation') in accordance with this section.

(2) Where the instrument of management in force at the relevant time relates –

(a) to a controlled community home; or
(b) to an assisted community home which, at any time before the instrument came into force, was a controlled community home,

the appropriate compensation is a sum equal to that part of the value of any premises which is attributable to expenditure incurred in relation to the premises, while the home was a controlled community home, by the authority who were then the responsible authority.

(3) Where the instrument of management in force at the relevant time relates –

(a) to an assisted community home; or

(b) to a controlled community home which, at any time before the instrument came into force, was an assisted community home,

the appropriate compensation is a sum equal to that part of the value of the premises which is attributable to the expenditure of money provided by way of grant under section 82, section 65 of the Children and Young Persons Act 1969 or section 82 of the Child Care Act 1980.

(4) Where the home is, at the relevant time, conducted in premises which formerly were used as an approved school or were an approved probation hostel or home, the appropriate compensation is a sum equal to that part of the value of the premises which is attributable to the expenditure –

(a) of sums paid towards the expenses of the managers of an approved school under section 104 of the Children and Young Persons Act 1933; ... [2]

(b) of sums paid under section 51(3)(c) of the Powers of Criminal Courts Act 1973 [or section 20(1)(c) of the Probation Service Act 1993][1] in relation to expenditure on approved probation hostels or homes [; or

(c) of sums paid under section 3, 5 or 9 of the Criminal Justice and Court Services Act 2000 in relation to expenditure on approved premises (within the meaning of Part I of that Act).][2]

(5) The appropriate compensation shall be paid –

(a) in the case of compensation payable under subsection (2), to the authority who were the responsible authority at the relevant time; and

(b) in any other case, to the Secretary of State.

(6) In this section –

'disposal' includes the grant of a tenancy and any other conveyance, assignment, transfer, grant, variation or extinguishment of an interest in or right over land, whether made by instrument or otherwise;

'premises' means any premises or part of premises (including land) used for the purposes of the home and belonging to the proprietor;

'the proprietor' means –

(a) the voluntary organisation by which the home is, at the relevant time, provided; or

(b) if the premises are not, at the relevant time, vested in that organisation, the persons in whom they are vested;

'the relevant time' means the time immediately before the liability to pay arises under subsection (1); and

'the responsible authority' means the local authority specified in the instrument of management in question.

(7) For the purposes of this section an event of a kind mentioned in subsection (1)(b) shall be taken to have occurred –

(a) in the case of a disposal, on the date on which the disposal was completed or, in the case of a disposal which is effected by a series of transactions, the date on which the last of those transactions was completed;

(b) in the case of premises which are put to different use, on the date on which they first begin to be put to their new use.

(8) The amount of any sum payable under this section shall be determined in accordance with such arrangements –

(a) as may be agreed between the voluntary organisation by which the home is, at the relevant time, provided and the responsible authority or (as the case may be) the Secretary of State; or

(b) in default of agreement, as may be determined by the Secretary of State.

(9) With the agreement of the responsible authority or (as the case may be) the Secretary of State, the liability to pay any sum under this section may be discharged, in whole or in part, by the transfer of any premises.

(10) This section has effect regardless of –

(a) anything in any trust deed for a controlled or assisted community home;
(b) the provisions of any enactment or instrument governing the disposition of the property of a voluntary organisation.

NOTES

Amendments. ¹ Words inserted: Probation Service Act 1993, s 32, Sch 3, para 9(2). ² Word omitted or words inserted: Criminal Justice and Court Services Act 2000, ss 74, 75, Sch 7, paras 87, 93, Sch 8. ³ Word repealed: Care Standards Act 2000, s 117, Sch 6.

Definitions. 'Appropriate compensation': s 58(1)–(4); 'assisted community home': s 53(5); 'community home': s 53(1); 'controlled community home': s 53(4); 'disposal': s 58(6); 'local authority': s 105(1); 'premises': s 58(6); 'the proprietor': s 58(6); 'the relevant time': s 58(6); 'the responsible authority': s 58(6); 'trust deed': s 55(6); 'voluntary organisation': s 105(1).

PART VII
VOLUNTARY HOMES AND VOLUNTARY ORGANISATIONS

59 Provision of accommodation by voluntary organisations

(1) Where a voluntary organisation provide accommodation for a child, they shall do so by –

(a) placing him (subject to subsection (2)) with –
    (i) a family;
    (ii) a relative of his; or
    (iii) any other suitable person,
    on such terms as to payment by the organisation and otherwise as the organisation may determine;
[(aa) maintaining him in an appropriate children's home;
(b)–(e) ...]¹
    (f) making such other arrangements (subject to subsection (3)) as seem appropriate to them.

[(1A) Where under subsection (1)(aa) a local authority maintains a child in a home provided, equipped and maintained by the Secretary of State under section 82(5), it shall do so on such terms as the Secretary of State may from time to time determine.]¹

(2) The Secretary of State may make regulations as to the placing of children with foster parents by voluntary organisations and the regulations may, in particular, make provision which (with any necessary modifications) is similar to the provision that may be made under section 23(2)(f).

(3) The Secretary of State may make regulations as to the arrangements which may be made under subsection (1)(f) and the regulations may in particular make provision which (with any necessary modifications) is similar to the provision that may be made under section 23(2)(f).

(4) The Secretary of State may make regulations requiring any voluntary organisation who are providing accommodation for a child –

(a) to review his case; and
(b) to consider any representations (including any complaint) made to them by any person falling within a prescribed class of person,

in accordance with the provisions of the regulations.

(5) Regulations under subsection (4) may in particular make provision which (with any necessary modifications) is similar to the provision that may be made under section 26.

(6) Regulations under subsections (2) to (4) may provide that any person who, without reasonable excuse, contravenes or fails to comply with a regulation shall be guilty of an offence and liable on summary conviction to a fine not exceeding level 4 on the standard scale.

NOTES

Amendments. [1] Paragraph (aa) substituted for paras (b)–(e) and subsection inserted: Care Standards Act 2000, s 116, Sch 4, para 14(8).

Definitions. 'Child': s 105(1); 'community home': s 53(1); 'registered children's home': s 63(8); 'relative': s 105(1); 'voluntary home': s 60(2); 'voluntary organisation': s 105(1).

60 [Voluntary homes][1]

(1), (2) ...[2]

[(3) In this Act 'voluntary home' means a children's home which is carried on by a voluntary organisation but does not include a community home.][1]

(4) Schedule 5 shall have effect for the purpose of supplementing the provisions of this Part.

NOTES

Amendments. [1] Section heading and subsection substituted: Care Standards Act 2000, s 116, Sch 4, para 14(9). [2] Subsections repealed: Care Standards Act 2000, s 117, Sch 6.

Definitions. 'Child': s 105(1); 'community home': s 53(1); 'health service hospital': s 105(1); 'mental nursing home': s 105(1); 'nursing home': s 105(1); 'residential care home': s 105(1); 'school': s 105(1); 'voluntary home': s 60(3); 'voluntary organisation': s 105(1).

61 Duties of voluntary organisations

(1) Where a child is accommodated by or on behalf of a voluntary organisation, it shall be the duty of the organisation –

(a) to safeguard and promote his welfare;
(b) to make such use of the services and facilities available for children cared for by their own parents as appears to the organisation reasonable in his case; and
(c) to advise, assist and befriend him with a view to promoting his welfare when he ceases to be so accommodated.

(2) Before making any decision with respect to any such child the organisation shall, so far as is reasonably practicable, ascertain the wishes and feelings of –

(a) the child;
(b) his parents;
(c) any person who is not a parent of his but who has parental responsibility for him; and

---

(d) any other person whose wishes and feelings the organisation consider to be relevant,

regarding the matter to be decided.

(3) In making any such decision the organisation shall give due consideration –

    (a) having regard to the child's age and understanding, to such wishes and feelings of his as they have been able to ascertain;

    (b) to such other wishes and feelings mentioned in subsection (2) as they have been able to ascertain; and

    (c) to the child's religious persuasion, racial origin and cultural and linguistic background.

NOTES

Definitions. 'Child': s 105(1); 'parental responsibility': s 3; 'voluntary organisation': s 105(1).

62 Duties of local authorities

(1) Every local authority shall satisfy themselves that any voluntary organisation providing accommodation –

    (a) within the authority's area for any child; or

    (b) outside that area for any child on behalf of the authority,

are satisfactorily safeguarding and promoting the welfare of the children so provided with accommodation.

(2) Every local authority shall arrange for children who are accommodated within their area by or on behalf of voluntary organisations to be visited, from time to time, in the interests of their welfare.

(3) The Secretary of State may make regulations –

    (a) requiring every child who is accommodated within a local authority's area, by or on behalf of a voluntary organisation, to be visited by an officer of the authority –

        (i) in prescribed circumstances; and

        (ii) on specified occasions or within specified periods; and

    (b) imposing requirements which must be met by any local authority, or officer of a local authority, carrying out functions under this section.

(4) Subsection (2) does not apply in relation to community homes.

(5) Where a local authority are not satisfied that the welfare of any child who is accommodated by or on behalf of a voluntary organisation is being satisfactorily safeguarded or promoted they shall –

    (a) unless they consider that it would not be in the best interests of the child, take such steps as are reasonably practicable to secure that the care and accommodation of the child is undertaken by –

        (i) a parent of his;

        (ii) any person who is not a parent of his but who has parental responsibility for him; or

        (iii) a relative of his; and

    (b) consider the extent to which (if at all) they should exercise any of their functions with respect to the child.

(6) Any person authorised by a local authority may, for the purpose of enabling the authority to discharge their duties under this section –

(a) enter, at any reasonable time, and inspect any premises in which children are being accommodated as mentioned in subsection (1) or (2);

(b) inspect any children there;

(c) require any person to furnish him with such records of a kind required to be kept by regulations made under [section 22 of the Care Standards Act 2000][1] (in whatever form they are held), or allow him to inspect such records, as he may at any time direct.

(7) Any person exercising the power conferred by subsection (6) shall, if asked to do so, produce some duly authenticated document showing his authority to do so.

(8) Any person authorised to exercise the power to inspect records conferred by subsection (6) –

(a) shall be entitled at any reasonable time to have access to, and inspect and check the operation of, any computer and any associated apparatus or material which is or has been in use in connection with the records in question; and

(b) may require –
   (i) the person by whom or on whose behalf the computer is or has been so used; or
   (ii) any person having charge of, or otherwise concerned with the operation of, the computer, apparatus or material,
   to afford him such assistance as he may reasonably require.

(9) Any person who intentionally obstructs another in the exercise of any power conferred by subsection (6) or (8) shall be guilty of an offence and liable on summary conviction to a fine not exceeding level 3 on the standard scale.

[(10) This section does not apply in relation to any voluntary organisation which is an institution within the further education sector, as defined in section 91 of the Further and Higher Education Act 1992, or a school.][2]

NOTES

Amendments. [1] Words substituted: Care Standards Act 2000, s 116, Sch 4, para 14(10). [2] Subsection inserted: Care Standards Act 2000, s 105(5).

Definitions. 'Child': s 105(1); 'community home': s 53(1); 'functions', 'local authority': s 105(1); 'parental responsibility': s 3; 'prescribed', 'relative', 'voluntary organisation': s 105(1).

PART VIII
REGISTERED CHILDREN'S HOMES

63 [Private children's homes etc][2]

(1)–(10) ...[1]

(11) Schedule 6 shall have effect with respect to [private][2] children's homes.

(12) Schedule 7 shall have effect for the purpose of setting out the circumstances in which a person may foster more than three children without being treated [, for the purposes of this Act and the Care Standards Act 2000,][2] as carrying on a children's home.

NOTES

Amendments. [1] Subsections repealed: Care Standards Act 2000, s 117, Sch 6. [2] Section heading substituted and words inserted: Care Standards Act 2000, s 116, Sch 4, para 14(1), (11).

Definitions. 'A privately fostered child': s 66(1); 'child': s 105(1); 'children's home': s 63(3); 'community home': s 53(1); 'health service hospital': s 105(1); 'home': s 63(9); 'independent school', 'mental nursing home', 'nursing home': s 105(1); 'parental responsibility': s 3; 'registered children's home': s 63(8); 'relative', 'residential care home', 'school': s 105(1); 'voluntary home': s 60(3); 'voluntary organisation': s 105(1).

64 Welfare of children in children's homes

(1) Where a child is accommodated in a [private][1] children's home, it shall be the duty of the person carrying on the home to –

    (a) safeguard and promote the child's welfare;

    (b) make such use of the services and facilities available for children cared for by their own parents as appears to that person reasonable in the case of the child; and

    (c) advise, assist and befriend him with a view to promoting his welfare when he ceases to be so accommodated.

(2) Before making any decision with respect to any such child the person carrying on the home shall, so far as is reasonably practicable, ascertain the wishes and feelings of –

    (a) the child;

    (b) his parents;

    (c) any other person who is not a parent of his but who has parental responsibility for him; and

    (d) any person whose wishes and feelings the person carrying on the home considers to be relevant,

regarding the matter to be decided.

(3) In making any such decision the person concerned shall give due consideration –

    (a) having regard to the child's age and understanding, to such wishes and feelings of his as he has been able to ascertain;

    (b) to such other wishes and feelings mentioned in subsection (2) as he has been able to ascertain; and

    (c) to the child's religious persuasion, racial origin and cultural and linguistic background.

(4) Section 62, except subsection (4), shall apply in relation to any person who is carrying on a [private][1] children's home as it applies in relation to any voluntary organisation.

NOTES

Amendments. [1] Word inserted: Care Standards Act 2000, s 116, Sch 4, para 14(12).

Definitions. 'Child': s 105(1); 'children's home': s 63(3); 'parental responsibility': s 3; 'voluntary organisation': s 105(1).

65 Persons disqualified from carrying on, or being employed in, children's homes

(1) A person who is disqualified (under section 68) from fostering a child privately shall not carry on, or be otherwise concerned in the management of, or have any financial interest in, a children's home unless he has –

    (a) disclosed to [the appropriate authority]¹ the fact that he is so disqualified; and

    (b) obtained [its]¹ written consent.

(2) No person shall employ a person who is so disqualified in a children's home unless he has –

    (a) disclosed to [the appropriate authority]¹ the fact that that person is so disqualified; and

    (b) obtained [its]¹ written consent.

(3) Where [the appropriate authority refuses to give its consent under this section, it]¹ shall inform the applicant by a written notice which states –

    (a) the reason for the refusal;

    [(b) the applicant's right to appeal under section 65A against the refusal to the Tribunal established under section 9 of the Protection of Children Act 1999]¹; and

    (c) the time within which he may do so.

(4) Any person who contravenes subsection (1) or (2) shall be guilty of an offence and liable on summary conviction to imprisonment for a term not exceeding six months or to a fine not exceeding level 5 on the standard scale or to both.

(5) Where a person contravenes subsection (2) he shall not be guilty of an offence if he proves that he did not know, and had no reasonable grounds for believing, that the person whom he was employing was disqualified under section 68.

[(6) In this section and section 65A 'appropriate authority' means–

    (a) in relation to England, the National Care Standards Commission; and

    (b) in relation to Wales, the National Assembly for Wales.]¹

NOTES

Amendments. ¹ Words substituted and subsection inserted: Care Standards Act 2000, s 116, Sch 4, para 14(13).

Definitions. 'Child': s 105(1); 'children's home': s 63(3); 'responsible authority': Sch 6, para 3(1); 'to foster a child privately': s 66(1)(b).

[65A Appeal against refusal of authority to give consent under section 65

(1) An appeal against a decision of an appropriate authority under section 65 shall lie to the Tribunal established under section 9 of the Protection of Children Act 1999.

(2) On an appeal the Tribunal may confirm the authority's decision or direct it to give the consent in question.]¹

NOTES

Amendments. ¹ Section inserted: Care Standards Act 2000, s 116, Sch 4, para 14(14).

PART IX
PRIVATE ARRANGEMENTS FOR FOSTERING CHILDREN

66 Privately fostered children

(1) In this Part –

    (a) 'a privately fostered child' means a child who is under the age of sixteen and who is cared for, and provided with accommodation [in their own home]¹ by, someone other than –

        (i) a parent of his;

        (ii) a person who is not a parent of his but who has parental responsibility for him; or

        (iii) a relative of his; and

    (b) 'to foster a child privately' means to look after the child in circumstances in which he is a privately fostered child as defined by this section.

(2) A child is not a privately fostered child if the person caring for and accommodating him –

    (a) has done so for a period of less than 28 days; and

    (b) does not intend to do so for any longer period.

(3) Subsection (1) is subject to –

    (a) the provisions of section 63; and

    (b) the exceptions made by paragraphs 1 to 5 of Schedule 8.

(4) In the case of a child who is disabled, subsection (1)(a) shall have effect as if for 'sixteen' there were substituted 'eighteen'.

[(4A) The Secretary of State may by regulations make provision as to the circumstances in which a person who provides accommodation to a child is, or is not, to be treated as providing him with accommodation in the person's own home.]¹

(5) Schedule 8 shall have effect for the purposes of supplementing the provision made by this Part.

NOTES

Amendments. ¹ Words and subsection inserted: Care Standards Act 2000, s 116, Sch 4, para 14(1), (15).

Definitions. 'Child': s 105(1); 'disabled': s 17(11); 'parental responsibility': s 3; 'privately fostered child': s 66(1); 'relative': s 105(1); 'to foster a child privately': s 66(1).

67 Welfare of privately fostered children

(1) It shall be the duty of every local authority to satisfy themselves that the welfare of children who are privately fostered within their area is being satisfactorily safeguarded and promoted and to secure that such advice is given to those caring for them as appears to the authority to be needed.

(2) The Secretary of State may make regulations –

    (a) requiring every child who is privately fostered within a local authority's area to be visited by an officer of the authority –

        (i) in prescribed circumstances; and

        (ii) on specified occasions or within specified periods; and

(b) imposing requirements which are to be met by any local authority, or officer of a local authority, in carrying out functions under this section.

(3) Where any person who is authorised by a local authority to visit privately fostered children has reasonable cause to believe that –

(a) any privately fostered child is being accommodated in premises within the authority's area; or
(b) it is proposed to accommodate any such child in any such premises,

he may at any reasonable time inspect those premises and any children there.

(4) Any person exercising the power under subsection (3) shall, if so required, produce some duly authenticated document showing his authority to do so.

(5) Where a local authority are not satisfied that the welfare of any child who is privately fostered within their area is being satisfactorily safeguarded or promoted they shall –

(a) unless they consider that it would not be in the best interests of the child, take such steps as are reasonably practicable to secure that the care and accommodation of the child is undertaken by –
    (i) a parent of his;
    (ii) any person who is not a parent of his but who has parental responsibility for him; or
    (iii) a relative of his; and
(b) consider the extent to which (if at all) they should exercise any of their functions under this Act with respect to the child.

NOTES

Definitions. 'Child': s 105(1); 'functions': s 105(1); 'local authority': s 105(1); 'parental responsibility': s 3; 'prescribed': s 105(1); 'privately fostered child': s 66(1); 'relative': s 105(1).

68 Persons disqualified from being private foster parents

(1) Unless he has disclosed the fact to the appropriate local authority and obtained their written consent, a person shall not foster a child privately if he is disqualified from doing so by regulations made by the Secretary of State for the purposes of this section.

(2) The regulations may, in particular, provide for a person to be so disqualified where –

(a) an order of a kind specified in the regulations has been made at any time with respect to him;
(b) an order of a kind so specified has been made at any time with respect to any child who has been in his care;
(c) a requirement of a kind so specified has been imposed at any time with respect to any such child, under or by virtue of any enactment;
(d) he has been convicted of any offence of a kind so specified, or [a probation order has been made in respect of him or he has been][1] discharged absolutely or conditionally for any such offence;
(e) a prohibition has been imposed on him at any time under section 69 or under any other specified enactment;
(f) his rights and powers with respect to a child have at any time been vested in a specified authority under a specified enactment.

(3) Unless he has disclosed the fact to the appropriate local authority and obtained their written consent, a person shall not foster a child privately if –

(a) he lives in the same household as a person who is himself prevented from fostering a child by subsection (1); or

(b) he lives in a household at which any such person is employed.

(4) Where an authority refuse to give their consent under this section, they shall inform the applicant by a written notice which states –

(a) the reason for the refusal;

(b) the applicant's right under paragraph 8 of Schedule 8 to appeal against the refusal; and

(c) the time within which he may do so.

(5) In this section –

'the appropriate authority' means the local authority within whose area it is proposed to foster the child in question; and

'enactment' means any enactment having effect, at any time, in any part of the United Kingdom.

NOTES

Amendments. [1] Words substituted: Criminal Justice and Court Services Act 2000, s 74, Sch 7, paras 87, 94.

Definitions. 'Appropriate authority': s 68(5); 'child': s 105(1); 'enactment': s 68(5); 'local authority': s 105(1); 'to foster a child privately': s 66(1).

69 Power to prohibit private fostering

(1) This section applies where a person –

(a) proposes to foster a child privately; or

(b) is fostering a child privately.

(2) Where the local authority for the area within which the child is proposed to be, or is being, fostered are of the opinion that –

(a) he is not a suitable person to foster a child;

(b) the premises in which the child will be, or is being, accommodated are not suitable; or

(c) it would be prejudicial to the welfare of the child for him to be, or continue to be, accommodated by that person in those premises,

the authority may impose a prohibition on him under subsection (3).

(3) A prohibition imposed on any person under this subsection may prohibit him from fostering privately –

(a) any child in any premises within the area of the local authority; or

(b) any child in premises specified in the prohibition;

(c) a child identified in the prohibition, in premises specified in the prohibition.

(4) A local authority who have imposed a prohibition on any person under subsection (3) may, if they think fit, cancel the prohibition –

(a) of their own motion; or

(b) on an application made by that person,

if they are satisfied that the prohibition is no longer justified.

(5) Where a local authority impose a requirement on any person under paragraph 6 of Schedule 8, they may also impose a prohibition on him under subsection (3).

(6) Any prohibition imposed by virtue of subsection (5) shall not have effect unless –

(a) the time specified for compliance with the requirement has expired; and
(b) the requirement has not been complied with.

(7) A prohibition imposed under this section shall be imposed by notice in writing addressed to the person on whom it is imposed and informing him of –

(a) the reason for imposing the prohibition;
(b) his right under paragraph 8 of Schedule 8 to appeal against the prohibition; and
(c) the time within which he may do so.

NOTES
Definitions. 'Child': s 105(1); 'local authority': s 105(1); 'to foster a child privately': s 66(1).

70 Offences

(1) A person shall be guilty of an offence if –

(a) being required, under any provision made by or under this Part, to give any notice or information –
    (i) he fails without reasonable excuse to give the notice within the time specified in that provision; or
    (ii) he fails without reasonable excuse to give the information within a reasonable time; or
    (iii) he makes, or causes or procures another person to make, any statement in the notice or information which he knows to be false or misleading in a material particular;
(b) he refuses to allow a privately fostered child to be visited by a duly authorised officer of a local authority;
(c) he intentionally obstructs another in the exercise of the power conferred by section 67(3);
(d) he contravenes section 68;
(e) he fails without reasonable excuse to comply with any requirement imposed by a local authority under this Part;
(f) he accommodates a privately fostered child in any premises in contravention of a prohibition imposed by a local authority under this Part;
(g) he knowingly causes to be published, or publishes, an advertisement which he knows contravenes paragraph 10 of Schedule 8.

(2) Where a person contravenes section 68(3), he shall not be guilty of an offence under this section if he proves that he did not know, and had no reasonable ground for believing, that any person to whom section 68(1) applied was living or employed in the premises in question.

(3) A person guilty of an offence under subsection (1)(a) shall be liable on summary conviction to a fine not exceeding level 5 on the standard scale.

(4) A person guilty of an offence under subsection (1)(b), (c) or (g) shall be liable on summary conviction to a fine not exceeding level 3 on the standard scale.

(5) A person guilty of an offence under subsection (1)(d) or (f) shall be liable on summary conviction to imprisonment for a term not exceeding six months, or to a fine not exceeding level 5 on the standard scale, or to both.

(6) A person guilty of an offence under subsection (1)(e) shall be liable on summary conviction to a fine not exceeding level 4 on the standard scale.

PART I

(7) If any person who is required, under any provision of this Part, to give a notice fails to give the notice within the time specified in that provision, proceedings for the offence may be brought at any time within six months from the date when evidence of the offence came to the knowledge of the local authority.

(8) Subsection (7) is not affected by anything in section 127(1) of the Magistrates' Courts Act 1980 (time limit for proceedings).

NOTES

Definitions. 'Child': s 105(1); 'local authority': s 105(1); 'privately fostered child': s 66(1).

PART X
CHILD MINDING AND DAY CARE FOR YOUNG CHILDREN

...[1]

NOTES

Amendments. [1] Part X repealed in relation to England and Wales: Care Standards Act 2000, s 79(5).

[PART XA
CHILD MINDING AND DAY CARE FOR CHILDREN IN
ENGLAND AND WALES

Introductory

79A Child minders and day care providers

(1) This section and section 79B apply for the purposes of this Part.

(2) 'Act as a child minder' means (subject to the following subsections) look after one or more children under the age of eight on domestic premises for reward; and 'child minding' shall be interpreted accordingly.

(3) A person who –

(a) is the parent, or a relative, of a child;
(b) has parental responsibility for a child;
(c) is a local authority foster parent in relation to a child;
(d) is a foster parent with whom a child has been placed by a voluntary organisation; or
(e) fosters a child privately,

does not act as a child minder when looking after that child.

(4) Where a person –

(a) looks after a child for the parents ('P1'), or
(b) in addition to that work, looks after another child for different parents ('P2'),

and the work consists (in a case within paragraph (a)) of looking after the child wholly or mainly in P1's home or (in a case within paragraph (b)) of looking after the children wholly or mainly in P1's home or P2's home or both, the work is not to be treated as child minding.

(5) In subsection (4), 'parent', in relation to a child, includes –

    (a) a person who is not a parent of the child but who has parental responsibility for the child;

    (b) a person who is a relative of the child.

(6) 'Day care' means care provided at any time for children under the age of eight on premises other than domestic premises.

(7) This Part does not apply in relation to a person who acts as a child minder, or provides day care on any premises, unless the period, or the total of the periods, in any day which he spends looking after children or (as the case may be) during which the children are looked after on the premises exceeds two hours.

(8) In determining whether a person is required to register under this Part for child minding, any day on which he does not act as a child minder at any time between 2 am and 6 pm is to be disregarded.

79B Other definitions, etc

(1) The registration authority in relation to England is Her Majesty's Chief Inspector of Schools in England (referred to in this Part as the Chief Inspector) and references to the Chief Inspector's area are references to England.

(2) The registration authority in relation to Wales is the National Assembly for Wales (referred to in this Act as 'the Assembly').

(3) A person is qualified for registration for child minding if –

    (a) he, and every other person looking after children on any premises on which he is or is likely to be child minding, is suitable to look after children under the age of eight;

    (b) every person living or employed on the premises in question is suitable to be in regular contact with children under the age of eight;

    (c) the premises in question are suitable to be used for looking after children under the age of eight, having regard to their condition and the condition and appropriateness of any equipment on the premises and to any other factor connected with the situation, construction or size of the premises; and

    (d) he is complying with regulations under section 79C and with any conditions imposed by the registration authority.

(4) A person is qualified for registration for providing day care on particular premises if –

    (a) every person looking after children on the premises is suitable to look after children under the age of eight;

    (b) every person living or working on the premises is suitable to be in regular contact with children under the age of eight;

    (c) the premises are suitable to be used for looking after children under the age of eight, having regard to their condition and the condition and appropriateness of any equipment on the premises and to any other factor connected with the situation, construction or size of the premises; and

    (d) he is complying with regulations under section 79C and with any conditions imposed by the registration authority.

(5) For the purposes of subsection (4)(b) a person is not treated as working on the premises in question if –

(a) none of his work is done in the part of the premises in which children are looked after; or

(b) he does not work on the premises at times when children are looked after there.

[(5A) Where, for the purposes of determining a person's qualification for registration under this Part –

(a) the registration authority requests any person ('A') to consent to the disclosure to the authority by another person ('B') of any information relating to A which is held by B and is of a prescribed description, and

(b) A does not give his consent (or withdraws it after having given it),

the registration authority may, if regulations so provide and it thinks it appropriate to do so, regard A as not suitable to look after children under the age of eight, or not suitable to be in regular contact with such children.]¹

(6) 'Domestic premises' means any premises which are wholly or mainly used as a private dwelling and 'premises' includes any area and any vehicle.

(7) 'Regulations' means –

(a) in relation to England, regulations made by the Secretary of State;

(b) in relation to Wales, regulations made by the Assembly.

(8) 'Tribunal' means the Tribunal established by section 9 of the Protection of Children Act 1999.

(9) Schedule 9A (which supplements the provisions of this Part) shall have effect.

NOTES

Amendments. ¹ Subsection inserted: Education Act 2002, s 152, Sch 13, para 1.

Regulations

79C Regulations etc governing child minders and day care providers

(1) The Secretary of State may, after consulting the Chief Inspector and any other person he considers appropriate, make regulations governing the activities of registered persons who act as child minders, or provide day care, on premises in England.

(2) The Assembly may make regulations governing the activities of registered persons who act as child minders, or provide day care, on premises in Wales.

(3) The regulations under this section may deal with the following matters (among others) –

(a) the welfare and development of the children concerned;

(b) suitability to look after, or be in regular contact with, children under the age of eight;

(c) qualifications and training;

(d) the maximum number of children who may be looked after and the number of persons required to assist in looking after them;

(e) the maintenance, safety and suitability of premises and equipment;

(f) the keeping of records;

(g) the provision of information.

(4) In relation to activities on premises in England, the power to make regulations under this section may be exercised so as to confer powers or impose duties on the Chief Inspector in the exercise of his functions under this Part.

(5) In particular they may be exercised so as to require or authorise the Chief Inspector, in exercising those functions, to have regard to or meet factors, standards and other matters prescribed by or referred to in the regulations.

(6) If the regulations require any person (other than the registration authority) to have regard to or meet factors, standards and other matters prescribed by or referred to in the regulations, they may also provide for any allegation that the person has failed to do so to be taken into account –

    (a) by the registration authority in the exercise of its functions under this Part, or
    (b) in any proceedings under this Part.

(7) Regulations may provide –

    (a) that a registered person who without reasonable excuse contravenes, or otherwise fails to comply with, any requirement of the regulations shall be guilty of an offence; and
    (b) that a person guilty of the offence shall be liable on summary conviction to a fine not exceeding level 5 on the standard scale.

Registration

79D Requirement to register

(1) No person shall –

    (a) act as a child minder in England unless he is registered under this Part for child minding by the Chief Inspector; or
    (b) act as a child minder in Wales unless he is registered under this Part for child minding by the Assembly.

(2) Where it appears to the registration authority that a person has contravened subsection (1), the authority may serve a notice ('an enforcement notice') on him.

(3) An enforcement notice shall have effect for a period of one year beginning with the date on which it is served.

(4) If a person in respect of whom an enforcement notice has effect contravenes subsection (1) without reasonable excuse (whether the contravention occurs in England or Wales), he shall be guilty of an offence.

(5) No person shall provide day care on any premises unless he is registered under this Part for providing day care on those premises by the registration authority.

(6) If any person contravenes subsection (5) without reasonable excuse, he shall be guilty of an offence.

(7) A person guilty of an offence under this section shall be liable on summary conviction to a fine not exceeding level 5 on the standard scale.

79E Applications for registration

(1) A person who wishes to be registered under this Part shall make an application to the registration authority.

(2) The application shall –

(a) give prescribed information about prescribed matters;

(b) give any other information which the registration authority reasonably requires the applicant to give.

(3) Where a person provides, or proposes to provide, day care on different premises, he shall make a separate application in respect of each of them.

(4) Where the registration authority has sent the applicant notice under section 79L(1) of its intention to refuse an application under this section, the application may not be withdrawn without the consent of the authority.

(5) A person who, in an application under this section, knowingly makes a statement which is false or misleading in a material particular shall be guilty of an offence and liable, on summary conviction, to a fine not exceeding level 5 on the standard scale.

79F Grant or refusal of registration

(1) If, on an application by a person for registration for child minding –

(a) the registration authority is of the opinion that the applicant is, and will continue to be, qualified for registration for child minding (so far as the conditions of section 79B(3) are applicable); and

(b) the applicant pays the prescribed fee,

the authority shall grant the application; otherwise, it shall refuse it.

(2) If, on an application by any person for registration for providing day care on any premises –

(a) the registration authority is of the opinion that the applicant is, and will continue to be, qualified for registration for providing day care on those premises (so far as the conditions of section 79B(4) are applicable); and

(b) the applicant pays the prescribed fee,

the authority shall grant the application; otherwise, it shall refuse it.

(3) An application may, as well as being granted subject to any conditions the authority thinks necessary or expedient for the purpose of giving effect to regulations under section 79C, be granted subject to any other conditions the authority thinks fit to impose.

(4) The registration authority may as it thinks fit vary or remove any condition to which the registration is subject or impose a new condition.

(5) Any register kept by a registration authority of persons who act as child minders or provide day care shall be open to inspection by any person at all reasonable times.

(6) A registered person who without reasonable excuse contravenes, or otherwise fails to comply with, any condition imposed on his registration shall be guilty of an offence.

(7) A person guilty of an offence under subsection (6) shall be liable on summary conviction to a fine not exceeding level 5 on the standard scale.

79G Cancellation of registration

(1) The registration authority may cancel the registration of any person if –

    (a) in the case of a person registered for child minding, the authority is of the opinion that the person has ceased or will cease to be qualified for registration for child minding;
    (b) in the case of a person registered for providing day care on any premises, the authority is of the opinion that the person has ceased or will cease to be qualified for registration for providing day care on those premises,

or if an annual fee which is due from the person has not been paid.

(2) Where a requirement to make any changes or additions to any services, equipment or premises has been imposed on a registered person under section 79F(3), his registration shall not be cancelled on the ground of any defect or insufficiency in the services, equipment or premises if –

    (a) the time set for complying with the requirements has not expired; and
    (b) it is shown that the defect or insufficiency is due to the changes or additions not having been made.

(3) Any cancellation under this section must be in writing.

79H Suspension of registration

(1) Regulations may provide for the registration of any person for acting as a child minder or providing day care to be suspended for a prescribed period by the registration authority in prescribed circumstances.

(2) Any regulations made under this section shall include provision conferring on the person concerned a right of appeal to the Tribunal against suspension.

[(3) A person registered under this Part for child minding by the Chief Inspector shall not act as a child minder in England at a time when that registration is suspended in accordance with regulations under this section.

(4) A person registered under this Part for child minding by the Assembly shall not act as a child minder in Wales at a time when that registration is so suspended.

(5) A person registered under this Part for providing day care on any premises shall not provide day care on those premises at any time when that registration is so suspended.

(6) If any person contravenes subsection (3), (4) or (5) without reasonable excuse, he shall be guilty of an offence and liable on summary conviction to a fine not exceeding level 5 on the standard scale.][1]

NOTES
   Amendments. [1] Subsections inserted: Education Act 2002, s 152, Sch 13, para 2.

79J Resignation of registration

(1) A person who is registered for acting as a child minder or providing day care may by notice in writing to the registration authority resign his registration.

(2) But a person may not give a notice under subsection (1) –

(a) if the registration authority has sent him a notice under section 79L(1) of its intention to cancel the registration, unless the authority has decided not to take that step; or

(b) if the registration authority has sent him a notice under section 79L(5) of its decision to cancel the registration and the time within which an appeal may be brought has not expired or, if an appeal has been brought, it has not been determined.

79K Protection of children in an emergency

(1) If, in the case of any person registered for acting as a child minder or providing day care –

    (a) the registration authority applies to a justice of the peace for an order –

        (i) cancelling the registration;

        (ii) varying or removing any condition to which the registration is subject; or

        (iii) imposing a new condition; and

    (b) it appears to the justice that a child who is being, or may be, looked after by that person, or (as the case may be) in accordance with the provision for day care made by that person, is suffering, or is likely to suffer, significant harm,

the justice may make the order.

(2) The cancellation, variation, removal or imposition shall have effect from the time when the order is made.

(3) An application under subsection (1) may be made without notice.

(4) An order under subsection (1) shall be made in writing.

(5) Where an order is made under this section, the registration authority shall serve on the registered person, as soon as is reasonably practicable after the making of the order –

    (a) a copy of the order;

    (b) a copy of any written statement of the authority's reasons for making the application for the order which supported that application; and

    (c) notice of any right of appeal conferred by section 79M.

(6) Where an order has been so made, the registration authority shall, as soon as is reasonably practicable after the making of the order, notify the local authority in whose area the person concerned acts or acted as a child minder, or provides or provided day care, of the making of the order.

79L Notice of intention to take steps

(1) Not less than 14 days before –

    (a) refusing an application for registration;

    (b) cancelling a registration;

    (c) removing or varying any condition to which a registration is subject or imposing a new condition; or

    (d) refusing to grant an application for the removal or variation of any condition to which a registration is subject,

the registration authority shall send to the applicant, or (as the case may be) registered person, notice in writing of its intention to take the step in question.

(2) Every such notice shall –

(a) give the authority's reasons for proposing to take the step; and
(b) inform the person concerned of his rights under this section.

(3) Where the recipient of such a notice informs the authority in writing of his desire to object to the step being taken, the authority shall afford him an opportunity to do so.

(4) Any objection made under subsection (3) may be made orally or in writing, by the recipient of the notice or a representative.

(5) If the authority, after giving the person concerned an opportunity to object to the step being taken, decides nevertheless to take it, it shall send him written notice of its decision.

(6) A step of a kind mentioned in subsection (1)(b) or (c) shall not take effect until the expiry of the time within which an appeal may be brought under section 79M or, where such an appeal is brought, before its determination.

(7) Subsection (6) does not prevent a step from taking effect before the expiry of the time within which an appeal may be brought under section 79M if the person concerned notifies the registration authority in writing that he does not intend to appeal.

79M Appeals

(1) An appeal against –

(a) the taking of any step mentioned in section 79L(1); ...[1]
(b) an order under section 79K, [or
(c) a determination made by the registration authority under this Part (other than one falling within paragraph (a) or (b)) which is of a prescribed description,][1]

shall lie to the Tribunal.

(2) On an appeal, the Tribunal may –

(a) confirm the taking of the step or the making of the order [or determination][1] or direct that it shall not have, or shall cease to have, effect; and
(b) impose, vary or cancel any condition.

NOTES

Amendments. [1] Words repealed and inserted (except in relation to Wales): Education Act 2002, ss 149(2), 152, 215(2), Sch 13, para 3, Sch 22, Pt 3.

Inspection: England

79N General functions of the Chief Inspector

(1) The Chief Inspector has the general duty of keeping the Secretary of State informed about the quality and standards of child minding and day care provided by registered persons in England.

(2) When asked to do so by the Secretary of State, the Chief Inspector shall give advice or information to the Secretary of State about such matters relating to the provision of child minding or day care by registered persons in England as may be specified in the Secretary of State's request.

(3) The Chief Inspector may at any time give advice to the Secretary of State, either generally or in relation to provision by particular persons or on particular premises, on any matter connected with the provision of child minding or day care by registered persons in England.

(4) The Chief Inspector may secure the provision of training for persons who provide or assist in providing child minding or day care, or intend to do so.

(5) Regulations may confer further functions on the Chief Inspector relating to child minding and day care provided in England.

(6) The annual reports of the Chief Inspector required by subsection (7)(a) of section 2 of the School Inspections Act 1996 to be made to the Secretary of State shall include an account of the exercise of the Chief Inspector's functions under this Part, and the power conferred by subsection (7)(b) of that section to make other reports to the Secretary of State includes a power to make reports with respect to matters which fall within the scope of his functions by virtue of this Part.

79P Early years child care inspectorate

(1) The Chief Inspector shall establish and maintain a register of early years child care inspectors for England.

(2) The register may be combined with the register maintained for England under paragraph 8(1) of Schedule 26 to the School Standards and Framework Act 1998 (register of nursery education inspectors).

(3) Paragraphs 8(2) [to (8)]¹, 9(1) to (4), 10 and 11 of that Schedule shall apply in relation to the register of early years child care inspectors as they apply in relation to the register maintained for England under paragraph 8(1) of that Schedule, but with the modifications set out in subsection (4).

(4) In the provisions concerned –

   (a) references to registered nursery education inspectors shall be read as references to registered early years child care inspectors;
   (b) references to inspections under paragraph 6 of that Schedule shall be read as references to inspections under section 79Q (and references to the functions of a registered nursery education inspector under paragraph 6 shall be interpreted accordingly);
   (c) references to the registration of a person under paragraph 6 of that Schedule shall be read as references to the registration of a person under subsection (1) (and references to applications made under paragraph 6 shall be interpreted accordingly); and
   (d) (*Not yet in force*)

(5) Registered early years child care inspectors are referred to below in this Part as registered inspectors.

NOTES

   Amendments. ¹ Words substituted (England only): Education Act 2002, s 152, Sch 14, para 4.

79Q Inspection of provision of child minding and day care in England

(1) The Chief Inspector may at any time require any registered person to provide him with any information connected with the person's activities as a child minder,

or provision of day care, which the Chief Inspector considers it necessary to have for the purposes of his functions under this Part.

(2) The Chief Inspector shall [at prescribed intervals inspect, or secure the inspection by a registered inspector of, any child minding provided in England by a registered person][1].

(3) The Chief Inspector shall [at prescribed intervals inspect, or secure the inspection by a registered inspector of, any day care provided by a registered person on any premises in England][1].

(4) The Chief Inspector may comply with subsection (2) or (3) either by organising inspections or by making arrangements with others for them to organise inspections.

(5) In prescribing the intervals mentioned in subsection (2) or (3) the Secretary of State may make provision as to the period within which the first inspection of child minding or day care provided by any person or at any premises is to take place.

(6) A person conducting an inspection under this section shall report on the quality and standards of the child minding or day care provided.

(7) The Chief Inspector may arrange for an inspection conducted by a registered inspector under this section to be monitored by another registered inspector.

NOTES

Amendments. [1] Words substituted (England only): Education Act 2002, s 152, Sch 13, para 4.

79R Reports of inspections

(1) A person who has conducted an inspection under section 79Q shall report in writing on the matters inspected to the Chief Inspector within the prescribed period.

(2) The period mentioned in subsection (1) may, if the Chief Inspector considers it necessary, be extended by up to three months.

(3) Once the report of an inspection has been made to the Chief Inspector under subsection (1) he –

  (a) may send a copy of it to the Secretary of State, and shall do so without delay if the Secretary of State requests a copy;
  (b) shall send a copy of it, or of such parts of it as he considers appropriate, to any prescribed authorities or persons; and
  (c) may arrange for the report (or parts of it) to be further published in any manner he considers appropriate.

(4) Subsections (2) to (4) of section 42A of the School Inspections Act 1996 shall apply in relation to the publication of any report under subsection (3) as they apply in relation to the publication of a report under any of the provisions mentioned in subsection (2) of section 42A.

Inspection: Wales

79S General functions of the Assembly

(1) The Assembly may secure the provision of training for persons who provide or assist in providing child minding or day care, or intend to do so.

PART I

(2) In relation to child minding and day care provided in Wales, the Assembly shall have any additional function specified in regulations made by the Assembly; but the regulations may only specify a function corresponding to a function which, by virtue of section 79N(5), is exercisable by the Chief Inspector in relation to child minding and day care provided in England.

79T Inspection: Wales

(1) The Assembly may at any time require any registered person to provide it with any information connected with the person's activities as a child minder or provision of day care which the Assembly considers it necessary to have for the purposes of its functions under this Part.

(2) The Assembly may by regulations make provision –

(a) for the inspection of the quality and standards of child minding provided in Wales by registered persons and of day care provided by registered persons on premises in Wales;

(b) for the publication of reports of the inspections in such manner as the Assembly considers appropriate.

(3) The regulations may provide for the inspections to be organised by –

(a) the Assembly; or

(b) Her Majesty's Chief Inspector of Education and Training in Wales, or any other person, under arrangements made with the Assembly.

(4) The regulations may provide for subsections (2) to (4) of section 42A of the School Inspections Act 1996 to apply with modifications in relation to the publication of reports under the regulations.

Supplementary

79U Rights of entry etc

(1) [Any person authorised for the purposes of this subsection by the registration authority][1] may at any reasonable time enter any premises in England or Wales on which child minding or day care is at any time provided.

(2) Where [a person authorised for the purposes of this subsection by the registration authority][1] has reasonable cause to believe that a child is being looked after on any premises in contravention of this Part, he may enter those premises at any reasonable time.

[(2A) Authorisation under subsection (1) or (2) –

(a) may be given for a particular occasion or period;

(b) may be given subject to conditions.][1]

(3) [A person entering premises under this section may (subject to any conditions imposed under subsection (2A)(b)][1] –

(a) inspect the premises;

(b) inspect, and take copies of –

(i) any records kept by the person providing the child minding or day care; and

(ii) any other documents containing information relating to its provision;

    (c) seize and remove any document or other material or thing found there which he has reasonable grounds to believe may be evidence of a failure to comply with any condition or requirement imposed by or under this Part;

    (d) require any person to afford him such facilities and assistance with respect to matters within the person's control as are necessary to enable him to exercise his powers under this section;

    (e) take measurements and photographs or make recordings;

    (f) inspect any children being looked after there, and the arrangements made for their welfare;

    (g) interview in private the person providing the child minding or day care; and

    (h) interview in private any person looking after children, or living or working, there who consents to be interviewed.

(4) Section 42 of the School Inspections Act 1996 (inspection of computer records for purposes of Part I of that Act) shall apply for the purposes of subsection (3) as it applies for the purposes of Part I of that Act.

(5) ...[1]

(6) A person exercising any power conferred by this section shall, if so required, produce some duly authenticated document showing his authority to do so.

(7) It shall be an offence wilfully to obstruct a person exercising any such power.

(8) Any person guilty of an offence under subsection (7) shall be liable on summary conviction to a fine not exceeding level 4 on the standard scale.

(9) In this section –

    ...[1]

    'documents' and 'records' each include information recorded in any form.

NOTES

    Amendments. [1] Words and subsection inserted, and subsection and definition repealed: Education Act 2002, s 152, Sch 13, para 5.

79V Function of local authorities

Each local authority shall, in accordance with regulations, secure the provision –

    (a) of information and advice about child minding and day care; and

    (b) of training for persons who provide or assist in providing child minding or day care.

Checks on suitability of persons working with children over the age of seven

79W Requirement for certificate of suitability

(1) This section applies to any person not required to register under this Part who looks after, or provides care for, children and meets the following conditions.

    References in this section to children are to those under the age of 15 or (in the case of disabled children) 17.

(2) The first condition is that the period, or the total of the periods, in any week which he spends looking after children or (as the case may be) during which the children are looked after exceeds five hours.

(3) The second condition is that he would be required to register under this Part (or, as the case may be, this Part if it were subject to prescribed modifications) if the children were under the age of eight.

(4) Regulations may require a person to whom this section applies to hold a certificate issued by the registration authority as to his suitability, and the suitability of each prescribed person, to look after children.

(5) The regulations may make provision about –

    (a) applications for certificates;

    (b) the matters to be taken into account by the registration authority in determining whether to issue certificates;

    (c) the information to be contained in certificates;

    (d) the period of their validity.

(6) The regulations may provide that a person to whom this section applies shall be guilty of an offence –

    (a) if he does not hold a certificate as required by the regulations; or

    (b) if, being a person who holds such a certificate, he fails to produce it when reasonably required to do so by a prescribed person.

(7) The regulations may provide that a person who, for the purpose of obtaining such a certificate, knowingly makes a statement which is false or misleading in a material particular shall be guilty of an offence.

(8) The regulations may provide that a person guilty of an offence under the regulations shall be liable on summary conviction to a fine not exceeding level 5 on the standard scale.

Time limit for proceedings

79X Time limit for proceedings

Proceedings for an offence under this Part or regulations made under it may be brought within a period of six months from the date on which evidence sufficient in the opinion of the prosecutor to warrant the proceedings came to his knowledge; but no such proceedings shall be brought by virtue of this section more than three years after the commission of the offence.][1]

NOTES

    Amendments. [1] Part inserted: Care Standards Act 2000, s 79(1).

PART XI
SECRETARY OF STATE'S SUPERVISORY FUNCTIONS AND RESPONSIBILITIES

80 Inspection of children's homes etc by persons authorised by Secretary of State

(1) The Secretary of State may cause to be inspected from time to time any –

    (a) [private][5] children's home;

    (b) premises in which a child who is being looked after by a local authority is living;

(c) premises in which a child who is being accommodated by or on behalf of a local education authority or voluntary organisation is living;

(d) premises in which a child who is being accommodated by or on behalf of a [Health Authority, Special Health Authority]³ [, Primary Care Trust]⁴ [or National Health Service trust]¹ is living;

(e) premises in which a child is living with a person with whom he has been placed by an adoption agency;

(f) premises in which a child who is a protected child is, or will be, living;

(g) premises in which a privately fostered child, or child who is treated as a foster child by virtue of paragraph 9 of Schedule 8, is living or in which it is proposed that he will live;

(h) premises on which any person is acting as a child minder;

(i) premises with respect to which a person is registered under section 71(1)(b) [or with respect to which a person is registered for providing day care under Part XA]⁵;

(j) [care home or independent hospital used to accommodate children;]⁵

(k) premises which are provided by a local authority and in which any service is provided by that authority under Part III;

(l) [school or college]⁶ providing accommodation for any child.

(2) An inspection under this section shall be conducted by a person authorised to do so by the Secretary of State.

(3) An officer of a local authority shall not be authorised except with the consent of that authority.

(4) The Secretary of State may require any person of a kind mentioned in subsection (5) to furnish him with such information, or allow him to inspect such records (in whatever form they are held), relating to –

(a) any premises to which subsection (1) or, in relation to Scotland, subsection (1)(h) or (i) applies;

(b) any child who is living in any such premises;

(c) the discharge by the Secretary of State of any of his functions under this Act;

(d) the discharge by any local authority of any of their functions under this Act,

as the Secretary of State may at any time direct.

(5) The persons are any –

(a) local authority;

(b) voluntary organisation;

(c) person carrying on a [private]⁵ children's home;

(d) proprietor of an independent school [or governing body of any other school]⁶;

[(da) governing body of an institution designated under section 28 of the Further and Higher Education Act 1992;

(db) further education corporation;]⁶

(e) person fostering any privately fostered child or providing accommodation for a child on behalf of a local authority, local education authority, [Health Authority, Special Health Authority]³ [, Primary Health Care Trust]⁴ [, National Health Service trust]² or voluntary organisation;

(f) local education authority providing accommodation for any child;

(g) person employed in a teaching or administrative capacity at any educational establishment (whether or not maintained by a local education authority) at which a child is accommodated on behalf of a local authority or local education authority;

  (h) person who is the occupier of any premises in which any person acts as a child minder (within the meaning of Part X) or provides day care for young children (within the meaning of that Part);

[(hh) person who is the occupier of any premises –

       (i) in which any person required to be registered for child minding under Part XA acts as a child minder (within the meaning of that Part); or

     (ii) with respect to which a person is required to be registered under that Part for providing day care;]⁵

  (i) person carrying on any home of a kind mentioned in subsection (1)(j);

 [(j) person carrying on a fostering agency.]⁶

(6) Any person inspecting any home or other premises under this section may –

  (a) inspect the children there; and

  (b) make such examination into the state and management of the home or premises and the treatment of the children there as he thinks fit.

(7) Any person authorised by the Secretary of State to exercise the power to inspect records conferred by subsection (4) –

  (a) shall be entitled at any reasonable time to have access to, and inspect and check the operation of, any computer and any associated apparatus or material which is or has been in use in connection with the records in question; and

  (b) may require –

       (i) the person by whom or on whose behalf the computer is or has been so used; or

     (ii) any person having charge of, or otherwise concerned with the operation of, the computer, apparatus or material,

to afford him such reasonable assistance as he may require.

(8) A person authorised to inspect any premises under this section shall have a right to enter the premises for that purpose, and for any purpose specified in subsection (4), at any reasonable time.

(9) Any person exercising that power shall, if so required, produce some duly authenticated document showing his authority to do so.

(10) Any person who intentionally obstructs another in the exercise of that power shall be guilty of an offence and liable on summary conviction to a fine not exceeding level 3 on the standard scale.

(11) The Secretary of State may by order provide for subsections (1), (4) and (6) not to apply in relation to such homes, or other premises, as may be specified in the order.

(12) Without prejudice to section 104, any such order may make different provision with respect to each of those subsections.

[(13) In this section –

  'college' means an institution within the further education sector as defined in section 91 of the Further and Higher Education Act 1992;

  'fostering agency' has the same meaning as in the Care Standards Act 2000;

  'further education corporation' has the same meaning as in the Further and Higher Education Act 1992.]⁶

Amendments. [1] Words inserted: National Health Service and Community Care Act 1990, s 66(1), Sch 9, para 36(4)(a). [2] Words inserted: National Health Service and Community Care Act 1990, s 66(1), Sch 9, para 36(4)(b). [3] Words substituted: Health Authorities Act 1995, s 2(1), Sch 1, Pt III, para 118(1), (9). [4] Words inserted: Health Act 1999 (Supplementary, Consequential etc Provisions) Order 2000, SI 2000/90. [5] Paragraph and words inserted or substituted: Care Standards Act 2000, ss 116, 117(2), Sch 4, paras 14(1), (16). [6] Subsection, paragraphs and words inserted or substituted: Care Standards Act 2000, s 109 (applies to England only).

Definitions. 'Adoption agency': s 105(1); 'child': s 105(1); 'child minder': s 71(2)(a); 'child who is looked after by a local authority': s 22(1); 'children's home': s 63(3); 'day care': ss 18, 71(2)(b); 'functions': s 105(1); 'health authority': s 105(1); 'independent school': s 105(1); 'local authority': s 105(1); 'local education authority': s 105(1); 'mental nursing home': s 105(1); 'nursing home': s 105(1); 'privately fostered child': s 105(1); 'residential care home': s 105(1); 'voluntary home': s 60(3); 'voluntary organisation': s 105(1).

81 Inquiries

(1) The Secretary of State may cause an inquiry to be held into any matter connected with –

    (a) the functions of [a local authority which are social services functions within the meaning of the Local Authority Social Services Act 1970][1], in so far as those functions relate to children;

    (b) the functions of an adoption agency;

    (c) the functions of a voluntary organisation, in so far as those functions relate to children;

    (d) a ...[1] [private][5] children's home or voluntary home;

    (e) [a care home or independent hospital][5], so far as it provides accommodation for children;

    (f) a home provided [in accordance with arrangements made][2] by the Secretary of State under section 82(5);

    (g) the detention of a child under [section 92 of the Powers of Criminal Courts (Sentencing) Act 2000][3].

(2) Before an inquiry is begun, the Secretary of State may direct that it shall be held in private.

(3) Where no direction has been given, the person holding the inquiry may if he thinks fit hold it, or any part of it, in private.

(4) Subsections (2) to (5) of section 250 of the Local Government Act 1972 (powers in relation to local inquiries) shall apply in relation to an inquiry under this section as they apply in relation to a local inquiry under that section.

(5) In this section 'functions' includes powers and duties which a person has otherwise than by virtue of any enactment.

Amendments. [1] Words repealed: Courts and Legal Services Act 1990, s 116, 125(7), Sch 16, para 21, Sch 20. [2] Words inserted: Courts and Legal Services Act 1990, s 116, Sch 16, para 21. [3] Words substituted: Powers of Criminal Courts (Sentencing) Act 2000, s 165(1), Sch 9, para 128. [4] Words substituted: Local Government Act 2000, s 107, Sch 5, para 21. [5] Words inserted and substituted: Care Standards Act 2000, s 116, Sch 4, para 14(17).

Definitions. 'Adoption agency': s 105(1); 'child': s 105(1); 'functions': ss 81(5), 105(1); 'local authority': s 105(1); 'mental nursing home': s 105(1); 'nursing home': s 105(1); 'registered children's home': s 63(8); 'residential care home': s 105(1); 'voluntary home': s 60(3); 'voluntary organisation': s 105(1).

82 Financial support by Secretary of State

(1) The Secretary of State may (with the consent of the Treasury) defray or contribute towards –

(a) any fees or expenses incurred by any person undergoing approved child care training;
(b) any fees charged, or expenses incurred, by any person providing approved child care training or preparing material for use in connection with such training; or
(c) the cost of maintaining any person undergoing such training.

(2) The Secretary of State may make grants to local authorities in respect of expenditure incurred by them in providing secure accommodation in community homes other than assisted community homes.

(3) Where –

(a) a grant has been made under subsection (2) with respect to any secure accommodation; but
(b) the grant is not used for the purpose for which it was made or the accommodation is not used as, or ceases to be used as, secure accommodation,

the Secretary of State may (with the consent of the Treasury) require the authority concerned to repay the grant, in whole or in part.

(4) The Secretary of State may make grants to voluntary organisations towards –

(a) expenditure incurred by them in connection with the establishment, maintenance or improvement of voluntary homes which, at the time when the expenditure was incurred –
    (i) were assisted community homes; or
    (ii) were designated as such; or
(b) expenses incurred in respect of the borrowing of money to defray any such expenditure.

(5) The Secretary of State may arrange for the provision, equipment and maintenance of homes for the accommodation of children who are in need of particular facilities and services which –

(a) are or will be provided in those homes; and
(b) in the opinion of the Secretary of State, are unlikely to be readily available in community homes.

(6) In this Part –

'child care training' means training undergone by any person with a view to, or in the course of –
    (a) his employment for the purposes of any of the functions mentioned in section 83(9) or in connection with the adoption of children or with the accommodation of children in a [care home or independent hospital][1]; or
    (b) his employment by a voluntary organisation for similar purposes;
'approved child care training' means child care training which is approved by the Secretary of State; and

'secure accommodation' means accommodation provided for the purpose of restricting the liberty of children.

(7) Any grant made under this section shall be of such amount, and shall be subject to such conditions, as the Secretary of State may (with the consent of the Treasury) determine.

NOTES

Amendments. [1] Words substituted: Care Standards Act 2000, s 116, Sch 4, para 14(18).

Definitions. 'Approved child care training': s 82(6); 'assisted community home': s 53(5); 'child': s 105(1); 'child care training': s 82(6); 'community home': s 53(1); 'functions': s 105(1); 'mental nursing home': s 105(1); 'nursing home': s 105(1); 'residential care home': s 105(1); 'secure accommodation': s 82(6); 'voluntary home': s 60(3); 'voluntary organisation': s 105(1).

83 Research and returns of information

(1) The Secretary of State may conduct, or assist other persons in conducting, research into any matter connected with –

(a) his functions, or the functions of local authorities, under the enactments mentioned in subsection (9);
(b) the adoption of children; or
(c) the accommodation of children in a [care home or independent hospital] [2].

(2) Any local authority may conduct, or assist other persons in conducting, research into any matter connected with –

(a) their functions under the enactments mentioned in subsection (9);
(b) the adoption of children; or
(c) the accommodation of children in a [care home or independent hospital] [2].

(3) Every local authority shall, at such times and in such form as the Secretary of State may direct, transmit to him such particulars as he may require with respect to –

(a) the performance by the local authority of all or any of their functions –
  (i) under the enactments mentioned in subsection (9); or
  (ii) in connection with the accommodation of children in a [care home or independent hospital][2]; and
(b) the children in relation to whom the authority have exercised those functions.

(4) Every voluntary organisation shall, at such times and in such form as the Secretary of State may direct, transmit to him such particulars as he may require with respect to children accommodated by them or on their behalf.

(5) The Secretary of State may direct the [justices' chief executive for][1] each magistrates' court to which the direction is expressed to relate to transmit –

(a) to such person as may be specified in the direction; and
(b) at such times and in such form as he may direct,

such particulars as he may require with respect to proceedings of the court which relate to children.

(6) The Secretary of State shall in each year lay before Parliament a consolidated and classified abstract of the information transmitted to him under subsections (3) to (5).

---

(7) The Secretary of State may institute research designed to provide information on which requests for information under this section may be based.

(8) The Secretary of State shall keep under review the adequacy of the provision of child care training and for that purpose shall receive and consider any information from or representations made by –

    (a) the Central Council for Education and Training in Social Work;

    (b) such representatives of local authorities as appear to him to be appropriate; or

    (c) such other persons or organisations as appear to him to be appropriate,

concerning the provision of such training.

(9) The enactments are –

    (a) this Act;

    (b) the Children and Young Persons Acts 1933 to 1969;

    (c) section 116 of the Mental Health Act 1983 (so far as it relates to children looked after by local authorities);

    (d) section 10 of the Mental Health (Scotland) Act 1984 (so far as it relates to children for whom local authorities have responsibility).

NOTES

Amendments. [1] Words substituted: Access to Justice Act 1999, s 90, Sch 13, paras 159, 160. [2] Words substituted: Care Standards Act 2000, s 116, Sch 4, para 14(19).

Definitions. 'Child': s 105(1); 'child care training': s 82(6); 'functions': s 105(1); 'local authority': s 105(1); 'mental nursing home': s 105(1); 'nursing home': s 105(1); 'residential care home': s 105(1); 'voluntary organisation': s 105(1).

84 Local authority failure to comply with statutory duty: default power of Secretary of State

(1) If the Secretary of State is satisfied that any local authority has failed, without reasonable excuse, to comply with any of the duties imposed on them by or under this Act he may make an order declaring that authority to be in default with respect to that duty.

(2) An order under subsection (1) shall give the Secretary of State's reasons for making it.

(3) An order under subsection (1) may contain such directions for the purpose of ensuring that the duty is complied with, within such period as may be specified in the order, as appear to the Secretary of State to be necessary.

(4) Any such direction shall, on the application of the Secretary of State, be enforceable by mandamus.

PART XII
MISCELLANEOUS AND GENERAL

Notification of children accommodated in certain establishments

85 Children accommodated by health authorities and local education authorities

(1) Where a child is provided with accommodation by any [Health Authority, Special Health Authority]², [Primary Care Trust,]³ [National Health Service trust]¹ or local education authority ('the accommodating authority') –

    (a) for a consecutive period of at least three months; or

    (b) with the intention, on the part of that authority, of accommodating him for such a period,

the accommodating authority shall notify the responsible authority.

(2) Where subsection (1) applies with respect to a child, the accommodating authority shall also notify the responsible authority when they cease to accommodate the child.

(3) In this section 'the responsible authority' means –

    (a) the local authority appearing to the accommodating authority to be the authority within whose area the child was ordinarily resident immediately before being accommodated; or

    (b) where it appears to the accommodating authority that a child was not ordinarily resident within the area of any local authority, the local authority within whose area the accommodation is situated.

(4) Where a local authority have been notified under this section, they shall –

    (a) take such steps as are reasonably practicable to enable them to determine whether the child's welfare is adequately safeguarded and promoted while he is accommodated by the accommodating authority; and

    (b) consider the extent to which (if at all) they should exercise any of their functions under this Act with respect to the child.

NOTES

Amendments. ¹ Words inserted: National Health Service and Community Care Act 1990, s 66(1), Sch 9, para 36(5). ² Words inserted: Health Authorities Act 1995, s 2(1), Sch 1, Pt III, para 118(1), (9). ³ Words inserted: Health Act 1999 (Supplementary, Consequential etc Provisions) Order 2000, SI 2000/90.

Definitions. 'Child': s 105(1); 'functions': s 105(1); 'health authority': s 105(1); 'local authority': s 105(1); 'local education authority': s 105(1); 'the accommodating authority': s 85(1); 'the responsible authority': s 85(3).

86 [Children accommodated in care homes or independent hospitals]¹

(1) Where a child is provided with accommodation in any [care home or independent hospital]¹ –

    (a) for a consecutive period of at least three months; or

    (b) with the intention, on the part of the person taking the decision to accommodate him, of accommodating him for such period,

the person carrying on the home shall notify the local authority within whose area the home is carried on.

(2) Where subsection (1) applies with respect to a child, the person carrying on the home shall also notify that authority when he ceases to accommodate the child in the home.

(3) Where a local authority have been notified under this section, they shall –

(a) take such steps as are reasonably practicable to enable them to determine whether the child's welfare is adequately safeguarded and promoted while he is accommodated in the home; and

(b) consider the extent to which (if at all) they should exercise any of their functions under this Act with respect to the child.

(4) If the person carrying on any home fails, without reasonable excuse, to comply with this section he shall be guilty of an offence.

(5) A person authorised by a local authority may enter any [care home or independent hospital][1] within the authority's area for the purpose of establishing whether the requirements of this section have been complied with.

(6) Any person who intentionally obstructs another in the exercise of the power of entry shall be guilty of an offence.

(7) Any person exercising the power of entry shall, if so required, produce some duly authenticated document showing his authority to do so.

(8) Any person committing an offence under this section shall be liable on summary conviction to a fine not exceeding level 3 on the standard scale.

NOTES

Amendments. [1] Words substituted: Care Standards Act 2000, s 116, Sch 4, para 14(20).

Definitions. 'Child': s 105(1); 'functions': s 105(1); 'local authority': s 105(1); 'mental nursing home': s 105(1); 'nursing home': s 105(1); 'residential care home': s 105(1).

87 [Welfare of children in boarding schools and colleges][1]

[(1) Where a school or college provides accommodation for any child, it shall be the duty of the relevant person to safeguard and promote the child's welfare.

(2) Subsection (1) does not apply in relation to a school or college which is a children's home or care home.

(3) Where accommodation is provided for a child by any school or college the appropriate authority shall take such steps as are reasonably practicable to enable them to determine whether the child's welfare is adequately safeguarded and promoted while he is accommodated by the school or college.

(4) Where the Commission are of the opinion that there has been a failure to comply with subsection (1) in relation to a child provided with accommodation by a school or college, they shall –

(a) in the case of a school other than an independent school or a special school, notify the local education authority for the area in which the school is situated;

(b) in the case of a special school which is maintained by a local education authority, notify that authority;

(c) in any other case, notify the Secretary of State.

(4A) Where the National Assembly for Wales are of the opinion that there has been a failure to comply with subsection (1) in relation to a child provided with accommodation by a school or college, they shall –

    (a) in the case of a school other than an independent school or a special school, notify the local education authority for the area in which the school is situated;

    (b) in the case of a special school which is maintained by a local education authority, notify that authority;

(5) Where accommodation is, or is to be, provided for a child by any school or college, a person authorised by the appropriate authority may, for the purpose of enabling that authority to discharge its duty under this section, enter at any time premises which are, or are to be, premises of the school or college.] [1]

(6) Any person [exercising] [1] the power conferred by subsection (5) may carry out such inspection of premises, children and records as is prescribed by regulations made by the Secretary of State for the purposes of this section.

(7) Any person exercising that power shall, if asked to do so, produce some duly authenticated document showing his authority to do so.

(8) Any person authorised by the regulations to inspect records –

    (a) shall be entitled at any reasonable time to have access to, and inspect and check the operation of, any computer and any associated apparatus or material which is or has been in use in connection with the records in question; and

    (b) may require –

        (i) the person by whom or on whose behalf the computer is or has been so used; or

        (ii) any person having charge of, or otherwise concerned with the operation of, the computer, apparatus or material,

    to afford him such assistance as he may reasonably require.

(9) Any person who intentionally obstructs another in the exercise of any power conferred by this section or the regulations shall be guilty of an offence and liable on summary conviction to a fine not exceeding level 3 on the standard scale.

[(10) In this section and sections 87A to 87D –

    'the 1992 Act' means the Further and Higher Education Act 1992;
    'appropriate authority' means –

        (a) in relation to England, the National Care Standards Commission;

        (b) in relation to Wales, the National Assembly for Wales;

    'college' means an institution within the further education sector as defined in section 91 of the 1992 Act;
    'the Commission' means the National Care Standards Commission;
    'further education corporation' has the same meaning as in the 1992 Act;
    'local education authority' and 'proprietor' have the same meanings as in the Education Act 1996.

(11) In this section and sections 87A and 87D 'relevant person' means –

    (a) in relation to an independent school, the proprietor of the school;

    (b) in relation to any other school, or an institution designated under section 28 of the 1992 Act, the governing body of the school or institution;

    (c) in relation to an institution conducted by a further education corporation, the corporation.

(12) Where a person other than the proprietor of an independent school is responsible for conducting the school, references in this section to the relevant person include references to the person so responsible.] [1]

PART I

NOTES

Amendments. [1] Subsections and words substituted: Care Standards Act 2000, ss 105, 116, Sch 4, para 14(1), (21).

Definitions. 'Child': s 105(1); 'children's home': s 63(3); 'independent school': s 105(1); 'local authority': s 105(1); 'proprietor': s 87(10); 'residential care home': s 105(1).

[87A Suspension of duty under section 87(3)

(1) The Secretary of State may appoint a person to be an inspector for the purposes of this section if –

    (a) that person already acts as an inspector for other purposes in relation to schools or colleges to which section 87(1) applies, and

    (b) the Secretary of State is satisfied that the person is an appropriate person to determine whether the welfare of children provided with accommodation by such schools or colleges is adequately safeguarded and promoted while they are accommodated by them.

(2) Where –

    (a) the relevant person enters into an agreement in writing with a person appointed under subsection (1),

    (b) the agreement provides for the person so appointed to have in relation to the school or college the function of determining whether section 87(1) is being complied with, and

    (c) the appropriate authority receive from the person mentioned in paragraph (b) ('the inspector') notice in writing that the agreement has come into effect,

the authority's duty under section 87(3) in relation to the school or college shall be suspended.

(3) Where the appropriate authority's duty under section 87(3) in relation to any school or college is suspended under this section, it shall cease to be so suspended if the appropriate authority receive –

    (a) a notice under subsection (4) relating to the inspector, or

    (b) a notice under subsection (5) relating to the relevant agreement.

(4) The Secretary of State shall terminate a person's appointment under subsection (1) if –

    (a) that person so requests, or

    (b) the Secretary of State ceases, in relation to that person, to be satisfied that he is such a person as is mentioned in paragraph (b) of that subsection,

and shall give notice of the termination of that person's appointment to the appropriate authority.

(5) Where –

    (a) the appropriate authority's duty under section 87(3) in relation to any school or college is suspended under this section, and

    (b) the relevant agreement ceases to have effect,

the inspector shall give to the appropriate authority notice in writing of the fact that it has ceased to have effect.

(6) In this section references to the relevant agreement, in relation to the suspension of the appropriate authority's duty under section 87(3) as regards any

school or college, are to the agreement by virtue of which the appropriate authority's duty under that provision as regards that school or college is suspended.]¹

NOTES
  Amendments. ¹ Section substituted: Care Standards Act 2000, s 106(1).

[87B Duties of inspectors under section 87A

(1) The Secretary of State may impose on a person appointed under section 87A(1) ('an authorised inspector') such requirements relating to, or in connection with, the carrying out under substitution agreements of the function mentioned in section 87A(2)(b) as the Secretary of State thinks fit.

(2) Where, in the course of carrying out under a substitution agreement the function mentioned in section 87A(2)(b), it appears to an authorised inspector that there has been a failure to comply with section 87(1) in the case of a child provided with accommodation by the school [or college]² to which the agreement relates, the inspector shall give notice of that fact –

  [(a) in the case of a school other than an independent school or a special school, to the local education authority for the area in which the school is situated;
  (b) in the case of a special school which is maintained by a local education authority, to that authority;
  (c) in any other case, to the Secretary of State.]²

(3) Where, in the course of carrying out under a substitution agreement the function mentioned in section 87A(2)(b), it appears to an authorised inspector that a child provided with accommodation by the school [or college]² to which the agreement relates is suffering, or is likely to suffer, significant harm, the inspector shall –

  (a) give notice of that fact to the local authority in whose area the school is situated, and
  (b) where the inspector is required to make inspection reports to the Secretary of State, supply that local authority with a copy of the latest inspection report to have been made by the inspector to the Secretary of State in relation to the school.

[(4) In this section 'substitution agreement' means an agreement by virtue of which the duty of the appropriate authority under section 87(3) in relation to a school or college is suspended.]²]¹

NOTES
  Commencement. 1 Jan 1996: SI 1995/2835.
  Amendments. ¹ Section inserted: Deregulation and Contracting Out Act 1994, s 38.
² Subsection substituted and words inserted: Care Standards Act 2000, s 106.

[87C Boarding schools: national minimum standards

(1) The Secretary of State may prepare and publish statements of national minimum standards for safeguarding and promoting the welfare of children for whom accommodation is provided in a school or college.

(2) The Secretary of State shall keep the standards set out in the statements under review and may publish amended statements whenever he considers it appropriate to do so.

(3) Before issuing a statement, or an amended statement which in the opinion of the Secretary of State effects a substantial change in the standards, the Secretary of State shall consult any persons he considers appropriate.

(4) The standards shall be taken into account –

(a) in the making by the appropriate authority of any determination under section 87(4) or (4A);

(b) in the making by a person appointed under section 87A(1) of any determination under section 87B(2); and

(c) in any proceedings under any other enactment in which it is alleged that the person has failed to comply with section 87(1).][1]

NOTES

Amendments. [1] Section inserted: Care Standards Act 2000, s 107.

[87D Annual fee for boarding school inspections

(1) Regulations under subsection (2) may be made in relation to any school or college in respect of which the appropriate authority is required to take steps under section 87(3).

(2) The Secretary of State may by regulations require the relevant person to pay the appropriate authority an annual fee of such amount, and within such time, as the regulations may specify.

(3) A fee payable by virtue of this section may, without prejudice to any other method of recovery, be recovered summarily as a civil debt.][1]

NOTES

Amendments. [1] Section inserted: Care Standards Act 2000, s 108.

Adoption

88 Amendments of adoption legislation

(1) The Adoption Act 1976 shall have effect subject to the amendments made by Part I of Schedule 10.

(2) The Adoption (Scotland) Act 1978 shall have effect subject to the amendments made by Part II of Schedule 10.

89 ...[1]

NOTES

Amendments. [1] Section repealed: Child Support, Pensions and Social Security Act 2000, s 85, Sch 9, Part IX.

Criminal care and supervision orders

90 Care and supervision orders in criminal proceedings

(1) The power of a court to make an order under subsection (2) of section 1 of the Children and Young Persons Act 1969 (care proceedings in [youth courts][1]) where it is of the opinion that the condition mentioned in paragraph (f) of that subsection ('the offence condition') is satisfied is hereby abolished.

(2) The powers of the court to make care orders –

    (a) under section 7(7)(a) of the Children and Young Persons Act 1969 (alteration in treatment of young offenders etc.); and

    (b) under section 15(1) of that Act, on discharging a supervision order made under section 7(7)(b) of that Act,

are hereby abolished.

(3) The powers given by that Act to include requirements in supervision orders shall have effect subject to amendments made by Schedule 12.

NOTES

    Amendments. [1] Words substituted: Criminal Justice Act 1991, s 100, Sch 11, para 40(1), (2)(r).

Effect and duration of orders etc

91 Effect and duration of orders etc

(1) The making of a residence order with respect to a child who is the subject of a care order discharges the care order.

(2) The making of a care order with respect to a child who is the subject of any section 8 order discharges that order.

(3) The making of a care order with respect to a child who is the subject of a supervision order discharges that other order.

(4) The making of a care order with respect to a child who is a ward of court brings that wardship to an end.

(5) The making of a care order with respect to a child who is the subject of a school attendance order made under [section 437 of the Education Act 1996][1] discharges the school attendance order.

(6) Where an emergency protection order is made with respect to a child who is in care, the care order shall have effect subject to the emergency protection order.

(7) Any order made under section 4(1) or 5(1) shall continue in force until the child reaches the age of eighteen, unless it is brought to an end earlier.

(8) Any –

    (a) agreement under section 4; or

    (b) appointment under section 5(3) or (4),

shall continue in force until the child reaches the age of eighteen, unless it is brought to an end earlier.

(9) An order under Schedule 1 has effect as specified in that Schedule.

(10) A section 8 order shall, if it would otherwise still be in force, cease to have effect when the child reaches the age of sixteen, unless it is to have effect beyond that age by virtue of section 9(6).

(11) Where a section 8 order has effect with respect to a child who has reached the age of sixteen, it shall, if it would otherwise still be in force, cease to have effect when he reaches the age of eighteen.

(12) Any care order, other than an interim care order, shall continue in force until the child reaches the age of eighteen, unless it is brought to an end earlier.

(13) Any order made under any other provision of this Act in relation to a child shall, if it would otherwise still be in force, cease to have effect when he reaches the age of eighteen.

(14) On disposing of any application for an order under this Act, the court may (whether or not it makes any other order in response to the application) order that no application for an order under this Act of any specified kind may be made with respect to the child concerned by any person named in the order without leave of the court.

(15) Where an application ('the previous application') has been made for –

    (a) the discharge of a care order;
    (b) the discharge of a supervision order;
    (c) the discharge of an education supervision order;
    (d) the substitution of a supervision order for a care order; or
    (e) a child assessment order,

no further application of a kind mentioned in paragraphs (a) to (e) may be made with respect to the child concerned, without leave of the court, unless the period between the disposal of the previous application and the making of the further application exceeds six months.

(16) Subsection (15) does not apply to applications made in relation to interim orders.

(17) Where –

    (a) a person has made an application for an order under section 34;
    (b) the application has been refused; and
    (c) a period of less than six months has elapsed since the refusal,

that person may not make a further application for such an order with respect to the same child, unless he has obtained the leave of the court.

NOTES

    Amendments. [1] Words substituted: Education Act 1996, s 582(1), Sch 37, Pt I, para 90.

    Definitions. 'A section 8 order': s 8(2); 'care order': ss 31(11), 105(1); 'child': s 105(1); 'child assessment order': s 43(2); 'education supervision order': s 36(2); 'emergency protection order': s 44(4); 'residence order': s 8(1); 'supervision order': s 31(11); 'the court': s 92(7).

Jurisdiction and procedure etc

92 Jurisdiction of courts

(1) The name 'domestic proceedings', given to certain proceedings in magistrates' courts, is hereby changed to 'family proceedings' and the names 'domestic court' and 'domestic court panel' are hereby changed to 'family proceedings court' and 'family panel', respectively.

(2) Proceedings under this Act shall be treated as family proceedings in relation to magistrates' courts.

(3) Subsection (2) is subject to the provisions of section 65(1) and (2) of the Magistrates' Courts Act 1980 (proceedings which may be treated as not being family proceedings), as amended by this Act.

(4) A magistrates' court shall not be competent to entertain any application, or make any order, involving the administration or application of –

    (a) any property belonging to or held in trust for a child; or

    (b) the income of any such property.

(5) The powers of a magistrates' court under section 63(2) of the Act of 1980 to suspend or rescind orders shall not apply in relation to any order made under this Act.

(6) Part I of Schedule 11 makes provision, including provision for the Lord Chancellor to make orders, with respect to the jurisdiction of courts and justices of the peace in relation to –

    (a) proceedings under this Act; and

    (b) proceedings under certain other enactments.

(7) For the purposes of this Act 'the court' means the High Court, a county court or a magistrates' court.

(8) Subsection (7) is subject to the provision made by or under Part I of Schedule 11 and to any express provision as to the jurisdiction of any court made by any other provision of this Act.

(9) The Lord Chancellor may by order make provision for the principal registry of the Family Division of the High Court to be treated as if it were a county court for such purposes of this Act, or of any provision made under this Act, as may be specified in the order.

(10) Any order under subsection (9) may make such provision as the Lord Chancellor thinks expedient for the purpose of applying (with or without modifications) provisions which apply in relation to the procedure in county courts to the principal registry when it acts as if it were a county court.

(11) Part II of Schedule 11 makes amendments consequential on this section.

NOTES

    Definitions. 'Family panel': s 92(1); 'family proceedings': s 92(2); 'family proceedings court': s 92(1); 'the court': s 92(7).

93 Rules of Court

(1) An authority having power to make rules of court may make such provision for giving effect to –

    (a) this Act;

    (b) the provisions of any statutory instrument made under this Act; or

    (c) any amendment made by this Act in any other enactment,

as appears to that authority to be necessary or expedient.

(2) The rules may, in particular, make provision –

(a) with respect to the procedure to be followed in any relevant proceedings (including the manner in which any application is to be made or other proceedings commenced);

(b) as to the persons entitled to participate in any relevant proceedings, whether as parties to the proceedings or by being given the opportunity to make representations to the court;

(c) with respect to the documents and information to be furnished, and notices to be given, in connection with any relevant proceedings;

(d) applying (with or without modification) enactments which govern the procedure to be followed with respect to proceedings brought on a complaint made to a magistrates' court to relevant proceedings in such a court brought otherwise than on a complaint;

(e) with respect to preliminary hearings;

(f) for the service outside [England and Wales][1], in such circumstances and in such manner as may be prescribed, of any notice of proceedings in a magistrates' court;

(g) for the exercise by magistrates' courts, in such circumstances as may be prescribed, of such powers as may be prescribed (even though a party to the proceedings in question is [or resides][1] outside England and Wales);

(h) enabling the court, in such circumstances as may be prescribed, to proceed on any application even though the respondent has not been given notice of the proceedings;

(i) authorising a single justice to discharge the functions of a magistrates' court with respect to such relevant proceedings as may be prescribed;

(j) authorising a magistrates' court to order any of the parties to such relevant proceedings as may be prescribed, in such circumstances as may be prescribed, to pay the whole or part of the costs of all or any of the other parties.

(3) In subsection (2) –

'notice of proceedings' means a summons or such other notice of proceedings as is required; and 'given', in relation to a summons, means 'served';
'prescribed' means prescribed by the rules; and
'relevant proceedings' means any application made, or proceedings brought, under any of the provisions mentioned in paragraphs (a) to (c) of subsection (1) and any part of such proceedings.

(4) This section and any other power in this Act to make rules of court are not to be taken as in any way limiting any other power of the authority in question to make rules of court.

(5) When making any rules under this section an authority shall be subject to the same requirements as to consultation (if any) as apply when the authority makes rules under its general rule making power.

NOTES

Amendments. [1] Words substituted and inserted: Courts and Legal Services Act 1990, s 116, Sch 16, para 22.

Definitions. 'Notice of proceedings': s 93(3); 'prescribed': s 93(3); 'relevant proceedings': s 93(3); 'the court': s 92(7).

94 Appeals

(1) [Subject to any express provision to the contrary made by or under this Act, an][1] appeal shall lie to the High Court against –

(a) the making by a magistrates' court of any order under this Act; or

(b) any refusal by a magistrates' court to make such an order.

(2) Where a magistrates' court has power, in relation to any proceedings under this Act, to decline jurisdiction because it considers that the case can more conveniently be dealt with by another court, no appeal shall lie against any exercise by that magistrates' court of that power.

(3) Subsection (1) does not apply in relation to an interim order for periodical payments made under Schedule 1.

(4) On an appeal under this section, the High Court may make such orders as may be necessary to give effect to its determination of the appeal.

(5) Where an order is made under subsection (4) the High Court may also make such incidental or consequential orders as appear to it to be just.

(6) Where an appeal from a magistrates' court relates to an order for the making of periodical payments, the High Court may order that its determination of the appeal shall have effect from such date as it thinks fit to specify in the order.

(7) The date so specified must not be earlier than the earliest date allowed in accordance with rules of court made for the purposes of this section.

(8) Where, on an appeal under this section in respect of an order requiring a person to make periodical payments, the High Court reduces the amount of those payments or discharges the order –

(a) it may order the person entitled to the payments to pay to the person making them such sum in respect of payments already made as the High Court thinks fit; and

(b) if any arrears are due under the order for periodical payments, it may remit payment of the whole, or part, of those arrears.

(9) Any order of the High Court made on an appeal under this section (other than one directing that an application be re-heard by a magistrates' court) shall, for the purposes –

(a) of the enforcement of the order; and

(b) of any power to vary, revive or discharge orders,

be treated as if it were an order of the magistrates' court from which the appeal was brought and not an order of the High Court.

(10) The Lord Chancellor may by order make provision as to the circumstances in which appeals may be made against decisions taken by courts on questions arising in connection with the transfer, or proposed transfer, of proceedings by virtue of any order under paragraph 2 of Schedule 11.

(11) Except to the extent provided for in any order made under subsection (10), no appeal may be made against any decision of a kind mentioned in that subsection.

NOTES

    Amendments. [1] Words inserted: Courts and Legal Services Act 1990, s 116, Sch 16, para 23.

95 Attendance of child at hearing under Part IV or V

(1) In any proceedings in which a court is hearing an application for an order under Part IV or V, or is considering whether to make any such order, the court

may order the child concerned to attend such stage or stages of the proceedings as may be specified in the order.

(2) The power conferred by subsection (1) shall be exercised in accordance with rules of court.

(3) Subsections (4) to (6) apply where –

    (a) an order under subsection (1) has not been complied with; or

    (b) the court has reasonable cause to believe that it will not be complied with.

(4) The court may make an order authorising a constable, or such person as may be specified in the order –

    (a) to take charge of the child and to bring him to the court; and

    (b) to enter and search any premises specified in the order if he has reasonable cause to believe that the child may be found on the premises.

(5) The court may order any person who is in a position to do so to bring the child to the court.

(6) Where the court has reason to believe that a person has information about the whereabouts of the child it may order him to disclose it to the court.

NOTES

Definitions. 'Child': s 105(1); 'the court': s 92(7).

96 Evidence given by, or with respect to, children

(1) Subsection (2) applies in any civil proceedings where a child who is called as a witness in any civil proceedings does not, in the opinion of the court, understand the nature of an oath.

(2) The child's evidence may be heard by the court if, in its opinion –

    (a) he understands that it is his duty to speak the truth; and

    (b) he has sufficient understanding to justify his evidence being heard.

(3) The Lord Chancellor may by order make provision for the admissibility of evidence which would otherwise be inadmissible under any rule of law relating to hearsay.

(4) An order under subsection (3) may only be made with respect to –

    (a) civil proceedings in general or such civil proceedings, or class of civil proceedings, as may be prescribed; and

    (b) evidence in connection with the upbringing, maintenance or welfare of a child.

(5) An order under subsection (3) –

    (a) may, in particular, provide for the admissibility of statements which are made orally or in a prescribed form or which are recorded by any prescribed method of recording;

    (b) may make different provision for different purposes and in relation to different descriptions of court; and

    (c) may make such amendments and repeals in any enactment relating to evidence (other than in this Act) as the Lord Chancellor considers necessary or expedient in consequence of the provision made by the order.

(6) Subsection (5)(b) is without prejudice to section 104(4).

(7) In this section –

['civil proceedings' means civil proceedings, before any tribunal, in relation to which the strict rules of evidence apply, whether as a matter of law or by agreement of the parties, and references to 'the court' shall be construed accordingly;][1] and

'prescribed' means prescribed by an order under subsection (3).

NOTES

Definitions. 'Child': s 105(1); 'civil proceedings': s 96(7); 'court': s 92(7); 'prescribed': s 96(7); 'upbringing': s 105(1).

Amendments. [1] Definition substituted: Civil Evidence Act 1995, s 15(1), Sch 1, para 16.

97 Privacy for children involved in certain proceedings

(1) Rules made under section 144 of the Magistrates' Courts Act 1980 may make provision for a magistrates' court to sit in private in proceedings in which any powers under this Act may be exercised by the court with respect to any child.

(2) No person shall publish any material which is intended, or likely, to identify –

(a) any child as being involved in any proceedings before [the High Court, a county court or][4] a magistrates' court in which any power under this Act may be exercised by the court with respect to that or any other child; or
(b) an address or school as being that of a child involved in any such proceedings.

(3) In any proceedings for an offence under this section it shall be a defence for the accused to prove that he did not know, and had no reason to suspect, that the published material was intended, or likely, to identify the child.

(4) The court or the [Lord Chancellor][3] may, if satisfied that the welfare of the child requires it, by order dispense with the requirements of subsection (2) to such extent as may be specified in the order.

(5) For the purposes of this section –

'publish' includes –
(a) include in a programme service (within the meaning of the Broadcasting Act 1990);][1] or
(b) cause to be published; and
'material' includes any picture or representation.

(6) Any person who contravenes this section shall be guilty of an offence and liable, on summary conviction, to a fine not exceeding level 4 on the standard scale.

(7) Subsection (1) is without prejudice to –

(a) the generality of the rule making power in section 144 of the Act of 1980; or
(b) any other power of a magistrates' court to sit in private.

(8) [Sections 69 (sittings of magistrates' courts for family proceedings) and 71 (newspaper reports of certain proceedings) of the Act of 1980][2] shall apply in relation to any proceedings [(before a magistrates' court)][4] to which this section applies subject to the provisions of this section.

NOTES
Amendments. [1] Words substituted: Broadcasting Act 1990, s 203(1), Sch 20, para 53. [2] Words substituted: Courts and Legal Services Act 1990, s 116, Sch 16, para 24. [3] Words substituted: Transfer of Functions (Magistrates' Courts and Family Law) Order 1992, SI 1992/709. [4] Words inserted: Access to Justice Act 1999, s 72.
Definitions. 'Child': s 105(1); 'material': s 97(5); 'publish': s 97(5); 'school': s 105(1); 'the court': s 92(7).

98 Self-incrimination

(1) In any proceedings in which a court is hearing an application for an order under Part IV or V, no person shall be excused from –

(a) giving evidence on any matter; or
(b) answering any question put to him in the course of his giving evidence,

on the ground that doing so might incriminate him or his spouse of an offence.

(2) A statement or admission made in such proceedings shall not be admissible in evidence against the person making it or his spouse in proceedings for an offence other than perjury.

99 ...[1]

NOTES
Amendments. [1] Section repealed: Access to Justice Act 1999, s 106, Sch 15, Pt I.

100 Restrictions on use of wardship jurisdiction

(1) Section 7 of the Family Law Reform Act 1969 (which gives the High Court power to place a ward of court in the care, or under the supervision, of a local authority) shall cease to have effect.

(2) No court shall exercise the High Court's inherent jurisdiction with respect to children –

(a) so as to require a child to be placed in the care, or put under the supervision, of a local authority;
(b) so as to require a child to be accommodated by or on behalf of a local authority;
(c) so as to make a child who is the subject of a care order a ward of court; or
(d) for the purpose of conferring on any local authority power to determine any question which has arisen, or which may arise, in connection with any aspect of parental responsibility for a child.

(3) No application for any exercise of the court's inherent jurisdiction with respect to children may be made by a local authority unless the authority have obtained the leave of the court.

(4) The court may only grant leave if it is satisfied that –

(a) the result which the authority wish to achieve could not be achieved through the making of any order of a kind to which subsection (5) applies; and

(b) there is reasonable cause to believe that if the court's inherent jurisdiction is not exercised with respect to the child he is likely to suffer significant harm.

(5) This subsection applies to any order –

(a) made otherwise than in the exercise of the court's inherent jurisdiction; and

(b) which the local authority is entitled to apply for (assuming, in the case of any application which may only be made with leave, that leave is granted).

NOTES

Definitions. 'Care order': ss 31(11), 105(1); 'child': s 105(1); 'harm': s 31(9); 'local authority': s 105(1); 'parental responsibility': s 3; 'significant harm': s 31(10); 'the court': s 92(7).

101 Effect of orders as between England and Wales and Northern Ireland, the Channel Islands or the Isle of Man

(1) The Secretary of State may make regulations providing –

(a) for prescribed orders which –
  (i) are made by a court in Northern Ireland; and
  (ii) appear to the Secretary of State to correspond in their effect to orders which may be made under any provision of this Act,
  to have effect in prescribed circumstances, for prescribed purposes of this Act, as if they were orders of a prescribed kind made under this Act;

(b) for prescribed orders which –
  (i) are made by a court in England and Wales; and
  (ii) appear to the Secretary of State to correspond in their effect to orders which may be made under any provision in force in Northern Ireland,
  to have effect in prescribed circumstances, for prescribed purposes of the law of Northern Ireland, as if they were orders of a prescribed kind made in Northern Ireland.

(2) Regulations under subsection (1) may provide for the order concerned to cease to have effect for the purposes of the law of Northern Ireland, or (as the case may be) the law of England and Wales, if prescribed conditions are satisfied.

(3) The Secretary of State may make regulations providing for prescribed orders which –

(a) are made by a court in the Isle of Man or in any of the Channel Islands; and

(b) appear to the Secretary of State to correspond in their effect to orders which may be made under this Act,
  to have effect in prescribed circumstances for prescribed purposes of this Act, as if they were orders of a prescribed kind made under this Act.

(4) Where a child who is in the care of a local authority is lawfully taken to live in Northern Ireland, the Isle of Man or in any of the Channel Islands, the care order in question shall cease to have effect if the conditions prescribed in regulations by the Secretary of State are satisfied.

(5) Any regulations made under this section may –

(a) make such consequential amendments (including repeals) in –
  (i) section 25 of the Children and Young Persons Act 1969 (transfers between England and Wales and Northern Ireland); or

PART I

(ii) section 26 (transfers between England and Wales and Channel Islands or Isle of Man) of that Act,

as the Secretary of State considers necessary or expedient; and

(b) modify any provision of this Act, in its application (by virtue of the regulations) in relation to an order made otherwise than in England and Wales.

NOTES

Definitions. 'Care order': ss 31(11), 105(1); 'child': s 105(1); 'local authority': s 105(1); 'prescribed': s 105(1); 'the court': s 92(7).

Search warrants

102 Power of constable to assist in exercise of certain powers to search for children or inspect premises

(1) Where, on an application made by any person for a warrant under this section, it appears to the court –

(a) that a person attempting to exercise powers under any enactment mentioned in subsection (6) has been prevented from doing so by being refused entry to the premises concerned or refused access to the child concerned; or

(b) that any such person is likely to be so prevented from exercising any such powers,

it may issue a warrant authorising any constable to assist that person in the exercise of those powers, using reasonable force if necessary.

(2) Every warrant issued under this section shall be addressed to, and executed by, a constable who shall be accompanied by the person applying for the warrant if –

(a) that person so desires; and

(b) the court by whom the warrant is issued does not direct otherwise.

(3) A court granting an application for a warrant under this section may direct that the constable concerned may, in executing the warrant, be accompanied by a registered medical practitioner, registered nurse or registered health visitor if he so chooses.

(4) An application for a warrant under this section shall be made in the manner and form prescribed by rules of court.

(5) Where –

(a) an application for a warrant under this section relates to a particular child; and

(b) it is reasonably practicable to do so,

the application and any warrant granted on the application shall name the child; and where it does not name him it shall describe him as clearly as possible.

(6) The enactments are –

(a) sections 62, 64, 67, 76, 80, 86 and 87;

(b) paragraph 8(1)(b) and (2)(b) of Schedule 3;

(c) section 33 of the Adoption Act 1976 (duty of local authority to secure that protected children are visited from time to time).

General

103 Offences by bodies corporate

(1) This section applies where any offence under this Act is committed by a body corporate.

(2) If the offence is proved to have been committed with the consent or connivance of or to be attributable to any neglect on the part of any director, manager, secretary or other similar officer of the body corporate, or any person who was purporting to act in any such capacity, he (as well as the body corporate) shall be guilty of the offence and shall be liable to be proceeded against and punished accordingly.

104 Regulations and orders

(1) Any power of the Lord Chancellor or the Secretary of State under this Act to make an order, regulations, or rules, except an order under section ...[1] 56(4)(a), 57(3), 84 or 97(4) or paragraph 1(1) of Schedule 4, shall be exercisable by statutory instrument.

(2) Any such statutory instrument, except one made under section 17(4), 107 or 108(2), shall be subject to annulment in pursuance of a resolution of either House of Parliament.

(3) An order under section 17(4) shall not be made unless a draft of it has been laid before, and approved by a resolution of, each House of Parliament.

(4) Any statutory instrument made under this Act may –

  (a) make different provision for different cases;
  (b) provide for exemptions from any of its provisions; and
  (c) contain such incidental, supplemental and transitional provisions as the person making it considers expedient.

105 Interpretation

(1) In this Act –

  'adoption agency' means a body which may be referred to as an adoption agency by virtue of section 1 of the Adoption Act 1976;
  ['appropriate children's home' has the meaning given by section 23;] [12]
  'bank holiday' means a day which is a bank holiday under the Banking and Financial Dealings Act 1971;
  ['care home' has the same meaning as in the Care Standards Act 2000;] [12]
  'care order' has the meaning given by section 31(11) and also includes any order which by or under any enactment has the effect of, or is deemed to be, a care order for the purposes of this Act; and any reference to a child who is in the care of an authority is a reference to a child who is in their care by virtue of a care order;

PART I

'child' means, subject to paragraph 16 of Schedule 1, a person under the age of eighteen;

'child assessment order' has the meaning given by section 43(2);

'child minder' has the meaning given by section 71;

'child of the family', in relation to the parties to a marriage, means –

    (a) a child of both of those parties;

    (b) any other child, not being a child who is placed with those parties as foster parents by a local authority or voluntary organisation, who has been treated by both of those parties as a child of their family;

['children's home', has the meaning given by section 23;][12]

'community home' has the meaning given by section 53;

'contact order' has the meaning given by section 8(1);

'day care' [(except in Part XA)][11] has the same meaning as in section 18;

'disabled', in relation to a child, has the same meaning as in section 17(11); ...[3]

'domestic premises' has the meaning given by section 71(12);

['dwelling-house' includes –

    (a) any building or part of a building which is occupied as a dwelling;

    (b) any caravan, house-boat or structure which is occupied as a dwelling; and any yard, garage or outhouse belonging to it and occupied with it;][6]

'education supervision order' has the meaning given in section 36;

'emergency protection order' means an order under section 44;

'family assistance order' has the meaning given in section 16(2);

'family proceedings' has the meaning given by section 8(3);

'functions' includes powers and duties;

'guardian of a child' means a guardian (other than a guardian of the estate of a child) appointed in accordance with the provisions of section 5;

'harm' has the same meaning as in section 31(9) and the question of whether harm is significant shall be determined in accordance with section 31(10);

['Health Authority' means a Health Authority established under section 8 of the National Health Services Act 1977;][3]

'health service hospital' has the same meaning as in the National Health Service Act 1977;

'hospital' [(except in Schedule 9A)][12] has the same meaning as in the Mental Health Act 1983, except that it does not include a [hospital at which high security psychiatric services within the meaning of that Act are provided][7];

'ill-treatment' has the same meaning as in section 31(9);

['income-based jobseeker's allowance' has the same meaning as in the Jobseekers Act 1995;][4]

['independent hospital' has the same meaning as in the Care Standards Act 2000;][12]

'independent school' has the same meaning as in [the Education Act 1996][5];

'local authority' means, in relation to England ...[2], the council of a county, a metropolitan district, a London Borough or the Common Council of the City of London [, in relation to Wales, the council of a county or a county borough][2] and, in relation to Scotland, a local authority within the meaning of section 1(2) of the Social Work (Scotland) Act 1968;

'local authority foster parent' has the same meaning as in section 23(3);

'local education authority' has the same meaning as in [the Education Act 1996][5];

'local housing authority' has the same meaning as in the Housing Act 1985; ...[12]

['officer of the Service' has the same meaning as in the Criminal Justice and
  Court Services Act 2000;][9]
'parental responsibility' has the meaning given in section 3;
'parental responsibility agreement' has the meaning given in section 4(1);
'prescribed' means prescribed by regulations made under this Act;
['private children's home' means a children's home in respect of which a
  person is registered under Part II of the Care Standards Act 2000 which is
  not a community home or a voluntary home;][12]
['Primary Care Trust' means a Primary Care Trust established under section
  16A of the National Health Service Act 1977;][7]
'privately fostered child' and 'to foster a child privately' have the same
  meaning as in section 66;
'prohibited steps order' has the meaning given by section 8(1);
'protected child' has the same meaning as in Part III of the Adoption Act 1976;
  ...[12]
'registered pupil' has the same meaning as in [the Education Act 1996][5];
'relative', in relation to a child, means a grandparent, brother, sister, uncle or
  aunt (whether of the full blood or half blood or by affinity) or step-parent;
'residence order' has the meaning given by section 8(1);
  ...[12]
'responsible person', in relation to a child who is the subject of a supervision
  order, has the meaning given in paragraph 1 of Schedule 3;
'school' has the same meaning as in [the Education Act 1996][5] or, in relation
  to Scotland, in the Education (Scotland) Act 1980;
'service', in relation to any provision made under Part III, includes any facility;
'signed', in relation to any person, includes the making by that person of his
  mark;
'special educational needs' has the same meaning as in [the Education Act
  1993][5];
['Special Health Authority' means a Special Health Authority established
  under section 11 of the National Health Service Act 1977;][3]
'specific issue order' has the meaning given by section 8(1);
['Strategic Health Authority' means a Strategic Health Authority established
  under section 8 of the National Health Service Act 1977;][13]
'supervision order' has the meaning given by section 31(11);
'supervised child' and 'supervisor', in relation to a supervision order or an
  education supervision order, mean respectively the child who is (or is to be)
  under supervision and the person under whose supervision he is (or is to be)
  by virtue of the order;
'upbringing', in relation to any child, includes the care of the child but not his
  maintenance;
'voluntary home' has the meaning given by section 60;
'voluntary organisation' means a body (other than a public or local authority)
  whose activities are not carried on for profit.

(2) References in this Act to a child whose father and mother were, or (as the case
may be) were not, married to each other at the time of his birth must be read with
section 1 of the Family Law Reform Act 1987 (which extends the meaning of such
references).

(3) References in this Act to –

(a) a person with whom a child lives, or is to live, as the result of a residence
  order; or

(b) a person in whose favour a residence order is in force,

shall be construed as references to the person named in the order as the person with whom the child is to live.

(4) References in this Act to a child who is looked after by a local authority have the same meaning as they have (by virtue of section 22) in Part III.

(5) References in this Act to accommodation provided by or on behalf of a local authority are references to accommodation so provided in the exercise of functions [of that or any other local authority which are social services functions within the meaning of][10] the Local Authority Social Services Act 1970.

[(5A) References in this Act to a child minder shall be construed –

    (a) ...[14]

    (b) in relation to England and Wales, in accordance with section 79A.] [11]

[(5B) (*Applies to Scotland only*)][14]

(6) In determining the 'ordinary residence' of a child for any purpose of this Act, there shall be disregarded any period in which he lives in any place –

    (a) which is a school or other institution;

    (b) in accordance with the requirements of a supervision order under this Act or an order under [section 63(1) of the Powers of Criminal Courts (Sentencing) Act 2000][8]; or

    (c) while he is being provided with accommodation by or on behalf of a local authority.

(7) References in this Act to children who are in need shall be construed in accordance with section 17.

(8) Any notice or other document required under this Act to be served on any person may be served on him by being delivered personally to him, or being sent by post to him in a registered letter or by the recorded delivery service at his proper address.

(9) Any such notice or other document required to be served on a body corporate or a firm shall be duly served if it is served on the secretary or clerk of that body or a partner of that firm.

(10) For the purposes of this section, and of section 7 of the Interpretation Act 1978 in its application to this section, the proper address of a person –

    (a) in the case of a secretary or clerk of a body corporate, shall be that of the registered or principal office of that body;

    (b) in the case of a partner of a firm, shall be that of the principal office of the firm; and

    (c) in any other case, shall be the last known address of the person to be served.

NOTES

Amendments. [1] Words inserted: Registered Homes (Amendment) Act 1991, s 2(6). [2] Words repealed or inserted: Local Government (Wales) Act 1994, Sch 10, para 13, Sch 18. [3] Definitions repealed or substituted: Health Authorities Act 1995, ss 2(1), 5(1), Sch 1, Pt III, para 118(1), (10). [4] Definition inserted: Jobseekers Act 1995, s 41(4), Sch 2, para 19. [5] Words substituted: Education Act 1996, s 582(1), Sch 37, Pt I, para 91. [6] Definition inserted: Family Law Act 1996, s 52, Sch 6, para 5. [7] Definitions inserted or amended: Health Act 1999 (Supplementary, Consequential etc Provisions) Order 2000, SI 2000/90. [8] Words substituted: Powers of Criminal Courts (Sentencing) Act 2000, s 165(1), Sch 9, para 128. [9] Definition inserted: Criminal Justice and Court Services Act 2000, s 74, Sch 7, paras 87, 95. [10] Words substituted: Local Government Act 2000, s 107, Sch 5, para 22. [11] Definition amended and subsection inserted: Care Standards

Act 2000, s 116, Sch 4, para 14(1), 23. [12] Definitions and words repealed, inserted and substituted: Care Standards Act 2000, s 116, Sch 4, para 14(23). [13] Definition inserted: National Health Service Reform and Health Care Professions Act 2002 (Supplementary, Consequential etc Provisions) Regulations 2002, SI 2002/2469. [14] Paragraph repealed and subsection inserted: Regulation of Care (Scotland) Act 2001, s 79, Sch 3, para 15.

106 Financial provisions

(1) Any –

(a) grants made by the Secretary of State under this Act; and
(b) any other expenses incurred by the Secretary of State under this Act,

shall be payable out of money provided by Parliament.

(2) Any sums received by the Secretary of State under section 58, or by way of the repayment of any grant made under section 82(2) or (4) shall be paid into the Consolidated Fund.

107 Application to the Channel Islands

Her Majesty may by Order in Council direct that any of the provisions of this Act shall extend to any of the Channel Islands with such exceptions and modifications as may be specified in the Order.

108 Short title, commencement, extent, etc

(1) This Act may be cited as the Children Act 1989.

(2) Sections 89 and 96(3) to (7), and paragraph 35 of Schedule 12, shall come into force on the passing of this Act and paragraph 36 of Schedule 12 shall come into force at the end of the period of two months beginning with the day on which this Act is passed but otherwise this Act shall come into force on such date as may be appointed by order made by the Lord Chancellor or the Secretary of State, or by both acting jointly.

(3) Different dates may be appointed for different provisions of this Act in relation to different cases.

(4) The minor amendments set out in Schedule 12 shall have effect.

(5) The consequential amendments set out in Schedule 13 shall have effect.

(6) The transitional provisions and savings set out in Schedule 14 shall have effect.

(7) The repeals set out in Schedule 15 shall have effect.

(8) An order under subsection (2) may make such transitional provisions or savings as appear to the person making the order to be necessary or expedient in connection with the provisions brought into force by the order, including –

(a) provisions adding to or modifying the provisions of Schedule 14; and
(b) such adaptations –
    (i) of the provisions brought into force by the order; and
    (ii) of any provisions of this Act then in force,
as appear to him necessary or expedient in consequence of the partial operation of this Act.

PART I

(9) The Lord Chancellor may by order make such amendments or repeals, in such enactments as may be specified in the order, as appear to him to be necessary or expedient in consequence of any provision of this Act.

(10) This Act shall, in its application to the Isles of Scilly, have effect subject to such exceptions, adaptations and modifications as the Secretary of State may by order prescribe.

(11) The following provisions of this Act extend to Scotland –

...²
section 25(8);
...²
section 88;
section 104 (so far as necessary);
section 105 (so far as necessary);
subsections (1) to (3), (8) and (9) and this subsection;
in Schedule 2, paragraph 24;
in Schedule 12, paragraphs 1, 7 to 10, 18, 27, 30(a) and 41 to 44;
in Schedule 13, paragraphs 18 to 23, 32, 46, 47, 50, 57, 62, 63, 68(a) and (b) and 71;
in Schedule 14, paragraphs 1, 33 and 34;
in Schedule 15, the entries relating to –
    (a) the Custody of Children Act 1891;
    (b) the Nurseries and Child Minders Regulation Act 1948;
    (c) section 53(3) of the Children and Young Persons Act 1963;
    (d) section 60 of the Health Services and Public Health Act 1968;
    (e) the Social Work (Scotland) Act 1968;
    (f) the Adoption (Scotland) Act 1978;
    (g) the Child Care Act 1980;
    (h) the Foster Children (Scotland) Act 1984;
    (i) the Child Abduction and Custody Act 1985; and
    (j) the Family Law Act 1986.

(12) The following provisions of this Act extend to Northern Ireland –

section 101(1)(b), (2) and (5)(a)(i);
subsections (1) to (3), (8) and (9) and this subsection;
in Schedule 2, paragraph 24;
in Schedule 12, paragraphs 7 to 10, 18 and 27;
in Schedule 13, paragraphs 21, 22, 46, 47, 57, 62, 63, 68(c) to (e) and 69 to 71;
in Schedule 14, paragraphs ...¹ 28 to 30 and 38(a); and
in Schedule 15, the entries relating to the Guardianship of Minors Act 1971, the Children Act 1975, the Child Care Act 1980, and the Family Law Act 1986.

NOTES

Amendments. ¹ Word repealed: Courts and Legal Services Act 1990, ss 116, 125(7), Sch 16, para 25, Sch 20. ² Words repealed: Regulation of Care (Scotland) Act 2001, s 80(1), Sch 4.

SCHEDULE 1

FINANCIAL PROVISION FOR CHILDREN

Section 15(1)

Orders for financial relief against parents

1. (1) On an application made by a parent or guardian of a child, or by any person in whose favour a residence order is in force with respect to a child, the court may –

- (a) in the case of an application to the High Court or a county court, make one or more of the orders mentioned in sub-paragraph (2);
- (b) in the case of an application to a magistrates' court, make one or both of the orders mentioned in paragraphs (a) and (c) of that sub-paragraph.

(2) The orders referred to in sub-paragraph (1) are –

- (a) an order requiring either or both parents of a child –
    - (i) to make to the applicant for the benefit of the child; or
    - (ii) to make to the child himself,
    such periodical payments, for such term, as may be specified in the order;
- (b) an order requiring either or both parents of a child –
    - (i) to secure to the applicant for the benefit of the child; or
    - (ii) to secure to the child himself,
    such periodical payments, for such term, as may be so specified;
- (c) an order requiring either or both parents of a child –
    - (i) to pay to the applicant for the benefit of the child; or
    - (ii) to pay to the child himself,
    such lump sum as may be so specified;
- (d) an order requiring a settlement to be made for the benefit of the child, and to the satisfaction of the court, of property –
    - (i) to which either parent is entitled (either in possession or in reversion); and
    - (ii) which is specified in the order;
- (e) an order requiring either or both parents of a child –
    - (i) to transfer to the applicant, for the benefit of the child; or
    - (ii) to transfer to the child himself,
    such property to which the parent is, or the parents are, entitled (either in possession or in reversion) as may be specified in the order.

(3) The powers conferred by this paragraph may be exercised at any time.

(4) An order under sub-paragraph (2)(a) or (b) may be varied or discharged by a subsequent order made on the application of any person by or to whom payments were required to be made under the previous order.

(5) Where a court makes an order under this paragraph –

- (a) it may at any time make a further such order under sub-paragraph (2)(a), (b) or (c) with respect to the child concerned if he has not reached the age of eighteen;
- (b) it may not make more than one order under sub-paragraph (2)(d) or (e) against the same person in respect of the same child.

PART I

(6) On making, varying or discharging a residence order the court may exercise any of its powers under this Schedule even though no application has been made to it under this Schedule.

[(7) Where a child is a ward of court, the court may exercise any of its powers under this Schedule even though no application has been made to it.]¹

NOTES

Amendments. ¹ Sub-paragraph added: Courts and Legal Services Act 1990, s 116, Sch 16, para 10(2).

Definitions. 'Child': s 105(1); 'parent': Sch 1, para 16(2); 'residence order': s 8(1); 'the court': s 92(7).

Orders for financial relief for persons over eighteen

2. (1) If, on an application by a person who has reached the age of eighteen, it appears to the court –

  (a) that the applicant is, will be or (if an order were made under this paragraph) would be receiving instruction at an educational establishment or undergoing training for a trade, profession or vocation, whether or not while in gainful employment; or
  (b) that there are special circumstances which justify the making of an order under this paragraph,

the court may make one or both of the orders mentioned in sub-paragraph (2).

(2) The orders are –

  (a) an order requiring either or both of the applicant's parents to pay to the applicant such periodical payments, for such term, as may be specified in the order;
  (b) an order requiring either or both of the applicant's parents to pay to the applicant such lump sum as may be so specified.

(3) An applicant may not be made under this paragraph by any person if, immediately before he reached the age of sixteen, a periodical payments order was in force with respect to him.

(4) No order shall be made under this paragraph at a time when the parents of the applicant are living with each other in the same household.

(5) An order under sub-paragraph (2)(a) may be varied or discharged by a subsequent order made on the application of any person by or to whom payments were required to be made under the previous order.

(6) In sub-paragraph (3) 'periodical payments order' means an order made under –

  (a) this Schedule;
  (b) ...¹
  (c) section 23 or 27 of the Matrimonial Causes Act 1973;
  (d) Part I of the Domestic Proceedings and Magistrates' Courts Act 1978, for the making or securing of periodical payments.

(7) The powers conferred by this paragraph shall be exercisable at any time.

(8) Where the court makes an order under this paragraph it may from time to time while that order remains in force make a further such order.

NOTES
Amendments. [1] Words repealed: Child Support Act 1991, s 58(14).
Definitions. 'Periodical payments order': Sch 1, para 2(6); 'the court': s 92(7).

Duration of orders for financial relief

3. (1) The term to be specified in an order for periodical payments made under paragraph 1(2)(a) or (b) in favour of a child may begin with the date of the making of an application for the order in question or any later date [or a date ascertained in accordance with sub-paragraph (5) or (6)][1] but –

    (a) shall not in the first instance extend beyond the child's seventeenth birthday unless the court thinks it right in the circumstances of the case to specify a later date; and

    (b) shall not in any event extend beyond the child's eighteenth birthday.

(2) Paragraph (b) of sub-paragraph (1) shall not apply in the case of a child if it appears to the court that –

    (a) the child is, or will be (if an order were made without complying with that paragraph) would be receiving instruction at an educational establishment or undergoing training for a trade, profession or vocation, whether or not while in gainful employment; or

    (b) there are special circumstances which justify the making of an order without complying with that paragraph.

(3) An order for periodical payments made under paragraph 1(2)(a) or 2(2)(a) shall, notwithstanding anything in the order, cease to have effect on the death of the person liable to make payments under the order.

(4) Where an order is made under paragraph 1(2)(a) or (b) requiring periodical payments to be made or secured to the parent of a child, the order shall cease to have effect if –

    (a) any parent making or securing the payments; and

    (b) any parent to whom the payments are made or secured,

live together for a period of more than six months.

[(5) Where –

    (a) a maintenance assessment ('the current assessment') is in force with respect to a child; and

    (b) an application is made for an order under paragraph 1(2)(a) or (b) of this Schedule for periodical payments in favour of that child –

        (i) in accordance with section 8 of the Child Support Act 1991; and

        (ii) before the end of the period of 6 months beginning with the making of the current assessment,

the term to be specified in any such order made on that application may be expressed to begin on, or at any time after, the earliest permitted date.

(6) For the purposes of subsection (5) above, 'the earliest permitted date' is whichever is the later of –

    (a) the date 6 months before the application is made; or

    (b) the date on which the current assessment took effect or, where successive maintenance assessments have been continuously in force with respect to a child, on which the first of those assessments took effect.

(7) Where –

- (a) a maintenance assessment ceases to have effect or is cancelled by or under any provision of the Child Support Act 1991, and
- (b) an application is made, before the end of the period of 6 months beginning with the relevant date, for an order for periodical payments under paragraph 1(2)(a) or (b) in favour of a child with respect to whom that maintenance assessment was in force immediately before it ceased to have effect or was cancelled,

the term to be specified in any such order, or in any interim order under paragraph 9, made on that application may begin with the date on which that maintenance assessment ceased to have effect or, as the case may be, the date with effect from which it was cancelled, or any later date.

(8) In sub-paragraph (7)(b) –

- (a) where the maintenance assessment ceased to have effect, the relevant date is the date on which it so ceased; and
- (b) where the maintenance assessment was cancelled, the relevant date is the later of –
    - (i) the date on which the person who cancelled it did so, and
    - (ii) the date from which the cancellation first had effect.][1]

NOTES

Amendments. [1] Words and subparagraphs inserted: Maintenance Orders (Backdating) Order 1993, SI 1993/623.

Matters to which court is to have regard in making orders for financial relief

4. (1) In deciding whether to exercise its powers under paragraph 1 or 2, and if so in what manner, the court shall have regard to all the circumstances including –

- (a) the income, earning capacity, property and other financial resources which each person mentioned in sub-paragraph (4) has or is likely to have in the foreseeable future;
- (b) the financial needs, obligations and responsibilities which each person mentioned in sub-paragraph (4) has or is likely to have in the foreseeable future;
- (c) the financial needs of the child;
- (d) the income, earning capacity (if any), property and other financial resources of the child;
- (e) any physical or mental disability of the child;
- (f) the manner in which the child was being, or was expected to be, educated or trained.

(2) In deciding whether to exercise its powers under paragraph 1 against a person who is not the mother or father of the child, and if so in what manner, the court shall in addition have regard to –

- (a) whether that person had assumed responsibility for the maintenance of the child, and, if so, the extent to which and basis on which he assumed that responsibility and the length of the period during which he met that responsibility;
- (b) whether he did so knowing that the child was not his child;
- (c) the liability of any other person to maintain the child.

(3) Where the court makes an order under paragraph 1 against a person who is not the father of the child, it shall record in the order that the order is made on the basis that the person against whom the order is made is not the child's father.

(4) The persons mentioned in sub-paragraph (1) are –

(a) in relation to a decision whether to exercise its powers under paragraph 1, any parent of the child;

(b) in relation to a decision whether to exercise its powers under paragraph 2, the mother and father of the child;

(c) the applicant for the order;

(d) any other person in whose favour the court proposes to make the order.

Provisions relating to lump sums

5. (1) Without prejudice to the generality of paragraph 1, an order under that paragraph for the payment of a lump sum may be made for the purpose of enabling any liabilities or expenses –

(a) incurred in connection with the birth of the child or in maintaining the child; and

(b) reasonably incurred before the making of the order,

to be met.

(2) The amount of any lump sum required to be paid by an order made by a magistrates' court under paragraph 1 or 2 shall not exceed £1000 or such larger amount as the [Lord Chancellor][1] may from time to time by order fix for the purposes of this sub-paragraph.

(3) The power of the court under paragraph 1 or 2 to vary or discharge an order for the making or securing of periodical payments by a parent shall include power to make an order under that provision for the payment of a lump sum by that parent.

(4) The amount of any lump sum which a parent may be required to pay by virtue of sub-paragraph (3) shall not, in the case of an order made by a magistrates' court, exceed the maximum amount that may at the time of the making of the order be required to be paid under sub-paragraph (2), but a magistrates' court may make an order for the payment of a lump sum not exceeding that amount even though the parent was required to pay a lump sum by a previous order under this Act.

(5) An order made under paragraph 1 or 2 for the payment of a lump sum may provide for the payment of that sum by instalments.

(6) Where the court provides for the payment of a lump sum by instalments the court, on an application made either by the person liable to pay or the person entitled to receive that sum, shall have power to vary that order by varying –

(a) the number of instalments payable;

(b) the amount of any instalment payable;

(c) the date on which any instalment becomes payable.

NOTES

Amendments. [1] Words substituted: Transfer of Functions (Magistrates' Courts and Family Law) Order 1992, SI 1992/709.

Definitions. 'Child': s 105(1), Sch 1, para 16(1); 'parent': Sch 1, para 16(2); 'the court': s 92(7).

Variation etc of orders for periodical payments

6. (1) In exercising its powers under paragraph 1 or 2 to vary or discharge an order for the making or securing of periodical payments the court shall have regard to all the circumstances of the case, including any change in any of the matters to which the court was required to have regard when making the order.

(2) The power of the court under paragraph 1 or 2 to vary an order for the making or securing of periodical payments shall include power to suspend any provision of the order temporarily and to revive any provision so suspended.

(3) Where on an application under paragraph 1 or 2 for the variation or discharge of an order for the making or securing of periodical payments the court varies the payments required to be made under that order, the court may provide that the payments as so varied shall be made from such date as the court may specify [except that, subject to sub-paragraph (9), the date shall not be]¹ earlier than the date of the making of the application.

(4) An application for the variation of an order made under paragraph 1 for the making or securing of periodical payments to or for the benefit of a child may, if the child has reached the age of sixteen, be made by the child himself.

(5) Where an order for the making or securing of periodical payments made under paragraph 1 ceases to have effect on the date on which the child reaches the age of sixteen, or at any time after that date but before or on the date on which he reaches the age of eighteen, the child may apply to the court which made the order for an order for its revival.

(6) If on such an application it appears to the court that –

(a) the child is, will be or (if an order were made under this sub-paragraph) would be receiving instruction at an educational establishment or undergoing training for a trade, profession or vocation, whether or not while in gainful employment; or

(b) there are special circumstances which justify the making of an order under this paragraph,

the court shall have power by order to revive the order from such date as the court may specify, not being earlier than the date of the making of the application.

(7) Any order which is revived by an order under sub-paragraph (5) may be varied or discharged under that provision, on the application of any person by whom or to whom payments are required to be made under the revived order.

(8) An order for the making or securing of periodical payments made under paragraph 1 may be varied or discharged, after the death of either parent, on the application of a guardian of the child concerned.

[(9) Where –

(a) an order under paragraph 1(2)(a) or (b) for the making or securing of periodical payments in favour of more than one child ('the order') is in force;

(b) the order requires payments specified in it to be made to or for the benefit of more than one child without apportioning those payments between them;

(c) a maintenance assessment ('the assessment') is made with respect to one or more, but not all, of the children with respect to whom those payments are to be made; and

(d)   an application is made, before the end of the period of 6 months beginning with the date on which the assessment was made, for the variation or discharge of the order,

the court may, in exercise of its powers under paragraph 1 to vary or discharge the order, direct that the variation or discharge shall take effect from the date on which the assessment took effect or any later date.]¹

NOTES

Amendments. ¹ Words substituted or subparagraph inserted: Maintenance Orders (Backdating) Order 1993, SI 1993/623.

[Variation of orders for periodical payments etc made by magistrates' courts

6A. (1) Subject to sub-paragraphs (7) and (8), the power of a magistrates' court –

(a)   under paragraph 1 or 2 to vary an order for the making of periodical payments, or
(b)   under paragraph 5(6) to vary an order for the payment of a lump sum by instalments,

shall include power, if the court is satisfied that payment has not been made in accordance with the order, to exercise one of its powers under paragraphs (a) to (d) of section 59(3) of the Magistrates' Courts Act 1980.

(2) In any case where –

(a)   a magistrates' court has made an order under this Schedule for the making of periodical payments or for the payment of a lump sum by instalments, and
(b)   payments under the order are required to be made by any method of payment falling within section 59(6) of the Magistrates' Courts Act 1980 (standing order, etc),

any person entitled to make an application under this Schedule for the variation of the order (in this paragraph referred to as 'the applicant') may apply to the clerk to the justices for the petty sessions area for which the court is acting for the order to be varied as mentioned in sub-paragraph (3).

(3) Subject to sub-paragraph (5), where an application is made under sub-paragraph (2), the clerk, after giving written notice (by post or otherwise) of the application to any interested party and allowing that party, within the period of 14 days beginning with the date of the giving of that notice, an opportunity to make written representations, may vary the order to provide that payments under the order shall be made [to the justices' chief executive for the court] ³.

(4) The clerk may proceed with an application under sub-paragraph (2) notwithstanding that any such interested party as is referred to in sub-paragraph (3) has not received written notice of the application.

(5) Where an application has been made under sub-paragraph (2), the clerk may, if he considers it inappropriate to exercise his power under sub-paragraph (3), refer the matter to the court which, subject to sub-paragraphs (7) and (8), may vary the order by exercising one of its powers under paragraphs (a) to (d) of section 59(3) of the Magistrates' Courts Act 1980.

(6) Subsection (4) of section 59 of the Magistrates' Courts Act 1980 (power of court to order that account be opened) shall apply for the purposes of sub-paragraphs (1) and (5) as it applies for the purposes of that section.

(7) Before varying the order by exercising one of its powers under paragraphs (a) to (d) of section 59(3) of the Magistrates' Courts Act 1980, the court shall have regard to any representations made by the parties to the application.

(8) If the court does not propose to exercise its power [under paragraph (c), (cc) or (d)][2] of subsection (3) of section 59 of the Magistrates' Courts Act 1980, the court shall, unless upon representations expressly made in that behalf by the applicant for the order it is satisfied that it is undesirable to do so, exercise its power under paragraph (b) of that subsection.

(9) None of the powers of the court, or of the clerk to the justices, conferred by this paragraph shall be exercisable in relation to an order under this Schedule for the making of periodical payments, or for the payment of a lump sum by instalments, which is not a qualifying maintenance order (within the meaning of section 59 of the Magistrates' Courts Act 1980).

(10) In sub-paragraphs (3) and (4) 'interested party', in relation to an application made by the applicant under sub-paragraph (2), means a person who would be entitled to be a party to an application for the variation of the order made by the applicant under any other provision of this Schedule if such an application were made.][1]

NOTES

Amendments. [1] Paragraph inserted: Maintenance Enforcement Act 1991, s 6. [2] Words substituted: Child Support Act 1991 (Consequential Amendments) Order 1994, SI 1994/731. [3] Words substituted: Access to Justice Act 1999, s 90, Sch 13, paras 159, 161.

Variation of orders for secured periodical payments after death of parent

7. (1) Where the parent liable to make payments under a secured periodical payments order has died, the persons who may apply for the variation or discharge of the order shall include the personal representatives of the deceased parent.

(2) No application for the variation of the order shall, except with the permission of the court, be made after the end of the period of six months from the date on which representation in regard to the estate of that parent is first taken out.

(3) The personal representatives of a deceased person against whom a secured periodical payments order was made shall not be liable for having distributed any part of the estate of the deceased after the end of the period of six months referred to in sub-paragraph (2) on the ground that they ought to have taken into account the possibility that the court might permit an application for variation to be made after that period by the person entitled to payments under the order.

(4) Sub-paragraph (3) shall not prejudice any power to recover any part of the estate so distributed arising by virtue of the variation of an order in accordance with this paragraph.

(5) Where an application to vary a secured periodical payments order is made after the death of the parent liable to make payments under the order, the circumstances to which the court is required to have regard under paragraph 6(1) shall include the changed circumstances resulting from the death of the parent.

(6) In considering for the purposes of sub-paragraph (2) the question when representation was first taken out, a grant limited to settled land or to trust property shall be left out of account and a grant limited to real estate or to personal estate shall be left out of account unless a grant limited to the remainder of the estate has previously been made or is made at the same time.

(7) In this paragraph 'secured periodical payments order' means an order for secured periodical payments under paragraph 1(2)(b).

NOTES

Definitions. 'Child': s 105(1), Sch 1, para 16(1); 'parent': Sch 1, para 16(2); 'secured periodical payments order': Sch 1, para 7(7); 'the court': s 92(7).

Financial relief under other enactments

8. (1) This paragraph applies where a residence order is made with respect to a child at a time when there is in force an order ('the financial relief order') made under any enactment other than this Act and requiring a person to contribute to the child's maintenance.

(2) Where this paragraph applies, the court may, on the application of –

    (a) any person required by the financial relief order to contribute to the child's maintenance; or

    (b) any person in whose favour a residence order with respect to the child is in force,

make an order revoking the financial relief order, or varying it by altering the amount of any sum payable under that order or by substituting the applicant for the person to whom any such sum is otherwise payable under that order.

Interim orders

9. (1) Where an application is made under paragraph 1 or 2 the court may, at any time before it disposes of the application, make an interim order –

    (a) requiring either or both parents to make such periodical payments, at such times and for such term as the court thinks fit; and

    (b) giving any direction which the court thinks fit.

(2) An interim order made under this paragraph may provide for payments to be made from such date as the court may specify [except that, subject to paragraph 3(5) and (6), the date shall not be][1] earlier than the date of the making of the application under paragraph 1 or 2.

(3) An interim order made under this paragraph shall cease to have effect when the application is disposed of or, if earlier, on the date specified for the purposes of this paragraph in the interim order.

(4) An interim order in which a date has been specified for the purposes of sub-paragraph (3) may be varied by substituting a later date.

NOTES

Amendments. [1] Words substituted: Maintenance Orders (Backdating) Order 1993, SI 1993/623.

Definitions. 'Child': s 105(1); 'parent': Sch 1, para 16(2); 'residence order': s 8(1); 'the court': s 92(7); 'the financial relief order': Sch 1, para 8(1).

Alteration of maintenance agreements

10. (1) In this paragraph and in paragraph 11 'maintenance agreement' means any agreement in writing made with respect to a child, whether before or after the commencement of this paragraph, which –

    (a) is or was made between the father and mother of the child; and

    (b) contains provision with respect to the making or securing of payments, or the disposition or use of any property, for the maintenance or education of the child,

and any such provisions are in this paragraph, and paragraph 11, referred to as 'financial arrangements'.

(2) Where a maintenance agreement is for the time being subsisting and each of the parties to the agreement is for the time being either domiciled or resident in England and Wales, then, either party may apply for an order under this paragraph.

(3) If the court to which the application is made is satisfied either –

    (a) that, by reason of a change in the circumstances in the light of which any financial arrangements contained in the agreement were made (including a change foreseen by the parties when making the agreement), the agreement should be altered so as to make different financial arrangements; or

    (b) that the agreement does not contain proper financial arrangements with respect to the child,

then that court may by order make such alterations in the agreement by varying or revoking any financial arrangements contained in it as may appear to it to be just having regard to all the circumstances.

(4) If the maintenance agreement is altered by an order under this paragraph, the agreement shall have effect thereafter as if the alteration had been made by agreement between the parties and for valuable consideration.

(5) Where a court decides to make an order under this paragraph altering the maintenance agreement –

    (a) by inserting provision for the making or securing by one of the parties to the agreement of periodical payments for the maintenance of the child; or

    (b) by increasing the rate of periodical payments required to be made or secured by one of the parties for the maintenance of the child,

then, in deciding the term for which under the agreement as altered by the order the payments or (as the case may be) the additional payments attributable to the increase are to be made or secured for the benefit of the child, the court shall apply the provisions of sub-paragraphs (1) and (2) of paragraph 3 as if the order were an order under paragraph 1(2)(a) or (b).

(6) A magistrates' court shall not entertain an application under sub-paragraph (2) unless both the parties to the agreement are resident in England and Wales and at least one of the parties is resident in the commission area ...[1] for which the court is appointed, and shall not have power to make any order on such an application except –

    (a) in a case where the agreement contains no provision for periodical payments by either of the parties, an order inserting provision for the making by one of the parties of periodical payments for the maintenance of the child;

(b) in a case where the agreement includes provision for the making by one of the parties of periodical payments, an order increasing or reducing the rate of, or terminating, any of those payments.

(7) For the avoidance of doubt it is hereby declared that nothing in this paragraph affects any power of a court before which any proceedings between the parties to a maintenance agreement are brought under any other enactment to make an order containing financial arrangements or any right of either party to apply for such an order in such proceedings.

11. (1) Where a maintenance agreement provides for the continuation, after the death of one of the parties, of payments for the maintenance of a child and that party dies domiciled in England and Wales, the surviving party or the personal representatives of the deceased party may apply to the High Court or a county court for an order under paragraph 10.

(2) If a maintenance agreement is altered by a court on an application under this paragraph, the agreement shall have effect thereafter as if the alteration had been made, immediately before the death, by agreement between the parties and for valuable consideration.

(3) An application under this paragraph shall not, except with leave of the High Court or a county court, be made after the end of the period of six months beginning with the day on which representation in regard to the estate of the deceased is first taken out.

(4) In considering for the purposes of sub-paragraph (3) the question when representation was first taken out, a grant limited to settled land or to trust property shall be left out of account and a grant limited to real estate or to personal estate shall be left out of account unless a grant limited to the remainder of the estate has previously been made or is made at the same time.

(5) A county court shall not entertain an application under this paragraph, or an application for leave to make an application under this paragraph, unless it would have jurisdiction to hear and determine proceedings for an order under section 2 of the Inheritance (Provision for Family and Dependants) Act 1975 in relation to the deceased's estate by virtue of section 25 of the County Courts Act 1984 (jurisdiction under the Act of 1975).

(6) The provisions of this paragraph shall not render the personal representatives of the deceased liable for having distributed any part of the estate of the deceased after the expiry of the period of six months referred to in sub-paragraph (3) on the ground that they ought to have taken into account the possibility that a court might grant leave for an application by virtue of this paragraph to be made by the surviving party after that period.

(7) Sub-paragraph (6) shall not prejudice any power to recover any part of the estate so distributed arising by virtue of the making of an order in pursuance of this paragraph.

NOTES
Amendments. [1] Words repealed: Access to Justice Act 1999, s 106, Sch 15, Pt V(1).
Definitions. 'Child': s 105(1); 'financial arrangements': Sch 1, para 10(1); 'maintenance agreement': Sch 1, para 10(1); 'the court': s 92(7).

Enforcement of orders for maintenance

12. (1) Any person for the time being under an obligation to make payments in pursuance of any order for the payment of money made by a magistrates' court under this Act shall give notice of any change of address to such person (if any) as may be specified in the order.

(2) Any person failing without reasonable excuse to give such a notice shall be guilty of an offence and liable on summary conviction to a fine not exceeding level 2 on the standard scale.

(3) An order for the payment of money made by a magistrates' court under this Act shall be enforceable as a magistrates' court maintenance order within the meaning of section 150(1) of the Magistrates' Courts Act 1980.

Direction for settlement of instrument by conveyancing counsel

13. Where the High Court or a county court decides to make an order under this Act for the securing of periodical payments or for the transfer or settlement of property, it may direct that the matter be referred to one of the conveyancing counsel of the court to settle a proper instrument to be executed by all necessary parties.

Financial provision for child resident in country outside England and Wales

14. (1) Where one parent of a child lives in England and Wales and the child lives outside England and Wales with –

(a) another parent of his;
(b) a guardian of his; or
(c) a person in whose favour a residence order is in force with respect to the child,

the court shall have power, on an application made by any of the persons mentioned in paragraphs (a) to (c), to make one or both of the orders mentioned in paragraph 1(2)(a) and (b) against the parent living in England and Wales.

(2) Any reference in this Act to the powers of the court under paragraph 1(2) or to an order made under paragraph 1(2) shall include a reference to the powers which the court has by virtue of sub-paragraph (1) or (as the case may be) to an order made by virtue of sub-paragraph (1).

Local authority contribution to child's maintenance

15. (1) Where a child lives, or is to live, with a person as the result of a residence order, a local authority may make contributions to that person towards the cost of the accommodation and maintenance of the child.

(2) Sub-paragraph (1) does not apply where the person with whom the child lives, or is to live, is a parent of the child or the husband or wife of a parent of the child.

Interpretation

16. (1) In this Schedule 'child' includes, in any case where an application is made under paragraph 2 or 6 in relation to a person who has reached the age of eighteen, that person.

PART I

(2) In this Schedule except paragraphs 2 and 15, 'parent' includes any party to a marriage (whether or not subsisting) in relation to whom the child concerned is a child of the family; and for this purpose any reference to either parent or both parents shall be construed as references to any parent of his and to all of his parents.

[(3) In this Schedule, 'maintenance assessment' has the same meaning as it has in the Child Support Act 1991 by virtue of section 54 of that Act as read with any regulations in force under that section.]¹

NOTES
Amendments. ¹ Words added: Maintenance Orders (Backdating) Order 1993, SI 1993/623.
Definitions. 'Child': s 105(1), Sch 1, para 16(1); 'child of the family': s 105(1); 'local authority': s 105(1); 'parent': Sch 1, para 16(2); 'residence order': s 8(1).

SCHEDULE 2

LOCAL AUTHORITY SUPPORT FOR CHILDREN AND FAMILIES

Sections 17, 23 and 29

PART I
PROVISION OF SERVICES FOR FAMILIES

Identification of children in need and provision of information

1. (1) Every local authority shall take reasonable steps to identify the extent to which there are children in need within their area.

(2) Every local authority shall –

(a) publish information
  (i) about services provided by them under sections 17, 18, [20, 23B to 23D, 24A and 24B]¹; and
  (ii) where they consider it appropriate, about the provision by others (including, in particular, voluntary organisations) of services which the authority have power to provide under those sections; and
(b) take such steps as are reasonably practicable to ensure that those who might benefit from the services receive the information relevant to them.

NOTES
Amendments. ¹ Words substituted: Children (Leaving Care) Act 2000, s 7(1), (4).

[Children's services plans

1A. (1) Every local authority shall, on or before 31st March 1997 –

(a) review their provision of services under sections 17, 20, 21, 23 and 24; and
(b) having regard to that review and to their most recent review under section 19, prepare and publish a plan for the provision of services under Part III.

(2) Every local authority –

    (a) shall, from time to time review the plan prepared by them under sub-paragraph (1)(b) (as modified or last substituted under this sub-paragraph), and

    (b) may, having regard to that review and to their most recent review under section 19, prepare and publish –

        (i) modifications (or, as the case may be, further modifications) to the plan reviewed; or

       (ii) a plan in substitution for that plan.

(3) In carrying out any review under this paragraph and in preparing any plan or modifications to a plan, a local authority shall consult –

    (a) every [Local Health Board,][4] [Health Authority [or][3] Primary Care Trust][2] the whole or any part of whose area lies within the area of the local authority;

    (b) every National Health Service trust which manages a hospital, establishment or facility (within the meaning of the National Health Service and Community Care Act 1990) in the authority's area;

    (c) if the local authority is not itself a local education authority, every local education authority the whole or any part of whose area lies within the area of the local authority;

    (d) any organisation which represents schools in the authority's area which are grant-maintained schools or grant-maintained special schools (within the meaning of the Education Act 1993);

    (e) the governing body of every such school in the authority's area which is not so represented;

    (f) such voluntary organisations as appear to the local authority –

        (i) to represent the interests of persons who use or are likely to use services provided by the local authority under Part III; or

       (ii) to provide services in the area of the local authority which, were they to be provided by the local authority, might be categorised as services provided under that Part;

    (g) the chief constable of the police force for the area;

    (h) the probation committee for the area;

    (i) such other persons as appear to the local authority to be appropriate; and

    (j) such other persons as the Secretary of State may direct.

(4) Every local authority shall, within 28 days of receiving a written request from the Secretary of State, submit to him a copy of –

    (a) the plan prepared by them under sub-paragraph (1); or

    (b) where that plan has been modified or substituted, the plan as modified or last substituted.][1]

NOTES

Amendments. [1] Paragraph inserted: Children Act 1989 (Amendment) (Children's Services Planning) Order 1996, SI 1996/785. [2] Words substituted: Health Act 1999 (Supplementary, Consequential etc Provisions) Order 2000, SI 2000/90. [3] Word substituted: National Health Service Reform and Health Care Professions Act 2002, s 2(5), Sch 2, Pt 2, para 52. [4] Words inserted (Wales only): Health, Social Care and Well-being Strategies (Wales) Regulations 2003, SI 2003/154.

Maintenance of a register of disabled children

2. (1) Every local authority shall open and maintain a register of disabled children within their area.

(2) The register may be kept by means of a computer.

Assessment of children's needs

3. Where it appears to a local authority that a child within their area is in need, the authority may assess his needs for the purposes of this Act at the same time as any assessment of his needs is made under –

    (a) the Chronically Sick and Disabled Persons Act 1970;
    (b) [Part IV of the Education Act 1996][1];
    (c) the Disabled Persons (Services, Consultation and Representation) Act 1986; or
    (d) any other enactment.

Prevention of neglect and abuse

4. (1) Every local authority shall take reasonable steps, through the provision of services under Part III of this Act, to prevent children within their area suffering ill-treatment or neglect.

(2) Where a local authority believe that a child who is at any time within their area –

    (a) is likely to suffer harm; but
    (b) lives or proposes to live in the area of another local authority they shall inform that other local authority.

(3) When informing that other local authority they shall specify –

    (a) the harm that they believe he is likely to suffer; and
    (b) (if they can) where the child lives or proposes to live.

Provision of accommodation in order to protect child

5. (1) Where –

    (a) it appears to a local authority that a child who is living on particular premises is suffering, or is likely to suffer, ill treatment at the hands of another person who is living on those premises; and
    (b) that other person proposes to move from the premises,

the authority may assist that other person to obtain alternative accommodation.

(2) Assistance given under this paragraph may be in cash.

(3) Subsections (7) to (9) of section 17 shall apply in relation to assistance given under this paragraph as they apply in relation to assistance given under that section.

Provision for disabled children

6. Every local authority shall provide services designed –

    (a) to minimise the effect on disabled children within their area of their disabilities; and

(b) to give such children the opportunity to lead lives which are as normal as possible.

Provision to reduce need for care proceedings etc.

7. Every local authority shall take reasonable steps designed –

(a) to reduce the need to bring –
   (i) proceedings for care or supervision orders with respect to children within their area;
   (ii) criminal proceedings against such children;
   (iii) any family or other proceedings with respect to such children which might lead to them being placed in the authority's care; or
   (iv) proceedings under the inherent jurisdiction of the High Court with respect to children;
(b) to encourage children within their area not to commit criminal offences; and
(c) to avoid the need for children within their area to be placed in secure accommodation.

Provision for children living with their families

8. Every local authority shall make such provision as they consider appropriate for the following services to be available with respect to children in need within their area while they are living with their families –

(a) advice, guidance and counselling;
(b) occupational, social, cultural or recreational activities;
(c) home help (which may include laundry facilities);
(d) facilities for, or assistance with, travelling to and from home for the purpose of taking advantage of any other service provided under this Act or of any similar service;
(e) assistance to enable the child concerned and his family to have a holiday.

Family centres

9. (1) Every local authority shall provide such family centres as they consider appropriate in relation to children within their area.

(2) 'Family centre' means a centre at which any of the persons mentioned in sub-paragraph (3) may –

(a) attend for occupational, social, cultural or recreational activities;
(b) attend for advice, guidance or counselling; or
(c) be provided with accommodation while he is receiving advice, guidance or counselling.

(3) The persons are –

(a) a child;
(b) his parents;
(c) any person who is not a parent of his but who has parental responsibility for him;
(d) any other person who is looking after him.

Maintenance of the family home

10. Every local authority shall take such steps as are reasonably practicable, where any child within their area who is in need and whom they are not looking after is living apart from his family –

(a) to enable him to live with his family; or

(b) to promote contact between him and his family,

if, in their opinion, it is necessary to do so in order to safeguard or promote his welfare.

Duty to consider racial groups to which children in need belong

11. Every local authority shall, in making any arrangements –

(a) for the provision of day care within their area; or

(b) designed to encourage persons to act as local authority foster parents,

have regard to the different racial groups to which children within their area who are in need belong.

NOTES

   Amendments. [1] Words substituted: Education Act 1996, s 582(1), Sch 37, Pt I, para 92.

   Definitions. 'Care order': ss 31(11), 105(1); 'child': s 105(1); 'child in need': s 17(10); 'day care': ss 18(4), 105(1); 'disabled': ss 17(11), 105(1); 'family': s 17(10); 'family centre': Sch 2, para 9(2); 'family proceedings': s 8(3); 'harm': ss 31(9), 105(1); 'ill-treatment': ss 31(9), 105(1); 'local authority': s 105(1); 'local authority foster parent': s 23(3); 'parental responsibility': s 3; 'secure accommodation': s 25(1); 'significant harm': ss 31(10), 105(1); 'supervision order': s 31(11); voluntary organisation': s 105(1).

PART II
CHILDREN LOOKED AFTER BY LOCAL AUTHORITIES

Regulations as to placing of children with local authority foster parents

12. Regulations under section 23(2)(a) may, in particular, make provision –

(a) with regard to the welfare of children placed with local authority foster parents;

(b) as to the arrangements to be made by local authorities in connection with the health and education of such children;

(c) as to the records to be kept by local authorities;

(d) for securing that a child is not placed with a local authority foster parent unless that person is for the time being approved as a local authority foster parent by such local authority as may be prescribed;

(e) for securing that where possible the local authority foster parent with whom a child is to be placed is –

  (i) of the same religious persuasion as the child; or

  (ii) gives an undertaking that the child will be brought up in that religious persuasion;

(f) for securing that children placed with local authority foster parents, and the premises in which they are accommodated, will be supervised and inspected by a local authority and that the children will be removed from those premises if their welfare appears to require it;

(g) as to the circumstances in which local authorities may make arrangements for duties imposed on them by the regulations to be discharged, on their behalf.

Regulations as to arrangements under section 23(2)(f)

13. Regulations under section 23(2)(f) may, in particular, make provision as to –

(a) the persons to be notified of any proposed arrangements;
(b) the opportunities such persons are to have to make representations in relation to the arrangements proposed;
(c) the persons to be notified of any proposed changes in arrangements;
(d) the records to be kept by local authorities;
(e) the supervision by local authorities of any arrangements made.

Regulations as to conditions under which child in care is allowed to live with parent, etc

14. Regulations under section 23(5) may, in particular, impose requirements on a local authority as to –

(a) the making of any decision by a local authority to allow a child to live with any person falling within section 23(4) (including requirements as to those who must be consulted before the decision is made, and those who must be notified when it has been made);
(b) the supervision or medical examination of the child concerned;
(c) the removal of the child, in such circumstances as may be prescribed, from the care of the person with whom he has been allowed to live.
[(d) the records to be kept by local authorities.]¹

Promotion and maintenance of contact between child and family

15. (1) Where a child is being looked after by a local authority, the authority shall, unless it is not reasonably practicable or consistent with his welfare, endeavour to promote contact between the child and –

(a) his parents;
(b) any person who is not a parent of his but who has parental responsibility for him; and
(c) any relative, friend or other person connected with him.

(2) Where a child is being looked after by a local authority –

(a) the authority shall take such steps as are reasonably practicable to secure that
(i) his parents; and
(ii) any person who is not a parent of his but who has parental responsibility for him,
are kept informed of where he is being accommodated; and
(b) every such person shall secure that the authority are kept informed of his or her address.

(3) Where a local authority ('the receiving authority') take over the provision of accommodation for a child from another local authority ('the transferring authority') under section 20(2) –

(a) the receiving authority shall (where reasonably practicable) inform
(i) the child's parents; and

       (ii) any person who is not a parent of his but who has parental responsibility for him;

  (b) sub-paragraph (2)(a) shall apply to the transferring authority, as well as the receiving authority, until at least one such person has been informed of the change; and

  (c) sub-paragraph (2)(b) shall not require any person to inform the receiving authority of his address until he has been so informed.

(4) Nothing in this paragraph requires a local authority to inform any person of the whereabouts of a child if –

  (a) the child is in the care of the authority; and

  (b) the authority has reasonable cause to believe that informing the person would prejudice the child's welfare.

(5) Any person who fails (without reasonable excuse) to comply with sub-paragraph (2)(b) shall be guilty of an offence and liable on summary conviction to a fine not exceeding level 2 on the standard scale.

(6) It shall be a defence in any proceedings under sub-paragraph (5) to prove that the defendant was residing at the same address as another person who was the child's parent or had parental responsibility for the child and had reasonable cause to believe that the other person had informed the appropriate authority that both of them were residing at that address.

Visits to or by children: expenses

16. (1) This paragraph applies where –

  (a) a child is being looked after by a local authority; and

  (b) the conditions mentioned in sub-paragraph (3) are satisfied.

(2) The authority may –

  (a) make payments to –

       (i) a parent of the child;

       (ii) any person who is not a parent of his but who has parental responsibility for him; or

       (iii) any relative, friend or other person connected with him,

    in respect of travelling, subsistence or other expenses incurred by that person in visiting the child; or

  (b) make payments to the child, or to any person on his behalf, in respect of travelling, subsistence or other expenses incurred by or on behalf of the child in his visiting –

       (i) a parent of his;

       (ii) any person who has parental responsibility for him; or

       (iii) any relative, friend or other person connected with him.

(3) The conditions are that –

  (a) it appears to the authority that the visit in question could not otherwise be made without undue financial hardship; and

  (b) the circumstances warrant the making of the payments.

Appointment of visitor for child who is not being visited

17. (1) Where it appears to a local authority in relation to any child that they are looking after that –

(a) communication between the child and –
    (i) a parent of his, or
    (ii) any person who is not a parent of his but who has parental responsibility for him,
has been infrequent; or

(b) he has not visited or been visited by (or lived with) any such person during the preceding twelve months,

and that it would be in the child's best interests for an independent person to be appointed to be his visitor for the purposes of this paragraph, they shall appoint such a visitor.

(2) A person so appointed shall –

(a) have the duty of visiting, advising and befriending the child; and
(b) be entitled to recover from the authority who appointed him any reasonable expenses incurred by him for the purposes of his functions under this paragraph.

(3) A person's appointment as a visitor in pursuance of this paragraph shall be determined if –

(a) he gives notice in writing to the authority who appointed him that he resigns the appointment; or
(b) the authority give him notice in writing that they have terminated it.

(4) The determination of such an appointment shall not prejudice any duty under this paragraph to make a further appointment.

(5) Where a local authority propose to appoint a visitor for a child under this paragraph, the appointment shall not be made if –

(a) the child objects to it; and
(b) the authority are satisfied that he has sufficient understanding to make an informed decision.

(6) Where a visitor has been appointed for a child under this paragraph, the local authority shall determine the appointment if –

(a) the child objects to its continuing; and
(b) the authority are satisfied that he has sufficient understanding to make an informed decision.

(7) The Secretary of State may make regulations as to the circumstances in which a person appointed as a visitor under this paragraph is to be regarded as independent of the local authority appointing him.

Power to guarantee apprenticeship deeds etc

18. (1) While a child is being looked after by a local authority, or is a person qualifying for advice and assistance, the authority may undertake any obligation by way of guarantee under any deed of apprenticeship or articles of clerkship which he enters into.

(2) Where a local authority have undertaken any such obligation under any deed or articles they may at any time (whether or not they are still looking after the person concerned) undertake the like obligation under any supplemental deed or articles.

Arrangements to assist children to live abroad

19. (1) A local authority may only arrange for, or assist in arranging for, any child in their care to live outside England and Wales with the approval of the court.

(2) A local authority may, with the approval of every person who has parental responsibility for the child arrange for, or assist in arranging for, any other child looked after by them to live outside England and Wales.

(3) The court shall not give its approval under sub-paragraph (1) unless it is satisfied that –

(a) living outside England and Wales would be in the child's best interests;
(b) suitable arrangements have been, or will be, made for his reception and welfare in the country in which he will live;
(c) the child has consented to living in that country; and
(d) every person who has parental responsibility for the child has consented to his living in that country.

(4) Where the court is satisfied that the child does not have sufficient understanding to give or withhold his consent, it may disregard sub-paragraph (3)(c) and give its approval if the child is to live in the country concerned with a parent, guardian, or other suitable person.

(5) Where a person whose consent is required by sub-paragraph (3)(d) fails to give his consent, the court may disregard that provision and give its approval if it is satisfied that that person –

(a) cannot be found;
(b) is incapable of consenting; or
(c) is withholding his consent unreasonably.

(6) Section 56 of the Adoption Act 1976 (which requires authority for the taking or sending abroad for adoption of a child who is a British subject) shall not apply in the case of any child who is to live outside England and Wales with the approval of the court given under this paragraph.

(7) Where a court decides to give its approval under this paragraph it may order that its decision is not to have effect during the appeal period.

(8) In sub-paragraph (7) 'the appeal period' means –

(a) where an appeal is made against the decision, the period between the making of the decision and the determination of the appeal; and
(b) otherwise, the period during which an appeal may be made against the decision.

[*Preparation for ceasing to be looked after*

19A. It is the duty of the local authority looking after a child to advise, assist and befriend him with a view to promoting his welfare when they have ceased to look after him.

19B. (1) A local authority shall have the following additional functions in relation to an eligible child whom they are looking after.

(2) In sub-paragraph (1) 'eligible child' means, subject to sub-paragraph (3), a child who –

(a) is aged sixteen or seventeen; and

(b) has been looked after by a local authority for a prescribed period, or periods amounting in all to a prescribed period, which began after he reached a prescribed age and ended after he reached the age of sixteen.

(3) The Secretary of State may prescribe –

(a) additional categories of eligible children; and
(b) categories of children who are not to be eligible children despite falling within sub-paragraph (2).

(4) For each eligible child, the local authority shall carry out an assessment of his needs with a view to determining what advice, assistance and support it would be appropriate for them to provide him under this Act –

(a) while they are still looking after him; and
(b) after they cease to look after him,

and shall then prepare a pathway plan for him.

(5) The local authority shall keep the pathway plan under regular review.

(6) Any such review may be carried out at the same time as a review of the child's case carried out by virtue of section 26.

(7) The Secretary of State may by regulations make provision as to assessments for the purposes of sub-paragraph (4).

(8) The regulations may in particular provide for the matters set out in section 23B(6).

Personal advisers

19C. A local authority shall arrange for each child whom they are looking after who is an eligible child for the purposes of paragraph 19B to have a personal adviser.][2]

Death of children being looked after by local authorities

20. (1) If a child who is being looked after by a local authority dies, the authority –

(a) shall notify the Secretary of State;
(b) shall, so far as is reasonably practicable, notify the child's parents and every person who is not a parent of his but who has parental responsibility for him;
(c) may, with the consent (so far as it is reasonably practicable to obtain it) of every person who has parental responsibility for the child, arrange for the child's body to be buried or cremated; and
(d) may, if the conditions mentioned in sub-paragraph (2) are satisfied, make payments to any person who has parental responsibility for the child, or any relative, friend or other person connected with the child, in respect of travelling, subsistence or other expenses incurred by that person in attending the child's funeral.

(2) The conditions are that –

(a) it appears to the authority that the person concerned could not otherwise attend the child's funeral without undue financial hardship; and
(b) that the circumstances warrant the making of the payments.

(3) Sub-paragraph (1) does not authorise cremation where it does not accord with the practice of the child's religious persuasion.

(4) Where a local authority have exercised their power under sub-paragraph (1)(c) with respect to a child who was under sixteen when he died, they may recover from any parent of the child any expenses incurred by them.

(5) Any sums so recoverable shall, without prejudice to any other method of recovery, be recoverable summarily as a civil debt.

(6) Nothing in this paragraph affects any enactment regulating or authorising the burial, cremation or anatomical examination of the body of a deceased person.

NOTES

Amendments. [1] Sub-paragraph added: Courts and Legal Services Act 1990, s 116, Sch 16, para 27. [2] Paragraphs inserted: Children (Leaving Care) Act 2000, s 1.

Definitions. 'Child': s 105(1); 'child who is looked after by a local authority': s 22(1); 'functions': s 105(1); 'local authority': s 105(1); 'local authority foster parent': s 23(3); 'parental responsibility': s 3; 'person qualifying for advice and assistance': s 24(2); 'prescribed': s 105(1); 'relative': s 105(1); 'receiving authority': Sch 2, para 15(3); 'the appeal period': Sch 2, para 19(8); 'the court': s 92(7); 'the transferring authority': Sch 2, para 15(3).

PART III
CONTIBUTIONS TOWARDS MAINTENANCE OF CHILDREN

Liability to contribute

21. (1) Where a local authority are looking after a child (other than in the cases mentioned in sub-paragraph (7)) they shall consider whether they should recover contributions towards the child's maintenance from any person liable to contribute ('a contributor').

(2) An authority may only recover contributions from a contributor if they consider it reasonable to do so.

(3) The persons liable to contribute are –

    (a) where the child is under sixteen, each of his parents;
    (b) where he has reached the age of sixteen, the child himself.

(4) A parent is not liable to contribute during any period when he is in receipt of income support [, working families' tax credit or disabled person's tax credit][3] under [Part VII of the Social Security Contributions and Benefits Act 1992][1] [or of an income-based jobseeker's allowance][2].

(5) A person is not liable to contribute towards the maintenance of a child in the care of a local authority in respect of any period during which the child is allowed by the authority (under section 23(5)) to live with a parent of his.

(6) A contributor is not obliged to make any contribution towards a child's maintenance except as agreed or determined in accordance with this Part of this Schedule.

(7) The cases are where the child is looked after by a local authority under –

    (a) section 21;
    (b) an interim care order;
    (c) [section 92 of the Powers of Criminal Courts (Sentencing) Act 2000][4].

PART I

NOTES

Amendments. [1] Words substituted: Social Security (Consequential Provisions) Act 1992, s 4, Sch 2, para 108. [2] Words inserted: Jobseekers Act 1995, s 41(4), Sch 2, para 19. [3] Words (as previously substituted by Disability Living Allowance and Disability Working Allowance Act 1991, s 7(2)) substituted: Tax Credits Act 1999, s 1(2), Sch 1, paras 1, 6(d)(iii). [4] Words substituted: Powers of Criminal Courts (Sentencing) Act 2000, s 165(1), Sch 9, para 131.

Agreed contributions

22. (1) Contributions towards a child's maintenance may only be recovered if the local authority have served a notice ('a contribution notice') on the contributor specifying –

    (a) the weekly sum which they consider that he should contribute; and

    (b) arrangements for payment.

(2) The contribution notice must be in writing and dated.

(3) Arrangements for payment shall, in particular, include –

    (a) the date on which liability to contribute begins (which must not be earlier than the date of the notice);

    (b) the date on which liability under the notice will end (if the child has not before that date ceased to be looked after by the authority); and

    (c) the date on which the first payment is to be made.

(4) The authority may specify in a contribution notice a weekly sum which is a standard contribution determined by them for all children looked after by them.

(5) The authority may not specify in a contribution notice a weekly sum greater than that which they consider –

    (a) they would normally be prepared to pay if they had placed a similar child with local authority foster parents; and

    (b) it is reasonably practicable for the contributor to pay (having regard to his means).

(6) An authority may at any time withdraw a contribution notice (without prejudice to their power to serve another).

(7) Where the authority and the contributor agree –

    (a) the sum which the contributor is to contribute; and

    (b) arrangements for payment,

(whether as specified in the contribution notice or otherwise) and the contributor notifies the authority in writing that he so agrees, the authority may recover summarily as a civil debt any contribution which is overdue and unpaid.

(8) A contributor may, by serving a notice in writing on the authority, withdraw his agreement in relation to any period of liability falling after the date of service of the notice.

(9) Sub-paragraph (7) is without prejudice to any other method of recovery.

Contribution orders

23. (1) Where a contributor has been served with a contribution notice and has –

(a) failed to reach any agreement with the local authority as mentioned in paragraph 22(7) within the period of one month beginning with the day on which the contribution notice was served; or

(b) served a notice under paragraph 22(8) withdrawing his agreement,

the authority may apply to the court for an order under this paragraph.

(2) On such an application the court may make an order ('a contribution order') requiring the contributor to contribute a weekly sum towards the child's maintenance in accordance with arrangements for payment specified by the court.

(3) A contribution order –

(a) shall not specify a weekly sum greater than that specified in the contribution notice; and

(b) shall be made with due regard to the contributor's means.

(4) A contribution order shall not –

(a) take effect before the date specified in the contribution notice; or

(b) have effect while the contributor is not liable to contribute (by virtue of paragraph 21); or

(c) remain in force after the child has ceased to be looked after by the authority who obtained the order.

(5) An authority may not apply to the court under sub-paragraph (1) in relation to a contribution notice which they have withdrawn.

(6) Where –

(a) a contribution order is in force;

(b) the authority serve another contribution notice; and

(c) the contributor and the authority reach an agreement under paragraph 22(7) in respect of that other contribution notice,

the effect of the agreement shall be to discharge the order from the date on which it is agreed that the agreement shall take effect.

(7) Where an agreement is reached under sub-paragraph (6) the authority shall notify the court –

(a) of the agreement; and

(b) of the date on which it took effect.

(8) A contribution order may be varied or revoked on the application of the contributor or the authority.

(9) In proceedings for the variation of a contribution order, the authority shall specify –

(a) the weekly sum which, having regard to paragraph 22, they propose that the contributor should contribute under the order as varied; and

(b) the proposed arrangements for payment.

(10) Where a contribution order is varied, the order –

(a) shall not specify a weekly sum greater than that specified by the authority in the proceedings for variation; and

(b) shall be made with due regard to the contributor's means.

(11) An appeal shall lie in accordance with rules of court from any order made under this paragraph.

Enforcement of contribution orders etc

24. (1) A contribution order made by a magistrates' court shall be enforceable as a magistrates' court maintenance order (within the meaning of section 150(1) of the Magistrates' Courts Act 1980).

(2) Where a contributor has agreed, or has been ordered, to make contributions to a local authority, any other local authority within whose area the contributor is for the time being living may –

    (a) at the request of the local authority who served the contribution notice; and

    (b) subject to agreement as to any sum to be deducted in respect of services rendered,

collect from the contributor any contributions due on behalf of the authority who served the notice.

(3) In sub-paragraph (2) the reference to any other local authority includes a reference to –

    (a) a local authority within the meaning of section 1(2) of the Social Work (Scotland) Act 1968; and

    (b) a Health and Social Services Board established under Article 16 of the Health and Personal Social Services (Northern Ireland) Order 1972.

(4) The power to collect sums under sub-paragraph (2) includes the power to –

    (a) receive and give a discharge for any contributions due; and

    (b) (if necessary) enforce payment of any contributions,

even though those contributions may have fallen due at a time when the contributor was living elsewhere.

(5) Any contributions collected under sub-paragraph (2) shall be paid (subject to any agreed deduction) to the local authority who served the contribution notice.

(6) In any proceedings under this paragraph, a document which purports to be –

    (a) a copy of an order made by a court under or by virtue of paragraph 23; and

    (b) certified as a true copy by the [justices' chief executive for][1] the court,

shall be evidence of the order.

(7) In any proceedings under this paragraph, a certificate which –

    (a) purports to be signed by the clerk or some other duly authorised officer of the local authority who obtained the contribution order; and

    (b) states that any sum due to the authority under the order is overdue and unpaid,

shall be evidence that the sum is overdue and unpaid.

Regulations

25. The Secretary of State may make regulations –

    (a) as to the considerations which a local authority must take into account in deciding –

(i) whether it is reasonable to recover contributions; and
(ii) what the arrangements for payment should be;
(b) as to the procedures they must follow in reaching agreements with –
(i) contributors (under paragraph 22 and 23); and
(ii) any other local authority (under paragraph 23).

NOTES

Amendments. [1] Words substituted: Access to Justice Act 1999, s 90, Sch 13, paras 159, 162.

Definitions. 'Child': s 105(1); 'child who is looked after by a local authority': s 22(1); 'contribution notice': Sch 2, para 22(1); 'contribution order': Sch 2, para 23(2); 'contributor': Sch 2, para 21(1); 'local authority': s 105(1); 'local authority foster parent': s 23(3); 'signed': s 105(1); 'the court': s 92(7).

SCHEDULE 3

SUPERVISION ORDERS

Sections 35 and 36

PART I
GENERAL

Meaning of 'responsible person'

1. In this Schedule, 'the responsible person', in relation to a supervised child, means –

(a) any person who has parental responsibility for the child; and
(b) any other person with whom the child is living.

Power of supervisor to give directions to supervised child

2. (1) A supervision order may require the supervised child to comply with any directions given from time to time by the supervisor which require him to do all or any of the following things –

(a) to live at a place or places specified in the directions for a period or periods so specified;
(b) to present himself to a person or persons specified in the directions at a place or places and on a day or days so specified;
(c) to participate in activities specified in the directions on a day or days so specified.

(2) It shall be for the supervisor to decide whether, and to what extent, he exercises his power to give directions and to decide the form of any directions which he gives.

(3) Sub-paragraph (1) does not confer on a supervisor power to give directions in respect of any medical or psychiatric examination or treatment (which are matters dealt with in paragraphs 4 and 5).

Imposition of obligations on responsible person

3. (1) With the consent of any responsible person, a supervision order may include a requirement –

  (a) that he take all reasonable steps to ensure that the supervised child complies with any direction given by the supervisor under paragraph 2;

  (b) that he take all reasonable steps to ensure that the supervised child complies with any requirement included in the order under paragraph 4 or 5;

  (c) that he comply with any directions given by the supervisor requiring him to attend at a place specified in the directions for the purpose of taking part in activities so specified.

(2) A direction given under sub-paragraph (1)(c) may specify the time at which the responsible person is to attend and whether or not the supervised child is required to attend with him.

(3) A supervision order may require any person who is a responsible person in relation to the supervised child to keep the supervisor informed of his address, if it differs from the child's.

Psychiatric and medical examinations

4. (1) A supervision order may require the supervised child –

  (a) to submit to a medical or psychiatric examination; or

  (b) to submit to any such examination from time to time as directed by the supervisor.

(2) Any such examination shall be required to be conducted –

  (a) by, or under the direction of, such registered medical practitioner as may be specified in the order;

  (b) at a place specified in the order and at which the supervised child is to attend as a non-resident patient; or

  (c) at –

    (i) a health service hospital; or

    (ii) in the case of a psychiatric examination, a hospital [, independent hospital or care home][1],

  at which the supervised child is, or is to attend as, a resident patient.

(3) A requirement of a kind mentioned in sub-paragraph (2)(c) shall not be included unless the court is satisfied, on the evidence of a registered medical practitioner, that –

  (a) the child may be suffering from a physical or mental condition that requires, and may be susceptible to, treatment; and

  (b) a period as a resident patient is necessary if the examination is to be carried out properly.

(4) No court shall include a requirement under this paragraph in a supervision order unless it is satisfied that –

  (a) where the child has sufficient understanding to make an informed decision, he consents to its inclusion; and

  (b) satisfactory arrangements have been, or can be, made for the examination.

Psychiatric and medical treatment

5. (1) Where a court which proposes to make or vary a supervision order is satisfied, on the evidence of a registered medical practitioner approved for the purposes of section 12 of the Mental Health Act 1983, that the mental condition of the supervised child –

(a) is such as requires, and may be susceptible to, treatment; but

(b) is not such as to warrant his detention in pursuance of a hospital order under Part III of that Act,

the court may include in the order a requirement that the supervised child shall, for a period specified in the order, submit to such treatment as is so specified.

(2) The treatment specified in accordance with sub-paragraph (1) must be –

(a) by, or under the direction of, such registered medical practitioner as may be specified in the order;

(b) as a non-resident patient at such a place as may be so specified; or

(c) as a resident patient in a hospital [, independent hospital or care home] [1].

(3) Where a court which proposes to make or vary a supervision order is satisfied, on the evidence of a registered medical practitioner, that the physical condition of the supervised child is such as requires, and may be susceptible to, treatment, the court may include in the order a requirement that the supervised child shall, for a period specified in the order, submit to such treatment as is so specified.

(4) The treatment specified in accordance with sub-paragraph (3) must be –

(a) by, or under the direction of, such registered medical practitioner as may be specified in the order;

(b) as a non-resident patient at such place as may be so specified; or

(c) as a resident patient in a health service hospital.

(5) No court shall include a requirement under this paragraph in a supervision order unless it is satisfied –

(a) where the child has sufficient understanding to make an informed decision, that he consents to its inclusion; and

(b) that satisfactory arrangements have been, or can be, made for the treatment.

(6) If a medical practitioner by whom or under whose direction a supervised person is being treated in pursuance of a requirement included in a supervision order by virtue of this paragraph is unwilling to continue to treat or direct the treatment of the supervised child or is of the opinion that –

(a) the treatment should be continued beyond the period specified in the order;

(b) the supervised child needs different treatment;

(c) he is not susceptible to treatment; or

(d) he does not require further treatment,

the practitioner shall make a report in writing to that effect to the supervisor.

(7) On receiving a report under this paragraph the supervisor shall refer it to the court, and on such a reference the court may make an order cancelling or varying the requirement.

NOTES

Amendments. [1] Words substituted: Care Standards Act 2000, s 116, Sch 4, para 14(24).

PART I

Definitions. 'Child': s 105(1); 'health service hospital': s 105(1); 'hospital': s 105(1); 'mental nursing home': s 105(1); 'parental responsibility': s 3; 'supervised child': s 105(1); 'supervision order': s 31(11); 'supervisor': s 105(1); 'the court': s 92(7); 'the responsible person': Sch 3, para 1.

PART II
MISCELLANEOUS

Life of supervision order

6. (1) Subject to sub-paragraph (2) and section 91, a supervision order shall cease to have effect at the end of the period of one year beginning with the date on which it was made.

(2) A supervision order shall also cease to have effect if an event mentioned in section 25(1)(a) or (b) of the Child Abduction and Custody Act 1985 (termination of existing orders) occurs with respect to the child.

(3) Where the supervisor applies to the court to extend, or further extend, a supervision order the court may extend the order for such period as it may specify.

(4) A supervision order may not be extended so as to run beyond the end of the period of three years beginning with the date on which it was made.

7. …¹

Information to be given to supervisor etc.

8. (1) A supervision order may require the supervised child –

(a) to keep the supervisor informed of any change in his address; and
(b) to allow the supervisor to visit him at the place where he is living.

(2) The responsible person in relation to any child with respect to whom a supervision order is made shall –

(a) if asked by the supervisor, inform him of the child's address (if it is known to him); and
(b) if he is living with the child, allow the supervisor reasonable contact with the child.

Selection of supervisor

9. (1) A supervision order shall not designate a local authority as the supervisor unless –

(a) the authority agree; or
(b) the supervised child lives or will live within their area.

(2)–(5) …³

Effect of supervision order on earlier orders

10. The making of a supervision order with respect to any child brings to an end any earlier care or supervision order which –

(a) was made with respect to that child; and
(b) would otherwise continue in force.

Local authority functions and expenditure

11. (1) The Secretary of State may make regulations with respect to the exercise by a local authority of their functions where a child has been placed under their supervision by a supervision order.

(2) Where a supervision order requires compliance with directions given by virtue of this section, any expenditure incurred by the supervisor for the purposes of the directions shall be defrayed by the local authority designated in the order.

NOTES

Amendments. [1] Paragraph repealed: Courts and Legal Services Act 1990, ss 116, 125(7), Sch 16, para 27, Sch 20. [2] Words substituted: Probation Service Act 1993, s 32, Sch 3, para 9(3). [3] Subparagraphs omitted: Criminal Justice and Court Services Act 2000, ss 74, 75, Sch 7, paras 87, 96, Sch 8.

Definitions. 'Care order': ss 31(11), 105(1); 'child': s 105(1); 'local authority': s 105(1); 'supervised child': s 105(1); 'supervision order': s 31(11); 'supervisor': s 105(1); 'the appropriate authority': Sch 3, para 9(3); 'the responsible person': Sch 3, para 1.

PART III
EDUCATION SUPERVISION ORDERS

Effect of orders

12. (1) Where an education supervision order is in force with respect to a child, it shall be the duty of the supervisor –

    (a) to advise, assist and befriend, and give directions to –
        (i) the supervised child; and
        (ii) his parents;
    in such a way as will, in the opinion of the supervisor, secure that he is properly educated;
    (b) where any such directions given to
        (i) the supervised child; or
        (ii) a parent of his,
    have not been complied with, to consider what further steps to take in the exercise of the supervisor's powers under this Act.

(2) Before giving any directions under sub-paragraph (1) the supervisor shall, so far as is reasonably practicable, ascertain the wishes and feelings of –

    (a) the child; and
    (b) his parents;

including, in particular, their wishes as to the place at which the child should be educated.

(3) When settling the terms of any such directions, the supervisor shall give due consideration –

    (a) having regard to the child's age and understanding, to such wishes and feelings of his as the supervisor has been able to ascertain; and
    (b) to such wishes and feelings of the child's parents as he has been able to ascertain.

(4) Directions may be given under this paragraph at any time while the education supervision order is in force.

PART I

13. (1) Where an education supervision order is in force with respect to a child, the duties of the child's parents under [sections 7 and 444 of the Education Act 1996 (duties to secure education of children and][1] to secure regular attendance of registered pupils) shall be superseded by their duty to comply with any directions in force under the education supervision order.

(2) Where an education supervision order is made with respect to a child –

    (a) any school attendance order –
        (i) made under [section 437 of the Education Act 1996][1] with respect to the child; and
        (ii) in force immediately before the making of the education supervision order,
    shall cease to have effect; and
    (b) while the education supervision order remains in force, the following provisions shall not apply with respect to the child –
        (i) [section 437][1] of that Act (school attendance orders);
        (ii) [section 9 of that Act][1] (pupils to be educated in accordance with wishes of their parents);
        (iii) [sections 411 and 423 of that Act][1] (parental preference and appeals against admission decisions);
    (c) a supervision order made with respect to the child in criminal proceedings, while the education supervision order is in force, may not include an education requirement of the kind which could otherwise be included under [paragraph 7 of Schedule 6 to the Powers of Criminal Courts (Sentencing) Act 2000][2];
    (d) any education requirement of a kind mentioned in paragraph (c), which was in force with respect to the child immediately before the making of the education supervision order, shall cease to have effect.

Effect where child also subject to supervision order

14. (1) This paragraph applies where an education supervision order and a supervision order, or order under [section 63(1) of the Powers of Criminal Courts (Sentencing) Act 2000][2], are in force at the same time with respect to the same child.

(2) Any failure to comply with a direction given by the supervisor under the education supervision order shall be disregarded if it would not have been reasonably practicable to comply with it without failing to comply with a direction given under the other order.

Duration of orders

15. (1) An education supervision order shall have effect for a period of one year, beginning with the date on which it is made.

(2) An education supervision order shall not expire if, before it would otherwise have expired, the court has (on the application of the authority in whose favour the order was made) extended the period during which it is in force.

(3) Such an application may not be made earlier than three months before the date on which the order would otherwise expire.

(4) The period during which an education supervision order is in force may be extended under sub-paragraph (2) on more than one occasion.

(5) No one extension may be for a period of more than three years.

(6) An education supervision order shall cease to have effect on –

(a) the child's ceasing to be of compulsory school age; or
(b) the making of a care order with respect to the child;

and sub-paragraphs (1) to (4) are subject to this sub-paragraph.

Information to be given to supervisor etc.

16. (1) An education supervision order may require the child –

(a) to keep the supervisor informed of any change in his address; and
(b) to allow the supervisor to visit him at the place where he is living.

(2) A person who is the parent of a child with respect to whom an education supervision order has been made shall –

(a) if asked by the supervisor, inform him of the child's address (if it is known to him); and
(b) if he is living with the child, allow the supervisor reasonable contact with the child.

Discharge of orders

17. (1) The court may discharge any education supervision order on the application of –

(a) the child concerned;
(b) a parent of his; or
(c) the local education authority concerned.

(2) On discharging an education supervision order, the court may direct the local authority within whose area the child lives, or will live, to investigate the circumstances of the child.

Offences

18. (1) If a parent of a child with respect to whom an education supervision order is in force persistently fails to comply with a direction given under the order he shall be guilty of an offence.

(2) It shall be a defence for any person charged with such an offence to prove that –

(a) he took all reasonable steps to ensure that the direction was complied with;
(b) the direction was unreasonable; or
(c) he had complied with –
  (i) a requirement included in a supervision order made with respect to the child; or
  (ii) directions given under such a requirement,
  and that it was not reasonably practicable to comply both with the direction and with the requirement or directions mentioned in this paragraph.

(3) A person guilty of an offence under this paragraph shall be liable on summary conviction to a fine not exceeding level 3 on the standard scale.

Persistent failure of child to comply with directions

19. (1) Where a child with respect to whom an education supervision order is in force persistently fails to comply with any direction given under the order, the local education authority concerned shall notify the appropriate local authority.

(2) Where a local authority have been notified under sub-paragraph (1) they shall investigate the circumstances of the child.

(3) In this paragraph 'the appropriate local authority' has the same meaning as in section 36.

Miscellaneous

20. The Secretary of State may by regulations make provision modifying, or displacing, the provisions of any enactment about education in relation to any child with respect to whom an education supervision order is in force to such extent as appears to the Secretary of State to be necessary or expedient in consequence of the provision made by this Act with respect to such orders.

Interpretation

21. In this part of this Schedule 'parent' has the same meaning as in [the Education Act 1996][1].

NOTES

Amendments. [1] Words substituted: Education Act 1996, s 582(1), Sch 37, Pt I, para 93. [2] Words substituted: Powers of Criminal Courts (Sentencing) Act 2000, s 165(1), Sch 9, para 131.

Definitions. 'Care order': ss 31(11), 105(1); 'child': s 105(1); 'education supervision order': s 36(2); 'local education authority': s 105(1); 'parent': Sch 3, para 21; 'supervised child': s 105(1); 'supervision order': s 31(11); 'supervisor': s 105(1); 'the appropriate local authority': Sch 3, para 19(3); 'the court': s 92(7).

SCHEDULE 4

MANAGEMENT AND CONDUCT OF COMMUNITY HOMES

Section 53(6)

PART I
INSTRUMENTS OF MANAGEMENT

Instruments of management for controlled and assisted community homes

1. (1) The Secretary of State may by order make an instrument of management providing for the constitution of a body of managers for any ...[1] home which is designated as a controlled or assisted community home.

(2) Sub-paragraph (3) applies where two or more ...[1] homes are designated as controlled community homes or as assisted community homes.

(3) If –

(a) those homes are, or are to be, provided by the same voluntary organisation; and

(b) the same local authority is to be represented on the body of managers for those homes,

a single instrument of management may be made by the Secretary of State under this paragraph constituting one body of managers for those homes or for any two or more of them.

(4) The number of persons who, in accordance with an instrument of management, constitute the body of managers for a ...[1] home shall be such number (which must be a multiple of three) as may be specified in the instrument.

(5) The instrument shall provide that the local authority specified in the instrument shall appoint –

(a) in the case of a ...[1] home which is designated as a controlled community home, two-thirds of the managers; and

(b) in the case of a ...[1] home which is designated as an assisted community home, one-third of them.

(6) An instrument of management shall provide that the foundation managers shall be appointed, in such manner and by such persons as may be specified in the instrument –

(a) so as to represent the interests of the voluntary organisation by which the home is, or is to be, provided; and

(b) for the purpose of securing that

(i) so far as is practicable, the character of the home ...[1] will be preserved; and

(ii) subject to paragraph 2(3), the terms of any trust deed relating to the home are observed.

(7) An instrument of management shall come into force on such date as it may specify.

(8) If an instrument of management is in force in relation to a ...[1] home the home shall be (and be known as) a controlled community home or an assisted community home, according to its designation.

(9) In this paragraph –

'foundation managers', in relation to a ...[1] home, means those of the managers of the home who are not appointed by a local authority in accordance with sub-paragraph (5); and

'designated' means designated in accordance with section 53.

2. (1) An instrument of management shall contain such provisions as the Secretary of State considers appropriate.

(2) Nothing in the instrument of management shall affect the purposes for which the premises comprising the home are held.

(3) Without prejudice to the generality of sub-paragraph (1), an instrument of management may contain provisions –

(a) specifying the nature and purpose of the home (or each of the homes) to which it relates;

(b) requiring a specified number or proportion of the places in that home (or those homes) to be made available to local authorities and to any other body specified in the instrument; and

(c) relating to the management of that home (or those homes) and the charging of fees with respect to –
  (i) children placed there; or
  (ii) places made available to any local authority or other body.

(4) Subject to sub-paragraphs (1) and (2), in the event of any inconsistency between the provisions of any trust deed and an instrument of management, the instrument of management shall prevail over the provisions of the trust deed in so far as they relate to the home concerned.

(5) After consultation with the voluntary organisation concerned and with the local authority specified in its instrument of management, the Secretary of State may by order vary or revoke any provisions of the instrument.

NOTES

Amendments. [1] Words repealed: Courts and Legal Services Act 1990, ss 116, 125(7), Sch 16, para 28, Sch 20.

Definitions. 'Assisted community home': s 53(5); 'child': s 105(1); 'community home': s 53(1); 'controlled community home': s 53(4); 'designated': Sch 4, para 1(9); 'foundation managers': Sch 4, para 1(9); 'local authority': s 105(1); 'trust deed': s 55(6); 'voluntary home': s 60(3); 'voluntary organisation': s 105(1).

PART II
MANAGEMENT OF CONTROLLED AND ASSISTED COMMUNITY HOMES

3. (1) The management, equipment and maintenance of a controlled community home shall be the responsibility of the local authority specified in its instrument of management.

(2) The management, equipment and maintenance of an assisted community home shall be the responsibility of the voluntary organisation by which the home is provided.

(3) In this paragraph –

'home' means a controlled community home or (as the case may be) assisted community home; and

'the managers', in relation to a home, means the managers constituted by its instrument of management; and

'the responsible body', in relation to a home, means the local authority or (as the case may be) voluntary organisation responsible for its management, equipment and maintenance.

(4) The functions of a home's responsible body shall be exercised through the managers [, except in so far as, under section 53(3B), any of the accommodation is to be managed by another person][1].

(5) Anything done, liability incurred or property acquired by a home's managers shall be done, incurred or acquired by them as agents of the responsible body [; and similarly, to the extent that a contract so provides, as respects anything done, liability incurred or property acquired by a person by whom, under section 53(3B), any of the accommodation is to be managed][1].

(6) In so far as any matter is reserved for the decision of a home's responsible body by –

(a) sub-paragraph (8);

(b) the instrument of management;

(c) the service by the body on the managers, or any of them, of a notice reserving any matter,

that matter shall be dealt with by the body and not by the managers.

(7) In dealing with any matter so reserved, the responsible body shall have regard to any representations made to the body by the managers.

(8) The employment of persons at a home shall be a matter reserved for the decision of the responsible body.

(9) Where the instrument of management of a controlled community home so provides, the responsible body may enter into arrangements with the voluntary organisation by which that home is provided whereby, in accordance with such terms as may be agreed

between them and the voluntary organisation, persons who are not in the employment of the responsible body shall undertake duties at that home.

(10) Subject to sub-paragraph (11) –

(a) where the responsible body for an assisted community home proposes to engage any person to work at that home or to terminate without notice the employment of any person at that home, it shall consult the local authority specified in the instrument of management and, if that authority so direct, the responsible body shall not carry out its proposal without their consent; and

(b) that local authority may, after consultation with the responsible body, require that body to terminate the employment of any person at that home.

(11) Paragraphs (a) and (b) of sub-paragraph (10) shall not apply –

(a) in such cases or circumstances as may be specified by notice in writing given by the local authority to the responsible body; and

(b) in relation to the employment of any persons or class of persons specified in the home's instrument of management.

(12) The accounting year of the managers of a home shall be such as may be specified by the responsible body.

(13) Before such date in each accounting year as may be so specified, the managers of a home shall submit to the responsible body estimates, in such form as the body may require, of expenditure and receipts in respect of the next accounting year.

(14) Any expenses incurred by the managers of a home with the approval of the responsible body shall be defrayed by that body.

(15) The managers of a home shall keep –

(a) proper accounts with respect to the home; and

(b) proper records in relation to the accounts.

(16) Where an instrument of management relates to more than one home, one set of accounts and records may be kept in respect of all the homes to which it relates.

NOTES

Amendments. [1] Words inserted: Criminal Justice and Public Order Act 1994, s 22.

Definitions. 'Assisted community home': s 53(5); 'community home': s 53(1); 'controlled community home': s 53(4); 'functions': s 105(1); 'home': Sch 4, para 3(3); 'local authority': s 105(1); 'the managers': Sch 4, para 3(3); 'the responsible body': Sch 4, para 3(3).

PART III
REGULATIONS

4. (1) The Secretary of State may make regulations –

(a) as to the placing of children in community homes;
(b), (c) ...[1]

(2), (3) ...[1]

NOTES
Amendments. [1] Paragraphs repealed: Care Standards Act 2000, s 117, Sch 6.

SCHEDULE 5
VOLUNTARY HOMES AND VOLUNTARY ORGANISATIONS

Section 60(4)

PART I
REGISTRATION OF VOLUNTARY HOMES

1.–6. ...[1]

NOTES
Amendments. [1] Paragraphs repealed: Care Standards Act 2000, s 117, Sch 6

PART II
REGULATIONS AS TO VOLUNTARY HOMES

Regulations as to conduct of voluntary homes

7. (1) The Secretary of State may make regulations –

(a) as to the placing of children in voluntary homes;
(b), (c) ...[1]

(2)–(4) ...[1]

8. ...[1]

NOTES
Amendments. [1] Paragraphs and sub-paragraphs repealed: Care Standards Act 2000, s 117, Sch 6.

SCHEDULE 6
[PRIVATE CHILDREN'S HOMES]¹

Section 63(11)

PART I
REGISTRATION

1.–9. ...²

NOTES

Amendments. ¹ Heading substituted: Care Standards Act 2000, s 116, Sch 4, para 14(1), (25)(a). ² Paragraphs repealed: Care Standards Act 2000, s 117, Sch 6.

PART II
REGULATIONS

10. (1) The Secretary of State may make regulations –

(a) as to the placing of children in [private]¹ children's homes;
(b), (c) ...²

(2) The regulations may in particular –

(a)–(k) ...²
(l) make provision similar to that made by regulations under section 26.

(3), (4) ...²

NOTES

Amendments. ¹ Word substituted: Care Standards Act 2000, s 116, Sch 4, para 14(25). ² Paragraphs and sub-paragraphs repealed: Care Standards Act 2000, s 117, Sch 6.

SCHEDULE 7
FOSTER PARENTS: LIMITS ON NUMBER OF FOSTER CHILDREN

Section 63(12)

Interpretation

1. For the purposes of this Schedule, a person fosters a child if –

(a) he is a local authority foster parent in relation to the child;
(b) he is a foster parent with whom the child has been placed by a voluntary organisation; or
(c) he fosters the child privately.

The usual fostering limit

2. Subject to what follows, a person may not foster more than three children ('the usual fostering limit').

Siblings

3. A person may exceed the usual fostering limit if the children concerned are all siblings with respect to each other.

Exemption by local authority

4. (1) A person may exceed the usual fostering limit if he is exempted from it by the local authority within whose area he lives.

(2) In considering whether to exempt a person, a local authority shall have regard, in particular, to –

    (a) the number of children whom the person proposes to foster;

    (b) the arrangements which the person proposes for the care and accommodation of the fostered children;

    (c) the intended and likely relationship between the person and the fostered children;

    (d) the period of time for which he proposes to foster the children; and

    (e) whether the welfare of the fostered children (and of any other children who are or will be living in the accommodation) will be safeguarded and promoted.

(3) Where a local authority exempt a person, they shall inform him by notice in writing –

    (a) that he is so exempted;

    (b) of the children, described by name, whom he may foster; and

    (c) of any condition to which the exemption is subject.

(4) A local authority may at any time by notice in writing –

    (a) vary or cancel an exemption; or

    (b) impose, vary or cancel a condition to which the exemption is subject,

and, in considering whether to do so, they shall have regard in particular to the considerations mentioned in sub-paragraph (2).

(5) The Secretary of State may make regulations amplifying or modifying the provisions of this paragraph in order to provide for cases where children need to be placed with foster parents as a matter of urgency.

Effect of exceeding fostering limit

5. (1) A person shall cease to be treated [, for the purposes of this Act and the Care Standards Act 2000][1] as fostering and shall be treated as carrying on a children's home if –

    (a) he exceeds the usual fostering limit; or

    (b) where he is exempted under paragraph 4 –

        (i) he fosters any child not named in the exemption; and

        (ii) in so doing, he exceeds the usual fostering limit.

(2) Sub-paragraph (1) does not apply if the children concerned are all siblings in respect of each other.

NOTES
   Amendments. [1] Words inserted: Care Standards Act 2000, s 116, Sch 4, para 14(26).

Complaints etc

6. (1) Every local authority shall establish a procedure for considering any representations (including any complaint) made to them about the discharge of their functions under paragraph 4 by a person exempted or seeking to be exempted under that paragraph.

(2) In carrying out any consideration of representations under subparagraph (1), a local authority shall comply with any regulations made by the Secretary of State for the purposes of this paragraph.

NOTES
   Definitions. 'Child': s 105(1); 'children's home': s 63(3); 'foster': Sch 7, para 1; 'local authority': s 105(1); 'local authority foster parent': s 23(3); 'the usual fostering limit': Sch 7, para 2; 'voluntary organisation': s 105(1).

SCHEDULE 8

PRIVATELY FOSTERED CHILDREN

Section 66(5)

Exemptions

1. A child is not a privately fostered child while he is being looked after by a local authority.

2. (1) A child is not a privately fostered child while he is in the care of any person –

    (a) in premises in which any –
        (i) parent of his;
        (ii) person who is not a parent of his but who has parental responsibility for him; or
        (iii) person who is a relative of his and who has assumed responsibility for his care,
      is for the time being living;
    (b) ...[1]
    (c) in accommodation provided by or on behalf of any voluntary organisation;
    (d) in any school in which he is receiving full-time education;
    (e) in any health service hospital;
    (f) [in any care home or independent hospital;][2]
    (g) in any home or institution not specified in this paragraph but provided, equipped and maintained by the Secretary of State.

(2) Sub-paragraph [(1)(c)][1] to (g) does not apply where the person caring for the child is doing so in his personal capacity and not in the course of carrying out his duties in relation to the establishment mentioned in the paragraph in question.

PART I

Amendments. [1] Sub-paragraph repealed and word substituted: Care Standards Act 2000, s 116, Sch 4, para 14(27). [2] Sub-paragraph substituted: Care Standards Act 2000, s 116, Sch 4, para 14(28).

3. A child is not a privately fostered child while he is in the care of any person in compliance with –

(a) an order under [section 63(1) of the Powers of Criminal Courts (Sentencing) Act 2000][2]; or

(b) a supervision requirement within the meaning of [Part II of the Children (Scotland) Act 1995][1].

NOTES
Amendments. [1] Words substituted: Children (Scotland) Act 1995, s 105(4), Sch 4, para 48(1), (5). [2] Words substituted: Powers of Criminal Courts (Sentencing) Act 2000, s 165(1), Sch 9, para 132.

4. A child is not a privately fostered child while he is liable to be detained, or subject to guardianship, under the Mental Health Act 1983.

5. A child is not a privately fostered child while –

(a) he is placed in the care of a person who proposes to adopt him under arrangements made by an adoption agency within the meaning of
  (i) section 1 of the Adoption Act 1976;
  (ii) section 1 of the Adoption (Scotland) Act 1978; or
  (iii) Article 3 of the Adoption (Northern Ireland) Order 1987; or

(b) he is a protected child.

Power of local authority to impose requirements

6. (1) Where a person is fostering any child privately, or proposes to foster any child privately, the appropriate local authority may impose on him requirements as to –

(a) the number, age and sex of the children who may be privately fostered by him;

(b) the standard of the accommodation and equipment to be provided for them;

(c) the arrangements to be made with respect to their health and safety; and

(d) particular arrangements which must be made with respect to the provision of care for them,

and it shall be his duty to comply with any such requirement before the end of such period as the authority may specify unless, in the case of a proposal, the proposal is not carried out.

(2) A requirement may be limited to a particular child, or class of child.

(3) A requirement (other than one imposed under sub-paragraph (1)(a)) may be limited by the authority so as to apply only when the number of children fostered by the person exceeds a specified number.

(4) A requirement shall be imposed by notice in writing addressed to the person on whom it is imposed and informing him of –

(a) the reason for imposing the requirement;

    (b) his right under paragraph 8 to appeal against it; and

    (c) the time within which he may do so.

(5) A local authority may at any time vary any requirement, impose any additional requirement or remove any requirement.

(6) In this Schedule –

    (a) 'the appropriate local authority' means –

        (i) the local authority within whose area the child is being fostered; or

       (ii) in the case of a proposal to foster a child, the local authority within whose area it is proposed that he will be fostered; and

    (b) 'requirement', in relation to any person, means a requirement imposed on him under this paragraph.

Regulations requiring notification of fostering etc

7. (1) The Secretary of State may by regulations make provision as to –

    (a) the circumstances in which notification is required to be given in connection with children who are, have been or are proposed to be fostered privately; and

    (b) the manner and form in which such notification is to be given.

(2) The regulations may, in particular –

    (a) require any person who is, or proposes to be, involved (whether or not directly) in arranging for a child to be fostered privately to notify the appropriate authority;

    (b) require any person who is –

        (i) a parent of a child; or

       (ii) a person who is not a parent of his but who has parental responsibility for a child,

    and who knows that it is proposed that the child should be fostered privately, to notify the appropriate authority;

    (c) require any parent of a privately fostered child, or person who is not a parent of such a child but who has parental responsibility for him, to notify the appropriate authority of any change in his address;

    (d) require any person who proposes to foster a child privately, to notify the appropriate authority of his proposal;

    (e) require any person who is fostering a child privately, or proposes to do so, to notify the appropriate authority of –

        (i) any offence of which he has been convicted;

       (ii) any disqualification imposed on him under section 68; or

      (iii) any prohibition imposed on him under section 69;

    (f) require any person who is fostering a child privately, to notify the appropriate authority of any change in his address;

    (g) require any person who is fostering a child privately to notify the appropriate authority in writing of any person who begins, or ceases, to be part of his household;

    (h) require any person who has been fostering a child privately, but has ceased to do so, to notify the appropriate authority (indicating, where the child has died, that that is the reason).

Appeals

8. (1) A person aggrieved by –

    (a) a requirement imposed under paragraph 6;

    (b) a refusal of consent under section 68;

    (c) a prohibition imposed under section 69;

    (d) a refusal to cancel such a prohibition;

    (e) a refusal to make an exemption under paragraph 4 of Schedule 7;

    (f) a condition imposed in such an exemption; or

    (g) a variation or cancellation of such an exemption,

may appeal to the court.

(2) The appeal must be made within fourteen days from the date on which the person appealing is notified of the requirement, refusal, prohibition, condition, variation or cancellation.

(3) Where the appeal is against –

    (a) a requirement imposed under paragraph 6;

    (b) a condition of an exemption imposed under paragraph 4 of Schedule 7; or

    (c) a variation or cancellation of such an exemption,

the requirement, condition, variation or cancellation shall not have effect while the appeal is pending.

(4) Where it allows an appeal against a requirement or prohibition, the court may, instead of cancelling the requirement or prohibition –

    (a) vary the requirement, or allow more time for compliance with it; or

    (b) if an absolute prohibition has been imposed, substitute for it a prohibition on using the premises after such time as the court may specify unless such specified requirements as the local authority had power to impose under paragraph 6 are complied with.

(5) Any requirement or prohibition specified or substituted by a court under this paragraph shall be deemed for the purposes of Part IX (other than this paragraph) to have been imposed by the local authority under paragraph 6 or (as the case may be) section 69.

(6) Where it allows an appeal against a refusal to make an exemption, a condition imposed in such an exemption or a variation or cancellation of such an exemption, the court may –

    (a) make an exemption;

    (b) impose a condition; or

    (c) vary the exemption.

(7) Any exemption made or varied under sub-paragraph (6), or any condition imposed under that sub-paragraph, shall be deemed for the purposes of Schedule 7 (but not for the purposes of this paragraph) to have been made, varied or imposed under that Schedule.

(8) Nothing in sub-paragraph (1)(e) to (g) confers any right of appeal on –

    (a) a person who is, or would be if exempted under Schedule 7, a local authority foster parent; or

    (b) a person who is, or would be if so exempted, a person with whom a child is placed by a voluntary organisation.

Extension of Part IX to certain school children during holidays

9. (1) Where a child under sixteen who is a pupil at a school ...[1] lives at the school during school holidays for a period of more than two weeks, Part IX shall apply in relation to the child as if –

    (a) while living at the school, he were a privately fostered child; and

    (b) paragraphs [2(1)(c) and (d)][2] and 6 were omitted.

[But this sub-paragraph does not apply to a school which is an appropriate children's home.][2]

(2) Sub-paragraph (3) applies to any person who proposes to care for and accommodate one or more children at a school in circumstances in which some or all of them will be treated as private foster children by virtue of this paragraph.

(3) That person shall, not less than two weeks before the first of those children is treated as a private foster child by virtue of this paragraph during the holiday in question, give written notice of his proposal to the local authority within whose area the child is ordinarily resident ('the appropriate authority'), stating the estimated number of the children.

(4) A local authority may exempt any person from the duty of giving notice under sub-paragraph (3).

(5) Any such exemption may be granted for a special period or indefinitely and may be revoked at any time by notice in writing given to the person exempted.

(6) Where a child who is treated as a private foster child by virtue of this paragraph dies, the person caring for him at the school shall, not later than 48 hours after the death, give written notice of it –

    (a) to the appropriate local authority; and

    (b) where reasonably practicable, to each parent of the child and to every person who is not a parent of his but who has parental responsibility for him.

(7) Where a child who is treated as a foster child by virtue of this paragraph ceases for any other reason to be such a child, the person caring for him at the school shall give written notice of the fact to the appropriate local authority.

NOTES

    Amendments. [1] Words repealed: Care Standards Act 2000, s 110. [2] Words inserted and substituted: Care Standards Act 2000, s 116, Sch 4, para 14(27).

Prohibition of advertisements relating to fostering

10. No advertisement indicating that a person will undertake, or will arrange for, a child to be privately fostered shall be published, unless it states that person's name and address.

Avoidance of insurances on lives of privately fostered children

11. A person who fosters a child privately and for reward shall be deemed for the purposes of the Life Assurance Act 1774 to have no interest in the life of the child.

PART I

NOTES
   Definitions. 'Child': s 105(1); 'child who is looked after by a local authority': s 22(1); 'children's home': s 63(3); 'health service hospital': s 105(1); 'local authority': s 105(1); 'local authority foster parent': s 23(3); 'local education authority': s 105(1); 'mental nursing home': s 105(1); 'nursing home': s 105(1); 'parental responsibility': s 3; 'privately fostered child': s 66; 'relative': s 105(1); 'requirement': Sch 8, para 6(6); 'residential care home': s 105(1); 'school': s 105(1); 'the appropriate local authority': Sch 8, para 6(6); 'the court': s 92(7); 'to foster a child privately': s 66; 'voluntary organisation': s 105(1).

[Schedule 9 ceases to extend to England and Wales.]

[SCHEDULE 9A
CHILD MINDING AND DAY CARE FOR YOUNG CHILDREN

Exemption of certain schools

1. (1) Except in prescribed circumstances, Part XA does not apply to provision of day care within sub-paragraph (2) for any child looked after in –

   (a) a maintained school;
   (b) a school assisted by a local education authority;
   (c) a school in respect of which payments are made by the Secretary of State or the Assembly under section 485 of the Education Act 1996;
   (d) an independent school.

(2) The provision mentioned in sub-paragraph (1) is provision of day care made by –

   (a) the person carrying on the establishment in question as part of the establishment's activities; or
   (b) a person employed to work at that establishment and authorised to make that provision as part of the establishment's activities.

(3) In sub-paragraph (1) –

   'assisted' has the same meaning as in the Education Act 1996;
   'maintained school' has the meaning given by section 20(7) of the School Standards and Framework Act 1998.

Exemption for other establishments

2. (1) Part XA does not apply to provision of day care within sub-paragraph (2) for any child looked after –

   (a) in an appropriate children's home;
   (b) in a care home;
   (c) as a patient in a hospital (within the meaning of the Care Standards Act 2000);
   (d) in a residential family centre.

(2) The provision mentioned in sub-paragraph (1) is provision of day care made by –

   (a) the department, authority or other person carrying on the establishment in question as part of the establishment's activities; or

(b) a person employed to work at that establishment and authorised to make that provision as part of the establishment's activities.

Exemption for occasional facilities

3. (1) Where day care is provided on particular premises on less than six days in any year, that provision shall be disregarded for the purposes of Part XA if the person making it has notified the registration authority in writing before the first occasion on which the premises concerned are so used in that year.

(2) In sub-paragraph (1) 'year' means the year beginning with the day (after the commencement of paragraph 5 of Schedule 9) on which the day care in question was or is first provided on the premises concerned and any subsequent year.

Disqualification for registration

4. (1) Regulations may provide for a person to be disqualified for registration for child minding or providing day care.

(2) The regulations may, in particular, provide for a person to be disqualified where –

    (a) he is included in the list kept under section 1 of the Protection of Children Act 1999;

    [(b) he is subject to a direction under section 142 of the Education Act 2002, given on the grounds that he is unsuitable to work with children][2];

    (c) an order of a prescribed kind has been made at any time with respect to him;

    (d) an order of a prescribed kind has been made at any time with respect to any child who has been in his care;

    (e) a requirement of a prescribed kind has been imposed at any time with respect to such a child, under or by virtue of any enactment;

    (f) he has at any time been refused registration under Part X or Part XA or any prescribed enactment or had any such registration cancelled;

    (g) he has been convicted of any offence of a prescribed kind, or has been placed on probation or discharged absolutely or conditionally for any such offence;

    (h) he has at any time been disqualified from fostering a child privately;

    (j) a prohibition has been imposed on him at any time under section 69, section 10 of the Foster Children (Scotland) Act 1984 or any prescribed enactment;

    (k) his rights and powers with respect to a child have at any time been vested in a prescribed authority under a prescribed enactment.

(3) Regulations may provide for a person who lives –

    (a) in the same household as a person who is himself disqualified for registration for child minding or providing day care; or

    (b) in a household at which any such person is employed,

to be disqualified for registration for child minding or providing day care.

[(3A) Regulations under this paragraph may provide for a person not to be disqualified for registration by reason of any fact which would otherwise cause him to be disqualified if –

    (a) he has disclosed the fact to the registration authority, and

    (b) the registration authority has consented in writing to his registration and has not withdrawn that consent.][1]

PART I

(4) A person who is disqualified for registration for providing day care shall not provide day care, or be concerned in the management of, or have any financial interest in, any provision of day care.

(5) No person shall employ, in connection with the provision of day care, a person who is disqualified for registration for providing day care.

(6) In this paragraph 'enactment' means any enactment having effect, at any time, in any part of the United Kingdom.

NOTES

Amendments. [1] Sub-paragraph inserted: Education Act 2002, s 152, Sch 13, para 6. [2] Sub-paragraph substituted: Education Act 2002, s 215(1), Sch 21, para 9.

5. (1) If any person –

  (a) acts as a child minder at any time when he is disqualified for registration for child minding; or
  (b) contravenes any of sub-paragraphs (3) to (5) of paragraph 4,

he shall be guilty of an offence.

(2) Where a person contravenes sub-paragraph (3) of paragraph 4, he shall not be guilty of an offence under this paragraph if he proves that he did not know, and had no reasonable grounds for believing, that the person in question was living or employed in the household.

(3) Where a person contravenes sub-paragraph (5) of paragraph 4, he shall not be guilty of an offence under this paragraph if he proves that he did not know, and had no reasonable grounds for believing, that the person whom he was employing was disqualified.

(4) A person guilty of an offence under this paragraph shall be liable on summary conviction to imprisonment for a term not exceeding six months, or to a fine not exceeding level 5 on the standard scale, or to both.

Certificates of registration

6. (1) If an application for registration is granted, the registration authority shall give the applicant a certificate of registration.

(2) A certificate of registration shall give prescribed information about prescribed matters.

(3) Where, due to a change of circumstances, any part of the certificate requires to be amended, the registration authority shall issue an amended certificate.

(4) Where the registration authority is satisfied that the certificate has been lost or destroyed, the authority shall issue a copy, on payment by the registered person of any prescribed fee.

(5) For the purposes of Part XA, a person is –

  (a) registered for providing child minding (in England or in Wales); or
  (b) registered for providing day care on any premises,

if a certificate of registration to that effect is in force in respect of him.

Annual fees

7. Regulations may require registered persons to pay to the registration authority at prescribed times an annual fee of a prescribed amount.

Co-operation between authorities

8. (1) Where it appears to the Chief Inspector that any local authority in England could, by taking any specified action, help in the exercise of any of his functions under Part XA, he may request the help of that authority specifying the action in question.

(2) Where it appears to the Assembly that any local authority in Wales could, by taking any specified action, help in the exercise of any of its functions under Part XA, the Assembly may request the help of that authority specifying the action in question.

(3) An authority whose help is so requested shall comply with the request if it is compatible with their own statutory or other duties and obligations and does not unduly prejudice the discharge of any of their functions.] [1]

NOTES

    Amendments. [1] Schedule inserted: Care Standards Act 2000, s 79(2), Sch 3.

SCHEDULE 10

AMENDMENTS OF ADOPTION LEGISLATION

[not reproduced]

SCHEDULE 11

JURISDICTION

Section 92

PART I
GENERAL

Commencement of proceedings

1. (1) The Lord Chancellor may by order specify proceedings under this Act or the Adoption Act 1976 which may only be commenced in –

    (a) a specified level of court;

    (b) a court which falls within a specified class of court; or

    (c) a particular court determined in accordance with, or specified in, the order.

(2) The Lord Chancellor may by order specify circumstances in which specified proceedings under this Act or the Adoption Act 1976 (which might otherwise be commenced elsewhere) may only be commenced in –

    (a) a specified level of court;

PART I

(b) a court which falls within a specified class of court; or

(c) a particular court determined in accordance with, or specified in, the order.

[(2A) Sub-paragraphs (1) and (2) shall also apply in relation to proceedings –

[(a) under section 55A of the Family Law Act 1986 (declarations of parentage); or]²

(b) which are to be dealt with in accordance with an order made under section 45 [of the Child Support Act 1991]² (jurisdiction of courts in certain proceedings under that Act).]¹

(3) The Lord Chancellor may by order make provision by virtue of which, where specified proceedings with respect to a child under –

(a) this Act;

(b) the Adoption Act 1976;

[(bb) section 20 (appeals) ...² of the Child Support Act 1991;]¹ or

(c) the High Court's inherent jurisdiction with respect to children,

have been commenced in or transferred to any court (whether or not by virtue of an order under this Schedule), any other specified family proceedings which may affect, or are otherwise connected with, the child may, in specified circumstances, only be commenced in that court.

(4) A class of court specified in an order under this Schedule may be described by reference to a description of proceedings and may include different levels of court.

Transfer of proceedings

2. (1) The Lord Chancellor may by order provide that in specified circumstances the whole, or any specified part of, specified proceedings to which this paragraph applies shall be transferred to –

(a) a specified level of court;

(b) a court which falls within a specified class of court; or

(c) a particular court determined in accordance with, or specified in, the order.

(2) Any order under this paragraph may provide for the transfer to be made at any stage, or specified stage, of the proceedings and whether or not the proceedings, or any part of them, have already been transferred.

(3) The proceedings to which this paragraph applies are –

(a) any proceedings under this Act;

(b) any proceedings under the Adoption Act 1976;

[(ba) any proceedings under section 55A of the Family Law Act 1986]²

[(bb) [any proceedings under]² section 20 (appeals) ...² of the Child Support Act 1991;]¹

(c) any other proceedings which –

(i) are family proceedings for the purposes of this Act, other than proceedings under the inherent jurisdiction of the High Court; and

(ii) may affect, or are otherwise connected with, the child concerned.

(4) Proceedings to which this paragraph applies by virtue of sub-paragraph (3)(c) may only be transferred in accordance with the provisions of an order made under this paragraph for the purpose of consolidating them with proceedings under –

(a) this Act;

(b) the Adoption Act 1976; or

(c) the High Court's inherent jurisdiction with respect to children.

(5) An order under this paragraph may make such provision as the Lord Chancellor thinks appropriate for excluding proceedings to which this paragraph applies from the operation of any enactment which would otherwise govern the transfer of those proceedings, or any part of them.

Hearings by single justice

3. (1) In such circumstances as the Lord Chancellor may by order specify –

(a) the jurisdiction of a magistrates' court to make an emergency protection order;

(b) any specified question with respect to the transfer of specified proceedings to or from a magistrates' court in accordance with the provisions of an order under paragraph 2,

may be exercised by a single justice.

(2) Any provision made under this paragraph shall be without prejudice to any other enactment or rule of law relating to the functions which may be performed by a single justice of the peace.

General

4. (1) For the purposes of this Schedule –

(a) the commencement of proceedings under this Act includes the making of any application under this Act in the course of proceedings (whether or not those proceedings are proceedings under this Act); and

(b) there are three levels of court, that is to say the High Court, any county court and any magistrates' court.

(2) In this Schedule 'specified' means specified by an order made under this Schedule.

(3) Any order under paragraph 1 may make provision as to the effect of commencing proceedings in contravention of any of the provisions of the order.

(4) An order under paragraph 2 may make provision as to the effect of a failure to comply with any of the provisions of the order.

(5) An order under this Schedule may –

(a) make such consequential, incidental or transitional provision as the Lord Chancellor considers expedient, including provision amending any other enactment so far as it concerns the jurisdiction of any court or justice of the peace;

(b) make provision for treating proceedings which are –
  (i) in part proceedings of a kind mentioned in paragraph (a) or (b) of paragraph 2(3); and
  (ii) in part proceedings of a kind mentioned in paragraph (c) of paragraph 2(3),
  as consisting entirely of proceedings of one or other of those kinds, for the purposes of the application of any order made under paragraph 2.

NOTES

Amendments. ¹ Words inserted: Child Support Act 1991, s 45(3)–(5). ² Words inserted, substituted or repealed: Child Support, Pensions and Social Security Act 2000, ss 83, 85, Sch 8, para 10(1)–(3), Sch 9, Part IX.

Definitions. 'Child': s 105(1); 'class of court': Sch 11, para 1(4); 'emergency protection order': s 44(4); 'family proceedings': s 8(3); 'functions': s 105(1); 'levels of court': Sch 11, para 4(1); 'specified': Sch 11, para 4(2); 'the commencement of proceedings under this Act': Sch 11, para 4(1).

PART II
CONSEQUENTIAL AMENDMENTS

[not reproduced]

SCHEDULE 12
MINOR AMENDMENTS

[not reproduced]

SCHEDULE 13
CONSEQUENTIAL AMENDMENTS

[not reproduced]

SCHEDULE 14
TRANSITIONALS AND SAVINGS

Section 108(6)

Pending Proceedings, etc

1. (1) [Subject to sub-paragraphs (1A) and (4)]¹, nothing in any provision of this Act (other than the repeals mentioned in sub-paragraph (2)) shall affect any proceedings which are pending immediately before the commencement of that provision.

[(1A) Proceedings pursuant to section 7(2) of the Family Law Reform Act 1969 (committal or wards of court to care of local authority) or in the exercise of the High Court's inherent jurisdiction with respect to children which are pending in relation to a child who has been placed or allowed to remain in the care of a local authority shall not be treated as pending proceedings after 13th October 1992 for the purposes of this Schedule if no final order has been made by that date pursuant to section 7(2) of the 1969 Act or in the exercise of the High Court's inherent jurisdiction in respect of the child's care.]¹

(2) The repeals are those of –

  (a) section 42(3) of the Matrimonial Causes Act 1973 (declaration by court that party to marriage unfit to have custody of children of family); and
  (b) section 38 of the Sexual Offences Act 1956 (power of court to divest person of authority over girl or boy in cases of incest).

(3) For the purposes of the following provisions of this Schedule, any reference to an order in force immediately before the commencement of a provision of this Act shall be construed as including a reference to an order made after that commencement in proceedings pending before that commencement.

(4) Sub-paragraph (3) is not to be read as making the order in question have effect from a date earlier than that on which it was made.

(5) An order under section 96(3) may make such provision with respect to the application of the order in relation to proceedings which are pending when the order comes into force as the Lord Chancellor considers appropriate.

2. Where, immediately before the day on which Part IV comes into force, there was in force an order under section 3(1) of the Children and Young Persons Act 1963 (order directing a local authority to bring a child or young person before a [youth court]⁶ under section 1 of the Children and Young Persons Act 1969), the order shall cease to have effect on that day.

CUSTODY ORDERS, ETC

Cessation of declarations of unfitness, etc.

3. Where, immediately before the day on which Parts I and II come into force, there was in force –

   (a) a declaration under section 42(3) of the Matrimonial Causes Act 1973 (declaration by court that party to marriage unfit to have custody of children of family); or
   (b) an order under section 38(1) of the Sexual Offences Act 1956 divesting a person of authority over a girl or boy in a case of incest;

the declaration or, as the case may be, the order shall cease to have effect on that day.

The Family Law Reform Act 1987 (c. 42)

Conversion of orders under section 4

4. Where, immediately before the day on which Parts I and II come into force, there was in force an order under section 4(1) of the Family Law Reform Act 1987 (order giving father parental rights and duties in relation to a child), then, on and after that day, the order shall be deemed to be an order under section 4 of this Act giving the father parental responsibility for the child.

Orders to which paragraphs 6 to 11 apply

5. (1) In paragraphs 6 to 11 'an existing order' means any order which –

   (a) is in force immediately before the commencement of Parts I and II;
   (b) was made under any enactment mentioned in sub-paragraph (2);
   (c) determines all or any of the following –
       (i) who is to have custody of a child;
       (ii) who is to have care and control of a child;
       (iii) who is to have access to a child;
       (iv) any matter with respect to a child's education or upbringing; and
   (d) is not an order of a kind mentioned in paragraph 15(1).

(2) The enactments are –

(a) the Domestic Proceedings and Magistrates' Courts Act 1978;
(b) the Children Act 1975;
(c) the Matrimonial Causes Act 1973;
(d) the Guardianship of Minors Acts 1971 and 1973;
(e) the Matrimonial Causes Act 1965;
(f) the Matrimonial Proceedings (Magistrates' Courts) Act 1960.

(3) For the purposes of this paragraph and paragraphs 6 to 11 'custody' includes legal custody and joint as well as sole custody but does not include access.

Parental responsibility of parents

6. (1) Where –

(a) a child's father and mother were married to each other at the time of his birth; and
(b) there is an existing order with respect to the child,

each parent shall have parental responsibility for the child in accordance with section 2 as modified by sub-paragraph (3).

(2) Where –

(a) a child's father and mother were not married to each other at the time of his birth; and
(b) there is an existing order with respect to the child,

section 2 shall apply as modified by sub-paragraphs (3) and (4).

(3) The modification is that for section 2(8) there shall be substituted –

'(8) The fact that a person has parental responsibility for a child does not entitle him to act in a way which would be incompatible with any existing order or any order made under this Act with respect to the child'.

(4) The modifications are that –

(a) for the purposes of section 2(2), where the father has custody or care and control of the child by virtue of any existing order, the court shall be deemed to have made (at the commencement of that section) an order under section 4(1) giving him parental responsibility for the child; and
(b) where by virtue of paragraph (a) a court is deemed to have made an order under section 4(1) in favour of a father who has care and control of a child by virtue of an existing order, the court shall not bring the order under section 4(1) to an end at any time while he has care and control of the child by virtue of the order.

Persons who are not parents but who have custody or care and control

7. (1) Where a person who is not the parent or guardian of a child has custody or care and control of him by virtue of an existing order, that person shall have parental responsibility for him so long as he continues to have that custody or care and control by virtue of the order.

(2) Where sub-paragraph (1) applies, [Parts I and II and paragraph 15 of Schedule 1][1] shall have effect as modified by this paragraph.

(3) The modifications are that –

(a) for section 2(8) there shall be substituted –

'(8) The fact that a person has parental responsibility for a child does not entitle him to act in a way which would be incompatible with any existing order or with any order made under this Act with respect to the child';

(b) at the end of section 9(4) there shall be inserted –

'(c) any person who has custody or care and control of a child by virtue of any existing order'; and

(c) at the end of section 34(1)(c) there shall be inserted –

'(cc) where immediately before the care order was made there was an existing order by virtue of which a person had custody or care and control of the child, that person.'

[(d) for paragraph 15 of Schedule I there shall be substituted –

'**15.** Where a child lives with a person as the result of a custodianship order within the meaning of section 33 of the Children Act 1975, a local authority may make contributions to that person towards the cost of the accommodation and maintenance of the child so long as that person continues to have legal custody of that child by virtue of the order.']¹

Persons who have care and control

8. (1) Sub-paragraphs (2) to (6) apply where a person has care and control of a child by virtue of an existing order, but they shall cease to apply when that order ceases to have effect.

(2) Section 5 shall have effect as if –

(a) for any reference to a residence order in favour of a parent or guardian there were substituted a reference to any existing order by virtue of which the parent or guardian has care and control of the child; and

(b) for subsection (9) there were substituted –

'(9) Subsections (1) and (7) do not apply if the existing order referred to in paragraph (b) of those subsections was one by virtue of which a surviving parent of the child also had care and control of him.'

(3) Section 10 shall have effect as if for subsection (5)(c)(i) there were substituted –

'(i) in any case where by virtue of an existing order any person or persons has or have care and control of the child, has the consent of that person or each of those persons'.

(4) Section 20 shall have effect as if for subsection (9)(a) there were substituted 'who has care and control of the child by virtue of an existing order.'

(5) Section 23 shall have effect as if for subsection (4)(c) there were substituted –

'(c) where the child is in care and immediately before the care order was made there was an existing order by virtue of which a person had care and control of the child, that person.'

(6) In Schedule 1, paragraphs 1(1) and 14(1) shall have effect as if for the words 'in whose favour a residence order is in force with respect to the child' there were substituted 'who has been given care and control of the child by virtue of an existing order'.

Persons who have access

9. (1) Sub-paragraphs (2) to (4) apply where a person has access by virtue of an existing order.

(2) Section 10 shall have effect as if after subsection (5) there were inserted –

'(5A) Any person who has access to a child by virtue of an existing order is entitled to apply for a contact order.'

(3) Section 16(2) shall have effect as if after paragraph (b) there were inserted –

'(bb) any person who has access to the child by virtue of an existing order.'

(4) Sections 43(11), 44(13) and 46(10), shall have effect as if in each case after paragraph (d) there were inserted –

'(dd) any person who has been given access to him by virtue of an existing order.'

Enforcement of certain existing orders

10. (1) Sub-paragraph (2) applies in relation to any existing order which, but for the repeal by this Act of –

(a) section 13(1) of the Guardianship of Minors Act 1971;
(b) section 43(1) of the Children Act 1975; or
(c) section 33 of the Domestic Proceedings and Magistrates' Courts Act 1978,

(provisions concerning the enforcement of custody orders) might have been enforced as if it were an order requiring a person to give up a child to another person.

(2) Where this sub-paragraph applies, the existing order may, after the repeal of the enactments mentioned in sub-paragraph (1)(a) to (c), be enforced under section 14 as if –

(a) any reference to a residence order were a reference to the existing order; and
(b) any reference to a person in whose favour the residence order is in force were a reference to a person to whom actual custody of the child is given by an existing order which is in force.

(3) In sub-paragraph (2) 'actual custody', in relation to a child, means the actual possession of his person.

Discharge of existing orders

11. (1) The making of a residence order or a care order with respect to a child who is the subject of an existing order discharges the existing order.

(2) Where the court makes any section 8 order (other than a residence order) with respect to a child with respect to whom any existing order is in force, the existing order shall have effect subject to the section 8 order.

(3) The court may discharge an existing order which is in force with respect to a child –

(a) in any family proceedings relating to the child or in which any question arises with respect to the child's welfare; or
(b) on the application of –
    (i) any parent or guardian of the child;

(ii) the child himself; or

(iii) any person named in the order.

(4) A child may not apply for the discharge of an existing order except with the leave of the court.

(5) The power in sub-paragraph (3) to discharge an existing order includes the power to discharge any part of the order.

(6) In considering whether to discharge an order under the power conferred by sub-paragraph (3) the court shall, if the discharge of the order is opposed by any party to the proceedings, have regard in particular to the matters mentioned in section 1(3).

GUARDIANS

Existing guardians to be guardians under this Act

12. (1) Any appointment of a person as guardian of a child which –

(a) was made –
   (i) under sections 3 to 5 of the Guardianship of Minors Act 1971;
   (ii) under section 38(3) of the Sexual Offences Act 1956; or
   (iii) under the High Court's inherent jurisdiction with respect to children; and

(b) has taken effect before the commencement of section 5(4),

shall (subject to sub-paragraph (2)) be deemed, on and after the commencement of section 5(4), to be an appointment made and having effect under that section.

(2) Where an appointment of a person as guardian of a child has effect under section 5 by virtue of sub-paragraph (1)(a)(ii), the appointment shall not have effect for a period which is longer than any period specified in the order.

Appointment of guardian not yet in effect

13. Any appointment of a person to be a guardian of a child –

(a) which was made as mentioned in paragraph 12(1)(a)(i); but

(b) which, immediately before the commencement of section 5(4), had not taken effect,

shall take effect in accordance with section 5 (as modified, where it applies, by paragraph 8(2)).

Persons deemed to be appointed as guardians under existing wills

14. For the purposes of the Wills Act 1837 and of this Act any disposition by will and testament or devise of the custody and tuition of any child, made before the commencement of section 5(4) and paragraph 1 of Schedule 13, shall be deemed to be an appointment by will of a guardian of the child.

CHILDREN IN CARE

Children in compulsory care

15. (1) Sub-paragraph (2) applies where, immediately before the day on which Part IV comes into force, a person was –

    (a) in care by virtue of –

        (i) a care order under section 1 of the Children and Young Persons Act 1969;

        (ii) a care order under section 15 of that Act, on discharging a supervision order made under section 1 of that Act; or

        (iii) an order or authorisation under section 25 or 26 of that Act;

    (b) ...⁵

    to be the subject of a care order under the Children and Young Persons Act 1969;

    (c) in care –

        (i) under section 2 of the Child Care Act 1980; or

        (ii) by virtue of paragraph 1 of Schedule 4 to that Act (which extends the meaning of a child in care under section 2 to include children in care under section 1 of the Children Act 1948),

    and a child in respect of whom a resolution under section 3 of the Act of 1980 or section 2 of the Act of 1948 was in force;

    (d) a child in respect of whom a resolution had been passed under section 65 of the Child Care Act 1980;

    (e) in care by virtue of an order under –

        (i) section 2(1)(e) of the Matrimonial Proceedings (Magistrates' Courts) Act 1960;

        (ii) section 7(2) of the Family Law Reform Act 1969;

        (iii) section 43(1) of the Matrimonial Causes Act 1973; or

        (iv) section 2(2)(b) of the Guardianship Act 1973;

        (v) section 10 of the Domestic Proceedings and Magistrates' Courts Act 1978,

    (orders having effect for certain purposes as if the child had been received into care under section 2 of the Child Care Act 1980);

    (f) in care by virtue of an order made, on the revocation of a custodianship order, under section 36 of the Children Act 1975; ... ²

    (g) in care by virtue of an order made, on the refusal of an adoption order, under section 26 of the Adoption Act 1976 or any order having effect (by virtue of paragraph 1 of Schedule 2 to that Act) as if made under that section [; or

    (h) in care by virtue of an order of the court made in the exercise of the High Court's inherent jurisdiction with respect to children.]²

(2) Where this sub-paragraph applies, then, on and after the day on which Part IV commences –

    (a) the order or resolution in question shall be deemed to be a care order;

    (b) the authority in whose care the person was immediately before that commencement shall be deemed to be the authority designated in that deemed care order; and

    (c) any reference to a child in the care of a local authority shall include a reference to a person who is the subject of such a deemed care order,

and the provisions of this Act shall apply accordingly, subject to paragraph 16.

Modifications

16. (1) Sub-paragraph (2) only applies where a person who is the subject of a care order by virtue of paragraph 15(2) is a person falling within sub-paragraph (1)(a) ...[5] of that paragraph.

(2) Where the person would otherwise have remained in care until reaching the age of nineteen, by virtue of –

> (a) section 20(3)(a) or 21(1) of the Children and Young Persons Act 1969;
> ...[5]
> (b) ...[5]

this Act applies as if in section 91(12) for the word 'eighteen' there were substituted 'nineteen'.

(3) ...[5]

[(3A) Where in respect of a child who has been placed or allowed to remain in the care of a local authority pursuant to section 7(2) of the Family Law Reform Act 1969 or in the exercise of the High Court's inherent jurisdiction and the child is still in the care of a local authority, proceedings have ceased by virtue of paragraph 1(1A) to be treated as pending, paragraph 15(2) shall apply on 14th October 1992 as if the child was in care pursuant to an order as specified in paragraph 15(1)(e)(ii) or (h) as the case may be.][1]

(4) [Sub-paragraphs (5) and (6) only apply][3] where a child who is the subject of a care order by virtue of paragraph 15(2) is a person falling within sub-paragraph (1)(e) to [(h)][2] of that paragraph.

(5) [Subject to sub-paragraph (6),][3] where a court, on making the order, or at any time thereafter, gave directions under –

> [(a) section 4(4)(a) of the Guardianship Act 1973;
> (b) section 43(5)(a) of the Matrimonial Causes Act 1973; or
> (c) in the exercise of the High Court's inherent jurisdiction with respect to children,][2]

as to the exercise by the authority of any powers, those directions shall [, subject to the provisions of section 25 of this Act and of any regulations made under that section,][3] continue to have effect (regardless of any conflicting provision in this Act [other than section 25][3]) until varied or discharged by a court under this sub-paragraph.

[(6) Where directions referred to in sub-paragraph (5) are to the effect that a child be placed in accommodation provided for the purpose of restricting liberty then the directions shall cease to have effect upon the expiry of the maximum period specified by regulations under section 25(2)(a) in relation to children of his description, calculated from 14th October 1991.][3]

Cessation of wardship where ward in care

[**16A.** (1) Where a child who is a ward of court is in care by virtue of –

(a) an order under section 7(2) of the Family Law Reform Act 1969; or

(b) an order made in the exercise of the High Court's inherent jurisdiction with respect to children,

he shall, on the day on which Part IV commences, cease to be a ward of court.]²

[(2) Where immediately before the day on which Part IV commences a child was in the care of a local authority and as the result of an order –

(a) pursuant to section 7(2) of the Family Law Reform Act 1969; or

(b) made in the exercise of the High Court's inherent jurisdiction with respect to children,

continued to be in the care of a local authority and was made a ward of court, he shall on the day on which Part IV commences, cease to be a ward of court.

(3) Sub-paragraphs (1) and (2) do not apply in proceedings which are pending.]¹

Children placed with parent etc. while in compulsory care

17. (1) This paragraph applies where a child is deemed by paragraph 15 to be in the care of a local authority under an order or resolution which is deemed by that paragraph to be a care order.

(2) If, immediately before the day on which Part III comes into force, the child was allowed to be under the charge and control of –

(a) a parent or guardian under section 21(2) of the Child Care Act 1980; or

(b) a person who, before the child was in the authority's care, had care and control of the child by virtue of an order falling within paragraph 5,

on and after that day the provision made by and under section 23(5) shall apply as if the child had been placed with the person in question in accordance with that provision.

Orders for access to children in compulsory care

18. (1) This paragraph applies to any access order –

(a) made under section 12C of the Child Care Act 1980 (access orders with respect to children in care of local authorities); and

(b) in force immediately before the commencement of Part IV

(2) On and after the commencement of Part IV, the access order shall have effect as an order made under section 34 in favour of the person named in the order.

[**18A.** (1) This paragraph applies to any decision of a local authority to terminate arrangements for access or to refuse to make such arrangements –

(a) of which notice has been given under, and in accordance with, section 12B of the Child Care Act 1980 (termination of access); and

(b) which is in force immediately before the commencement of Part IV.

(2) On and after the commencement of Part IV, a decision to which this paragraph applies shall have effect as a court order made under section 34(4) authorising the local authority to refuse to allow contact between the child and the person to whom notice was given under section 12B of the Child Care Act 1980.]³

19. (1) This paragraph applies where, immediately before the commencement of Part IV, an access order made under section 12C of the Act of 1980 was suspended by virtue of an order made under section 12E of that Act (suspension of access orders in emergencies).

(2) The suspending order shall continue to have effect as if this Act had not been passed.

(3) If –

    (a) before the commencement of Part IV; and

    (b) during the period for which the operation of the access order is suspended,

the local authority concerned made an application for its variation or discharge to an appropriate juvenile court, its operation shall be suspended until the date on which the application to vary or discharge it is determined or abandoned.

Children in voluntary care

20. (1) This paragraph applies where, immediately before the day on which Part III comes into force –

    (a) a child was in the care of a local authority –

        (i) under section 2(1) of the Child Care Act 1980; or

        (ii) by virtue of paragraph 1 of Schedule 4 to that Act (which extends the meaning of references to children in care under section 2 to include references to children in care under section 1 of the Children Act 1948); and

    (b) he was not a person in respect of whom a resolution under section 3 of the Act of 1980 or section 2 of the Act of 1948 was in force.

(2) Where this paragraph applies, the child shall, on and after the day mentioned in sub-paragraph (1), be treated for the purposes of this Act as a child who is provided with accommodation by the local authority under Part III, but he shall cease to be so treated once he ceases to be so accommodated in accordance with the provisions of Part III.

(3) Where –

    (a) this paragraph applies; and

    (b) the child, immediately before the day mentioned in sub-paragraph (1), was (by virtue of section 21(2) of the Act of 1980) under the charge and control of a person falling within paragraph 17(2)(a) or (b),

the child shall not be treated for the purposes of this Act as if he were being looked after by the authority concerned.

Boarded out children

21. (1) Where, immediately before the day on which Part III comes into force, a child in the care of a local authority –

(a) was –
   (i) boarded out with a person under section 21(1)(a) of the Child Care Act 1980; or
   (ii) placed under the charge and control of a person, under section 21(2) of that Act; and
(b) the person with whom he was boarded out, or (as the case may be) placed, was not a person falling within paragraph 17(2)(a) or (b),

on and after that day, he shall be treated (subject to sub-paragraph (2)) as having been placed with a local authority foster parent and shall cease to be so treated when he ceases to be placed with that person in accordance with the provisions of this Act.

(2) Regulations made under section 23(2)(a) shall not apply in relation to a person who is a local authority foster parent by virtue of sub-paragraph (1) before the end of the period of twelve months beginning with the day on which Part III comes into force and accordingly that person shall for that period be subject –

(a) in a case falling within sub-paragraph (1)(a)(i), to terms and regulations mentioned in section 21(1)(a) of the Act of 1980; and
(b) in a case falling within sub-paragraph (1)(a)(ii), to terms fixed under section 21(2) of that Act and regulations made under section 22A of that Act,

as if that Act had not been repealed by this Act.

Children in care to qualify for advice and assistance

22. Any reference in Part III to a person qualifying for advice and assistance shall be construed as including a reference to a person within the area of the local authority in question who is under twenty-one and who was, at any time after reaching the age of sixteen but while still a child –

(a) a person falling within –
   (i) any of paragraphs (a) to [(h)]² of paragraph 15(1); or
   (ii) paragraph 20(1); or
(b) the subject of a criminal care order (within the meaning of paragraph 34).

Emigration of children in care

23. Where –

(a) the Secretary of State has received a request in writing from a local authority that he give his consent under section 24 of the Child Care Act 1980 to the emigration of a child in their care; but
(b) immediately before the repeal of the Act of 1980 by this Act, he has not determined whether or not to give his consent,

section 24 of the Act of 1980 shall continue to apply (regardless of that repeal) until the Secretary of State has determined whether or not to give his consent to the request.

Contributions for maintenance of children in care

24. (1) Where, immediately before the day on which Part III of Schedule 2 comes into force, there was in force an order made (or having effect as if made) under any of the enactments mentioned in sub-paragraph (2), then, on and after that day –

    (a) the order shall have effect as if made under paragraph 23(2) of Schedule 2 against a person liable to contribute; and

    (b) Part III of Schedule 2 shall apply to the order, subject to the modifications in sub-paragraph (3).

(2) The enactments are –

    (a) section 11(4) of the Domestic Proceedings and Magistrates' Courts Act 1978;

    (b) section 26(2) of the Adoption Act 1976;

    (c) section 36(5) of the Children Act 1975;

    (d) section 2(3) of the Guardianship Act 1973;

    (e) section 2(1)(h) of the Matrimonial Proceedings (Magistrates' Courts) Act 1960,

(provisions empowering the court to make an order requiring a person to make periodical payments to a local authority in respect of a child in care).

(3) The modifications are that, in paragraph 23 of Schedule 2 –

    (a) in sub-paragraph (4), paragraph (a) shall be omitted;

    (b) for sub-paragraph (6) there shall be substituted –

'(6) Where –

    (a) a contribution order is in force;

    (b) the authority serve a contribution notice under paragraph 22; and

    (c) the contributor and the authority reach an agreement under paragraph 22(7) in respect of the contribution notice,

the effect of the agreement shall be to discharge the order from the date on which it is agreed that the agreement shall take effect'; and

    (c) at the end of sub-paragraph (10) there shall be inserted –
'and

    (c) where the order is against a person who is not a parent of the child, shall be made with due regard to –

        (i) whether that person had assumed responsibility for the maintenance of the child, and, if so, the extent to which and basis on which he assumed that responsibility and the length of the period during which he met that responsibility;

       (ii) whether he did so knowing that the child was not his child;

     (iii) the liability of any other person to maintain the child.'

SUPERVISION ORDERS

Orders under section 1(3)(b) or 21(2) of the 1969 Act

25. (1) This paragraph applies to any supervision order –

    (a) made –

        (i) under section 1(3)(b) of the Children and Young Persons Act 1969; or

       (ii) under section 21(2) of that Act on the discharge of a care order made under section 1(3)(c) of that Act; and

(b) in force immediately before the commencement of Part IV.

(2) On and after the commencement of Part IV, the order shall be deemed to be a supervision order made under section 31 and –

(a) any requirement of the order that the child reside with a named individual shall continue to have effect while the order remains in force, unless the court otherwise directs

(b) any other requirement imposed by the court, or directions given by the supervisor, shall be deemed to have been imposed or given under the appropriate provisions of Schedule 3.

(3) Where, immediately before the commencement of Part IV, the order had been in force for a period of [six months or more]³, it shall cease to have effect at the end of the period of six months beginning with the day on which Part IV comes into force unless –

(a) the court directs that it shall cease to have effect at the end of a different period (which shall not exceed three years);

(b) it ceased to have effect earlier in accordance with section 91; or

(c) it would have ceased to have had effect earlier had this Act not been passed.

(4) Where sub-paragraph (3) applies, paragraph 6 of Schedule 3 shall not apply.

(5) Where, immediately before the commencement of Part IV, the order had been in force for less than six months it shall cease to have effect in accordance with section 91 and paragraph 6 of Schedule 3 unless –

(a) the court directs that it shall cease to have effect at the end of a different period (which shall not exceed three years); or

(b) it would have ceased to have had effect earlier had this Act not been passed.

Other supervision orders

26. (1) This paragraph applies to any order for the supervision of a child which was in force immediately before the commencement of Part IV and was made under –

(a) section 2(1)(f) of the Matrimonial Proceedings (Magistrates' Courts) Act 1960;

(b) section 7(4) of the Family Law Reform Act 1969;

(c) section 44 of the Matrimonial Causes Act 1973;

(d) section 2(2)(a) of the Guardianship Act 1973;

(e) section 34(5) or 36(3)(b) of the Children Act 1975;

(f) section 26(1)(a) of the Adoption Act 1976; or

(g) section 9 of the Domestic Proceedings and Magistrates' Courts Act 1978.

(2) The order shall not be deemed to be a supervision order made under any provision of this Act but shall nevertheless continue in force for a period of one year beginning with the day on which Part IV comes into force unless –

(a) the court directs that it shall cease to have effect at the end of a lesser period; or

(b) it would have ceased to have had effect earlier had this Act not been passed.

PLACE OF SAFETY ORDERS

27. (1) This paragraph applies to –

(a) any order or warrant authorising the removal of a child to a place of safety which –
    (i) was made, or issued, under any of the enactments mentioned in sub-paragraph (2); and
    (ii) was in force immediately before the commencement of Part IV; and

(b) any interim order made under section 23(5) of the Children and Young Persons Act 1963 or section 28(6) of the Children and Young Persons Act 1969.

(2) The enactments are –

(a) section 40 of the Children and Young Persons Act 1933 (warrant to search for or remove child);

(b) section 28(1) of the Children and Young Persons Act 1969 (detention of child in place of safety);

(c) section 34(1) of the Adoption Act 1976 (removal of protected children from unsuitable surroundings);

(d) section 12(1) of the Foster Children Act 1980 (removal of foster children kept in unsuitable surroundings).

(3) The order or warrant shall continue to have effect as if this Act had not been passed.

(4) Any enactment repealed by this Act shall continue to have effect in relation to the order or warrant so far as is necessary for the purposes of securing that the effect of the order is what it would have been had this Act not been passed.

(5) Sub-paragraph (4) does not apply to the power to make an interim order or further interim order given by section 23(5) of the Children and Young Persons Act 1963 or section 28(6) of the Children and Young Persons Act 1969.

(6) Where, immediately before section 28 of the Children and Young Persons Act 1969 is repealed by this Act, a child is being detained under the powers granted by that section, he may continue to be detained in accordance with that section but subsection (6) shall not apply.

RECOVERY OF CHILDREN

28. The repeal by this Act of subsection (1) of section 16 of the Child Care Act 1980 (arrest of child absent from compulsory care) shall not affect the operation of that section in relation to any child arrested before the coming into force of the repeal.

29. (1) This paragraph applies where –

(a) a summons has been issued under section 15 or 16 of the Child Care Act 1980 (recovery of children in voluntary or compulsory care); and

(b) the child concerned is not produced in accordance with the summons before the repeal of that section by this Act comes into force.

(2) The summons, any warrant issued in connection with it and section 15 or (as the case may be) section 16, shall continue to have effect as if this Act had not been passed.

30. The amendment by paragraph 27 of Schedule 12 of section 32 of the Children and Young Persons Act 1969 (detention of absentees) shall not affect the operation of that section in relation to –

(a) any child arrested; or
(b) any summons or warrant issued,
under that section before the coming into force of that paragraph.

PART I

VOLUNTARY ORGANISATIONS: PARENTAL RIGHTS RESOLUTIONS

31. (1) This paragraph applies to a resolution –

(a) made under section 64 of the Child Care Act 1980 (transfer of parental rights and duties to voluntary organisations); and
(b) in force immediately before the commencement of Part IV.

(2) The resolution shall continue to have effect until the end of the period of six months beginning with the day on which Part IV comes into force unless it is brought to an end earlier in accordance with the provisions of the Act of 1980 preserved by this paragraph.

(3) While the resolution remains in force, any relevant provisions of, or made under, the Act of 1980 shall continue to have effect with respect to it.

(4) Sub-paragraph (3) does not apply to –

(a) section 62 of the Act of 1980 and any regulations made under that section (arrangements by voluntary organisations for emigration of children); or
(b) section 65 of the Act of 1980 (duty of local authority to assume parental rights and duties).

(5) Section 5(2) of the Act of 1980 (which is applied to resolutions under Part VI of that Act by section 64(7) of that Act) shall have effect with respect to the resolution as if the reference in paragraph (c) to an appointment of a guardian under section 5 of the Guardianship of Minors Act 1971 were a reference to an appointment of a guardian under section 5 of this Act.

FOSTER CHILDREN

32. (1) This paragraph applies where –

(a) immediately before the commencement of Part VIII, a child was a foster child within the meaning of the Foster Children Act 1980; and
(b) the circumstances of the case are such that, had Parts VIII and IX then been in force, he would have been treated for the purposes of this Act as a child who was being provided with accommodation in a children's home and not as a child who was being privately fostered.

(2) If the child continues to be cared for and provided with accommodation as before, section 63(1) and (10) shall not apply in relation to him if –

(a) an application for registration of the home in question is made under section 63 before the end of the period of three months beginning with the day on which Part VIII comes into force; and
(b) the application has not been refused or, if it has been refused –
(i) the period for an appeal against the decision has not expired; or
(ii) an appeal against the refusal has been made but has not been determined or abandoned.

(3) While section 63(1) and (10) does not apply, the child shall be treated as a privately fostered child for the purposes of Part IX.

NURSERIES AND CHILD MINDING

33. (1) Sub-paragraph (2) applies where, immediately before the commencement of Part X, any premises are registered under section 1(1)(a) of the Nurseries and Child-Minders Regulation Act 1948 (registration of premises, other than premises wholly or mainly used as private dwellings, where children are received to be looked after).

(2) During the transitional period, the provisions of the Act of 1948 shall continue to have effect with respect to those premises to the exclusion of Part X.

(3) Nothing in sub-paragraph (2) shall prevent the local authority concerned from registering any person under section 71(1)(b) with respect to the premises.

(4) In this paragraph 'the transitional period' means the period ending with –

(a) the first anniversary of the commencement of Part X; or
(b) if earlier, the date on which the local authority concerned registers any person under section 71(1)(b) with respect to the premises.

34. (1) Sub-paragraph (2) applies where, immediately before the commencement of Part X –

(a) a person is registered under section 1(1)(b) of the Act of 1948 (registration of persons who for reward receive into their homes children under the age of five to be looked after); and
(b) all the children looked after by him as mentioned in section 1(1)(b) of that Act are under the age of five.

(2) During the transitional period, the provisions of the Act of 1948 shall continue to have effect with respect to that person to the exclusion of Part X.

(3) Nothing in sub-paragraph (2) shall prevent the local authority concerned from registering that person under section 71(1)(a).

(4) In this paragraph 'the transitional period' means the period ending with –

(a) the first anniversary of the commencement of Part X; or
(b) if earlier, the date on which the local authority concerned registers that person under section 71(1)(a).

CHILDREN ACCOMMODATED IN CERTAIN ESTABLISHMENTS

35. In calculating, for the purposes of section 85(1)(a) or 86(1)(a), the period of time for which a child has been accommodated any part of that period which fell before the day on which that section came into force shall be disregarded.

CRIMINAL CARE ORDERS

36. (1) This paragraph applies where, immediately before the commencement of section 90(2) there was in force an order ('a criminal care order') made –

(a) under section 7(7)(a) of the Children and Young Persons Act 1969 (alteration in treatment of young offenders etc.); or

(b) under section 15(1) of that Act, on discharging a supervision order made under section 7(7)(b) of that Act.

(2) The criminal care order shall continue to have effect until the end of the period of six months beginning with the day on which section 90(2) comes into force unless it is brought to an end earlier in accordance with –

(a) the provisions of the Act of 1969 preserved by sub-paragraph (3)(a); or
(b) this paragraph.

(3) While the criminal care order remains in force, any relevant provisions –

(a) of the Act of 1969; and
(b) of the Child Care Act 1980,

shall continue to have effect with respect to it.

(4) While the criminal care order remains in force, a court may, on the application of the appropriate person, make –

(a) a residence order;
(b) a care order or a supervision order under section 31;
(c) an education supervision order under section 36 (regardless of subsection (6) of that section); or
(d) an order falling within sub-paragraph (5),

and shall, on making any of those orders, discharge the criminal care order.

(5) The order mentioned in sub-paragraph (4)(d) is an order having effect as if it were a supervision order of a kind mentioned in section 12AA of the Act of 1969 (as inserted by paragraph 23 of Schedule 12), that is to say, a supervision order –

(a) imposing a requirement that the child shall live for a specified period in local authority accommodation; but
(b) in relation to which the conditions mentioned in [subsection (6)]² of section 12AA are not required to be satisfied.

(6) The maximum period which may be specified in an order made under sub-paragraph (4)(d) is six months and such an order may stipulate that the child shall not live with a named person.

(7) Where this paragraph applies, section 5 of the Rehabilitation of Offenders Act 1974 (rehabilitation periods for particular sentences) shall have effect regardless of the repeals in it made by this Act.

(8) In sub-paragraph (4) 'appropriate person' means –

(a) in the case of an application for a residence order, any person (other than a local authority) who has the leave of the court;
(b) in the case of an application for an education supervision order, a local education authority; and
(c) in any other case, the local authority to whose care the child was committed by the order.

MISCELLANEOUS

Consents under the Marriage Act 1949 (c. 76)

37. (1) In the circumstances mentioned in sub-paragraph (2), section 3 of and Schedule 2 to the Marriage Act 1949 (consents to marry) shall continue to have effect regardless of the amendment of that Act by paragraph 5 of Schedule 12.

(2) The circumstances are that –

    (a) immediately before the day on which paragraph 5 of Schedule 12 comes into force, there is in force –
        (i) an existing order, as defined in paragraph 5(1); or
        (ii) an order of a kind mentioned in paragraph 16(1); and
    (b) section 3 of and Schedule 2 to the Act of 1949 would, but for this Act, have applied to the marriage of the child who is the subject of the order.

The Children Act 1975 (c. 72)

38. The amendments of other enactments made by the following provisions of the Children Act 1975 shall continue to have effect regardless of the repeal of the Act of 1975 by this Act –

    (a) section 68(4), (5) and (7) (amendments of section 32 of the Children and Young Persons Act 1969); and
    (b) in Schedule 3 –
        (i) paragraph 13 (amendments of Births and Deaths Registration Act 1953);
        (ii) paragraph 43 (amendment of Perpetuities and Accumulations Act 1964);
        (iii) paragraphs 46 and 47 (amendments of Health Services and Public Health Act 1968); and
        (iv) paragraph 77 (amendment of Parliamentary and Other Pensions Act 1972).

The Child Care Act 1980 (c. 5)

39. The amendment made to section 106(2)(a) of the Children and Young Persons Act 1933) by paragraph 26 of Schedule 5 to the Child Care Act 1980 shall continue to have effect regardless of the repeal of the Act of 1980 by this Act.

Legal aid

40. ...[7]

NOTES

Amendments. [1] Words inserted or substituted: SI 1991/1990, amending SI 1991/828. [2] Words repealed, inserted or substituted: Courts and Legal Services Act 1990, ss 116, 125(7), Sch 16, para 33, Sch 20. [3] Words inserted or substituted: Children Act 1989 (Commencement and Transitional Provisions) Order 1991, SI 1991/828, art 4, Sch. [4] References in paras 12, 13 and 14 to 'the commencement of section 5' shall be construed as references to the commencement of sub-ss (1)–(10) and (13) of that section (14 Oct 1991) except in relation to the appointment of a guardian of the estate of any child in which case they shall be construed as a reference to the commencement of sub-ss (11) and (12) of that section (1 Feb 1992): SI 1991/1990, amending SI 1991/828. [5] Words repealed: Armed Forces Act 1991, s 26(2), Sch 3. [6] Words substituted: Criminal Justice Act 1991, s 100, Sch 11, para 40(2)(r). [7] Paragraph repealed: Access to Justice Act 1999, s 106, Sch 15, Pt I.

Definitions. 'A section 8 order': s 8(2); 'actual custody': Sch 14, para 10(3); 'appropriate person': Sch 14, para 36(8); 'care order': ss 31(11), 105(1); 'child': s 105(1); 'children's home': s 63(3); 'contact order': s 8(1); 'contribution notice': Sch 2, para 22(1); 'contribution order': Sch 2, para 23(2); 'contributor': Sch 2, para 21(1); 'criminal care order': Sch 14, para 36(1); 'custody': Sch 14, para 5(3); 'education supervision order': s 36(2); 'existing order': Sch 14, para 5(1), (2); 'family proceedings': s 8(3); 'local authority': s 105(1); 'local authority foster parent': s 23(3); 'local education authority': s 105(1); 'order in force immediately before the commencement of … this Act': Sch 14, para (1), (3), (4); 'parental responsibility': s 3; 'privately fostered child': s 66(1); 'residence order': s 8(1); 'supervision order': s 31(11); 'supervisor': s 105(1); 'the transitional period': Sch 14, para 33(4); 'upbringing': s 105(1).

PART II

Statutory Instruments

Children (Allocation of Proceedings) Order 1991, SI 1991/1677

ARRANGEMENT OF ARTICLES

1 Citation, commencement and interpretation

(1) This Order may be cited as the Children (Allocation of Proceedings) Order 1991 and shall come into force on 14th October 1991.

(2) In this Order, unless the context otherwise requires –

'child' –

    (a) means, subject to sub-paragraph (b), a person under the age of 18 with respect to whom proceedings are brought, and

    (b) where the proceedings are under Schedule 1, also includes a person who has reached the age of 18,

'London commission area' has the meaning assigned to it by section 2(1) of the Justices of the Peace Act 1979;

'petty sessions area' has the meaning assigned to it by section 4 of the Justices of the Peace Act 1979; and

'the Act' means the Children Act 1989, and a section, Part or Schedule referred to by number alone means the section, Part or Schedule so numbered in that Act.

2 Classes of county court

For the purposes of this Order there shall be the following classes of county court –

(a) divorce county courts, being those courts designated for the time being as divorce county courts by an order under section 33 of the Matrimonial and Family Proceedings Act 1984;

(b) family hearing centres, being those courts set out in Schedule 1 to this Order;

(c) care centres, being those courts set out in column (ii) of Schedule 2 to this Order.

Commencement of proceedings

3 Proceedings to be commenced in magistrates' court

(1) Subject to paragraphs (2) and (3) and to article 4, proceedings under any of the following provisions shall be commenced in a magistrates' court –

(a) section 25 (use of accommodation for restricting liberty);

(b) section 31 (care and supervision orders);

(c) section 33(7) (leave to change name of or remove from United Kingdom child in care);

(d) section 34 (parental contact);

(e) section 36 (education supervision orders);

(f) section 43 (child assessment orders);

(g) section 44 (emergency protection orders);

(h) section 45 (duration of emergency protection orders etc);

(i) section 46(7) (application for emergency protection order by police officer);

(j) section 48 (powers to assist discovery of children etc);

(k) section 50 (recovery orders);

(l) section 75 (protection of children in an emergency);

(m) section 77(6) (appeal against steps taken under section 77(1));

(n) section 102 (powers of constable to assist etc);

(o) paragraph 19 of Schedule 2 (approval of arrangements to assist child to live abroad);

(p) paragraph 23 of Schedule 2 (contribution orders);

(q) paragraph 8 of Schedule 8 (certain appeals);

(r) section 21 of the Adoption Act 1976;

[(s) ...[3]

(t) section 20 of the Child Support Act 1991 (appeals) where the appeals are to be dealt with in accordance with the Child Support Appeals (Jurisdiction of Courts) Order 1993;][1]

[(u) section 30 of the Human Fertilisation and Embryology Act 1990 (parental orders in favour of gamete donors).][2]

(2) Notwithstanding paragraph (1) and subject to paragraph (3), proceedings of a kind set out in sub-paragraph (b), (e), (f), (g), (i) or (j) of paragraph (1), and which arise out of an investigation directed, by the High Court or a county court, under section 37(1), shall be commenced –

(a) in the court which directs the investigation, where that court is the High Court or a care centre, or

(b) in such care centre as the court which directs the investigation may order.

(3) Notwithstanding paragraphs (1) and (2), proceedings of a kind set out in sub-paragraph (a) to (k), (n) or (o) of paragraph (1) shall be [commenced in]¹ a court in which are pending other proceedings, in respect of the same child, which are also of a kind set out in those sub-paragraphs.

PART II

NOTES
Amendments. ¹ Words inserted or substituted: SI 1993/624. ² Words inserted: SI 1994/2164.
³ Sub-paragraph deleted: SI 2001/775.

4 Application to extend, vary or discharge order

(1) Subject to paragraphs (2) and (3), proceedings under the Act, or under the Adoption Act 1976 –

(a) to extend, vary or discharge an order, or

(b) the determination of which may have the effect of varying or discharging an order,

shall be [commenced in]¹ the court which made the order.

(2) Notwithstanding paragraph (1), an application for an order under section 8 which would have the effect of varying or discharging an order made, by a county court, in accordance with section 10(1)(b) shall be made to a divorce county court.

(3) Notwithstanding paragraph (1), an application to extend, vary or discharge an order made, by a county court, under section 38, or for an order which would have the effect of extending, varying or discharging such an order, shall be made to a care centre.

(4) A court may transfer proceedings [commenced]¹ in accordance with paragraph (1) to any other court in accordance with the provisions of articles 5 to 13.

NOTES
Amendments. ¹ Words substituted: SI 1993/624.

Transfer of proceedings

5 Disapplication of enactments about transfer

Sections 38 and 39 of the Matrimonial and Family Proceedings Act 1984 shall not apply to proceedings under the Act or under the Adoption Act 1976.

6 Transfer from one magistrates' court to another

[(1)]¹ A magistrates' court (the 'transferring court') shall transfer proceedings [to which this article applies]¹ to another magistrates' court (the 'receiving court') where –

    (a) having regard to the principle set out in section 1(2), the transferring court considers that the transfer is in the interests of the child –

        (i) because it is likely significantly to accelerate the determination of the proceedings,

        (ii) because it would be appropriate for those proceedings to be heard together with other family proceedings which are pending in the receiving court, or

        (iii) for some other reason, and

    (b) the receiving court, by its justices' clerk (as defined by rule 1(2) of the Family Proceedings Courts (Children Act 1989) Rules 1991), consents to the transfer.

[(2) This article applies to proceedings –

    (a) under the Act;

    (b) under the Adoption Act 1976;

    (c) of the kind mentioned in sub-paragraphs [...[4] (t) or (u)][2] of article 3(1) [and under section 55A of the Family Law Act 1986][4]][1];

    [(d) under section 11 of the Crime and Disorder Act 1998 (child safety orders).][3]

NOTES

Amendments. [1] Words inserted or substituted and paragraph added: SI 1993/624. [2] Words substituted: SI 1994/2164. [3] Sub-paragraph inserted: SI 1998/2166. [4] Sub-paragraph reference deleted and words inserted: SI 2001/775.

7 Transfer from magistrates' court to county court by magistrates' court

(1) Subject to paragraphs (2), (3) and (4) and to articles 15 to 18, a magistrates' court may, upon application by a party or of its own motion, transfer to a county court proceedings of any of the kinds mentioned in article 3(1) [or proceedings under section 55A of the Family Law Act 1986][1] where it considers it in the interests of the child to do so having regard, first, to the principle set out in section 1(2) and, secondly, to the following questions –

    (a) whether the proceedings are exceptionally grave, important or complex, in particular –

        (i) because of complicated or conflicting evidence about the risks involved to the child's physical or moral well-being or about other matters relating to the welfare of the child;

        (ii) because of the number of parties;

        (iii) because of a conflict with the law of another jurisdiction;

        (iv) because of some novel and difficult point of law; or

        (v) because of some question of general public interest;

    (b) whether it would be appropriate for those proceedings to be heard together with other family proceedings which are pending in another court; and

    (c) whether transfer is likely significantly to accelerate the determination of the proceedings, where –

        (i) no other method of doing so, including transfer to another magistrates' court, is appropriate, and

        (ii) delay would seriously prejudice the interests of the child who is the subject of the proceedings.

(2) Notwithstanding paragraph (1), proceedings of the kind mentioned in sub-paragraphs (g) to (j), (l), (m), (p) or (q) of article 3(1) should not be transferred from a magistrates' court.

(3) Notwithstanding paragraph (1), proceedings of the kind mentioned in sub-paragraph (a) or (n) of article 3(1) shall only be transferred from a magistrates' court to a county court in order to be heard together with other family proceedings which arise out of the same circumstances as gave rise to the proceedings to be transferred and which are pending in another court.

(4) Notwithstanding paragraphs (1) and (3), proceedings of the kind mentioned in article 3(1)(a) shall not be transferred from a magistrates' court which is not a family proceedings court within the meaning of section 92(1).

NOTES

Amendments. [1] Words inserted: SI 2001/775.

8 Subject to articles 15 to 18, a magistrates' court may transfer to a county court proceedings under the Act or under the Adoption Act 1976, being proceedings to which article 7 does not apply, where, having regard to the principle set out in section 1(2), it considers that in the interests of the child the proceedings can be dealt with more appropriately in that county court.

9 Transfer from magistrates' court following refusal of magistrates' court to transfer

(1) Where a magistrates' court refuses to transfer proceedings under article 7, a party to those proceedings may apply to the care centre listed in column (ii) of Schedule 2 to this Order against the entry in column (i) for the petty sessions area or London commission area in which the magistrates' court is situated for an order under paragraph (2).

(2) Upon hearing an application under paragraph (1) the court may transfer the proceedings to itself where, having regard to the principle set out in section 1(2) and the questions set out in article 7(1)(a) to (c), it considers it in the interests of the child to do so.

(3) Upon hearing an application under paragraph (1) the court may transfer the proceedings to the High Court where, having regard to the principle set out in section 1(2), it considers –

(a) that the proceedings are appropriate for determination in the High Court, and

(b) that such determination would be in the interests of the child.

[(4) This article shall apply (with the necessary modifications) to proceedings brought under Parts I and II as it applies where a magistrates' court refuses to transfer proceedings under article 7.][1]

NOTES

Amendments. [1] Paragraph inserted: SI 1997/1897.

10 Transfer from one county court to another

[(1)]¹ Subject to articles 15 to 17, a county court (the 'transferring court') shall transfer proceedings [to which this article applies]¹ to another county court (the 'receiving court') where –

    (a) the transferring court, having regard to the principle set out in section 1(2), considers the transfer to be in the interests of the child, and

    (b) the receiving court is –

        (i) of the same class or classes, within the meaning of article 2, as the transferring court, or

        (ii) to be presided over by a judge or district judge who is specified by directions under section 9 of the Courts and Legal Services Act 1990, for the same purposes as the judge or district judge presiding over the transferring court.

[(2) This article applies to proceedings –

    (a) under the Act;

    (b) under the Adoption Act 1976;

    (c) of the kind mentioned in sub-paragraphs [...³ (t) or (u)]² of article 3(1) [and under section 55A of the Family Law Act 1986]³.]¹

NOTES

Amendments. ¹ Words inserted or substituted and paragraph added: SI 1993/624. ² Words substituted: SI 1994/2164. ³ Sub-paragraph reference deleted and words inserted: SI 2001/775.

11 Transfer from county court to magistrates' court by county court

[(1)]¹ A county court may transfer to a magistrates' court before trial proceedings which were transferred under article 7(1) where the county court, having regard to the principle set out in section 1(2) and the interests of the child, considers that the criterion cited by the magistrates' court as the reason for transfer –

    (a) in the case of the criterion in article 7(1)(a), does not apply,

    (b) in the case of the criterion in article 7(1)(b), no longer applies, because the proceedings with which the transferred proceedings were to be heard have been determined,

    (c) in the case of the criterion in article 7(1)(c), no longer applies.

[(2) Paragraph (1) shall apply (with the necessary modifications) to proceedings under Parts I and II brought in, or transferred to, a county court as it applies to proceedings transferred to a county court under article 7(1).]¹

NOTES

Amendments. ¹ Paragraph numbering and paragraph inserted: SI 1997/1897.

12 Transfer from county court to High Court by county court

[(1)]¹ A county court may transfer proceedings [to which this article applies]¹ to the High Court where, having regard to the principle set out in section 1(2), it considers –

    (a) that the proceedings are appropriate for determination in the High Court, and

    (b) that such determination would be in the interests of the child.

[(2) This article applies to proceedings –

    (a) under the Act;
    (b) under the Adoption Act 1976;
    (c) of the kind mentioned in sub-paragraphs [...[3] (t) or (u)][2] of article 3(1) [and under section 55A of the Family Law Act 1986][3].][1]

NOTES

Amendments. [1] Words inserted or substituted and paragraph added: SI 1993/624. [2] Words substituted: SI 1994/2164. [3] Sub-paragraph reference deleted and words inserted: SI 2001/775.

13 Transfer from High Court to county court

[(1)][1] Subject to articles 15, 16 and 18, the High Court may transfer to a county court proceedings [to which this article applies][1] where, having regard to the principle set out in section 1(2), it considers that the proceedings are appropriate for determination in such a court and that such determination would be in the interests of the child.

(2) This article applies to proceedings –

    (a) under the Act;
    (b) under the Adoption Act 1976;
    (c) of the kind mentioned in sub-paragraphs [...[3] (t) or (u)][2] of article 3(1) [and under section 55A of the Family Law Act 1986][3].][1]

NOTES

Amendments. [1] Words inserted or substituted and paragraph added: SI 1993/624. [2] Words substituted: SI 1994/2164. [3] Sub-paragraph reference deleted and words inserted: SI 2001/775.

Allocation of proceedings to particular county courts

14 Commencement

Subject to articles 18, 19 and 20 and to rule 2.40 of the Family Proceedings Rules 1991 (Application under Part I or II of the Children Act 1989 where matrimonial cause is pending), an application under the Act or under the Adoption Act 1976 which is to be [made to][1] a county court shall be [made to][1] a divorce county court.

NOTES

Amendments. [1] Words substituted: SI 1993/624.

15 Proceedings under Part I or II or Schedule 1

(1) Subject to paragraph (3), where an application under Part I or II or Schedule 1 is to be transferred from a magistrates' court to a county court, it shall be transferred to a divorce county court.

(2) Subject to paragraph (3), where an application under Part I or II or Schedule 1, other than an application for an order under section 8, is to be transferred from the High Court to a county court, it shall be transferred to a divorce county court.

(3) Where an application under Part I or II or Schedule 1, other than an application for an order under section 8, is to be transferred to a county court for the purpose of consolidation with other proceedings, it shall be transferred to the court in which those other proceedings are pending.

PART II

16 Orders under section 8 of the Children Act 1989

(1) An application for an order under section 8 in a divorce county court, which is not also a family hearing centre, shall, if the court is notified that the application will be opposed, be transferred for trial to a family hearing centre.

(2) Subject to paragraph (3), where an application for an order under section 8 is to be transferred from the High Court to a county court it shall be transferred to a family hearing centre.

(3) Where an application for an order under section 8 is to be transferred to a county court for the purpose of consolidation with other proceedings, it may be transferred to the court in which those other proceedings are pending whether or not it is a family hearing centre; but paragraph (1) shall apply to the application following the transfer.

17 Application for adoption or freeing for adoption

(1) Subject to article 22, proceedings in a divorce county court, which is not also a family hearing centre, under section 12 or 18 of the Adoption Act 1976 shall, if the court is notified that the proceedings will be opposed, be transferred for trial to a family hearing centre.

(2) Where proceedings under the Adoption Act 1976 are to be transferred from a magistrates' court to a county court, they shall be transferred to a divorce county court.

18 Applications under Part III, IV or V

(1) An application under Part III, IV or V, if it is to be [made to]¹ a county court, shall be [made to]¹ a care centre.

(2) An application under Part III, IV or V which is to be transferred from the High Court to a county court shall be transferred to a care centre.

(3) An application under Part III, IV or V which is to be transferred from a magistrates' court to a county court shall be transferred to the care centre listed against the entry in column (i) of Schedule 2 to this Order for the petty sessions area or London commission area in which the relevant magistrates' court is situated.

NOTES
  Amendments. ¹ Words substituted: SI 1993/624.

19 Principal Registry of the Family Division

The principal registry of the Family Division of the High Court shall be treated, for the purposes of this Order, as if it were a divorce county court, a family hearing centre and a care centre listed against every entry in column (i) of Schedule 2 to this Order (in addition to the entries against which it is actually listed).

[20 Lambeth, Shoreditch and Woolwich County Courts

Notwithstanding articles 14, 16 and 17, an application for an order under section 4 or 8 or under the Adoption Act 1976 may be made to and tried in Lambeth, Shoreditch or Woolwich County Court.]¹

NOTES
   Amendments. [1] Article substituted: SI 1997/1897.

Miscellaneous

21 Contravention of provisions of this Order

Where proceedings are commenced or transferred in contravention of a provision of this Order, the contravention shall not have the effect of making the proceedings invalid; and no appeal shall lie against the determination of proceedings on the basis of such contravention alone.

22 Transitional provision – proceedings under Adoption Act 1976

Proceedings under the Adoption Act 1976 which are commenced in a county court prior to the coming into force of this Order may, notwithstanding article 17(1), remain in that court for trial.

SCHEDULE 1

FAMILY HEARING CENTRES

Article 2

Midland ...[6] Circuit

Birmingham County Court	Coventry County Court
Derby County Court	[Dudley County Court][1]
[...[6]][1]	Leicester County Court
Lincoln County Court	Mansfield County Court
Northampton County Court	Nottingham County Court
...[6]	...[6]
Stafford County Court	Stoke-on-Trent County Court
Telford County Court	Walsall County Court
Wolverhampton County Court	Worcester County Court

Northern Circuit

Blackburn County Court	Bolton County Court
Carlisle County Court	Lancaster County Court
Liverpool County Court	Manchester County Court
[Oldham County Court][4]	Stockport County Court

North Eastern Circuit

Barnsley County Court	Bradford County Court
Darlington County Court	Dewsbury County Court
Doncaster County Court	Durham County Court

PART II

[Grimsby County Court][6]

Halifax County Court

Harrogate County Court

Huddersfield County Court

Keighley County Court

Kingston-upon-Hull County Court

Leeds County Court

Newcastle-upon-Tyne County Court

Pontefract County Court

Rotherham County Court

Scarborough County Court

Sheffield County Court

Skipton County Court

Sunderland County Court

Teesside County Court

Wakefield County Court

York County Court

South Eastern Circuit

[Barnet County Court][5]

[Bedford County Court][1]

Bow County Court

Brentford County Court

Brighton County Court

Bromley County Court

Cambridge County Court

Canterbury County Court

Chelmsford County Court

Chichester County Court

Colchester and Clacton County Court

Croydon County Court

[Dartford County Court][1]

Edmonton County Court

Guildford County Court

Hitchin County Court

Ilford County Court

Ipswich County Court

[King's Lynn County Court][1]

Kingston-upon-Thames County Court

Luton County Court

Maidstone County Court

Medway County Court

Milton Keynes County Court

Norwich County Court

[Oxford County Court][6]

[Peterborough County Court][6]

Reading County Court

Romford County Court

Slough County Court

Southend County Court

Wandsworth County Court

Watford County Court

Willesden County Court

Wales and Chester Circuit

Aberystwyth County Court

Caernarfon County Court

Cardiff County Court

Carmarthen County Court

Chester County Court

Crewe County Court

Haverfordwest County Court

Llangefni County Court

Macclesfield County Court

Merthyr Tydfil County Court

Newport (Gwent) County Court

[Pontypridd County Court][2]

Rhyl County Court

Swansea County Court

Warrington County Court

Welshpool and Newtown County Court

Wrexham County Court

Western Circuit

[Barnstaple County Court][4]	Basingstoke County Court
[Bath County Court][1]	Bournemouth County Court
Bristol County Court	Exeter County Court
Gloucester County Court	Plymouth County Court
Portsmouth County Court	[Salisbury County Court][3]
Southampton County Court	Swindon County Court
Taunton County Court	Truro County Court
[Weymouth County Court][1]	[Yeovil County Court][7]

NOTES

Amendments. [1] Words inserted: SI 1994/3138. [2] Words inserted: SI 1995/1649. [3] Words inserted: SI 1997/1897. [4] Words inserted: SI 1999/524. [5] Words inserted: SI 2000/2670. [6] Entries deleted or inserted: SI 2001/775. [7] Entry inserted: SI 2001/1656.

SCHEDULE 2
CARE CENTRES

Article 2

(i)	**(ii)**
Petty Sessions Areas	**Care Centres**
	Midland ...[5] Circuit
...[5]	
Aldridge and Brownhills	Wolverhampton County Court
Alfreton and Belper	Derby County Court
Ashby-De-La-Zouch	Leicester County Court
Atherstone and Coleshill	Coventry County Court
...[5]	
Bewdley and Stourport	Worcester County Court
...[5]	
Birmingham	Birmingham County Court
Boston	Lincoln County Court
Bourne and Stamford	Lincoln County Court
Bridgnorth	Telford County Court
...[5]	
Bromsgrove	Worcester County Court
Burton-upon-Trent	[Derby County Court][2]
Caistor	Lincoln County Court
Cannock	Wolverhampton County Court
...[5]	

(i)	(ii)
Petty Sessions Areas	**Care Centres**
Cheadle	Stoke-on-Trent County Court
Chesterfield	Derby County Court
City of Hereford	Worcester County Court
Congleton	Stoke-on-Trent County Court
Corby	Northampton County Court
Coventry	Coventry County Court
Crewe and Nantwich	Stoke-on-Trent County Court
Daventry	Northampton County Court
Derby and South Derbyshire ...⁵	Derby County Court
Drayton	Telford County Court
Dudley	Wolverhampton County Court
East Retford ...⁵	Nottingham County Court
Eccleshall	Stoke-on-Trent County Court
Elloes ...⁵ ...⁵	Lincoln County Court
Gainsborough	Lincoln County Court
Glossop	Derby County Court
Grantham ...⁵	Lincoln County Court
Halesowen ...⁵	Wolverhampton County Court
High Peak ...⁵	Derby County Court
Ilkeston	Derby County Court
Kettering	Northampton County Court
Kidderminster	Worcester County Court
Leek	Stoke-on-Trent County Court
Leicester (City)	Leicester County Court
Leicester (County)	Leicester County Court
Lichfield	Stoke-on-Trent County Court
Lincoln District	Lincoln County Court
Loughborough	Leicester County Court
Louth	Lincoln County Court
Ludlow	Telford County Court

(i)	(ii)
Petty Sessions Areas	**Care Centres**
Lutterworth	Leicester County Court
Malvern Hills	Worcester County Court
Mansfield	Nottingham County Court
Market Bosworth	Leicester County Court
Market Harborough	Leicester County Court
Market Rasen	Lincoln County Court
Melton and Belvoir	Leicester County Court
Mid-Warwickshire	Coventry County Court
Mid-Worcestershire	Worcester County Court
Newark and Southwell	Nottingham County Court
Newcastle-under-Lyme	Stoke-on-Trent County Court
...[5]	
Northampton	Northampton County Court
North Herefordshire	Worcester County Court
...[5]	
...[5]	
Nottingham	Nottingham County Court
Nuneaton	Coventry County Court
Oswestry	Telford County Court
...[5]	
...[5]	
Pirehill North	Stoke-on-Trent County Court
Redditch	Worcester County Court
Rugby	Coventry County Court
Rugeley	Wolverhampton County Court
Rutland	Leicester County Court
...[5]	
Seisdon	Wolverhampton County Court
Sleaford	Lincoln County Court
Shrewsbury	Telford County Court
Solihull	Birmingham County Court
South Herefordshire	Worcester County Court
South Warwickshire	Coventry County Court
Spilsby and Skegness	Lincoln County Court
Stoke-on-Trent	Stoke-on-Trent County Court
Stone	Stoke-on-Trent County Court
Stourbridge	Wolverhampton County Court

PART II

(i)	(ii)
Petty Sessions Areas	**Care Centres**
Sutton Coldfield	Birmingham County Court
Tamworth	Stoke-on-Trent County Court
Telford	Telford County Court
...5	
Towcester	Northampton County Court
Uttoxeter	Stoke-on-Trent County Court
Vale of Evesham	Worcester County Court
Warley	Wolverhampton County Court
Walsall	Wolverhampton County Court
Wellingborough	Northampton County Court
West Bromwich	Wolverhampton County Court
West Derbyshire	Derby County Court
...5	
...5	
Wolds	Lincoln County Court
Wolverhampton	Wolverhampton County Court
...5	
Worcester City	Worcester County Court
Worksop	Nottingham County Court
	Northern Circuit
Appleby	Carlisle County Court
Ashton-under-Lyne	Manchester County Court
Barrow with Bootle	Lancaster County Court
Blackburn	Blackburn County Court
Blackpool	Lancaster County Court
Bolton	Manchester County Court
Burnley	Blackburn County Court
Bury	Manchester County Court
Carlisle	Carlisle County Court
Chorley	Blackburn County Court
Darwen	Blackburn County Court
Eccles	Manchester County Court
Fylde	Lancaster County Court
Hyndburn	Blackburn County Court
Kendal and Lonsdale	Lancaster County Court
Keswick	Carlisle County Court

(i)	(ii)
Petty Sessions Areas	**Care Centres**
Knowsley	Liverpool County Court
Lancaster	Lancaster County Circuit
Leigh	Manchester County Court
Liverpool	Liverpool County Court
Manchester	Manchester County Court
Middleton and Heywood	Manchester County Court
North Lonsdale	Lancaster County Court
North Sefton	Liverpool County Court
Oldham	Manchester County Court
Ormskirk	Liverpool County Court
Pendle	Blackburn County Court
Penrith and Alston	Carlisle County Court
Preston	Blackburn County Court
Ribble Valley	Blackburn County Court
Rochdale	Manchester County Court
Rossendale	Blackburn County Court
St Helens	Liverpool County Court
Salford	Manchester County Court
South Lakes	Lancaster County Court
South Ribble	Blackburn County Court
South Sefton	Liverpool County Court
South Tameside	Manchester County Court
Stockport	Manchester County Court
Trafford	Manchester County Court
West Allerdale	Carlisle County Court
Whitehaven	Carlisle County Court
Wigan	Liverpool County Court
Wigton	Carlisle County Court
Wirral	Liverpool County Court
Wyre	Lancaster County Court

PART II

North Eastern Circuit

Bainton Beacon	Kingston-upon-Hull County Court
Barnsley	Sheffield County Court
Batley and Dewsbury	Leeds County Court
Berwick-upon-Tweed	Newcastle-upon-Tyne County Court
Beverley	Kingston-upon-Hull County Court

(i)	(ii)
Petty Sessions Areas	**Care Centres**
Blyth Valley	Newcastle-upon-Tyne County Court
Bradford	Leeds County Court
Brighouse	Leeds County Court
Calder	Leeds County Court
Chester-le-Street	Newcastle-upon-Tyne County Court
Claro	York County Court
Coquetdale	Newcastle-upon-Tyne County Court
Darlington	Teesside County Court
Derwentside	Newcastle-upon-Tyne County Court
Dickering	Kingston-upon-Hull County Court
Doncaster	Sheffield County Court
Durham	Newcastle-upon-Tyne County Court
Easington	Sunderland County Court
Easingwold	York County Court
Gateshead	Newcastle-upon-Tyne County Court
[Grimsby and Cleethorpes	Kingston-upon-Hull County Court
Goole and Howdenshire	Kingston-upon-Hull County Court][5]
Hartlepool	Teesside County Court
Holme Beacon	Kingston-upon-Hull County Court
Houghton-le-Spring ...[5]	Sunderland County Court
Huddersfield	Leeds County Court
Keighley	Leeds County Court
Kingston-upon-Hull	Kingston-upon-Hull County Court
Langbaurgh East	Teesside County Court
Leeds	Leeds County Court
Middle Holderness	Kingston-upon-Hull County Court
Morley	Leeds County Court
Morpeth Ward	Newcastle-upon-Tyne County Court
Newcastle-upon-Tyne	Newcastle-upon-Tyne County Court
Northallerton	Teesside County Court
North Holderness	Kingston-upon-Hull County Court
[North Lincolnshire	Kingston-upon-Hull County Court][5]
North Tyneside	Newcastle-upon-Tyne County Court
Pontefract	Leeds County Court
Pudsey and Otley	Leeds County Court
Richmond	Teesside County Court

(i)	(ii)
Petty Sessions Areas	**Care Centres**
Ripon Liberty	York County Court
Rotherham	Sheffield County Court
Ryedale	York County Court
Scarborough	York County Court
Sedgefield	Newcastle-upon-Tyne County Court
Selby	York County Court
Sheffield	Sheffield County Court
Skyrack and Wetherby	Leeds County Court
South Holderness	Kingston-upon-Hull County Court
South Hunsley Beacon	Kingston-upon-Hull County Court
South Tyneside	Sunderland County Court
Staincliffe	Leeds County Court
Sunderland	Sunderland County Court
Teesdale and Wear Valley	Newcastle-upon-Tyne County Court
Teesside	Teesside County Court
Todmorden	Leeds County Court
Tynedale	Newcastle-upon-Tyne County Court
Wakefield	Leeds County Court
Wansbeck	Newcastle-upon-Tyne County Court
Whitby Strand	Teesside County Court
Wilton Beacon	Kingston-upon-Hull County Court
York	York County Court

	South Eastern Circuit
[Abingdon	Oxford County Court][5]
Ampthill	Luton County Court
Arundel	Brighton County Court
Ashford and Tenterden	[Canterbury County Court][1]
Aylesbury	Milton Keynes County Court
Barnet	Principal Registry of the Family Division
Barking and Dagenham	Principal Registry of the Family Division
Basildon	Chelmsford County Court
Battle and Rye	Brighton County Court
…[6]	
Bedford	Luton County Court

(i)	(ii)
Petty Sessions Areas	**Care Centres**
Bexhill	Brighton County Court
Bexley	Principal Registry of the Family Division
[Bicester	Oxford County Court][5]
Biggleswade	Luton County Court
Bishop's Stortford	Watford County Court
Brent	Principal Registry of the Family Division
Brentwood	Chelmsford County Court
Brighton	Brighton County Court
Bromley	Principal Registry of the Family Division
Buckingham	Milton Keynes County Court
Burnham	Milton Keynes County Court
Cambridge	[Cambridge County Court][6]
Canterbury and St Augustine	[Canterbury County Court][1]
Chelmsford	Chelmsford County Court
Chertsey	Guildford County Court
Cheshunt	Watford County Court
Chichester and District	Brighton County Court
Chiltern	Milton Keynes County Court
Colchester	Chelmsford County Court
Crawley	Brighton County Court
Cromer	Norwich County Court
Crowborough	Brighton County Court
Croydon	Principal Registry of the Family Division
Dacorum	Watford County Court
Dartford	Medway County Court
[Didcot and Wantage	Oxford County Court][5]
Diss	Norwich County Court
Dorking	Guildford County Court
Dover and East Kent	[Canterbury County Court][1]
Downham Market	Norwich County Court
Dunmow	Chelmsford County Court
Dunstable	Luton County Court
Ealing	Principal Registry of the Family Division

(i)	(ii)
Petty Sessions Areas	**Care Centres**
Eastbourne	Brighton County Court
[East Cambridgeshire	Cambridge County Court][6]
East Dereham	Norwich County Court
[East Oxfordshire	Oxford County Court][5]
…[6]	
Enfield	Principal Registry of the Family Division
Epping and Ongar	Chelmsford County Court
Epsom	Guildford County Court
Esher and Walton	Guildford County Court
Fakenham	Norwich County Court
Farnham	Guildford County Court
Faversham and Sittingbourne	Medway County Court
[Fenland	Peterborough County Court][6]
Folkestone and Hythe	[Canterbury County Court][1]
The Forest	Reading County Court
Freshwell and South Hinckford	Chelmsford County Court
Godstone	Guildford County Court
Guildford	Guildford County Court
Gravesham	Medway County Court
Great Yarmouth	Norwich County Court
Hailsham	Brighton County Court
Halstead and Hedingham	Chelmsford County Court
Harlow	Chelmsford County Court
Harrow Gore	Principal Registry of the Family Division
Haringey	Principal Registry of the Family Division
Harwich	Chelmsford County Court
Hastings	Brighton County Court
[Haverhill and Sudbury	Ipswich County Court][6]
Havering	Principal Registry of the Family Division
[Henley	Oxford County Court][5]
Hertford and Ware	Watford County Court
Hillingdon	Principal Registry of the Family Division
Horsham	Brighton County Court

PART II

(i)	(ii)
Petty Sessions Areas	**Care Centres**
Hounslow	Principal Registry of the Family Division
Hove	Brighton County Court
Hunstanton	Norwich County Court
[Huntingdonshire ...[6]	Peterborough County Court][6]
King's Lynn	Norwich County Court
Kingston-upon-Thames	Principal Registry of the Family Division
Leighton Buzzard	Luton County Court
Lewes ...[6]	Brighton County Court
Luton	Luton County Court
Maidenhead	Reading County Court
Maidstone	Medway County Court
Maldon and Witham ...[1]	Chelmsford County Court
Medway	Medway County Court
Merton	Principal Registry of the Family Division
Mid-Hertfordshire	Watford County Court
Mid-Sussex ...[6]	Brighton County Court
Milton Keynes	Milton Keynes County Court
Newham	Principal Registry of the Family Division
[North East Suffolk	Ipswich County Court][6]
North Hertfordshire	Watford County Court
[North Oxfordshire and Chipping Norton	Oxford County Court][5]
North Walsham	Norwich County Court
[North West Suffolk	Ipswich County Court][6]
Norwich	Norwich County Court
[Oxford	Oxford County Court][5]
Peterborough ...[1]	Peterborough County Court
Reading and Sonning	Reading County Court
Redbridge	Principal Registry of the Family Division

(i)	(ii)
Petty Sessions Areas	**Care Centres**
Reigate	Guildford County Court
Richmond-upon-Thames	Principal Registry of the Family Division
...[6]	
Rochford and Southend-on-Sea	Chelmsford County Court
Saffron Walden	Chelmsford County Court
St Albans	Watford County Court
[St Edmundsbury and Stowmarket ...[6]	Ipswich County Court][6]
Sevenoaks	Medway County Court
Slough	Reading County Court
[South East Suffolk	Ipswich County Court][6]
South Mimms	Watford County Court
Staines and Sunbury	Guildford County Court
Stevenage	Watford County Court
Steyning	Brighton County Court
...[6]	
Sutton	Principal Registry of the Family Division
Swaffham	Norwich County Court
Tendring	Chelmsford County Court
[Thanet	Canterbury County Court][1]
Thetford	Norwich County Court
Thurrock	Chelmsford County Court
Tonbridge and Malling ...[6]	Medway County Court
Tunbridge Wells and Cranbrook	Medway County Court
Waltham Forest	Principal Registry of the Family Division
Watford	Watford County Court
West Berkshire	Reading County Court
Windsor ...[6]	Reading County Court
[Witney	Oxford County Court][5]
Woking ...[6]	Guildford County Court
[Woodstock	Oxford County Court][5]
Worthing	Brighton County Court

PART II

(i) Petty Sessions Areas	(ii) Care Centres
Wycombe	Milton Keynes County Court
Wymondham	Norwich County Court
	Wales and Chester Circuit
Ardudwy-is-Artro	[Caernarfon County Court][1]
Ardudwy-uwch-Artro	[Caernarfon County Court][1]
Bangor	[Caernarfon County Court][1]
Bedwellty	Newport (Gwent) County Court
Berwyn	Rhyl County Court
Brecon	[Pontypridd County Court][3]
Caernarfon and Gwyrfai	[Caernarfon County Court][1]
Cardiff	Cardiff County Court
Carmarthen North	Swansea County Court
Carmarthen South	Swansea County Court
Ceredigion Ganol	Swansea County Court
Chester	Chester County Court
Cleddau	Swansea County Court
Colwyn	Rhyl County Court
Congleton	Stoke-on-Trent County Court
Conwy and Llandudno	[Caernarfon County Court][1]
Crewe and Nantwich	Stoke-on-Trent County Court
Cynon Valley	[Pontypridd County Court][3]
De Ceredigion	Swansea County Court
Dinefwr	Swansea County Court
Dyffryn Clywd	Rhyl County Court
East Gwent	Newport (Gwent) County Court
Eifionydd	[Caernarfon County Court][1]
Ellesmere Port and Neston	Chester County Court
Estimaner	[Caernarfon County Court][1]
Flint	Rhyl County Court
Gogledd Ceredigion	Swansea County Court
Gogledd Preseli	Swansea County Court
Halton	Warrington County Court
Hawarden	Rhyl County Court
Llandrindod Wells	[Pontypridd County Court][3]
Llanelli	Swansea County Court
Lliw Valley	Swansea County Court

(i)	(ii)
Petty Sessions Areas	**Care Centres**
Lower Rhymney Valley	Cardiff County Court
Macclesfield	Warrington County Court
Machynlleth	[Chester County Court][1]
Merthyr Tydfil	[Pontypridd County Court][3]
Miskin	[Pontypridd County Court][3]
Mold	Rhyl County Court
Nant Conwy	[Caernarfon County Court][1]
Neath	Swansea County Court
Newcastle and Ogmore	Cardiff County Court
Newport	Newport (Gwent) County Court
Newtown	[Chester County Court][1]
North Anglesey	[Caernarfon County Court][1]
Penllyn	[Caernarfon County Court][1]
Port Talbot	Swansea County Court
Pwllheli	[Caernarfon County Court][1]
Rhuddlan	Rhyl County Court
South Anglesey	[Caernarfon County Court][1]
South Pembrokeshire	Swansea County Court
Swansea	Swansea County Court
Talybont	[Caernarfon County Court][1]
Upper Rhymney Valley	[Pontypridd County Court][3]
Vale of Glamorgan	Cardiff County Court
Vale Royal	Chester County Court
Warrington	Warrington County Court
Welshpool	[Chester County Court][1]
Wrexham Maelor	Rhyl County Court
Ystradgynlais	Swansea County Court
	Western Circuit
Alton	Portsmouth County Court
Andover	Portsmouth County Court
Axminster	Taunton County Court
Barnstaple	Taunton County Court
Basingstoke	Portsmouth County Court
Bath and Wansdyke	Bristol County Court
Bideford and Great Torrington	Taunton County Court
Blandford and Sturminster	Bournemouth County Court

PART II

(i) **Petty Sessions Areas**	(ii) **Care Centres**
Bodmin	Truro County Court
Bournemouth	Bournemouth County Court
Bristol	Bristol County Court
Bridport	Bournemouth County Court
Cheltenham	Bristol County Court
Christchurch	Bournemouth County Court
Cirencester, Fairford and Tetbury	[Swindon County Court][1]
Cullompton	Taunton County Court
Dorchester	Bournemouth County Court
Droxford	Portsmouth County Court
Dunheved and Stratton	Truro County Court
Eastleigh	Portsmouth County Court
East Penwith	Truro County Court
East Powder	Truro County Court
Exeter	Plymouth County Court
Exmouth	Plymouth County Court
Falmouth and Kerrier	Truro County Court
Fareham	Portsmouth County Court
Forest of Dean	Bristol County Court
Gloucester	Bristol County Court
Gosport	Portsmouth County Court
Havant	Portsmouth County Court
Honiton	Taunton County Court
Hythe	Bournemouth County Court
Isle of Wight	Portsmouth County Court
Isles of Scilly	Truro County Court
Kennet	[Swindon County Court][1]
Kingsbridge	Plymouth County Court
Long Ashton	Bristol County Court
Lymington	Bournemouth County Court
Mendip	Taunton County Court
North Avon	Bristol County Court
North Cotswold	Bristol County Court
North Wiltshire	[Swindon County Court][1]
Odiham	Portsmouth County Court
Okehampton	Plymouth County Court
Penwith	Truro County Court

(i)	(ii)
Petty Sessions Areas	**Care Centres**
Petersfield	Portsmouth County Court
Plymouth	Plymouth County Court
Plympton	Plymouth County Court
Portsmouth	Portsmouth County Court
Poole	Bournemouth County Court
Pydar	Truro County Court
Ringwood	Bournemouth County Court
Romsey	Bournemouth County Court
Salisbury	[Swindon County Court][4]
Sedgemoor	Taunton County Court
Shaftesbury	Bournemouth County Court
Sherborne	Bournemouth County Court
Southampton	Portsmouth County Court
South East Cornwall	Plymouth County Court
South Gloucestershire	Bristol County Court
South Molton	Taunton County Court
South Somerset	Taunton County Court
Swindon	[Swindon County Court][1]
Taunton Deane	Taunton County Court
Tavistock	Plymouth County Court
Teignbridge	Plymouth County Court
Tewkesbury	Bristol County Court
Tiverton	Taunton County Court
Torbay	Plymouth County Court
Totnes	Plymouth County Court
Totton and New Forest	Bournemouth County Court
Truro and South Powder	Truro County Court
Wareham and Swanage	Bournemouth County Court
West Somerset	Taunton County Court
Weston-Super-Mare	Bristol County Court
West Wiltshire	[Swindon County Court][1]
Weymouth and Portland	Bournemouth County Court
Wimborne	Bournemouth County Court
Winchester	Portsmouth County Court
Wonford	Plymouth County Court

PART II

(i)	(ii)
London Commission Area	**Care Centre**
Inner London Area and City of London	Principal Registry of the Family Division

NOTES

Amendments. [1] Words inserted, repealed or substituted: SI 1994/3138. [2] Words substituted: SI 1994/2164. [3] Words substituted: SI 1995/1649. [4] Words substituted: SI 1997/1897. [5] Entries inserted or entries or words deleted: SI 2001/775. [6] Entries revoked and words inserted and substituted: Children (Allocation of Proceedings) (Amendment) Order 2003, SI 2003/331.

Children (Allocation of Proceedings) (Appeals) Order 1991, SI 1991/1801

1 Citation, commencement and interpretation

(1) This Order may be cited as the Children (Allocation of Proceedings) (Appeals) Order 1991 and shall come into force on 14th October 1991.

(2) In this Order –

'district judge' includes an assistant district judge and a deputy district judge; and

'circuit judge' means any person who is capable of sitting as a judge for a county court district and who is allocated to hear appeals permitted by this Order in accordance with directions given under section 9 of the Courts and Legal Services Act 1990.

2 Appeals

Where a district judge orders the transfer of proceedings to a magistrates' court in accordance with article 11 of the Children (Allocation of Proceedings) Order 1991 an appeal may be made against that decision –

(a) to a judge of the Family Division of the High Court, or

(b) except where the order was made by a district judge or deputy district judge of the principal registry of the Family Division, to a circuit judge.

Family Proceedings Rules 1991, SI 1991/1247

ARRANGEMENT OF RULES

PART I
PRELIMINARY

PART II
MATRIMONIAL CAUSES

PART III
OTHER MATRIMONIAL ETC PROCEEDINGS

PART II

PART V
WARDSHIP

PART VI
CHILD ABDUCTION AND CUSTODY

PART VII
ENFORCEMENT OF ORDERS

Chapter 1. General

Chapter 3. Registration and Enforcement of Custody Orders

PART VIII
APPEALS

PART IX
DISABILITY

PART X
PROCEDURE (GENERAL)

NOTES

Commencement. 14 Oct 1991.

Enabling power. Matrimonial and Family Proceedings Act 1984, s 40(1).

PART I
PRELIMINARY

1.1 Citation and commencement

These rules may be cited as the Family Proceedings Rules 1991 and shall come into force on 14th October 1991.

1.2 Interpretation

(1) In these rules, unless the context otherwise requires –

'the Act of 1973' means the Matrimonial Causes Act 1973;
'the Act of 1984' means the Matrimonial and Family Proceedings Act 1984;
'the Act of 1986' means the Family Law Act 1986;
'the Act of 1989' means the Children Act 1989;
['the Act of 1991' means the Child Support Act 1991;]²
'ancillary relief ' means –

    (a) an avoidance of disposition order,
    (b) a financial provision order,
    (c) an order for maintenance pending suit,
    (d) a property adjustment order, ...⁵
    (e) a variation order; [or
    (f) a pension sharing order;]⁶

'avoidance of disposition order' means an order under section 37(2)(b) or (c) of the Act of 1973;
'business day' has the meaning assigned to it by rule 1.5(6);
'cause' means a matrimonial cause as defined by section 32 of the Act of 1984 or proceedings under section 19 of the Act of 1973 (presumption of death and dissolution of marriage);
'child' and 'child of the family' have, except in Part IV, the meanings respectively assigned to them by section 52(1) of the Act of 1973;
'consent order' means an order under section 33A of the Act of 1973;
['Contracting State' means –

    (a) one of the original parties to the Council Regulation, that is to say Belgium, Germany, Greece, Spain, France, Ireland, Italy, Luxembourg, the Netherlands, Austria, Portugal, Finland, Sweden and the United Kingdom, and
    (b) a party which has subsequently adopted the Council Regulation;]⁷

['the Council Regulation' means Council Regulation (EC) No 1347/2000 of 29th May 2000 on jurisdiction and the recognition and enforcement of judgments in matrimonial matters and in matters of parental responsibility for children of both spouses;]⁷
'court' means a judge or the district judge;
'court of trial' means a divorce county court designated by the Lord Chancellor as a court of trial pursuant to section 33(1) of the Act of 1984 and, in relation to matrimonial proceedings pending in a divorce county court, the principal registry shall be treated as a court of trial having its place of sitting at the Royal Courts of Justice;
'defended cause' means a cause not being an undefended cause;
'district judge', in relation to proceedings in the principal registry, a district registry or a county court, means the district judge or one of the district judges of that registry or county court, as the case may be;
'district registry' [, except in rule 4.22(2A),]¹ means any district registry having a divorce county court within its district;

'divorce county court' means a county court so designated by the Lord Chancellor pursuant to section 33(1) of the Act of 1984;

'divorce town', in relation to any matrimonial proceedings, means a place at which sittings of the High Court are authorised to be held outside the Royal Courts of Justice for the hearing of such proceedings or proceedings of the class to which they belong;

'document exchange' means any document exchange for the time being approved by the Lord Chancellor;

'family proceedings' has the meaning assigned to it by section 32 of the Act of 1984;

'financial provision order' means any of the orders mentioned in section 21(1) of the Act of 1973 except an order under section 27(6) of that Act;

'financial relief' has the same meaning as in section 37 of the Act of 1973;

'judge' does not include a district judge;

'notice of intention to defend' has the meaning assigned to it by rule 10.8;

['officer of the service' has the same meaning as in the Criminal Justice and Court Services Act 2000;][7]

'order for maintenance pending suit' means an order under section 22 of the Act of 1973;

'person named' includes a person described as 'passing under the name of A.B.';

'the President' means the President of the Family Division or, in the case of his absence or incapacity through illness or otherwise or of a vacancy in the office of President, the senior puisne judge of that Division;

'principal registry' means the Principal Registry of the Family Division;

'proper officer' means –

(a) in relation to the principal registry, the [family proceedings department manager][3], and

(b) in relation to any other court or registry, the [court manager][3],

or other officer of the court or registry acting on his behalf in accordance with directions given by the Lord Chancellor;

'property adjustment order' means any of the orders mentioned in section 21(2) of the Act of 1973;

'registry for the divorce town' shall be construed in accordance with rule 2.32(6);

'Royal Courts of Justice', in relation to matrimonial proceedings pending in a divorce county court, means such place, being the Royal Courts of Justice or elsewhere, as may be specified in directions given by the Lord Chancellor pursuant to section 42(2)(a) of the Act of 1984;

'senior district judge' means the senior district judge of the Family Division or, in his absence from the principal registry, the senior of the district judges in attendance at the registry;

'special procedure list' has the meaning assigned to it by rule 2.24(3);

'undefended cause' means –

(i) a cause in which no answer has been filed or any answer filed has been struck out, or

(ii) a cause which is proceeding only on the respondent's answer and in which no reply or answer to the respondent's answer has been filed or any such reply or answer has been struck out, or

(iii) a cause to which rule 2.12(4) applies and in which no notice has been given under that rule or any notice so given has been withdrawn, or

(iv) a cause in which an answer has been filed claiming relief but in which no pleading has been filed opposing the grant of a decree on the petition or answer or any pleading or part of a pleading opposing the grant of such relief has been struck out, or

(v) any cause not within (i) to (iv) above in which a decree has been pronounced;

'variation order' means an order under section 31 of the Act of 1973.

(2) Unless the context otherwise requires, a cause begun by petition shall be treated as pending for the purposes of these rules notwithstanding that a final decree or order has been made on the petition.

(3) Unless the context otherwise requires, a rule or Part referred to by number means the rule or Part so numbered in these rules.

(4) In these rules a form referred to by number means the form so numbered in Appendix 1 [or 1A][4] to these rules with such variation as the circumstances of the particular case may require.

(5) In these rules any reference to an Order and rule is –

(a) if prefixed by the letters 'CCR', a reference to that Order and rule in the County Court Rules 1981, and

(b) if prefixed by the letters 'RSC', a reference to that Order and rule in the Rules of the Supreme Court 1965.

[(5A) In these rules a reference to a Part or rule, if prefixed by the letters 'CPR' is a reference to that Part or rule in the Civil Procedure Rules 1998.][4]

(6) References in these rules to a county court shall, in relation to matrimonial proceedings, be construed as reference to a divorce county court.

(7) In this rule and in rule 1.4, 'matrimonial proceedings' means proceedings of a kind with respect to which divorce county courts have jurisdiction by or under section 33, 34 or 35 of the Act of 1984.

NOTES

Amendments. [1] Words inserted: SI 1992/2067. [2] Definition inserted: SI 1993/295. [3] Definition amended: SI 1997/1056. [4] Words and paragraph inserted: SI 1999/3491. [5] Word omitted: SI 2000/2267. [6] Definition inserted: SI 2000/2267. [7] Definition inserted: SI 2001/821.

References. References in para (5) to the County Court Rules 1981 and the Rules of the Supreme Court 1965 are references to the County Court Rules and the Rules of the Supreme Court in force immediately before 26 April 1999 and references to provisions of those Rules in the Family Proceedings Rules 1991 shall be read accordingly.

1.3 Application of other rules

(1) Subject to the provisions of these rules and of any enactment the County Court Rules 1981 and the Rules of the Supreme Court 1965 shall [continue to][1] apply, with the necessary modifications, to family proceedings in a county court and the High Court respectively.

(2) For the purposes of paragraph (1) any provision of these rules authorising or requiring anything to be done in family proceedings shall be treated as if it were, in the case of proceedings pending in a county court, a provision of the County Court Rules 1981 and, in the case of proceedings pending in the High Court, a provision of the Rules of the Supreme Court 1965.

NOTES

Amendments. [1] Words inserted: SI 1999/1012.

References. References in this rule to the County Court Rules 1981 and the Rules of the Supreme Court 1965 are references to the County Court Rules and the Rules of the Supreme Court in force immediately before 26 April 1999 and references to provisions of those Rules in the Family Proceedings Rules 1991 shall be read accordingly.

1.4 County court proceedings in principal registry

(1) Subject to the provisions of these rules, matrimonial proceedings pending at any time in the principal registry which, if they had been begun in a divorce county court, would be pending at that time in such a court, shall be treated, for the purposes of these rules and of any provision of the County Court Rules 1981 and the County Courts Act 1984, as pending in a divorce county court and not in the High Court.

(2) Unless the context otherwise requires, any reference to a divorce county court in any provision of these rules which relates to the commencement or prosecution of proceedings in a divorce county court, or the transfer of proceedings to or from such a court, includes a reference to the principal registry.

NOTES

References. Reference in this rule to the County Court Rules 1981 is a reference to the County Court Rules in force immediately before 26 April 1999 and references to provisions of those Rules in the Family Proceedings Rules 1991 shall be read accordingly.

1.5 Computation of time

(1) Any period of time fixed by these rules, or by any rules applied by these rules, or by any decree, judgment, order or direction for doing any act shall be reckoned in accordance with the following provisions of this rule.

(2) Where the act is required to be done not less than a specified period before a specified date, the period starts immediately after the date on which the act is done and ends immediately before the specified date.

(3) Where the act is required to be done within a specified period after or from a specified date, the period starts immediately after that date.

(4) Where, apart from this paragraph, the period in question, being a period of seven days or less, would include a day which is not a business day, that day shall be excluded.

(5) Where the time so fixed for doing an act in the court office expires on a day on which the office is closed, and for that reason the act cannot be done on that day, the act shall be in time if done on the next day on which the office is open.

(6) In these rules 'business day' means any day other than –

    (a) a Saturday, Sunday, Christmas Day or Good Friday; or
    (b) a bank holiday under the Banking and Financial Dealings Act 1971, in England and Wales.

****

PART II
MATRIMONIAL CAUSES

****

2.38 Respondent's statement as to arrangements for children

(1) A respondent on whom there is served a statement in accordance with rule 2.2(2) may, whether or not he agreed that statement, file in the court office a written statement of his views on the present and proposed arrangements for the children, and on receipt of such a statement from the respondent the proper officer shall send a copy to the petitioner.

(2) Any such statement of the respondent's views shall, if practicable, be filed within the time limited for giving notice of intention to defend and in any event before the district judge considers the arrangements or proposed arrangements for the upbringing and welfare of the children of the family under section 41(1) of the Act of 1973.

2.39 Procedure for complying with section 41 of Act of 1973

(1) Where no such application as is referred to in rule 2.40(1) is pending the district judge shall, after making his certificate under rule 2.36(1)(a) or after the provision of evidence pursuant to a direction under rule 2.24(4), as the case may be, proceed to consider the matters specified in section 41(1) of the Act of 1973 in accordance with the following provisions of this rule.

(2) Where, on consideration of the relevant evidence, including any further evidence or report provided pursuant to this rule and any statement filed by the respondent under rule 2.38, the district judge is satisfied that –

- (a) there are no children of the family to whom section 41 of the Act of 1973 applies, or
- (b) there are such children but the court need not exercise its powers under the Act of 1989 with respect to any of them or give any direction under section 41(2) of the Act of 1973,

the district judge shall certify accordingly and, in a case to which sub-paragraph (b) applies, the petitioner and the respondent shall each be sent a copy of the certificate by the proper officer.

(3) Where the district judge is not satisfied as mentioned in paragraph (2) above he may, without prejudice to his powers under the Act of 1989 or section 41(2) of the Act of 1973, give one or more of the following directions –

- (a) that the parties, or any of them, shall file further evidence relating to the arrangements for the children (and the direction shall specify the matters to be dealt with in further evidence);
- (b) that a welfare report on the children, or any of them, be prepared;
- (c) that the parties, or any of them, shall attend before him at the date, time and place specified in the direction;

and the parties shall be notified accordingly.

(4) Where the court gives a direction under section 41(2) of the Act of 1973, notice of the direction shall be given to the parties.

(5) In this rule 'parties' means the petitioner, the respondent and any person who appears to the court to have the care of the child.

2.40 Applications relating to children of the family

(1) Where a cause is pending, an application by a party to the cause or by any other person for an order under any provision of Part I or Part II of the Act of 1989 in relation to a child of the family shall be made in the cause; and where the applicant is not a party and has obtained such leave as is required under the Act of 1989 to make the application, no leave to intervene in the cause shall be necessary.

(2) If, while a cause is pending, proceedings relating to any child of the family are begun in any other court, a concise statement of the nature of the proceedings shall forthwith be filed by the person beginning the proceedings or, if he is not a party to the cause, by the petitioner.

[(3) A cause shall be treated as pending for the purposes of this rule for a period of one year after the last hearing or judicial intervention in the cause and rule 1.2(2) shall not apply.][1]

NOTES
    Amendments. [1] Paragraph added: SI 1997/1893.

****

2.57 Children to be separately represented on certain applications

(1) Where an application is made to the High Court or a divorce county court for an order for a variation of settlement, the court shall, unless it is satisfied that the proposed variation does not adversely affect the rights or interests of any children concerned, direct that the children be separately represented on the application, either by a solicitor or by a solicitor and counsel, and may appoint the Official Solicitor or other fit person to be guardian ad litem of the children for the purpose of the application.

(2) On any other application for ancillary relief the court may give such a direction or make such appointment as it is empowered to give or make by paragraph (1).

(3) Before a person other than the Official Solicitor is appointed guardian ad litem under this rule there shall be filed a certificate by the solicitor acting for the children that the person proposed as guardian has no interest in the matter adverse to that of the children and that he is a proper person to be such guardian.

PART III
OTHER MATRIMONIAL ETC PROCEEDINGS

3.1 Application in case of failure to provide reasonable maintenance

(1) Every application under section 27 of the Act of 1973 shall be made by originating application in Form M19.

(2) The application may be made to any divorce county court and there shall be filed with the application an affidavit by the applicant and also a copy of the application and of the affidavit for service on the respondent.

---

(3) The affidavit shall state –

   (a) the same particulars regarding the marriage, the court's jurisdiction, the children and the previous proceedings as are required in the case of a petition by sub-paragraphs (a), (c), (d), (f) and (i) of paragraph 1 of Appendix 2;

   (b) particulars of the respondent's failure to provide reasonable maintenance for the applicant, or, as the case may be, of the respondent's failure to provide, or to make a proper contribution towards, reasonable maintenance for the children of the family; and

   (c) full particulars of the applicant's property and income and of the respondent's property and income, so far as may be known to the applicant.

(4) A copy of the application and of the affidavit referred to in paragraph (2) shall be served on the respondent, together with a notice in Form M20 with Form M6.

(5) Subject to paragraph (6), the respondent shall, within 14 days after the time allowed for sending the acknowledgement of service, file an affidavit stating –

   (a) whether the alleged failure to provide, or to make proper contribution towards, reasonable maintenance is admitted or denied, and, if denied, the grounds on which he relies;

   (b) any allegation which he wishes to make against the applicant; and

   (c) full particulars of his property and income, unless otherwise directed.

(6) Where the respondent challenges the jurisdiction of the court to hear the application he shall, within 14 days after the time allowed for sending the acknowledgement of service, file an affidavit setting out the grounds of the challenge; and the obligation to file an affidavit under paragraph (5) shall not arise until 14 days after the question of jurisdiction has been determined and the court has decided that the necessary jurisdiction exists.

(7) Where the respondent's affidavit contains an allegation of adultery or of an improper association with a person named, the provisions of rule 2.60 (which deal with service on, and [filing of a statement in answer by][1], a named person) shall apply.

(8) If the respondent does not file an affidavit in accordance with paragraph (5), the court may order him to file an affidavit containing full particulars of his property and income, and in that case the respondent shall serve a copy of any such affidavit on the applicant.

(9) Within 14 days after being served with a copy of any affidavit filed by the respondent, the applicant may file a further affidavit as to means and as to any fact in the respondent's affidavit which is disputed, and in that case the applicant shall serve a copy on the respondent.

No further affidavit shall be filed without leave.

(10) Rules 2.61 to 2.66 and rule 10.10 shall apply, with such modifications as may be appropriate, to an application for an order under section 27 of the Act of 1973 as if the application were an application for ancillary relief.

NOTES

   Amendments. [1] Words inserted: SI 1999/3491.

   References. References to rules 2.52 to 2.70 shall be read as references to those rules before SI 1999/3491 introducing the new ancillary relief rules came into force.

3.2 Application for alteration of maintenance agreement during lifetime of parties

(1) An application under section 35 of the Act of 1973 for the alteration of a maintenance agreement shall be made by originating application containing, unless otherwise directed, the information required by Form M21.

(2) The application may be made to any divorce county court and may be heard and determined by the district judge.

(3) There shall be filed with the application an affidavit by the applicant exhibiting a copy of the agreement and verifying the statements in the application and also a copy of the application and of the affidavit for service on the respondent.

(4) A copy of the application and of the affidavit referred to in paragraph (3) shall be served on the respondent, together with a notice in Form M20 with Form M6 attached.

(5) The respondent shall, within 14 days after the time limited for giving notice of intention to defend, file an affidavit in answer to the application containing full particulars of his property and income and, if he does not do so, the court may order him to file an affidavit containing such particulars.

(6) A respondent who files an affidavit under paragraph (5) shall at the same time file a copy which the proper officer shall serve on the applicant.

3.3 Application for alteration of maintenance agreement after death of one party

(1) An application under section 36 of the Act of 1973 for the alteration of a maintenance agreement after the death of one of the parties shall be made –

    (a) in the High Court, by originating summons out of the principal registry or any district registry, or
    (b) in a county court, by originating application,

in Form M22.

(2) There shall be filed in support of the application an affidavit by the applicant exhibiting a copy of the agreement and an official copy of the grant of representation to the deceased's estate and of every testamentary document admitted to proof and stating –

    (a) whether the deceased died domiciled in England and Wales;
    (b) the place and date of the marriage between the parties to the agreement and the name and status of the wife before the marriage;
    (c) the name of every child of the family and of any other child for whom the agreement makes financial arrangements, and –
        (i) the date of birth of each such child who is still living (or, if it be the case, that he has attained 18) and the place where and the person with whom any such minor child is residing,
        (ii) the date of death of any such child who has died since the agreement was made;
    (d) whether there have been in any court any, and if so what, previous proceedings with reference to the agreement or to the marriage or to the children of the family or any other children for whom the agreement makes financial arrangements, and the date and effect of any order or decree made in such proceedings;

(e) whether there have been in any court any proceedings by the applicant against the deceased's estate under the Inheritance (Provision for Family and Dependants) Act 1975 or any Act repealed by that Act and the date and effect of any order made in such proceedings;

(f) in the case of an application by the surviving party, the applicant's means;

(g) in the case of an application by the personal representatives of the deceased, the surviving party's means, so far as they are known to the applicants, and the information mentioned in sub-paragraphs (a), (b) and (c) of rule 3.4(4);

(h) the facts alleged by the applicant as justifying an alteration in the agreement and the nature of the alteration sought;

(i) if the application is made after the end of the period of six months from the date on which representation in regard to the deceased's estate was first taken out, the grounds on which the court's permission to entertain the application is sought.

(3) CCR Order 48, rules 3(1), 7 and 9 shall apply to an originating application under the said section 36 as they apply to an application under section 1 of the Inheritance (Provision for Family and Dependants) Act 1975.

(4) In this rule and the next following rule 'the deceased' means the deceased party to the agreement to which the application relates.

3.4 Further proceedings on application under rule 3.3

(1) Without prejudice to his powers under RSC Order 15 (which deals with parties and other matters), the district judge may at any stage of the proceedings direct that any person be added as a respondent to an application under rule 3.3.

(2) RSC Order 15, rule 13 (which enables the court to make representation orders in certain cases), shall apply to the proceedings as if they were mentioned in paragraph (1) of the said rule 13.

(3) Where the application is in a county court, the references in paragraphs (1) and (2) to RSC Order 15 and Order 15, rule 13 shall be construed as references to CCR Order 5 and Order 5, rule 6 respectively.

(4) A respondent who is a personal representative of the deceased shall, within 14 days after the time limited for giving notice of intention to defend, file an affidavit in answer to the application stating –

(a) full particulars of the value of the deceased's estate for probate, after providing for the discharge of the funeral, testamentary and administration expenses, debts and liabilities payable thereout, including the amount of the [inheritance tax or any other tax replaced by that tax][1] and interest thereon;

(b) the persons or classes of persons beneficially interested in the estate (giving the names and addresses of all living beneficiaries) and the value of their interests so far as ascertained, and

(c) if such be the case, that any living beneficiary (naming him) is a minor or a patient within the meaning of rule 9.1.

(5) If a respondent who is a personal representative of the deceased does not file an affidavit stating the matters mentioned in paragraph (4) the district judge may order him to do so.

(6) A respondent who is not a personal representative of the deceased may, within 14 days after the time limited for giving notice of intention to defend, file an affidavit in answer to the application.

(7) Every respondent who files an affidavit in answer to the application shall at the same time lodge a copy, which the proper officer shall serve on the applicant.

NOTES
Amendments. [1] Words substituted: SI 1991/2113.

3.5 Application of other rules to proceedings under section 35 or 36 of Act of 1973

(1) The following rules shall apply, with the necessary modifications, to an application under section 35 or 36 of the Act of 1973, as if it were an application for ancillary relief –

  (a) in the case of an application under either section, rules 2.60, 2.62(4) to (6), 2.63, 2.64, 2.65 and 10.10;
  (b) in the case of an application under section 35, rule 2.66; and
  (c) in the case of an application under section 36, rule 2.66(1) and (2).

(2) Subject to paragraph (1) and to the provisions of rules 3.2 to 3.4, these rules shall, so far as applicable, apply with the necessary modifications to an application under section 35 or section 36 (as the case may be) of the Act of 1973, as if the application were a cause, the originating application or summons a petition, and the applicant the petitioner.

3.6 Married Women's Property Act 1882

(1) Subject to paragraph (2) below, an application under section 17 of the Married Women's Property Act 1882 (in this and the next following rule referred to as 'section 17') shall be made –

  (a) in the High Court, by originating summons, which may be issued out of the principal registry or any district registry, or
  (b) in a county court, by originating application,

in Form M23 and shall be supported by affidavit.

(2) An order under section 17 may be made in any ancillary relief proceedings upon the application of any party thereto in Form M11 by notice of application or summons.

(3) An application under section 17 to a county court shall be filed –

  (a) subject to sub-paragraph (b), in the court for the district in which the applicant or respondent resides, or
  (b) in the divorce county court in which any pending matrimonial cause has been commenced by or on behalf of either the applicant or the respondent, or in which any matrimonial cause is intended to be commenced by the applicant.

(4) Where the application concerns the title to or possession of land, the originating summons or application shall –

  (a) state whether the title to the land is registered or unregistered and, if registered, the Land Registry title number; and

(b) give particulars, so far as known to the applicant, of any mortgage of the land or any interest therein.

(5) The application shall be served on the respondent, together with a copy of the affidavit in support and an acknowledgement of service in Form M6.

(6) Where particulars of a mortgage are given pursuant to paragraph (4), the applicant shall file a copy of the originating summons or application, which shall be served on the mortgagee; and any person so served may apply to the court in writing, within 14 days after service, for a copy of the affidavit in support; and within 14 days of receiving such affidavit may file an affidavit in answer and shall be entitled to be heard on the application.

(7) If the respondent intends to contest the application, he shall, within 14 days after the time allowed for sending the acknowledgement of service, file an affidavit in answer to the application setting out the grounds on which he relies, and lodge in the court office a copy of the affidavit for service on the applicant.

(8) If the respondent fails to comply with paragraph (7), the applicant may apply for directions; and the district judge may give such directions as he thinks fit, including a direction that the respondent shall be debarred from defending the application unless an affidavit is filed within such time as the district judge may specify.

(9) A district judge may grant an injunction in proceedings under section 17 if, but only so far as, the injunction is ancillary or incidental to any relief sought in those proceedings.

(10) Rules 2.62(4) to (6) and 2.63 to 2.66 shall apply, with the necessary modifications, to an application under section 17 as they apply to an application for ancillary relief.

(11) Subject to the provisions of this rule, these rules shall apply, with the necessary modifications, to an application under section 17 as if the application were a cause, the originating summons or application a petition, and the applicant a petitioner.

3.7 Exercise in principal registry of county court jurisdiction under section 17 of Married Women's Property Act 1882

(1) Where any proceedings for divorce, nullity or judicial separation which are either pending in the principal registry, or are intended to be commenced there by the applicant, are or will be treated as pending in a divorce county court, an application under section 17 by one of the parties to the marriage may be made to the principal registry as if it were a county court.

(2) In relation to proceedings commenced or intended to be commenced in the principal registry under paragraph (1) of this rule or transferred from the High Court to the principal registry by an order made under section 38 of the Act of 1984 –

(a) section 42 of the Act of 1984 and the rules made thereunder shall have effect, with the necessary modifications, as they have effect in relation to proceedings commenced in or transferred to the principal registry under that section; and

(b) CCR Order 4, rule 8 and rule 3.6(3) (which relate to venue) shall not apply.

(3) Rule 1.4(1) shall apply, with the necessary modifications, to proceedings in, or intended to be commenced in, the principal registry under paragraph (1) of this rule as it applies to matrimonial proceedings.

[3.8 Applications under Part IV of the Family Law Act 1996 (Family Homes and Domestic Violence)

(1) An application for an occupation order or a non-molestation order under Part IV of the Family Law Act 1996 shall be made in Form FL401.

(2) An application for an occupation order or a non-molestation order made by a child under the age of sixteen shall be made in Form FLA401 but shall be treated, in the first instance, as an application to the High Court for leave.

(3) An application for an occupation order or a non-molestation order which is made in other proceedings which are pending shall be made in Form FL401.

(4) An application in Form FL401 shall be supported by a statement which is signed by the applicant and is sworn to be true.

(5) Where an application is made without giving notice, the sworn statement shall state the reasons why notice was not given.

(6) An application made on notice (together with the sworn statement and a notice in Form FL402) shall be served by the applicant on the respondent personally not less than 2 days before the date on which the application will be heard.

(7) The court may abridge the period specified in paragraph (6).

(8) Where the applicant is acting in person, service of the application shall be effected by the court if the applicant so requests.

This does not affect the court's power to order substituted service.

(9) Where an application for an occupation order or a non-molestation order is pending, the court shall consider (on the application of either party or of its own motion) whether to exercise its powers to transfer the hearing of that application to another court and shall make an order for transfer in Form FL417 if it seems necessary or expedient to do so.

(10) Rule 9.2A shall not apply to an application for an occupation order or a non-molestation order under Part IV of the Family Law Act 1996.

(11) A copy of an application for an occupation order under section 33, 35 or 36 of the Family Law Act 1996 shall be served by the applicant by first-class post on the mortgagee or, as the case may be, the landlord of the dwelling-house in question, with a notice in Form FL416 informing him of his right to make representations in writing or at any hearing.

(12) Where the application is for the transfer of a tenancy, notice of the application shall be served by the applicant on the other cohabitant or spouse and on the landlord (as those terms are defined by paragraph 1 of Schedule 7 to the Family Law Act 1996) and any person so served shall be entitled to be heard on the application.

(13) Rules 2.62(4) to (6) and 2.63 (investigation, requests for further information) shall apply, with the necessary modifications, to –

    (a) an application for an occupation order under section 33, 35 or 36 of the Family Law Act 1996, and
    (b) an application for the transfer of a tenancy,

as they apply to an application for ancillary relief.

(14) Rule 3.6(7) to (9) (Married Women's Property Act 1882) shall apply, with the necessary modifications, to an application for the transfer of a tenancy, as they apply to an application under rule 3.6.

(15) The applicant shall file a statement in Form FL415 after he has served the application.

3.9 Hearing of applications under Part IV of the Family Law Act 1996

(1) An application for an occupation order or a non-molestation order under Part IV of the Family Law Act 1996 shall be dealt with in chambers unless the court otherwise directs.

(2) Where an order is made on an application made ex parte, a copy of the order together with a copy of the application and of the sworn statement in support shall be served by the applicant on the respondent personally.

(3) Where the application is for an occupation order under section 33, 35 or 36 of the Family Law Act 1996, a copy of any order made on the application shall be served by the applicant by first-class post on the mortgagee or, as the case may be, the landlord of the dwelling-house in question.

(4) A copy of an order made on an application heard inter partes shall be served by the applicant on the respondent personally.

(5) Where the applicant is acting in person, service of a copy of any order made on the hearing of the application shall be effected by the court if the applicant so requests.

(6) The following forms shall be used in connection with hearings of applications under Part IV of the Family Law Act 1996 –

(a) a record of the hearing shall be made on Form FL405, and
(b) any order made on the hearing shall be issued in Form FL404.

(7) The court may direct that a further hearing be held in order to consider any representations made by a mortgagee or a landlord.

(8) An application to vary, extend or discharge an order made under Part IV of the Family Law Act 1996 shall be made in Form FL403 and this rule shall apply to the hearing of such an application.

3.9A Enforcement of orders made on applications under Part IV of the Family Law Act 1996

(1) Where a power of arrest is attached to one or more of the provisions ('the relevant provisions') of an order made under Part IV of the Family Law Act 1996 –

(a) the relevant provisions shall be set out in Form FL406 and the form shall not include any provisions of the order to which the power of arrest was not attached; and
(b) a copy of the form shall be delivered to the officer for the time being in charge of any police station for the applicant's address or of such other police station as the court may specify.

The copy of the form delivered under sub-paragraph (b) shall be accompanied by a statement showing that the respondent has been served with the order or informed of its terms (whether by being present when the order was made or by telephone or otherwise).

(2) Where an order is made varying or discharging the relevant provisions, the proper officer shall –

(a) immediately inform the officer who received a copy of the form under paragraph (1) and, if the applicant's address has changed, the officer for the time being in charge of the police station for the new address; and

(b) deliver a copy of the order to any officer so informed.

(3) An application for the issue of a warrant for the arrest of the respondent shall be made in Form FL407 and the warrant shall be issued in Form FL408

(4) The court before whom a person is brought following his arrest may –

(a) determine whether the facts, and the circumstances which led to the arrest, amounted to disobedience of the order, or

(b) adjourn the proceedings and, where such an order is made, the arrested person may be released and –

(i) be dealt with within 14 days of the day on which he was arrested; and

(ii) be given not less than 2 days' notice of the adjourned hearing.

Nothing in this paragraph shall prevent the issue of a notice under CCR Order 29, rule 1(4) if the arrested person is not dealt with within the period mentioned in sub-paragraph (b)(i) above.

(5) The following provisions shall apply, with the necessary modifications, to the enforcement of orders made on applications under Part IV of the Family Law Act 1996 –

(a) RSC Order 52, rule 7 (powers to suspend execution of committal order);

(b) (in a case where an application for an order of committal is made to the High Court) RSC Order 52, rule 2 (application for leave);

(c) CCR Order 29, rule 1 (committal for breach of order);

(d) CCR Order 29, rule 1A (undertakings);

(e) CCR Order 29, rule 3 (discharge of person in custody); and CCR Order 29, rule 1 shall have effect, as if for paragraph (3), there were substituted the following –

'(3) At the time when the order is drawn up, the proper officer shall –

(a) where the order made is (or includes) a non-molestation order and

(b) where the order made is an occupation order and the court so directs,

issue a copy of the order, indorsed with or incorporating a notice as to the consequences of disobedience, for service in accordance with paragraph (2).'.

(6) The court may adjourn consideration of the penalty to be imposed for contempts found provided and such consideration may be restored if the respondent does not comply with any conditions specified by the court.

(7) Where the court makes a hospital order in Form FL413 or a guardianship order in Form FL414 under the Mental Health Act 1983, the proper officer shall –

(a) send to the hospital any information which will be of assistance in dealing with the patient;

(b) inform the applicant when the respondent is being transferred to hospital.

(8) Where a transfer direction given by the Secretary of State under section 48 of the Mental Health Act 1983 is in force in respect of a person remanded in custody

by the court under Schedule 5 to the Family Law Act 1996, the proper officer shall notify –

    (a) the governor of the prison to which that person was remanded; and

    (b) the hospital where he is detained,

of any committal hearing which that person is required to attend and the proper officer shall give notice in writing to the hospital where that person is detained of any further remand under paragraph 3 of Schedule 5 to the Family Law Act 1996.

(9) An order for the remand of the respondent shall be in form FL409.

(10) In paragraph (4) 'arrest' means arrest under a power of arrest attached to an order or under a warrant of arrest.

3.10 Applications under Part IV of the Family Law Act 1996: bail

(1) An application for bail made by a person arrested under a power of arrest or a warrant of arrest may be made either orally or in writing.

(2) Where an application is made in writing, it shall contain the following particulars –

    (a) the full name of the person making the application;

    (b) the address of the place where the person making the application is detained at the time when the application is made;

    (c) the address where the person making the application would reside if he were to be granted bail;

    (d) the amount of the recognizance in which he would agree to be bound; and

    (e) the grounds on which the application is made and, where a previous application has been refused, full particulars of any change in circumstances which has occurred since that refusal.

(3) An application made in writing shall be signed by the person making the application or by a person duly authorised by him in that behalf or, where the person making the application is a minor or is for any reason incapable of acting, by a guardian ad litem acting on his behalf and a copy shall be served by the person making the application on the applicant for the Part IV order.

(4) The persons prescribed for the purposes of paragraph 4 of Schedule 5 to the Family Law Act 1996 (postponement of taking of recognizance) are –

    (a) a district judge,

    (b) a justice of the peace,

    (c) a justices' clerk,

    (d) a police officer of the rank of inspector or above or in charge of a police station, and

    (e) (where the person making the application is in his custody) the governor or keeper of a prison.

(5) The person having custody of the person making the application shall –

    (a) on receipt of a certificate signed by or on behalf of the district judge stating that the recognizance of any sureties required have been taken, or on being otherwise satisfied that all such recognizances have been taken; and

    (b) on being satisfied that the person making the application has entered into his recognizance,

release the person making the application.

PART II

(6) The following forms shall be used –

    (a) the recognizance of the person making the application shall be in Form FL410 and that of a surety in Form FL411;

    (b) a bail notice in Form FL412 shall be given to the respondent where he is remanded on bail.][1]

NOTES
Amendments. [1] Rules substituted: SI 1997/1893.

3.11 Proceedings in respect of polygamous marriage

(1) The provisions of this rule shall have effect where a petition, originating application or originating summons asks for matrimonial relief within the meaning of section 47(2) of the Act of 1973 in respect of a marriage [where either party to the marriage is, or has during the subsistence of the marriage been, married to more than one person][1] (in this rule referred to as a polygamous marriage).

(2) The petition, originating application or originating summons –

    (a) shall state that the marriage in question is polygamous;

    (b) shall state whether or not there is, to the knowledge of the petitioner or applicant, any living spouse of his or hers additional to the respondent or, as the case may be, any living spouse of the respondent additional to the petitioner or applicant (in this rule referred to as an additional spouse); and

    (c) if there is any additional spouse, shall give his or her full name and address and the date and place of his or her marriage to the petitioner or applicant or, as the case may be, to the respondent, or state, so far as may be applicable, that such information is unknown to the petitioner or applicant.

(3) Without prejudice to its powers under RSC Order 15 (which deals with parties) or CCR Order 15 (which deals with amendment) the court may order that any additional spouse –

    (a) be added as a party to the proceedings; or

    (b) be given notice of –

        (i) the proceedings; or

        (ii) of any application in the proceedings for any such order as is mentioned in section 47(2)(d) of the Act of 1973.

(4) Any order under paragraph (3) may be made at any stage of the proceedings and either on the application of any party or by the court of its own motion and, where an additional spouse is mentioned in a petition or an acknowledgement of service of a petition, the petitioner shall, on making any application in the proceedings or, if no previous application has been made in the proceedings, on making a request for directions for trial, ask for directions as to whether an order should be made under paragraph (3).

(5) Any person to whom notice is given pursuant to an order under paragraph (3) shall be entitled, without filing an answer or affidavit, to be heard in the proceedings or on the application to which the notice relates.

NOTES
Amendments. [1] Words substituted: SI 1996/816.

3.12 Application under section 55 of Act of 1986 for declaration as to marital status

(1) Unless otherwise directed, a petition by which proceedings are begun under section 55 of the Act of 1986 for a declaration as to marital status shall state –

    (a) the names of the parties to the marriage to which the application relates and the residential address of each of them at the date of the presentation of the petition;

    (b) the place and date of any ceremony of marriage to which the application relates;

    (c) the grounds on which the application is made and all other material facts alleged by the petitioner to justify the making of the declaration;

    (d) whether there have been or are continuing any proceedings in any court, tribunal or authority in England and Wales or elsewhere between the parties which relate to, or are capable of affecting, the validity or subsistence of the marriage, divorce, annulment or legal separation to which the application relates, or which relate to the matrimonial status of either of the parties, and, if so –

        (i) the nature, and either the outcome or present state of those proceedings,

        (ii) the court, tribunal or authority before which they were begun,

        (iii) the date when they were begun,

        (iv) the names of the parties to them,

        (v) the date or expected date of the trial,

        (vi) any other facts relevant to the question whether the petition should be stayed under Schedule 1 to the Domicile and Matrimonial Proceedings Act of 1973;

    and any such proceedings shall include any which are instituted otherwise than in a court of law in any country outside England and Wales, if they are instituted before a tribunal or other authority having power under the law having effect there to determine questions of status, and shall be treated as continuing if they have begun and have not been finally disposed of;

    (e) where it is alleged that the court has jurisdiction based on domicile, which of the parties to the marriage to which the application relates is domiciled in England and Wales on the date of the presentation of the petition, or died before that date and was at death domiciled in England and Wales.

    (f) where it is alleged that the court has jurisdiction based on habitual residence, which of the parties to the marriage to which the application relates has been habitually resident in England and Wales, or died before that date and had been habitually resident in England and Wales throughout the period of one year ending with the date of death;

    (g) where the petitioner was not a party to the marriage to which the application relates, particulars of his interest in the determination of the application.

(2) Where the proceedings are for a declaration that the validity of a divorce, annulment or legal separation obtained in any country outside England or Wales in respect of the marriage either is or is not entitled to recognition in England and Wales, the petition shall in addition state the date and place of the divorce, annulment or legal separation.

(3) There shall be annexed to the petition a copy of the certificate of any marriage to which the application relates, or, as the case may be, a certified copy of any

PART II

decree of divorce, annulment or order for legal separation to which the application relates.

(4) Where a document produced by virtue of paragraph (3) is not in English it shall, unless otherwise directed, be accompanied by a translation certified by a notary public or authenticated by affidavit.

(5) The parties to the marriage in respect of which a declaration is sought shall be petitioner and respondent respectively to the application, unless a third party is applying for a declaration, in which case he shall be the petitioner and the parties to the marriage shall be respondents to the application.

[3.13 Application under section 55A of Act of 1986 for declaration of parentage

(1) Unless otherwise directed, a petition by which proceedings are begun under section 55A of the Act of 1986 for a declaration of parentage shall state –

    (a) the full name and the sex, date and place of birth and residential address of the petitioner (except where the petitioner is the Secretary of State);

    (b) where the case is not an excepted case within section 55A(4) of the Act of 1986, either the petitioner's interest in the determination of the application, or that section 27(2) of the Act of 1991 applies;

    (c) if they are known, the full name and the sex, date and place of birth and residential address of each of the following persons (unless that person is the petitioner) –

        (i) the person whose parentage is in issue;

        (ii) the person whose parenthood is in issue; and

        (iii) any person who is acknowledged to be the father or mother of the person whose parentage is in issue;

    (d) if the petitioner, the person whose parentage is in issue or the person whose parenthood is in issue, is known by a name other than that which appears in the certificate of his birth, that other name shall also be stated in the petition and in any decree made thereon;

    (e) if it is known, the full name of the mother, or alleged mother, of the person whose parentage is in issue, at the date of –

        (i) her birth;

        (ii) her first marriage;

        (iii) the birth of the person whose parentage is in issue; and

        (iv) her most recent marriage;

    if it was at any of those times different from her full name at the date of the presentation of the petition;

    (f) the grounds on which the petitioner relies and all other material facts alleged by him to justify the making of the declaration;

    (g) whether there are or have been any other proceedings in any court, tribunal or authority in England or Wales or elsewhere relating to the parentage of the person whose parentage is in issue or to the parenthood of the person whose parenthood is in issue, and, if so –

        (i) particulars of the proceedings, including the court, tribunal or authority before which they were begun, and their nature, outcome or present state;

        (ii) the date they were begun;

        (iii) the names of the parties; and

        (iv) the date or expected date of any trial in the proceedings;

    (h) that either the person whose parentage is in issue or the person whose parenthood is in issue –

   (i)   is domiciled in England and Wales on the date of the presentation of
         the petition;
   (ii) has been habitually resident in England and Wales throughout the
         period of one year ending with that date; or
   (iii) died before that date and either was at death domiciled in England
         and Wales or had been habitually resident in England and Wales
         throughout the period of one year ending with the date of death; and
  (i)   the nationality, citizenship or immigration status of the person whose
        parentage is in issue and of the person whose parenthood is in issue, and
        the effect which the granting of a declaration of parentage would have
        upon the status of each of them as regards his nationality, citizenship or
        right to be in the United Kingdom.

(2) Unless otherwise directed, there shall be annexed to the petition a copy of the
birth certificate of the person whose parentage is in issue.

(3) The respondents to the application shall be –

   (i)   the person whose parentage is in issue; and
   (ii) any person who is, or who is alleged to be, the mother or father of the
         person whose parentage is in issue;

excluding the petitioner.

[(4) The prescribed officer for the purposes of section 55A(7) of the Act of 1986
shall be the proper officer within the meaning of rule 1.2(1).]²

(5) Within 21 days after a declaration of parentage has been made, the prescribed
officer shall send to the Registrar General a copy of the declaration in Form M30
and the petition.]¹

NOTES

Amendments. ¹ Rule substituted: SI 2001/821. ² Paragraph substituted: Family Proceedings
(Amendment) Rules 2003, SI 2003/184.

3.14 Application under section 56(1)(b) and (2) of Act of 1986 for a declaration of legitimacy or legitimation

(1) Unless otherwise directed, a petition by which proceedings are begun under
section 56(1)(b) and (2) of the Act of 1986 for a declaration of legitimacy or
legitimation shall state –

   (a) the name of the petitioner, and if the petitioner is known by a name other
        than that which appears in the certificate of his birth, that other name shall
        be stated in the petition and in any decree made thereon;
   (b) the date and place of birth of the petitioner;
   (c) if it is known, the name of the petitioner's father and the maiden name of
        the petitioner's mother and, if it is different, her current name, and the
        residential address of each of them at the time of the presentation of the
        petition;
   (d) the grounds on which the petitioner relies and all other material facts
        alleged by him to justify the making of the declaration; and
   (e) either that the petitioner is domiciled in England and Wales on the date of
        the presentation of the petition or that he has been habitually resident in
        England and Wales throughout the period of one year ending with that
        date.

(2) Unless otherwise directed, there shall be annexed to the petition a copy of the petitioner's birth certificate.

(3) The petitioner's father and mother, or the survivor of them, shall be respondents to the application.

3.15 Application under section 57 of Act of 1986 for declaration as to adoption effected overseas

(1) Unless otherwise directed, a petition by which proceedings are begun under section 57 of the Act of 1986 for a declaration as to an adoption effected overseas shall state –

- (a) the names of those persons who are to be respondents pursuant to paragraph (4) and the residential address of each of them at the date of the presentation of the petition;
- (b) the date and place of the petitioner's birth;
- (c) the date and place of the adoption order and the court or other tribunal or authority which made it;
- (d) all other material facts alleged by the petitioner to justify the making of the declaration and the grounds on which the application is made;
- (e) either that the petitioner is domiciled in England and Wales on the date of the presentation of the petition or that he has been habitually resident in England and Wales throughout the period of one year ending with that date.

(2) There shall be annexed to the petition a copy of the petitioner's birth certificate (if it is available this certificate should be the one made after the adoption referred to in the petition) and, unless otherwise directed, a certified copy of the adoption order effected under the law of any country outside the British Islands.

(3) Where a document produced by virtue of paragraph (2) is not in English, it shall, unless otherwise directed, be accompanied by a translation certified by a notary public or authenticated by affidavit.

(4) The following shall, if alive, be respondents to the application, either –

- (a) those whom the petitioner claims are his adoptive parents for the purposes of section 39 of the Adoption Act 1976; or
- (b) those whom the petitioner claims are not his adoptive parents for the purposes of that section.

3.16 General provisions as to proceedings under rules 3.12, 3.13, 3.14 and 3.15

(1) A petition under rule 3.12, 3.13, 3.14 or 3.15 shall be supported by an affidavit by the petitioner verifying the petition and giving particulars of every person whose interest may be affected by the proceedings and his relationship to the petitioner.

Provided that if the petitioner is under the age of 18, the affidavit shall, unless otherwise directed, be made by his next friend.

(2) Where the jurisdiction of the court to entertain a petition is based on habitual residence the petition shall include a statement of the addresses of the places of residence of the person so resident and the length of residence at each place either during the period of one year ending with the date of the presentation of the petition or, if that person is dead, throughout the period of one year ending with the date of death.

(3) An affidavit for the purposes of paragraph (1) may contain statements of information or belief with the sources and grounds thereof.

(4) [Except in the case of a petition under rule 3.13, a copy of the petition][1] and every document accompanying it shall be sent by the petitioner to the Attorney General at least one month before the petition is filed and it shall not be necessary thereafter to serve these documents upon him.

[(5) If the Attorney General has notified the court that he wishes to intervene in the proceedings, the proper officer shall send to him a copy of any answer and, in the case of a petition under rule 3.13, of the petition and every document accompanying it.][1]

(6) When all answers to the petition have been filed the petitioner shall issue and serve on all respondents to the application a request for directions as to any other persons who should be made respondents to the petition or given notice of the proceedings.

(7) When giving directions in accordance with paragraph (6) the court shall consider whether it is [desirable][1] that the Attorney General should argue before it any question relating to the proceedings, and if it does so consider [and the Attorney General agrees to argue that question][1], the Attorney General need not file an answer and the court shall give directions requiring him to serve on all parties to the proceedings a summary of his argument.

(8) Persons given notice of proceedings pursuant to directions given in accordance with paragraph (6) shall within 21 days after service of the notice upon them be entitled to apply to the court to be joined as parties.

(9) The Attorney General may file an answer to the petition within 21 days after directions have been given under paragraph (7) and no directions for trial shall be given until that period and the period referred to in paragraph (8) have expired.

(10) The Attorney General, in deciding whether it is necessary or expedient to intervene in the proceedings, may have a search made for, and may inspect and bespeak a copy of, any document filed or lodged in the court offices which relates to any other family proceedings referred to in proceedings.

(11) Declarations made in accordance with section 55, section 56(1)(a), section 56(1)(b) and (2) and section 57 of the Act of 1986 shall be in the forms prescribed respectively in Forms M29, M30, M31 and M32.

(12) Subject to rules 3.12, 3.13, 3.14 and 3.15 and this rule, these rules shall, so far as applicable and with the exception of rule 2.6(1), apply with the necessary modifications to the proceedings as if they were a cause.

NOTES
Amendments. [1] Text substituted or inserted: SI 2001/821.

3.17 Application for leave under section 13 of Act of 1984

(1) An application for leave to apply for an order for financial relief under Part III of the Act of 1984 shall be made ex parte by originating summons issued in Form M25 out of the principal registry and shall be supported by an affidavit by the applicant stating the facts relied on in support of the application with particular reference to the matters set out in section 16(2) of that Act.

(2) The affidavit in support shall give particulars of the judicial or other proceedings by means of which the marriage to which the application relates was

PART II

dissolved or annulled or by which the parties to the marriage were legally separated and shall state, so far as is known to the applicant –

(a) the names of the parties to the marriage and the date and place of the marriage;

(b) the occupation and residence of each of the parties to the marriage;

(c) whether there are any living children of the family and, if so, the number of such children and the full names (including surname) of each and his date of birth or, if it be the case, that he is over 18;

(d) whether either party to the marriage has remarried;

(e) an estimate in summary form of the appropriate amount or value of the capital resources and net income of each party and of any minor child of the family;

(f) the grounds on which it is alleged that the court has jurisdiction to entertain an application for an order for financial relief under Part III of the Act of 1984.

(3) The proper officer shall fix a date, time and place for the hearing of the application by a judge in chambers and give notice thereof to the applicant.

3.18 Application for order for financial relief or avoidance of transaction order under Part III of Act of 1984

(1) An application for an order for financial relief under Part III of the Act of 1984 shall be made by originating summons issued in Form M26 out of the principal registry and at the same time the applicant, unless otherwise directed, shall file an affidavit in support of the summons giving full particulars of his property and income.

(2) The applicant shall serve a sealed copy of the originating summons on the respondent and shall annex thereto a copy of the affidavit in support, if one has been filed, and a notice of proceedings and acknowledgement of service in Form M28, and rule 10.8 shall apply to such an acknowledgement of service as if the references in paragraph (1) of that rule to Form M6 and in paragraph (2) of that rule to seven days were, respectively, references to Form M28 and 31 days.

(3) Rules 2.57, 2.59, 2.61, 2.62(5) and (6), 2.63 and 2.66(1) and (2) shall apply, with the necessary modifications, to an application for an order for financial relief under this rule as they apply to an application for ancillary relief made by notice in Form M11 and the court may order the attendance of any person for the purpose of being examined or cross-examined and the discovery and production of any document.

(4) An application for an interim order for maintenance under section 14 or an avoidance of transaction order under section 23 of the Act of 1984 may be made, unless the court otherwise directs, in the originating summons under paragraph (1) or by summons in accordance with rule 10.9(1) and an application for an order under section 23 shall be supported by an affidavit, which may be the affidavit filed under paragraph (1), stating the facts relied on.

(5) If the respondent intends to contest the application he shall, within 28 days after the time limited for giving notice to defend, file an affidavit in answer to the application setting out the grounds on which he relies and shall serve a copy on the applicant.

(6) In respect of any application for an avoidance of transaction order the court may give such a direction or make such appointment as it is empowered to give or make by paragraph (3) and rule 2.59 shall apply, with the necessary modifications,

to an application for an avoidance of transaction order as it applies to an application for an avoidance of disposition order.

(7) Where the originating summons contains an application for an order under section 22 of the Act of 1984 the applicant shall serve a copy on the landlord of the dwelling house and he shall be entitled to be heard on the application.

(8) An application for an order for financial relief under Part III of the Act of 1984 or for an avoidance of transaction order shall be determined by a judge.

3.19 Application for order under section 24 of Act of 1984 preventing transaction

(1) An application under section 24 of the Act of 1984 for an order preventing a transaction shall be made by originating summons issued in Form M27 out of the principal registry and shall be supported by an affidavit by the applicant stating the facts relied on in support of the application.

(2) The applicant shall serve a sealed copy of the originating summons on the respondent and shall annex thereto a copy of the affidavit in support and a notice of proceedings and acknowledgement of service in Form M28 and rule 10.8 shall apply to such an acknowledgement of service as if the references in paragraph (1) of that rule to Form M6 and in paragraph (2) of that rule to seven days were, respectively, references to Form M28 and 31 days.

(3) If the respondent intends to contest the application he shall, within 28 days after the time limited for giving notice of intention to defend, file an affidavit in answer to the application setting out the grounds on which he relies and shall serve a copy on the applicant.

(4) The application shall be determined by a judge.

(5) Rule 2.66 (except paragraph (3)) shall apply, with the necessary modifications, to the application as if it were an application for ancillary relief.

3.20 Consent to marriage of minor

(1) An application under section 3 of the Marriage Act 1949 (in this rule referred to as 'section 3') for the consent of the court to the marriage of a minor shall be dealt with in chambers unless the court otherwise directs.

(2) The application may be heard and determined by a district judge.

(3) An application under section 3 may be brought without the intervention of the applicant's next friend, unless the court otherwise directs.

(4) Where an application under section 3 follows a refusal to give consent to the marriage every person who has refused consent shall be made a defendant to the summons or a respondent to the application, as appropriate.

(5) The application shall, unless the court orders otherwise, be served not less than seven days before the date upon which the application is to be heard.

[3.21 Application under section 27 of the Act of 1991 for declaration of parentage

(1) Rule 4.6 shall apply to an application under [section 55A of the Act of 1986 (declarations of parentage)][2] as it applies to an application under the Act of 1989.

(2) Where an application under [section 55A of the Act of 1986][2] has been transferred to the High Court or a county court the court shall, as soon as practicable after a transfer has occurred, consider what directions to give for the conduct of the proceedings.

(3) Without prejudice to the generality of paragraph (2), the court may, in particular, direct that –

    (a) the proceedings shall proceed as if they had been commenced by originating summons or originating application;

    (b) any document served or other thing done while the proceedings were pending in another court, including a magistrates' court, shall be treated for such purposes as may be specified in the direction as if it had been such document or other thing, being a document or other thing provided for by the rules of court applicable in the court to which the proceedings have been transferred, as may be specified in the direction and had been served or done pursuant to any such rule;

    (c) a pre-trial hearing shall be held to determine what further directions, if any, should be given.

(4) The application may be heard and determined by a district judge.][1]

NOTES
    Amendments. [1] Rule inserted: SI 1993/295. [2] Words substituted: SI 2001/821.

[3.22 Appeal under section 20 of the Act of 1991 ...[2]

(1) Rule 4.6 shall apply to an appeal under section 20 of the Act of 1991 ([appeals to appeal tribunals][2]) as it applies to an application under the Act of 1989.

(2) Where an appeal under section 20 of the Act of 1991 is transferred to the High Court or a county court, Rule 3.21(2) and (3) shall apply to the appeal as it applies to an application under [section 55A of the Act of 1986] [2].][1]

NOTES
    Amendments. [1] Rule inserted: SI 1993/295. [2] Words deleted or substituted: SI 2001/821.

[3.23 Appeal from Child Support Commissioner

(1) This rule shall apply to any appeal to the Court of Appeal under section 25 of the Act of 1991 (appeal from Child Support Commissioner on question of law).

(2) Where leave to appeal is granted by the Commissioner, the notice of appeal must be served within 6 weeks from the date on which notice of the grant was given in writing to the appellant.

(3) Where leave to appeal is granted by the Court of Appeal upon an application made within 6 weeks of the date on which notice of the Commissioner's refusal of leave to appeal was given in writing to the appellant, the notice of appeal must be served –

    (a) before the end of the said period of 6 weeks; or

    (b) within 7 days after the date on which leave is granted,

whichever is the later, or within such other period as the Court of Appeal may direct.][1]

NOTES
Amendments. ¹ Rule inserted: SI 1993/295.

PART IV
PROCEEDINGS UNDER THE CHILDREN ACT 1989

4.1 Interpretation and application

(1) In this Part of these rules, unless a contrary intention appears –

a section or schedule referred to means the section or schedule so numbered in the Act of 1989;

'a section 8 order' has the meaning assigned to it by section 8(2);

'application' means an application made under or by virtue of the Act of 1989 or under these rules, and 'applicant' shall be construed accordingly;

'child', in relation to proceedings to which this Part applies –

    (a) means, subject to sub-paragraph (b), a person under the age of 18 with respect to whom the proceedings are brought, and

    (b) where the proceedings are under Schedule 1, also includes a person who has reached the age of 18;

['children and family reporter' means an officer of the service who has been asked to prepare a welfare report under section 7(1)(a);]²

['children's guardian' –

    (a) means an officer of the service appointed under section 41 for the child with respect to whom the proceedings are brought; but

    (b) does not include such an officer appointed in relation to proceedings specified by Part IVA;]²

'directions appointment' means a hearing for directions under rule 4.14(2);

'emergency protection order' means an order under section 44;

…²

'leave' includes permission and approval;

'note' includes a record made by mechanical means;

'parental responsibility' has the meaning assigned to it by section 3;

'recovery order' means an order under section 50;

'specified proceedings' has the meaning assigned to it by section 41(6) and rule 4.2(2); and

'welfare officer' means a person who has been asked to prepare a welfare report under [section 7(1)(b)]².

(2) Except where the contrary intention appears, the provisions of this Part apply to proceedings in the High Court and the county courts –

    (a) on an application for a section 8 order;

    (b) on an application for a care order or a supervision order;

    (c) on an application under section 4(1)(a), 4(3), 5(1), 6(7), 13(1), 16(6), 33(7), 34(2), 34(3), 34(4), 34(9), 36(1), 38(8)(b), 39(1), 39(2), 39(3), 39(4), 43(1), 43(12), 44, 45, 46(7), 48(9) [, 50(1) or 102(1)]; ¹

    (d) under Schedule 1, except where financial relief is also sought by or on behalf of an adult;

    (e) on an application under paragraph 19(1) of Schedule 2;

    (f) on an application under paragraph 6(3), 15(2) or 17(1) of Schedule 3;

    (g) on an application under paragraph 11(3) or 16(5) of Schedule 14; or

    (h) under section 25.

NOTES

Amendments. ¹ Words substituted: SI 1991/2113. ² Definition inserted or deleted, or words substituted: SI 2001/821.

4.2 Matters prescribed for the purposes of the Act of 1989

(1) The parties to proceedings in which directions are given under section 38(6), and any person named in such a direction, form the prescribed class for the purposes of section 38(8) (application to vary directions made with interim care or interim supervision order).

(2) The following proceedings are specified for the purposes of section 41 in accordance with subsection (6)(i) thereof –

    (a) proceedings under section 25;
    (b) applications under section 33(7);
    (c) proceedings under paragraph 19(1) of Schedule 2;
    (d) applications under paragraph 6(3) of Schedule 3.
    [(e) appeals against the determination of proceedings of a kind set out in sub-paragraphs (a) to (d).]¹

(3) The applicant for an order that has been made under section 43(1) and the persons referred to in section 43(11) may, in any circumstances, apply under section 43(12) for a child assessment order to be varied or discharged.

(4) The following persons form the prescribed class for the purposes of section 44(9) (application to vary directions) –

    (a) the parties to the application for the order in respect of which it is sought to vary the directions;
    (b) the [children's guardian]²;
    (c) the local authority in whose area the child concerned is ordinarily resident;
    (d) any person who is named in the directions.

NOTES

Amendments. ¹ Words inserted: SI 1991/2113. ² Words substituted: SI 2001/821.

4.3 Application for leave to commence proceedings

(1) Where the leave of the court is required to bring any proceedings to which this Part applies, the person seeking leave shall file –

    (a) a written request for leave [in Form C2]¹ setting out the reasons for the application; and
    [(b) a draft of the application (being the documents referred to in rule 4.4 (1A)) for the making of which leave is sought together with sufficient copies for one to be served on each respondent.]¹

(2) On considering a request for leave filed under paragraph (1), the court shall –

    (a) grant the request, whereupon the proper officer shall inform the person making the request of the decision, or
    (b) direct that a date be fixed for the hearing of the request, whereupon the proper officer shall fix such a date and give such notice as the court directs to the person making the request and such other persons as the court requires to be notified, of the date so fixed.

(3) Where leave is granted to bring proceedings to which this Part applies the application shall proceed in accordance with rule 4.4; but paragraph (1)(a) of that rule shall not apply.

(4) In the case of a request for leave to bring proceedings under Schedule 1, the draft application under paragraph (1) shall be accompanied by a statement setting out the financial details which the person seeking leave believes to be relevant to the request and containing a declaration that it is true to the maker's best knowledge and belief, together with sufficient copies for one to be served on each respondent.

NOTES
Amendments. ¹ Words inserted or substituted: SI 1994/3155.

4.4 Application

(1) Subject to paragraph (4), an applicant shall –

    [(a) file the documents referred to in paragraph (1A) below (which documents shall together be called the 'application') together with sufficient copies for one to be served on each respondent, and] ³

    (b) serve a copy of the application, [together with Form C6 and such (if any) of Forms C7 and C10A as are given to him by the proper officer under paragraph (2)(b)]³ on each respondent such number of days prior to the date fixed under paragraph (2)(a) as is specified for that application in column (ii) of Appendix 3 to these rules.

[(1A) the documents to be filed under paragraph (1)(a) above are –

    (a) (i) whichever is appropriate of Forms C1 to C4 or C51, and
        (ii) such of the supplemental Forms C10 or C11 to C20 as may be appropriate, or

    (b) where there is no appropriate form a statement in writing of the order sought,

and where the application is made in respect of more than one child, all the children shall be included in one application.] ³

(2) On receipt of the documents filed under paragraph (1)(a) the proper officer shall –

    (a) fix the date for a hearing or a directions appointment, allowing sufficient time for the applicant to comply with paragraph (1)(b),

    (b) endorse the date so fixed upon [Form C6 and, where appropriate, Form C6A]³, and

    [(c) return forthwith to the applicant the copies of the application and Form C10A if filed with it, together with Form C6 and such of Forms C6A and C7 as are appropriate.]³

[(3) The applicant shall, at the same time as complying with paragraph (1)(b), serve Form C6A on the persons set out for the relevant class of proceedings in column (iv) of Appendix 3 to these rules.]³

(4) An application for –

    (a) a [section 8 order]²,
    (b) an emergency protection order,
    (c) a warrant under section 48(9), ...¹
    (d) a recovery order, [or

(e) a warrant under section 102(1)][1]

may be made ex parte in which case the applicant shall –

    (i) file the application ...[1] in the appropriate form in Appendix 1 to these rules –
        (a) where the application is made by telephone, within 24 hours after the making of the application, or
        (b) in any other case, at the time when the application is made, and
    (ii) in the case of an application for a [section 8 order][2] or an emergency protection order, serve a copy of the application on each respondent within 48 hours after the making of the order.

(5) Where the court refuses to make an order on an ex parte application it may direct that the application be made inter partes.

(6) In the case of proceedings under Schedule 1, the application under paragraph (1) shall be accompanied by a statement [in Form C10A][3] setting out the financial details which the applicant believes to be relevant to the application ...[3], together with sufficient copies for one to be served on each respondent.

NOTES

Amendments. [1] Words revoked or inserted: SI 1991/2113. [2] Words substituted: SI 1992/2067. [3] Words inserted, repealed or substituted: SI 1994/3155.

4.5 Withdrawal of application

(1) An application may be withdrawn only with leave of the court.

(2) Subject to paragraph (3), a person seeking leave to withdraw an application shall file and serve on the parties a written request for leave setting out the reasons for the request.

(3) The request under paragraph (2) may be made orally to the court if the parties and either the [children's guardian][1] or the [welfare officer or children and family reporter][1] are present.

(4) Upon receipt of a written request under paragraph (2) the court shall –

    (a) if –
        (i) the parties consent in writing,
        (ii) the [children's guardian][1] has had an opportunity to make representations, and
        (iii) the court thinks fit,
    grant the request, in which case the proper officer shall notify the parties, the [children's guardian][1] and the [welfare officer or children and family reporter][1] of the granting of the request, or
    (b) direct that a date be fixed for the hearing of the request in which case the proper officer shall give at least 7 days' notice to the parties, the [children's guardian][1] and the [welfare officer or children and family reporter][1], of the date fixed.

NOTES
Amendments. [1] Words substituted: SI 2001/821.

4.6 Transfer

(1) Where an application is made, in accordance with the provisions of [the Allocation Order][1], to a county court for an order transferring proceedings from a magistrates' court following the refusal of the magistrates' court to order such a transfer, the applicant shall –

    (a) file the application in Form [C2][2], together with a copy of the certificate issued by the magistrates' court, and

    (b) serve a copy of the documents mentioned in sub-paragraph (a) personally on all parties to the proceedings which it is sought to have transferred,

within 2 days after receipt by the applicant of the certificate.

(2) Within 2 days after receipt of the documents served under paragraph (1)(b), any party other than the applicant may file written representations.

(3) The court shall, not before the fourth day after the filing of the application under paragraph (1), unless the parties consent to earlier consideration, consider the application and either –

    (a) grant the application, whereupon the proper officer shall inform the parties of that decision, or

    (b) direct that a date be fixed for the hearing of the application, whereupon the proper officer shall fix such a date and give not less than 1 day's notice to the parties of the date so fixed.

(4) Where proceedings are transferred from a magistrates' court to a county court in accordance with the provisions of [the Allocation Order][1], the county court shall consider whether to transfer those proceedings to the High Court in accordance with that Order and either –

    (a) determine that such an order need not be made,

    (b) make such an order,

    (c) order that a date be fixed for the hearing of the question whether such an order should be made, whereupon the proper officer shall give such notice to the parties as the court directs of the date so fixed, or

    (d) invite the parties to make written representations, within a specified period, as to whether such an order should be made; and upon receipt of the representations the court shall act in accordance with sub-paragraph (a), (b) or (c).

(5) The proper officer shall notify the parties of an order transferring the proceedings from a county court or from the High Court made in accordance with the provisions of [the Allocation Order][1].

[(6) Before ordering the transfer of proceedings from a county court to a magistrates' court in accordance with the Allocation Order, the county court shall notify the magistrates' court of its intention to make such an order and invite the views of the clerk to the justices on whether such an order should be made.

(7) An order transferring proceedings from a county court to a magistrates' court in accordance with the Allocation Order shall –

    (a) be in form [C49][2], and

    (b) be served by the court on the parties.

(8) In this rule 'the Allocation Order' means the Children (Allocation of Proceedings) Order 1991 or any Order replacing that Order.][1]

PART II

NOTES
    Amendments. [1] Words substituted or inserted: SI 1991/2113. [2] Words substituted: SI 1994/3155.

4.7 Parties

(1) The respondents to proceedings to which this Part applies shall be those persons set out in the relevant entry in [column (iii)][1] of Appendix 3 to these rules.

(2) In proceedings to which this Part applies, a person may file a request [in Form C2][2] that he or another person –

   (a) be joined as a party, or
   (b) cease to be a party.

(3) On considering a request under paragraph (2) the court shall, subject to paragraph (4) –

   (a) grant it without a hearing or representations, save that this shall be done only in the case of a request under paragraph (2)(a), whereupon the proper officer shall inform the parties and the person making the request of that decision, or
   (b) order that a date be fixed for the consideration of the request, whereupon the proper officer shall give notice of the date so fixed, together with a copy of the request –
       (i) in the case of a request under paragraph (2)(a), to the applicant, and
       (ii) in the case of a request under paragraph (2)(b), to the parties, or
   (c) invite the parties or any of them to make written representations, within a specified period, as to whether the request should be granted; and upon the expiry of the period the court shall act in accordance with sub-paragraph (a) or (b).

(4) Where a person with parental responsibility requests that he be joined under paragraph (2)(a), the court shall grant his request.

(5) In proceedings to which this Part applies the court may direct –

   (a) that a person who would not otherwise be a respondent under these rules be joined as a party to the proceedings, or
   (b) that a party to the proceedings cease to be a party.

NOTES
    Amendments. [1] Words substituted: SI 1992/2067. [2] Words substituted: SI 1994/3155.

4.8 Service

(1) Subject to the requirement in rule 4.6(1)(b) of personal service, where service of a document is required under this Part (and not by a provision to which section 105(8) (Service of notice or other document under the Act) applies) it may be effected –

   (a) if the person to be served is not known by the person serving to be acting by solicitor –
       (i) by delivering it to him personally, or
       (ii) by delivering it at, or by sending it by first-class post to, his residence or his last known residence, or

(b) if the person to be served is known by the person serving to be acting by solicitor –

    (i) by delivering the document at, or sending it by first-class post to, the solicitor's address for service,

    (ii) where the solicitor's address for service includes a numbered box at a document exchange, by leaving the document at that document exchange or at a document exchange which transmits documents on every business day to that document exchange, or

    (iii) by sending a legible copy of the document by facsimile transmission to the solicitor's office.

(2) In this rule 'first-class post' means first-class post which has been pre-paid or in respect of which pre-payment is not required.

(3) Where a child who is a party to proceedings to which this Part applies [is not prosecuting or defending them without a next friend or guardian ad litem under rule 9.2A and][1] is required by these rules or other rules of court to serve a document, service shall be effected by –

(a) the solicitor acting for the child, or

(b) where there is no such solicitor, [the children's guardian or][4] the guardian ad litem, or

(c) where there is neither such a solicitor [nor a children's guardian][4] nor a guardian ad litem, the court.

(4) Service of any document on a child [who is not prosecuting or defending the proceedings concerned without a next friend or guardian ad litem under rule 9.2A][1] shall, subject to any direction of the court, be effected by service on –

(a) the solicitor acting for the child, or

(b) where there is no such solicitor, [the children's guardian or][4] the guardian ad litem, or

(c) where there is neither such a solicitor [nor a children's guardian][4] nor a guardian ad litem, with leave of the court, the child.

(5) Where the court refuses leave under paragraph (4)(c) it shall give a direction under paragraph (8).

(6) A document shall, unless the contrary is proved, be deemed to have been served –

(a) in the case of service by first-class post, on the second business day after posting, and

(b) in the case of service in accordance with paragraph (1)(b)(ii), on the second business day after the day on which it is left at the document exchange.

(7) At or before the first directions appointment in, or hearing of, proceedings to which this Part applies the applicant shall file a statement [in Form C9][3] that service of –

(a) a copy of the application [and other documents referred to in rule 4.4(1)(b)][3] has been effected on each respondent, and

(b) notice of the proceedings has been effected under rule 4.4(3);

and the statement shall indicate –

    (i) the manner, date, time and place of service, or

    (ii) where service was effected by post, the date, time and place of posting.

[(8) In proceedings to which this Part applies, where these rules or other rules of court require a document to be served, the court may, without prejudice to any power under rule 4.14, direct that –

    (a) the requirement shall not apply;

    (b) the time specified by the rules for complying with the requirement shall be abridged to such extent as may be specified in the direction;

    (c) service shall be effected in such manner as may be specified in the direction.][2]

NOTES

    Amendments. [1] Words inserted: SI 1992/456. [2] Words substituted: SI 1992/2067. [3] Words inserted: SI 1994/3155. [3] Words inserted: SI 2001/821.

4.9 Answer to application

(1) Within 14 days of service of an application for a section 8 order [or an application under Schedule 1][1], each respondent shall file, and serve on the parties, an [acknowledgement of][1] the application in Form [C7][1].

(2) ...[1]

(3) Following service of an application to which this Part applies, other than an application under rule 4.3 or for a section 8 order, a respondent may, subject to paragraph (4), file a written answer, which shall be served on the other parties.

(4) An answer under paragraph (3) shall, except in the case of an application under section 25, 31, 34, 38, 43, 44, 45, 46, 48 or 50, be filed, and served, not less than 2 days before the date fixed for the hearing of the application.

NOTES

    Amendments. [1] Words inserted, repealed or substituted: SI 1994/3155.

4.10 Appointment of [children's guardian][2]

(1) As soon as practicable after the commencement of specified proceedings, or the transfer of such proceedings to the court, the court shall appoint a [children's guardian][2], unless –

    (a) such an appointment has already been made by the court which made the transfer and is subsisting, or

    (b) the court considers that such an appointment is not necessary to safeguard the interests of the child.

(2) At any stage in specified proceedings a party may apply, without notice to the other parties unless the court directs otherwise, for the appointment of a [children's guardian][2].

(3) The court shall grant an application under paragraph (2) unless it considers such an appointment not to be necessary to safeguard the interests of the child, in which case it shall give its reasons; and a note of such reasons shall be taken by the proper officer.

(4) At any stage in specified proceedings the court may, of its own motion, appoint a [children's guardian][2].

[(4A) The court may, in specified proceedings, appoint more than one children's guardian in respect of the same child.][2]

(5) The proper officer shall, as soon as practicable, notify the parties and any [welfare officer or children and family reporter]² of an appointment under this rule or, as the case may be, of a decision not to make such an appointment.

(6) Upon the appointment of a [children's guardian]² the proper officer shall, as soon as practicable, notify him of the appointment and serve on him copies of the application and of documents filed under rule 4.17(1).

[(7) A children's guardian appointed by the court under this rule shall not –

   (a) be a member, officer or servant of a local authority which, or an authorised person (within the meaning of section 31(9)) who, is a party to the proceedings;

   (b) be, or have been, a member, officer or servant of a local authority or voluntary organisation (within the meaning of section 105(1)) who has been directly concerned in that capacity in arrangements relating to the care, accommodation or welfare of the child during the five years prior to the commencement of the proceedings; or

   (c) be a serving probation officer who has, in that capacity, been previously concerned with the child or his family.]²

(8) When appointing a [children's guardian]² the court shall consider the appointment of anyone who has previously acted as [children's guardian]² of the same child.

(9) The appointment of a [children's guardian]² under this rule shall continue for such time as is specified in the appointment or until terminated by the court.

(10) When terminating an appointment in accordance with paragraph (9), the court shall give its reasons in writing for so doing.

(11) Where the court appoints a [children's guardian]² in accordance with this rule or refuses to make such an appointment, the court or the proper officer shall record the appointment or refusal in Form [C47]¹.

NOTES

   Amendments. ¹ Word substituted: SI 1994/3155. ² Words inserted or substituted: SI 2001/821.

[4.11 Powers and duties of officers of the service

(1) In carrying out his duty under section 7(1)(a) or section 41(2), the officer of the service shall have regard to the principle set out in section 1(2) and the matters set out in section 1(3)(a) to (f) as if for the word 'court' in that section there were substituted the words 'officer of the service'.

(2) The officer of the service shall make such investigations as may be necessary for him to carry out his duties and shall, in particular–

   (a) contact or seek to interview such persons as he thinks appropriate or as the court directs;

   (b) obtain such professional assistance as is available to him which he thinks appropriate or which the court directs him to obtain.

(3) In addition to his duties, under other paragraphs of this rule, or rules 4.11A and 4.11B, the officer of the service shall provide to the court such other assistance as it may require.

(4) A party may question the officer of the service about oral or written advice tendered by him to the court.]¹

NOTES
   Amendments. ¹ Rule substituted: SI 2001/821.

[4.11A Additional powers and duties of children's guardian

(1) The children's guardian shall–

(a) appoint a solicitor to represent the child unless such a solicitor has already been appointed; and

(b) give such advice to the child as is appropriate having regard to his understanding and, subject to rule 4.12(1)(a), instruct the solicitor representing the child on all matters relevant to the interests of the child including possibilities for appeal, arising in the course of proceedings.

(2) Where the children's guardian is an officer of the service authorised by the Service in the terms mentioned by and in accordance with section 15(1) of the Criminal Justice and Court Services Act 2000, paragraph (1)(a) shall not require him to appoint a solicitor for the child if he intends to have conduct of the proceedings on behalf of the child unless–

(a) the child wishes to instruct a solicitor direct; and

(b) the children's guardian or the court considers that he is of sufficient understanding to do so.

(3) Where it appears to the children's guardian that the child–

(a) is instructing his solicitor direct; or

(b) intends to conduct and is capable of conducting the proceedings on his own behalf,

he shall inform the court and from then he–

(i) shall perform all of his duties set out in rule 4.11 and this rule, other than those duties under paragraph (1)(a) of this rule, and such other duties as the court may direct;

(ii) shall take such part in the proceedings as the court may direct; and

(iii) may, with the leave of the court, have legal representation in the conduct of those duties.

(4) Unless excused by the court, the children's guardian shall attend all directions appointments in and hearings of the proceedings and shall advise the court on the following matters–

(a) whether the child is of sufficient understanding for any purpose including the child's refusal to submit to a medical or psychiatric examination or other assessment that the court has the power to require, direct or order.

(b) the wishes of the child in respect of any matter relevant to the proceedings including his attendance at court;

(c) the appropriate forum for the proceedings;

(d) the appropriate timing of the proceedings or any part of them;

(e) the options available to it in respect of the child and the suitability of each such option including what order should be made in determining the application; and

(f) any other matter concerning which the court seeks his advice or concerning which he considers that the court should be informed.

(5) The advice given under paragraph (4) may, subject to any order of the court, by given orally or in writing; and if the advice be given orally, a note of it shall be taken by the court or the proper officer.

(6) The children's guardian shall, where practicable, notify any person whose joinder as a party to those proceedings would be likely, in the opinion of the children's guardian, to safeguard the interests of the child of that person's right to apply to be joined under rule 4.7(2) and shall inform the court–

(a) of any such notification given;
(b) of anyone whom he attempted to notify under this paragraph but was unable to contact; and
(c) of anyone whom he believes may wish to be joined to the proceedings.

(7) The children's guardian shall, unless the court otherwise directs, not less than 14 days before the date fixed for the final hearing of the proceedings–

(a) file a written report advising on the interests of the child; and
(b) serve a copy of the filed report on the other parties.

(8) The children's guardian shall serve and accept service of documents on behalf of the child in accordance with rule 4.8(3)(b) and (4)(b) and, where the child has not himself been served, and has sufficient understanding, advise the child of the contents of any document so served.

(9) If the children's guardian inspects records of the kinds referred to in section 42, he shall bring to the attention of–

(a) the court; and
(b) unless the court otherwise directs, the other parties to the proceedings,

all records and documents which may, in his opinion, assist in the proper determination of the proceedings.

(10) The children's guardian shall ensure that, in relation to a decision made by the court in the proceedings–

(a) if he considers it appropriate to the age and understanding of the child, the child is notified of that decision; and
(b) if the child is notified of the decision, it is explained to the child in a manner appropriate to his age and understanding.][1]

NOTES
Amendments. [1] Rule inserted: SI 2001/821.

[4.11B Additional powers and duties of a children and family reporter

(1) The children and family reporter shall–

(a) notify the child of such contents of his report (if any) as he considers appropriate to the age and understanding of the child, including any reference to the child's own views on the application and the recommendation of the children and family reporter; and
(b) if he does notify the child of any contents of his report, explain them to the child in a manner appropriate to his age and understanding.

(2) Where the court has–

(a) directed that a written report be made by a children and family reporter; and

(b) notified the children and family reporter that his report is to be considered at a hearing,

the children and family reporter shall–

      (i) file the report; and

      (ii) serve a copy on the other parties and on the children's guardian (if any),

by such time as the court may direct, and if no direction is given, not less than 14 days before that hearing.

(3) The court may direct that the children and family reporter attend any hearing at which his report is to be considered.

(4) The children and family reporter shall advise the court if he considers that the joinder of a person as a party to the proceedings would be likely to safeguard the interests of the child.

(5) The children and family reporter shall consider whether it is in the best interests of the child for the child to be made a party to the proceedings.

(6) If the children and family reporter considers the child should be made a party to the proceedings he shall notify the court of his opinion together with the reasons for that opinion.][1]

NOTES

Amendments. [1] Rule inserted: SI 2001/821.

4.12 Solicitor for child

(1) A solicitor appointed under section 41(3) or in accordance with [rule 4.11A(1)(a)][2] shall represent the child –

    (a) in accordance with instructions received from the [children's guardian][2] (unless the solicitor considers, having taken into account the views of the [children's guardian][2] and any direction of the court under [rule 4.11A(3)][2], that the child wishes to give instructions which conflict with those of the [children's guardian][2] and that he is able, having regard to his understanding, to give such instructions on his own behalf in which case he shall conduct the proceedings in accordance with instructions received from the child), or

    (b) where no [children's guardian][2] has been appointed for the child and the condition in section 41(4)(b) is satisfied, in accordance with instructions received from the child, or

    (c) in default of instructions under (a) or (b), in furtherance of the best interests of the child.

(2) A solicitor appointed under section 41(3) or in accordance with [rule 4.11A(1)(a)][2] shall serve and accept service of documents on behalf of the child in accordance with rule 4.8(3)(a) and (4)(a) and, where the child has not himself been served and has sufficient understanding, advise the child of the contents of any document so served.

(3) Where the child wishes an appointment of a solicitor under section 41(3) or in accordance with [rule 4.11A(1)(a)][2] to be terminated, he may apply to the court for an order terminating the appointment; and the solicitor and the [children's guardian][2] shall be given an opportunity to make representations.

(4) Where the [children's guardian]² wishes an appointment of a solicitor under section 41(3) to be terminated, he may apply to the court for an order terminating the appointment; and the solicitor and, if he is of sufficient understanding, the child, shall be given an opportunity to make representations.

(5) When terminating an appointment in accordance with paragraph (3) or (4), the court shall give its reasons for so doing, a note of which shall be taken by the court or the proper officer.

(6) Where the court appoints a solicitor under section 41(3) or refuses to make such an appointment, the court or the proper officer shall record the appointment or refusal in Form [C48]¹.

NOTES

Amendments. ¹ Word substituted: SI 1994/3155. ² Words substituted: SI 2001/821.

[4.13 Welfare officer

(1) Where the court has directed that a written report be made by a welfare officer [in accordance with section 7(1)(b)]², the report shall be filed at or by such time as the court directs or, in the absence of such a direction, at least 14 days before a relevant hearing; and the proper officer shall, as soon as practicable, serve a copy of the report on the parties and any [children's guardian]².

(2) In paragraph (1), a hearing is relevant if the proper officer has given the welfare officer notice that his report is to be considered at it.

(3) After the filing of a report by a welfare officer, the court may direct that the welfare officer attend any hearing at which the report is to be considered; and

    (a) except where such a direction is given at a hearing attended by the welfare officer, the proper officer shall inform the welfare officer of the direction; and

    (b) at the hearing at which the report is considered any party may question the welfare officer about his report.

[(3A) The welfare officer shall consider whether it is in the best interests of the child for the child to be made a party to the proceedings.

(3B) If the welfare officer considers the child should be made a party to the proceedings he shall notify the court of his opinion together with the reasons for that opinion.]²

(4) This rule is without prejudice to any power to give directions under rule 4.14.]¹

NOTES

Amendments. ¹ Rule substituted: SI 1992/2067, except in relation to a written report the making of which was directed before 5 October 1992. ² Words inserted or substituted: SI 2001/821.

4.14 Directions

(1) In this rule, 'party' includes the [children's guardian]² and, where a request or a direction concerns a report under section 7, the [welfare officer or children and family reporter]².

(2) In proceedings to which this Part applies the court may, subject to paragraph (3), give, vary or revoke directions for the conduct of the proceedings, including –

PART II

  (a) the timetable for the proceedings;
  (b) varying the time within which or by which an act is required, by these rules or by other rules of court, to be done;
  (c) the attendance of the child;
  [(d) the appointment of a children's guardian, a guardian ad litem, or a solicitor under section 41(3);]²
  (e) the service of documents;
  (f) the submission of evidence including experts' reports;
  (g) the preparation of welfare reports under section 7;
  (h) the transfer of the proceedings to another court;
  (i) consolidation with other proceedings.

(3) Directions under paragraph (2) may be given, varied or revoked either –

  (a) of the court's own motion having given the parties notice of its intention to do so, and an opportunity to attend and be heard or to make written representations,
  (b) on the written request [in Form C2]¹ of a party specifying the direction which is sought, filed and served on the other parties, or
  (c) on the written request [in Form C2]¹ of a party specifying the direction which is sought, to which the other parties consent and which they or their representatives have signed.

(4) In an urgent case the request under paragraph (3)(b) may, with the leave of the court, be made –

  (a) orally, or
  (b) without notice to the parties, or
  (c) both as in sub-paragraph (a) and as in sub-paragraph (b).

(5) On receipt of a written request under paragraph (3)(b) the proper officer shall fix a date for the hearing of the request and give not less than 2 days' notice [in Form C6]¹ to the parties of the date so fixed.

(6) On considering a request under paragraph (3)(c) the court shall either –

  (a) grant the request, whereupon the proper officer shall inform the parties of the decision, or
  (b) direct that a date be fixed for the hearing of the request, whereupon the proper officer shall fix such a date and give not less than 2 days' notice to the parties of the date so fixed.

(7) A party may apply for an order to be made under section 11(3) or, if he is entitled to apply for such an order, under section 38(1) in accordance with paragraph (3)(b) or (c).

(8) Where a court is considering making, of its own motion, a section 8 order, or an order under section 31, 34 or 38, the power to give directions under paragraph (2) shall apply.

(9) Directions of a court which are still in force immediately prior to the transfer of proceedings to which this Part applies to another court shall continue to apply following the transfer, subject to any changes of terminology which are required to apply those directions to the court to which the proceedings are transferred, unless varied or discharged by directions under paragraph (2).

(10) The court or the proper officer shall take a note of the giving, variation or revocation of a direction under this rule and serve, as soon as practicable, a copy of the note on any party who was not present at the giving, variation or revocation.

NOTES

Amendments. [1] Words inserted: SI 1994/3155. [2] Words substituted: SI 2001/821.

4.15 Timing of proceedings

(1) Where these rules or other rules of court provide a period of time within which or by which a certain act is to be performed in the course of proceedings to which this Part applies, that period may not be extended otherwise than by direction of the court under rule 4.14.

(2) At the –

    (a) transfer to a court of proceedings to which this Part applies,

    (b) postponement or adjournment of any hearing or directions appointment in the course of proceedings to which this Part applies, or

    (c) conclusion of any such hearing or directions appointment other than one at which the proceedings are determined, or so soon thereafter as is practicable, the court or the proper officer shall –

    (i) fix a date upon which the proceedings shall come before the court again for such purposes as the court directs, which date shall, where paragraph (a) applies, be as soon as possible after the transfer, and

    (ii) give notice to the parties, the [children's guardian][1] or the [welfare officer or children and family reporter][1] of the date so fixed.

NOTES

Amendments. [1] Words substituted: SI 2001/821.

4.16 Attendance at directions appointment and hearing

(1) Subject to paragraph (2), a party shall attend a directions appointment of which he has been given notice in accordance with rule 4.14(5) unless the court otherwise directs.

(2) Proceedings or any part of them shall take place in the absence of any party, including the child, if –

    (a) the court considers it in the interests of the child, having regard to the matters to be discussed or the evidence likely to be given, and

    (b) the party is represented by a [children's guardian][1] or solicitor;

and when considering the interests of the child under sub-paragraph (a) the court shall give the [children's guardian][1], the solicitor for the child and, if he is of sufficient understanding, the child an opportunity to make representations.

(3) Subject to paragraph (4), where at the time and place appointed for a hearing or directions appointment the applicant appears but one or more of the respondents do not, the court may proceed with the hearing or appointment.

(4) The court shall not begin to hear an application in the absence of a respondent unless –

    (a) it is proved to the satisfaction of the court that he received reasonable notice of the date of the hearing; or

    (b) the court is satisfied that the circumstances of the case justify proceeding with the hearing.

(5) Where, at the time and place appointed for a hearing or directions appointment one or more of the respondents appear but the applicant does not, the court may

PART II

refuse the application or, if sufficient evidence has previously been received, proceed in the absence of the applicant.

(6) Where at the time and place appointed for a hearing or directions appointment neither the applicant nor any respondent appears, the court may refuse the application.

(7) Unless the court otherwise directs, a hearing of, or directions appointment in, proceedings to which this Part applies shall be in chambers.

NOTES
  Amendments. [1] Words substituted: SI 2001/821.

4.17 Documentary evidence

(1) Subject to paragraphs (4) and (5), in proceedings to which this Part applies a party shall file and serve on the parties, any [welfare officer or children and family reporter][2] and any [children's guardian][2] of whose appointment he has been given notice under rule 4.10(5) –

  (a) written statements of the substance of the oral evidence which the party intends to adduce at a hearing of, or a directions appointment in, those proceedings, which shall –
    (i) be dated,
    (ii) be signed by the person making the statement, ...[1]
    (iii) contain a declaration that the maker of the statement believes it to be true and understands that it may be placed before the court; and
    [(iv) show in the top right hand corner of the first page –
      (a) the initials and surname of the person making the statement,
      (b) the number of the statement in relation to the maker,
      (c) the date on which the statement was made, and
      (d) the party on whose behalf it is filed; and][1]
  (b) copies of any documents, including experts' reports, upon which the party intends to rely at a hearing of, or a directions appointment in, those proceedings,

at or by such time as the court directs or, in the absence of a direction, before the hearing or appointment.

(2) A party may, subject to any direction of the court about the timing of statements under this rule, file and serve on the parties a statement which is supplementary to a statement served under paragraph (1).

(3) At a hearing or a directions appointment a party may not, without the leave of the court –

  (a) adduce evidence, or
  (b) seek to rely on a document,

in respect of which he has failed to comply with the requirements of paragraph (1).

(4) In proceedings for a section 8 order a party shall –

  (a) neither file nor serve any document other than as required or authorised by these rules, and
  (b) in completing a form prescribed by these rules, neither give information, nor make a statement, which is not required or authorised by that form,

without the leave of the court.

---

(5) In proceedings for a section 8 order no statement or copy may be filed under paragraph (1) until such time as the court directs.

NOTES
Amendments. ¹ Words inserted or revoked: SI 1992/2067. ² Words substituted: SI 2001/821.

4.18 Expert evidence – examination of child

(1) No person may, without the leave of the court, cause the child to be medically or psychiatrically examined, or otherwise assessed, for the purpose of the preparation of expert evidence for use in the proceedings.

(2) An application for leave under paragraph (1) shall, unless the court otherwise directs, be served on all parties to the proceedings and on the [children's guardian]¹.

(3) Where the leave of the court has not been given under paragraph (1), no evidence arising out of an examination or assessment to which that paragraph applies may be adduced without the leave of the court.

NOTES
Amendments. ¹ Words substituted: SI 2001/821.

4.19 Amendment

(1) Subject to rule 4.17(2), a document which has been filed or served in proceedings to which this Part applies, may not be amended without the leave of the court which shall, unless the court otherwise directs, be requested in writing.

(2) On considering a request for leave to amend a document the court shall either –

    (a) grant the request, whereupon the proper officer shall inform the person making the request of that decision, or

    (b) invite the parties or any of them to make representations, within a specified period, as to whether such an order should be made.

(3) A person amending a document shall file it and serve it on those persons on whom it was served prior to amendment; and the amendments shall be identified.

4.20 Oral evidence

The court or the proper officer shall keep a note of the substance of the oral evidence given at a hearing of, or directions appointment in, proceedings to which this Part applies.

4.21 Hearing

(1) The court may give directions as to the order of speeches and evidence at a hearing, or directions appointment, in the course of proceedings to which this Part applies.

(2) Subject to directions under paragraph (1), at a hearing of, or directions appointment in, proceedings to which this Part applies, the parties and the [children's guardian]⁴ shall adduce their evidence in the following order –

    (a) the applicant,

    (b) any party with parental responsibility for the child,

    (c) other respondents,

    (d) the [children's guardian][4],

    (e) the child, if he is a party to the proceedings and there is no [children's guardian][4].

(3) After the final hearing of proceedings to which this Part applies, the court shall deliver its judgment as soon as is practicable.

[(4) When making an order or when refusing an application, the court shall –

    (a) where it makes a finding of fact state such finding and complete Form C22; and

    (b) state the reasons for the court's decision.][3]

(5) An order made in proceedings to which this Part applies shall be recorded, by the court or the proper officer, either in the appropriate form in Appendix 1 to these rules or, where there is no such form, in writing.

(6) Subject to paragraph (7), a copy of an order made in accordance with paragraph (5) shall, as soon as practicable after it has been made, be served by the proper officer on the parties to the proceedings in which it was made [and][1] on any person with whom the child is living.

(7) Within 48 hours after the making ex parte of –

    (a) a [section 8 order][2], or

    (b) an order under section 44, 48(4), 48(9) or 50,

the applicant shall serve a copy of the order in the appropriate form in Appendix 1 to these Rules on –

    (i) each party,

    (ii) any person who has actual care of the child or who had such care immediately prior to the making of the order, and

    (iii) in the case of an order referred to in sub-paragraph (b), the local authority in whose area the child lives or is found.

(8) At a hearing of, or directions appointment in, an application which takes place outside the hours during which the court office is normally open, the court or the proper officer shall take a note of the substance of the proceedings.

NOTES

Amendments. [1] Word inserted: SI 1992/456. [2] Words substituted: SI 1992/2067. [3] Words inserted: SI 1994/3155. [4] Words substituted: SI 2001/821.

[4.21A Attachment of penal notice to section 8 order

CCR Order 29, rule 1 (committal for breach of order or undertaking) shall apply to section 8 orders as if for paragraph (3) of that rule there were substituted the following –

    '(3) In the case of a section 8 order (within the meaning of section 8(2) of the Children Act 1989) enforceable by committal order under paragraph (1), the judge or the district judge may, on the application of the person entitled to enforce the order, direct that the proper officer issue a copy of the order, indorsed with or incorporating a notice as to the consequences of disobedience, for service in accordance with paragraph (2); and no copy of the order shall be issued with any such notice indorsed or incorporated save in accordance with such a direction.']¹

NOTES

Amendments. Rule inserted: SI 1992/2067.

4.22 Appeals

(1) Where an appeal lies –

- (a) to the High Court under section 94, or
- (b) from any decision of a district judge to the judge of the court in which the decision was made,

it shall be made in accordance with the following provisions; and references to 'the court below' are references to the court from which, or person from whom, the appeal lies.

(2) The appellant shall file and serve on the parties to the proceedings in the court below, and on any [children's guardian]² –

- (a) notice of the appeal in writing, setting out the grounds upon which he relies;
- (b) a certified copy of the summons or application and of the order appealed against, and of any order staying its execution;
- (c) a copy of any notes of the evidence;
- (d) a copy of any reasons given for the decision.

[(2A) In relation to an appeal to the High Court under section 94, the documents required to be filed by paragraph (2) shall, –

- (a) where the care centre listed in column (ii) of Schedule 2 to the Children (Allocation of Proceedings) Order 1991 against the entry in column (i) relating to the petty sessions area or London commission area in which the court below is situated –
  - (i) is the principal registry, or
  - (ii) has a district registry in the same place,
  be filed in that registry, and
- (b) in any other case, be filed in the district registry, being in the same place as a care centre within the meaning of article 2(c) of the said Order, which is nearest to the court below.]¹

(3) The notice of appeal shall be filed and served in accordance with paragraph (2)(a) –

- (a) within 14 days after the determination against which the appeal is brought, or
- (b) in the case of an appeal against an order under section 38(1), within 7 days after the making of the order, or
- (c) with the leave of the court to which, or judge to whom, the appeal is to be brought, within such other time as that court or judge may direct.

(4) The documents mentioned in paragraph (2)(b) to (d) shall, subject to any direction of the court to which, or judge to whom, the appeal is to be brought, be filed and served as soon as practicable after the filing and service of the notice of appeal under paragraph (2)(a).

(5) Subject to paragraph (6), a respondent who wishes –

PART II

(a) to contend on the appeal that the decision of the court below should be varied, either in any event or in the event of the appeal being allowed in whole or in part, or

(b) to contend that the decision of the court below should be affirmed on grounds other than those relied upon by that court, or

(c) to contend by way of cross-appeal that the decision of the court below was wrong in whole or in part,

shall, within 14 days of receipt of notice of the appeal, file and serve on all other parties to the appeal a notice in writing, setting out the grounds upon which he relies.

(6) No notice under paragraph (5) may be filed or served in an appeal against an order under section 38.

(7) In the case of an appeal mentioned in paragraph (1)(a), an application to –

(a) withdraw the appeal,

(b) have the appeal dismissed with the consent of all the parties, or

(c) amend the grounds of appeal,

may be heard by a district judge.

(8) An appeal of the kind mentioned in paragraph (1)(a) shall, unless the President otherwise directs, be heard and determined by a single judge.

NOTES
Amendments. [1] Words inserted: SI 1992/2067. [2] Words substituted: SI 2001/821.

4.23 Confidentiality of documents

(1) Notwithstanding any rule of court to the contrary, no document, other than a record of an order, held by the court and relating to proceedings to which this Part applies shall be disclosed, other than to –

(a) a party,

(b) the legal representative of a party,

(c) the [children's guardian][1],

(d) the Legal Aid Board, or

(e) a [welfare officer or children and family reporter][1],

[(f) an expert whose instruction by a party has been authorised by the court,][1]

without leave of the judge or district judge.

(2) Nothing in this rule shall prevent the notification by the court or the proper officer of a direction under section 37(1) to the authority concerned.

[(3) Nothing in this rule shall prevent the disclosure of a document prepared by an officer of the service for the purpose of–

(a) enabling a person to perform functions required under section 62(3A) of the Justices of the Peace Act 1997;

(b) assisting an officer of the service who is appointed by the court under any enactment to perform his functions.][1]

[(4) Nothing in this rule shall prevent the disclosure of any document relating to proceedings by an officer of the service to any other officer of the service unless that other officer is involved in the same proceedings but on behalf of a different party.][1]

NOTES
Amendments. [1] Words substituted or inserted: SI 2001/821.

4.24 Notification of consent

[(1)][2] Consent for the purposes of –

    (a) section 16(3), [or][1]
    (b) [section 38A(2)(b)(ii) or 44A(2)(b)(ii), or][2]
    (c) paragraph 19(3)(c) or (d) of Schedule 2,

shall be given either –

    (i) orally in court, or
    (ii) in writing to the court signed by the person giving his consent.

[(2) Any written consent given for the purposes of subsection (2) of section 38A or section 44A, shall include a statement that the person giving consent –

    (a) is able and willing to give to the child the care which it would be reasonable to expect a parent to give him; and
    (b) understands that the giving of consent could lead to the exclusion of the relevant person from the dwelling-house in which the child lives.][2]

NOTES
Amendments. [1] Words inserted and repealed: SI 1992/456. [2] Paragraph numbering, words and paragraph inserted: SI 1997/1893.

[4.24A Exclusion requirements: interim care orders and emergency protection orders

(1) This rule applies where the court includes an exclusion requirement in an interim care order or an emergency protection order.

(2) The applicant for an interim care order or emergency protection order shall –

    (a) prepare a separate statement of the evidence in support of the application for an exclusion requirement;
    (b) serve the statement personally on the relevant person with a copy of the order containing the exclusion requirement (and of any power of arrest which is attached to it);
    (c) inform the relevant person of his right to apply to vary or discharge the exclusion requirement.

(3) Where a power of arrest is attached to an exclusion requirement in an interim care order or an emergency protection order, a copy of the order shall be delivered to the officer for the time being in charge of the police station for the area in which the dwelling-house in which the child lives is situated (or of such other station as the court may specify) together with a statement showing that the relevant person has been served with the order or informed of its terms (whether by being present when the order was made or by telephone or otherwise).

(4) Rules 3.9(5), 3.9A (except paragraphs (1) and (3)) and 3.10 shall apply, with the necessary modifications, for the service, variation, discharge and enforcement of any exclusion requirement to which a power of arrest is attached as they apply to an order made on an application under Part IV of the Family Law Act 1996.

(5) The relevant person shall serve the parties to the proceedings with any application which he makes for the variation or discharge of the exclusion requirement.

(6) Where an exclusion requirement ceases to have effect whether –

    (a) as a result of the removal of a child under section 38A(10) or 44A(10),

    (b) because of the discharge of the interim care order or emergency protection order, or

    (c) otherwise,

the applicant shall inform –

    (i) the relevant person,

    (ii) the parties to the proceedings,

    (iii) any officer to whom a copy of the order was delivered under paragraph (3), and

    (iv) (where necessary) the court.

(7) Where the court includes an exclusion requirement in an interim care order or an emergency protection order of its own motion, paragraph (2) shall apply with the omission of any reference to the statement of the evidence.] [1]

NOTES
Amendments. [1] Rule inserted: SI 1997/1893.

4.25 Secure accommodation – evidence

In proceedings under section 25, the court shall, if practicable, arrange for copies of all written reports before it to be made available before the hearing to –

    (a) the applicant;

    (b) the parent or guardian of the child;

    (c) any legal representative of the child;

    (d) the [children's guardian] [1]; and

    (e) the child, unless the court otherwise directs;

and copies of such reports may, if the court considers it desirable, be shown to any person who is entitled to notice of the proceedings in accordance with these rules.

NOTES
Amendments. [1] Words substituted: SI 2001/821.

4.26 Investigation under section 37

(1) This rule applies where a direction is given to an appropriate authority by the High Court or a county court under section 37(1).

(2) On giving a direction the court shall adjourn the proceedings and the court or the proper officer shall record the direction [in Form C40] [1].

(3) A copy of the direction recorded under paragraph (2) shall, as soon as practicable after the direction is given, be served by the proper officer on the parties to the proceedings in which the direction is given and, where the appropriate authority is not a party, on that authority.

(4) When serving the copy of the direction on the appropriate authority the proper officer shall also serve copies of such of the documentary evidence which has been, or is to be, adduced in the proceedings as the court may direct.

(5) Where a local authority informs the court of any of the matters set out in section 37(3)(a) to (c) it shall do so in writing.

NOTES
Amendments. [1] Words substituted: SI 1994/3155.

4.27 Direction to local education authority to apply for education supervision order

(1) For the purposes of section 40(3) and (4) of the Education Act 1944 a direction by the High Court or a county court to a local education authority to apply for an education supervision order shall be given [in writing] [1].

(2) Where, following such a direction, a local education authority informs the court that they have decided not to apply for an education supervision order, they shall do so in writing.

NOTES
Amendments. [1] Words substituted: SI 1997/1893.

4.28 Transitional provision

Nothing in any provision of this Part of these rules shall affect any proceedings which are pending (within the meaning of paragraph 1 of Schedule 14 to the Act of 1989) immediately before these rules come into force.

[PART IVA
PROCEEDINGS UNDER SECTION 30 OF THE HUMAN FERTILISATION AND EMBRYOLOGY ACT 1990

4A.1 Interpretation

(1) In this Part of these Rules –

'the 1990 Act' means the Human Fertilisation and Embryology Act 1990;
'the birth father' means the father of the child, including a person who is treated as being the father of the child by section 28 of the 1990 Act where he is not the husband within the meaning of section 30 of the 1990 Act;
'the birth mother' means the woman who carried the child;
'the birth parents' means the birth mother and the birth father;
...[1]
'the husband and wife' means the persons who may apply for a parental order where the conditions set out in section 30(1) of the 1990 Act are met;
'parental order' means an order under section 30 of the 1990 Act (parental orders in favour of gamete donors) providing for a child to be treated in law as a child of the parties to a marriage.
['parental order reporter' means an officer of the service appointed under section 41 of the Children Act 1989 in relation to proceedings specified by paragraph (2);] [1]

PART II

(2) Applications under section 30 of the 1990 Act are specified proceedings for the purposes of section 41 of the Children Act 1989 in accordance with section 41(6)(i) of that Act.

NOTES
Amendments. 1 Definition omitted or inserted: SI 2001/821.

4A.2 Application of Part IV

Subject to the provisions of this Part, the provisions of Part IV of these Rules shall apply as appropriate with any necessary modifications to proceedings under this Part except that rules 4.7(1), 4.9, 4.10(1)(b), 4.10(11), [4.11A(1)]¹, [4.11A(3)]¹ and 4.12 shall not apply.

NOTES
Amendments. 1 References substituted: SI 2001/821.

4A.3 Parties

The applicants shall be the husband and wife and the respondents shall be the persons set out in the relevant entry in column (iii) of Appendix 3.

4A.4 [Acknowledgement]¹

Within 14 days of the service of an application for a parental order, each respondent shall file and serve on all the other parties an [acknowledgement in Form C52].¹

NOTES
Amendments. 1 Words substituted: SI 1994/3155.

4A.5 Appointment and duties of the [parental order reporter]¹

(1) As soon as practicable after the application has been filed the court shall consider the appointment of a [parental order reporter]¹ in accordance with section 41(1) of the Children Act 1989.

(2), (3) ...¹

(4) In addition to such of the matters set out in [rules 4.11 and 4.11A]¹ as are appropriate to the proceedings, the [parental order reporter]¹ shall –

(i) investigate the matters set out in section 30(1) to (7) of the 1990 Act;
(ii) so far as he considers necessary, investigate any matter contained in the application form or other matter which appears relevant to the making of a parental order;
(iii) advise the court on whether there is any reason under section 6 of the Adoption Act 1976, as applied with modifications by the Parental Orders (Human Fertilisation and Embryology) Regulations 1994, to refuse the parental order.

NOTES
Amendments. 1 Words substituted or omitted: SI 2001/821.

4A.6 Personal attendance of applicants

The court shall not make a parental order except upon the personal attendance before it of the applicants.

4A.7 Copies of orders

(1) Where a parental order is made by a court sitting in Wales in respect of a child who was born in Wales and the applicants so request before the order is drawn up, the proper officer shall obtain a translation into Welsh of the particulars set out in the order.

(2) Within 7 days after the making of a parental order, the proper officer shall send a copy of the order to the Registrar General.

(3) A copy of any parental order may be supplied to the Registrar General at his request.

4A.8 Amendment and revocation of orders

(1) An application under paragraph 4 of Schedule 1 to the Adoption Act 1976 as modified by the Parental Orders (Human Fertilisation and Embryology) Regulations 1994 for the amendment of a parental order or the revocation of a direction to the Registrar General may be made ex parte in the first instance but the court may require notice of the application to be served on such persons as it thinks fit.

(2) Where the application is granted, the proper officer shall send to the Registrar General a notice specifying the amendments or informing him of the revocation and shall give sufficient particulars of the order to enable the Registrar General to identify the case.

4A.9 Custody, inspection and disclosure of documents and information

(1) All documents relating to proceedings for a parental order shall, while they are in the custody of the court, be kept in a place of special security.

(2) Any person who obtains any information in the course of, or relating to proceedings for a parental order shall treat that information as confidential and shall only disclose it if –

    (a) the disclosure is necessary for the proper exercise of his duties, or
    (b) the information is requested –
        (i) by a court or public authority (whether in Great Britain or not) having power to determine proceedings for a parental order and related matters, for the purpose of discharge of its duties in that behalf, or
        (ii) by a person who is authorised in writing by the Secretary of State to obtain the information for the purposes of research.

4A.10 Application for removal, return etc of child

(1) An application under sections 27(1), 29(1) or 29(2) of the Adoption Act 1976 as applied with modifications by the Parental Orders (Human Fertilisation and Embryology) Regulations 1994 shall be made on notice in proceedings under section 30 of the 1990 Act.

PART II

(2) The proper officer shall serve a copy of the application and a notice of the date of the hearing on all the parties to the proceedings under section 30, on the guardian ad litem and on any other person or body, not being the child, as the court thinks fit.

(3) The court may at any time give directions as to the conduct of the application under this rule.][1]

NOTES
Amendments. [1] Part inserted: SI 1994/2165.

PART V
WARDSHIP

5.1 Application to make a minor a ward of court

(1) An application to make a minor a ward of court shall be made by originating summons and, unless the court otherwise directs, the plaintiff shall file an affidavit in support of the application when the originating summons is issued.

(2) Rule 4.3 shall, so far as applicable, apply to an application by a local authority for the leave of the court under section 100(3) of the Act of 1989.

(3) Where there is no person other than the minor who is a suitable defendant, an application may be made ex parte to a district judge for leave to issue either an ex parte originating summons or an originating summons with the minor as defendant thereto; and, except where such leave is granted, the minor shall not be made a defendant to an originating summons under this rule in the first instance.

(4) Particulars of any summons issued under this rule in a district registry shall be sent by the proper officer to the principal registry for recording in the register of wards.

(5) The date of the minor's birth shall, unless otherwise directed, be stated in the summons, and the plaintiff shall –

    (a) on issuing the summons or before or at the first hearing thereof lodge in the registry out of which the summons issued a certified copy of the entry in the Register of Births or, as the case may be, in the Adopted Children Register relating to the minor, or

    (b) at the first hearing of the summons apply for directions as to proof of birth of the minor in some other manner.

(6) The name of each party to the proceedings shall be qualified by a brief description, in the body of the summons, of his interest in, or relation to, the minor.

(7) Unless the court otherwise directs, the summons shall state the whereabouts of the minor or, as the case may be, that the plaintiff is unaware of his whereabouts.

(8) Upon being served with the summons, every defendant other than the minor shall forthwith lodge in the registry out of which the summons issued a notice stating the address of the defendant and the whereabouts of the minor or, as the case may be, that the defendant is unaware of his whereabouts and, unless the court otherwise directs, serve a copy of the same upon the plaintiff.

(9) Where any party other than the minor changes his address or becomes aware of any change in the whereabouts of the minor after the issue or, as the case may be, service of the summons, he shall, unless the court otherwise directs, forthwith

lodge notice of the change in the registry out of which the summons issued and serve a copy of the notice on every other party.

(10) The summons shall contain a notice to the defendant informing him of the requirements of paragraphs (8) and (9).

(11) In this rule any reference to the whereabouts of a minor is a reference to the address at which and the person with whom he is living and any other information relevant to the question where he may be found.

5.2 Enforcement of order by tipstaff

The power of the High Court to secure, through an officer attending upon the court, compliance with any direction relating to a ward of court may be exercised by an order addressed to the tipstaff.

5.3 Where minor ceases to be a ward of court

(1) A minor who, by virtue of section 41(2) of the Supreme Court Act 1981, becomes a ward of court on the issue of a summons under rule 5.1 shall cease to be a ward of court –

    (a) if an application for an appointment for the hearing of the summons is not made within the period of 21 days after the issue of the summons, at the expiration of that period;

    (b) if an application for such an appointment is made within that period, on the determination of the application made by the summons unless the court hearing it orders that the minor be made a ward of court.

(2) Nothing in paragraph (1) shall be taken as affecting the power of the court under section 41(3) of the said Act to order that any minor who is for the time being a ward of court shall cease to be a ward of court.

(3) If no application for an appointment for the hearing of a summons under rule 5.1 is made within the period of 21 days after the issue of the summons, a notice stating whether the applicant intends to proceed with the application made by the summons must be left at the registry in which the matter is proceeding immediately after the expiration of that period.

5.4 Adoption of minor who is a ward of court

(1) An application for leave –

    (a) to commence proceedings to adopt a minor who is a ward or

    (b) to commence proceedings to free such a minor for adoption,

may be ex parte to a district judge.

(2) Where a local authority has been granted leave to place a minor who is a ward with foster parents with a view to adoption it shall not be necessary for an application to be made for leave under paragraph (1)(a) or (b) unless the court otherwise directs.

(3) If the applicant for leave under paragraph (1)(a) or (b), or a local authority which has applied for leave as referred to in paragraph (2), or a foster parent so requests, the district judge may direct that any subsequent proceedings shall be conducted with a view to securing that the proposed adopter is not seen by or made known to any respondent or prospective respondent who is not already aware of his identity except with his consent.

(4) In paragraphs (1) and (3) 'proceedings' means proceedings in the High Court or in a county court.

[5.5 Orders for use of secure accommodation

No order shall be made with the effect of placing or keeping a minor in secure accommodation, within the meaning of section 25(1) of the Act of 1989 [unless the minor has been made a party to the summons.]².]¹

NOTES
Amendments. ¹ Rule inserted: SI 1991/2113. ² Words substituted: SI 1992/456.

[5.6 Notice to provider of refuge

Where a child is staying in a refuge which is certified under section 51(1) or 51(2) of the Act of 1989, the person who is providing that refuge shall be given notice of any application under this Part of these rules in respect of that child.] ¹

NOTES
Amendments. ¹ Rule inserted: SI 1991/2113.

PART VI
CHILD ABDUCTION AND CUSTODY ...¹

NOTES
Amendments. ¹ Words repealed: SI 1994/3155.

6.1 Interpretation

In this Part, unless the context otherwise requires –

  (a) 'the Act' means the Child Abduction and Custody Act 1985 and words or expressions bear the same meaning as in that Act;
  (b) 'the Hague Convention' means the convention defined in section 1¹ of the Act and 'the European Convention' means the convention defined in section 12¹ of the Act 1965.

6.2 Mode of application

(1) Except as otherwise provided by this Part, every application under the Hague Convention and the European Convention shall be made by originating summons, which shall be in Form No. 10 in Appendix A to the Rules of the Supreme Court [and issued out of the principal registry]¹.

(2) An application in custody proceedings for a declaration under section 23(2) of the Act shall be made by summons in those proceedings.

NOTES
Amendments. ¹ Words inserted: SI 1997/1893.

6.3 Contents of originating summons: general provisions

(1) The originating summons under which any application is made under the Hague Convention or the European Convention shall state –

    (a) the name and date of birth of the child in respect of whom the application is made;

    (b) the names of the child's parents or guardians;

    (c) the whereabouts or suspected whereabouts of the child;

    (d) the interest of the plaintiff in the matter and the grounds of the application; and

    (e) particulars of any proceedings (including proceedings out of the jurisdiction and concluded proceedings) relating to the child,

and shall be accompanied by all relevant documents including but not limited to the documents specified in Article 8 of the Hague Convention or, as the case may be, Article 13 of the European Convention.

6.4 Contents of originating summons: particular provisions

(1) In applications under the Hague Convention, in addition to the matters specified in rule 6.3 –

    (a) the originating summons under which an application is made for the purposes of Article 8 for the return of a child shall state the identity of the person alleged to have removed or retained the child and, if different, the identity of the person with whom the child is presumed to be;

    (b) the originating summons under which an application is made for the purposes of Article 15 for a declaration shall identify the proceedings in which the request that such a declaration be obtained was made.

(2) In applications under the European Convention, in addition to the matters specified in rule 6.3, the originating summons shall identify the decision relating to custody or rights of access which is sought to be registered or enforced or in relation to which a declaration that it is not to be recognised is sought.

6.5 Defendants

The defendants to an application under the Act shall be –

    (a) the person alleged to have brought into the United Kingdom the child in respect of whom an application under the Hague Convention is made;

    (b) the person with whom the child is alleged to be;

    (c) any parent or guardian of the child who is within the United Kingdom and is not otherwise a party;

    (d) the person in whose favour a decision relating to custody has been made if he is not otherwise a party; and

    (e) any other person who appears to the court to have a sufficient interest in the welfare of the child.

6.6 Acknowledgement of service

The time limited for acknowledging service of an originating summons by which an application is made under the Hague Convention or the European Convention shall be seven days after service of the originating summons (including the day of service) or, in the case of a defendant referred to in rule 6.5(d) or (e), such further time as the Court may direct.

6.7 Evidence

(1) The plaintiff, on issuing an originating summons under the Hague Convention or the European Convention, may lodge affidavit evidence in the principal registry in support of his application and serve a copy of the same on the defendant with the originating summons.

(2) A defendant to an application under the Hague Convention or the European Convention may lodge affidavit evidence in the principal registry and serve a copy of the same on the plaintiff within seven days after service of the originating summons on him.

(3) The plaintiff in an application under the Hague Convention or the European Convention may within seven days thereafter lodge in the principal registry a statement in reply and serve a copy thereof on the defendant.

6.8 Hearing

Any application under the Act (other than an application (a) to join a defendant, (b) to dispense with service or extend the time for acknowledging service, or (c) for the transfer of proceedings) shall be heard and determined by a judge and shall be dealt with in chambers unless the court otherwise directs.

6.9 Dispensing with service

The court may dispense with service of any summons (whether originating or ordinary) in any proceedings under the Act.

6.10 Adjournment of summons

The hearing of the originating summons under which an application under the Hague Convention or the European Convention is made may be adjourned for a period not exceeding 21 days at any one time.

6.11 Stay of proceedings

(1) A party to proceedings under the Hague Convention shall, where he knows that an application relating to the merits of rights of custody is pending in or before a relevant authority, file in the principal registry a concise statement of the nature of the application which is pending, including the authority before which it is pending.

(2) A party –

   (a) to pending proceedings under section 16 of the Act, or
   (b) to proceedings as a result of which a decision relating to custody has been
        registered under section 16 of the Act,

shall, where he knows that such an application as is specified in section 20(2) of the Act [or section 42(2) of the Child Custody Act 1987 (an Act of Tynwald)][1] is pending in or before a relevant authority, file a concise statement of the nature of the application which is pending.

(3) The proper officer shall on receipt of such a statement as is mentioned in paragraph (1) or (2) notify the relevant authority in which or before whom the application is pending and shall subsequently notify it or him of the result of the proceedings.

(4) On the court receiving notification under paragraph (3) above or equivalent notification from the Court of Session [, the High Court in Northern Ireland or the High Court of Justice of the Isle of Man][1] –

    (a) where the application relates to the merits of rights of custody, all further proceedings in the action shall be stayed unless and until the proceedings under the Hague Convention in the High Court, Court of Session [, High Court in Northern Ireland or the High Court of Justice of the Isle of Man,][1], as the case may be, are dismissed, and the parties to the action shall be notified by the proper officer of the stay and of any such dismissal accordingly, and

    (b) where the application is such a one as is specified in section 20(2) of the Act, the proper officer shall notify the parties to the action.

(5) In this rule 'relevant authority' includes the High Court, a county court, a magistrates' court, the Court of Session, a sheriff court, a children's hearing within the meaning of Part III of the Social Work (Scotland) Act 1968, [the High Court in Northern Ireland or the High Court of Justice of the Isle of Man][1], a county court in Northern Ireland, a court of summary jurisdiction in Northern Ireland [, the High Court of Justice of the Isle of Man, a court of summary jurisdiction in the Isle of Man][1] or the Secretary of State.

NOTES

    Amendments. [1] Words inserted or substituted: SI 1994/2890.

6.12 Transfer of proceedings

(1) At any stage in the proceedings under the Act the court may, of its own motion or on the application by summons of any party to the proceedings issued on two days' notice, order that the proceedings be transferred to the Court of Session [, the High Court in Northern Ireland or the High Court of Justice of the Isle of Man][1].

(2) Where an order is made under paragraph (1) the proper officer shall send a copy of the order, which shall state the grounds therefor, together with the originating summons, the documents accompanying it and any evidence, to the Court of Session [, the High Court in Northern Ireland or the High Court of Justice of the Isle of Man][1], as the case may be.

(3) Where proceedings are transferred to the Court of Session [, the High Court in Northern Ireland or the High Court of Justice of the Isle of Man][1] the costs of the whole proceedings both before and after the transfer shall be at the discretion of the Court to which the proceedings are transferred.

(4) Where proceedings are transferred to the High Court from the Court of Session [, the High Court in Northern Ireland or the High Court of Justice of the Isle of Man][1] the proper officer shall notify the parties of the transfer and the proceedings shall continue as if they had begun by originating summons under rule 6.2.

NOTES

    Amendments. [1] Words substituted: SI 1994/2890.

6.13 Interim directions

An application for interim directions under section 5 or section 19 of the Act may where the case is one of urgency be made ex parte on affidavit but shall otherwise be made by summons.

6.14 ...[1]

NOTES
Amendments. [1] Rule revoked: SI 1992/2067.

6.15 Revocation and variation of registered decisions

(1) This rule applies to decisions which have been registered under section 16 of the Act and are subsequently varied or revoked by an authority in the Contracting State in which they were made.

(2) The court shall, on cancelling the registration of a decision which has been revoked, notify –

  (a) the person appearing to the court to have care of the child,
  (b) the person on whose behalf the application for registration of the decision was made, and
  (c) any other party to that application,

of the cancellation.

(3) The court shall, on being notified of the variation of a decision, notify –

  (a) the person appearing to the court to have care of the child, and
  (b) any party to the application for registration of the decision

of the variation and any such person may apply by summons in the proceedings for the registration of the decision, for the purpose of making representations to the court before the registration is varied.

(4) Any person appearing to the court to have an interest in the matter may apply by summons in the proceedings for the registration of a decision for the cancellation or variation of the registration.

6.16 Orders for disclosure of information

At any stage in proceedings under the European Convention the court may, if it has reason to believe that any person may have relevant information about the child who is the subject of those proceedings, order that person to disclose such information and may for that purpose order that the person attend before it or file affidavit evidence.

[6.17 Applications and orders under sections 33 and 34 of the Family Law Act 1986

(1) In this rule 'the 1986 Act' means the Family Law Act 1986.

(2) An application under section 33 of the 1986 Act shall be in Form C4 and an order made under that section shall be in Form C30.

(3) An application under section 34 of the 1986 Act shall be in Form C3 and an order made under that section shall be in Form C31.

(4) An application under section 33 or section 34 of the 1986 Act may be made ex parte in which case the applicant shall file the application –

  (a) where the application is made by telephone, within 24 hours after the making of the application, or
  (b) in any other case at the time when the application is made,

and shall serve a copy of the application on each respondent 48 hours after the making of the order.

(5) Where the court refuses to make an order on an ex parte application it may direct that the application be made inter partes.][1]

NOTES
    Amendments. [1] Rule inserted: SI 1994/3155.

PART VII
ENFORCEMENT OF ORDERS

Chapter 1. General

7.1 Enforcement of order for payment of money etc

(1) Before any process is issued for the enforcement of an order made in family proceedings for the payment of money to any person, an affidavit shall be filed verifying the amount due under the order and showing how that amount is arrived at.

In a case to which CCR Order 25 rule 11 (which deals with the enforcement of a High Court judgment in the county court) applies, the information required to be given in an affidavit under this paragraph may be given in the affidavit filed pursuant to that rule.

(2) Except with the leave of the district judge, no writ of fieri facias or warrant of execution shall be issued to enforce payment of any sum due under an order for ancillary relief or an order made under the provisions of section 27 of the Act of 1973 where an application for a variation order is pending.

(3) Where a warrant of execution has been issued to enforce an order made in family proceedings pending in the principal registry which are treated as pending in a divorce county court, the goods and chattels against which the warrant has been issued shall, wherever they are situate, be treated for the purposes of section 103 of the County Courts Act 1984 as being out of the jurisdiction of the principal registry.

(4) The Attachment of Earnings Act 1971 and CCR Order 27 (which deals with attachment of earnings) shall apply to the enforcement of an order made in family proceedings in the principal registry which are treated as pending in a divorce county court as if the order were an order made by such a court.

(5) Where an application under CCR Order 25, rule 3 (which deals with the oral examination of a judgment debtor) relates to an order made by a divorce county court –

   (a) the application shall be made to such divorce county court as in the opinion of the applicant is nearest to the place where the debtor resides or carries on business, and
   (b) there shall be filed with the application the affidavit required by paragraph (1) of this rule and, except where the application is made to the court in which the order sought to be enforced was made, a copy of the order shall be exhibited to the affidavit;

and accordingly paragraph (2) of the said rule 3 shall not apply.

7.2 Committal and injunction

(1) Subject to RSC Order 52, rule 6 (which, except in certain cases, requires an application for an order of committal to be heard in open court) an application for an order of committal in family proceedings pending in the High Court shall be made by summons.

(2) Where no judge is conveniently available to hear the application, then, without prejudice to CCR Order 29, rule 3(2) (which in certain circumstances gives jurisdiction to a district judge) an application for –

    (a) the discharge of any person committed, or
    (b) the discharge by consent of an injunction granted by a judge,

may be made to the district judge who may, if satisfied of the urgency of the matter and that it is expedient to do so, make any order on the application which a judge could have made.

(3) Where an order or warrant for the committal of any person to prison has been made or issued in family proceedings pending in the principal registry which are treated as pending in a divorce county court [or a county court][1], that person shall, wherever he may be, be treated for the purposes of section 122 of the County Courts Act 1984 as being out of the jurisdiction of the principal registry; but if the committal is for failure to comply with the terms of an injunction, the order or warrant may, if [the court][1] so directs, be executed by the tipstaff within any county court district.

[(3A) Where an order or warrant for the arrest or committal of any person has been made or issued in proceedings under Part IV of the Family Law Act 1996 pending in the principal registry which are treated as pending in a county court, the order or warrant may, if the court so directs, be executed by the tipstaff within any county court district.][1]

(4) For the purposes of section 118 of the County Courts Act 1984 in its application to the hearing of family proceedings at the Royal Courts of Justice [or the principal registry][1], the tipstaff shall be deemed to be an officer of the court.

NOTES

    Amendments. [1] Words inserted or substituted and paragraph inserted: SI 1997/1893.

7.3 Transfer of county court order to High Court

(1) Any person who desires the transfer to the High Court of any order made by a divorce county court in family proceedings except an order for periodical payments or for the recovery of arrears of periodical payments shall apply to the court ex parte by affidavit stating the amount which remains due under the order, and on the filing of the application the transfer shall have effect.

(2) Where an order is so transferred, it shall have the same force and effect and the same proceedings may be taken on it as if it were an order of the High Court.

****

Chapter 3. Registration and Enforcement of Custody Orders

7.7 Registration under Family Law Act 1986

(1) In this Chapter, unless the context otherwise requires –

'the appropriate court', means in relation to Scotland, the Court of Session and, in relation to Northern Ireland, the High Court [and, in relation to a specified dependent territory, the corresponding court in that territory][1];

['the appropriate officer' means, in relation to the Court of Session, the Deputy Principal Clerk of Session, in relation to the High Court in Northern Ireland, the Master (Care and Protection) of that court and, in relation to the appropriate court in a specified dependent territory, the corresponding officer of that court;][1]

…[1]

'Part I order' means an order under Part I of the Act of 1986;

…[1]

'registration' means registration under Part I of the Act of 1986, and 'register' and 'registered' shall be construed accordingly;

['specified dependent territory' means a dependent territory specified in column 1 of Schedule 1 to the Family Law Act 1986 (Dependent Territories) Order 1991.][1]

(2) The prescribed officer for the purposes of sections 27(4) and 28(1) of the Act shall be the [family proceedings department manager][2] of the principal registry and the functions of the court under sections 27(3) and 28(1) of the Act of 1986 shall be performed by the proper officer.

PART II

NOTES

Amendments. [1] Words inserted or repealed: SI 1994/2890. [2] Words substituted: SI 1997/1056.

7.8 Application to register English Part I order

(1) An application under section 27 of the Act of 1986 for the registration of a Part I order made by the High Court shall be made by lodging in the principal registry or the district registry, as the case may be, a certified copy of the order, together with a copy of any order which has varied any of the terms of the original order and an affidavit by the applicant in support of his application, with a copy thereof.

(2) An application under section 27 of the Act of 1986 for the registration of a Part I order made by a county court shall be made by filing in that court a certified copy of the order, together with a certified copy of any order which has varied any of the terms of the original order and an affidavit in support of the application, with a copy thereof.

(3) The affidavit in support under paragraphs (1) and (2) above shall state –

(a) the name and address of the applicant and his interest under the order;

(b) the name and date of birth of the child in respect of whom the order was made, his whereabouts or suspected whereabouts and the name of any person with whom he is alleged to be;

(c) the name and address of any other person who has an interest under the order and whether it has been served on him;

[(d) in which of the jurisdictions of Scotland, Northern Ireland or a specified dependent territory the order is to be registered;][1]

(e) that, to the best of the applicant's information and belief, the order is in force;

(f) whether, and if so where, the order is already registered; and

(g) details of any order known to the applicant which affects the child and is in force in the jurisdiction in which the Part I order is to be registered;

and there shall be exhibited to the affidavit any document relevant to the application.

(4) Where the documents referred to in paragraphs (1) and (3), or (2) and (3), as the case may be are to be sent to the appropriate court, the proper officer shall –

(a) retain the original affidavit and send the other documents to [the appropriate officer][1];

(b) record the fact of transmission in the records of the court; and

(c) file a copy of the documents.

(5) On receipt of notice of the registration of a Part I order in the appropriate court the proper officer shall record the fact of registration in the records of the court.

(6) If it appears to the proper officer that the Part I is no longer in force or that the child has attained the age of 16, he shall refuse to send the documents to the appropriate court and shall within 14 days of such refusal give notice of it, and the reason for it, to the applicant.

(7) If the proper officer refuses to send the documents to the appropriate court, the applicant may apply to the judge in chambers for an order that the documents (or any of them) be sent to the appropriate court.

NOTES
Amendments. [1] Words substituted: SI 1994/2890.

7.9 [Registration of orders made in Scotland, Northern Ireland or a specified dependent territory][1]

On receipt of a certified copy of an order made in [Scotland, Northern Ireland or a specified dependent territory][1] for registration, the prescribed officer shall –

(a) record the order in the register by entering particulars of –
   (i) the name and address of the applicant and his interest under the order;
   (ii) the name and whereabouts or suspected whereabouts of the child, his date of birth, and the date on which he will attain the age of 16; and
   (iii) the terms of the order, its date and the court which made it;
(b) file the certified copy and accompanying documents; and
(c) give notice to the court which sent the certified copy and to the applicant for registration that the order has been registered.

NOTES
Amendments. [1] Words substituted: SI 1994/2890.

7.10 Revocation and variation of English order

(1) Where a Part I order which is registered in the appropriate court is revoked or varied, the proper officer of the court making the subsequent order shall –

(a) send a certified copy of that order to [the appropriate officer]¹, as the case may be, and to the court which made the Part I order, if that court is different from the court making the subsequent order, for filing by that court;

(b) record the fact of transmission in the records of the court; and

(c) file a copy of the order.

(2) On receipt of notice from the appropriate court of the amendment of its register, the proper officer in the court which made the Part I order and in the court which made the subsequent order shall each record the fact of amendment.

NOTES
Amendments. ¹ Words substituted: SI 1994/2890.

7.11 [Registration of revoked, recalled or varied orders made in Scotland, Northern Ireland or a specified dependent territory]¹

(1) On receipt of a certified copy of an order made in [Scotland, Northern Ireland or a specified dependent territory]¹ which revokes, recalls or varies a registered Part I order, the proper officer shall enter particulars of the revocation, recall or variation, as the case may be, in the register, and give notice of the entry to –

(a) the court which sent the certified copy,

(b) if different, the court which made the Part I order,

(c) the applicant for registration, and

(d) if different, the applicant for the revocation, recall or variation of the order.

(2) An application under section 28(2) of the Act of 1986 shall be made by summons and may be heard and determined by a district judge.

(3) If the applicant for the Part I order is not the applicant under section 28(2) of the Act of 1986 he shall be made a defendant to the application.

(4) Where the court cancels a registration of its own motion or on an application under paragraph (2), the proper officer shall amend the register accordingly and shall give notice of the amendment to the court which made the Part I order.

NOTES
Amendments. ¹ Words substituted: SI 1994/2890.

7.12 Interim directions

(1) An application for interim directions under section 29 of the Act of 1986 may be heard and determined by a district judge.

(2) The parties to the proceedings for enforcement and, if he is not a party thereto, the applicant for the Part I order, shall be made parties to the application.

7.13 Staying and dismissal of enforcement proceedings

(1) An application under section 30(1) or 31(1) of the Act of 1986 may be heard and determined by a district judge.

(2) The parties to the proceedings for enforcement which are sought to be stayed and, if he is not a party thereto, the applicant for the Part I order shall be made parties to an application under either of the said sections.

PART II

(3) Where the court makes an order under section 30(2) or (3) or section 31(3) of the Act of 1986, the proper officer shall amend the register accordingly and shall give notice of the amendment to the court which made the Part I order and to the applicants for registration, for enforcement and for the stay or dismissal of the proceedings for enforcement.

7.14 Particulars of other proceedings

A party to proceedings for or relating to a Part I order who knows of other proceedings (including proceedings out of the jurisdiction and concluded proceedings) which relate to the child concerned shall file an affidavit stating –

    (a) in which jurisdiction and court the other proceedings were instituted;

    (b) the nature and current state of such proceedings and the relief claimed or granted;

    (c) the names of the parties to such proceedings and their relationship to the child; and

    (d) if applicable, and if known, the reasons why the relief claimed in the proceedings for or relating to the Part I order was not claimed in the other proceedings.

7.15 Inspection of register

The following persons, namely –

    (a) the applicant for registration of a registered Part I order,

    (b) any person who satisfies a district judge that he has an interest under the Part I order, and

    (c) any person who obtains the leave of a district judge,

may inspect any entry in the register relating to the order and may bespeak copies of the order and of any document relating thereto.

****

PART VIII
APPEALS

8.1 Appeals from district judges

(1) Except where paragraph (2) applies, any party may appeal from an order or decision made or given by the district judge in family proceedings in a county court to a judge on notice; and in such a case –

    (a) CCR Order 13 rule 1(10) (which enables the judge to vary or rescind an order made by the district judge in the course of proceedings), and

    (b) CCR Order 37 rule 6 (which gives a right of appeal to the judge from a judgment or final decision of the district judge),

shall not apply to the order or decision.

(2) Any order or decision granting or varying an order (or refusing to do so) –

    (a) on an application for ancillary relief, or

    (b) in proceedings to which rules 3.1, 3.2, 3.3, [or 3.6] [1] apply,

shall be treated as a final order for the purposes of CCR Order 37, rule 6.

[(3) On any appeal to which paragraph (2) applies–

(a) the appeal shall be limited to a review of the decision or order of the district judge unless the judge considers that in the circumstances of the case it would be in the interests of justice to hold a rehearing;

(b) oral evidence or evidence which was not before the district judge may be admitted if in all circumstances of the case it would be in the interests of justice to do so, irrespective of whether the appeal be by way of review or rehearing.]²

(4) Unless the court otherwise orders, any notice under this rule must be issued within 14 days of the order or decision appealed against and served not less than 14 days before the day fixed for the hearing of the appeal.

(5) Appeals under this rule shall be heard in chambers unless the judge otherwise directs.

(6) Unless the court otherwise orders, an appeal under this rule shall not operate as a stay of proceedings on the order or decision appealed against.

[(7) This rule does not apply to any appeal by a party to proceedings for the assessment of costs against a decision in those proceedings.]

NOTES

Amendments. ¹ Words substituted: SI 1997/1893. ² Paragraphs substituted and inserted: Family Proceedings (Amendment) Rules 2003, SI 2003/184.

[8.1A Appeals from orders made under Part IV of the Family Law Act 1996

(1) This rule applies to all appeals from orders made under Part IV of the Family Law Act 1996 and on such an appeal –

(a) paragraphs (2), (3), (4), (5), (7) and (8) of rule 4.22,
(b) paragraphs (5) and (6) of rule 8.1, and
(c) paragraphs (4)(e) and (6) of rule 8.2,

shall apply subject to the following provisions of this rule and with the necessary modifications.

(2) The [justices' chief executive for]² the magistrates' court from which an appeal is brought shall be served with the documents mentioned in rule 4.22(2).

(3) Where an appeal lies to the High Court, the documents required to be filed by rule 4.22(2) shall be filed in the registry of the High Court which is nearest to the magistrates' court from which the appeal is brought.

(4) Where the appeal is brought against the making of a hospital order or a guardianship order under the Mental Health Act 1983, a copy of any written evidence considered by the magistrates' court under section 37(1)(a) of the 1983 Act shall be sent by the [justices' chief executive]² to the registry of the High Court in which the documents relating to the appeal are filed in accordance with paragraph (3).

(5) A district judge may dismiss an appeal to which this rule applies for want of prosecution and may deal with any question of costs arising out of the dismissal or withdrawal of an appeal.

(6) Any order or decision granting or varying an order (or refusing to do so) in proceedings in which an application is made in accordance with rule 3.8 for –

    (a) an occupation order as described in section 33(4) of the Family Law Act 1996,

    (b) an occupation order containing any of the provisions specified in section 33(3) where the applicant or the respondent has matrimonial home rights, or

    (c) a transfer of tenancy,

shall be treated as a final order for the purposes of CCR Order 37, rule 6 and, on an appeal from such an order, the judge may exercise his own discretion in substitution for that of the district judge and the provisions of CCR Order 37, rule 6 shall apply.][1]

NOTES

    Amendments. [1] Rule inserted: SI 1997/1893. [2] Words substituted: SI 2001/821.

8.2 Appeals under Domestic Proceedings and Magistrates' Courts Act 1978

(1) Subject to paragraph (9) below, every appeal to the High Court under the Domestic Proceedings and Magistrates' Courts Act 1978 shall be heard by a Divisional Court of the Family Division and shall be entered by lodging three copies of the notice of motion in the principal registry.

(2) The notice must be served, and the appeal entered, within 6 weeks after the date of the order appealed against.

(3) Notice of the motion may be served in accordance with RSC Order 65, rule 5.

(4) On entering the appeal, or as soon as practicable thereafter, the appellant shall, unless otherwise directed, lodge in the principal registry –

    (a) three certified copies of the summons and of the order appealed against, and of any order staying its execution,

    (b) three copies of the clerk's notes of the evidence,

    (c) three copies of the justices' reasons for their decision,

    (d) a certificate that notice of the motion has been duly served on the clerk and on every party affected by the appeal, and

    (e) where the notice of the motion includes an application to extend the time for bringing the appeal, a certificate (and a copy thereof) by the appellant's solicitor, or the appellant if he is acting in person, setting out the reasons for the delay and the relevant dates.

(5) If the clerk's notes of the evidence are not produced, the court may hear and determine the appeal on any other evidence or statement of what occurred in the proceedings before the magistrates' court as appears to the court to be sufficient.

(6) The court shall not be bound to allow the appeal on the ground merely of misdirection or improper reception or rejection of evidence unless, in the opinion of the court, substantial wrong or miscarriage of justice has been thereby occasioned.

(7) A district judge may dismiss an appeal to which this rule applies for want of prosecution or, with the consent of the parties, may dismiss the appeal or give leave for it to be withdrawn, and may deal with any question of costs arising out of the dismissal or withdrawal.

(8) Any interlocutory application in connection with or for the purpose of any appeal to which this rule applies may be heard and disposed of before a single judge.

(9) Where an appeal to which this rule applies relates only to the amount of any periodical or lump sum payment ordered to be made, it shall, unless the President otherwise directs, be heard and determined by a single judge, and in that case –

    (a) for the references in paragraphs (1) and (4)(a), (b) and (c) to three copies of the documents therein mentioned there shall be substituted references to one copy;

    (b) the parties may agree in writing or the President may direct that the appeal be heard and determined at a divorce town.

[8.3 Appeals under section 13 of the Administration of Justice Act 1960

Proceedings within paragraph 3(d) of Schedule 1 to the Supreme Court Act 1981 shall be heard and determined by a Divisional Court of the Family Division and rule 8.2(4) shall apply, with the necessary modifications, to such proceedings.] [1]

NOTES
    Amendments. [1] Rule inserted: SI 1991/2113.

PART II

PART IX
DISABILITY

9.1 Interpretation and scope of Part IX

(1) In this Part –

    'patient' means a person who, by reason of mental disorder within the meaning of the Mental Health Act 1983, is incapable of managing and administering his property and affairs;
    'person under disability' means a person who is a minor or a patient;
    'Part VII' means Part VII of the Mental Health Act 1983.

(2) So far as they relate to minors [who are the subject of applications],[1] the provisions of this Part of these rules shall not apply to proceedings which are specified proceedings within the meaning of section 41(6) of the Children Act 1989 and, with respect to proceedings which are dealt with together with specified proceedings, this Part shall have effect subject to the said section 41 and Part IV of these rules.

[(3) Rule 9.2A shall apply only to proceedings under the Act of 1989 or the inherent jurisdiction of the High Court with respect to minors.] [2]

NOTES
    Amendments. [1] Words inserted: SI 1991/2113. [2] Words inserted: SI 1992/456.

9.2 Person under disability must sue by next friend etc

(1) [Except where rule 9.2A or any other rule otherwise provides, a person under disability may begin and prosecute any family proceedings only by his next friend and may defend any such proceedings only][2] by his guardian ad litem and, except

as otherwise provided by this rule, it shall not be necessary for a guardian ad litem to be appointed by the court.

(2) No person's name shall be used in any proceedings as next friend of a person under disability unless he is the Official Solicitor or the documents mentioned in paragraph (7) have been filed.

(3) Where a person is authorised under Part VII to conduct legal proceedings in the name of a patient or on his behalf, that person shall, subject to [paragraph (2)]¹ be entitled to be next friend or guardian ad litem of the patient in any family proceedings to which his authority extends.

(4) Where a person entitled to defend any family proceedings is a patient and there is no person authorised under Part VII to defend the proceedings in his name or on his behalf, then –

> (a) the Official Solicitor shall, if he consents, be the patient's guardian ad litem, but at any stage of the proceedings an application may be made on not less than four days' notice to the Official Solicitor, for the appointment of some other person as guardian;
> (b) in any other case, an application may be made on behalf of the patient for the appointment of a guardian ad litem;

and there shall be filed in support of any application under this paragraph the documents mentioned in paragraph (7).

(5) Where a petition, answer, originating application or originating summons has been served on a person whom there is reasonable ground for believing to be a person under disability and no notice of intention to defend has been given, or answer or affidavit in answer filed, on his behalf, the party at whose instance the document was served shall, before taking any further steps in the proceedings, apply to a district judge for directions as to whether a guardian ad litem should be appointed to act for that person in the cause, and on any such application the district judge may, if he considers it necessary in order to protect the interests of the person served, order that some proper person be appointed his guardian ad litem.

(6) [Except where a minor is prosecuting or defending proceedings under rule 9.2A, no]² notice of intention to defend shall be given, or answer or affidavit in answer filed, by or on behalf of a person under disability unless the person giving the notice or filing the answer or affidavit –

> (a) is the Official Solicitor or, in a case to which paragraph (4) applies, is the Official Solicitor or has been appointed by the court to be guardian ad litem; or
> (b) in any other case, has filed the documents mentioned in paragraph (7).

(7) The documents referred to in paragraphs (2), (4) and (6) are –

> (a) a written consent to act by the proposed next friend or guardian ad litem;
> (b) where the person under disability is a patient and the proposed next friend or guardian ad litem is authorised under Part VII to conduct the proceedings in his name or on his behalf, an office copy, sealed with the seal of the Court of Protection, of the order or other authorisation made or given under Part VII; and
> (c) except where the proposed next friend or guardian ad litem is authorised as mentioned in sub-paragraph (b), a certificate by the solicitor acting for the person under disability –

    (i) that he knows or believes that the person to whom the certificate relates is a minor or patient, stating (in the case of a patient) the grounds of his knowledge or belief and, where the person under disability is a patient, that there is no person authorised as aforesaid, and

    (ii) that the person named in the certificate as next friend or guardian ad litem has no interest in the cause or matter in question adverse to that of the person under disability and that he is a proper person to be next friend or guardian.

NOTES

  Amendments. ¹ Words substituted: SI 1991/2113. ² Words substituted: SI 1992/456.

[9.2A Certain minors may sue without next friend etc

(1) Where a person entitled to begin, prosecute or defend any proceedings to which this rule applies, is a minor to whom this Part applies, he may subject to paragraph (4), begin, prosecute or defend, as the case may be, such proceedings without a next friend or guardian ad litem –

  (a) where he has obtained the leave of the court for that purpose; or

  (b) where a solicitor –

    (i) considers that the minor is able, having regard to his understanding, to give instructions in relation to the proceedings; and

    (ii) has accepted instructions from the minor to act for him in the proceedings and, where the proceedings have begun, is so acting.

(2) A minor shall be entitled to apply for the leave of the court under paragraph (1)(a) without a next friend or guardian ad litem either –

  (a) by filing a written request for leave setting out the reasons for the application, or

  (b) by making an oral request for leave at any hearing in the proceedings.

(3) On considering a request for leave filed under paragraph (2)(a), the court shall either –

  (a) grant the request, whereupon the proper officer shall communicate the decision to the minor and, where the leave relates to the prosecution or defence of existing proceedings, to the other parties to those proceedings, or

  (b) direct that the request be heard ex parte, whereupon the proper officer shall fix a date for such a hearing and give to the minor making the request such notice of the date so fixed as the court may direct.

(4) Where a minor has a next friend or guardian ad litem in proceedings and the minor wishes to prosecute or defend the remaining stages of the proceedings without a next friend or guardian ad litem, the minor may apply to the court for leave for that purpose and for the removal of the next friend or guardian ad litem; and paragraph (2) shall apply to the application as if it were an application under paragraph (1)(a).

(5) On considering a request filed under paragraph (2) by virtue of paragraph (4), the court shall either –

  (a) grant the request, whereupon the proper officer shall communicate the decision to the minor and next friend or guardian ad litem concerned and to all other parties to the proceedings, or

   (b) direct that the request be heard, whereupon the proper officer shall fix a date for such a hearing and give to the minor and next friend or guardian ad litem concerned such notice of the date so fixed as the court may direct;

provided that the court may act under sub-paragraph (a) only if it is satisfied that the next friend or guardian ad litem does not oppose the request.

(6) Where the court is considering whether to –

   (a) grant leave under paragraph (1)(a), or

   (b) grant leave under paragraph (4) and remove a next friend or guardian ad litem,

it shall grant the leave sought and, as the case may be, remove the next friend or guardian ad litem if it considers that the minor concerned has sufficient understanding to participate as a party in the proceedings concerned or proposed without a next friend or guardian ad litem.

[(6A) In exercising its powers under paragraph (6) the court may order the next friend or guardian ad litem to take such part in the proceedings as the court may direct.][2]

(7) Where a request for leave is granted at a hearing fixed under paragraph (3)(b) (in relation to the prosecution or defence of proceedings already begun) or (5)(b), the proper officer shall forthwith communicate the decision to the other parties to the proceedings.

(8) The court may revoke any leave granted under paragraph (1)(a) where it considers that the child does not have sufficient understanding to participate as a party in the proceedings concerned without a next friend or guardian ad litem.

(9) Without prejudice to any requirement of CCR Order 50, rule 5 or RSC Order 67, where a solicitor is acting for a minor in proceedings which the minor is prosecuting or defending without a next friend or guardian ad litem by virtue of paragraph (1)(b) and either of the conditions specified in the paragraph (1)(b)(i) and (ii) cease to be fulfilled, he shall forthwith so inform the court.

(10) Where –

   (a) the court revokes any leave under paragraph (8), or

   (b) either of the conditions specified in paragraph (1)(b)(i) and (ii) is no longer fulfilled,

the court may, if it considers it necessary in order to protect the interests of the minor concerned, order that some proper person be appointed his next friend or guardian ad litem.

(11) Where a minor is of sufficient understanding to begin, prosecute or defend proceedings without a next friend or guardian ad litem –

   (a) he may nevertheless begin, prosecute or defend them by his next friend or guardian ad litem; and

   (b) where he is prosecuting or defending proceedings by his next friend or guardian ad litem, the respective powers and duties of the minor and next friend or guardian ad litem, except those conferred or imposed by this rule, shall not be affected by the minor's ability to dispense with a next friend or guardian ad litem under the provisions of this rule.][1]

NOTES

Amendments. [1] Rule inserted: SI 1992/456. [2] Paragraph inserted: SI 1997/1893.

9.3 Service on person under disability

(1) Where a document to which rule 2.9 applies is required to be served on a person under disability ...[1], it shall be served –

    (a) in the case of a minor who is not also a patient, on his father or guardian or, if he has no father or guardian, on the person with whom he resides or in whose care he is;

    (b) in the case of a patient –

        (i) on the person (if any) who is authorised under Part VII to conduct in the name of the patient or on his behalf the proceedings in connection with which the document is to be served, or

        (ii) if there is no person so authorised, on the Official Solicitor if he has consented under rule 9.2(4) to be the guardian ad litem of the patient, or

        (iii) in any other case, on the person with whom the patient resides or in whose care he is –

    Provided that the court may order that a document which has been, or is to be, served on the person under disability or on a person other than one mentioned in sub-paragraph (a) or (b) shall be deemed to be duly served on the person under disability.

(2) Where a document is served in accordance with paragraph (1) it shall be indorsed with a notice in Form M24; and after service has been effected the person at whose instance the document was served shall, unless the Official Solicitor is the guardian ad litem of the person under disability or the court otherwise directs, file an affidavit by the person on whom the document was served stating whether the contents of the document were, or its purport was, communicated to the person under disability and, if not, the reasons for not doing so.

NOTES
   Amendments. [1] Words revoked: SI 1992/2067.

9.4 Petition for nullity on ground of mental disorder

(1) Where a petition for nullity has been presented on the ground that at the time of the marriage the respondent was suffering from mental disorder within the meaning of the Mental Health Act 1983 of such a kind or to such an extent as to be unfitted for marriage, then, whether or not the respondent gives notice of intention to defend, the petitioner shall not proceed with the cause without the leave of the district judge.

(2) The district judge by whom an application for leave is heard may make it a condition of granting leave that some proper person be appointed to act as guardian ad litem of the respondent.

9.5 Separate representation of children

[(1) Without prejudice to rules 2.57 and 9.2A, if in any family proceedings it appears to the court that it is in the best interest of any child to be made a party to the proceedings, the court may appoint –

    (a) an officer of the service;

    (b) (if he consents) the Official Solicitor; or

    (c) (if he consents) some other proper person,

PART II

to be the guardian ad litem of the child with authority to take part in the proceedings on the child's behalf.] [1]

(2) An order under paragraph (1) may be made by the court of its own motion or on the application of a party to the proceedings or of the proposed guardian ad litem.

(3) The court may at any time direct that an application be made by a party for an order under paragraph (1) and may stay the proceedings until the application has been made.

(4) ...[1]

(5) Unless otherwise directed, a person appointed under this rule or rule 2.57 to be the guardian ad litem of a child in any family proceedings shall be treated as a party for the purpose of any provision of these rules requiring a document to be served on or notice to be given to a party to the proceedings.

[(6) Where the guardian ad litem appointed under this rule is an officer of the service, rules 4.11 and 4.11A shall apply to him as they apply to a children's guardian appointed under section 41 of the Children Act 1989.] [1]

NOTES
   Amendments. [1] Paragraph substituted, omitted or inserted: SI 2001/821.

PART X
PROCEDURE (GENERAL)

10.1 Application

The provisions of this Part apply to all family proceedings, but have effect subject to the provisions of any other Part of these rules.

10.2 Service on solicitors

(1) Where a document is required by these rules to be sent to any person who is acting by a solicitor, service shall, subject to any other direction or order, be effected –

   (a) by sending the document by first class post to the solicitor's address for service; or
   (b) where that address includes a numbered box at a document exchange, at that document exchange or at a document exchange which transmits documents every business day to that document exchange; or
   (c) by FAX (as defined by RSC Order 1, rule 4(1)) in accordance with the provisions of RSC Order 65, rule 5(2B).

(2) Any document which is left at a document exchange in accordance with paragraph (1)(b) shall, unless the contrary is proved, be deemed to have been served on the second day after the day on which it is left.

(3) Where no other mode of service is prescribed, directed or ordered, service may additionally be effected by leaving the document at the solicitor's address.

10.3 Service on person acting in person

(1) Subject to paragraph (3) and to any other direction or order, where a document is required by these rules to be sent to any person who is acting in person, service shall be effected by sending the document by first class post to the address given by him or, if he has not given an address for service, to his last known address.

(2) Subject to paragraph (3), where no other mode of service is prescribed, directed or ordered, service may additionally be effected by delivering the document to him or by leaving it at the address specified in paragraph (1).

(3) Where it appears to the district judge that it is impracticable to deliver the document to the person to be served and that, if the document were left at, or sent by post to, the address specified in paragraph (1), it would be unlikely to reach him, the district judge may dispense with service of the document.

10.4 Service by bailiff in proceedings in principal registry

Where, in any proceedings pending in the principal registry which are treated as pending in a divorce county court, a document is to be served by bailiff, it shall be sent for service to the proper officer of the county court within the district of which the document is to be served.

10.5 Proof of service by officer of court etc

(1) Where a petition is sent to any person by an officer of the court, he shall note the date of posting in the records of the court.

(2) Without prejudice to section 133 of the County Court Act 1984 (proof of service of summonses etc) a record made pursuant to paragraph (1) shall be evidence of the facts stated therein.

(3) Where the court has authorised notice by advertisement to be substituted for service and the advertisement has been inserted by some person other than the proper officer, that person shall file copies of the newspapers containing the advertisement.

10.6 Service out of England and Wales

(1) Any document in family proceedings may be served out of England and Wales without leave either in the manner prescribed by these rules or –

- (a) where the proceedings are pending in the High Court, in accordance with RSC Order 11, rules 5 and 6 (which relates to the service of a writ abroad); or
- (b) where the proceedings are pending in a divorce county court, in accordance with CCR Order 8, rules 8 to 10 (which relate to the service of process abroad).

(2) Where the document is served in accordance with RSC Order 11, rules 5 and 6, those rules and rule 8 of the said Order 11 (which deals with the expenses incurred by the Secretary of State) shall have effect in relation to service of the document as they have effect in relation to service of notice of a writ, except that the official certificate of service referred to in paragraph (5) of the said rule 5 shall, if the document was served personally, show the server's means of knowledge of the identity of the person served.

(3) Where the document is served in accordance with CCR Order 8, rules 8 to 10, those rules shall have effect subject to the following modifications –

    (a) the document need not be served personally on the person required to be served so long as it is served in accordance with the law of the country in which service is effected;

    (b) the official certificate or declaration with regard to service referred to in paragraph (6) of the said rule 10 shall, if the document was served personally, show the server's means of knowledge of the identity of the person served; and

    (c) in paragraph (7) of the said rule 10 the words 'or in the manner in which default summonses are required to be served' shall be omitted.

(4) Where a petition is to be served on a person out of England and Wales, then –

    (a) the time within which that person must give notice of intention to defend shall be determined having regard to the practice adopted under RSC Order 11, rule 4(4) (which requires an order for leave to serve a writ out of the jurisdiction to limit the time for appearance) and the notice in Form M5 shall be amended accordingly;

    (b) if the petition is to be served otherwise than in accordance with RSC Order 11, rules 5 and 6, or CCR Order 8, rules 8 to 10, and there is reasonable ground for believing that the person to be served does not understand English, the petition shall be accompanied by a translation, approved by the district judge, of the notice in Form M5, in the official language of the country in which service is to be effected or, if there is more than one official language of that country, in any one of those languages which is appropriate to the place where service is to be effected; but this sub-paragraph shall not apply in relation to a document which is to be served in a country in which the official language, or one of the official languages, is English.

(5) Where a document specifying the date of hearing of any proceedings is to be served out of England and Wales, the date shall be fixed having regard to the time which would be limited under paragraph (4)(a) for giving notice of intention to defend if the document were a petition.

10.7 Mode of giving notice

Unless otherwise directed, any notice which is required by these rules to be given to any person shall be in writing, and may be given in any manner in which service may be effected under RSC Order 65, rule 5.

10.8 Notice of intention to defend

(1) In these rules any reference to a notice of intention to defend is a reference to an acknowledgment of service in Form M6 containing a statement to the effect that the person by whom or on whose behalf it is signed intends to defend the proceedings to which the acknowledgment relates, and any reference to giving notice of intention to defend is a reference to returning such a notice to the court office.

(2) In relation to any person on whom there is served a document requiring or authorising an acknowledgment of service to be returned to the court office, references in these rules to the time limited for giving notice of intention to defend are references –

(a) to seven days after service of the document, in the case of notice of intention to defend a petition under Part II of these rules, and

(b) in any other case, to 14 days or such other time as may be fixed.

(3) Subject to paragraph (2) a person may give notice of intention to defend notwithstanding that he has already returned to the court office an acknowledgment of service not constituting such a notice.

10.9 Mode of making applications

Except where these rules, or any rules applied by these rules, otherwise provide, every application in family proceedings –

(a) shall be made to a district judge;

(b) shall, if the proceedings are pending in the High Court, be made by summons or, if the proceedings are pending in a divorce county court, be made in accordance with CCR Order 13, rule 1 (which deals with applications in the course of proceedings).

10.10 Orders for transfer of family proceedings

(1) Where a cause is pending in the High Court, the district judge of the registry in which the cause is pending or a judge may order that the cause be transferred to another registry.

(2) Where a cause is pending in a divorce county court, the court may order that the cause be transferred to another divorce county court.

(3) Paragraphs (1) and (2) shall apply to applications in causes as they apply to causes; but before making an order for transfer of an application the court shall consider whether it would be more convenient to transfer the cause under paragraph (1) or (2), as the case may be.

(4) The court shall not, either of its own motion or on the application of any party, make an order under paragraph (1), (2) or (3) unless the parties have either –

(a) had an opportunity of being heard on the question, or

(b) consented to such an order.

(5) Where the parties, or any of them, desire to be heard on the question of a transfer, the court shall give the parties notice of a date, time and place at which the question will be considered.

(6) Paragraphs (4) and (5) shall apply with the necessary modifications to an order for the transfer of family proceedings under section 38 or 39 of the Act of 1984 as they apply to an order under paragraph (1) or (2) of this rule.

(7) Paragraphs (4) and (5) shall not apply where the court makes an order for transfer under paragraphs (1), (2) or (3) in compliance with the provisions of any Order made under Part I of Schedule 11 to the Children Act 1989.

10.11 Procedure on transfer of cause or application

(1) Where any cause or application is ordered to be transferred from one court or registry to another, the proper officer of the first-mentioned court or registry shall, unless otherwise directed, give notice of the transfer to the parties.

(2) Any provision in these rules, or in any order made or notice given pursuant to these rules, for the transfer of proceedings between a divorce county court and the

PART II

High Court shall, in relation to proceedings which, after the transfer, are to continue in the principal registry, be construed –

    (a) in the case of a transfer from the High Court to a divorce county court, as a provision for the proceedings to be treated as pending in a divorce county court, and

    (b) in the case of a transfer from a divorce county court to the High Court, as a provision for the proceedings no longer to be treated as pending in a divorce county court.

(3) Proceedings transferred from a divorce county court to the High Court pursuant to any provision in these rules shall, unless the order of transfer otherwise directs, proceed in the registry nearest to the divorce county court from which they are transferred, but nothing in this paragraph shall prejudice any power under these rules to order the transfer of the proceedings to a different registry.

10.12 Evidence by affidavit

On any application made –

    (a) in a county court, by originating application or in accordance with CCR Order 13, rule 1 (which deals with applications in the course of proceedings) or

    (b) in the High Court, by originating summons, notice or motion,

evidence may be given by affidavit unless these rules otherwise provide or the court otherwise directs, but the court may, on the application of any party, order the attendance for cross-examination of the person making any such affidavit; and where, after such an order has been made, that person does not attend, his affidavit shall not be used as evidence without the leave of the court.

10.13 Taking of affidavit in county court proceedings

In relation to family proceedings pending or treated as pending in a divorce county court, section 58(1) of the County Courts Act 1984 shall have effect as if after paragraph (c) there were inserted the following words –

    'or

    (d) a district judge of the principal registry; or

    (e) any officer of the principal registry authorised by the President under section 2 of the Commissioners for Oaths Act 1889; or

    (f) any clerk in the Central Office of the Royal Courts of Justice authorised to take affidavits for the purposes of proceedings in the Supreme Court.'.

10.14 Evidence of marriage outside England and Wales

(1) The celebration of a marriage outside England and Wales and its validity under the law of the country where it was celebrated may, in any family proceedings in which the existence and validity of the marriage is not disputed, be proved by the evidence of one of the parties to the marriage and the production of a document purporting to be –

    (a) a marriage certificate or similar document issued under the law in force in that country; or

    (b) a certified copy of an entry in a register of marriages kept under the law in force in that country.

(2) Where a document produced by virtue of paragraph (1) is not in English it shall, unless otherwise directed, be accompanied by a translation certified by a notary public or authenticated by affidavit.

(3) This rule shall not be construed as precluding the proof of a marriage in accordance with the Evidence (Foreign, Dominion and Colonial Documents) Act 1933 or in any other manner authorised apart from this rule.

[10.14A Power of court to limit cross-examination

The court may limit the issues on which an officer of the service may be cross-examined.][1]

NOTES
  Amendments. [1] Rule inserted: SI 2001/821.

10.15 Official shorthand note etc of proceedings

(1) Unless the judge otherwise directs, an official shorthand note shall be taken of the proceedings at the trial in open court of every cause pending in the High Court.

(2) An official shorthand note may be taken of any other proceedings before a judge or district judge if directions for the taking of such a note are given by the Lord Chancellor.

(3) The shorthand writer shall sign the note and certify it to be a correct shorthand note of the proceedings and shall retain the note unless he is directed by the district judge to forward it to the court.

(4) On being so directed the shorthand writer shall furnish the court with a transcript of the whole or such part as may be directed of the shorthand note.

(5) Any party, any person who has intervened in a cause, the Queen's Proctor or, where a declaration of parentage has been made under [section 55A][1] of the Act of 1986, the Registrar General shall be entitled to require from the shorthand writer a transcript of the shorthand note, and the shorthand writer shall, at the request of any person so entitled, supply that person with a transcript of the whole or any part of the note on payment of the shorthand writer's charges authorised by any scheme in force providing for the taking of official shorthand notes of legal proceedings.

(6) Except as aforesaid, the shorthand writer shall not, without the permission of the court, furnish the shorthand note or a transcript of the whole or any part thereof to anyone.

(7) In these Rules references to a shorthand note include references to a record of the proceedings made by mechanical means and in relation to such a record references to the shorthand writer shall have effect as if they were references to the person responsible for transcribing the record.

NOTES
  Amendments. [1] Text substituted: SI 2001/821.

10.16 Copies of decrees and orders

(1) A copy of every decree shall be sent by the proper officer to every party to the cause.

(2) A sealed or other copy of a decree or order made in open court shall be issued to any person requiring it on payment of the prescribed fee.

10.17 Service of order

(1) Where an order made in family proceedings has been drawn up, the proper officer of the court where the order is made shall, unless otherwise directed, send a copy of the order to every party affected by it.

(2) Where a party against whom the order is made is acting by a solicitor, a copy may, if the district judge thinks fit, be sent to that party as if he were acting in person, as well as to his solicitor.

(3) It shall not be necessary for the person in whose favour the order was made to prove that a copy of the order has reached any other party to whom it is required to be sent.

(4) This rule is without prejudice to RSC Order 45, rule 7 (which deals with the service of an order to do or abstain from doing an act), CCR Order 29 rule 1 (which deals with orders enforceable by committal) and any other rule or enactment for the purposes of which an order is required to be served in a particular way.

10.18 No notice of intention to proceed after year's delay

RSC Order 3, rule 6 (which requires a party to give notice of intention to proceed after a year's delay) shall not apply to any proceedings pending in the High Court.

10.19 Filing of documents at place of hearing etc

Where the file of any family proceedings has been sent from one divorce county court or registry to another for the purpose of a hearing or for some other purpose, any document needed for that purpose and required to be filed shall be filed in the other court or registry.

10.20 Inspection etc of documents retained in court

(1) Subject to rule 10.21, a party to any family proceedings or his solicitor or the Queen's Proctor or a person appointed under rule 2.57 or 9.5 to be the guardian ad litem of a child in any family proceedings may have a search made for, and may inspect and bespeak a copy of, any document filed or lodged in the court office in those proceedings.

(2) Any person not entitled to a copy of a document under paragraph (1) above who intends to make an application under the Hague Convention (as defined in section 1(1) of the Child Abduction and Custody Act 1985) in a Contracting State (as defined in section 2 of that Act) other than the United Kingdom shall, if he satisfies the [court][1] that he intends to make such an application, be entitled to obtain a copy bearing the seal of the court of any order relating to the custody of the child in respect of whom the application is to be made.

(3) Except as provided by rules 2.36(4) and 3.16(10) and paragraphs (1) and (2) of this rule, no document filed or lodged in the court office other than a decree or order made in open court shall be open to inspection by any person without the leave of the district judge, and no copy of any such document, or of an extract from any such document, shall be taken by, or issued to, any person without such leave.

NOTES
Amendments. [1] Word substituted: SI 1992/2067.

10.21 Disclosure of addresses

(1) [Subject to rule 2.3][1] nothing in these rules shall be construed as requiring any party to reveal the address of their private residence (or that of any child) save by order of the court.

(2) Where a party declines to reveal an address in reliance upon paragraph (1) above, he shall give notice of that address to the court in Form [C8][2] and that address shall not be revealed to any person save by order of the court.

NOTES
Amendments. [1] Words inserted: SI 1991/2113. [2] Words substituted: SI 1994/3155.

[10.21A Disclosure of information under the Act of 1991

Where the Secretary of State requires a person mentioned in regulation 2(2) or (3)(a) of the Child Support (Information, Evidence and Disclosure) Regulations 1992 to furnish information or evidence for a purpose mentioned in regulation 3(1) of those Regulations, nothing in rules 4.23 (confidentiality of documents), 10.20 (inspection etc of documents in court) or 10.21 (disclosure of addresses) shall prevent that person from furnishing the information or evidence sought or require him to seek leave of the court before doing so.] [1]

NOTES
Amendments. [1] Rule inserted: SI 1993/295.

10.22 Practice to be observed in district registries and divorce county courts

(1) The President and the senior district judge may, with the concurrence of the Lord Chancellor, issue directions for the purpose of securing in the district registries and the divorce county courts due observance of statutory requirements and uniformity of practice in family proceedings.

(2) RSC Order 63, rule 11 (which requires the practice of the Central Office to be followed in the district registries) shall not apply to family proceedings.

10.23 Transitional provisions

(1) Subject to paragraph (2) below, these rules shall apply, so far as practicable, to any proceedings pending on the day on which they come into force.

(2) Rule 8.1 shall not apply to an appeal from an order or decision made or given by a district judge in matrimonial proceedings in a divorce county court where notice of appeal has been filed before the day on which these rules come into force.

(3) Where, by reason of paragraph (1) above, these rules do not apply to particular proceedings pending on the day on which they come into force, the rules in force immediately before that day shall continue to apply to those proceedings.

(4) Nothing in this rule shall be taken as prejudicing the operation of the provisions of the Interpretation Act 1978 as regards the effect of repeals.

(5) Without prejudice to the generality of paragraph (1) above (and for the avoidance of doubt) rule 2.39 shall not apply to any proceedings which are pending within the meaning of paragraph 1(1) of Schedule 14 to the Children Act 1989.

[10.24 Applications for relief which is precluded by the Act of 1991

(1) Where an application is made for an order which, in the opinion of the district judge, the court would be prevented from making by section 8 or 9 of the Act of 1991, the proper officer may send a notice in Form M34 to the applicant.

(2) In the first instance, the district judge shall consider the matter under paragraph (1) himself, without holding a hearing.

(3) Where a notice is sent under paragraph (1), no requirement of these rules, except for those of this rule, as to the service of the application by the proper officer or as to any other procedural step to follow the making of an application of the type in question, shall apply unless and until the court directs that they shall apply or that they shall apply to such extent and subject to such modifications as may be specified in the direction.

(4) Where an applicant who has been sent a notice under paragraph (1) informs the proper officer in writing, within 14 days of the date of the notice, that he wishes to persist with his application, the proper officer shall refer the matter to the district judge for action in accordance with paragraph (5).

(5) Where the district judge acts in accordance with this paragraph, he shall give such directions as he considers appropriate for the matter to be heard and determined by the court and, without prejudice to the generality of the foregoing, such directions may provide for the hearing to be ex parte.

(6) Where directions are given under paragraph (5), the proper officer shall inform the applicant of the directions and, in relation to the other parties, –
    (a) send them a copy of the application;
    (b) where the hearing is to be ex parte, inform them briefly –
        (i) of the nature and effect of the notice under this rule,
        (ii) that the matter is being resolved ex parte, and
        (iii) that they will be informed of the result in due course; and
    (c) where the hearing is to be inter partes, inform them of –
        (i) the circumstances which led to the directions being given, and
        (ii) the directions.

(7) Where a notice has been sent under paragraph (1) and the proper officer is not informed under paragraph (4), the application shall be treated as having been withdrawn.

(8) Where the matter is heard pursuant to directions under paragraph (5) and the court determines that it would be prevented by section 8 or 9 of the Act of 1991 from making the order sought by the application, it shall dismiss the application.

(9) Where the court dismisses an application under this rule it shall give its reasons in writing, copies of which shall be sent to the parties by the proper officer.

(10) In this rule, 'the matter' means the question whether the making of an order in the terms sought by the application would be prevented by section 8 or 9 of the Act of 1991.][1]

[10.25 Modification of rule 10.24 in relation to non-free-standing applications

Where a notice is sent under rule 10.24(1) in respect of an application which is contained in a petition or other document ('the document') which contains material extrinsic to the application –

    (a) the document shall, until the contrary is directed under sub-paragraph (c) of this rule, be treated as if it did not contain the application in respect of which the notice was served;

    (b) the proper officer shall, when he sends copies of the document to the respondents under any provision of these rules, attach a copy of the notice under rule 10.24(1) and a notice informing the respondents of the effect of sub-paragraph (a) of this paragraph; and

    (c) if it is determined, under rule 10.24, that the court would not be prevented, by section 8 or 9 of the Act of 1991, from making the order sought by the application, the court shall direct that the document shall be treated as if it contained the application, and it may give such directions as it considers appropriate for the conduct of the proceedings in consequence of that direction.]¹

[10.26 Human Rights Act 1998

(1) In this rule –

'originating document' means a petition, application, originating application, originating summons or other originating process;
'answer' means an answer or other document filed or served by a party in reply to an originating document (but not an acknowledgement of service);
'Convention right' has the same meaning as in the Human Rights Act 1998;
'declaration of incompatibility' means a declaration of incompatibility under section 4 of the Human Rights Act 1998.

(2) A party who seeks to rely on any provision of or right arising under the Human Rights Act 1998 or seeks a remedy available under that Act –

    (a) shall state that fact in his originating document or (as the case may be) answer; and

    (b) shall in his originating document or (as the case may be) answer –
        (i) give precise details of the Convention right which it is alleged has been infringed and details of the alleged infringement;
        (ii) specify the relief sought;
        (iii) state if the relief sought includes a declaration of incompatibility.

(3) A party who seeks to amend his originating document (as the case may be) answer to include the matters referred to in paragraph (2) shall, unless the court orders otherwise, do so as soon as possible and in any event not less than 28 days before the hearing.

(4) The court shall not make a declaration of incompatibility unless 21 days' notice, or such other period of notice as the court directs, has been given to the Crown.

(5) Where notice has been given to the Crown a Minister, or other person permitted by the Human Rights Act 1998, shall be joined as a party on giving notice to the court.

(6) Where a party has included in his originating document or (as the case may be) answer:

    (a) a claim for a declaration of incompatibility, or
    (b) an issue for the court to decide which may lead to the court considering making a declaration of incompatibility,

then the court may at any time consider whether notice should be given to the Crown as required by the Human Rights Act 1998 and give directions for the content and service of the notice.

(7) In the case of an appeal for which permission to appeal is required, the court shall, unless it decides that it is appropriate to do so at another stage in the proceedings, consider the issues and give the directions referred to in paragraph (6) when deciding whether to give such permission.

(8) If paragraph (7) does not apply, and a hearing for directions would, but for this rule, be held, the court shall unless it decides that it is appropriate to do so at another stage in the proceedings, consider the issues and give the directions referred to in paragraph (6) at the hearing for directions.

(9) If neither paragraph (7) nor paragraph (8) applies, the court shall consider the issues and give the directions referred to in paragraph (6) when it considers it appropriate to do so, and may fix a hearing for this purpose.

(10) Where a party amends his originating document or (as the case may be) answer to include any matter referred to in paragraph (6)(a), then the court will consider whether notice should be given to the Crown and give directions for the content and service of the notice.

(11) In paragraphs (12) to (16), 'notice' means the notice given under paragraph (4).

(12) The notice shall be served on the person named in the list published under section 17 of the Crown Proceedings Act 1947.

(13) The notice shall be in the form directed by the court.

(14) Unless the court orders otherwise, the notice shall be accompanied by the directions given by the court and the originating document and any answers in the proceedings.

(15) Copies of the notice shall be served on all the parties.

(16) The court may require the parties to assist in the preparation of the notice.

(17) Unless the court orders otherwise, the Minister or other person permitted by the Human Rights Act 1998 to be joined as a party shall, if he wishes to be joined, give notice of his intention to be joined as a party to the court and every other party, and where the Minister has nominated a person to be joined as a party the notice must be accompanied by the written nomination.

(18) Where a claim is made under [section 7(1)][2] of the Human Rights Act 1998 in respect of a judicial act the procedure in paragraphs (6) to (17) shall also apply, but the notice to be given to the Crown:

(a) shall be given to the Lord Chancellor and shall be served on the Treasury Solicitor on his behalf; and

(b) shall also give details of the judicial act which is the subject of the claim and of the court that made it.

(19) Where in any appeal a claim is made [under section 7(1) of that Act and section 9(3) and (4) applies][2] –

(a) that claim must be set out in the notice of appeal; and

(b) notice must be given to the Crown in accordance with paragraph (18).

(20) The appellant must in a notice of appeal to which paragraph (19)(a) applies –

(a) state that a claim is being made under [section 7(1)][2] of the Human Rights Act 1998 [in respect of a judicial act and section 9(3) applies] [2]; and

(b) give details of –

(i) the Convention right which it is alleged has been infringed;

(ii) the infringement;

(iii) the judicial act complained of; and

(iv) the court which made it.

(21) Where paragraph (19) applies and the appropriate person (as defined in section 9(5) of the Human Rights Act 1998) has not applied within 21 days, or such other period as the court directs, after the notice is served to be joined as a party, the court may join the appropriate person as a party.

(22) On any application or appeal concerning –

(a) a committal order;

(b) a refusal to grant habeas corpus; or

(c) a secure accommodation order made under section 25 of the Act of 1989,

if the court ordering the release of the person concludes that his Convention rights have been infringed by the making of the order to which the application or appeal relates, the judgment or order should so state, but if the court does not do so, that failure will not prevent another court from deciding the matter.] [1]

NOTES

Amendments. [1] Rule inserted: SI 2000/2267. [2] Words substituted or inserted: SI 2001/821.

[10.27 Costs

(1) Order 38 of the County Court Rules 1981 and Order 62 of the Rules of the Supreme Court 1965 shall not apply to costs in family proceedings, and CPR Parts 43, 44 (except rules 44.9 to 44.12), 47 and 48 shall apply to costs in those proceedings, with the following modifications –

(a) in CPR rule 43.2(1)(c)(ii), 'district judge' includes a district judge of the Principal Registry of the Family Division;

(b) CPR rule 44.3(2) (costs follow the event) shall not apply.

(2) Except in the case of an appeal against a decision of an authorised court officer (to which CPR rules 47.20 to 47.23 apply), an appeal against a decision in assessment proceedings relating to costs in family proceedings shall be dealt with in accordance with the following paragraphs of this rule.

(3) An appeal within paragraph (2) above shall lie as follows –

    (a) where the decision appealed against was made by a district judge of the High Court or a costs judge (as defined by CPR rule 43.2(1)(b)), to a judge of the High Court;

    (b) where the decision appealed against was made by a district judge of a county court, to a judge of that court.

(4) CPR Part 52 applies to every appeal within paragraph (2) above, and any reference in CPR Part 52 to a judge or a district judge shall be taken to include a district judge of the Principal Registry of the Family Division.

(5) The Civil Procedure Rules 1998 shall apply to an appeal to which CPR Part 52 or CPR rules 47.20 to 47.23 apply in accordance with paragraph (2) above in the same way as they apply to any other appeal within CPR Part 52 or CPR rules 47.20 to 47.23 as the case may be; accordingly the Rules of the Supreme Court 1965 and the County Court Rules 1981 shall not apply to any such appeal.][1]

NOTES

    Amendment. [1] Rule inserted: Family Proceedings (Amendment) Rules 2003, SI 2003/184.

APPENDIX 1

FORMS

M1	Statement of Information for a Consent Order
M2	General Heading of Proceedings
M3	Certificate with Regard to Reconciliation
[M4	Statement of Arrangements for Children][4]
[M5	Notice of Proceedings][4, 7]
[M6	Acknowledgment of Service][4]
M7	Affidavit by Petitioner in Support of Petition
M8	Notice of Application for Decree Nisi to be made Absolute
M9	Certificate of Making Decree Nisi Absolute (Divorce)
M10	Certificate of Making Decree Nisi Absolute (Nullity)
	...[8]
M16	Request for Issue of Judgment Summons
M17	Judgment Summons
	...[6]
[M19	Originating Application on Ground of Failure to Provide Reasonable Maintenance][4]
M20	Notice of Application Under Rule 3.1 or 3.2
[M21	Originating Application for Alteration of Maintenance Agreement during Parties' Lifetime][4]

M22   Originating Application for Alteration of Maintenance Agreement after Death of One of the Parties

M23   Originating Summons Under Section 17 of the Married Women's Property Act 1882 or Section 1 of the Matrimonial Homes Act 1967

M24   Notice to be Indorsed on Document Served in Accordance with Rule 9.3

M25   Ex Parte Originating Summons Under Section 13 of the Matrimonial and Family Proceedings Act 1984

M26   Originating Summons Under Section 12 of the Matrimonial and Family Proceedings Act 1984

M27   Originating Summons Under Section 24 of the Matrimonial and Family Proceedings Act 1984

M28   Notice of Proceedings and Acknowledgment of Service

M29   Declaration as to Marital Status Under Section 55 of the Family Law Act 1986

M30   Declaration as to Parentage Under [Section 55A] of the Family Law Act 1986

M31   Declaration as to Legitimacy or Legitimation Under Section 56(1)(b) and (2) of the Family Law Act 1986

[M32   Declaration as to an Adoption Effected Overseas under Section 57 of the Family Law Act 1986][1]

[M33   Application for registration of Maintenance Order in a Magistrates' Court][3]

[M34   Notice under rule 10.24(1)][4]

[[C1	Application	for an order][9]
C2	Application	for an order or directions in existing family proceedings
	Application	to be joined as, or cease to be, a party in existing family proceedings
	Application	for leave to commence proceedings
C3	Application	for an order authorising search for, taking charge of, and delivery of a child
C4	Application	for an order for disclosure of a child's whereabouts
C6	Notice	of proceedings [Hearing] [Directions Appointment] *(Notice to parties)*
C6A	Notice	of proceedings [Hearing] [Directions Appointment] (Notice to non-parties)
[C7		Acknowledgement][9]
C8		Confidential Address
[C9	Statement	of Service][9]

C10	Supplement	for an application for financial provision for a child or for variation of financial provision for a child
C10A	Statement	of Means
[C11	Supplement	for an application for an Emergency Protection Order][6]
C12	Supplement	for an application for a Warrant to assist a person authorised by an Emergency Protection Order
C13	Supplement	for an application for a Care or Supervision Order
C14	Supplement	for an application for authority to refuse contact with a child in care
C15	Supplement	for an application for contact with a child in care
C16	Supplement	for an application for a Child Assessment Order
C17	Supplement	for an application for an Education Supervision Order
C17A	Supplement	for an application for an extension of an Education Supervision Order
C18	Supplement	for an application for a Recovery Order
C19	Supplement	for a Warrant of Assistance
C20	Supplement	for an application for an order to hold a child in Secure Accommodation
C21	Order or direction	Blank
C22	Record	of hearing
[C23	Order	Emergency Protection Order][6]
C24	Order	Variation of an Emergency Protection Order
		Extension of an Emergency Protection Order
		Discharge of an Emergency Protection Order
C25	Warrant	To assist a person authorised by an Emergency Protection Order
C26	Order	Authority to keep a child in Secure Accommodation
C27	Order	Authority to search for another child
C28	Warrant	To assist a person to gain access to a child or entry to premises
C29	Order	Recovery of a child
C30	Order	To disclose information about the whereabouts of a missing child

C31	Order	Authorising search for, taking charge of, and delivery of a child
C32	Order	Care Order
		Discharge of a Care Order
[C33	Order	Interim Care Order][6]
C34	Order	Contact with a child in care
		Authority to refuse contact with a child in care
C35	Order	Supervision Order
		Interim Supervision Order
C36	Order	Substitution of a Supervision Order for a Care Order
		Discharge of a Supervision Order
		Variation of a Supervision Order
		Extension of a Supervision Order
C37	Order	Education Supervision Order
C38	Order	Discharge of an Education Supervision Order
		Extension of an Education Supervision Order
C39	Order	Child Assessment Order
C40	Direction	To undertake an investigation
[C42	Order	Family Assistance Order][9]
C43	Order	Residence Order
		Contact Order
		Specific Issue Order
		Prohibited Steps Order
C44	Order	Leave to change the surname by which a child is known
		Leave to remove a child from the United Kingdom
C45	Order	Parental Responsibility Order
		Termination of a Parental Responsibility Order
C46	Order	Appointment of a guardian
		Termination of the appointment of a guardian
[C47	Order	Making or refusing the appointment of a children's guardian
		Termination of the appointment of a children's guardian][9]
[C48	Order	Appointment of a solicitor for a child

PART II

		Refusal of the appointment of a solicitor for a child
		Termination of the appointment of a solicitor for a child][9]
C49	Order	Transfer of Proceedings to [the High Court] [a county court] [a family proceedings court]
C51		Application for a Parental Order
C52		Acknowledgement of an application for a Parental Order
C53	Order	Parental Order
C54	Notice	of Refusal of a Parental Order][5]
[FL401		Application for a non-molestation order/an occupation order
FL402		Notice of Proceedings [Hearing] [Directions Appointment]
FL403		Application to vary, extend or discharge an order in existing proceedings
FL404		Order or Direction
FL405		Record of Hearing
FL406		Power of Arrest
FL407		Application for a Warrant of Arrest
FL408		Warrant of Arrest
FL409		Remand Order
FL410		Recognizance of respondent
FL411		Recognizance of respondent's surety
FL412		Bail Notice
FL413		Hospital Order/Interim Hospital Order
FL414		Guardianship Order
FL415		Statement of Service
FL416		Notice to Mortgagees and Landlords
FL417		Transfer of proceedings to [the High Court] [a county court] [a family proceedings court]][6]

NOTES

Amendments. [1] Forms substituted or inserted: SI 1991/2113. [2] Forms amended: SI 1992/456. [3] Forms substituted, inserted or amended: SI 1992/2067. [4] Forms substituted, inserted or amended: SI 1993/295. [5] Forms substituted: SI 1994/3155. [6] Forms deleted, substituted or inserted: SI 1997/1893. [7] Form amended: SI 1998/1901. [8] Forms omitted: SI 1999/3491. [9] Forms substituted or inserted: SI 2001/821.

****

[APPENDIX 3
NOTICES AND RESPONDENTS

Rules 4.4 and 4.7

(i) Provision under which proceedings brought	(ii) Minimum number of days prior to hearing or directions appointment for service under rule 4.4(1)(b)	(iii) Respondents	(iv) Persons to whom notice is to be given
All applications.	See separate entries below.	Subject to separate entries below: every person whom the applicant believes to have parental responsibility for the child; where the child is the subject of a care order, every person whom the applicant believes to have had parental responsibility immediately prior to the making of the care order; in the case of an application to extend, vary or discharge an order, the parties to the proceedings leading to the order which it is sought to have extended, varied or discharged; in the case of specified proceedings, the child.	Subject to separate entries below: local authority providing accommodation for the child; persons who are caring for the child at the time when the proceedings are commenced; in the case of proceedings brought in respect of a child who is alleged to be staying in a refuge which is certified under section 51(1) or (2), the person who is providing the refuge.

PART II

(i) *Provision under which proceedings brought*	(ii) *Minimum number of days prior to hearing or directions appointment for service under rule 4.4(1)(b)*	(iii) *Respondents*	(iv) *Persons to whom notice is to be given*
Section 4(1)(a), 4(3), 5(1), 6(7), 8, 13(1), 16(6), 33(7), Schedule 1, paragraph 19(1) of Schedule 2, or paragraph 11(3) or 16(5) of Schedule 14.	14 days.	As for 'all applications' above, and: in the case of proceedings under Schedule 1, those persons whom the applicant believes to be interested in or affected by the proceedings; in the case of an application under paragraph 11(3)(b) or 16(5) of Schedule 14, any person, other than the child, named in the order or directions which it is sought to discharge or vary.	As for 'all applications' above, and: in the case of an application for a section 8 order, every person whom the applicant believes – (i) to be named in a court order with respect to the same child, which has not ceased to have effect, (ii) to be a party to pending proceedings in respect of the same child, or (iii) to be a person with whom the child has lived for at least 3 years prior to the application, unless, in a case to which (i) or (ii) applies, the applicant believes that the court order or pending proceedings are not relevant to the application; in the case of an application under paragraph 19(1) of Schedule 2, the parties to the proceedings leading to the care order;

(i) *Provision under which proceedings brought*	(ii) *Minimum number of days prior to hearing or directions appointment for service under rule 4.4(1)(b)*	(iii) *Respondents*	(iv) *Persons to whom notice is to be given*
			in the case of an application under section 5(1), the father of the child if he does not have parental responsibility.
Section 36(1), 39(1), 39(2), 39(3), 39(4), 43(1), or paragraph 6(3), 15(2) or 17(1) of Schedule 3.	7 days.	As for 'all applications' above, and: in the case of an application under section 39(2) or (3), the supervisor; in the case of proceedings under paragraph 17(1) of Schedule 3, the local education authority concerned; in the case of proceedings under section 36 or paragraph 15(2) or 17(1) of Schedule 3, the child.	As for 'all applications' above, and: in the case of an application for an order under section 43(1) – (i) every person whom the applicant believes to be a parent of the child, (ii) every person whom the applicant believes to be caring for the child, (iii) every person in whose favour a contact order is in force with respect to the child, and (iv) every person who is allowed to have contact with the child by virtue of an order under section 34.

PART II

(i) *Provision under which proceedings brought*	(ii) *Minimum number of days prior to hearing or directions appointment for service under rule 4.4(1)(b)*	(iii) *Respondents*	(iv) *Persons to whom notice is to be given*
Section 31, 34(2), 34(3), 34(4), 34(9) or 38(8)(b).	3 days.	As for 'all applications' above, and; in the case of an application under section 34, the person whose contact with the child is the subject of the application.	As for 'all applications' above, and; in the case of an application under section 31 – (i) every person whom the applicant believes to be a party to pending relevant proceedings in respect of the same child, and (ii) every person whom the applicant believes to be a parent without parental responsibility for the child.
Section 43(12).	2 days.	As for 'all applications' above.	Those of the persons referred to in section 43(11)(a) to (e) who were not party to the application for the order which it is sought to have varied or discharged.

(i) *Provision under which proceedings brought*	(ii) *Minimum number of days prior to hearing or directions appointment for service under rule 4.4(1)(b)*	(iii) *Respondents*	(iv) *Persons to whom notice is to be given*
Section 25, 44(1), 44(9)(b), 45(4), 45(8), 46(7), 48(9), 50(1), or 102(1).	1 day.	As for 'all applications' above, and: in the case of an application under section 44(9)(b) – (i) the parties to the application for the order in respect of which it is sought to vary the directions; (ii) any person who was caring for the child prior to the making of the order, and (iii) any person whose contact with the child is affected by the direction which it is sought to have varied; in the case of an application under section 50, the person whom the applicant alleges to have effected or to have been or to be responsible for the taking or keeping of the child.	Except for applications under section 102(1), as for 'all applications' above, and: in the case of an application under section 44(1), every person whom the applicant believes to be a parent of the child; in the case of an application under section 44(9)(b) – (i) the local authority in whose area the child is living, and (ii) any person whom the applicant believes to be affected by the direction which it is sought to have varied; in the case of an application under section 102(1), the person referred to in section 102(1) and any person preventing or likely to prevent such a person from exercising powers under enactments mentioned in subsection (6) of that section.][1]

PART II

(i) Provision under which proceedings brought	(ii) Minimum number of days prior to hearing or directions appointment for service under rule 4.4(1)(b)	(iii) Respondents	(iv) Persons to whom notice is to be given
[Section 30 of the Human Fertilisation and Embryology Act 1990.	14 days.	The birth parents (except where the applicants seek to dispense with their agreement under section 30(6) of the Human Fertilisation and Embryology Act 1990) and any other persons or body with parental responsibility for the child at the date of the application.	Any local authority or voluntary organisation that has at any time provided accommodation for the child.]²

NOTES

Amendments. ¹ Appendix substituted: SI 1992/2067. ² Words inserted: SI 1994/2165.

Family Proceedings Courts (Children Act 1989) Rules 1991, SI 1991/1395

ARRANGEMENT OF RULES

PART II

PART III
MISCELLANEOUS

NOTES

Commencement. 14 October 1991.

Enabling power. Magistrates' Courts Act 1980, s 144.

PART I
INTRODUCTORY

1 Citation, commencement and interpretation

(1) These Rules may be cited as the Family Proceedings Courts (Children Act 1989) Rules 1991 and shall come into force on 14th October 1991.

(2) Unless a contrary intention appears –

a section or schedule referred to means the section or schedule in the Act of 1989,

'application' means an application made under or by virtue of the Act of 1989 or under these Rules, and 'applicant' shall be construed accordingly,

'business day' means any day other than –

    (a) a Saturday, Sunday, Christmas Day or Good Friday; or

    (b) a bank holiday, that is to say, a day which is, or is to be observed as, a bank holiday, or a holiday, under the Banking and Financial Dealings Act 1971, in England and Wales,

'child'

    (a) means, in relation to any relevant proceedings, subject to sub-paragraph (b), a person under the age of 18 with respect to whom the proceedings are brought, and

    (b) where paragraph 16(1) of Schedule 1 applies, also includes a person who has reached the age of 18,

['children and family reporter' means an officer of the service who has been asked to prepare a welfare report under section 7(1)(a);][1]

['children's guardian'–

    (a) means an officer of the service appointed under section 41 for the child with respect to whom the proceedings are brought; but

    (b) does not include such an officer appointed in relation to proceedings specified by rule 21A;][1]

'contribution order' has the meaning assigned to it by paragraph 23(2) of Schedule 2,

'court' means a family proceedings court constituted in accordance with sections 66 and 67 of the Magistrates' Courts Act 1980 or, in respect of those proceedings prescribed in rule 2(5), a single justice who is a member of a family panel,

'directions appointment' means a hearing for directions under rule 14(2),

'emergency protection order' means an order under section 44,

'file' means deposit with the [justices' chief executive][2],

'form' means a form in Schedule 1 to these Rules with such variation as the circumstances of the particular case may require,

…[1]

['justices' chief executive' means a justices' chief executive appointed under section 40 of the Justices of the Peace Act 1997;][2]

'leave' includes approval,

'note' includes a record made by mechanical means,

['officer of the service' has the same meaning as in the Criminal Justice and Court Services Act 2000;][1]

'parental responsibility' has the meaning assigned to it by section 3,

'parties' in relation to any relevant proceedings means the respondents specified for those proceedings in the third column of Schedule 2 to these Rules, and the applicant,

'recovery order' means an order under section 50,

'relevant proceedings' has the meaning assigned to it by section 93(3),

'section 8 order' has the meaning assigned to it by section 8(2),

'specified proceedings' has the meaning assigned to it by section 41(6) and rule 2(2),

'the 1981 rules' means the Magistrates' Courts Rules 1981,

'the Act of 1989' means the Children Act 1989,

'welfare officer' means a person who has been asked to prepare a welfare report under [section 7(1)(b)][1].

NOTES

    Amendments. [1] Words inserted or omitted: SI 2001/818. [2] Words substituted: SI 2001/615.

2 Matters prescribed for the purposes of the Act of 1989

(1) The parties to proceedings in which directions are given under section 38(6), and any person named in such a direction, form the prescribed class for the purposes of section 38(8)(b) (application to vary directions made with interim care or interim supervision order).

(2) The following proceedings are specified for the purposes of section 41 in accordance with subsection (6)(i) thereof –

    (a) proceedings [(in a family proceedings court)][1] under section 25;

PART II

(b) applications under section 33(7);

(c) proceedings under paragraph 19(1) of Schedule 2;

(d) applications under paragraph 6(3) of Schedule 3.

(3) The applicant for an order that has been made under section 43(1) and the persons referred to in section 43(11) may, in any circumstances, apply under section 43(12) for a child assessment order to be varied or discharged.

(4) The following persons form the prescribed class for the purposes of section 44(9)(b) (application to vary directions) –

(a) the parties to the application for the order in respect of which it is sought to vary the directions;

(b) the [children's guardian]²;

(c) the local authority in whose area the child concerned is ordinarily resident;

(d) any person who is named in the directions.

(5) The following proceedings are prescribed for the purposes of section 93(2)(i) as being proceedings with respect to which a single justice may discharge the functions of a family proceedings court, that is to say, proceedings –

(a) where an ex parte application is made, under sections 10, 44(1), 48(9), 50(1), 75(1) or 102(1),

(b) subject to rule 28, under sections 11(3) or 38(1),

(c) under sections 4(3)(b), 7, 14, 34(3)(b), 37, 41, 44(9)(b) and (11)(b)(iii), 48(4), 91(15) or (17), or paragraph 11(4) of Schedule 14,

(d) in accordance with any Order made by the Lord Chancellor under Part I of Schedule 11, and

(e) in accordance with rules 3 to 8, 10 to 19, 21, 22, or 27.

NOTES

Amendments. ¹ Words inserted: SI 1991/1991. ² Words substituted: SI 2001/818.

PART II
GENERAL

3 Application for leave to commence proceedings

(1) Where the leave of the court is required to bring any relevant proceedings, the person seeking leave shall file –

(a) a written request for leave [in Form C2]¹ setting out the reasons for the application, and

[(b) a draft of the application (being the documents referred to in rule 4(1A)) for the making of which leave is sought together with sufficient copies for one to be served on each respondent.]¹

(2) On considering a request for leave filed under paragraph (1), the court shall –

(a) grant the request, whereupon the [justices' chief executive]² shall inform the person making the request of the decision, or

(b) direct that a date be fixed for a hearing of the request, whereupon the justices' clerk shall fix such a date and [the justices' chief executive shall]² give such notice as the court directs to the person making the request and to such other persons as the court requires to be notified, of the date so fixed.

(3) Where leave is granted to bring any relevant proceedings, the application shall proceed in accordance with rule 4; but paragraph (1)(a) of that rule shall not apply.

NOTES

Amendments. [1] Words inserted or substituted: SI 1994/3156. [2] Words inserted or substituted: SI 2001/615.

4 Application

(1) Subject to paragraph (4), an applicant shall –

   [(a) file the documents referred to in paragraph (1A) below (which documents shall together be called the 'application') together with sufficient copies for one to be served on each respondent, and] [2]

   (b) serve a copy of the application [together with Form C6 and such (if any) of Forms C7 and C10A as are given to him by the [justices' chief executive] [3] under paragraph 2(b)] [2] on each respondent such minimum number of days prior to the date fixed under paragraph (2)(a) as is specified in relation to that application in column (ii) of Schedule 2 to these Rules.

[(1A) the documents to be filed under paragraph (1)(a) above are –

   (a) (i) whichever is appropriate of Forms C1 to C5 or C51, and

   (ii) such of the supplemental Forms C10 or C11 to C20 as may be appropriate, or

   (b) where there is no appropriate form a statement in writing of the order sought,

and where the application is made in respect of more than one child, all the children shall be included in one application.] [2]

[(2) On receipt by the justices' chief executive of the documents filed under paragraph (1)(a) –

   (a) the justices' clerk shall fix the date, time and place for a hearing or a directions appointment, allowing sufficient time for the applicant to comply with paragraph (1)(b), and

   (b) the justices' chief executive shall –

      (i) endorse the date, time and place so fixed upon Form C6, and where appropriate, Form C6A, and

      (ii) return forthwith to the applicant the copies of the application and Form C10A if filed with it, together with Form C6, and such of Forms C6A and C7 as are appropriate.] [3]

[(3) The applicant shall, at the same time as complying with paragraph (1)(b), serve Form C6A on the persons set out in relation to the relevant class of proceedings in column (iv) of Schedule 2 to these Rules.] [2]

(4) An application for –

   (a) a [section 8 order] [1],

   (b) an emergency protection order,

   (c) a warrant under section 48(9),

   (d) a recovery order, or

   (e) a warrant under section 102(1),

may, with leave of the justices' clerk, be made ex parte in which case the applicant shall –

> (i) file with the [justices' chief executive][3] or the court the application
> ...[2] in the appropriate form in Schedule 1 to these Rules at the time
> when the application is made or as directed by the justices' clerk,
> and
>
> (ii) in the case of an application for a prohibited steps order, or a
> specific issue order, under section 8 or an emergency protection
> order, and also in the case of an application for an order under
> section 75(1) where the application is ex parte, serve a copy of the
> application on each respondent within 48 hours after the making of
> the order.

(5) Where the court refuses to make an order on an ex parte application it may
direct that the application be made inter partes.

(6) In the case of proceedings under Schedule 1, the application under paragraph
(1) shall be accompanied by a statement [in Form C10A][2] setting out the financial
details which the applicant believes to be relevant to the application ...[2], together
with sufficient copies for one to be served on each respondent.

NOTES
Amendments. [1] Words substituted: SI 1992/2068. [2] Words inserted, repealed or substituted: SI
1994/3156. [3] Words or paragraphs substituted: SI 2001/615.

5 Withdrawal of application

(1) An application may be withdrawn only with leave of the court.

(2) Subject to paragraph (3), a person seeking leave to withdraw an application
shall file and serve on the parties a written request for leave setting out the reasons
for the request.

(3) The request under paragraph (2) may be made orally to the court if the parties
and, if appointed, the [children's guardian][1] or the [welfare officer or children and
family reporter][1] are present.

(4) Upon receipt of a written request under paragraph (2), the court shall –

> (a) if –
> > (i) the parties consent in writing,
> > (ii) any [children's guardian][1] has had an opportunity to make
> > representations, and
> > (iii) the court thinks fit,
> > grant the request; in which case the [justices' chief executive][2] shall notify
> > the parties, the [children's guardian][1] and the [welfare officer or children
> > and family reporter][1] of the granting of the request; or
> (b) the justices' clerk shall fix a date for the hearing of the request and [the
> justices' chief executive shall][2] give at least 7 days' notice to the parties,
> the [children's guardian][1] and the [welfare officer or children and family
> reporter][1] of the date fixed.

NOTES
Amendments. [1] Words substituted: SI 2001/818. [2] Words substituted or inserted: SI 2001/615.

6 Transfer of proceedings

(1) Where, in any relevant proceedings, the [justices' chief executive][2] or the court
receives a request in writing from a party that the proceedings be transferred to

another family proceedings court or to a county court, the [justices' chief executive]² or court shall issue [an order or certificate]¹ in the appropriate form in Schedule 1 to these Rules, granting or refusing the request in accordance with any Order made by the Lord Chancellor under Part I of Schedule 11.

(2) Where a request is granted under paragraph (1), the [justices' chief executive]² shall send a copy of the [order]¹ –

(a) to the parties,
(b) to any [children's guardian]³, and
(c) to the family proceedings court or to the county court to which the proceedings are to be transferred.

(3) Any consent given or refused by a justices' clerk in accordance with any Order made by the Lord Chancellor under Part I of Schedule 11 shall be recorded in writing by the justices' clerk at the time it is given or refused or as soon as practicable thereafter.

(4) Where a request to transfer proceedings to a county court is refused under paragraph (1), the person who made the request may apply in accordance with rule 4.6 of the Family Proceedings Rules 1991 for an order under any Order made by the Lord Chancellor under Part I of Schedule 11.

NOTES

Amendments. ¹ Words substituted: SI 1994/3156. ² Words substituted: SI 2001/615. ³ Words substituted: SI 2001/818.

7 Parties

(1) The respondents to relevant proceedings shall be those persons set out in the relevant entry in column (iii) of Schedule 2 to these Rules.

(2) In any relevant proceedings a person may file a request [in Form C2]¹ that he or another person –

(a) be joined as a party, or
(b) cease to be a party.

(3) On considering a request under paragraph (2) the court shall, subject to paragraph (4) –

(a) grant it without a hearing or representations, save that this shall be done only in the case of a request under paragraph (2)(a), whereupon the [justices' chief executive]² shall inform the parties and the person making the request of that decision, or
(b) order that a date be fixed for the consideration of the request, whereupon the [justices' chief executive]² shall give notice of the date so fixed, together with a copy of the request –
    (i) in the case of a request under paragraph (2)(a), to the applicant, and
    (ii) in the case of a request under paragraph (2)(b), to the parties, or
(c) invite the parties or any of them to make written representations, within a specified period, as to whether the request should be granted; and upon the expiry of the period the court shall act in accordance with sub-paragraph (a) or (b).

(4) Where a person with parental responsibility requests that he be joined under paragraph (2)(a), the court shall grant his request.

(5) In any relevant proceedings the court may direct –

> (a) that a person who would not otherwise be a respondent under these Rules be joined as a party to the proceedings, or
> (b) that a party to the proceedings cease to be a party.

NOTES
Amendments. [1] Words substituted: SI 1994/3156. [2] Words substituted: SI 2001/615.

8 Service

(1) Where service of a document is required by these Rules (and not by a provision to which section 105(8) (service of notice or other document under the Act) applies) it may be effected –

> (a) if the person to be served is not known by the person serving to be acting by solicitor –
>> (i) by delivering it to him personally, or
>> (ii) by delivering it at, or by sending it by first-class post to, his residence or his last known residence, or
> (b) if the person to be served is known by the person serving to be acting by solicitor –
>> (i) by delivering the document at, or sending it by first-class post to, the solicitor's address for service,
>> (ii) where the solicitor's address for service includes a numbered box at a document exchange, by leaving the document at that document exchange or at a document exchange which transmits documents on every business day to that document exchange, or
>> (iii) by sending a legible copy of the document by facsimile transmission to the solicitor's office.

(2) In this rule, 'first-class post' means first-class post which has been pre-paid or in respect of which pre-payment is not required.

(3) Where a child who is a party to any relevant proceedings is required by these Rules to serve a document, service shall be effected by –

> (a) the solicitor acting for the child,
> (b) where there is no such solicitor, the [children's guardian] [3], or
> (c) where there is neither such a solicitor nor a [children's guardian] [3], the [justices' chief executive] [4].

(4) Service of any document on a child shall, subject to any direction of the justices' clerk or the court, be effected by service on –

> (a) the solicitor acting for the child,
> (b) where there is no such solicitor, the [children's guardian] [3], or
> (c) where there is neither such a solicitor nor a [children's guardian] [3], with leave of the justices' clerk or the court, the child.

(5) Where the justices' clerk or the court refuses leave under paragraph (4)(c), a direction shall be given under paragraph (8).

(6) A document shall, unless the contrary is proved, be deemed to have been served –

> (a) in the case of service by first-class post, on the second business day after posting, and
> (b) in the case of service in accordance with paragraph (1)(b)(ii), on the second business day after the day on which it is left at the document exchange.

(7) At or before the first directions appointment in, or hearing of, relevant proceedings, whichever occurs first, the applicant shall file a statement [in Form C9]² that service of –

    (a) a copy of the application [and other documents referred to in rule 4(1)(b)]² has been effected on each respondent, and

    (b) notice of the proceedings has been effected under rule 4(3);

and the statement shall indicate –

       (i) the manner, date, time and place of service, or

      (ii) where service was effected by post, the date, time and place of posting.

[(8) In any relevant proceedings, where these rules require a document to be served, the court or the justices' clerk may, without prejudice to any power under rule 14, direct that –

    (a) the requirement shall not apply;

    (b) the time specified by the rules for complying with the requirement shall be abridged to such extent as may be specified in the direction;

    (c) service shall be effected in such manner as may be specified in the direction.]¹

NOTES

Amendments. ¹ Words substituted: SI 1992/2068. ² Words inserted: SI 1994/3156. ³ Words substituted: SI 2001/818. ⁴ Words substituted: SI 2001/615.

[9 Acknowledgement of application

Within 14 days of service of an application for a section 8 order or an application under Schedule 1, each respondent shall file and serve on the parties an acknowledgement of the application in Form C7.]¹

NOTES

Amendments. ¹ Rule substituted: SI 1994/3156.

10 Appointment of [children's guardian]¹

(1) As soon as practicable after the commencement of specified proceedings or the transfer of such proceedings to the court, the justices' clerk or the court shall appoint a [children's guardian]¹ unless –

    (a) such an appointment has already been made by the court which made the transfer and is subsisting, or

    (b) the justices' clerk or the court considers that such an appointment is not necessary to safeguard the interests of the child.

(2) At any stage in specified proceedings a party may apply, without notice to the other parties unless the justices' clerk or the court otherwise directs, for the appointment of a [children's guardian]¹.

(3) The justices' clerk or the court shall grant an application under paragraph (2) unless it is considered that such an appointment is not necessary to safeguard the interests of the child, in which case reasons shall be given; and a note of such reasons shall be taken by the justices' clerk.

(4) At any stage in specified proceedings the justices' clerk or the court may appoint a [children's guardian]¹ even though no application is made for such an appointment.

[(4A) The justices' chief executive or the court may, in specified proceedings, appoint more than one children's guardian in respect of the same child.] ¹

(5) The [justices' chief executive]² shall, as soon as practicable, notify the parties and any [welfare officer or children and family reporter]¹ of an appointment under this rule or, as the case may be, of a decision not to make such an appointment.

(6) Upon the appointment of a [children's guardian]¹ the [justices' chief executive]² shall, as soon as practicable, notify him of the appointment and serve on him copies of the application and of documents filed under rule 17(1).

[(7) A children's guardian appointed by the justices' chief executive or by the court under this rule shall not –

> (a) be a member, officer or servant of a local authority which, or an authorised person (within the meaning of section 31(9)) who, is a party to the proceedings;
> (b) be, or have been, a member, officer or servant of a local authority or voluntary organisation (within the meaning of section 105(1)) who has been directly concerned in that capacity in arrangements relating to the care, accommodation or welfare of the child during the five years prior to the commencement of the proceedings; or
> (c) be a serving probation officer who has, in that capacity, been previously concerned with the child or his family.]¹

(8) When appointing a [children's guardian]¹, the justices' clerk or the court shall consider the appointment of anyone who has previously acted as [children's guardian]¹ of the same child.

(9) The appointment of a [children's guardian]¹ under this rule shall continue for such time as is specified in the appointment or until terminated by the court.

(10) When terminating an appointment in accordance with paragraph (9), the court shall give reasons in writing for so doing, a note of which shall be taken by the justices' clerk.

(11) Where the justices' clerk or the court appoints a [children's guardian]¹ in accordance with this rule or refuses to make such an appointment, the justices' clerk shall record the appointment or refusal in the appropriate form in Schedule 1 to these Rules.

NOTES
   Amendments. ¹ Words substituted or inserted: SI 2001/818. ² Words substituted: SI 2001/615.

[11 Powers and duties of officers of the service

(1) In carrying out his duty under section 7(1)(a) or section 41(2), the officer of the service shall have regard to the principle set out in section 1(2) and the matters set out in section 1(3)(a) to (f) as if for the word 'court' in that section there were substituted the words 'officer of the service'.

(2) The officer of the service shall make such investigations as may be necessary for him to carry out his duties and shall, in particular–

(a) contact or seek to interview such persons as he thinks appropriate or as the court directs;

(b) obtain such professional assistance as is available to him which he thinks appropriate or which the justices' clerk or the court directs him to obtain.

(3) In addition to his duties, under other paragraphs of this rule, or rules 11A or 11B, the officer of the service shall provide to the justices' chief executive, the justices' clerk and the court such other assistance as he or it may require.

(4) A party may question the officer of the service about oral or written advice tendered by him to the justices' chief executive, the justices' clerk or the court.][1]

NOTES

Amendments. [1] Rule substituted: SI 2001/818.

[11A Additional powers and duties of children's guardian

(1) The children's guardian shall –

(a) appoint a solicitor to represent the child unless such a solicitor has already been appointed; and

(b) give such advice to the child as is appropriate having regard to his understanding and, subject to rule 12(1)(a), instruct the solicitor representing the child on all matters relevant to the interests of the child including possibilities for appeal, arising in the course of proceedings.

(2) Where it appears to the children's guardian that the child –

(a) is instructing his solicitor direct; or

(b) intends to conduct and is capable of conducting the proceedings on his own behalf,

he shall inform the court through the justices' chief executive and from then he –

(i) shall perform all of his duties set out in rule 11 and this rule, other than those duties under paragraph (1)(a) of this rule, and such other duties as the justices' clerk or the court may direct;

(ii) shall take such part in the proceedings as the justices' clerk or the court may direct; and

(iii) may, with the leave of the justices' clerk or the court, have legal representation in the conduct of those duties.

(3) Unless excused by the justices' clerk or the court, the children's guardian shall attend all directions appointments in and hearings of the proceedings and shall advise the court on the following matters –

(a) whether the child is of sufficient understanding for any purpose including the child's refusal to submit to a medical or psychiatric examination or other assessment that the court has the power to require, direct or order;

(b) the wishes of the child in respect of any matter relevant to the proceedings including his attendance at court;

(c) the appropriate forum for the proceedings;

(d) the appropriate timing of the proceedings or any part of them;

(e) the options available to it in respect of the child and the suitability of each such option including what order should be made in determining the application; and

(f) any other matter concerning which the justices' chief executive, the justices' clerk or the court seeks his advice or concerning which he considers that the justices' chief executive, the justices' clerk or the court should be informed.

(4) The advice given under paragraph (3) may, subject to any order of the court, be given orally or in writing; and if the advice be given orally, a note of it shall be taken by the justices' clerk or the court.

(5) The children's guardian shall, where practicable, notify any person whose joinder as a party to those proceedings would be likely, in the opinion of the officer of the service, to safeguard the interests of the child of that person's right to apply to be joined under rule 7(2) and shall inform the justices' chief executive or the court –

(a) of any such notification given;
(b) of anyone whom he attempted to notify under this paragraph but was unable to contact; and
(c) of anyone whom he believes may wish to be joined to the proceedings.

(6) The children's guardian shall, unless the justices' clerk or the court otherwise directs, not less than 14 days before the date fixed for the final hearing of the proceedings –

(a) file a written report advising on the interests of the child;
(b) serve a copy of the filed report on the other parties.

(7) The children's guardian shall serve and accept service of documents on behalf of the child in accordance with rule 8(3)(b) and (4)(b) and, where the child has not himself been served, and has sufficient understanding, advise the child of the contents of any document so served.

(8) If the children's guardian inspects records of the kinds referred to in section 42, he shall bring to the attention of –

(a) the court, through the justices' chief executive; and
(b) unless the court or the justices' clerk otherwise directs, the other parties to the proceedings,

all records and documents which may, in his opinion, assist in the proper determination of the proceedings.

(9) The children's guardian shall ensure that, in relation to a decision made by the justices' clerk or the court in the proceedings –

(a) if he considers it appropriate to the age and understanding of the child, the child is notified of that decision; and
(b) if the child is notified of the decision, it is explained to the child in a manner appropriate to his age and understanding.]¹

NOTES
Amendments. ¹ Rule inserted: SI 2001/818.

[11B Additional powers and duties of a children and family reporter

(1) In addition to his duties under rule 11, the children and family reporter shall –

(a) notify the child of such contents of his report (if any) as he considers appropriate to the age and understanding of the child, including any reference to the child's own views on the application and the recommendation of the children and family reporter; and

(b) if he does notify the child of any contents of his report, explain them to the child in a manner appropriate to his age and understanding.

(2) Where the court has –

(a) directed that a written report be made by a children and family reporter; and

(b) notified the children and family reporter that his report is to be considered at a hearing,

the children and family reporter shall –

(i) file his report; and

(ii) serve a copy on the other parties and on the children's guardian (if any),

by such time as the court may direct and if no direction is given, not less than 14 days before that hearing.

(3) The court may direct that the children and family reporter attend any hearing at which his report is to be considered.

(4) The children and family reporter shall advise the court if he considers that the joinder of a person as a party to the proceedings would be likely to safeguard the interests of the child.

(5) The children and family reporter shall consider whether it is in the best interests of the child for the child to be made a party to the proceedings.

(6) If the children and family reporter considers the child should be made a party to the proceedings he shall notify the court of his opinion together with the reasons for that opinion.][1]

NOTES

Amendments. [1] Rule inserted: SI 2001/818.

12 Solicitor for child

(1) A solicitor appointed under section 41(3) or in accordance with [rule 11A(1)(a)][1] shall represent the child –

(a) in accordance with instructions received from the [children's guardian][1] (unless the solicitor considers, having taken into account the views of the [children's guardian][1] and any direction of the court under [rule 11A(2)][1], that the child wishes to give instructions which conflict with those of the [children's guardian][1] and that he is able, having regard to his understanding, to give such instructions on his own behalf in which case he shall conduct the proceedings in accordance with instructions received from the child), or

(b) where no [children's guardian][1] has been appointed for the child and the condition in section 41(4)(b) is satisfied, in accordance with instructions received from the child, or

(c) in default of instructions under (a) or (b), in furtherance of the best interests of the child.

(2) A solicitor appointed under section 41(3) or in accordance with [rule 11A(1)(a)][1] shall serve and accept service of documents on behalf of the child in accordance with rule 8(3)(a) and (4)(a) and, where the child has not himself been

served and has sufficient understanding, advise the child of the contents of any document so served.

(3) Where the child wishes an appointment of a solicitor under section 41(3) or in accordance with [rule 11A(1)(a)]¹ to be terminated, he may apply to the court for an order terminating the appointment; and the solicitor and the [children's guardian]¹ shall be given an opportunity to make representations.

(4) Where the [children's guardian]¹ wishes an appointment of a solicitor under section 41(3) to be terminated, he may apply to the court for an order terminating the appointment; and the solicitor and, if he is of sufficient understanding, the child, shall be given an opportunity to make representations.

(5) When terminating an appointment in accordance with paragraph (3) or (4), the court shall give reasons for so doing, a note of which shall be taken by the justices' clerk.

(6) Where the justices' clerk or the court appoints a solicitor under section 41(3) or refuses to make such an appointment, the justices' clerk shall record the appointment or refusal in the appropriate form in Schedule 1 to these Rules and [the justices' chief executive shall]² serve a copy on the parties and, where he is appointed, on the solicitor.

NOTES
Amendments. ¹ Words substituted: SI 2001/818. ² Words inserted: SI 2001/615.

[13 Welfare officer

(1) Where the court or a justices' clerk has directed that a written report be made by a welfare officer [in accordance with section 7(1)(b)]², the report shall be filed at or by such time as the court or justices' clerk directs or, in the absence of such a direction, at least 14 days before a relevant hearing; and the [justices' chief executive]³ shall, as soon as practicable, serve a copy of the report on the parties and any [children's guardian]².

(2) In paragraph (1), a hearing is relevant if the[justices' chief executive]³ has given the welfare officer notice that his report is to be considered at it.

(3) After the filing of a written report by a welfare officer, the court or the justices' clerk may direct that the welfare officer attend any hearing at which the report is to be considered; and

   (a) except where such a direction is given at a hearing attended by the welfare officer, the [justices' chief executive]³ shall inform the welfare officer of the direction; and
   (b) at the hearing at which the report is considered any party may question the welfare officer about his report.

[(3A) The welfare officer shall consider whether it is in the best interests of the child for the child to be made a party to the proceedings.

(3B) If the welfare officer considers the child should be made a party to the proceedings he shall notify the court of his opinion together with the reasons for that opinion.]²

(4) This rule is without prejudice to the court's power to give directions under rule 14.]¹

NOTES

Amendments. [1] Rule substituted: SI 1992/2068, except in relation to a written report the making of which was directed before 5 October 1992. [2] Words substituted or inserted: SI 2001/818. [3] Words substituted: SI 2001/615.

14 Directions

(1) In this rule, 'party' includes the [children's guardian][3] and, where a request or direction concerns a report under section 7, the [welfare officer or children and family reporter][3].

(2) In any relevant proceedings the justices' clerk or the court may, subject to paragraph (5), give, vary or revoke directions for the conduct of the proceedings, including –

    (a) the timetable for the proceedings;
    (b) varying the time within which or by which an act is required, by these Rules, to be done;
    (c) the attendance of the child;
    (d) the appointment of a [children's guardian][3] ...[3], or of a solicitor under section 41(3);
    (e) the service of documents;
    (f) the submission of evidence including experts' reports;
    (g) the preparation of welfare reports under section 7;
    (h) the transfer of the proceedings to another court in accordance with any Order made by the Lord Chancellor under Part I of Schedule 11;
    (i) consolidation with other proceedings;

and the justices' clerk shall, on receipt of an application [by the justices' chief executive][4], or where proceedings have been transferred to his court, consider whether such directions need to be given.

(3) Where the justices' clerk or a single justice who is holding a directions appointment considers, for whatever reason, that it is inappropriate to give a direction on a particular matter, he shall refer the matter to the court which may give any appropriate direction.

(4) Where a direction is given under paragraph (2)(h), [an order][2] shall be issued in the appropriate form in Schedule 1 to these Rules and the [justices' chief executive][4] shall follow the procedure set out in rule 6(2).

(5) Directions under paragraph (2) may be given, varied or revoked either –

    (a) of the justices' clerk's or the court's own motion [the justices' chief executive][4] having given the parties notice of the intention to do so and an opportunity to attend and be heard or to make written representations,
    (b) on the written request [in Form C2][2] of a party specifying the direction which is sought, filed and served on the other parties, or
    (c) on the written request [in Form C2][2] of a party specifying the direction which is sought, to which the other parties consent and which they or their representatives have signed.

(6) In an urgent case, the request under paragraph (5)(b) may, with the leave of the justices' clerk or the court, be made –

    (a) orally,
    (b) without notice to the parties, or
    (c) both as in sub-paragraph (a) and as in sub-paragraph (b).

PART II

(7) On receipt of a request [by the justices' chief executive][4] under paragraph (5)(b) the justices' clerk shall fix a date for the hearing of the request and [the justices' chief executive shall][4] give not less than 2 days' notice [in Form C6][2] to the parties of the date so fixed.

(8) On considering a request under paragraph (5)(c) the justices' clerk or the court shall either –

    (a) grant the request, whereupon the [justices' chief executive][4] shall inform the parties of the decision, or

    (b) direct that a date be fixed for the hearing of the request, whereupon the justices' clerk shall fix such a date and [the justices' chief executive shall][4] give not less than 2 days' notice to the parties of the date so fixed.

(9) Subject to rule 28, a party may request, in accordance with paragraph 5(b) or (c), that an order be made under section 11(3) or, if he is entitled to apply for such an order, under section 38(1), and paragraphs (6), (7) and (8) shall apply accordingly.

(10) Where, in any relevant proceedings, the court has power to make an order of its own motion, the power to give directions under paragraph (2) shall apply.

(11) Directions of the justices' clerk or a court which are still in force immediately prior to the transfer of relevant proceedings to another court shall continue to apply following the transfer, subject to any changes of terminology which are required to apply those directions to the court to which the proceedings are transferred, unless varied or discharged by directions under paragraph (2).

(12) The justices' clerk or the court shall [record][1] the giving, variation or revocation of a direction under this rule [in the appropriate form in Schedule 1 to these Rules][1] and [the justices' chief executive shall][4] serve, as soon as practicable, a copy of [the form][1] on any party who was not present at the giving, variation or revocation.

NOTES

    Amendments. [1] Words inserted or substituted: SI 1991/1991. [2] Words inserted or substituted: SI 1994/3156. [3] Words substituted or omitted: SI 2001/818. [4] Words inserted or substituted: SI 2001/615.

15 Timing of proceedings

(1) Any period of time fixed by these Rules, or by any order or direction, for doing any act shall be reckoned in accordance with this rule.

(2) Where the period, being a period of 7 days or less, would include a day which is not a business day, that day shall be excluded.

(3) Where the time fixed for filing a document with the [justices' chief executive][1] expires on a day on which the [office of the justices' chief executive][1] is closed, and for that reason the document cannot be filed on that day, the document shall be filed in time if it is filed on the next day on which the [office of the justices' chief executive][1] is open.

(4) Where these Rules provide a period of time within which or by which a certain act is to be performed in the course of relevant proceedings, that period may not be extended otherwise than by a direction of the justices' clerk or the court under rule 14.

(5) At the –

(a) transfer to a court of relevant proceedings,
(b) postponement or adjournment of any hearing or directions appointment in the course of relevant proceedings, or
(c) conclusion of any such hearing or directions appointment other than one at which the proceedings are determined, or so soon thereafter as is practicable,

> [(i) the justices' clerk shall fix a date upon which the proceedings shall come before him or the court again for such purposes as he or the court directs, which date shall, where paragraph (a) applies, be as soon as possible after the transfer, and
>
> (ii) the justices' chief executive shall give notice to the parties and to the [children's guardian]² or the [welfare officer or children and family reporter]² of the date so fixed.]¹

NOTES

Amendments. ¹ Words substituted: SI 2001/615. ² Words substituted: SI 2001/818.

16 Attendance at directions appointment and hearing

(1) Subject to paragraph (2), a party shall attend a directions appointment of which he has been given notice in accordance with rule 14(5) unless the justices' clerk or the court otherwise directs.

(2) Relevant proceedings shall take place in the absence of any party including the child if –

(a) the court considers it in the interests of the child, having regard to the matters to be discussed or the evidence likely to be given, and
(b) the party is represented by a [children's guardian]¹ or solicitor;

and when considering the interests of the child under sub-paragraph (a) the court shall give the [children's guardian]¹, solicitor for the child and, if he is of sufficient understanding, the child, an opportunity to make representations.

(3) Subject to paragraph (4) below, where at the time and place appointed for a hearing or directions appointment the applicant appears but one or more of the respondents do not, the justices' clerk or the court may proceed with the hearing or appointment.

(4) The court shall not begin to hear an application in the absence of a respondent unless –

(a) it is proved to the satisfaction of the court that he received reasonable notice of the date of the hearing; or
(b) the court is satisfied that the circumstances of the case justify proceeding with the hearing.

(5) Where, at the time and place appointed for a hearing or directions appointment, one or more respondents appear but the applicant does not, the court may refuse the application or, if sufficient evidence has previously been received, proceed in the absence of the applicant.

(6) Where at the time and place appointed for a hearing or directions appointment neither the applicant nor any respondent appears, the court may refuse the application.

(7) If the court considers it expedient in the interests of the child, it shall hear any relevant proceedings in private when only the officers of the court, the parties, their legal representatives and such other persons as specified by the court may attend.

NOTES
Amendments. [1] Words substituted: SI 2001/818.

17 Documentary evidence

(1) Subject to paragraphs (4) and (5), in any relevant proceedings a party shall file and serve on the parties, any [welfare officer or children and family reporter][2] and any [children's guardian][2] of whose appointment he has been given notice under rule 10(5) –

    (a) written statements of the substance of the oral evidence which the party intends to adduce at a hearing of, or a directions appointment in, those proceedings, which shall –
        (i) be dated,
        (ii) be signed by the person making the statement, ...[1]
        (iii) contain a declaration that the maker of the statement believes it to be true and understands that it may be placed before the court, and
      [(iv) show in the top right hand corner of the first page –
        (a) the initials and surname of the person making the statement,
        (b) the number of the statement in relation to the maker,
        (c) the date on which the statement was made, and
        (d) the party on whose behalf it is filed; and][1]
    (b) copies of any documents, including, subject to rule 18(3), experts' reports, upon which the party intends to rely, at a hearing of, or a directions appointment in, those proceedings,

at or by such time as the justices' clerk or the court directs or, in the absence of a direction, before the hearing or appointment.

(2) A party may, subject to any direction of the justices' clerk or the court about the timing of statements under this rule, file and serve on the parties a statement which is supplementary to a statement served under paragraph (1).

(3) At a hearing or directions appointment a party may not, without the leave of the justices' clerk, in the case of a directions appointment, or the court –

    (a) adduce evidence, or
    (b) seek to rely on a document,

in respect of which he has failed to comply with the requirements of paragraph (1).

(4) In proceedings for a section 8 order a party shall –

    (a) neither file nor serve any document other than as required or authorised by these Rules, and
    (b) in completing a form prescribed by these Rules, neither give information, nor make a statement, which is not required or authorised by that form,

without the leave of the justices' clerk or the court.

(5) In proceedings for a section 8 order, no statement or copy may be filed under paragraph (1) until such time as the justices' clerk or the court directs.

NOTES
Amendments. [1] Words revoked or inserted: SI 1992/2068. [2] Words substituted: SI 2001/818.

18 Expert evidence – examination of child

(1) No person may, without the leave of the justices' clerk or the court, cause the child to be medically or psychiatrically examined, or otherwise assessed, for the purpose of the preparation of expert evidence for use in the proceedings.

(2) An application for leave under paragraph (1) shall, unless the justices' clerk or the court otherwise directs, be served on all the parties to the proceedings and on the [children's guardian][1].

(3) Where the leave of the justices' clerk or the court has not been given under paragraph (1), no evidence arising out of an examination or assessment to which that paragraph applies may be adduced without the leave of the court.

NOTES
   Amendments. [1] Words substituted: SI 2001/818.

19 Amendment

(1) Subject to rule 17(2), a document which has been filed or served in any relevant proceedings may not be amended without the leave of the justices' clerk or the court which shall, unless the justices' clerk or the court otherwise directs, be requested in writing.

(2) On considering a request for leave to amend a document the [justices' chief executive][1] or the court shall either –

   (a) grant the request, whereupon the justices' clerk shall inform the person making the request of that decision, or
   (b) invite the parties or any of them to make representations, within a specified period, as to whether such an order should be made.

(3) A person amending a document shall file it with the [justices' chief executive] [1] and serve it on those persons on whom it was served prior to amendment; and the amendments shall be identified.

NOTES
   Amendments. [1] Words substituted: SI 2001/615.

20 Oral evidence

The justices' clerk or the court shall keep a note of the substance of the oral evidence given at a hearing of, or directions appointment in, relevant proceedings.

21 Hearing

(1) Before the hearing, the justice or justices who will be dealing with the case shall read any documents which have been filed under rule 17 in respect of the hearing.

(2) The justices' clerk at a directions appointment, or the court at a hearing or directions appointment, may give directions as to the order of speeches and evidence.

(3) Subject to directions under paragraph (2), at a hearing of, or directions appointment in, relevant proceedings, the parties and the [children's guardian][3] shall adduce their evidence in the following order –

    (a) the applicant,

    (b) any party with parental responsibility for the child,

    (c) other respondents,

    (d) the [children's guardian][3],

    (e) the child if he is a party to the proceedings and there is no [children's guardian][3].

(4) After the final hearing of relevant proceedings, the court shall make its decision as soon as is practicable.

(5) Before the court makes an order or refuses an application or request, the justices' clerk shall record in writing –

    (a) the names of the justice or justices constituting the court by which the decision is made, and

    (b) in consultation with the justice or justices, the reasons for the court's decision and any findings of fact.

[(6) When making an order or when refusing an application, the court, or one of the justices constituting the court by which the decision is made shall

    (a) where it makes a finding of fact state such finding and complete Form C22; and

    (b) state the reasons for the court's decision.][2]

[(7) As soon as practicable after the court announces its decision –

    (a) the justices' clerk shall make a record of any order made in the appropriate form in Schedule 1 to these Rules or, where there is no such form, in writing; and

    (b) subject to paragraph (8), the justices' chief executive shall serve a copy of any order made on the parties to the proceedings and on any person with whom the child is living.][4]

(8) Within 48 hours after the making of an order under section 48(4) or the making, ex parte, of –

    (a) a [section 8 order][1], or

    (b) an order under section 44, 48(9), 50 [or][1] 75(1) ...[1],

the applicant shall serve a copy of the order in the appropriate form in Schedule 1 to these Rules on –

    (i)   each party,

    (ii) any person who has actual care of the child, or who had such care immediately prior to the making of the order, and

    (iii) in the case of an order referred to in sub-paragraph (b), the local authority in whose area the child lives or is found.

NOTES

    Amendments. [1] Words inserted, substituted or revoked: SI 1992/2068. [2] Words substituted: SI 1994/3156. [3] Words substituted: SI 2001/818. [4] Words substituted: SI 2001/615.

[PART IIA
PROCEEDINGS UNDER SECTION 30 OF THE HUMAN
FERTILISATION AND EMBRYOLOGY ACT 1990

21A Interpretation

(1) In this Part of these Rules –

'the 1990 Act' means the Human Fertilisation and Embryology Act 1990;

'the birth father' means the father of the child, including a person who is treated as being the father of the child by section 28 of the 1990 Act where he is not the husband within the meaning of section 30 of the 1990 Act;

'the birth mother' means the woman who carried the child;

'the birth parents' means the birth mother and the birth father;

…¹

'the husband and wife' means the persons who may apply for a parental order where the conditions set out in section 30(1) of the 1990 Act are met;

'parental order' means an order under section 30 of the 1990 Act (parental orders in favour of gamete donors) providing for a child to be treated in law as a child of the parties to a marriage.

['parental order reporter' means an officer of the service appointed under section 41 of the Children Act 1989 in relation to proceedings specified by paragraph (2).]¹

(2) Applications under section 30 of the 1990 Act are specified proceedings for the purposes of section 41 of the Children Act 1989 in accordance with section 41(6)(i) of that Act.

NOTES
Amendments. ¹ Definition omitted or inserted: SI 2001/818.

21B Application of the remaining provisions of these Rules

Subject to the provisions of this Part, the remaining provisions of these Rules shall apply as appropriate with any necessary modifications to proceedings under this Part except that rules 7(1), 9, 10(1)(b), 10(11), [11A(1)]¹, [11A(2)]¹ and 12 shall not apply.

NOTES
Amendments. ¹ Text substituted: SI 2001/818.

21C Parties

The applicants shall be the husband and wife and the respondents shall be the persons set out in the relevant entry in column (iii) of Schedule 2.

21D [Acknowledgement]¹

Within 14 days of the service of an application for a parental order, each respondent shall file and serve on all the other parties an [acknowledgement in Form C52.]¹

NOTES
Amendments. ¹ Words substituted: SI 1994/3156.

21E Appointment and duties of the [parental order reporter][1]

(1) As soon as practicable after the application has been filed, the justices' clerk shall consider the appointment of a [parental order reporter][1] in accordance with section 41(1) of the Children Act 1989.

(2) ...[1]

(3) In addition to such of the matters set out in [rules 11 and 11A][1] as are appropriate, the [parental order reporter][1] shall –

  (i) investigate the matters set out in section 30(1) to (7) of the 1990 Act;
  (ii) so far as he considers necessary, investigate any matter contained in the application form or other matter which appears relevant to the making of a parental order;
  (iii) advise the court on whether there is any reason under section 6 of the Adoption Act 1976, as applied with modifications by the Parental Orders (Human Fertilisation and Embryology) Regulations 1994, to refuse the parental order.

NOTES
Amendments. [1] Words substituted or omitted: SI 2001/818.

21F Personal attendance of applicants

The court shall not make a parental order except upon the personal attendance before it of the applicants.

21G Copies of orders

(1) Where a parental order is made by a court sitting in Wales in respect of a child who was born in Wales and the applicants so request before the order is drawn up, the [justices' chief executive][1] shall obtain a translation into Welsh of the particulars set out in the order.

(2) Within 7 days after the making of a parental order, the [justices' chief executive][1] shall send a copy of the order to the Registrar General.

(3) A copy of any parental order may be supplied to the Registrar General at his request.

NOTES
Amendments. [1] Words substituted: SI 2001/615.

21H Amendment and revocation of orders

(1) Any application made under paragraph 4 of Schedule 1 to the Adoption Act 1976 as modified by the Parental Orders (Human Fertilisation and Embryology) Regulations 1994 for the amendment of a parental order or for the revocation of a direction to the Registrar General shall be made to a family proceedings court for the same petty sessions area as the family proceedings court which made the parental order, by delivering it or sending it by post to the [justices' chief executive][1].

(2) Notice of the application shall be given by the [justices' chief executive][1] to such persons (if any) as the court thinks fit.

(3) Where the application is granted, the [justices' chief executive][1] shall send to the Registrar General a notice specifying the amendments or informing him of the revocation and shall give sufficient particulars of the order to enable the Registrar General to identify the case.

NOTES
   Amendments. [1] Words substituted: SI 2001/615.

21I Keeping of registers, custody, inspection and disclosure of documents and information

(1) Such part of the register kept in pursuance of rules made under the Magistrates' Courts Act 1980 as relates to proceedings for parental orders shall be kept in a separate book and the book shall not contain particulars of any other proceedings.

(2) The book kept in pursuance of paragraph (1) and all other documents relating to the proceedings for a parental order shall, while they are in the custody of the court, be kept in a place of special security.

(3) Any person who obtains information in the course of, or relating to proceedings for a parental order, shall treat that information as confidential and shall only disclose it if –

   (a) the disclosure is necessary for the proper exercise of his duties, or
   (b) the information is requested –
      (i) by a court or public authority (whether in Great Britain or not) having the power to determine proceedings for a parental order and related matters, for the purpose of the discharge of its duties in that behalf, or
      (ii) by a person who is authorised in writing by the Secretary of State to obtain the information for the purposes of research.

21J Application for removal, return etc of child

(1) An application under sections 27(1), 29(1) or 29(2) of the Adoption Act 1976 as applied with modifications by the Parental Orders (Human Fertilisation and Embryology) Regulations 1994 shall be made by complaint to the family proceedings court in which the application under section 30 of the 1990 Act is pending.

(2) The respondents shall be all the parties to the proceedings under section 30 and such other person or body, not being the child, as the court thinks fit.

(3) The [justices' chief executive][2] shall serve notice of the time fixed for the hearing, together with a copy of the complaint on the guardian ad litem who may attend on the hearing of the application and be heard on the question of whether the application should be granted.

(4) The court may at any time give directions as to the conduct of the application under this rule.

(5) Where an application under this rule is determined, the [justices' chief executive][2] shall serve notice of the determination on all the parties.

(6) A search warrant issued by a justice of the peace under section 29(4) of the Adoption Act 1976 (applied as above) (which relates to premises specified in an information to which an order made under the said section 29(1) relates,

PART II

authorising a constable to search the said premises and if he finds the child to return the child to the person on whose application the said order was made) shall be in a warrant form as if issued under section 102 of the Children Act 1989 (warrant to search for or remove a child) or a form to the like effect.]¹

PART III
MISCELLANEOUS

22 Costs

(1) In any relevant proceedings, the court may, at any time during the proceedings in that court, make an order that a party pay the whole or any part of the costs of any other party.

(2) A party against whom the court is considering making a costs order shall have an opportunity to make representations as to why the order should not be made.

[22A Power of court to limit cross-examination

The court may limit the issues on which an officer of the service may be cross-examined.]¹

23 Confidentiality of documents

(1) No document, other than a record of an order, held by the court and relating to relevant proceedings shall be disclosed, other than to –

    (a) a party,
    (b) the legal representative of a party,
    (c) the [children's guardian]¹,
    (d) the Legal Aid Board, or
    (e) a [welfare officer or children and family reporter]¹, [or
    (f) an expert whose instruction by a party has been authorised by the court,]¹

without leave of the justices' clerk or the court.

(2) Nothing in this rule shall prevent the notification by the court or the [justices' chief executive]² of a direction under section 37(1) to the authority concerned.

[(3) Nothing in this rule shall prevent the disclosure of a document prepared by an officer of the service for the purpose of –

    (a) enabling a person to perform functions required under section 62(3A) of the Justices of the Peace Act 1997;
    (b) assisting an officer of the service who is appointed by the court under any enactment to perform his functions.]¹

[(4) Nothing in this rule shall prevent the disclosure of any document relating to proceedings by an officer of the service to any other officer of the service unless that other officer is involved in the same proceedings but on behalf of a different party.]¹

NOTES
Amendments. ¹ Words substituted or inserted: SI 2001/818. ² Words substituted: SI 2001/615.

24 Enforcement of residence order

Where a person in whose favour a residence order is in force wishes to enforce it he shall file a written statement describing the alleged breach of the arrangements settled by the order, whereupon the justices' clerk shall fix a date, time and place for a hearing of the proceedings and [the justices' chief executive shall]¹ give notice, as soon as practicable, to the person wishing to enforce the residence order and to any person whom it is alleged is in breach of the arrangements settled by that order, of the date fixed.

NOTES
Amendments. ¹ Words inserted: SI 2001/615.

25 Notification of consent

[(1)]² Consent for the purposes of –

    (a) section 16(3), [or]¹
    (b) [section 38A(2)(b)(ii) or 44A(2)(b)(ii), or]²
    (c) paragraph 19(1) of Schedule 2,

shall be given either –

      (i) orally in court, or
     (ii) in writing to the [justices' chief executive]³ or the court and signed by the person giving his consent.

[(2) Any written consent given for the purposes of subsection (2) of section 38A or section 44A, shall include a statement that the person giving consent –

    (a) is able and willing to give to the child the care which it would be reasonable to expect a parent to give him; and
    (b) understands that the giving of consent could lead to the exclusion of the relevant person from the dwelling-house in which the child lives.]²

NOTES
Amendments. ¹ Words inserted or revoked: SI 1992/2068. ² Paragraph numbering and paragraph inserted and words substituted: SI 1997/1895. ³ Words substituted: SI 2001/615.

[25A Exclusion requirements: interim care orders and emergency protection orders

(1) This rule applies where the court includes an exclusion requirement in an interim care order or an emergency protection order.

(2) The applicant for an interim care order or emergency protection order shall –

    (a) prepare a separate statement of the evidence in support of the application for an exclusion requirement;

(b) serve the statement personally on the relevant person with a copy of the order containing the exclusion requirement (and of any power of arrest which is attached to it);

(c) inform the relevant person of his right to apply to vary or discharge the exclusion requirement.

(3) Where a power of arrest is attached to an exclusion requirement in an interim care order or an emergency protection order, a copy of the order shall be delivered to the officer for the time being in charge of the police station for the area in which the dwelling-house in which the child lives is situated (or of such other station as the court may specify) together with a statement that the relevant person has been served with the order or informed of its terms (whether by being present when the order was made or by telephone or otherwise).

(4) Rules 12A(3), 20 (except paragraphs (1) and (3)) and 21 of the Family Proceedings Courts (Matrimonial Proceedings etc) Rules 1991 shall apply, with the necessary modifications, for the service, variation, discharge and enforcement of any exclusion requirement to which a power of arrest is attached as they apply to an order made on an application under Part IV of the Family Law Act 1996.

(5) The relevant person shall serve the parties to the proceedings with any application which he makes for the variation or discharge of the exclusion requirement.

(6) Where an exclusion requirement ceases to have effect whether –

(a) as a result of the removal of a child under section 38A(10) or 44A(10),

(b) because of the discharge of the interim care order or emergency protection order, or

(c) otherwise,

the applicant shall inform –

(i) the relevant person,

(ii) the parties to the proceedings,

(iii) any officer to whom a copy of the order was delivered under paragraph (3), and

(iv) (where necessary) the court.

(7) Where the court includes an exclusion requirement in an interim care order or an emergency protection order of its own motion, paragraph (2) shall apply with the omission of any reference to the statement of the evidence.][1]

NOTES

Amendments. [1] Rule inserted: SI 1997/1895.

26 Secure accommodation

In proceedings under section 25, the [justices' chief executive][1] shall, if practicable, arrange for copies of all written reports before the court to be made available before the hearing to –

(a) the applicant,

(b) the parent or guardian of the child,

(c) any legal representative of the child,

(d) the [children's guardian][2], and

(e) the child, unless the justices' clerk or the court otherwise directs;

and copies of such reports may, if the court considers it desirable, be shown to any person who is entitled to notice of the proceedings in accordance with these Rules.

NOTES
Amendments. [1] Words substituted: SI 2001/615. [2] Words substituted: SI 2001/818.

27 Investigation under section 37

(1) This rule applies where a direction is given to an appropriate authority by a family proceedings court under section 37(1).

(2) On giving a direction the court shall adjourn the proceedings and the justices' clerk or the court shall record the direction [in Form C40][1].

(3) A copy of the direction recorded under paragraph (2) shall, as soon as practicable after the direction is given, be served by the [justices' chief executive][2] on the parties to the proceedings in which the direction is given and, where the appropriate authority is not a party, on that authority.

(4) When serving the copy of the direction on the appropriate authority the [justices' chief executive][2] shall also serve copies of such of the documentary evidence which has been, or is to be, adduced in the proceedings as the court may direct.

(5) Where a local authority informs the court of any of the matters set out in section 37(3)(a) to (c) it shall do so in writing.

NOTES
Amendments. [1] Words substituted: SI 1994/3156. [2] Words substituted: SI 2001/615.

28 Limits on the power of a justices' clerk or a single justice to make an order under section 11(3) or section 38(1)

A justices' clerk or single justice shall not make an order under section 11(3) or section 38(1) unless –

(a) a written request for such an order has been made to which the other parties and any [children's guardian][1] consent and which they or their representatives have signed,

(b) a previous such order has been made in the same proceedings, and

(c) the terms of the order sought are the same as those of the last such order made.

NOTES
Amendments. [1] Words substituted: SI 2001/818.

29 Appeals to a family proceedings court under section 77(6) and paragraph 8(1) of Schedule 8

(1) An appeal under section 77(6) or paragraph 8(1) of Schedule 8 shall be by application in accordance with rule 4.

(2) An appeal under section 77(6) shall be brought within 21 days from the date of the step to which the appeal relates.

30 Contribution orders

(1) An application for a contribution order under paragraph 23(1) of Schedule 2 shall be accompanied by a copy of the contribution notice served in accordance with paragraph 22(1) of that Schedule and a copy of any notice served by the contributor under paragraph 22(8) of that Schedule.

(2) Where a local authority notifies the court of an agreement reached under paragraph 23(6) of Schedule 2, it shall do so in writing through the [justices' chief executive][1].

(3) An application for the variation or revocation of a contribution order under paragraph 23(8) of Schedule 2 shall be accompanied by a copy of the contribution order which it is sought to vary or revoke.

NOTES
Amendments. [1] Words substituted: SI 2001/615.

31 Direction to local education authority to apply for education supervision order

(1) For the purposes of section 40(3) and (4) of the Education Act 1944, a direction by a magistrates' court to a local education authority to apply for an education supervision order shall be given [in writing][1].

(2) Where, following such a direction, a local education authority informs the court that they have decided not to apply for an education supervision order, they shall do so in writing.

NOTES
Amendments. [1] Words substituted: SI 1997/1895.

[31A Applications and orders under sections 33 and 34 of the Family Law Act 1986

(1) In this rule 'the 1986 Act' means the Family Law Act 1986.

(2) An application under section 33 of the 1986 Act shall be in Form C4 and an order made under that section shall be in Form C30.

(3) An application under section 34 of the 1986 Act shall be in Form C3 and an order made under that section shall be in Form C31.

(4) An application under section 33 or section 34 of the 1986 Act may be made ex parte in which case the applicant shall file the application –

    (a) where the application is made by telephone, within 24 hours after the making of the application, or
    (b) in any other case at the time when the application is made,

and shall serve a copy of the application on each respondent 48 hours after the making of the order.

(5) Where the court refuses to make an order on an ex parte application it may direct that the application be make inter partes.][1]

NOTES
Amendments. [1] Rule inserted: SI 1994/3156.

32 Delegation by justices' clerk

(1) In this rule, 'employed as a clerk in court' has the same meaning as in rule 2(1) of the Justices' Clerks (Qualifications of Assistants) Rules 1979.

(2) Anything authorised to be done by, to or before a justices' clerk under these Rules, or under paragraphs 13 to 15C of the Justices' Clerks Rules 1970 as amended by Schedule 3 to these Rules, may be done instead by, to or before a person employed as a clerk in court where that person is appointed by the magistrates' courts committee to assist him and where that person has been specifically authorised by the justices' clerk for that purpose.

(3) Any authorisation by the justices' clerk under paragraph (2) shall be recorded in writing at the time the authority is given or as soon as practicable thereafter.

33 Application of section 97 of the Magistrates' Courts Act 1980

Section 97 of the Magistrates' Courts Act 1980 shall apply to relevant proceedings in a family proceedings court as it applies to a hearing of a complaint under that section.

[33A Disclosure of addresses

(1) Nothing in these rules shall be construed as requiring any party to reveal the address of their private residence (or that of any child) except by order of the court.

(2) Where a party declines to reveal an address in reliance upon paragraph (1) he shall give notice of that address to the court in Form C8 and that address shall not be revealed to any person except by order of the court.][1]

NOTES
    Amendments. [1] Rule inserted: SI 1994/3156.

[33B Setting aside on failure of service

Where an application has been sent to a respondent in accordance with rule 8(1) and, after an order has been made on the application, it appears to the court that the application did not come to the knowledge of the respondent in due time, the court may of its own motion set aside the order and may give such directions as it thinks fit for the rehearing of the application.][1]

NOTES
    Amendments. [1] Rule inserted: SI 1997/1895.

34 Consequential and minor amendments, savings and transitionals

(1) Subject to paragraph (3) the consequential and minor amendments in Schedule 3 to these Rules shall have effect.

(2) Subject to paragraph (3), the provisions of the 1981 rules shall have effect subject to these Rules.

(3) Nothing in these Rules shall affect any proceedings which are pending (within the meaning of paragraph 1 of Schedule 14 to the Act of 1989) immediately before these Rules come into force.

****

SCHEDULE 1
FORMS

[C1	Application	for an order
C2	Application	for an order or directions in existing family proceedings
	Application	to be joined as, or cease to be, a party in existing family proceedings
	Application	for leave to commence proceedings
C3	Application	for an order authorising search for, taking charge of, and delivery of a child
C4	Application	for an order for disclosure of a child's whereabouts
C5	Application	concerning the registration of a child-minder or a provider of day care
C6	Notice	of proceedings [Hearing] [Directions Appointment] (*Notice to parties*)
C6A	Notice	of proceedings [Hearing] [Directions Appointment] (*Notice to non-parties*)
C7		Acknowledgement
C8		Confidential Address
C9	Statement	of Service
C10	Supplement	for an application for financial provision for a child or for variation of financial provision for a child
C10A	Statement	of Means
[C11	Supplement	for an application for an Emergency Protection Order][2]
C12	Supplement	for an application for a Warrant to assist a person authorised by an Emergency Protection Order
C13	Supplement	for an application for a Care or Supervision Order
C14	Supplement	for an application for authority to refuse contact with a child in care

C15	Supplement	for an application for contact with a child in care
C16	Supplement	for an application for a Child Assessment Order
C17	Supplement	for an application for an Education Supervision Order
C17A	Supplement	for an application for an extension of an Education Supervision Order
C18	Supplement	for an application for a Recovery Order
C19	Supplement	for a Warrant of Assistance
C20	Supplement	for an application for an order to hold a child in Secure Accommodation
C21	Order or direction	Blank
C22	Record	of hearing
[C23	Order	Emergency Protection Order][2]
C24	Order	Variation of an Emergency Protection Order
		Extension of an Emergency Protection Order
		Discharge of an Emergency Protection Order
C25	Warrant	To assist a person authorised by an Emergency Protection Order
C26	Order	Authority to keep a child in Secure Accommodation
C27	Order	Authority to search for another child
C28	Warrant	To assist a person to gain access to a child or entry to premises
C29	Order	Recovery of a child
C30	Order	To disclose information about the whereabouts of a missing child
C31	Order	Authorising search for, taking charge of, and delivery of a child
C32	Order	Care Order
		Discharge of a Care Order
[C33	Order	Interim Care Order][2]
C34	Order	Contact with a child in care
		Authority to refuse contact with a child in care
C35	Order	Supervision Order

PART II

		Interim Supervision Order
C36	Order	Substitution of a Supervision Order for a Care Order
		Discharge of a Supervision Order
		Variation of a Supervision Order
		Extension of a Supervision Order
C37	Order	Education Supervision Order
C38	Order	Discharge of an Education Supervision Order
		Extension of an Education Supervision Order
C39	Order	Child Assessment Order
C40	Direction	To undertake an investigation
C41	Order	Cancellation of the registration of a child-minder or a provider of day care
		Removal, Variation or Imposition of a requirement on a child-minder or a provider of day care
C42	Order	Family Assistance Order
C43	Order	Residence Order
		Contact Order
		Specific Issue Order
		Prohibited Steps Order
C44	Order	Leave to change the surname by which a child is known
		Leave to remove a child from the United Kingdom
C45	Order	Parental Responsibility Order
		Termination of a Parental Responsibility Order
C46	Order	Appointment of a guardian
		Termination of the appointment of a guardian
C47	Order	Making or refusing the appointment of a [children's guardian][3]
		Termination of the appointment of a [children's guardian][3]
C48	Order	Appointment of a solicitor for a child
		Refusal of the appointment of a solicitor for a child

		Termination of the appointment of a solicitor for a child
C49	Order	Transfer of Proceedings to [the High Court] [a county court] [a family proceedings court]
C50	Certificate	Refusal to transfer proceedings
C51	Application	for a Parental Order
C52		Acknowledgement of an application for a Parental Order
C53	Order	Parental Order
C54	Notice	of Refusal of a Parental Order][1]

NOTES

Amendments. [1] Forms substituted: SI 1994/3156. [2] Form substituted: SI 1997/1895. [3] Words substituted: SI 2001/818.

SCHEDULE 2

RESPONDENTS AND NOTICE

Rules 4 and 7

(i) Provision under which proceedings brought	(ii) Minimum number of days prior to hearing or directions appointment for service under rule 4(1)(b)	(iii) Respondents	(iv) Persons to whom notice is to be given
All applications.	See separate entries below.	Subject to separate entries below. every person whom the applicant believes to have parental responsibility for the child; where the child is the subject of a care order, every person whom the applicant believes to have had parental	Subject to separate entries below, the local authority providing accommodation for the child; persons who are caring for the child at the time when the proceedings are commenced; in the case of proceedings brought

(i) *Provision under which proceedings brought*	(ii) *Minimum number of days prior to hearing or directions appointment for service under rule 4(1)(b)*	(iii) *Respondents*	(iv) *Persons to whom notice is to be given*
		responsibility immediately prior to the making of the care order; in the case of an application to extend, vary or discharge an order, the parties to the proceedings leading to the order which it is sought to have extended, varied or discharged;	in respect of a child who is alleged to be staying in a refuge which is certificated under section 51(1) or (2), the person who is providing the refuge.
...[1]		in the case of specified proceedings, the child.	
Section 4(1)(a), 4(3), 5(1), 6(7), [8,][1] 13(1), 16(6), 33(7), 77(6), [Schedule 1,][1] paragraph 19(1), 23(1) or 23(8) of Schedule 2, paragraph 8(1) of Schedule 8, or paragraph 11(3) or 16(5) of Schedule 14.	14 days.	Except for proceedings under section 77(6), Schedule 2, or paragraph 8(1) of Schedule 8, as for 'all applications' above, and – in the case of an application under paragraph 11(3)(b) or 16(5) of Schedule 14, any person, other than the child, named in the order or directions which it is sought to discharge or vary; [in the case of proceedings][1] under section 77(6), the	As for 'all applications' above, and – in the case of an application under paragraph 19(1) of Schedule 2, the parties to the proceedings leading to the care order; in the case of an application under section 5(1), the father of the child if he does not have parental responsibility.

(i) *Provision under which proceedings brought*	(ii) *Minimum number of days prior to hearing or directions appointment for service under rule 4(1)(b)*	(iii) *Respondents*	(iv) *Persons to whom notice is to be given*
		local authority against whose decision the appeal is made; [in the case of proceedings under Schedule 1, those persons whom the applicant believes to be interested in or affected by the proceedings;][1] in the case of an application under paragraph 23(1) of Schedule 2, the contributor; in the case of an application under paragraph 23(8) of Schedule 2 – (i) if the applicant is the local authority, the contributor, and (ii) if the applicant is the contributor, the local authority. In the case of an application under paragraph 8(1) of Schedule 8, the local authority against whose decision the appeal is made.	

PART II

(i) *Provision under which proceedings brought*	(ii) *Minimum number of days prior to hearing or directions appointment for service under rule 4(1)(b)*	(iii) *Respondents*	(iv) *Persons to whom notice is to be given*
		[in the case of an application for a section 8 order, every person whom the applicant believes — (i) to be named in a court order with respect to the same child, which has not ceased to have effect, (ii) to be a party to pending proceedings in respect of the same child, or (iii) to be a person with whom the child has lived for at least three years prior to the application, unless, in a case to which (i) or (ii) applies, the applicant believes that the court order or pending proceedings are not relevant to the application.][1]	

(i) Provision under which proceedings brought	(ii) Minimum number of days prior to hearing or directions appointment for service under rule 4(1)(b)	(iii) Respondents	(iv) Persons to whom notice is to be given
Section 36(1), 39(1), 39(2), 39(3), 39(4), 43(1), or paragraph 6(3), 15(2) or 17(1) of Schedule 3.	7 days.	As for 'all applications' above, and – in the case of an application under section 39(2) or (3), the supervisor; in the case of proceedings under paragraph 17(1) of Schedule 3, the local education authority concerned; in the case of proceedings under section 36 or paragraph 15(2) or 17(1) of Schedule 3, the child.	As for 'all applications' above, and – in the case of an application for an order under section 43(1) – (i) every person whom the applicant believes to be a parent of the child, (ii) every person whom the applicant believes to be caring for the child, (iii) every person in whose favour a contact order is in force with respect to the child, and (iv) every person who is allowed to have contact with the child by virtue of an order under section 34.

(i) *Provision under which proceedings brought*	(ii) *Minimum number of days prior to hearing or directions appointment for service under rule 4(1)(b)*	(iii) *Respondents*	(iv) *Persons to whom notice is to be given*
Section 31, 34(2), 34(3), 34(4), 34(9) or 38(8)(b).	3 days.	As for 'all applications' above, and – in the case of an application under section 34, the person whose contact with the child is the subject of the application.	As for 'all applications' above, and – in the case of application under section 31 – (i) every person whom the applicant believes to be a party to pending relevant proceedings in respect of the same child, and (ii) every person whom the applicant believes to be a parent without parental responsibility for the child.
Section 43(12).	2 days.	As for 'all applications' above.	Those of the persons referred to in section 43(11)(a) to (e) who were not party to the application for the order which it is sought to have varied or discharged.

(i) Provision under which proceedings brought	(ii) Minimum number of days prior to hearing or directions appointment for service under rule 4(1)(b)	(iii) Respondents	(iv) Persons to whom notice is to be given
Section 25, 44(1), 44(9)(b), 45(4), 45(8), 46(7), 48(9), 50(1), 75(1) or 102(1).	1 day.	Except for applications under section 75(1) or 102(1), as for 'all applications' above, and – in the case of an application under section 44(9)(b) – (i) the parties to the application for the order in respect of which it is sought to vary the directions; (ii) any person who was caring for the child prior to the making of the order; and (iii) any person whose contact with the child is affected by the direction which it is sought to have varied; in the case of an application under section 50, the person whom the applicant alleges to have effected or to have been or to be responsible for the taking or keeping of the child;	As for 'all applications' above and – in the case of an application under section 44(1), every person whom the applicant believes to be a parent of the child; in the case of an application under section 44(9)(b) – (i) the local authority in whose area the child is living, and (ii) any person whom the applicant believes to be affected by the direction which it is sought to have varied.

PART II

(i) *Provision under which proceedings brought*	(ii) *Minimum number of days prior to hearing or directions appointment for service under rule 4(1)(b)*	(iii) *Respondents*	(iv) *Persons to whom notice is to be given*
		in the case of an application under section 75(1), the registered person; in the case of an application under section 102(1), the person referred to in section 102(1) and any person preventing or likely to prevent such a person from exercising powers under enactments mentioned in subsection (6) of that section.	
[Section 30 of the Human Fertilisation and Embryology Act 1990.	14 days.	The birth parents (except where the applicants seek to dispense with their agreement under section 30(6) of the Human Fertilisation and Embryology Act 1990) and any other persons or body with parental responsibility for the child at the date of the application.	Any local authority or voluntary organisation that has at any time provided accommodation for the child.][2]

NOTES

Amendments. [1] Words substituted, revoked or inserted: SI 1992/2068. [2] Words inserted: SI 1994/2166.

****

PART III

Practice Directions and Guidance

Practice Note
11 November 1993

Citations: [1994] 1 FLR 323

B v B (Court Bundles: Video Evidence)

After consultation with the President and with his approval Wall J made the following statement about the efficient preparation of court bundles.

1 Careful thought should always be given by the solicitors carrying the burden of the litigation to the preparation of the bundles to be used in court. This should preferably be done in consultation with counsel who is to have the conduct of the case in court and should certainly be done in consultation with the solicitors for the other parties. There should always be liaison and co-operation between the parties' legal advisers in the preparation of documents for use in court. This should be done in good time before the trial: documents which arrive late or at the last minute can then be added to existing bundles or bundled separately.

2 Where the mechanical task of putting bundles together is delegated to a clerk or junior member of staff it remains the responsibility of the solicitor or managing clerk who has the conduct of the case to check the bundles before they leave the solicitors' offices to ensure that they are in order.

3 In particular, a check should be made to ensure that all the documents copied are legible and that the photocopying process has not truncated any document so that part of it is missing. Elementary as this may sound, illegible or truncated documents are frequently found in court bundles. Where a document is found to be illegible or will not copy properly (for example because it is itself a copy or because it is an original which has been highlighted over the text) a typed version of the document should be made and inserted in the bundle next to the illegible copy.

4 Documents should be presented in a logical (usually chronological) order. The preparer of the bundles should attempt to put himself or herself in the position of the judge who is coming to the papers for the first time. Nothing is more frustrating than to open a bundle of documents and to read 'I make this statement further to my previous statement of such and such a date and in answer to the respondent's statement'. The judge then has the choice either of reading something which answers an allegation he has yet to read or searching the bundle for the document to which it is a reply. For these reasons it is not appropriate to bundle each party's evidence separately in different bundles or in different sections of a bundle. A chronological presentation enables the judge to read a bundle through from beginning to end without the distraction of having to search for documents which are out of sequence.

5 All bundles should be properly indexed with a description of each document and the page number at which it begins and ends.

6 Bundles should be individually paginated, and the pagination should be continuous throughout each bundle. A master bundle should be prepared and copy bundles should only be made after the master bundle has been paginated, not before. By these means only can it be ensured that everyone in court has the same document with identical pagination. Equally documents should not be presented with generalised numbering – for example, document 1 is the applicant's statement, document 2 is the respondent's statement, and so on. The aim in court is

to be able to refer to bundle A page x, not bundle A, document 2, and page x of that document. The latter process is very time-wasting.

7 It is common practice for solicitors to prepare bundles for their own use and for the use of the court and to provide indices only to the solicitors for the other parties. In my judgement it is preferable for the solicitors having the conduct of the litigation to prepare all the bundles and distribute them after making a charge for photocopying. Where, however, indices only are supplied, it is the duty of the recipient solicitors to ensure that the bundles which they make up from the indices have identical pagination to the master bundles. A simple telephone call should obviate any difficulty in this regard.

8 Whilst each case varies in relation to the issues which arise from it, thought should always be given to the categorisation of documents and their distribution into individual bundles. Usually it is sensible to have a bundle of statements or affidavits (chronologically arranged) another for formal court documents and interlocutory court orders (also in chronological order) another for bundles of expert or medical reports (likewise arranged in chronological sequence) and so on.

9 Where medical records are relevant and reproduced every effort should be made to ensure that the copies are legible and photocopied in the correct order and are presented the right way up. In rare cases where a bundle of solicitors' correspondence is relevant, that correspondence should likewise be presented in chronological order. Where there are documents in manuscript (such as letters between the parties) typed copies should be provided unless the manuscript is clearly legible.

10 Rigorous pruning of unnecessary material should take place and duplication should be avoided. If a document is exhibited to an affidavit or statement and should more logically appear elsewhere (for example as a medical report in a medical bundle) a page can be inserted in the bundle from which it has been removed stating where it is to be found.

11 Wherever possible the chronology prepared by the applicant should be cross-referenced to the relevant page in the relevant bundle. Such a process can only be achieved if the person preparing the chronology has access to the bundles in their final state, but the process is of enormous assistance to the judge. Equally a dramatis personae which identifies the parties and the principal witnesses and where their evidence is to be found is extremely useful to the judge.

12 There should always be a 'witness bundle' that is to say a spare bundle for use by witnesses in the witness box. When a document needs to be put to a witness it is at the very least a discourtesy to the witness if the document has to be retrieved from a solicitor's file or counsel's papers. It is also time wasting. Moreover, the witness bundles must be kept up to date during the trial. It is the duty of the advocate having the conduct of the proceedings to ensure that this is done.

13 Bundles should be presented in a way which enables them to lie flat when opened. It is very irritating when cross-referencing documentation or making a note if the bundle snaps shut as soon as the hand is taken off it. Furthermore, staples, treasury tags or other means of holding papers together should be removed once the papers are in a file or ring binder.

14 Documents frequently arrive or emerge during the course of a trial. Provided there is agreement for their inclusion in the court bundles they should be paginated, photocopied, hole punched and inserted in the relevant bundle at the relevant place and, if possible, the index to the particular bundle amended to cover their inclusion.

15 Where videos of interviews with children form part of the evidence in the case there should either be a directions appointment at which their use is discussed and directions about their use given, alternatively the parties' respective solicitors should attempt to agree about the manner in which they are to be used. Thus:

(a) where there is to be a challenge to the technique used or debate as to the interpretation of what the child or interviewer has said, transcripts should be obtained and placed in a separate bundle;

(b) if the judge is to be asked to view the videos in private before the trial begins:
  (i) the agreement of all the parties to this course should be obtained,
  (ii) the parties should endeavour to agree those parts of the interviews which the judge should look at,
  (iii) a transcript should be provided to the judge;

(c) where it is intended that the video should be played in court in addition or as an alternative to a private viewing made by the judge, early arrangements should be made for the provision of the relevant equipment, agreement reached on the parts of the interviews which are to be played and transcripts provided.

PART III

Practice Direction
31 January 1995

Citations: [1995] 1 FLR 456; [1995] 1 WLR 332; [1995] 1 All ER 586

Case Management

1 The importance of reducing the cost and delay of civil litigation makes it necessary for the court to assert greater control over the preparation for and conduct of hearings than has hitherto been customary. Failure by practitioners to conduct cases economically will be visited by appropriate orders for costs, including wasted costs orders.

2 The court will accordingly exercise its discretion to limit –

  (a) discovery;
  (b) the length of opening and closing oral submissions;
  (c) the time allowed for the examination and cross-examination of witnesses;
  (d) the issues on which it wishes to be addressed;
  (e) reading aloud from documents and authorities.

3 Unless otherwise ordered, every witness statement or affidavit shall stand as the evidence in chief of the witness concerned. The substance of the evidence which a party intends to adduce at the hearing must be sufficiently detailed, but without prolixity; it must be confined to material matters of fact, not (except in the case of the evidence of professional witnesses) of opinion; and if hearsay evidence is to be adduced, the source of the information must be declared or good reason given for not doing so.

4 It is a duty owed to the court both by the parties and by their legal representatives to give full and frank disclosure in ancillary relief applications and also in all matters in respect of children. The parties and their advisers must also use their best endeavours:

  (a) to confine the issues and the evidence called to what is reasonably considered to be essential for the proper presentation of their case;
  (b) to reduce or eliminate issues for expert evidence;
  (c) in advance of the hearing to agree which are the issues or the main issues.

5 *(ceased to have effect – see President's Direction of 10 March 2000)*

6 In cases estimated to last for five days or more and in which no pre-trial review has been ordered, application should be made for a pre-trial review. It should when practicable be listed at least three weeks before the hearing and be conducted by the judge or district judge before whom the case is to be heard and should be attended by the advocates who are to represent the parties at the hearing. Whenever possible, all statements of evidence and all reports should be filed before the date of the review and in good time for them to have been considered by all parties.

7 Whenever practicable and in any matter estimated to last five days or more, each party should, not less than two clear days before the hearing, lodge with the court, or the Clerk of the Rules in matters in the Royal Courts of Justice in London, and deliver to other parties, a chronology and a skeleton argument concisely summarising that party's submissions in relation to each of the issues, and citing the main authorities relied upon. It is important that skeleton arguments should be brief.

8 *(ceased to have effect – see President's Direction of 10 March 2000)*

9 The opening speech should be succinct. At its conclusion other parties may be invited briefly to amplify their skeleton arguments. In a heavy case the court may in conjunction with final speeches require written submissions, including the findings of fact for which each party contends.

10 This practice direction which follows *Practice Direction (Civil Litigation: Case Management)* [1995] 1 WLR 262 handed down by Lord Taylor of Gosforth CJ and Sir Richard Scott V-C to apply in the Queen's Bench and Chancery Divisions, shall apply to all family proceedings in the High Court and in all care centres, family hearing centres and divorce county courts.

11 Issued with the concurrence of the Lord Chancellor.

Sir Stephen Brown P

Best Practice Guidance
June 1997

Note: the following materials are taken from the *Children Act Advisory Committee Handbook of Best Practice in Children Act cases*, and are reproduced with the kind permission of the President of the Family Division.

Handbook of Best Practice in Children Act cases

INTRODUCTION

When writing its final report, the Committee thought it might be helpful to gather together in a separate document the guidance available on best practice in Children Act proceedings with a view to providing a useful tool for the conscientious but busy practitioner. Some of this material is newly written and some is a compendium of guidance from our earlier reports updated both by experience and authoritative reported decisions. It follows that some of this guidance is firmly authoritative (deriving from binding decisions or practice directions) whilst much remains advisory, but based on accumulated experience of what works best.

The basic message of this Handbook is that the earlier matters are considered and acted upon by the parties and their advisers, and the more that can be done jointly with other parties, the better the court process can serve the interests of children. Work done in preparation, and in liaison with other parties, is rarely wasted and indeed is almost always productive in terms of avoiding, or at least reducing, the trial process which is after all both the most costly and certainly the most stressful part of the whole proceedings.

We hope that all practitioners (and not just the lawyers) will find this Handbook useful as we try to translate into practice in each case the obligation to promote the welfare of the children with whom we are dealing. We have set out this Handbook with a view primarily to ease of reference in the hope that it will find widespread use in practice.

SECTION 1 – PREPARATION FOR COURT IN CARE PROCEEDINGS

Local authority solicitors

1 At the earliest stage, when first consulted, focus on:

    (a) the issues;
    (b) the legal framework;
    (c) the evidence needed to support an application;
    (d) the proposed care plan;
    (e) the appropriate level of court; and
    (f) the likely time scale for concluding the court case in the light of:
        (i) the complexities involved, and
        (ii) the ages and needs of the children.

2 If counsel is to be instructed, do so at an early stage. Consider together the preparation for trial and whether transfer to the care centre is appropriate.

PART III

All parties and their legal advisers

3 By the first directions hearing, consider whether the issues of fact are stark enough to justify a split hearing, with an early resolution of factual disputes to enable a definitive care plan to be formulated and to enable the guardian ad litem to make recommended actions as to outcome. For example, this is likely to arise in cases of alleged non-accidental injury where different persons are in the frame as possible perpetrators and/or accomplices, and in cases of sexual abuse.

4 Use directions hearings imaginatively. Anticipate problems and address them in advance.

(a) Ensure strict compliance with timetables for filing evidence and documents.

(b) Inform the court, as a matter of urgency, if the timetable cannot be met for any reason.

(c) Be prepared in advance with dates and availability of witnesses and time needed to adduce evidence.

(d) Liaise with other parties to ensure that all issues are addressed at an early stage, for example:
   (i) whether transfer to the care centre would be appropriate;
   (ii) which other persons are seeking party status;
   (iii) issues of disclosure and confidentiality; or
   (iv) any assessments or experts' reports sought by any party.

(e) Fix the final hearing, even if only provisionally.

5 All parties, and in particular the guardian ad litem, have a duty to:

(a) advise the court on the timetable appropriate to the issues and timescale of the child concerned;

(b) keep the timetable under constant review throughout the preparation for the hearing; and

(c) bring to the attention of the court promptly any significant developments and seek further directions.

Instruction of experts

6 See **Section 5** below.

The care plan

7 Ensure that the issues raised by the local authority are clearly set out with a fully researched care plan, to enable the parties to know what case they have to meet.

8 If permanent placement in an alternative family is the plan, prepare the ground as far as possible without pre-empting the court's decision.

9 If the plan is for an adoptive placement, the court will be handicapped in assessing the plan and the timescale, unless the child concerned has already been considered and approved by the adoption and fostering panel, and potential suitable adoptive families have been identified. It is not good practice to await the making of a care order before obtaining such information, because the court is deprived of important background information and significant delay can occur in placing the child in the event of the court approving the plan.

10 If the plan involves a specialist placement with therapy and/or further assessment, identify the placement and any professionals involved, together with the timescale and the availability of appropriate funding.

11 If the plan depends upon the finding of facts or determination of particular issues by the court, state why and set out clear alternative proposals.

12 If no firm proposal can be made, that should be made clear and explained.

Preparing the evidence

13 Check source material and ensure that the case presented is balanced and fair.

14 If research material is to be relied upon, ensure that it is relevant and cogent.

15 Prepare a chronology and statement of issues as the case proceeds, in order to assist the court at directions hearings.

Preparation for the hearing

16 In advance of the final directions hearing, or pre-hearing review before trial, discuss with all parties whether threshold criteria are admitted and if so on what basis, so as to be able to present:

  (a) a statement of agreed facts relevant to the threshold criteria and outcome, and a statement of remaining issues;
  (b) a chronology; and
  (c) a paginated bundle (core bundle if appropriate).

17 In reaching the final estimate of length of hearing:

  (a) establish what evidence is to be called on behalf of any party;
  (b) use the attached template or similar document, in consultation with all parties, so as to timetable the attendance of witnesses at court throughout the hearing; and
  (c) allow time for speeches and judgment in the estimate; and
  (d) keep the time estimate under constant review and inform the court immediately of any change.

18 In preparing the bundle for the final hearing, help the judge, parties and witnesses by:

  (a) providing separate sections for experts' reports and interlocutory orders;
  (b) not keeping rigidly to chronological order if it would result in documents dealing with one particular issue being scattered throughout the bundle;
  (c) ensuring photocopied material is legible and
  (d) having relevant handwritten documents typed.

19 Consider whether a skeleton argument will be of assistance to the court and other parties.

20 Lodge skeleton arguments with the bundle of documents. (They must *not* be handed in on the day of the hearing.)

The court

21 It is essential that judges have the opportunity to read the papers in advance of all directions appointments, and in particular before the final directions hearing, so

PART III

as to ensure that all relevant matters are addressed. It is desirable and saving of court time if the judge who is listed for the full hearing also determines the final directions appointment.

SECTION 2 – RENEWAL OF INTERIM CARE ORDERS

Introduction

22 When an interim care order is made, it is normally necessary for the making of a further interim care order to be considered on at least one occasion before the final hearing. It appears that there is a variety of local practices for dealing with such cases, and, while it is not intended to encourage courts to depart unnecessarily from well-established local arrangements (particularly those which approximate closely to what is recommended below), it is thought that some guidance should be given to ensure some degree of uniformity. Although the making of further interim care orders is here described as 'renewal', it must be remembered that the proper form of order is that the whole application is adjourned to the next date for further consideration.

23 The issue of renewal of interim care orders should normally be addressed at the first directions hearing. An interim care order made at the first hearing will expire after 56 days. In a majority of cases, the reality is that, once an interim care order has been made, the position is unlikely to change before the final hearing. In such cases it would be wasteful of legal costs to require all parties to attend a further hearing.

24 A court may not renew an interim care order as a matter of course, and without reconsideration. At the expiration of every interim care order, the granting of any further interim care order must be considered independently on its merits. It can never be right for a court granting an interim care order at one sitting to attempt to lay down a policy which might fetter the discretion of any future sitting in regard to the grant or refusal of a further interim care order – see *Re P (Minors) (Interim Order)* [1993] 2 FLR 742, CA.

25 It is, therefore, necessary for the court to make a judgment regarding renewal on each occasion, and the court should treat each further hearing as an opportunity to monitor the progress of the application. This does not necessarily mean that all parties should be required to attend a hearing on each occasion. The court is entitled to deal with the matter on the basis of attendance by the local authority only, provided that written consents of the other parties are produced and no party objects.

26 It is therefore suggested that, provided the parents of any child concerned (or any other party with whom the child has been living) are legally represented, provision may be made in the first directions order for a further interim care order to be made without the need for the personal attendance of all parties.

27 When any party objects to the renewal:

(a) that party shall set out the change of circumstances relied upon, and then:
(b) the court must direct an inter partes hearing, allowing sufficient time for the arguments to be heard;
(c) the local authority must inform the court of any objection which it receives; and
(d) the local authority should be prepared to report as to progress and all parties' compliance with directions.

28 The procedure would therefore be as follows.

(a) At the first hearing the court would make the interim care order and further order that:

'The application is adjourned to [date] when the court will consider whether a further interim care order should be made. Provided consents to the making of a further interim care order have been received, and no notice of objection has been received by the [applicant local authority] by 4.00 p.m. on [48 hours before the hearing date] no party other than the applicant need attend.'

(b) Court staff should then list the date for the judge, district judge, or justices' clerk to deal with the application. The appointment should be allowed only a short time; if there are several such appointments, they could be blocklisted.

(c) If any objection is received, the court and, if appropriate, the local authority, must notify all parties urgently that they must attend. In the event of there being inadequate time to hear a contested hearing, the court must urgently fix a date for hearing and make a short term interim care order to cover the interim period.

29 Where a local authority:

(a) produces consents from all parties;

(b) confirms that all directions have been complied with; and

(c) considers that it might be unduly onerous to require the personal attendance of its representative, then there is no reason in principle why the court should not permit the local authority to make a written application for renewal. In such a case, responsibility would rest with the local authority to ensure that a written application was acceptable to the court, and that all parties concerned were satisfied that the papers would reach the court file in time for the hearing.

30 A suggested draft certificate is set out on the following pages.

31 This procedure should not be adopted where any party is in breach of any direction.

32 Where any parent, or other person who has had or who seeks care of the child, is unrepresented, the court should make a tailor-made order, depending on that party's significance in the case, and give notice of every hearing to that person.

[see following page for Draft application for further interim care order]

PART III

Draft application for further interim care order

APPLICATION for further Interim Care Order

Date present order due to expire:

Date of Final Directions/PTR:

Date of Final Hearing:

Estimated length of Final Hearing:

Respondents' representatives:

1   Name:

    Address:

    Telephone number:

2   Name:

    Address:

    Telephone number:

3   Name:

    Address:

    Telephone number:

Child/guardian ad litem's representative:

Name:

Address:

Telephone number:

Nature of current placement:

Has placement changed since last order?	YES/NO
Is change proposed during this order?	YES/NO

Extent of contact offered:

Has this been taken up?	FULL/PARTIAL/NONE

Timetable

has the timetable been complied with to date?	YES/NO
can all outstanding orders be met?	YES/NO
are there any on-going assessments?	YES/NO
is it expected they will affect the timetable?	YES/NO

(If there has been any actual change in placement or any is proposed, please attach a short report addressing that matter.)

As solicitors for the [local authority] we enclose copies of consents received, and certify that we have received no notice of objection to the making of a further interim care order from any party. We apply for a further interim care order to remain in force until [date]:

signed:

date:

SECTION 3 – FIRST APPOINTMENTS IN PUBLIC LAW CASES IN THE COUNTY COURTS: THE ROLE OF THE COURT

Introduction

33 Nominated care district and Circuit judges who deal with directions appointments in public law cases have a vital role in ensuring that the case is

properly brought on for hearing. Such matters as renewal of interim care orders, decisions on split hearings, joinder of parties and timetabling are of the utmost importance and may have a crucial effect on the outcome of the case. It is, therefore, essential that the judge should have been able to read and absorb the papers in the case before the hearing otherwise it will be very difficult for him to challenge anything which the parties' representatives tell him.

The role of the family proceedings court in cases to be transferred

34 It is inevitable that first appointments are listed at very short notice. The clerk of the family proceedings court should:

(a) notify the care centre of the transfer by telephone and ask the date of the first appointment before the judge;
(b) inform all parties of the directions appointment in the care centre;
(c) ensure that the file of papers reaches the care centre not later than midday on the day before the hearing, using a courier service if necessary; and
(d) alert the district judge, by telephone if necessary, to any unusual factor in the case.

The role of the care centre

35 Listing staff in the care centre *must*:

(a) on the telephone, give the clerk of the family proceedings court a date for a directions hearing within two working days;
(b) place the file before the judge on the afternoon before the hearing;
(c) inform the judge of the listing of the application;
(d) (wherever possible) make listed time available for the judge to read the papers; and
(e) (wherever possible) list appointments subsequent to the first appointment before the same judge to ensure continuity of approach.

SECTION 4 – PRIVATE LAW CASES

Introduction

36 The following is a brief guide to best practice in applications made under section 8 of the Children Act. This guidance may need to be tailored to deal with cases involving unrepresented litigants.

37 Specific good practice for cases involving allegations of sexual abuse is set out in the Annex to this section.

Before proceedings

38 Consider whether the dispute between the parties could be resolved in any way other than litigation. Most areas have a mediation service which would be able to attempt to deal with disputes by way of negotiation and agreement. There is rarely anything to be lost, and normally much to be gained, by mediation.

39 At the earliest stage, if it becomes clear that negotiated or mediated settlement will not be possible, focus on:

(a) the issues, including the question of how crucial facts are to be proved;
(b) the legal framework; and
(c) the evidence needed to support the case to be put forward.

Issue of proceedings

40 Ensure that form C1 contains all relevant information, including a brief outline of the case (but not a detailed statement by the applicant).

41 To prevent unnecessary delay at the first directions appointment, prepare at least draft statements by:

(a) the applicant, and
(b) any witnesses who it is known will have to give evidence.

The first directions appointment

The role of the court
42 The court will fix a first directions appointment when an application is issued. The task of the court at the first appointment is to:

(a) investigate the issues;
(b) inquire into the possibility of settlement; and
(c) give directions in any case which has to proceed.

43 When giving directions, the court will normally:

(a) consider the appropriate tier of court;
(b) order the filing of witness statements;
(c) consider whether there are circumstances justifying sequential rather than simultaneous exchange;
(d) express times for filing (for example, of witness statements or the court welfare officer's report) by fixing a date, eg 'by 28 April 1997' and not 'within 14 days'; and
(e) include in the order the date for the next appointment and, even if only provisionally, the final hearing.

44 An order should not provide for an application to be adjourned generally unless the parties consider that it will not be necessary to return to court. In that event the order should also provide for the application to stand dismissed if not restored by a certain date.

45 The order should provide that any letter of instructions to experts (to be joint instructions wherever possible) is to be filed at court.

46 A paginated bundle of documents and chronology should be normal practice except in the simplest case.

The role of the parties
47 Parties and their legal representatives must attend directions appointments unless specifically excused.

48 A party's legal representative must have both sufficient knowledge and authority to take any necessary decisions.

49 Use the first appointment imaginatively, anticipating problems and addressing them in advance, and dealing with questions of expert evidence. (See **Section 5**)

50 When it is to be suggested that there should be contact at a contact centre or supervised contact by an individual, make enquiries to ensure that the centre or individual will be available to provide the service.

Welfare reports

51 Parties should have access to a court welfare officer, or other person qualified to assist them, at or before the first appointment. Some courts achieve this by requiring a court welfare officer to attend the first appointment, others by referring the parties to the welfare officer before the date of the first appointment. Ask about the practice of the local court if you are in any doubt.

52 If a welfare officer has attempted to mediate between the parties, he should not be involved in the case in any other way.

53 When ordering a welfare report, the guidance as to best practice under 'Welfare Reports' at *Best Practice Note of January 1995* should be followed. In particular:

(a) the request for a report should state the issue giving rise to the request;
(b) addendum reports should not normally be ordered, and should not be necessary for the hearing if timetabling has been effective;
(c) any request for the court welfare officer to attend the final hearing should be examined carefully, and not granted as a matter of course;
(d) when a court requires the court welfare officer to attend a hearing, enquiry should be made to ensure that he is available; and
(e) the court hearing the case should allow the officer to give evidence first and then to be released.

Final directions appointments or pre-trial reviews

54 The final directions appointment, or pre-trial review, should be timetabled to take place when any welfare report and all evidence has been filed.

55 The applicant's solicitor must prepare an agreed and paginated bundle of documents, containing an index and a chronology, not less than 24 hours before the hearing.

56 The court will expect the parties' advisers to have addressed the question of what evidence can be agreed and what is in dispute. An order will be made accordingly.

57 The counsel or solicitor who will attend the final hearing should attend the pre-trial review. If this is not possible, the person attending must be thoroughly conversant with the case and competent to make any necessary concessions or admissions and to advise the lay client in respect of settlement.

The final hearing

58 Except by direction of the court, children should not attend a hearing.

59 Consider how the decision of the court is to be communicated to the children. In some cases, particularly where the court's decision is contrary to the reported wishes of the child, it may be appropriate for the court welfare officer to see the child to explain what has happened.

Annex: Flawed sexual abuse investigation

Despite the guidance in *B v B (Sexual Abuse: Procedural Delay)* [1994] 1 FLR 323 and *Re A and B (Minors) (No 2)* [1995] 1 FLR 351, problems continue to occur in private law cases where allegations of sexual abuse of a child are investigated by the police and/or social services. Frequently the cases involve an application for contact with a child, where the primary carer has refused contact on the ground that the child has been sexually abused by the applicant. Such cases cause particular difficulties where the applicant denies the allegation, and alleges that the other parent has either invented the sexual abuse or has brainwashed the child into believing that sexual abuse has occurred. The parent opposing contact may be obstructive and use delaying tactics in order to prevent contact taking place, even under supervision. If such cases are not strictly timetabled, resulting delays can achieve the object of frustrating resumption of contact, even if the court finds that sexual abuse is not proved. Good practice requires as follows:

(a) The legal representatives have a duty, irrespective of whether or not delay might be tactically of advantage to their client, to ensure that a case does not drift and is resolved with the minimum of delay.

(b) The timetable must be strictly controlled by the court and must never be left to the parties. As in public law cases, the court must monitor the procedural steps ordered, building in reviews of progress and setting stringent time limits and return dates.

(c) When the local authority is involved with a concurrent, but independent investigation, the principal co-ordinating agency for the determination of issues is the court, using section 7 of the Children Act 1989 which enables the court to require the local authority to report to the court on the nature, progress and outcome of the child protection investigation. Section 7 should be used to keep the parties informed of progress and material available.

(d) The local authority should make available a social worker to give evidence on the report and to be cross examined if so required.

(e) Any joint child abuse interview conducted by police and social services must follow the memorandum of good practice. Otherwise not only is the resulting interview of no forensic value, but it may impede or contaminate any further assessment of the child ordered by the court.

(f) The court has power to compel discovery of documents held by local authorities or the police, eg videos of interview with the child. If any arguments arise as to confidentiality, or public interest immunity, they should be determined at an early stage at a directions hearing.

(g) Although the court cannot compel a prosecuting authority to reach decisions speedily, the court can and should bring to the attention of the authority the need for a timely decision on criminal prosecution.

(h) Even when there is a police investigation, there is no good legal or social work reason why the social worker should not make contact with the parent under investigation, so that information can be given and exchanged which is relevant to the welfare of the child. The social worker should make it clear that until the police investigation is complete, the specific allegation cannot be discussed. Many parents under police investigation suffer a sense of grievance when no reason is given for denial of contact, with the result that the parent perceives the local authority as pursuing investigations with a closed mind and a presumption of guilt.

(i) The issue whether or not a child has been sexually abused is for decision by the court and it is essential that other agencies await that decision

PART III

before introducing management, counselling or therapy that pre-judges the issue. Therefore, the welfare of the child demands speedy resolution of issues.

(j) If leave is sought to instruct an expert, it is essential to define the issues, to establish the area of expertise required and the proposed timetable, to consider joint instruction and to follow the guidance in **Section 5**. In deciding whether to grant leave for a child to be assessed the court should consider carefully the issues, and whether the court is likely to be assisted in determining whether sexual abuse has been established, as opposed to outcome, by the contribution from an expert in the field of psychological medicine.

(k) There is often a tension between a positive clinical finding of sexual abuse, and judicial findings that abuse has not occurred. In contested cases clinical methods will inevitably be subjected to scrutiny. Any investigation which focuses attention on the statements of the child runs the risk of producing a false result if what the child says is unreliable or if the child's primary caretaker is unreliable, particularly where the allegation emerges in bitterly contested section 8 proceedings. The dangers of a false conclusion are enhanced if the alleged perpetrator is excluded from clinical investigation. It is vital to approach a child abuse investigation with an open mind.

(l) Where possible directions appointments should be heard by the judge who is likely to determine the substantive issues.

(m) In cases in which there is a stark factual issue to be determined the court will need to consider carefully whether it is appropriate to obtain a section 7 report clarifying the issues before ordering a welfare report, whether factual issues need to be determined by the court before a welfare report is ordered as to outcome, or whether a report should be ordered at an early stage in the proceedings. Each case needs to be considered on its merits, and the court welfare service should be invited to make representations.

SECTION 5 – EXPERTS AND THE COURTS

Introduction

60 The guidance in this section applies equally to public and private law cases in which experts are instructed.

61 It is of critical importance to distinguish the respective functions of expert and judge.

(a) The expert forms an assessment, and expresses an opinion within the area of his expertise. This may include an opinion on the issues in the case, but the judge decides particular issues in individual cases.

(b) It is not for the judge to become involved in medical controversy, except in the rare case where such controversy is an issue in the case.

62 The court depends on the skill, knowledge, and above all, the professional and intellectual integrity of the expert witness.

Leave to instruct experts

The role of the instructing parties
63 Applications for leave to instruct experts should be considered by each party at the earliest possible stage of the proceedings in order to avoid serial applications by different parties seeking to counter opinions from experts which do not support their case. Such applications are likely to be refused – see *H v Cambridgeshire County Council* [1997] 1 FCR 569.

64 Advocates who seek such leave have a positive duty to place all relevant information before the court at the earliest opportunity. Applications are unlikely to succeed unless they specify:

(a) the category of expert evidence sought to be adduced;
(b) the name of the expert;
(c) his availability for reporting, meeting with other experts and attendance at court;
(d) the relevance of the expert evidence to the issues in the case;
(e) whether evidence can properly be obtained by both parties jointly instructing one expert; and
(f) whether expert evidence may properly be adduced by one party only, eg the guardian ad litem.

The role of the court
65 The court has a positive duty to enquire into the information provided by the party or parties seeking leave to instruct an expert.

66 The court should never make a generalised order for leave to disclose papers to an expert. The order should specify:

(a) the area of expertise;
(b) the issues to be addressed;
(c) the identity of the expert;
(d) the date by which the letter of instruction is to be sent;
(e) the documents to be released to the expert;
(f) the date for filing the expert's report with the court;
(g) a provision for experts of like discipline to communicate (as discussed below) to agree facts and define issues, together with responsibility for fixing the agenda and chairing the meeting; and
(h) the availability of the expert to give oral evidence, if required.

67 Expert reports based solely upon leave to disclose documents in a 'paper exercise' are rarely as persuasive as those reports based on interviews and assessment as well as the documentation. *Re C (Expert Evidence: Disclosure Practice)* [1995] 1 FLR 204 provides guidance on experts, in contested cases, meeting in advance of the hearing. It should be a condition of appointment of any expert that he should be required to hold discussions with other experts instructed in the same field of expertise, in advance of the hearing, in order to identify areas of agreement and dispute, which should be incorporated into a schedule for the court. Such discussion should be chaired by a co-ordinator, such as the guardian ad litem if there is consent so to act. In advance of the meeting, the co-ordinator should prepare and circulate to all experts a schedule of issues and questions to be addressed at the meeting. The schedule should be prepared in co-operation with all parties, so that all relevant matters are considered by the experts.

68 Problems may arise when an expert's conclusion is unfavourable to the instructing party's case. The court may need to give consideration as to how that expert's evidence is to be adduced.

Letters of instruction and provision of information to experts

69 The letter of instruction should:

(a) define the context in which the opinion is sought;

(b) set out specific questions for the expert to address;

(c) identify any relevant issues of fact to enable each expert to give an opinion on each set of competing issues;

(d) specify any examinations to be permitted;

(e) list the documents to be sent to the expert, which should be presented in a sorted bundle and include an agreed chronology and background history; and

(f) require, as a condition of appointment, that the expert must, in advance of the hearing, hold discussions with other experts appointed in the same field of expertise, and produce a statement of agreement and disagreement on the issues by a specified date.

70 Always disclose the letter of instruction to the other parties, and invite them to contribute to defining the appropriate issues, relevant documentation, history, and questions to be addressed. Include the resulting letter in the bundle of documents for use in court.

71 Doctors who have clinical experience of a child before the commencement of proceedings should have all clinical material made available for inspection by the court and other experts, eg medical notes, hospital records, x-rays, photographs, and correspondence.

72 It is the instructing solicitor's duty to ensure that an expert who is to give oral evidence is kept up to date with relevant developments in the case.

73 It is the duty of the advocate calling an expert to ensure that the witness, in advance of giving oral evidence, has seen all fresh relevant material, and is aware of new developments.

Duties of experts

74 The role of the expert is to provide independent assistance to the court by way of objective, unbiased opinion, in relation to matters within his expertise. Expert evidence presented to the court must be, and be seen to be, the independent product of the expert, uninfluenced by the instructing party.

75 Acceptance of instructions imposes an obligation to

(a) comply with the court's timetable and

(b) notify the instructing solicitors promptly if there is any risk that the timetable cannot be adhered to.

76 Experts should not hesitate to seek further information and documentation when this is required. Such requests should form part of the court bundle.

77 In his report, an expert should:

(a) state the facts or assumptions on which his opinion is based, and not omit to consider material facts which detract from his concluded opinion;

(b)   make it clear when a particular aspect of the case is outside his expertise;

(c)   indicate, if appropriate, that his opinion is not properly researched because of insufficient data, and is therefore provisional; and

(d)   inform the other parties, and, when appropriate, the court if at any time he changes his opinion on a material matter.

78 If an opinion is based, wholly or in part, on research conducted by others, the expert must:

(a)   set this out clearly in the report;

(b)   identify the research relied on;

(c)   state its relevance to the points at issue; and

(d)   be prepared to justify the opinions expressed.

79 It is unacceptable for any expert in a child case, whose evidence is relevant to the outcome, to give evidence without having read, in advance, the report of the guardian ad litem.

Assisting the experts

80 Legal advisers for the parties should co-operate, at an early stage in the preparation for trial, to ensure availability of the experts to give evidence in a logical sequence.

81 It is helpful to timetable experts, in a difficult case, to give evidence one after another, so that each can listen to the evidence of other experts, and comment on that evidence.

82 Child proceedings are non-adversarial, and it is not necessary that witnesses are called in conventional order.

83 Where it becomes clear that an expert's opinion is uncontentious, and that the expert will not be required to attend court, he must be notified at the earliest opportunity. Whenever attendance at court is necessary, the court must always try to accommodate the expert by interposing the evidence at a given time.

84 In order that all relevant matters are fully considered at the appropriate time in advance of the hearing, it is essential that advocates who will appear at the hearing are involved at the earliest stage in order to consider how the case should be prepared and progressed.

The Expert Witness Group

85 The Expert Witness Group has been active in developing an 'Expert Witness Pack', which it hopes to have published in the autumn of 1997. The pack, which will be available for purchase and will be cited in bibliographies, etc, will include several pro formas and:

(a)   draft letters of instruction and acceptance;

(b)   a checklist for both solicitor and expert;

(c)   guidelines and a model curriculum vitae for expert witnesses; and

(d)   a model format for experts' reports.

86 Further information about the Expert Witness Group and the Expert Witness Pack may be obtained from: Dr Eileen Vizard, Consultant Child and Adolescent Psychiatrist, Camden and Islington Community Health Services NHS Trust, Simmons House Adolescent Unit, St. Luke's-Woodside Hospital, Woodside Avenue, London N10 3HU (Telephone: 0181 219 1883).

SECTION 6 – APPEALS FROM THE FAMILY PROCEEDINGS COURTS UNDER SECTION 94 OF THE CHILDREN ACT 1989

87 Appeals lie to a single judge of the Family Division unless the President otherwise directs. The procedure on appeal is set out in Rule 4.22 of the Family Proceedings Rules 1991.

88 Despite guidance in reported cases, problems continue to arise in the preparation and determination of such appeals.

89 Compliance with the rules and good practice requires the following.

(a) The merits of an appeal must be carefully and expeditiously considered. Dissatisfaction with the decision of the family proceedings court will not justify an appeal, unless the court erred in the exercise of discretion within the meaning of *G v G* [1985] FLR 894. An appeal is not a rehearing.

(b) Time limits are strict. An appeal must be commenced by filing and serving the notice of appeal on all parties and on any guardian ad litem within 14 days of the decision, unless the appeal is against an interim care order or interim supervision order, in which event the time limit is 7 days. The period for service may be altered by the High Court on application, to a longer or shorter period, under Rule 4.22(3)(*c*). The High Court will not grant an extension of time without good reason and advocates must be prepared to justify such applications.

(c) The documents set out in Rule 4.22(2) must be filed in the nearest district registry which is a care centre to the court in which the order appealed from was made. Good practice requires that all reports and witness statements filed in the proceedings should be filed for the appeal in addition to the documents identified in Rule 4.22(2).

(d) The family proceedings court must as a matter of urgency supply to the appellant a typed copy of the notes of evidence and of the reasons for the decision. It is detrimental to the welfare of the child concerned if there is any delay in the production of these documents.

(e) Strict time limits are laid down for a respondent who wishes to cross appeal, or to seek a variation, or an affirmation of the decision on grounds other than those relied upon by the family proceedings court. Within 14 days of receipt of the notice of appeal the respondent must file and serve on all parties to the appeal, a notice in writing setting out the grounds relied on. No notice may be filed or served in an appeal against an order under section 38.

90 The appeal should be set down promptly. Where it is unlikely that a case can be listed without delay on Circuit, arrangements will be made for the appeal to be heard in London.

91 In advance of the hearing the appellant must file a paginated bundle with a chronology and in all save the most simple cases, each party must file a skeleton argument. There is a duty upon advocates to file in advance an accurate time estimate of the length of hearing, and to keep the court informed of any change to that estimate.

92 Any application for a stay pending appeal must be made to the High Court. The family proceedings court has no power to grant a stay.

SECTION 7 – DISCLOSURE OF LOCAL AUTHORITY DOCUMENTS

Early consideration

93 Crown Prosecution Service and defence solicitors should give early consideration whether disclosure of records held in the possession of a local authority may be required. The appropriate time for such consideration will be at the commencement of the 4 weeks period (custody cases) or 6 weeks period (bail cases) between committal or transfer and the plea and directions hearing.

94 The parties should inform the judge of the steps that have been taken so that, if necessary, directions may be given and noted on the questionnaire.

95 Requests by the Crown Prosecution Service or the defence solicitor for disclosure should:

(a) be made in writing to the legal services department of the local authority who will nominate a lawyer to deal with the matter;

(b) provide specific details of the information required and an explanation as to why it is relevant to the proceedings, identifying as precisely as possible the category and nature of the documents for which disclosure is sought and

(c) be accompanied by a copy of the indictment or of the schedule of charges upon committal.

96 If the defence solicitors request information, they should notify the Crown Prosecution Service of the request and vice versa.

97 Case records will be examined by legal services and the appropriate officer to identify whether they contain the information which is sought.

98 Information which is disclosed to the defence solicitors will also be disclosed to the Crown Prosecution Service and vice versa.

99 If the case records do *not* contain the requested information, the requester will be so informed by legal services which, subject to relevance and the principle of confidentiality, may be able (but is not bound) to provide a summary of the type of information which is on file.

100 If the requester is not satisfied with the response, legal services, after appropriate consultation, will provide the name of a person to be witness summonsed to attend court with the records.

101 Where the case records do contain the information requested, legal services will disclose it so long as it is not protected by public interest immunity, legal privilege or statutory confidentiality.

102 If the local authority wishes to assert protection from disclosure for the records requested or any of them, legal services, after appropriate consultation, will provide the name of a person to be witness summonsed to attend court with the records.

103 If the local authority wishes to make representations as to why the records requested should not be disclosed, it will inform:

(a) the requester;

(b) the opposing party's representative and

(c) the court listing officer,

and a convenient date for listing, before a judge will be set.

PART III

104 The local authority should provide a skeleton argument and serve it on the parties and the court.

105 At the hearing:

(a) the witness must produce the records to the judge;

(b) files must be flagged to identify the documents for which immunity from disclosure is sought;

(c) representations will be made on behalf of the parties; and

(d) the judge will give appropriate directions.

106 Whenever possible, the hearing will be before the judge who will be conducting the trial. If the trial judge has not been nominated, then the hearing judge may determine the issue of disclosure.

107 The judge will give his decision in court or chambers, in the presence of the parties' representatives.

108 The judge may also give direction as to the custody of the records pending trial and as to any copies to be obtained on behalf of the parties.

109 The hearing referred to above should take place not less than 4 weeks before trial.

110 Where the requester has reasonable grounds to believe that a witness or a defendant has been involved with social services, information may be obtained by writing to the relevant department stating the witness's or defendant's name, date of birth and address.

Confidentiality of records

111 The court will normally conduct the hearing at which public interest immunity is claimed in chambers, where the local authority may be represented by a solicitor.

112 When records are disclosed to the parties by order of the court, it is on the undertaking that:

(a) they will only be used for the purpose of the criminal proceedings before the court; and

(b) their contents are revealed only to the parties and their legal representatives. (Leave of the court must be obtained for wider disclosure, eg to an expert witness.)

Costs

113 An officer of the local authority who necessarily attends court for the purpose of the proceedings otherwise than as a witness may be allowed expenses (Regulation 18(2) within Costs in Criminal Cases (General) Regulations 1986).

114 The court has no power to order payment from central funds of the cost of a search or legal costs.

115 If the court rules that the application for disclosure is frivolous or by way of a fishing expedition, it may order that costs be paid by the applicant or his legal advisers.

APPENDIX A

GUIDANCE, BEST PRACTICE NOTES AND PRO FORMAS FROM THE
COMMITTEE'S PREVIOUS ANNUAL REPORTS

I Best practice guidance on section 37(1) directions
Set out in the notes to CA 1989, s 37(1).

**II Urgent hearings on Circuit before Family Division judges: standby
procedure**
Set out as *President's Guidance of 17 December 1993*.

[*see following page for Questionnaire on guardian ad litem performance*]

III Questionnaire on guardian ad litem performance

Name of Guardian

Name of case: No:

Part one *(To be completed by the staff)*

1. Did the GAL appoint a solicitor for the first hearing?   Yes/No
2. Did the GAL attend all directions and interim hearings as appropriate?   Yes/No
3. Did the GAL adhere to the court timetable?   Yes/No
4. Did the GAL respond to telephone calls and letters satisfactorily?   Yes/No

Part two *(To be completed by the Judge/Magistrates)*

5.Did you consider the report to be *(Tick as appropriate)*   Good

Adequate

˜Poor

6. Did the GAL give oral evidence *(Tick as appropriate)*   Well

Adequately

Inadequately

7. Did the GAL's argument / evidence justify the recommendation
made? *(Tick as appropriate)*   Well

Adequately

Inadequately

8. If you have any further comments as to any aspects of the GAL's work please
state them:

Name of court:

Date:

Signed:

Name:

Please return to:

IV Local authority assessments

Special considerations arise where the local authority wish to carry out an assessment eg a Section 37 assessment or family assessment.

In such cases the court should:

(i) Identify the purpose of the assessment.

(ii) Specify the time in which the assessment is to be carried out and direct that evidence of the outcome of the assessment be filed by a given date.

(iii) Fix a directions hearing for a date immediately after the date fixed for the completion of the assessment.

(iv) At the directions hearing the court should consider what evidence is needed to bring the case speedily and fairly to final or substantive hearing.

(v) Where the court exercises its discretion to grant leave for the papers to be shown to a particular expert, the court should go on to give directions.

These should:

– State the timescale in which the evidence in question should be produced.

– Provide for the disclosure of any written expert report both to all parties and to the other experts in the case. When a report is disclosed it should include a copy of the letter of instruction.

– Provide for discussion between experts following mutual disclosure of reports and for the filing of further evidence by the experts stating the areas of agreement and disagreement between the experts. Parties should only instruct experts who are willing to meet in advance of the hearing. When granting leave, the court must make this a condition of the appointment.

Where it proves impracticable to give such directions at the time when leave to disclose the report is granted, the court must set a date for a further directions hearing at which such directions can be given.

V Bundles of documents

Set out as *Practice Note of 11 November 1993*.

VI Best practice note for the judiciary and family proceedings courts when ordering a court welfare officer's report

1 A welfare report may only be ordered pursuant to Section 7 of the Children Act 1989 ie when a court "considering any question with respect to a child under [the] Act 'requires a report' on such matters relating to the welfare of that child as are required to be dealt with in the report". A report may not be ordered for any other purpose.

2 Before a welfare report is ordered consideration should be given to the court's power to refer parties to mediation (with the consent of the parties). This may be a mediation service or the court welfare officer, depending on local arrangements. It is important that this should not be confused with a welfare report and that any court welfare officer who may have been involved in any privileged mediation proceedings should not be the officer who undertakes the preparation of a welfare report.

3 The ordering of a welfare officer's report is a judicial act requiring inquiry into the circumstances of the child. A report should never be ordered when there is no live issue under the Children Act before the court; for example, a report must not be ordered when no formal proceedings have yet been instituted. Furthermore, save in exceptional circumstances, a report should not be ordered in response to a written request by the parties.

4 Although the exact procedures in different courts vary, there will always be some kind of preliminary appointment or hearing before the district judge, justices' clerk or family proceedings court in children's cases. This is normally the occasion on which a welfare report should be ordered. The attendance of the parties and their solicitors is required at this time to enable the court properly to inquire into the issues to be covered in the report. When a court welfare officer is present, or otherwise available, the court may consider inviting the parties to have a preliminary discussion with him or her.

5 When a welfare report is ordered the judge, district judge or justices' clerk should explain briefly to the parties what will be involved and should emphasize the need to cooperate with the welfare officer and specifically to keep any appointments made. In particular, when the principle of contact is in dispute the parties should be told that the welfare officer will probably wish to see the applicant parent alone with the child. It should also be emphasised that the report, when received, is a confidential document and must not be shown to anyone who is not a named party to the application.

6 The order for the report should specify the time by which the report should be filed and, if possible, indicate the date of the substantive hearing. The solicitors for the applicant should be handed a pro forma in the form of the model attached and asked to complete details such as name, address and telephone number on the front of the form. The judge, district judge or justices' clerk should complete the rear of the pro forma which sets out the reasons for the report and the concern of the court; this should set out succinctly the issues on which the officer is being asked to report. This part of the form should specify any documents which are to be sent to the welfare officer. This form must be fully completed and attached to the court file before the court disposes of the case.

7 An addendum report may be ordered eg for the purpose of testing an agreement between the parties or where there has been a substantial change in circumstances. However, an addendum report should not be ordered merely because of a delay or adjournment in the listing of the substantive hearing.

8 The court will not order both a welfare report and Section 37 report.

9 It should be noted that the court welfare officers do not travel outside the United Kingdom; International Social Services are available to meet this need.

10 A court welfare officer will not attend a hearing unless specifically directed to do so by the court (Family Proceedings Rules 1991 rule 4.13 and Family Proceedings Courts (Children Act 1989) Rules 1991 rule 13). When such a direction is given the court should ensure that the officer gives evidence as soon as possible after the case has opened (and in any event on the first day) and is released after that evidence has been completed.

VII Best practice note to court staff when welfare reports have been ordered

1 Staff should ensure that the pro forma on the court file has been fully completed by the solicitors and the judge, district judge or justices' clerk on the day that a welfare report is ordered. When this has not been done the file should be immediately referred back to the judge or, when he or she is not immediately available, to another family judge or authorised clerk.

2 A copy of the order and of the pro forma should be sent by the court to the court welfare office within whose area the child lives within 48 hours of the order being made. Copies of all documents specified on the pro forma should accompany the order. The pro forma should be date stamped with the date of despatch.

3 When a welfare report is received, it should immediately be date stamped and copies should be sent by the court to the solicitors for the parties immediately (or faxed when there is less than 7 days before the hearing) usually without reference back to the judge. Where a party acts in person a letter should be sent by the court inviting that party to call to collect the report.

4 When a hearing date (or change of date) is being considered and it appears that the parties will require the court welfare officer to attend, he or she should be consulted before the date is fixed.

VIII Welfare report referral form

[see following page for Welfare Report Referral]

Welfare Report Referral
About this form

- The solicitor for the applicant must fill in Part 1 (below)

- A judge or a justices' clerk will fill in Part 2 (overleaf)

- The court office will then send a copy of this form and any other papers to the court welfare office within whose area the child lives. This will be done within 48 hours.

For the use of the court office

Court

Case Number

Name of judge or clerk to the justices

Date of case review

Date of final hearing

Report ordered on

This form sent on

Report to be filed by

Part 1
The Applicant

Full name (surname in BLOCK LETTERS)
Date of birth & Relationship to the child
Address

| Date of Birth | Relationship |

Daytime Telephone Number
The Applicant's Solicitor
Name and Reference
Address

| Home | Work |
| Ref. |

Telephone & FAX numbers

| Telephone | FAX |

The Respondent

Full name (surname in BLOCK LETTERS)
Date of birth & Relationship to the child
Address

| Date of Birth | Relationship |

Daytime Telephone Number
The Respondent's Solicitor
Name and Reference
Address

| Home | Work |
| Ref. |

Telephone & FAX numbers

| Telephone | FAX |

Other relevant parties

Full name (surname in BLOCK LETTERS)
Date of birth
Address

Children

	Name	Date of Birth	Residing with	School Attended
1				
2				
3				
4				

Part 2

The nature of the application

For example: residence, contact, parental responsibility, prohibited steps, specific issue, (or other)

The welfare report

Give, in detail
- *the reason(s) for the Court ordering the report*
- *particular areas of concern which are to be reported on.*

About the parties

Were they interviewed at court? No ☐ Yes ☐ The Family Court Welfare Officer *(name)*

Was a settlement or mediation attempted? No ☐ Yes ☐ The Family Court Welfare Officer *(name)*

Have the parties been given copies of the information leaflet? No ☐ Yes ☐

Are there any dates when the parties will **not** be available? No ☐ Yes ☐ The dates _____

Will an interpreter be needed? No ☐ Yes ☐ The language(s) *(including signing)*

Are there any issues of culture or religion which the Family Court Welfare Officer should be aware of? No ☐ Yes ☐ The issue(s) _____

Are other papers attached to this form? *For example: statements, directions* No ☐ Yes ☐ The papers are **the Court Order +** _____

Is there a Child Protection issue? No ☐ Yes ☐

The Court Welfare Officer is

Give the name and address

Part 2 completed by

Name:		Date:
[District] Judge	Justices' Clerk	
☐	☐	

IX Receipt and undertaking for video recordings

Name of solicitor   Name of firm

Address

Telephone   Solicitor's reference

I, the above named solicitor, hereby confirm that I am acting for (insert name of client):

who is a party to the proceedings currently before the court concerning (insert name of child or children):

I acknowledge receipt of the recording marked "Evidence of   "

I acknowledge that this recording is and will remain the property of the Chief Constable of .... Police notwithstanding the fact that I agree to pay the reasonable expenses incurred by .... Police in providing me with this recording on loan.

I undertake that whilst the recording is in my possession I shall:
(a) not make or permit any other person to make a copy of the recording;
(b) not make or permit any disclosure of the recording or its contents to any person except when in my opinion it is strictly necessary in the interests of the child and / or the interests of justice;
(c) not part with possession of the recording to anyone other than to counsel instructed by me or to an expert witness authorised by the court, and in particular
(d) NOT PART WITH POSSESSION OF THE RECORDING TO *(insert name of client)*

(e) at all times (except whilst being played) keep the recording in a locked, secure container and not leave it unattended in vehicles or otherwise unprotected;
(f) record details of the name of any person allowed access to the recording and produce such record to an officer of .... Police upon request;
(g) ensure that any person who takes possession of the recording under paragraph (c) above is supplied with a copy of this undertaking and agrees to be bound by its terms;
(h) return the recording to .... Police immediately upon the conclusion of the proceedings or when I am no longer professionally instructed in the matter whichever is sooner;
(i) give notice to .... Police of any application to the court which may result in the variation of the terms set out in this undertaking.

Signed:
Dated:

X Guidance as to preparation of the justices' written findings and reasons – The Honourable Mr Justice Cazalet

General

1 The obligations placed upon justices and their clerks are set out succinctly in Rules 21(5) and (6) of the Family Proceedings Courts (Children Act 1989) Rules 1991. Stated summarily these require that before the court makes an order or refuses an application or request, the justices' clerk shall record in writing, in consultation with the justices, the reason for the court's decision and any finding of fact. Furthermore, when justices make an order or refuse an application, the court, or one of the justices constituting the court by which the decision is made, shall state any finding of fact or reasons for the court's decision. These provisions are straightforward and are expressed in terminology which is unequivocal. They must be interpreted literally and strictly.

2 The justices and their clerks must ensure that the reasons and findings of fact are stated at the time the order is made. They cannot be added to subsequently. The written reasons and findings of fact must accord with what is stated in court. Justices cannot make an order and then reserve judgment (a luxury which the Court of Appeal is permitted). Justices must give their reasons, and any findings made, each time they make an order or decline to make an order.

3 There can be no 'back door' process. That is to say that if, on appeal, a point is taken which the justices did consider in their deliberations but omitted to put in their reasons, they cannot formally make a subsequent addendum to those reasons and supply them to the appeal court.

4 Even when the parties are agreed, there is, none the less, an overriding duty in the court to investigate the proposals advanced by the parties. However, the extent of the investigation must reflect reality and so, when an agreed order is sought, the investigation of the evidence need not and should not be dealt with in full detail unless there are concerns as to the propriety of the order. Nevertheless, it is particularly important that in cases where a care order is made by consent the basis upon which the care order is made is clearly stated, for example because of a failure to protect from an abusive spouse or an agreed non-accidental injury as set out in some statement identified in the proceedings. If this step is taken it will avoid a long and perhaps inconclusive later trawl through the evidence in the earlier case in an attempt to establish what the actual finding then was and its relevance to a different child or new family situation. Also, justices must bear in mind that it will always be important for the child's wishes (given that the child is of sufficient age and maturity for those wishes to be relevant) to be taken into consideration. A consent order sought by the parents may not always properly reflect this.

5 The Children Act has brought two fundamental changes in the way that justices conduct hearings. First they must read all the papers before coming to court (that is to say they must come into court 'hot'); second they must give their reasons and findings of fact in writing. It is essential that justices are fully conversant with the written documents before the case starts. This will have one advantage in particular. The justices will know when to intervene to stop evidence being led which simply repeats what has already been stated, usually in a statement of evidence in chief. This unnecessary repetition can be extremely time wasting.

6 It is vital to remember that the findings of fact and reasons will form the basis of any appeal accordingly they must be clearly stated. In order to avoid pressure of

time when reasons are being prepared it may be appropriate to release the parties for a period or to require them to come back the next day. In this event only one of the justices concerned need attend and read out the written reasons and findings.

7 Clarity in findings and reasons is important not only so that the appeal court knows the basis on which the decision has been made but also so that the losing party knows why the decision has gone against him. It is worth remembering that decisions in family cases, unlike most other decisions in the courts, concern the future. If the losing party leaves court without understanding properly why the order has been made against him because the court has not clearly explained the reason for its decision then this will not augur well for later hearings and may well give rise to a sense of grievance which impedes the working of the order.

8 Do not be afraid to raise points with advocates during their speeches. This should help to clarify difficult points.

9 When justices make an order which differs from the advice or conclusion reached in the report of the court welfare officer or guardian ad litem it is imperative for them to set out in clear terms why they have done so. This need not be stated at great length but it must be possible for the parties (and if there is an appeal, for the appellate court) to follow the process whereby the different conclusion was reached.

10 When the arguments of the losing party are being dealt with in the findings state these first before the arguments of the party in whose favour the decision is to be made.

11 When you intervene because an advocate is being too long winded, repetitious or adversarial you will carry much more authority if you have read and fully understood the papers in the case. When you do intervene be firm, courteous and controlled.

12 When you are dealing with a care case it is usually helpful to require the advocate when opening the case for the local authority to state specifically the facts upon which he relies as establishing that the threshold criteria apply. This will enable the court to direct its mind to the material evidence as it emerges and should help to clarify at an early stage the findings which will have to be made to support a care order.

More specific guidelines in setting out reasons and findings of fact

There are a number of different proformas used by different justices for the purposes of setting out their reasons and findings of fact. Once a particular system which works satisfactorily has evolved then it would be a mistake to interfere with it in any fundamental way. I accordingly set out below some guidelines which may be of assistance in formulating reasons and findings.

1 At the start state brief details about the child, parents and any other party (this includes dealing with family, siblings and where the child makes his/her home etc).

2 State, in concise form, the competing applications (ie the orders which each party is seeking).

3 State the relevant facts not in dispute, including appropriate background details (this will include stating physical injuries, emotional or educational problems from which the child may have suffered and which are not in dispute. This will *not* deal with the cause of such injuries unless that also is not in dispute). Keep this short.

4 Set out in general form the facts in dispute (for example the cause of a non-accidental injury). This will normally involve a short statement of the competing assertions by the parties concerned.

5 State your findings of fact including in particular, where appropriate, whose evidence was preferred. In general terms you should state the reasons for preferring one witness to another (for example because he or she was more convincing, because there was corroboration, or because one witness clearly had a better recollection than another and so forth). Be careful before you call a witness a liar. We are not infallible!

6 An appellate court cannot write into justices' reasons inference and findings working backwards from their conclusions. The material findings of fact must be stated so be as firm as you feel you can be when stating your findings.

7 State concisely any relevant law, and refer to the threshold criteria. Refer to any *relevant* passage of legal authority cited.

8 State your conclusions from the facts found. In particular, if you are dealing with a care case you should state why you consider the threshold criteria to apply.

9 State your decision and reasons for it, making clear that you have taken into account the welfare checklist by going through the relevant provisions.

Conclusion

The sequence stated above is the one that I usually follow. It matters not if you vary it somewhat or if your proforma follows a somewhat different sequence. The importance is that you should deal with all those particular headings.

The clerk is under a legal duty to record your findings and reasons in consultation with you. Once you have completed your deliberations you should call in the clerk and go through the record of your findings of fact and reasons. On the back of the proforma your clerk will enter the details of all the documentary evidence which was considered by the court.

Provided you follow these various heads you should cover all essential matters. The important thing is to get a system a sequence of headings under which you deal with the evidence and any submissions made by the advocates which lead on to your decision. Once you have learned to work within a particular framework, the preparation of the written findings and reasons will come much more easily.

APPENDIX B

THE OFFICIAL SOLICITOR: APPOINTMENT IN FAMILY PROCEEDINGS
(PRACTICE NOTE)

Appointment as guardian ad litem of child subject of proceedings
[Editorial note: the *Practice Note of 8 September 1995* has been superseded – see now *Practice Note of 2 April 2001 (Official Solicitor: Appointment in Family Proceedings)* [2001] 2 FLR 155.]

APPENDIX C

PRACTICE DIRECTIONS BY THE PRESIDENT OF THE FAMILY DIVISION

I Applications by children

Under s 10 of the Children Act 1989, the prior leave of the court is required in respect of applications by the child concerned for s 8 orders (contact, prohibited steps, residence and specific issue orders). Rule 4.3 of the Family Proceedings Rules 1991 and r 3 of the Family Proceedings Courts (Children Act 1989) Rules 1991 set out the procedure to be followed when applying for leave.

Such applications raise issues which are more appropriate for determination in the High Court and should be transferred there for hearing.

Issued with the concurrence of the Lord Chancellor.

II Case management

Set out as *Practice Direction of 31 January 1995*.

Family Proceedings (Allocation to Judiciary) Directions 1999

Citations: [1999] 2 FLR 799

The Lord Chancellor, in exercise of the powers conferred on him by section 9 of the Courts and Legal Services Act 1990 and with the concurrence of the President of the Family Division, hereby gives the following Directions:

1 (1) These Directions shall come into force on 1 May 1999.

(2) Subject to paragraph (3), these Directions shall have effect in relation to proceedings which are pending immediately before 1st May 1999 as if the Family Proceedings (Allocation to Judiciary) Directions 1993 had not been made.

(3) Nothing in these Directions shall affect the provisions of paragraph 1 of the Family Proceedings (Allocation to Judiciary) Directions 1991 in relation to proceedings which were pending immediately before 14th October 1991.

[**2** In these Directions, in the absence of a contrary implication –

'family proceedings' and 'judge' bear the meanings assigned to them in s 9 of the Courts and Legal Services Act 1990;
'nominated' in relation to a judge means a judge who has been approved as one to whom family proceedings may be allocated by the President of the Family Division;
'opposed hearing' includes an application made ex parte; and
'Schedule' means the Schedule to these Directions.] [1]

NOTES

Amendment. [1] Paragraph substituted: *Lord Chancellor's Direction (Family Proceedings (Allocation to Judiciary) (Amendment) Directions 2002)* [2002] 2 FLR 692.

3 These Directions shall apply where proceedings of a class specified in column (i) of the Schedule are pending in a county court or, by virtue of section 42 of the Matrimonial and Family Proceedings Act 1984, a provision of the Children (Allocation of Proceedings) Order 1991 or of the Family Law Act 1996 (Part IV) (Allocation of Proceedings) Order 1997, treated as pending in a county court in the Principal Registry of the Family Division of the High Court.

4 Subject to the following paragraphs of these Directions, the proceedings in column (i) of the Schedule may be allocated to a judge of the description specified in the corresponding entry in column (ii), in the circumstances specified in the corresponding entry in column (iii).

5 Without prejudice to the provisions of the Schedule, any of the proceedings in column (i) of the Schedule may be allocated to –

(a) a judge of the Family Division of the High Court;
(b) a person acting as a judge of the Family Division of the High Court in pursuance of a request made under section 9(1) of the Supreme Court Act

PART III

1981 other than a former judge of the Court of [Appeal or a former puisne judge of the High Court][1]; but public family law proceedings shall be allocated only to a judge who has been nominated for them;

(c) a person sitting as a recorder ...[1] who has been authorised to act as a judge of the Family Division of the High Court under section 9(4) of the Supreme Court Act 1981.

(d) a person sitting as a recorder ...[1] who is a [district judge (Magistrates' Courts)][1] and who is nominated for public family law proceedings in the county court.

[(e) a person sitting as a recorder who is a district judge of the Principal Registry of the Family Division.][1]

NOTES

Amendment. [1] Words substituted, deleted and inserted: *Lord Chancellor's Direction (Family Proceedings (Allocation to Judiciary) (Amendment) Directions 2002)* [2002] 2 FLR 692.

5A When a person sitting as a recorder ...[1] is also a district judge nominated for public family law proceedings, any proceedings may be allocated to him which, under these Directions, may be allocated to a district judge nominated for public family law proceedings.

NOTES

Amendment. [1] Words deleted: *Lord Chancellor's Direction (Family Proceedings (Allocation to Judiciary) (Amendment) Directions 2002)* [2002] 2 FLR 692.

6 Where any family proceedings include proceedings of more than one class specified in column (i) of the Schedule, the Schedule shall apply to those classes as if they did not form part of the same proceedings.

7 For the purposes of paragraphs (f), (g), (h) and (i) of the Schedule, where –

(a) unopposed proceedings become opposed during the course of the hearing; and

(b) the judge before whom the hearing takes place does not fall within a description of judge to whom the proceedings would have been allocated if the proceedings had been opposed at the commencement of the trial, he shall adjourn the hearing to a judge to whom such a hearing would be allocated by these Directions.

THE SCHEDULE
ALLOCATION OF PROCEEDINGS

(i) DESCRIPTION OF PROCEEDINGS	(ii) DESCRIPTION OF JUDGE	(iii) CIRCUMSTANCES IN WHICH ALLOCATION APPLIES
(a) Family proceedings for which no express provision is made in this Schedule.	A circuit judge, deputy circuit judge or recorder nominated for private or public family law proceedings; a district judge of the Principal Registry of the Family Division of the High Court; or a district judge or deputy district judge.	All circumstances
(b) Non-contentious or common form probate business within the meaning of s 128 of the Supreme Court Act 1981.	A judge	All circumstances
(c) Proceedings under any of the provisions in Part IV of the Family Law Act 1996 (c 27).	A circuit judge or deputy circuit judge nominated for private or public family law proceedings;	All circumstances
	a recorder nominated for public family law proceedings; or	All circumstances
	a district judge of the Principal Registry of the Family Division of the High Court; or	All circumstances
	a district judge;	All circumstances
	a recorder nominated for private family law proceedings, a recorder or a deputy district judge.	All circumstances except proceedings to enforce an order made under Part IV.

PART III

(i)	(ii)	(iii)
DESCRIPTION OF PROCEEDINGS	**DESCRIPTION OF JUDGE**	**CIRCUMSTANCES IN WHICH ALLOCATION APPLIES**
(d) Hearing of contested petition for a decree of divorce, nullity or judicial separation.	A circuit judge, deputy circuit judge or a recorder nominated for private or public family law proceedings.	All circumstances
(e) Proceedings under any of the following provisions of the Adoption Act 1976 (c 36):	A circuit judge nominated for adoption proceedings; or	All circumstances
[s 14 (adoption by married couple); s 15 (adoption by one person);	a deputy circuit judge or recorder nominated for adoption proceedings;	All circumstances
s 18 (freeing child for adoption); s 20 (revocation of order under s 18);	a district judge of the Principal Registry of the Family Division of the High Court; or	Interlocutory matters
ss 27, 28 or 29 (restrictions on removal of child);	a district judge nominated for adoption proceedings; or	Interlocutory matters
s 55 (adoption of children abroad)].	a deputy district judge nominated for adoption proceedings.	Interlocutory matters
(f) Proceedings under any of the following provisions of the Children Act 1989 (c 41):	A circuit judge nominated for private or public family law proceedings; or	All circumstances
[s 4(1)(a) (applications for parental responsibility by father);	a deputy circuit judge or recorder nominated for private or public family law proceedings; or	All circumstances
s 4(3) (termination of parental responsibility);	a district judge of the Principal Registry of the Family Division of the High Court; or	All circumstances

(i)	(ii)	(iii)
DESCRIPTION OF PROCEEDINGS	DESCRIPTION OF JUDGE	CIRCUMSTANCES IN WHICH ALLOCATION APPLIES

s 5(1) (appointment of guardian);
 	
s 6(7) (termination of guardianship);
	a district judge nominated for private or public family law proceedings;	All circumstances

para 11(3) of Sch 14 (discharge of existing custody etc orders)].	a district judge or deputy district judge.	(1) Interlocutory matters; or (2) unopposed hearings.
(g) Proceedings under any of the following provisions of the Children Act 1989 (c 41);	A circuit judge nominated for private or public family law proceedings; or	All circumstances
[s 13(1) (change of child's name or removal from jurisdiction);	a deputy circuit judge or recorder nominated for private or public family law proceedings; or	All circumstances
s 16(6) reference of question of variation or discharge of s 8 order);	a district judge of the Principal Registry of the Family Division of the High Court; or	All circumstances
applications under s 10 of the Children Act 1989 (c 41) for an order under s 8.]	a district judge nominated for private or public family law proceedings;	All circumstances
	a district judge;	(1) Interlocutory matters; (2) unopposed hearings; or (3) opposed hearings where

PART III

(i)	(ii)	(iii)
DESCRIPTION OF PROCEEDINGS	DESCRIPTION OF JUDGE	CIRCUMSTANCES IN WHICH ALLOCATION APPLIES
		(a) the application is for a contact order and the principle of contact with the applicant is unopposed; or (b) the order (i) is (or is one of a series of orders which is) to be limited in time until the next hearing or order, and (ii) the substantive application is returnable before a judge within column (ii) of this paragraph who has full jurisdiction in all circumstances.
	a deputy district judge.	(1) Interlocutory matters; or
		(2) unopposed hearings.
(h) Proceedings under any of the following provisions of the Children Act 1989 (c 41):	A circuit judge nominated for public family law proceedings; or	All circumstances
[s 25 (secure accommodation); s 31 (care and supervision orders);	a district judge of the Principal Registry of the Family Division of the High Court;	All circumstances
s 33(7) (change of child's name or removal from jurisdiction); s 39(1), (2) or (4) (discharge and variation of care and supervision orders); para 6 of Sch 3 (supervision order); s 34 (parental contact etc with child in care); para 19(1) of Sch 2 (arrangements to assist children to live abroad)].	a district judge nominated for public family law proceedings.	(1) Interlocutory matters; or (2) unopposed hearings; or (3) opposed hearings where the application is for an order under s 34 (a contact order) and the principle of contact is unopposed.

(i)	(ii)	(iii)
DESCRIPTION OF PROCEEDINGS	DESCRIPTION OF JUDGE	CIRCUMSTANCES IN WHICH ALLOCATION APPLIES
(i) Proceedings under s 38 of the Children Act 1989 (c 41) (interim care or supervision orders).	A circuit judge nominated for public family law proceedings;	All circumstances
	a district judge of the Principal Registry of the Family Division of the High Court; or	All circumstances
	a district judge nominated for public family law proceedings.	All circumstances
(j) Proceedings under any of the following provisions of the Children Act 1989 (c 41):	A circuit judge nominated for public family law proceedings;	All circumstances
[s 39(3) (variation of supervision order); s 36(1) (education supervision order);	a district judge of the Principal Registry of the Family Division of the High Court; or	All circumstances
para 15(2), or 17(1) of Sch 3 (extension and discharge of education supervision order);	a district judge nominated for public family law proceedings.	All circumstances
s 43 (child assessment order);		
ss 44, 45(4), 45(8), 46(7), 48(9) (order for emergency protection of child);		
s 50 (recovery order);		
applications for leave under s 91(14), (15) or (17) further applications);		
applications under s 21 of the Adoption Act 1976 (c 36) (substitution of adoption agencies)].		

PART III

(i)	(ii)	(iii)
DESCRIPTION OF PROCEEDINGS	DESCRIPTION OF JUDGE	CIRCUMSTANCES IN WHICH ALLOCATION APPLIES
(k) Proceedings under the following provisions of the Child Support Act 1991 (c 48):	a circuit judge nominated for private or public family law proceedings; or	All circumstances
s 20 (appeals).	a district judge of the Principal Registry of the Family Division of the High Court.	All circumstances
(l) The hearing of an appeal under: (i) r 8.1 of the Family Proceedings Rules 1991; (ii) Ord 37, r 6 of the County Court Rules 1981 as applied by the said r 8.1; or (iii) the Children (Allocation of Proceedings) (Appeals) Order 1991 (the 1991 Order).	A person capable of sitting as a judge of a county court district and nominated for private or public family law proceedings.	Where, under these directions such person would have been able to hear the matter at first instance but subject to the exception contained in Art 2(b) of the 1991 Order.
(m) Proceedings under s 30 of the Human Fertilisation and Embryology Act 1990 (c 37).	A circuit judge nominated for private or public family law proceedings; or	All circumstances
	A district judge of the Principal Registry of the Family Division of the High Court; or	Interlocutory matters
	a district judge.	Interlocutory matters
(n) Proceedings under any of the following provisions of the Family Law Act 1986 (c 55) in respect of proceedings or orders made under s 8 of the Children Act 1989 (c 41):	A circuit judge nominated for private or public family law proceedings; or	All circumstances

(i)	(ii)	(iii)
DESCRIPTION OF PROCEEDINGS	DESCRIPTION OF JUDGE	CIRCUMSTANCES IN WHICH ALLOCATION APPLIES
[s 33 (power to order disclosure of child's whereabouts);	a district judge of the Principal Registry of the Family Division of the High Court; or	All circumstances
s 34 (power to order recovery of child); s 37 (surrender of passports)].	a district judge nominated for private or public family law proceedings.	All circumstances
(o) Proceedings under any of the following provisions of the Family Law Act 1986 (c 55):	A circuit judge nominated for private or public family law proceedings; or	All circumstances
[s 55 (declaration as to marital status)	A district judge of the Principal Registry of the Family Division of the High Court; or	Interlocutory matters
s 55A (declarations of parentage)	A district judge.	Interlocutory matters
s 56 (declarations of legitimacy or legitimation)		
s 57 (declarations as to adoptions effected overseas).]		

NOTES

    Amendments. [1] Schedule substituted: *Lord Chancellor's Direction (Family Proceedings (Allocation to Judiciary) (Amendment) Directions 2002)* [2002] 2 FLR 692.

PART III

President's Direction
10 March 2000

Citations: [2000] 1 FLR 536; [2000] 1 WLR 737; [2000] 2 All ER 287

Family Proceedings: Court Bundles

1 The following practice applies to all hearings in family proceedings in the High Court, to all hearings of family proceedings in the Royal Courts of Justice and to hearings with a time estimate of half a day or more in all care centres, family hearing centres and divorce county courts (including the Principal Registry of the Family Division when so treated), except as specified in paragraph 2.3 below, and subject to specific directions given in any particular case. 'Hearing' extends to all hearings before judges and district judges and includes the hearing of any application.

2.1 A bundle for the use of the court at the hearing shall be provided by the party in the position of applicant at the hearing or by any other party who agrees to do so. It shall contain copies of all documents relevant to the hearing in chronological order, paginated and indexed and divided into separate sections, as follows:

    (a) applications and orders;

    (b) statements and affidavits;

    (c) experts' reports and other reports including those of a guardian ad litem; and

    (d) other documents, divided into further sections as may be appropriate.

2.2 Where the nature of the hearing is such that a complete bundle of all documents is unnecessary, the bundle may comprise only those documents necessary for the hearing but the summary (paragraph 3.1(a) below) must commence with a statement that the bundle is limited or incomplete. The summary should be limited to those matters which the court needs to know for the purpose of the hearing and for management of the case.

2.3 The requirement to provide a bundle shall not apply to the hearing of any urgent application where the circumstances are such that it is not reasonably practicable for a bundle to be provided.

3.1 At the commencement of the bundle there shall be:

    (a) a summary of the background to the hearing limited, if practicable, to one A4 page;

    (b) a statement of the issue or issues to be determined;

    (c) a summary of the order or directions sought by each party;

    (d) a chronology if it is a final hearing or if the summary under (a) is insufficient;

    (e) skeleton arguments as may be appropriate, with copies of all authorities relied on.

3.2 If possible the bundle shall be agreed. In all cases, the party preparing the bundle shall paginate it and provide an index to all other parties prior to the hearing.

3.3 The bundle should normally be contained in a ring binder or lever arch file (limited to 350 pages in each file). Where there is more than one bundle, each should be clearly distinguishable. Bundles shall be lodged, if practicable, 2 clear days prior to the hearing. For hearings in the Royal Courts of Justice bundles shall be lodged with the Clerk of the Rules. All bundles shall have clearly marked on the outside, the title and number of the case, the hearing date and time and, if known, the name of the judge hearing the case.

4 After each hearing which is not a final hearing, the party responsible for the bundle shall retrieve it from the court. The bundle with any additional documents shall be re-lodged for further hearings in accordance with the above provisions.

5 This direction replaces paragraphs 5 and 8 of *Practice Direction (Case Management)* [1995] 1 FLR 456 dated 31 January 1995 and shall have effect from 2 May 2000.

6 Issued with the approval and concurrence of the Lord Chancellor.

Dame Elizabeth Butler-Sloss
President

President's Direction
24 July 2000

Citations: [2000] 2 FLR 429

Human Rights Act 1998

1 It is directed that the following practice shall apply as from 2 October 2000 in all family proceedings:

Citation of authorities
2 When an authority referred to in s 2 of the Human Rights Act 1998 ('the Act') is to be cited at a hearing:

- (a) the authority to be cited shall be an authoritative and complete report;
- (b) the court must be provided with a list of authorities it is intended to cite and copies of the reports:
    - (i) in cases to which *Practice Direction (Family Proceedings: Court Bundles)* (10 March 2000) [2000] 1 FLR 536 applies, as part of the bundle;
    - (ii) otherwise, not less than 2 clear days before the hearing; and
- (c) copies of the complete original texts issued by the European Court and Commission, either paper based or from the Court's judgment database (HUDOC) which is available on the internet, may be used.

Allocation to judges
3(1) The hearing and determination of the following will be confined to a High Court judge:

- (a) a claim for a declaration of incompatibility under s 4 of the Act; or
- (b) an issue which may lead to the court considering making such a declaration.
- (2) The hearing and determination of a claim made under the Act in respect of a judicial act shall be confined in the High Court to a High Court judge and in county courts to a circuit judge.

Issued with the concurrence and approval of the Lord Chancellor.

Dame Elizabeth Butler-Sloss
President

PART III

Protocol for Judicial Case Management in Public Law Children Act Cases

June 2003

Foreword

by the President of the Family Division, the Lord Chancellor and the Secretary of State for Education and Skills

After over a decade of otherwise successful implementation of the Children Act there remains a large cloud in the sky in the form of delay. Delay in care cases has persisted for too long. The average care case lasts for almost a year. This is a year in which the child is left uncertain as to his or her future, is often moved between several temporary care arrangements, and the family and public agencies are left engaged in protracted and complex legal wranglings. Though a fair and effective process must intervene before a child is taken from its parents, we believe it is essential that unnecessary delay is eliminated and that better outcomes for children and families are thereby achieved. This protocol sets a guideline of 40 weeks for the conclusion of care cases. Some cases will need to take longer than this, but many more cases should take less.

The causes of delay have become clear from the Scoping Study published by the Department in March 2002, and through the work of the Advisory Committee that finalised this protocol. There is now a real enthusiasm among all the agencies involved for tackling these causes. Other work has begun and the momentum is building. Overt efforts have been made locally, both by Care Centres and by Family Proceedings Courts. Additional judicial sitting days for care work are being found. Measures are being taken to help improve the performance of CAFCASS. This protocol will form the backbone of these other efforts.

The Advisory Committee has involved all of the agencies and organisations that have a significant role to play in the care process and has striven to produce a consensus as to the content of this protocol. We are grateful to all the members of the Committee and to everyone else who engaged with the consultation process.

This protocol has been prepared on the basis that a change in the whole approach to case management and a clarification of focus, among all those involved in care cases, is the best way forward. This protocol is not a fresh start – it is a collation and distillation of best practice – we do ask you to engage it wholeheartedly with all your usual enthusiasm and dedication.

Dame Elizabeth Butler-Sloss
President

Lord Falconer of Thoroton
The Secretary of State for Constitutional Affairs and Lord Chancellor

Rt Hon Charles Clarke MP
Secretary of State for Education and Skills

Protocol for Judicial Case Management in Public Law Children Act Cases

Contents

The Protocol

The Appendices

1	2	3
The Application	**The First Hearing in the FPC**	**Allocation Hearing & Directions**
Day 1 to Day 3	**On (or before) Day 6**	**By Day 11 (CC) 15(HC)**
Objective: LA to provide sufficient information to identify issues/make early welfare and case management decisions	**Objective:** To decide what immediate steps are necessary/contested ICO/preventing delay/appropriate court	**Objective:** To make provision for continuous/consistent judicial case management

Action:
 • LA file Application in Form C1/C3 *on Day 1* [1.1]
 • Directions on Issue by Court
  - fixing the hearing
  - Appointment of Guardian *on Day 1* [1.2]
 • Allocation of Guardian by Cafcass *by Day 3* [1.2-3]
 • Appointment of Solicitor for the child
  - no appointment of Guardian
  - Notification to parties of name of Guardian/solicitor *on Day 3* [1.4]
 • LA File and serve Documents *by Day 3* [1.5]
	Action:
	 • Parties [2.2]
	 • Contested Interim Care Orders [2.3]
	 • Transfer [2.4] and transfer arrangements [2.5]
	
	 Initial Case Management and Checklist [2.6] including:
	  - Case Management Conference
	  - Final Hearing
	  - Pre-Hearing Review
	  - Evidence
	  - Disclosure
	  - Core Assessment
	  - Standard Directions Form
	
	 by Day 6
		Action:
		
		 Care Centre court officer shall:
		 • Allocate 1-2 Judges (including final hearing judge) [3.2]
		 • Attach SDF with proposed date for CMC, Final Hearing and PHR *by Day 8* [3.2]:
		
		 Judge (at Allocation Hearing) considers:
		 • Transfer, ICO, CM Checklist, dates for CMC, Final Hearing, PHR, Disclosure, Core Assessment, SDF *by Day 11* [3.4]
		 • Case Management Documents [3.4]

5 days

▼ **1 Day** ▼

In High Court:
• Court Officer *by Day 12* [3.6]
• Case Management Judge *by Day 15* [3.7]

Within 54 days

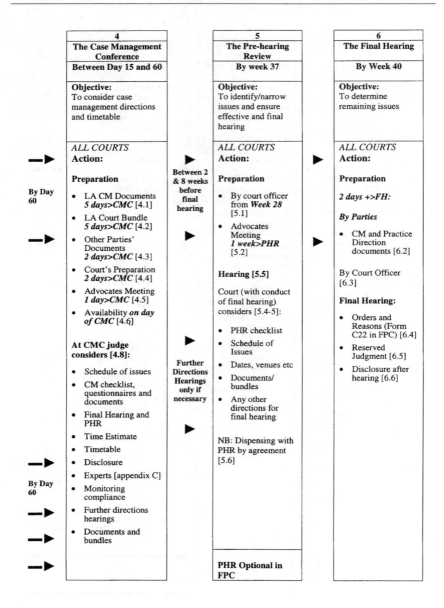

4	5	6
The Case Management Conference	**The Pre-hearing Review**	**The Final Hearing**
Between Day 15 and 60	**By week 37**	**By Week 40**
Objective: To consider case management directions and timetable	**Objective:** To identify/narrow issues and ensure effective and final hearing	**Objective:** To determine remaining issues

By Day 60

4 — ALL COURTS
Action:

Preparation

- LA CM Documents *5 days>CMC* [4.1]
- LA Court Bundle *5 days>CMC* [4.2]
- Other Parties' Documents *2 days>CMC* [4.3]
- Court's Preparation *2 days>CMC* [4.4]
- Advocates Meeting *1 day>CMC* [4.5]
- Availability *on day of CMC* [4.6]

At CMC judge considers [4.8]:

- Schedule of issues
- CM checklist, questionnaires and documents
- Final Hearing and PHR
- Time Estimate
- Timetable
- Disclosure
- Experts [appendix C]

By Day 60

- Monitoring compliance
- Further directions hearings
- Documents and bundles

Between 2 & 8 weeks before final hearing

5 — ALL COURTS
Action:

Preparation

- By court officer from *Week 28* [5.1]
- Advocates Meeting *1 week>PHR* [5.2]

Hearing [5.5]

Court (with conduct of final hearing) considers [5.4-5]:

- PHR checklist
- Schedule of Issues
- Dates, venues etc
- Documents/ bundles
- Any other directions for final hearing

Further Directions Hearings only if necessary

NB: Dispensing with PHR by agreement [5.6]

PHR Optional in FPC

6 — ALL COURTS
Action:

Preparation

2 days +>FH:

By Parties

- CM and Practice Direction documents [6.2]

By Court Officer [6.3]

Final Hearing:

- Orders and Reasons (Form C22 in FPC) [6.4]
- Reserved Judgment [6.5]
- Disclosure after hearing [6.6]

Days

Where target times are expressed in days, the days are "court business days" in accordance with the Rules (principles of application para 10)

STEP 1: The Application

Objective   **Target time:**
                                                by DAY 3

To provide sufficient information about the Local
Authority's (LA) case to enable:
*   The parties and the Court to identify the issues
*   The Court to make early welfare and case
    management decisions about the child

Action	Party and Timing
1.1 **LA Application**	LA on **DAY 1**

When a decision is made to apply for a care or
supervision order the **LA** shall:

*   File with the Court an application in **form
    C1**

*   Set out in **form C13** under 'Reasons' a
    summary of all facts and matters relied
    upon, in particular, those necessary to
    satisfy the threshold criteria and/or

*   Refer in the Reasons to any annexed
    schedules setting out the facts and matters
    relied upon

*   **Not** state that the Reasons are those
    contained in the evidence filed or to be
    filed.

1.2 **Directions on Issue**	Court on **DAY 1**

On the day the application is filed (**DAY 1**) the
Court shall:

*   Issue the application

*   Issue a notice in **form C6** to the LA
    fixing a time and a date for the First
    Hearing which shall be not later than on
    DAY 6

*   Appoint a Guardian (unless satisfied that
    it is not necessary to do so to safeguard
    the child's interests)

Action	Party and Timing
• Inform CAFCASS of the decision to appoint and the request to allocate a Guardian	
1.3 Allocation of the Guardian by CAFCASS	CAFCASS **by DAY 3**
Within **2 days** of issue (by **DAY 3**) **CAFCASS** shall inform the Court of:	
• The name of the allocated Guardian or	
• The likely date upon which an application will be made.	
1.4 Appointment of the Solicitor for the Child	Guardian **on DAY 3**
When a Guardian is allocated the **Guardian** shall on that day:	
• Appoint a solicitor for the child	
• Inform the Court of the name of the solicitor appointed	
• In the event that the Guardian's allocation is delayed and the Court has already appointed a solicitor, ensure that effective legal representation is maintained	
Where a Guardian is not allocated within **2 days** of issue, the **Court** shall on **DAY 3:**	FPC **on DAY 3**
• Consider when a Guardian will be allocated	
• Decide whether to appoint a solicitor for the child	
In any event on the day the appointment is made the **Court** shall:	FPC **on DAY 3**

Action	Party and Timing
• Notify all parties on **form C46** of the names of the Guardian and/o4r the solicitor for the child who have been appointed.	

1.5	**LA Documents**	LA **by DAY 3**

Within **2 days** of issue (by **DAY 3**) the **LA** shall file and serve on all parties, the solicitor for the child and CAFCASS the following documents:

- The **forms C1 and C13** and any supplementary forms and notices issued by the Court

- Any relevant **court orders** relating to the child (together with the relevant Justices Facts and Reasons in **form C22** and any relevant **judgments** that exist)

- The **initial social work statement (appendix B/3)**

- The **social work chronology (appendix B/2)**

- The **core or initial assessment** reports **(appendix F)**

- Any other **additional evidence** including specialist assessments or reports which then exist and which are relied upon by the LA.

STEP 2: The First Hearing in the FPC

Objective   **Target time: by DAY 6**

To decide what immediate steps are necessary to
safeguard the welfare of the child by:
- Determining contested interim care order
  applications/with whom the child will live
- Identifying how to prevent delay
- Identifying the appropriate Court
- Transferring to the appropriate Court

Action	Party and Timing
2.1 The First Hearing	FPC on DAY 6

The First Hearing shall take place in the Family
Proceedings Court (FPC) on or before **DAY 6**.
At every First Hearing the **FPC** shall:

- Consider who should be a **party** to the
  proceedings (step 2.2)
- Make arrangements for contested **interim
  care applications** to be determined (step
  2.3)
- Consider whether the proceedings should
  be **transferred** to the Care Centre or
  another FPC (step 2.4)
- Where the proceedings are not transferred,
  make **initial case management** decisions
  (step 2.6).

Action	Party and Timing
2.2 Parties and Service	FPC on DAY 6

At the First Hearing the **FPC** shall:

- Obtain confirmation that all those who are
  entitled to be parties have been served
- Consider whether any other person should
  be joined as a party
- Give directions relating to party status and
  the service of documents upon parties.

Action	Party and Timing
2.3 Contested Interim Care Orders	FPC **on DAY 6**

In any proceedings where the application for an
interim care order (ICO) is not agreed at the
First Hearing, the **FPC** shall:

- Decide whether to grant an order and if so
  what order; or
- List the application for an urgent contested
  interim hearing in an FPC prior to the
  Case Management Conference (CMC);
  and
- Give such case management directions as
  are necessary to ensure that the interim
  hearing will be effective; or
- Transfer the proceedings to be heard at the
  Care Centre.

Action	Party and Timing
2.4 Urgency and Transfer	FPC **on DAY 6**

At the First Hearing the **FPC** shall:

- Hear submissions as to complexity, gravity
  and urgency
- Consider whether transfer to another Court
  is appropriate and in any event determine
  any application made by a party for
  transfer
- Give reasons for any transfer decision
  made and record the information provided
  by the parties relating to transfer on **form
  C22** (including any intention to apply for
  transfer to the High Court)
- Send the court file and the Order of
  transfer in **form C49** to the receiving court
  within **1 day** of the First Hearing (by
  DAY 7)

Action	Party and Timing
2.5 **Proceedings Transferred to the Care Centre**	FPC **on DAY 6**

Where a decision is made to transfer to the Care Centre, the **FPC** shall:

- In accordance with the arrangements set out in the **Care Centre Plan** (CCP) and the **FPC Plan** (FPCP) **(appendix E)**, immediately inform the court officer at the Care Centre of the transfer and of the reasons set out on **form C22**

- Obtain a date and time from the court officer for an **Allocation Hearing**/contested interim hearing in the Care Centre which shall be between **3** and **5** days of the decision to transfer (by **DAY 11**)

- Notify the parties of the Care Centre to which the proceedings are transferred and of the date and time of the Allocation Hearing/contested interim hearing

- Direct the LA or the child's solicitor to prepare a **case synopsis (appendix B/1)** which shall be filed with the Care Centre and served within **2 days** of the First Hearing in the FPC (by **DAY 8**)

- Except as to disclosure of documents, make only those **case management directions upon transfer** as are agreed with the Care Centre as set out in the CCP and the FPCP.

2.6 **Case Management in the FPC**	FPC **on DAY 6**

In any case where the proceedings are **NOT** transferred to the care centre the **FPC** shall at the First Hearing:

- Consider the **case management checklist (appendix A/3)**

Action	Party and Timing

- Fix a date and time for a **Case Management Conference** (CMC) in the FPC within **54 days** of the First Hearing (between **DAYS 15 and 60**) unless all of the case management decisions set out at step 4.8 of this protocol can be taken at the First Hearing and the application can be listed for Final Hearing

- Fix a date for the **Final Hearing** or if it is not possible to do so fix a hearing window (either of which shall be not later than in the **3 week** period commencing the **37th WEEK** after the application was issued)

- Consider whether a **Pre Hearing Review** (PHR) is necessary and if so fix a PHR not later than **2 weeks** and no earlier than **8 weeks** before the Final Hearing date/window

- Give such **case management directions** as are necessary to ensure that all steps will have been taken prior to the CMC to enable it to be effective, in particular:
  - that a **statement of evidence** from each party (including the child where of sufficient age and understanding, but excluding the child's Guardian) is filed and served replying to the facts alleged and the proposals made by the LA in the initial social work statement
  - whether directions as to full and frank **disclosure** of all relevant documents need to be given and in any event give directions where necessary to ensure that the disclosure of relevant documents by the LA occurs within **20 days** of the First Hearing (by **DAY 26**)
  - whether a **core assessment** (**appendix F**) exists or should be directed to be undertaken by the LA before the CMC
  - Record on the **Standard Directions Form (SDF)** (**appendix A/1**) the Court's case management decisions and reasons and serve the directions given on the parties

Action	Party and Timing
2.7 The **FPC** shall give a direction at the First Hearing that **no further documents** shall be filed without the Court's permission unless in support of a new application or in accordance with case management directions given at that hearing (the Court will consider directions relating to the filing of comprehensive evidence and documents at the CMC)	

STEP 3: Allocation Hearing & Directions

Objective

To make provision for continuous and consistent judicial case management

Target time: by DAY 11

	Action	Party and Timing	
3.1	**Following Transfer**	Care Centre	**from DAY 6**

Following transfer to the **Care Centre** or to the **High Court** all further hearings in the proceedings shall be conducted:

- So as to ensure **judicial continuity of case management** in accordance with the protocol;
- By one or not more than 2 judges who are identified as **case management judges** in the CCP (**appendix E/1**), one of whom may be and where possible should be the judge who will conduct the Final Hearing

	Action	Party and Timing	
3.2	**Allocation in the Care Centre**	Court Officer	**by DAY 8**

Within **2 days** of the order transferring proceedings to the Care Centre (normally by **DAY 8**) the **court officer** shall:

- Allocate one and not more than two **case management judges** (one of whom may be and where possible should be the Judge who will conduct the Final Hearing) to case manage the proceedings in accordance with the protocol and the CCP
- Where possible, identify the judge who is to be the **Final Hearing judge**

Action	Party and Timing

• Upon receipt of the court file from the FPC, attach to the file the **form C22** issued by the FPC, the **case synopsis (appendix B/1)** and a **Standard Directions Form (SDF) (appendix A/1)** and complete the SDF to the extent only of:
  • the names of the **allocated and identified judges**
  • the proposed date of the **CMC** (which shall be within **54 days** of the date of the First Hearing in the FPC ie between **DAYS 15 and 60**)
  • the proposed **Final Hearing** date or hearing window (which shall be not later than in the **3 week** period commencing the **37th WEEK** after the application was issued)
  • the proposed date of the **PHR** (which shall be not later than **2 weeks** and no earlier than **8 weeks** before the Final Hearing/trial window)
 	
• Inform the case management judge in writing:
  • of any other circumstances of **urgency**
  • of any contested interim hearing for an **ICO**
  • of any application to **transfer to the High Court**
  • of the date and time of the **Allocation Hearing** (which shall be between **3 and 5 days** of the First Hearing in the FPC ie by **DAY 11**)
 	
• Notify the parties of the date, time and venue fixed for the Allocation Hearing, together with the identity of the allocated/nominated judges	

3.3 **Section 37 Request for a Report and Transfer to a Care Centre**	Court Officer **within 2 days of the order of transfer**

Where in any family proceedings a Court decides to direct an appropriate LA to investigate a child's circumstances, the Court shall follow the guidance set out at **appendix G**.

Action	Party and Timing

Where, following a section 37 request for a report, proceedings are transferred to the Care Centre:

- The **transferring court** shall make a record of the Court's reasons for the transfer on **form C22** and the **court officer** of the transferring court shall send the court file, the order of transfer in **form C49** and the record of reasons to the Care Centre within **1 day** of the order

- The **court officer** in the care centre shall within **2 days** of the order transferring the proceedings take the steps set out at paragraph 3.2 and shall also:
    - inform the case management judge in writing of the transfer (and such circumstances as are known)
    - request the case management judge to consider giving directions as to the **appointment of a Guardian and/or a solicitor for the child** at or before the Allocation Hearing
    - notify all parties on **form C46** of the names of the Guardian and/or the solicitor for the child when they are appointed
    - inform the LA solicitor or the child's solicitor of the requirement that a **case synopsis (appendix B/1)** be prepared which shall be filed with the care centre and served not later than **2 days** before the date fixed for the Allocation Hearing.

3.4 **Allocation Hearing**	Case Management Judge	**by DAY 11**

The Allocation Hearing in the Care Centre shall take place between **3 and 5 days** of the First Hearing in the FPC (by **DAY 11**). At the Allocation Hearing the **case management judge** shall:

Action	Party and Timing

- Consider whether the proceedings should be **transferred to the High Court or re-transferred to the FPC**

- Determine any **contested interim application** for a care or supervision order

- Where **the proceedings have been transferred from a court following a section 37 request** consider:
  - whether directions should be given to appoint a Guardian and/or a solicitor for the child in accordance with steps 1.2 to 1.4 of the protocol
  - whether any directions need to be given for the filing and service of LA documents in accordance with step 1.5 of the protocol

- Consider the **case management checklist (appendix A/3)**

- Fix a date and time for a **CMC** which shall be within **54 days** of the First Hearing in the FPC (between **DAYS 15 and 60**)

- Fix a date for the **Final Hearing** and confirm the identity of the Final Hearing judge or if it is not possible to do so fix a hearing window (either of which shall be not later than in the **3 week** period commencing the **37th WEEK** after the application was issued)

- Fix a date and time for a **PHR** which shall be not later than **2 weeks** and no earlier than **8 weeks** before the Final Hearing date or window

- Give such **case management directions** as are necessary to ensure that all steps will have been taken prior to the CMC to enable it to be effective, in particular:
  - that a **statement of evidence from each party** (including the child where of sufficient age and understanding, but excluding the child's Guardian) is filed and served replying to the facts alleged and the proposals made by the LA in the initial social work statement

Action	Party and Timing
• whether directions as to full and frank **disclosure** of all relevant documents need to be given and in any event give directions where necessary to ensure that the disclosure of relevant documents by the LA occurs within **20 days** of the First Hearing (by **DAY 26**) • whether a **core assessment (appendix F)** exists or should be directed to be undertaken by the LA before the CMC	
• Having regard to the *Practice Direction (Family Proceedings: Court Bundles)* [2000] 1 FLR 536 (**appendix D**), if applicable, give directions to the LA setting out which of the following **case management documents** in addition to the **case management questionnaire** (**appendix A/2**) are to be filed and served for use at the CMC: • a **schedule of findings of fact** which the Court is invited to make (in particular so as to satisfy the threshold criteria) • any update to the **social work chronology (appendix B/2)** that may be required • the **initial care plan (appendix F)** • if there is a question of law; a **skeleton argument with authorities** • a **summary of the background** (only if necessary to supplement the case synopsis) • an **advocate's chronology** (only if necessary to supplement the social work chronology or the case synopsis)	
• Having regard to **appendix D**, give directions to the LA setting out the form of **bundle or documents index** that the Court requires	
• Complete the **SDF (appendix A/1)** to record the Court's case management decisions and reasons.	

	Action	Party and Timing
3.5	**Case Management Questionnaire**	Court on **DAY 12** Officer

Within **1 day** of the Allocation Hearing (on **DAY 12**) the **court officer** shall serve on each party:

- the completed **SDF** together with a
- **case management questionnaire (appendix A/2)**.

	Action	Party and Timing
3.6	**Allocation in the High Court**	Court on **DAY 12** Officer

Where an application is transferred to the High Court, the **court officer** shall within **1 day** of the Allocation Hearing (on **DAY 12**):

- In consultation with the Family Division Liaison Judge (or if the proceedings are transferred to the RCJ, the Clerk of the Rules) allocate a judge of the High Court who shall be the **case management judge** (and who may be the judge who will conduct the final hearing) to case manage the proceedings in accordance with the protocol and the CCP

- If necessary to accord with the CCP, allocate a **second case management judge** in the Care Centre who shall be responsible to the allocated High Court judge for case management of the proceedings

- Where possible, identify a judge of the High Court to be the **Final Hearing judge**

- Attach to the court file the **form C22** issued by the FPC, the **case synopsis (appendix B/1)** and a **SDF (appendix A/1)** and complete the SDF to the extent only of:
  - the names of the **allocated judges**
  - the date of the **CMC** (which shall be within **54 days** of the date of the First Hearing in the FPC ie between **DAYS 15 and 60**)

Action	Party and Timing
• the proposed **Final Hearing** date or window (which shall be not later than in the **3 week** period commencing the **37th WEEK** after the application was issued) Action • the proposed date of the **PHR** (which shall be not later than **2 weeks** and no earlier than **8 weeks** before the Final Hearing or window)	

• Inform the case management judge in writing of:
    • any other circumstance of **urgency**
    • any contested hearing for an **ICO**	

• Within **1 day** of receipt of the court file and **completed SDF** from the allocated High Court judge (by **DAY 16**), send to each party a copy of the completed SDF together with a **case management questionnaire (appendix A/2)**	Court Officer **on DAY 16**

3.7 **Allocation Directions in the High Court**	Case Manage-ment Judge **by DAY 15**

Within **3 days** of receipt of the court file (by **DAY 15**) the allocated **case management judge** shall:

• Consider the **case management checklist (appendix A/3)**

• Complete the **SDF (appendix A/1)** having regard to those matters set out at step 3.4

• Return the court file and the completed SDF to the court officer.

STEP 4: The Case Management Conference

Objective

Target time: between DAYS 15 and 60

To consider what case management directions are necessary
- To ensure that a fair hearing of the proceedings takes place
- To timetable the proceedings so that the Final Hearing is completed within or before the recommended hearing window

Action	Party and Timing
4.1 **LA Case Management Documents** In every case the **LA** shall not later than **5 days** before the CMC prepare, paginate, index, file and serve: • The **case management documents** for the CMC that have been directed at the Allocation Hearing/Directions (step 3.4) and • A **case management questionnaire** (**appendix A/2**)	LA **not later than 5 days before the CMC**
4.2 **The Court Bundle** Not later than **5 days** before the date fixed for the CMC, the **LA** shall: • For hearings to which the *Practice Direction* (*Family Proceedings: Court Bundles*) [2000] 1 FLR 536 (**appendix D**) applies or in accordance with any direction given at a First Hearing or Allocation Hearing, file with the Court a **bundle** • Serve on each of the represented parties an **index** to the bundle • Serve on any un-represented party a copy indexed bundle	LA **not later than 5 days before the CMC**

Action	Party and Timing	
• For hearings to which **appendix D does not apply**, serve on all parties an **index** of the documents that have been filed		
4.3 **Other Party's Case Management Documents**	All Parties except the LA	**not later than 2 days before the CMC**
Not later than **2 days** before the date of the CMC **each party other than the LA** shall:		
• File with the court and serve on the parties the following **case management documents** • a **position statement** which sets out that party's response to the case management documents filed by the LA indicating the issues that are agreed and those that are not agreed. (A Guardian's position statement on behalf of the child should comment on the LA's arrangements and plans for the child) • a completed **case management questionnaire (appendix A/2)**		
• **Not** file any **other case management documents** without the prior direction of the Court		
4.4 **The Court's Preparation**	Court Officer	**not later than 2 days before the CMC**
Not later than 2 days before the CMC the court officer shall:		
• Place the **case management documents of all parties** at the front of the court file and at the front of any bundle that is filed by the LA		
• Deliver the court file and bundle to the case management judge who is to conduct the CMC		
• Ensure that any arrangements for video and telephone conferencing and with criminal and civil listing officers have been made		

Action	Party and Timing
4.5 **Advocates Meeting**	Advocates **on or before the day of the CMC**

Before **the day** fixed for the **CMC** or (where it has not been practicable to have an earlier meeting) not later than **1 hour** before the time fixed for the CMC, the **parties and/or their lawyers** shall:

- Meet to **identify and narrow the issues** in the case

- Consider the **case management checklist (appendix A/3)**

- Consider the **case management questionnaires (appendix A/2)**

- Consider in accordance with the **experts code of guidance (appendix C)** whether and if so why any application is to be made to instruct an **expert**

- Consider whether full and frank **disclosure** of all relevant documents has taken place — All Parties **on DAY 34**

- Draft a composite **schedule of issues (appendix B/4)** which identifies:
  - a summary of the issues in the case
  - a summary of issues for determination at the CMC by reference to the case management questionnaires/case management checklist
  - the timetable of legal and social work steps proposed
  - the estimated length of hearing of the PHR and of the Final Hearing
  - the order which the Court will be invited to make at the CMC

Action	Party and Timing

4.6 Availability

On **the day** of the CMC **the parties** shall complete and file with the Court:

- **witness non-availability form (appendix A/4)**
- A schedule (so far as it is known) of the names and contact details (professional address, telephone, fax, DX and e-mail) of:
  - the lead social worker and team manager
  - the Guardian
  - solicitors and counsel/advocates for each party
  - un-represented litigants
  - any experts upon whose evidence it is proposed to rely

4.7 Conduct of the CMC

The CMC shall be conducted by one of the allocated case management judges or as directed by the FPC case management legal adviser in accordance with the protocol. It is the essence of the protocol that case management through to Final Hearing must be consistently provided by the same case management judges/legal advisers/FPCs.

All advocates who are retained to have conduct of the final hearing shall:

- Use their best endeavours to attend the CMC and must do so if directed by the Court
- Bring to the CMC details of their own availability for the 12 month period following the CMC
- Attend the advocates meeting before the CMC

Action	Party and Timing
4.8 **The Hearing**	Case Manage- ment Judge

At the CMC the **case management judge/court** shall:

- Consider the parties' composite **schedule of issues (appendix B/4)**

- Consider the **case management checklist (appendix A/3)**

- Consider the parties' **case management questionnaires (appendix A/2)** and **case management documents** (steps 3.4 and 4.3)

- If not already fixed at the First or Allocation Hearing, fix the date of the **Final Hearing** which shall be not later than in the **3 week** period commencing the **37th WEEK** after the application was issued

- If not already fixed, fix the date and time of the **PHR** which shall be not later than **2 weeks** before and no earlier than **8 weeks** before the Final Hearing

- Give a **time estimate** for each hearing that has been fixed

  Consider whether any hearing can take place using video, telephone or other **electronic means**

- Consider any outstanding application of which notice has been given to the Court and to the parties in accordance with the rules

- Give all necessary **case management directions** to:
  - **timetable** all remaining legal and social work steps
  - ensure that full and frank **disclosure** of all relevant documents is complete
  - ensure that a **core assessment (appendix F)** or other appropriate assessments materials will be available to the Court

Action	Party and Timing
• ensure that if any **expert** is to be instructed the expert and the parties will complete their work for the Court within the Court's timetable and in accordance with the **experts code of guidance (appendix C)**	
• provide for **regular monitoring** of the Court's case management directions to include certification of compliance at each ICO renewal and the notification to the Court by the Guardian and by each responsible party of any material non compliance	
• permit a **further directions hearing** before the allocated case management judge in the event of a change of circumstances or significant non compliance with the directions of the Court	
• update, file and serve such of the **existing case management documents** as are necessary	
• update, file and serve a **court bundle/index** for the PHR and for the final Hearing	
• ensure that the PHR and Final Hearing will be effective	

STEP 5: The Pre-Hearing Review

Objective	Target time: by **WEEK 37**
To identify and narrow the remaining issues between the parties and ensure that the Final Hearing is effective	

Action	Party and Timing
5.1 **The Court's Preparation** The **court officer** shall:	Court Officer **from WEEK 28**

- In circumstances where **no PHR direction** has been given, send the court file/bundle to the case management judge during **WEEK 28** with a request for confirmation that no PHR is necessary or for a direction that a PHR be listed

- **Notify** the parties of any **PHR direction** given by the case management judge

- **List a PHR** where directions have been given by the case management judge (not earlier than **8 weeks** and not later than **2 weeks** before the Final Hearing ie between **WEEKS 29 and 37**)

- Not later than **2 days** before the PHR:
  - place the **updated case management documents** directed at the CMC (if any) at the front of the court file and at the front of any bundle that is filed by the LA
  - deliver the court file/bundle to the judge/FPC nominated to conduct the PHR
  - ensure that any arrangements for video and telephone conferencing and with criminal and civil listing officers have been made

5.2 **Advocates Meeting**	Advocates **in the week before the PHR**

In the **week** before the PHR **the advocates** who have conduct of the **Final Hearing** shall:

Action	Party and Timing

- Communicate with each other and if necessary meet to **identify and narrow the issues** to be considered by the Court at the PHR and the Final Hearing

- Consider the **pre-hearing review checklist (appendix A/5)**

- **2 days** before the PHR file a composite **schedule of issues (appendix B/4)** which shall set out:
  - a summary of issues in the case
  - a summary of issues for determination at the PHR
  - a draft witness template
  - the revised estimated length of hearing of the Final Hearing
  - whether the proceedings are ready to be heard and if not, what steps need to be taken at the PHR to ensure that the proceedings can be heard on the date fixed for the Final Hearing
  - the order which the Court will be invited to make at the PHR

5.3	**Case Management Documents**	Advocates **between WEEKS 29 and 30**
	No case management documents are to be filed for use at a PHR except:	

- Any **updated case management documents** directed by the case management judge at the CMC (step 4.8)

- The composite **schedule of issues (appendix B/4)**

- Documents in support of a **new application**.

5.4 **Conduct of the PHR**

The **PHR** (or any directions hearing in the FPC which immediately precedes a Final Hearing) shall be listed before the judge/FPC nominated to conduct the Final Hearing. In exceptional circumstances the Court may in advance approve the release of the PHR but only to one of the allocated case management judges.

Action	Party and Timing
The **advocates** who are retained to have conduct of the Final Hearing shall:	

- Use their best endeavours to secure their release from any other professional obligation to enable them to attend the PHR
- Update the case management documents as directed at the CMC
- Attend the advocates meeting.

5.5	**The Hearing**	Court **at the PHR**

At the PHR the **Court** shall:

- Consider the **pre-hearing review checklist (appendix A/5)**
- Consider the parties' composite **schedule of issues (appendix B/4)**
- Confirm or give a **revised time estimate** for the Final Hearing
- Confirm the **fixed dates, venues and the nominated judge** for the Final Hearing
- Give such directions as are necessary to **update the existing case management documents** and the Court **bundle/index** having regard to the application of the *Practice Direction (Family Proceedings: Court Bundles)* [2000] 1 FLR 536 **(appendix D)**
- Give such directions as are necessary to ensure that the Final Hearing will be effective

5.6	**Dispensing with the PHR**	All Parties **before the PHR**

Where the requirements of an advocates meeting have been complied with and all parties certify (in the composite **schedule of issues**) that:

Action	Party and Timing
• The proceedings are ready to be heard	
• There has been compliance with the directions of the Court and	
• There is agreement by all parties to all of the directions proposed having regard to the **pre-hearing review checklist (appendix A/5)**	
The Court may decide to **dispense with the PHR** or deal with it on paper or by electronic means, including computer, video or telephone conferencing	

STEP 6: The Final Hearing

Objective   **Target time:**
                                                 by WEEK 40

To determine the remaining issues between the parties

Action	Party and Timing	
6.1	**The Hearing** • The judge or FPC identified in the allocation directions as confirmed at the PHR Where one of the allocated case management judges or an FPC has heard a substantial factual issue or there has been a 'preliminary hearing' to determine findings of fact it is necessary for the same judge/magistrates who conducted the preliminary hearing to conduct the Final Hearing.	Judge/FPC nominated for the Final Hearing	
6.2	**Case Management and Practice Direction Documents** Not later than **2 days** before the Final Hearing **the parties** shall: • Prepare, file and serve the **case management documents** for the Final Hearing as directed by the Court at the PHR • Prepare, file and serve the **court bundle or index of court documents** as directed by the Court at the PHR	All Parties	**not later than 2 days before the Final Hearing**
6.3	**The Court's Preparation** Not later than 2 days before the Final Hearing the Court officer shall: • Place any **case management documents** at the front of the court file and at the front of any bundle that is filed by the LA • Deliver the **court file/bundle** to the judge/FPC nominated to conduct the Final Hearing	Court Officer	**not later than 2 days before the Final Hearing**

Action	Party and Timing
• Ensure that any arrangements for the reception of evidence by video link and telephone conferencing, interpreters, facilities for disabled persons and special measures for vulnerable or intimidated witnesses have been made	
6.4 **Orders and Reasons**	Court **at the Final Hearing**
At the conclusion of the Final Hearing the **Court** shall: • Set out the basis/reasons for the orders made or applications refused in a **judgment** and where appropriate in the form of **recitals** to the order or in the case of an FPC in **form C22** • Annexe to the order the **agreed or approved documents** setting out the threshold criteria and the care plan for the child • Where the judgment is not in writing give consideration to whether there should be a **transcript** and if so who will obtain and pay for it	
6.5 **Reserved judgment**	Judge **at the end of submissions**
In a complex case a judge (but not an FPC) may decide to reserve judgment and take time for consideration. Where judgment is reserved the Court will endeavour to fix a date for judgment to be given or handed down within **20 days** (4 weeks) of the conclusion of submissions. Advocates may be invited to make oral or written submissions as to consequential orders and directions at the conclusion of submissions or when the draft judgment is released.	

Action	Party and Timing
6.6 Disclosure	Court **at the end of the Final Hearing**

At the end of every Final Hearing the **Court** shall consider whether to give directions for **disclosure of documents**, for example:

- In any case where it is proposed that the child should be placed for adoption and so that subsequent adoption proceedings are not delayed, to the LA adoption panel, specialist adoption agency and/or proposed adopters and their legal advisers for use in subsequent adoption proceedings

- For any medical or therapeutic purpose

- For a claim to be made to the CICA

APPENDIX A/1:

Standard Directions Form

IN THE HIGH COURT OF JUSTICE
FAMILY DIVISION

COUNTY COURT/FPC

Case Number

Application of

Local Authority

Re

Child(ren)

Standard directions by Case Management Judge/Magistrates/Legal Adviser

Date of this order

Upon reading the papers filed by the applicant:

IT IS ORDERED by   **The Honourable**
His/Her Honour
District Judge
Magistrates/Justices Clerk

Allocation Directions

This case is allocated for case management to:

The Honourable
His/Her Honour   and
District Judge
Magistrates/Justices Clerk

Contact Telephone No
(Judge's Clerk/Court Officer/Legal Adviser)

The allocated judge(s) will be responsible for the continuous case management of this case

All future hearings in this case will be conducted by one of the allocated judges and *not* by the urgent applications judge or by any other judge unless on application to one of the allocated judges (if necessary in case of urgency by telephone) the allocated judge releases the case to another judge.
(Where it is possible to identify the Final Hearing Judge/Magistrates).

The judge who will be responsible for the PHR and the conduct of the Final Hearing is:

Case Management Conference

There will be a Case Management Conference before	**The Honourable His/Her Honour District Judge Magistrates/Justices Clerk**	

at   venue

on the   date

at   time

The parties and their lawyers shall consider each of the matters set out at Steps 1 to 4 of the Protocol and in the CMC Checklist.

The parties shall prepare, file and serve **the Evidence and Case Management Documents** listed below. No documents other than those identified shall thereafter be filed with the Court without the Court's permission, unless in support of a new application.

Local Authority Preparation for the CMC

The **LOCAL AUTHORITY** shall not later than **2pm 5 days before** the date of the Case Management Conference prepare and file with the Court the following:
(Delete as appropriate)

(a) a Bundle prepared in accordance with the [*Practice Direction (Family Proceedings: Court Bundles) [2000] 1 FLR 536] [....or specify the form].* The Local Authority shall at the same time serve on each of the Respondents an Index to the Bundle and on any unrepresented party a copy of the bundle;

(b) an Index of the Documents filed with the Court. The Local Authority shall at the same time serve on each of the Respondents a copy of the Index;

(c) the following case management documents *(delete if not required)*:

* A **case management questionnaire**
* A schedule of the **findings of fact** which the Court is to be invited to make (in particular so as to satisfy the threshold criteria)
* Any update to the **social work chronology**
* The **interim care plan**(s)
* A **skeleton argument** limited to legal questions with accompanying authorities.
* A clear and concise **summary of the background** on one page of A4 paper (only where necessary to supplement the Case Synopsis)
* An **advocates** chronology (only where necessary to supplement the Case Synopsis or the social work chronology)

Respondent's Preparation for the CMC

The **RESPONDENTS** shall not later than **2pm 2 working days before** the date of the Case Management Conference prepare and file with the Court and serve on the Local Authority copies of:

- A statement of evidence in **reply to** the local authorities **initial social work statement** (unless already filed).
- A **case management questionnaire**.
- A **position statement** (setting out what is agreed and what is not agreed).

The Advocates Meeting

The parties lawyers and any un-represented party shall attend an **Advocates Meeting**:

at	venue
on the	date
at	time

to discuss those matters set out at Step 4.5 of the Protocol and shall prepare a composite **schedule of issues** which shall be filed with the Court:

not later than	time
on the	date

in default of the advocates meeting taking place and in any event, the lawyers for all parties and any un-represented party shall attend at Court on the day of the Case Management Conference NOT LATER THAN **1 hour before** the time fixed for the hearing so that they can all meet together to discuss the issues and draft the composite **schedule of issues**.

Experts

Any party that proposes to ask the Court's permission to instruct an **expert witness** shall comply with the **experts code of guidance** and shall set out the required particulars in their case management questionnaire

Availability and Contact Details

The parties' legal representatives shall bring to the advocates meeting and to the CMC:

- Their professional diaries for the next 12 months.
- Details (so far as can be known) of the names and the availability of anybody who it is proposed should conduct any assessment or provide any expert evidence so that a **witness availability form** can be prepared and filed at the CMC.

- Details (so far as can be known) of the names and contact details (professional addresses and telephone / fax / DX / e-mail numbers for) so that a **schedule** can be prepared and filed at the CMC with particulars of:
  - the lead social worker
  - the Children's Guardian
  - the solicitors and counsel/advocates for each party
  - any experts and assessors who have been or may be instructed

Disclosure of Documents

Any outstanding disclosure of relevant documents between the parties shall take place:

by date

Pre-Hearing Review

There will be a PHR before the Final Hearing Judge:

at venue

on the date

at time

with a time estimate of time estimate

Final Hearing

The Final Hearing will take place before the Final Hearing Judge

at venue

on the date

at time

with a time estimate of time estimate

ADDITIONAL DIRECTIONS (if any)

OBSERVATIONS

Signed

APPENDIX A/2:

Case Management Questionnaire

This questionnaire is completed [by][on behalf of],

Note:
Please state your party status.

who is the [ ] [Applicant] [Respondent]
[   ] [other]
in these proceedings.

In the

[Family Proceedings Court]
[District Registry] [County Court]
[Principal Registry of the Family Division]
[The High Court of Justice]

Case Number

Please read the following notes before completing the Case Management Questionnaire.

• **The Local Authority** must file and serve this questionnaire (together with the other case management documents directed at steps 3.4 and 4.1 of the protocol) **not later than 5 days** before the date fixed for the Case Management Conference.

• **All other parties** must file and serve this questionnaire (together with the other case management documents listed at step 4.3 of the protocol) **not later than 2 days** before the date fixed for the Case Management Conference.

• Your answers to the following questions should be given **in summary form only**. However, if you need more space for your answers use a separate sheet of paper. Please put your full name and case number at the top of any additional sheet and mark clearly which question the information refers to. Please ensure that any additional sheets are firmly attached to the questionnaire.

Have you served a copy of the completed questionnaire [and the other documents required by the protocol] on the other [party][parties]?

Yes [ ]   No [ ]

A. Complexity/Urgency

Are the proceedings complex?   Yes [ ]   No [ ]

Are there are any urgent features that the Court should know about?   Yes [ ]   No [ ]

If **'Yes'**, to either question please explain briefly why the proceedings are complex and or what urgent features the Court should be aware of:

B. Urgent/Preliminary Hearings

Do you wish there to be an urgent hearing?   Yes ☐   No ☐

Do you wish there to be a preliminary hearing?   Yes ☐   No ☐

If **'Yes'**, to either question please explain briefly why such a hearing is required and what question(s) the Court will be asked to answer at that hearing.

C. Evidence

Part 1 – Witnesses/Reports

Are there any **witness statements** or **clinical reports** upon which you intend to rely?

Yes ☐   No ☐

If 'Yes', please provide the information requested in the box below:

Author	Date of Report:	Nature of Evidence:

Part 2 – Further Assessments/Expert Evidence

Do you propose to ask for a further assessment?   Yes ☐   No ☐

Do you propose to seek permission to use expert evidence?   Yes ☐   No ☐

If you answer 'Yes' to either of the above questions, for each further assessment or expert you propose please give those details required by the Experts Code of Guidance (step 2.3) on a separate sheet and attach it to this questionnaire.

D. Other Evidence including Evidence of Ethnicity, Language, Religion, Culture, Gender and Vulnerability

Is any other evidence needed for example, relating to the ethnicity, language, religion, culture, gender and vulnerability of the child or other significant person?   Yes ☐   No ☐

If '**Yes**', please give brief details of the evidence that you propose:

E. Legal and Social Work Timetable

Please give details of the Legal and Social Work timetable that is proposed:

Date Proposed:	Step Proposed:	Party Responsible:

F. Hearing and Reading Time

How long do you think the Case Management Conference will take? [ ] hour(s) [ ] minutes

How long do you think the Pre-Hearing Review will take? [ ] hour(s) [ ] minutes

How long do you think the Final Hearing will take? [ ] day(s) [ ] hour(s)

Give details of the recommended reading list for the Case Management Conference:

G. Proposed Directions

(Parties should agree directions at the Advocates Meeting. A list of proposed directions or orders should be attached to this questionnaire using the standard variable directions forms wherever possible.)

Have you attached a list of the directions (or orders)
you wish the Court to consider at the CMC:

(a) to ensure that the matters set out in the protocol   Yes ☐   No ☐
     are complied with; and

(b) that are required for any other purpose, in particular,   Yes ☐   No ☐
     compliance with the Experts Code of Guidance (Step 2.4)
     and to ensure that disclosure of relevant documents takes place.

H. Other Information

In the space below, set out any other information you consider will help the judge or court to manage this case.

Signed [   ]   date [   ]

[Counsel] [Solicitor] for the
[   ][Applicant] [Respondent] [   ][other]

Please enter your contact name, reference number and full postal address including
(if appropriate) details of DX, fax or e-mail.

Name:	Reference:
Address:	Telephone number:
	Fax number:
	DX number:
	e-mail:

APPENDIX A/3

Case Management Checklist

Objective

The following checklist is to be used for the First Hearing in the FPC, the Allocation Hearing in the Care Centre, Allocation Directions in the High Court and for the CMC

Representation of the Child

1   Has CAFCASS been notified of any decision to appoint a Guardian? If so, has a Guardian been allocated or is the likely date of allocation known? ☐

2   Are there any other relevant proceedings? If so, was a Guardian appointed and has CAFCASS been informed of the nature/number of the other/previous proceedings and the identity of the Guardian? ☐

3   If a decision has been made to appoint a Guardian but no allocation has yet taken place by CAFCASS: are any directions necessary for the representation of the child including the appointment of a solicitor? ☐

4   Have the parties been notified of the names of the Guardian and of the solicitor appointed in form C46? ☐

5   Should consideration be given to the separate representation of the child? ☐

Parties

6   Have all significant persons involved in the child's care been identified, in particular those persons who are automatically Respondents to the application? Are any directions required to ensure service upon a party? ☐

7   Has consideration been given to notifying a father without parental responsibility and informing other significant adults in the extended family of the proceedings? ☐

8   Should any other person be joined as a party to the proceedings (whether upon application or otherwise)? Are any directions necessary for the service of documents. If so, which documents? ☐

ICO

9   Are the grounds for making an ICO agreed? Have they been recorded on form C22 or in a document approved by the Court? ☐

10   If the grounds for making an ICO are not agreed has a date been fixed for an urgent hearing of the contested interim application or are the proceedings to be transferred to the Care Centre? ☐

11   Have all case management directions been given to ensure that the contested interim hearing will be effective? ☐

Urgency, Transfer and Re-Transfer

12   Are there any features of particular urgency and if so what directions are necessary to provide for that urgency or to minimise delay eg lateral or upwards transfer? ☐

13   Have any circumstances of complexity, gravity and urgency been considered and has any decision to transfer the proceedings to the Care Centre/High Court been made and notified to the parties? ☐

14   Have the directions that are set out in the CCP and the FPCP been made upon transfer? ☐

15   After transfer, have the circumstances of complexity, gravity and urgency that remain been re-considered and is it appropriate to transfer back to the Care Centre or FPC? ☐

16   In relation to any question of re-transfer, has the availability of the Court been ascertained and have the parties been notified? ☐

Protocol Documents

17   **LA Documents on Issue of Application.** Are any directions necessary relating to the preparation, filing and service of those LA documents that are required by the protocol within 2 days of the proceedings being issued? ☐

18   **Case Synopsis.** Are any directions necessary to ensure that the LA or the Child's solicitor prepares, files and serves a case synopsis? ☐

19   **The Court Bundle/Index.** Are any directions necessary to ensure that a court bundle is prepared and filed or that an index to the Court documents is prepared, filed and served? ☐

20   Have directions been given to update the court bundle/index, in particular the responsibility for, the format of and arrangements for updating (or the compilation of an application bundle) and whether updates can be provided to the Court/judge by e-mail? ☐

21   **Local Authority Case Management Documents.** Are any directions necessary to ensure that the LA case management documents are prepared, filed and served? ☐

| 22 | **Other Party's Case Management Documents.** Are any directions necessary to ensure that the case management documents of other parties are prepared, filed and served? | ☐ |

| 23 | **Case Management Questionnaires.** Are any directions necessary to ensure that the parties prepare, file and serve case management questionnaires? | ☐ |

| 24 | **Recommended Reading List.** For any hearing where no case management questionnaire or schedule of issues will be available, are any directions necessary for the parties to provide the Court with a joint reading list? | ☐ |

| 25 | **Witness Non-Availability Form.** Are any directions necessary to ensure that a witness availability form and schedule of contact details are completed/updated? | ☐ |

Preliminary Directions

| 26 | **Statements of Evidence from Each Party.** Have directions been given for the parties other than the LA to prepare, file and serve evidence in reply to the LA's initial social work statement? | ☐ |

| 27 | **Disclosure.** Have directions been given to ensure that all relevant documents are disclosed by the LA within 20 days of the First Hearing? | ☐ |

| 28 | **Allocation.** Have all allocation directions been given? | ☐ |

| 29 | **Standard Directions Form.** Has the SDF been completed and served? | ☐ |

Listing

| 30 | **CMC.** Has a date and time been fixed for the CMC (between days 15 and 60)? Is the date, time and time estimate recorded on the draft SDF? | ☐ |

| 31 | If a CMC is not to be listed have all case management directions been given for the Final Hearing and are they recorded on the draft SDF? | ☐ |

| 32 | **PHR.** Is a PHR necessary? Is the date, time and time estimate recorded on the draft SDF (not later than 2 weeks and no earlier than 8 weeks before the Final Hearing)? | ☐ |

| 33 | If a PHR is not necessary have all case management directions set out in the PHR checklist been considered in giving directions for the Final Hearing? | ☐ |

| 34 | **Final Hearing.** Has a date or hearing window been fixed for the Final Hearing (not later than in the 3 weeks commencing the 37th week after issue) and are the dates recorded on the draft SDF together with the time estimate? | ☐ |

35	**Venue/Technology.** Have directions been given for the venue of each hearing and whether video link, telephone conferencing or electronic communication with the Court can be used? If so, have arrangements been made for the same?	☐

Evidence

36	**Other Proceedings.** Has consideration been given to the relevance of any other/previous proceedings and as to whether the Judgment/Reasons given or evidence filed should be admitted into evidence?	☐
37	**Disclosure.** Has the Guardian read the social work files? If not when will that task be complete? Having read the files has the Guardian confirmed that either they contain no other relevant documents or that an application for specific disclosure is necessary?	☐
38	Are there any applications relating to the disclosure of documents?	☐
39	**The Child's Evidence.** Should evidence be prepared, filed and served concerning the child's wishes and feelings?	☐
40	**The Issues.** What are the issues in the case?	☐
41	Are any directions necessary for the filing of further factual evidence (including clinical evidence of treatment) by any party and if so to which issue(s) is such evidence to be directed?	☐
42	Are any directions necessary for any party to respond to the LA's factual evidence and/or to the LA's proposed threshold criteria and schedule of findings of fact sought?	☐
43	**LA Core Assessment.** Has a core assessment been completed? If not, are any directions necessary for the preparation, service and filing of an assessment?	☐
44	**Additional Assessments and Expert Evidence.** In respect of every question relating to a request for expert evidence, is the request in accordance with the Experts Code of Guidance?	☐
45	What are the issues to which it is proposed expert evidence or further assessment should be directed?	☐
46	Who is to conduct the assessment or undertake the report, what is the expert's discipline, has the expert confirmed availability, what is the timetable for the report, the responsibility for instruction and the likely costs on both an hourly and global basis, what is the proposed responsibility for or apportionment of costs of jointly instructed experts as between the LA and the publicly funded parties (including whether there should be a section 38(6) direction?	☐
47	Are any consequential directions necessary (eg to give permission for examination or interview)?	☐

| 48 | Are any directions necessary to provide the expert with the documents/further documents? | ☐ |

| 49 | Are any directions necessary for the conduct of experts meetings/discussions and the preparation, filing and service of statements of agreement and disagreement? | ☐ |

| 50 | **Ethnicity, Language, Religion and Culture.** Has consideration been given to the ethnicity, language, religion and culture of the child and other significant persons and are any directions necessary to ensure that evidence about the same is available to the Court? | ☐ |

Care Plans and Final Evidence

| 51 | **LA.** Have directions been given for the preparation, filing and service of the final proposals of the LA and in particular its final statements of evidence and care plan? | ☐ |

| 52 | **Other Parties.** Have directions been given for the preparation, filing and service of the parents' and other parties responses to the LA's proposals? | ☐ |

| 53 | **Guardian.** Are any directions necessary for the preparation, filing and service of the Guardian's report? | ☐ |

Other Case Management Steps

| 54 | **Advocates Meetings and Schedules of Issue.** Are any directions necessary to ensure that an advocates meeting takes place and that a composite Schedule of Issues is drafted? | ☐ |

| 55 | **Preliminary/Split Hearing.** Is a finding of fact hearing necessary and if so, what is the discrete issue of fact that is to be determined, by whom and when? | ☐ |

| 56 | **Family Group Conference/ADR.** Has consideration been given to whether a family group conference or alternative dispute resolution can be held and would any directions assist to facilitate the conference resolution? | ☐ |

| 57 | **Twin Track Planning.** Are any directions necessary to ensure that in the appropriate case twin track planning has been considered and where appropriate, directions given in relation to any concurrent freeing for adoption proceedings and for the filing and service of evidence relating to placement options and their feasibility? In particular have dates been fixed for the filing of the parallel plan and in respect of the Adoption/Fostering/Permanent Placement Panel timetable? | ☐ |

| 58 | **Adoption Directions.** Are any directions necessary to ensure that the Adoption Practice Direction is complied with and in particular that any proposed (concurrent) freeing proceedings have been commenced? | ☐ |

59	**Placement.** Are any directions necessary for the filing and service of evidence relating to placement options including extended family placements and their feasibility, information about the timetable for the assessment and planning processes and any proposed referrals to Adoption/Fostering and/or Permanence Panels?	☐
60	**Court's Timetable.** Has a timetable of all legal and social work steps been agreed and is the timetable set out in the Court order or as an approved document annexed to the order?	☐
61	**Monitoring and Compliance.** What directions are necessary to ensure that the Court's timetable and directions are monitored and complied with, in particular have directions been given for the certification of compliance upon ICO renewals and for any further directions or a return to Court in the event of a significant non-compliance?	☐
62	**Change of Circumstance.** What directions are necessary to make provision for the parties to return to court in the event of a significant change of circumstance?	☐
63	**Preparation for Final Hearing.** Is any consideration necessary of the case management directions set out in the PHR checklist in particular:	☐

- Use of interpreters?

- Special Measures for Vulnerable or intimidated witnesses?

- Children's evidence or attendance at court?

- Facilities for persons with a disability?

- Evidence or submissions by video or telephone conference or on paper or by e-mail?

- Video and audio recordings and transcripts?

APPENDIX A/4:
Witness Non-Availability

This questionnaire is completed [by][on behalf of],   In the

Note:
Please state
your party
status.

who is the [ ] [Applicant] [Respondent]
[   ] [other]
in these proceedings.

[Family Proceedings Court]
[District Registry] [County Court]
[Principal Registry of the Family Division]
[The High Court of Justice]

Case Number

Sheet No.   of

Note: This form may be used for a maximum of six witnesses. If you intend to ask for more than six witnesses to give evidence on your behalf, please continue on a second sheet. You should indicate how many sheets you have used by completing the box above.

Date of Final Hearing (where known)

Location of Final Hearing (where known)

Witness Details:

Witness Number: Witness Name: Description:

1.

2

3.

4.

5.

6.

Completion of the Non-Availability Grid:

NOTE:

Mark dates when Experts and other witnesses are <u>NOT</u> available. Codes for use in the grid are as follows: H = Holiday, C = Course, S = Sickness or medical appointment, T = Attendance at another trial/hearing, O = Other

The person signing this form must be fully familiar with all the details of non-availability given on the Grid overleaf. If there are other issues the Court should be aware of concerning witness availability please state these below:

Signed: Date:

    [Counsel] [Solicitor] for the
    [   ] [Applicant] [Respondent] [   ]

Date	MONTH — Witness Number				
1					
2					
3					
4					
5					
6					
7					
8					
9					
10					
11					
12					
13					
14					
15					
16					
17					
18					
19					
20					
21					
22					
23					
24					
25					
26					
27					
28					
28					
29					
30					
31					

Date	MONTH — Witness Number				
1					
2					
3					
4					
5					
6					
7					
8					
9					
10					
11					
12					
13					
14					
15					
16					
17					
18					
19					
20					
21					
22					
23					
24					
25					
26					
27					
28					
28					
29					
30					
31					

Date	MONTH — Witness Number				
1					
2					
3					
4					
5					
6					
7					
8					
9					
10					
11					
12					
13					
14					
15					
16					
17					
18					
19					
20					
21					
22					
23					
24					
25					
26					
27					
28					
28					
29					
30					
31					

Date	MONTH — Witness Number				
1					
2					
3					
4					
5					
6					
7					
8					
9					
10					
11					
12					
13					
14					
15					
16					
17					
18					
19					
20					
21					
22					
23					
24					
25					
26					
27					
28					
28					
29					
30					
31					

Date	MONTH — Witness Number				
1					
2					
3					
4					
5					
6					
7					
8					
9					
10					
11					
12					
13					
14					
15					
16					
17					
18					
19					
20					
21					
22					
23					
24					
25					
26					
27					
28					
28					
29					
30					
31					

Date	MONTH — Witness Number				
1					
2					
3					
4					
5					
6					
7					
8					
9					
10					
11					
12					
13					
14					
15					
16					
17					
18					
19					
20					
21					
22					
23					
24					
25					
26					
27					
28					
28					
29					
30					
31					

APPENDIX A/5

PHR Checklist

Objective

The following checklist is to be used for the Pre-Hearing Review

1	Have the protocol and other practice direction steps been complied with?	☐
2	Have each of the directions given at the CMC and any subsequent hearing been complied with?	☐
3	Have the issues to be determined at the Final Hearing been identified and recorded in the draft PHR order?	☐
4	Which witnesses are to be called, by whom and in relation to what issue(s)?	☐
5	Are any experts required to give oral evidence, if so why and in relation to what issue(s)?	☐
6	What is the extent of the examination in chief and cross-examination of each witness that is proposed?	☐
7	Has a witness template been completed and agreed?	☐
8	What, if any, of the written evidence is agreed or not in issue (and accordingly is to be read by the Court on that basis)?	☐
9	Are interpretation facilities necessary and if so have they been directed and/or arranged (Note the special arrangements to be made for deaf signing)?	☐
10	Are any facilities needed for a party or witness with a disability? If so have arrangements been made?	☐
11	Are any special measures or security measures applied for in relation to vulnerable or intimidated witnesses including, for example, live video link, screens or witness support? If so what are the arrangements, if any, that are directed to be made?	☐
12	Is it intended that the child will attend to see the judge and/or give evidence at the Final Hearing and have the arrangements been agreed and made?	☐
13	Is any evidence is to be taken indirectly by live video link eg for an expert or witness who is overseas or otherwise unable to attend Court. If so have the arrangements been made?	☐

14   Are any video or audio recordings to be used and if so: ☐

    (a)   have the relevant excerpts of the recordings been agreed?

    (b)   have agreed transcripts been obtained and?

    (c)   have the arrangements been made to view/listen to the recordings?

15   Are there questions of law to be determined, and if so when should the submissions be heard and what provision should be made for the consideration of the authorities and skeleton arguments that will be required?   ☐

16   Is there a recommended reading list for the Court?   ☐

17   What is the timetable for the final hearing including opening and closing submissions and judgment/reasons?   ☐

18   What is the estimated length of the Final Hearing?   ☐

19   Who is/are the judge/magistrates nominated to conduct the Final Hearing?   ☐

20   Where is the venue for the Final Hearing?   ☐

21   Does the *Practice Direction (Family Proceedings: Court Bundles)* [2000] 1 FLR 536 apply to the Final Hearing and/or are any other case management documents to be updated, prepared, filed and served by the parties and if so: by whom and when?   ☐

22   Are the proceedings ready for Final Hearing and have all steps and directions been complied with so that the PHR can be dispensed with or considered by the Court in the absence of the parties?   ☐

APPENDIX B

Standard Documents

Objective

The following documents are identified in the protocol and their contents are prescribed below

1   **Case Synopsis** shall contain such of the following information as is known in summary form for use at the Allocation Hearing and shall normally be limited to 2 sides of A4:

- The identities of the parties and other significant persons

- The applications that are before the Court

- A very brief summary of the precipitating incident(s) and background circumstances

- Any particular issue that requires a direction to be given at the Allocation Hearing (eg relating to a social services core assessment)

- Any intention to apply to transfer the proceedings to the High Court

- The parties interim proposals in relation to placement and contact

- The estimated length of the Allocation Hearing (to include a separate estimate relating to a contested ICO where relevant)

- A recommended reading list and a suggested reading time for the Allocation Hearing

- Advance notice of any other decisions or proceedings that may be relevant, to include: criminal prosecutions, family law proceedings, disciplinary, immigration and mental health adjudications

2   **Social Work Chronology** is a schedule containing a succinct summary of the significant dates and events in the child's life in chronological order. It is a running record ie it is to be updated during the proceedings. The schedule headings are:

- serial number

- date

- event-detail

- witness or document reference (where applicable)

3   **Initial Social Work Statement**. The initial social work statement filed by the LA within 2 days of the issue of an application is strictly limited to the following evidence:

- The precipitating incident(s) and background circumstances relevant to the grounds and reasons for making the application including a brief description of any referral and assessment processes that have already occurred

- Any facts and matters that are within the social worker's personal knowledge

- Any emergency steps and previous court orders that are relevant to the application

- Any decisions made by the LA that are relevant to the application

- Information relevant to the ethnicity, language, religion, culture, gender and vulnerability of the child and other significant persons in the form of a 'family profile' together with a narrative description and details of the social care services that are relevant to the same

- Where the LA is applying for an ICO and/or is proposing to remove or seeking to continue the removal of a child under emergency protection: the LA's initial proposals for the child including placement, contact with parents and other significant persons and the social care services that are proposed

- The LA's initial proposals for the further assessment of the parties during the proceedings including twin track planning

- The social work timetable, tasks and responsibilities so far as they are known.

4   **Schedule of Issues**. The composite schedule of issues produced by the advocates at the end of the advocates' meetings prior to the CMC and the PHR should be agreed so far as is possible and where not agreed should set out the differing positions as to the following:

- A summary of the issues in the case (including any diverse cultural or religious contexts)

- A summary of issues for determination of the CMC/PHR by reference to the questionnaires/checklists

- For the CMC: the timetable of legal and social work steps proposed

- The estimated length of hearing of the PHR and the Final Hearing

- For the PHR: whether the Final Hearing is ready to be heard and if not, what steps need to be taken

- The order which the Court will be invited to make at the CMC/PHR

APPENDIX C

Code of Guidance for Expert Witnesses in Family Proceedings

Objective

The objective of this Code of Guidance is to provide the Court with early information to enable it to determine whether it is necessary and/or practicable to ask an expert to assist the Court:

- To identify, narrow and where possible agree the issues between the parties

- To provide an opinion about a question that is not within the skill and experience of the Court

- To encourage the early identification of questions that need to be answered by an expert

- To encourage disclosure of full and frank information between the parties, the Court and any expert instructed

Action	Party and Timing
1 **The Duties of Experts**	
1.1 **Overriding Duty:** An **expert in family proceedings has an overriding duty to** the Court that takes precedence over any obligation to the person from whom he has received instructions or by whom he is paid.	

1.2   **Particular Duties:** Among any other duties an expert may have, **an expert shall** have regard to the following duties:
 	
   • To assist the Court in accordance with the overriding duty
 	
   • To provide an opinion that is independent of the party or parties instructing the expert
 	
   • To confine an opinion to matters material to the issues between the parties and in relation only to questions that are within the expert's expertise (skill and experience). If a question is put which falls outside that expertise the expert must say so	

Action	Party and Timing	

- In expressing an opinion take into consideration all of the material facts including any relevant factors arising from diverse cultural or religious contexts at the time the opinion is expressed, indicating the facts, literature and any other material that the expert has relied upon in forming an opinion

- To indicate whether the opinion is provisional (or qualified, as the case may be) and the reason for the qualification, identifying what further information is required to give an opinion without qualification

- Inform those instructing the expert without delay of any change in the opinion and the reason for the change

2	**Preparation for the CMC**	Solicitor instructing the expert
2.1	**Preliminary Enquiries of the Expert**: Not later than 10 days before the CMC the solicitor for the party proposing to instruct the expert (or lead solicitor/solicitor for the child if the instruction proposed is joint) shall approach the expert with the following information:	**10 days before the CMC**

- The nature of the proceedings and the issues likely to require determination by the Court;

- The questions about which the expert is to be asked to give an opinion (including any diverse cultural or religious contexts)

- When the Court is to be asked to give permission for the instruction (if unusually permission has already been given the date and details of that permission)

- Whether permission is asked of the Court for the instruction of another expert in the same or any related field (ie to give an opinion on the same or related questions)

- The volume of reading which the expert will need to undertake

- Whether or not (in an appropriate case) permission has been applied for or given for the expert to examine the child

Action	Party and Timing
• Whether or not (in an appropriate case) it will be necessary for the expert to conduct interviews (and if so with whom)	
• The likely timetable of legal and social work steps	
• When the expert's opinion is likely to be required	
• Whether and if so what date has been fixed by the Court for any hearing at which the expert may be required to give evidence (in particular the Final Hearing).	
2.2 **Expert's Response:** Not later than 5 days before the CMC the solicitors intending to instruct the expert shall obtain the following information from the expert:	Solicitor instructing the expert **5 days before the CMC**
• That the work required is within the expert's expertise	
• That the expert is available to do the relevant work within the suggested time scale	
• When the expert is available to give evidence, the dates and/or times to avoid, and, where a hearing date has not been fixed, the amount of notice the expert will require to make arrangements to come to Court without undue disruption to their normal clinical routines.	
• The cost, including hourly and global rates, and likely hours to be spent, of attending at experts/professionals meetings, attending court and writing the report (to include any examinations and interviews).	
2.3 **Case Management Questionnaire:** **Any party** who proposes to ask the Court for permission to instruct an expert shall not later than 2 days before the CMC (or any hearing at which the application is to be made) file and serve a case management questionnaire setting out the proposal to instruct the expert in the following detail:	The Party proposing to instruct the expert **not later than 2 days before the CMC**
• The name, discipline, qualifications and expertise of the expert (by way of CV where possible)	

Action	Party and Timing
• The expert's availability to undertake the work	
• The relevance of the expert evidence sought to be adduced to the issues in the proceedings and the specific questions upon which it is proposed the expert should give an opinion (including the relevance of any diverse cultural or religious contexts)	
• The timetable for the report	
• The responsibility for instruction	
• Whether or not the expert evidence can properly be obtained by the joint instruction of the expert by two or more of the parties.	
• Whether the expert evidence can properly be obtained by only one party (eg on behalf of the child)	
• Whether it is necessary for more than one expert in the same discipline to be instructed by more than one party	
• Why the expert evidence proposed cannot be given by social services undertaking a core assessment or by the Guardian in accordance with their different statutory duties	
• The likely cost of the report on both an hourly and global basis.	
• The proposed apportionment of costs of jointly instructed experts as between the Local Authority and the publicly funded parties.	

2.4 Draft Order for the CMC:

Any party proposing to instruct an **expert** shall in the draft order submitted at the CMC request the Court to give directions (among any others) as to the following:

Any Party **not later than 2 days before the CMC**

- The party who is to be responsible for drafting the letter of instruction and providing the documents to the expert

- The issues identified by the Court and the questions about which the expert is to give an opinion

- The timetable within which the report is to be prepared, filed and served

Action	Party and Timing
• The disclosure of the report to the parties and to any other expert	
• The conduct of an experts' discussion	
• The preparation of a statement of agreement and disagreement by the experts following an experts discussion	
• The attendance of the expert at the Final Hearing unless agreement is reached at or before the PHR about the opinions given by the expert.	

	Action	Party and Timing
3	**Letter of Instruction**	Solicitor **within 5**
3.1	**The solicitor instructing the expert** shall within 5 days of the CMC prepare (agree with the other parties where appropriate) file and serve a letter of instruction to the expert which shall:	instructing **days of** the expert **the CMC**

- Set out the context in which the expert's opinion is sought (including any diverse ethnic, cultural, religious or linguistic contexts)
- Define carefully the specific questions the expert is required to answer ensuring
  - **that they are within the ambit of the expert's area of expertise and**
  - **that they do not contain unnecessary or irrelevant detail**
  - **that the questions addressed to the expert are kept to a manageable number and are clear, focused and direct**
  - **that the questions reflect what the expert has been requested to do by the Court**
- List the documentation provided or provide for the expert an indexed and paginated bundle which shall include:
  - **a copy of the order (or those parts of the order) which gives permission for the instruction of the expert immediately the order becomes available**
  - **an agreed list of essential reading**
  - **all new documentation when it is filed and regular updates to the list of documents provided or to the index to the paginated bundle**
  - **a copy of this code of guidance and of the protocol**

Action	Party and Timing
• Identify the relevant lay and professional people concerned with the proceedings (eg the treating clinicians) and inform the expert of his/her right to talk to the other professionals provided an accurate record is made of the discussion	
• Identify any other expert instructed in the proceedings and advise the expert of his/her right to talk to the other experts provided an accurate record is made of the discussion	
• Define the contractual basis upon which the expert is retained and in particular the funding mechanism including how much the expert will be paid (an hourly rate and overall estimate should already have been obtained) when the expert will be paid, and what limitation there might be on the amount the expert can charge for the work which he/she will have to do. There should also be a brief explanation of the 'detailed assessment process' in cases proceeding in the Care Centre or the High Court which are not subject to a high cost case contract	
• In default of agreement the format of the letter of instruction shall be determined by the Court, which may determine the issue upon written application with representations from each party.	

4   The Expert's Report

Content of the Report:

4.1   The expert's report shall be addressed to the Court and shall:

The Expert **in accordance with the Court's timetable**

- • Give details of the expert's qualifications and experience

- • Contain a statement setting out the substance of all material instructions (whether written or oral) summarising the facts stated and instructions given to the expert which are material to the conclusions and opinions expressed in the report

- • Give details of any literature or other research material upon which the expert has relied in giving an opinion

Action	Party and Timing
• State who carried out any test, examination or interview which the expert has used for the report and whether or not the test, examination or interview has been carried out under the expert's supervision.	
• Give details of the qualifications of any person who carried out the test, examination or interview	

• Where there is a range of opinion on the question to be answered by the expert:
  • summarise the range of opinion and
  • give reasons for the opinion expressed	

• Contain a summary of the expert's conclusions and opinions	
• Contain a statement that the expert understands his duty to the Court and has complied with that duty	
• Where appropriate be verified by a statement of truth.	

Action	Party and Timing	
4.2 **Supplementary Questions:** Any party wishing to ask supplementary questions of an expert for the purpose of clarifying the expert's report must put those questions in writing to the parties not later than 5 days after receipt of the report. Only those questions that are agreed by the parties or in default of agreement approved by the Court may be put to the expert The Court may determine the issue upon written application with representations from each party.	Any party	**within 5 days of the receipt of the report**

Action	Party and Timing	
5 **Experts Discussion (Meeting)**	The Court	**at the CMC**
5.1 **Purpose:** The Court will give directions for the experts to meet or communicate:		
• To identify and narrow the issues in the case.		
• To reach agreement on the expert questions		
• To identify the reasons for disagreement on any expert question and to identify what if any action needs to be taken to resolve any outstanding disagreement/question		

Action	Party and Timing
• To obtain elucidation or amplification of relevant evidence in order to assist the Court to determine the issues	
• To limit, wherever possible, the need for experts to attend Court to give oral evidence.	

	Action		Party and Timing
5.2	**The Arrangements for a Discussion/Meeting: In accordance with the directions given by** the Court **at the CMC,** the solicitor for the child or such other professional who is given the responsibility by the Court shall make arrangements for there to be a discussion between the experts within 10 days of the filing of the experts reports. The following matters should be considered:	Child's Solicitor	**within 10 days of the filing of the experts' reports**

 • Where permission has been given for the instruction of experts from different disciplines a global discussion may be held relating to those questions that concern all or most of them.

 • Separate discussions may have to be held among experts from the same or related disciplines but care should be taken to ensure that the discussions complement each other so that related questions are discussed by all relevant experts

 • 7 days prior to a discussion or meeting the solicitor for the child or other nominated professional should formulate an agenda to include a list of the questions for consideration. This may usefully take the form of a list of questions to be circulated among the other parties in advance. The agenda should comprise all questions that each party wishes the experts to consider. The agenda and list of questions should be sent to each of the experts not later than 2 days before the discussion

Action	Party and Timing
• The discussion should usually be chaired by the child's solicitor or in exceptional cases where the parties have applied to the Court at the CMC, by an independent professional identified by the parties or the Court. In complex medical cases it may be necessary for the discussion to be jointly chaired by an expert. A minute must be taken of the questions answered by the experts, and a Statement of Agreement and Disagreement must be prepared which should be agreed and signed by each of the experts who participated in the discussion. The statement should be served and filed not later than 5 days after the discussion has taken place	
• Consideration should be given in each case to whether some or all of the experts participate by telephone conference or video link to ensure that minimum disruption is caused to clinical schedules.	

5.3	**Positions of the Parties:** Where any party refuses to be bound by an agreement that has been reached at an experts' discussion that party must inform the Court at or before the PHR of the reasons for refusing to accept the agreement.	Any Party	**at the PHR**

5.4	**Professionals Meetings:** In proceedings where the Court gives a direction that a professionals meeting shall take place between the Local Authority and any relevant named professionals for the purpose of providing assistance to the Local Authority in the formulation of plans and proposals for the child, the meeting shall be arranged, chaired and minuted in accordance with directions given by the Court.		

6	**Arranging for the Expert to attend Court**	Every Party responsible for the instruction of an expert	**by the PHR**
6.1	**Preparation:** The party who is responsible for the instruction of an expert witness shall ensure:		

Action	Party and Timing
• That a date and time is fixed for the Court to hear the expert's evidence that is if possible convenient to the expert and that the fixture is made substantially in advance of the Final Hearing and no later than at the PHR (ie no later than 2 weeks before the Final Hearing)	
• That if the expert's oral evidence is not required the expert is notified as soon as possible	
• That the witness template accurately indicates how long the expert is likely to be giving evidence, in order to avoid the inconvenience of the expert being delayed at Court.	

6.2 All parties shall ensure: — All Parties **at the PHR**

• That where expert witnesses are to be called the advocates attending the PHR have identified at the advocates meeting the issues which the experts are to address

• That wherever possible a logical sequence to the evidence is arranged with experts of the same discipline giving evidence on the same day(s)

• That at the PHR the Court is informed of any circumstance where all experts agree but a party nevertheless does not accept the agreed opinion so that directions can be given for the proper consideration of the experts' evidence and the parties reasons for not accepting the same

• That in the exceptional case the Court is informed of the need for a witness summons.

7   Post Hearing Action   — Solicitor instructing the expert   **within 10 days of the Final Hearing**

7.1 Within 10 days of the Final Hearing the solicitor instructing the expert should provide feedback to the expert by way of a letter informing the expert of the outcome of the case, and the use made by the Court of the expert's opinion. Where the Court directs that a copy of the transcript can be sent to the expert, the solicitor instructing the expert should obtain the transcript within 10 days of the Final Hearing.

APPENDIX D

Practice Direction (Family Proceedings: Court Bundles)

[Editorial note: This Practice Direction is reproduced as *President's Direction (Family Proceedings: Court Bundles) (10 March 2000)* at p 413 of this Handbook.]

APPENDIX E/1

The Care Centre Plan

Objective

To implement the protocol (without modification) on a local basis and to ensure that in each Care Centre judicial and administrative resources are deployed in order to achieve the highest practical level of continuity of judicial case management and the earliest possible resolution of cases

1   **Responsibility for the Preparation and Operation of the CCP:** The Designated Family Judge (DFJ) in each Care Centre shall be responsible for the preparation and operation of the CCP

2   **Consultees:** When preparing the CCP the DFJ shall consult fully with each of the Circuit and District Judges nominated to do Public Law work at the Care Centre as well as with:

- The Court Service

- All relevant Family Proceedings Courts (FPCs)

- CAFCASS

- All relevant Local Authorities

- Other local professional bodies

3   **Contents of the CCP:** The CCP shall provide for the following:

(a)   The arrangements for transfer and retransfer of cases between the FPCs and the Care Centre and the job title and contact particulars of the person responsible for administering transfers at each court

(b)   How and when cases will be allocated to one and not more than two case management judges (one of whom may be and where possible should be the judge who will conduct the Final Hearing) to case manage the proceedings in accordance with the protocol and the CCP

(c)   Where two judges are allocated, for the division of work between them

(d)   Where the case management judge or judges are not able to be the Final Hearing judge, how and when the Final Hearing judge for the case is to be identified

(e)   Wherever possible, for the release of the allocated judges from other business to hear applications and the arrangements for the case to follow the allocated judge or to be heard by telephone conferencing or video link.

(f)   Where, exceptionally, no allocated judge is available to hear an application, for the referral of the proceedings to one of the allocated judges or the DFJ before it is listed before another judge

(g)   The identity of the DFJ, the judges to whom cases may be allocated for case management and the other Nominated Circuit Judges and Nominated District Judges at the Care Centre (All judges of the Family Division of the High Court are available to act as case management judges)

(h)   The local agreement with each MCC as to the directions to be given by FPCs on the transfer of cases to the Care Centre

(i)   The local arrangements for joint directions in cases where there are concurrent relevant criminal proceedings

(j)   The arrangements in the Care Centre for the allocation of the judiciary to conduct Public Law Children Act cases

(k)   The arrangements for the monitoring by the local Family Court Business Committee of the implementation of the protocol and the CCP

(l)   The arrangements for active liaison between the Care Centre and the FPCs

4   **Authorisation of the Care Centre Plan:** Each CCP shall be subject to the final approval of the Family Division Liaison Judge (FDLJ) of the relevant Circuit before implementation.

5   **Timetable for Preparation and Lodging of the CCP:** The first CCP for each Care Centre shall be submitted to the FDLJ by the DFJ by the 1st October 2003. The CCP as approved by the FDLJ shall be lodged at the office of the President of the Family Division by the 31st October 2003.

6   **Review and Amendment of the CCP:** Not later than 1st October 2004 the first CCP shall be reviewed in the same way as it was prepared. Thereafter the CCP shall be reviewed in the same way every 2 years unless the DFJ determines that it is necessary to do so earlier or the President or the FDLJ so direct. Revised or updated plans shall be lodged at the President's office within 10 days of their approval by the FDLJ.

APPENDIX E/2

The Family Proceedings Court Plan

Objective

To implement the protocol (without modification) on a local basis and to ensure that in each Family Proceedings Court (FPC) and administrative centre resources are deployed in order to achieve the highest practical level of continuity of case management and the earliest possible resolution of cases

1 **Responsibility for the Preparation and Operation of the FPCP:** The Justices' Chief Executive (JCE) for each Magistrates Courts Committee (MCC) area shall be responsible for arranging for the preparation and administrative operation of the Family Proceedings Court Plan (FPCP).

2 **Consultees:** When preparing the FPCP the JCE should consult fully with each of the Chairs of the Family Panels, the District Judges (Magistrates Courts) nominated to do Public Law cases in the MCC area and the Justices Clerk(s) as well as with:

   • The Court Service

   • CAFCASS

   • All relevant Local Authorities

   • Other local professional bodies.

3 **Contents of the FPCP:** The FPCP shall provide for the following:

   (a) The arrangements for transfer and retransfer of cases between the FPCs and between FPCs and the Care Centre and the job title and contact particulars of the court officers responsible for administering transfers at each court

   (b) The local arrangements with the Care Centre as to the directions to be given by FPCs on the transfer of cases to the Care Centre

   (c) The best practical arrangements to maximise effective and continuous case management. Where practicable within existing resources, this could include allocation to no more than 2 legal advisers and to no more than 6 identified magistrates (or 2 DJs(MC)); or to a team of specialist family legal advisers. If possible, however, the objective of continuous case management by allocation of each case to a single legal adviser and to a single bench for case management and Final Hearing should be pursued.

   (d) Arrangements for active liaison between the FPCs and the Care Centre.

4 **Authorisation of the FPC Plan:** The FPCP for each MCC shall be subject to the final approval of the JCE after consultation with the relevant Designated Family Judge(s) (DFJ) and the Family Division Liaison Judge (FDLJ) of the relevant Circuit before implementation.

5   **Timetable for Preparation and Lodging of the FPCP:** The first FPCP for each MCC area should be returned to the FDLJ by the JCE by the 1st October 2003. The FPCP should be lodged at the office of the President of the Family Division by the 31st October 2003.

6   **Review and Amendment of the FPCP:** Not later than the 1st April 2004 the first FPCP shall be reviewed in the same way as it was prepared. Thereafter the FPCP shall be reviewed in the same way every year unless the JCE determines that it is necessary to do so earlier (in consultation with the FDLJ). Revised or updated plans shall be lodged at the President's office within 28 days of their submission to the FDLJ.

APPENDIX F

Social Services Assessment and Care Planning Aide-Memoire

Days

The reference in this appendix to "DAYS" is independent of the "DAYS" referred to in The 6 Steps

	Recommended Guidance	Recommended timetable
1	**Referral** A referral to a Council with Social Services Responsibilities (CSSR) in England and a Local Authority in Wales (ie a request for services including child protection) triggers the following Government guidance:	**On DAY 1**
2	**Initial Decision** Within 1 working day of a referral social services should make a decision about what response is required including a decision to take no action or to undertake an initial assessment. The parents or carers (the family), where appropriate, the child and (unless inappropriate) the referrer should be informed of the initial decision and its reasons by social services	**On DAY 2**
3	**Initial Assessment** An initial assessment (if undertaken) should be completed by social services within a maximum of 7 working days of the date of the referral (ie 6 working days from the date of the decision about how to respond to a referral)	**By DAY 7**
4	As part of an initial assessment social services should: • Obtain and collate information and reports from other agencies • Interview family members and the child • In any event, see the child	

	Recommended Guidance	**Recommended timetable**
5	At the conclusion of an initial assessment social services will make a decision about whether the child is a child in need and about further action including whether to undertake a core assessment. It will inform the family, the child and other relevant agencies of the decision and its reasons. Social services will record the response of each person and agency consulted	
6	**Initial Assessment Record** Social services will make and keep a record of the initial assessment and decision making process. The Department of Health (DH) and Welsh Assembly Government (WAG) publish an 'Initial Assessment Record' for this purpose.	
7	**Child in Need Plan** Where social services decide that the child is a child in need they will make a plan which sets out the services to be provided to meet the child's needs.	
8	**Strategy Discussion/Record** Where social services has evidence that the child is suspected to be suffering or is likely to suffer significant harm it should ensure that an inter agency strategy discussion takes place to decide whether to initiate an enquiry under section 47 of the Children Act. This should also result in the child in need plan being updated. A record of the strategy discussion will be made.	
9	**Achieving Best Evidence in Criminal Proceedings** Where a child is the victim of or witness to a suspected crime the strategy discussion shall include a discussion about how any interviews are to be conducted with the child. These may be as part of a police investigation and /or a section 47 enquiry initiated by social services, These interviews should be undertaken in accordance with Government guidance 'Achieving Best Evidence in Criminal Proceedings'.	

	Recommended Guidance	Recommended timetable
10	**Complex Child Abuse Investigations** Where a complex child abuse investigation has been initiated by social services or the police there will be inter agency strategy discussions to make recommendations relating to the planning, co-ordination and management of the investigation and assessment processes in accordance with the guidance given in 'Working Together', 'Complex Child Abuse Investigations: Inter Agency Issues' (England only - to be published in Wales, Summer 2003)	
11	**Section 47 Enquiries** If during a strategy discussion it is decided that there is reasonable cause to suspect that the child is suffering or is likely to suffer significant harm, section 47 enquiries will be initiated by social services. This means that a core assessment will be commenced under section 47 of the Children Act 1989. It should be completed within 35 working days of the completion of the initial assessment or the strategy discussion at which it was decided to initiate section 47 enquiries.	**By DAY 42 or within 35 days of the last strategy discussion**
12	**Core Assessment** Where social services decides to undertake a core assessment it should be completed within 35 working days of the initial assessment or the date of the subsequent strategy discussion A timetable for completion of specialist assessments should be agreed with social services	**By DAY 42 or within 15 days of the last strategy discussion**
13	At the conclusion of a core assessment social services should consult with the family, the child and all relevant agencies before making decisions about the plan for the child. Social Services will record the response of each person and agency consulted.	
14	**Core Assessment Record** Social services will make and keep a record of the core assessment and decision making process. The DH and WAG publish a 'Core Assessment Record' for this purpose.	

Recommended Guidance	Recommended timetable
15 **Child Protection Conferences** Where social services undertakes section 47 enquiries and it is concluded that a child is at continuing risk of suffering or is likely to suffer significant harm, social services will consider whether to convene a child protection conference. A child protection conference determines whether the child is at continuing risk of significant harm and therefore requires a child protection plan to be put in place when determining whether to place the child's name on the child protection register. It agrees an outline child protection plan. An initial child protection conference should take place within 15 working days of the last strategy discussion (ie by day 22) in accordance with the Government guidance given in 'Working Together to Safeguard Children: a guide to inter-agency working to safeguard and promote the welfare of children'	**By DAY 22 or within 15 days of the end of the last strategy discussion**

16 **Decision to Apply for a Care Order** At the conclusion of the core assessment which may have been undertaken under section 47 of the Children Act and where no earlier decision has been made social services should decide whether to apply for a statutory order and should be able to identify by reference to the conclusions in the core assessment

- The needs of the child (including for protection),

- The services that will be provided,

- The role of other professionals and agencies,

- Whether additional specialist assessments are to be undertaken,

- The timetable and

- The responsibilities of those involved.

17 **Plans** At the conclusion of a core assessment social services will prepare one or more of the following plans:

- A children in need plan

Recommended Guidance	Recommended timetable
• A child protection plan for a child whose name is on the child protection register • A care plan (where the child is a looked after child) The DH and WAG publish formats and/or guidance for each of these plans.	
18 **Interim Care Plans** Where social services decide to make an application to the Court it will be necessary to satisfy the Court that an order would be better for the child than making no order at all. An interim care plan should be prepared, filed and served so as to be available to the Court for the CMC in accordance with steps 3.4 and 4.1 of the protocol.	
19 In cases where no core assessment has been undertaken (eg because the interim care order had to be taken quickly before one could be begun/completed) it should be begun/completed as soon as possible. The interim care plan should be developed from the initial assessment information	

20 **Care Plans** Care Plans should be written so as to comply with the Government guidance given in **LAC(99) 29** in England and *Care Plans and Care Proceedings under the CA 1989* **NAFWC 1/2000** in Wales. While interim care plans will necessarily be in outline and contain less comprehensive information, the plan should include details of the following:
 	
 • The aim of the plan and a summary of the social work timetable
 	
 • A summary of the child's needs and how these are to be met including
    • placement
    • contact with family and other significant persons
    • education, healthcare and social care services
    • the role of parents and other significant persons
    • the views of others
 	
 • Implementation and management of the plan	

	Recommended Guidance	Recommended timetable
21	**Emergency Protection** Where at any time there is reasonable cause to believe that a child is suffering or is likely to suffer significant harm, an application for a child assessment order or an emergency protection order may be made (among others) by social services. The child may be removed or remain in a safe place under police powers of protection. In each case agency and/or court records of the application and reasons will exist.	
22	**Adoption** Government guidance is given on the assessment and decision making process relating to adoption in England in **LAC (2001) 33** which from the 1st April 2003 incorporates the 'National Adoption Standards for England'. The processes and timescales of assessment and decision making for a child for whom adoption is identified as an option are set out in detail in the Standards.	

APPENDIX G:

Section 37 Request

Objective	**Target time: by DAY 40**

To provide a recommended procedure within the existing rules for the timely determination of section 37 requests by the Court

Days

The reference in this appendix to **"DAYS"** is independent of the **"DAYS"** referred to in The 6 Steps

Action	Party and Timing	
1	**The Test** Where, in any family proceedings in which a question arises with respect to the welfare of any child, it appears to the Court that it may be appropriate for a care or supervision order to be made with respect to the child, the **Court** may direct the appropriate local authority (LA) to undertake an investigation of the child's circumstances.	Court	**on DAY 1**
	The Court's Request On the same day the **Court** shall: • Identify the LA that is to prepare the s 37 report • Fix the date for the next hearing • Specify the date for the s 37 report to be filed by the LA • Direct the court officer to give notice of the order and the form C40 to the LA court liaison manager/lawyer (as set out in the CCP) by fax on the day the order is made • Direct each party to serve upon the LA all further documents filed with the Court.	Court	**on DAY 1**
3	Where a s 37 report is required in less than 8 weeks, the **Court** should make direct enquiries of the Court liaison manager/lawyer of the LA to agree the period within which a report can be written.	Court	**on DAY 1**
4	Within 24 hours of the order being made (on **DAY 2**) the **court officer** shall serve on the LA a sealed copy of the order and such other documents as the Court has directed.	Court Officer	**on DAY 1**
5	**LA Responsibility** Within 24 hours of the receipt of the sealed order (on **DAY 3**) the Court liaison manager/lawyer of the **LA** shall ensure that the request is allocated to a social services team manager who shall:	LA	**on DAY 3**

Action	Party and Timing	
• Be responsible for the preparation of the report and the allocation of a social worker/team to carry out any appropriate assessment		
• Ensure that the request is treated and recorded as a formal referral by social services in respect of each child named in the order		
• Notify the Court and the lawyers acting for all parties of his/her identity and contact details and the identity of the team that has been allocated		
• Follow Government guidance in relation to referral and assessment processes (see appendix F).		
6 Any **assessment** including a core assessment that is undertaken by social services should be completed within 35 days of the allocation above ie within 36 days of the service of the sealed court order.	Social Services	**by DAY 38**
7 At the conclusion of the social services enquiries **social services** shall:	Social Services	**between DAYS 38 and 40**
• Consult with the family, the child and all relevant agencies before making decisions about a plan for the child. The LA will record the response of each person and agency consulted		
• Decide whether to apply to the Court for a statutory order		
• File the section 37 report with the Court and serve it upon the parties on or before the date specified in the Court's order.		
8 Where social services decide not to apply for a care or supervision order they should as part of their report set out the decisions they have made and the reasons for those decisions and any plan they have made for the child (including the services to be provided) in accordance with Government guidance (see appendix F).		

PRACTICE DIRECTION

Practice Direction (Care Cases: Judicial Continuity and Judicial Case Management)

1.1   This Practice Direction, which includes the annexed Principles and the annexed Protocol, is issued by the President of the Family Division with the concurrence of the Lord Chancellor. It is intended to implement the recommendations of the Final Report, published in May 2003, of the Lord Chancellor's Advisory Committee on Judicial Case Management in Public Law Children Act Cases chaired by Munby and Coleridge JJ.

1.2   The Practice Direction, Principles and Protocol apply to all Courts, including Family Proceedings Courts, hearing applications issued by local authorities under Part IV (Care and Supervision) of the Children Act 1989 ("care cases") where

(a)   the application is issued on or after 1 November 2003; or

(b)   the proceedings are transferred on or after 1 November 2003 from the Family Proceedings Court to a Care Centre, or from a County Court to a Care Centre or from a Care Centre to the High Court.

1.3   *Practice Direction (Family Proceedings: Court Bundles)* [2000] 1 WLR 737, [2000] 1 FLR 536, remains in force and is to be complied with in all cases to which it applies, subject only to the Protocol and to any directions which may be given, in any particular care case by the case management judge.

1.4   Paragraph 2 of the *President's Direction (Judicial Continuity)* [2002] 2 FLR 367 shall cease to have effect in any case to which this Practice Direction applies.

2   **Purpose of the Practice Direction, Principles and Protocol**

2.1   The purpose of the Practice Direction, Principles and Protocol is to ensure consistency in the application of best practice by all Courts dealing with care cases and, in particular, to ensure:

(a)   that care cases are dealt with in accordance with the overriding objective;

(b)   that there are no unacceptable delays in the hearing and determination of care cases; and

(c)   that save in exceptional or unforeseen circumstances every care case is finally determined within 40 weeks of the application being issued.

2.2   The Principles are the principles which govern the application of the Practice Direction and Protocol by the Courts and the parties.

3   **The Overriding Objective**

3.1   The overriding objective is to enable the Court to deal with every care case

(a)   justly, expeditiously, fairly and with the minimum of delay;

(b) in ways which ensure, so far as is practicable, that
    (i) the parties are on an equal footing;
    (ii) the welfare of the children involved is safeguarded; and
    (iii) distress to all parties is minimised;

(c) so far as is practicable, in ways which are proportionate
    (i) to the gravity and complexity of the issues; and
    (ii) to the nature and extent of the intervention proposed in the private family life of the children and adults involved.

3.2	The Court should seek to give effect to the overriding objective when it exercises any power given to it by the Family Proceedings Courts (Children Act 1989) Rules 1991 or the Family Proceedings Rules 1991 (as the case may be) or interprets any rule.
3.3	The parties are required to help the Court to further the overriding objective.
3.4	The Court will further the overriding objective by actively managing cases as required by sections 11 and 32 of the Children Act 1989 and in accordance with the Practice Direction, Principles and Protocol.

4   Avoiding Delay

4.1	Section 1(2) of the Children Act 1989 requires the Court to "have regard to the general principle that any delay in determining any question is likely to prejudice the welfare of the child".
4.2	Decisions of the European Court of Human Rights emphasise the need under article 6 of the European Convention for the Protection of Human Rights and Fundamental Freedoms for "exceptional diligence" in this context: *Johansen v Norway* (1996) 23 EHRR 33, para [88].
4.3	One of the most effective means by which unnecessary delay can be avoided in care cases is by active case management by a specialist judiciary.

5   Judicial Case Management

5.1   The key principles underlying the Practice Direction, Principles and Protocol are

(a) **judicial continuity**: each care case will be allocated to one or not more than two case management judges, who will be responsible for every stage in the proceedings down to the final hearing and one of whom may be, and where possible should be, the judge who will conduct the final hearing;

(b) **active case management**: each care case will be actively case managed by the case management judge(s) with a view at all times to furthering the overriding objective;

(c) **consistency by standardisation** of steps: each care case will so far as possible be managed in a consistent way
    (i) in accordance with the standardised procedures laid down in the Protocol; and
    (ii) using, wherever possible, standardised forms of order and other standardised documents;

(d) **the case management conference**: in each care case there will be a case management conference to enable the case management judge to actively case manage the case and, at the earliest practicable opportunity, to
 (i) identify the relevant issues; and
 (ii) fix the timetable for all further directions and other hearings (including the date of the final hearing).

6 **Implementing the Protocol**

6.1 The Protocol is based on, and is intended to promote the adoption in all Courts and in all care cases of, the best practice currently adopted by Courts dealing with care cases.

6.2 The Protocol will be implemented:

(a) in each Care Centre by reference to the Care Centre Plan which will be drafted locally (see appendix E/1 to the Protocol); and

(b) in each Family Proceedings Court by reference to the FPC Plan which will be drafted locally (see appendix E/2 to the Protocol).

6.3 The target times specified in the Protocol for the taking of each step should be adhered to wherever possible and treated as the maximum permissible time for the taking of that step. Save in exceptional or unforeseen circumstances every care case should be finally determined within 40 weeks of the application being issued. Simpler cases can often be finally determined within a shorter time.

6.4 Unless the case management judge is satisfied that some other direction is necessary in order to give effect to the overriding objective, the case management judge should, and, unless the case management judge has otherwise ordered, the parties and any expert who may be instructed in the case must (as the case may be):

(a) use or require the parties to use the forms and standard documents referred to in Appendix A to the Protocol;

(b) prepare or require the parties to prepare the documents referred to in Appendix B to the Protocol in accordance with that Appendix;

(c) comply or require the parties and every expert to comply with the Code of Guidance for Expert Witnesses in Family Proceedings contained in Appendix C to the Protocol; and

(d) make every order and direction in the form of any relevant form which may from time to time be approved by the President of the Family Division for this purpose.

6.5 Appendix D to the Protocol contains the text of the President's *Practice Direction (Family Proceedings: Court Bundles)* [2000] 1 WLR 737, [2000] 1 FLR 536.

6.6 Appendix F to the Protocol contains the Social Services Assessment and Care Planning Aide-Memoire, which is a summary of existing guidance relating to assessment and care planning.

6.7 Appendix G to the Protocol is a summary of best practice guidance relating to requests made under section 37 of the Children Act 1989.

6.8   Cases in which there are concurrent care proceedings and criminal proceedings are to be dealt with in accordance with the Care Centre Plan.

7   **Monitoring and Compliance**

7.1   It is the responsibility of the Designated Family Judge in conjunction with the Court Service and in consultation with the Family Division Liaison Judge

(a)   to monitor the extent to which care cases in the Courts for which he is responsible are being conducted in compliance with the protocol and with directions previously given by the Court;

(b)   to arrange for the collection and collation of such statistical and other information and in such form as the Family Division Liaison Judge and the President of the Family Division may from time to time direct.

ANNEX TO THE PRACTICE DIRECTION

Principles of Application

The principles which govern the application of the Practice Direction and Protocol by the Courts and the parties

1   The **Aim** of the Practice Direction and Protocol is to reduce delay and improve the quality of justice for children and families by the following means:

- Proper Court control of proceedings

- Identifying and promoting best practice

- The consistent application of best practice by all Courts

- Providing predictable standards which the Courts will treat as the normal and reasonable approach to the conduct of proceedings by parties

2   In order to achieve the **Aim** the Practice Direction gives effect to:

- A **protocol** which sets out predictable standards as specific steps to be taken in all care proceedings by reference to identified best practice

- An **overriding objective** to provide consistency of case management decisions

- **Court plans** to maximise the use of judicial and administrative resources

- Best practice **guidance**

3   **Court Control:** Proper Court control of care proceedings requires forward planning so that:

- A specialist judiciary is identified and trained

- Arrangements are made for continuous case management in the High Court, and in each Care Centre and Family Proceedings Court

- The arrangements for continuous case management are supervised by the specialist judiciary in conjunction with dedicated court officers, in particular
  - the matching and allocation of judicial and administrative resources to cases; and
  - the allocation and listing of cases,

- There is continuous and active case management of each case by allocated case management judges/benches

- There is continuous monitoring of the progress of all proceedings against target times to help minimise delay

4   **Continuity of Case Management:** The continuity of case management is to be achieved:

- In the Care Centre and the High Court by a **care centre plan** (CCP); and

- In the Family Proceedings Courts, by a **family proceedings courts plan** (FPCP)

- By the **identification of the specialist judiciary** and the **dedicated court officers** in the plans

Guidelines for the preparation and implementation of the plans are set out at appendix E to the protocol.

5   **Active Case Management:** Active case management is to be achieved by giving directions to ensure that the determination of proceedings occurs quickly, efficiently and with the minimum of delay and risk to the child (and where appropriate other persons) by:

- Identifying the appropriate Court to conduct the proceedings and transferring the proceedings as early as possible to that Court

- Identifying all facts and matters that are in issue at the earliest stage and then at each case management step in the proceedings

- Deciding which issues need full investigation and hearing and which do not

- Considering whether the likely benefits of taking a particular social work or legal step justify the delay which will result and the cost of taking it

- Encouraging the parties to use an alternative dispute resolution procedure such as a family group conference and facilitating the use of such a procedure

- Helping the parties to reach agreement in relation to the whole or part of a case, quickly, fairly and with the minimum of hostility

- Encouraging the parties to co-operate with each other in the conduct of the proceedings

- Identifying the timetable for all legal and social work steps

- Fixing the dates for all appointments and hearings

- Standardising, simplifying and regulating:
  - the use of case management documentation and forms
  - the court's orders and directions
- Controlling:
  - the use and cost of experts
  - the nature and extent of the documents which are to be disclosed to the parties and presented to the Court
  - whether and if so in what manner the documents disclosed are to be presented to the Court

- Monitoring the Court's timetable and directions against target times for the completion of each protocol step to prevent delay and non-compliance

6   **Standard Directions, Forms and Documents:** In order to simplify and provide consistency in the exchange of information: such standard variable directions, forms (appendix A) and standard documents (appendix B) as may be approved from time to time by the President are to be used unless otherwise directed by the Court.

7   **Controlling the Use and Cost of Experts:** Expert evidence should be proportionate to the issues in question and should relate to questions that are outside the skill and experience of the Court. To assist the Court in its control of the use and cost of experts a Code of Guidance is incorporated as appendix C to the protocol. The Code of Guidance is to be followed by the parties when a party proposes that the court gives permission for the use of an expert. The Code of Guidance should form part of every letter of instruction so that experts can adopt best practice guidance in the formulation of their reports and advices to the Court.

8   **Disclosure:** Disclosure of relevant documents should be encouraged at the earliest opportunity. Where disclosure is in issue the Court's control of the extent of disclosure will have regard to whether the disclosure proposed is proportionate to the issues in question and the continuing duty of each party to give *full* and frank disclosure of information to each other and the Court.

9   **Inter-Disciplinary Good Practice:** The Court's process and its reliance upon best practice should acknowledge and encourage inter-disciplinary best practice and in particular pre-application investigation, assessment, consultation and planning by statutory agencies (including local authorities) and other potential parties (an aide-memoire of local authority guidance is annexed to the protocol at appendix F).

10   **Target Time:** The target times specified in the protocol for the taking of each step should be adhered to wherever possible and treated as the maximum permissible time for the taking of that step. Where target times are expressed in days, the days are 'court business days' in accordance with the Rules. Save in exceptional or unforeseen circumstances every care case should be finally determined within 40 weeks of the application being issued. Simpler cases can often be finally determined within a shorter time. Target times should only be departed from at the direction of the Court and for good reason in accordance with the overriding objective.

11   **Monitoring and Compliance:** To facilitate directions being given to deal with a change of circumstances or to remedy a material non-compliance at the earliest opportunity the Court should consider requiring regular certification of compliance with the Court's timetable and directions by the parties, for example on interim care order renewal certificates. In addition the Court might consider other mechanisms to monitor the progress of a case without the need for the parties or their representatives to attend Court.

12   **Technology:** Where the facilities are available to the Court and the parties, the Court should consider making *full* use of technology including electronic information exchange and video or telephone conferencing.

LORD CHANCELLOR'S ADVISORY COMMITTEE ON JUDICIAL CASE MANAGEMENT IN PUBLIC LAW CHILDREN ACT CASES

Final Report

May 2003

1. Introduction

1.1. This is the final report of the Lord Chancellor's Advisory Committee on Judicial Case Management in Public Law Children Act Cases ("the committee"). It has been chaired by the Hon. Mr Justice Munby and The Hon. Mr Justice Coleridge. A list of the Committee members and other consultees is given in the Annex.

1.2. The committee was established in May 2002 by the Lord Chancellor at the instigation of the President of the Family Division. Its purpose was to consider the whole question of case management in Public Law Children Act cases (PLCACs). Its specific terms of reference were:

> "to consider and approve a draft protocol based on the models of best practice collated from Care Centres and Family Proceedings Courts and agree on target time-scales for each stage of the Public Law Children Act process"

1.3. The committee had four plenary sessions (beginning in November 2002) but sub-groups representing particular interests met on a number of other occasions as did the core judicial group concerned with detailed drafting.

1.4. As can be seen from the list of represented organisations and consultees, this large committee drew on the experience and expertise of all those agencies which participate at any stage in PLCACs which, by their nature, often involve many parties and are complex. At all times the intention has been to achieve complete consensus amongst participants to ensure the maximum level of voluntary and whole-hearted co-operation after implementation.

1.5. We are very happy to record the overwhelming and enthusiastic support which this project and the resulting Protocol has attracted from all participants. This degree of support undoubtedly reflects the dedication of each individual organisation to doing the best for the children involved in the process and the desire to make improvements whenever possible and within the constraints created by lack of public resources (for which, of course, there is predictably an incessant demand) in a number of related areas.

2. Background

2.1. Section 1(2) of the Children Act 1989 requires the Court to "have regard to the general principle that any delay in determining any question is likely to prejudice the welfare of the child".

2.2. Decisions of the European Court of Human Rights emphasise the need under article 6 of the European Convention for the Protection of Human Rights and Fundamental Freedoms for "exceptional diligence" in this context: see *Johansen v Norway* (1996) 23 EHRR 33, para [88]

2.3. The problem of delay in care cases has long been recognised and specifically considered on previous occasions including:

(a)   by Dame Margaret Booth in her report in July 1996 'Avoiding Delay in Children Act Cases';

(b)   by the Lord Chancellor's Department in its March 2002 'Scoping Study on the Causes of Delay'.

2.4.   The Lord Chancellor's Department has been pursuing a programme of work to reduce delay in these cases since the publication of the Scoping Study. That study identified case management as an area which, if improved, could have a substantial impact on delay. And all members of the Committee are agreed that one of the surest means by which unnecessary delay can be avoided in PLCACs is by the proper management and control of cases by a specialist judiciary.

2.5.   Many Care Centres around the country and the Family Division of the High Court in London have, over the last few years, established protocols/best practice guides/practice directions for improving case management. They have emerged partly as a result of a need to tackle serious issues of localised delay and partly as a result of the national civil case management protocols (following the introduction of the CPR reforms). Similarly, the successful introduction of the new Family Proceedings Rules governing the procedure for ancillary relief cases has demonstrated how court-led case management can alleviate delay and make significant savings in both court time and cost per case.

2.6.   The protocol (agreed by the Advisory Committee at its final meeting on 6 March 2003) represents a collation of the best practice from around the country and is the first National statement of common practice and solutions. The annexes have, in addition, been drafted partly by those with specialised experience in particular areas.

2.7.   It is proposed that the protocol will be introduced by attachment to a President's Practice Direction in May or June 2003 with a view to National implementation on 1 November 2003. The period between May/June and November has been provided to enable familiarisation and training to be achieved amongst all potential users.

3.   Format and content

3.1.   The format of the protocol is designed to be as simple and user friendly as possible recognising the fact that it will be used by staff in all agencies (legal and non legal) and at all levels of the process. It is the culmination of a process of reduction to six essential steps covering all the stages of a case, from issue of the application to conclusion of the final hearing.

3.2.   The time periods for each stage are expressed as "target times" to reflect the fact that some degree of limited flexibility is necessary and desirable and also that resource limitations in certain areas, at present, do not admit of the imposition of a more stringently enforceable timetable. However, it is hoped and expected that every reasonable effort will be made not to exceed them and wherever possible to improve upon them.

4.   Paramount objective

4.1.   **The paramount objective** of the protocol has been to **improve the outcomes for children by reducing unnecessary delay** in PLCACs and, to this end, to achieve the completion of all cases within an overall timetable of **not more than 40 weeks** (save in exceptional or unforeseen circumstances).

4.2.   The following **key elements** have been identified to the achievement of that paramount objective:

4.2.1. The highest practical level of judicial continuity and case management by one or not more than two judges per case. The precise achievement of this key element will be by:
- **Care Centre Plans** drafted by individual Designated Family Judges in consultation with all local judiciary and local agencies. These plans will be finally approved by Family Division Liaison Judges and then lodged with the President. The plans will be periodically reviewed to ensure they remain current.
- **Family Proceedings Court Plans** similarly drafted by the Justices Chief Executive in consultation with Family Panels, Justices Clerks and other local agencies and also lodged with the President.
- **Improved listing arrangements**

4.2.2. **Consistency** of all aspects of case management at all levels of court together with identification of cases requiring "transfer up" at the earliest opportunity.

4.2.3. **Time-tabling to final hearing** at the earliest practical stage and the reduction of intermediate hearings to no more than four (First Hearing, Allocation Hearing, Case Management Conference and Pre Hearing Review) save in exceptional or unforeseen circumstances.

4.2.4. A more rigorous control of the use of experts.

4.2.5. A more rigorous **control of the content and quantity of Court documentation** including standardisation where possible.

4.3.   The Protocol has been produced to assist all participants in the process (including judges, lawyers, guardians, social workers and other experts) by providing them with a common, timed framework for the case management of every case at every stage and every level. To this end, it sets out the "Six Steps" that every PLCAC should go through and includes guidance on and documentation for the conduct of each of the steps. As is apparent the protocol does not radically change the procedure (no rule changes are required), rather it seeks to distil and streamline the process to its essentials and change the culture within which the proceedings takes place.

4.4.   Although the paramount objective of the protocol has been to improve outcomes for children by reducing delay, the Committee believes also that it has a very real potential for reducing the cost (per case) to the public purse. Certain figures were shown to us during the period when the Committee was deliberating. These figures suggested that there might be (on a worst case basis) a small increase in overall cost. However, on a best case basis the savings were evidently very considerable. Our experience of the High Court London Practice Direction is that it is already delivering higher settlement rates (and at an earlier stage in the process) and shorter final hearings. If this is replicated nationwide, savings of both time and money will follow. For our part we are unable to envisage a situation where better managed cases could cost more than the present less formalised, drawn out procedures. Similarly, our experience in the parallel ancillary relief field is entirely supportive of the assertion that savings of time and money result from a properly managed and disciplined system of case handling.

4.5.   Apart from direct cost savings, there is also potential for indirect savings where cases take less time and children are eg. retained for less time within the care system.

5.   Major obstacles to success

5.1.   PLCACs are complex and involve many agencies, all of them publicly funded in one way or another. The Committee was able to resolve many current concerns and other issues that arose during its deliberations from different quarters on its way to achieving consensus. However, there remains an overarching concern that better outcomes for children and further reductions in delay require further work and investment to complement and reinforce the efficacy of the Protocol.

5.2.   The Protocol is an essential step forward, but the Committee would like to record the following major obstacles to real success in this area:

5.2.1. **Social services departments** continue to be seriously understaffed, suffering both recruitment and retention of staff problems. This critically limits their ability to speed up the pre-application stages in the care process. It also has the effect that, were they to focus more of their precious human resources on the actual litigation stage, their other roles in care, prevention and education would be likely to be compromised

5.2.2. **CAFCASS** has a shortage of guardians which, in parts of the country, remains significant. Effective case management within the Courts and CAFCASS will alleviate some of the pressure. Increased funding for the next financial year is obviously welcome and helpful. However, until guardians can be promptly allocated at the start of each case throughout England and Wales neither the children nor the Courts will be receiving the essential and proper service.

5.2.3. **Publicly funded remuneration** for the legal profession must reflect the fact that PLCACs require the full input and co-operation of experienced, specialist practitioners. Without such practitioners the protocol will not work to its best advantage. Underpayment of the practitioners who do this work will inevitably lead to a shortage of such specialist lawyers (and accordingly in the future to a shortage of specialist judges, both part and full time) as the brightest and best turn to better remunerated fields of practice. Remuneration must also be structured to reflect the fact that the Protocol requires advocates to do considerably more work at the early stages of a case to ensure the early identification and narrowing of issues.

5.2.4. The need for significantly more **family sitting days** in some areas

5.2.5. A **shortage of experts** in a number of fields prevents the swift hearing of cases in some areas. The Protocol should help but the problem persists.

5.2.6. **Local listing practices** in some places call for a radical change of culture. Specialist judges are at the heart of the Protocol's success but even those judges cannot case manage effectively if the listing arrangements do not accommodate the need for continuity and also allow for a sensible amount of reading time prior to hearings. In less busy courts and rural areas this is sometimes hard to achieve and requires special attention. The proper exploitation, at the case management stage, of the available expertise of many District Judges is also sometimes overlooked. Finally, proper training and support from all departments of the Lord Chancellor's Department and the Court Service is essential.

6.   The introduction of the protocol should lead to better use of available resources and so reduction of unnecessary delay. However, it must be remembered and emphasised that PLCACs, by their very nature, sometimes call for flexibility and delay. The target in every case is to get the best possible outcome for the child concerned. There will always remain cases where there is a need for adapting or

prolonging the procedure to fit changing circumstances or allow for constructive delay. The right answer cannot be sacrificed on the altar of speed and efficiency.

7. Conclusion

7.1.   The work of the Committee has been facilitated by an exceptional level of commitment to the cause of improving the use of available resources, reducing delay and an overwhelming consensus on the need for better and more effective continuous case management by specialist judges. The Committee is confident that this consensus and commitment will be transmitted through the organisations represented on the Committee, through the Court system and through Government and that this will result in real reductions in delay and corresponding cost savings.

7.2.   We have from time to time expressed anxiety at the suggestion that the Protocol might be introduced initially on a pilot basis. We repeat that we believe that to be an unnecessary and retrograde step. We strongly recommend that the Protocol be implemented nationally in accordance with the timetable set out in para 2.7 of this report. At the same time on-going careful but simple monitoring by the Care Centres and FPCs to measure the effect of the Protocol should be put in place (as is already happening in the High Court in London).

7.3.   We would like to express our most sincere gratitude to all the members of the Committee for the enormous amounts of both time and effort they have invested in this project. Many of them are from the private sector and gave much precious time without reward. In this regard Ernest Ryder QC calls for special mention. He has been the "drafter-in-chief" without whose encyclopaedic knowledge and dedication to the cause this Protocol would not have finally emerged. His Honour Judge Cryan's input on the Care Centre and FPC Plans and other ancillary documents has also been particularly demanding of time and sensitivity.

Hon Mr Justice Munby

Hon Mr Justice Coleridge

Annex to the Report
The members of the Advisory Committee:

The Honourable Mr Justice Munby (Chair)
The Honourable Mr Justice Coleridge (Chair)
His Honour Judge Cryan
Senior District Judge Angel, Principal Registry of the Family Division
District Judge Harrison CBE (Association of District Judges)
District Judge Rawkins (Association of District Judges) District Judge
(Magistrates' Courts) Crichton
Ernest Ryder QC
Mark Camley, Court Service
Bruce Clark, Department of Health
Audrey Damazer, Justices' Clerks' Society
Nigel Druce, Association of Directors of Social Services
Julia Eeles, Association of Justices' Chief Executives
Christine Field JP, Magistrates' Association
Sally Field, Lord Chancellor's Department
Katherine Gieve, Solicitors Family Law Association
Liz Goldthorpe, Association of Lawyers for Children
Jane Held, Association of Directors of Social Services
Derek Hill, Public Legal Services Division, Lord Chancellor's Department
Sheri Holland, Child Care Law Joint Liaison Group
Elaine Laken, Justices' Clerks' Society
Elizabeth Lawson QC, FLBA
Angela Nield, Association of Lawyers for Children
Andrew MacFarlane QC, Family Law Bar Association
Pat Monro, The Law Society
Charles Prest, CAFCASS
Rachel Rogers, The Law Society
Philip Thomson, Child Care Law Joint Liaison Group
John Briden, Lord Chancellor's Department
Emran Mian, Lord Chancellor's Department
Dave Berry, Lord Chancellor's Department (Secretary)

The Advisory Committee is indebted to the following people for their contributions:

The Right Honourable The President of the Family Division
The Honourable Mr Justice Wall, on behalf of the expert witness group of the President's Interdisciplinary Committee
The Honourable Mrs Justice Black, Family Division Liaison Judge, Northern Circuit, on behalf of the Northern Circuit Family Law Seminar
Her Honour Judge Andrew
His Honour Judge Iain Hamilton
District Judge Caddick
June Ackers, Solicitor, Manchester City Council
Fay Barrett, Court Service
Dr Julia Brophy, University of Oxford
Helen Bateman, Public Legal Services Division, Lord Chancellor's Department
Lucy Cheetham, Barrister
Alex Collishaw, Court Service
John Crosse, Solicitor, City of Wakefield Metropolitan District Council
Malcolm Dodds, Justices' Clerk, Medway
Adrian Donaghey, Court Service
Hazel Edwards, Lord Chancellor's Department

Ruth Few, Clerk of the Rules, Royal Courts of Justice
Amanda Finlay, Director of Public and Private Rights, Lord Chancellor's Department
Ananda Hall, Family Division Lawyer
Helen Jones, Department of Health
Mike Lauerman, Department of Health
Chris Longbottom, Solicitor, Leeds City Council
Professor Judith Masson, University of Warwick
Katherine Randall, Lord Chancellor's Department
Malcolm Richardson JP, Magistrates' Association
David Ryden, Solicitor, City of Bradford Metropolitan District Council
William Simmonds, Child Care Law Joint Liaison Group
Sam Sprague, Senior Private Secretary to the President
Robert Tapsfield, Family Rights Group
Steve Taylor, Court Service West Yorkshire Authorities
Margaret Wilson JP, Magistrates' Association

The Advisory Committee also received invaluable contributions from the Family Division Liaison Judges, the Designated Family Judges, the Family Committee of the Judicial Studies Board and a number of Magistrates' Courts Committees, for which it is very grateful.

PART IV

Miscellaneous

Miscellaneous

2001

JANUARY	FEBRUARY	MARCH
M T W T F S S	M T W T F S S	M T W T F S S
1 2 3 4 5 6 7	1 2 3 4	1 2 3 4
8 9 10 11 12 13 14	5 6 7 8 9 10 11	5 6 7 8 9 10 11
15 16 17 18 19 20 21	12 13 14 15 16 17 18	12 13 14 15 16 17 18
22 23 24 25 26 27 28	19 20 21 22 23 24 25	19 20 21 22 23 24 25
29 30 31	26 27 28	26 27 28 29 30 31

APRIL	MAY	JUNE
M T W T F S S	M T W T F S S	M T W T F S S
30 1	1 2 3 4 5 6	1 2 3
2 3 4 5 6 7 8	7 8 9 10 11 12 13	4 5 6 7 8 9 10
9 10 11 12 13 14 15	14 15 16 17 18 19 20	11 12 13 14 15 16 17
16 17 18 19 20 21 22	21 22 23 24 25 26 27	18 19 20 21 22 23 24
23 24 25 26 27 28 29	28 29 30 31	25 26 27 28 29 30

JULY	AUGUST	SEPTEMBER
M T W T F S S	M T W T F S S	M T W T F S S
30 31 1	1 2 3 4 5	1 2
2 3 4 5 6 7 8	6 7 8 9 10 11 12	3 4 5 6 7 8 9
9 10 11 12 13 14 15	13 14 15 16 17 18 19	10 11 12 13 14 15 16
16 17 18 19 20 21 22	20 21 22 23 24 25 26	17 18 19 20 21 22 23
23 24 25 26 27 28 29	27 28 29 30 31	24 25 26 27 28 29 30

OCTOBER	NOVEMBER	DECEMBER
M T W T F S S	M T W T F S S	M T W T F S S
1 2 3 4 5 6 7	1 2 3 4	31 1 2
8 9 10 11 12 13 14	5 6 7 8 9 10 11	3 4 5 6 7 8 9
15 16 17 18 19 20 21	12 13 14 15 16 17 18	10 11 12 13 14 15 16
22 23 24 25 26 27 28	19 20 21 22 23 24 25	17 18 19 20 21 22 23
29 30 31	26 27 28 29 30	24 25 26 27 28 29 30

2002

JANUARY	FEBRUARY	MARCH
M T W T F S S	M T W T F S S	M T W T F S S
1 2 3 4 5 6	1 2 3	1 2 3
7 8 9 10 11 12 13	4 5 6 7 8 9 10	4 5 6 7 8 9 10
14 15 16 17 18 19 20	11 12 13 14 15 16 17	11 12 13 14 15 16 17
21 22 23 24 25 26 27	18 19 20 21 22 23 24	18 19 20 21 22 23 24
28 29 30 31	25 26 27 28	25 26 27 28 29 30 31

APRIL	MAY	JUNE
M T W T F S S	M T W T F S S	M T W T F S S
1 2 3 4 5 6 7	1 2 3 4 5	1 2
8 9 10 11 12 13 14	6 7 8 9 10 11 12	3 4 5 6 7 8 9
15 16 17 18 19 20 21	13 14 15 16 17 18 19	10 11 12 13 14 15 16
22 23 24 25 26 27 28	20 21 22 23 24 25 26	17 18 19 20 21 22 23
29 30	27 28 29 30 31	24 25 26 27 28 29 30

JULY	AUGUST	SEPTEMBER
M T W T F S S	M T W T F S S	M T W T F S S
1 2 3 4 5 6 7	1 2 3 4	30 1
8 9 10 11 12 13 14	5 6 7 8 9 10 11	2 3 4 5 6 7 8
15 16 17 18 19 20 21	12 13 14 15 16 17 18	9 10 11 12 13 14 15
22 23 24 25 26 27 28	19 20 21 22 23 24 25	16 17 18 19 20 21 22
29 30 31	26 27 28 29 30 31	23 24 25 26 27 28 29

OCTOBER	NOVEMBER	DECEMBER
M T W T F S S	M T W T F S S	M T W T F S S
1 2 3 4 5 6	1 2 3	30 31 1
7 8 9 10 11 12 13	4 5 6 7 8 9 10	2 3 4 5 6 7 8
14 15 16 17 18 19 20	11 12 13 14 15 16 17	9 10 11 12 13 14 15
21 22 23 24 25 26 27	18 19 20 21 22 23 24	16 17 18 19 20 21 22
28 29 30 31	25 26 27 28 29 30	23 24 25 26 27 28 29

2003

JANUARY

M	T	W	T	F	S	S
		1	2	3	4	5
6	7	8	9	10	11	12
13	14	15	16	17	18	19
20	21	22	23	24	25	26
27	28	29	30	31		

FEBRUARY

M	T	W	T	F	S	S
					1	2
3	4	5	6	7	8	9
10	11	12	13	14	15	16
17	18	19	20	21	22	23
24	25	26	27	28		

MARCH

M	T	W	T	F	S	S
31					1	2
3	4	5	6	7	8	9
10	11	12	13	14	15	16
17	18	19	20	21	22	23
24	25	26	27	28	29	30

APRIL

M	T	W	T	F	S	S
	1	2	3	4	5	6
7	8	9	10	11	12	13
14	15	16	17	18	19	20
21	22	23	24	25	26	27
28	29	30				

MAY

M	T	W	T	F	S	S
			1	2	3	4
5	6	7	8	9	10	11
12	13	14	15	16	17	18
19	20	21	22	23	24	25
26	27	28	29	30	31	

JUNE

M	T	W	T	F	S	S
30						1
2	3	4	5	6	7	8
9	10	11	12	13	14	15
16	17	18	19	20	21	22
23	24	25	26	27	28	29

JULY

M	T	W	T	F	S	S
	1	2	3	4	5	6
7	8	9	10	11	12	13
14	15	16	17	18	19	20
21	22	23	24	25	26	27
28	29	30	31			

AUGUST

M	T	W	T	F	S	S
				1	2	3
4	5	6	7	8	9	10
11	12	13	14	15	16	17
18	19	20	21	22	23	24
25	26	27	28	29	30	31

SEPTEMBER

M	T	W	T	F	S	S
1	2	3	4	5	6	7
8	9	10	11	12	13	14
15	16	17	18	19	20	21
22	23	24	25	26	27	28
29	30					

OCTOBER

M	T	W	T	F	S	S
		1	2	3	4	5
6	7	8	9	10	11	12
13	14	15	16	17	18	19
20	21	22	23	24	25	26
27	28	29	30	31		

NOVEMBER

M	T	W	T	F	S	S
					1	2
3	4	5	6	7	8	9
10	11	12	13	14	15	16
17	18	19	20	21	22	23
24	25	26	27	28	29	30

DECEMBER

M	T	W	T	F	S	S
1	2	3	4	5	6	7
8	9	10	11	12	13	14
15	16	17	18	19	20	21
22	23	24	25	26	27	28
29	30	31				

2004

JANUARY

M	T	W	T	F	S	S
			1	2	3	4
5	6	7	8	9	10	11
12	13	14	15	16	17	18
19	20	21	22	23	24	25
26	27	28	29	30	31	

FEBRUARY

M	T	W	T	F	S	S
						1
2	3	4	5	6	7	8
9	10	11	12	13	14	15
16	17	18	19	20	21	22
23	24	25	26	27	28	29

MARCH

M	T	W	T	F	S	S
1	2	3	4	5	6	7
8	9	10	11	12	13	14
15	16	17	18	19	20	21
22	23	24	25	26	27	28
29	30	31				

APRIL

M	T	W	T	F	S	S
			1	2	3	4
5	6	7	8	9	10	11
12	13	14	15	16	17	18
19	20	21	22	23	24	25
26	27	28	29	30		

MAY

M	T	W	T	F	S	S
31					1	2
3	4	5	6	7	8	9
10	11	12	13	14	15	16
17	18	19	20	21	22	23
24	25	26	27	28	29	30

JUNE

M	T	W	T	F	S	S
	1	2	3	4	5	6
7	8	9	10	11	12	13
14	15	16	17	18	19	20
21	22	23	24	25	26	27
28	29	30				

JULY

M	T	W	T	F	S	S
			1	2	3	4
5	6	7	8	9	10	11
12	13	14	15	16	17	18
19	20	21	22	23	24	25
26	27	28	29	30	31	

AUGUST

M	T	W	T	F	S	S
30	31					1
2	3	4	5	6	7	8
9	10	11	12	13	14	15
16	17	18	19	20	21	22
23	24	25	26	27	28	29

SEPTEMBER

M	T	W	T	F	S	S
		1	2	3	4	5
6	7	8	9	10	11	12
13	14	15	16	17	18	19
20	21	22	23	24	25	26
27	28	29	30			

OCTOBER

M	T	W	T	F	S	S
				1	2	3
4	5	6	7	8	9	10
11	12	13	14	15	16	17
18	19	20	21	22	23	24
25	26	27	28	29	30	31

NOVEMBER

M	T	W	T	F	S	S
1	2	3	4	5	6	7
8	9	10	11	12	13	14
15	16	17	18	19	20	21
22	23	24	25	26	27	28
29	30					

DECEMBER

M	T	W	T	F	S	S
		1	2	3	4	5
6	7	8	9	10	11	12
13	14	15	16	17	18	19
20	21	22	23	24	25	26
27	28	29	30	31		

CONVERSION TABLES

Length

kilometres (km)	km or miles	miles
1.609	1	0.621
3.219	2	1.243
4.828	3	1.864
6.437	4	2.485
8.047	5	3.107
9.656	6	3.728
11.265	7	4.350
12.875	8	4.971
14.484	9	5.592
16.093	10	6.214
32.187	20	12.427
48.280	30	18.641
64.374	40	24.855
80.467	50	31.069
96.561	60	37.282
112.654	70	43.496
128.758	80	49.710
144.841	90	55.923
160.934	100	62.137

Area

hectares (ha)	ha or acres	acres
0.405	1	2.471
0.809	2	4.942
1.214	3	7.413
1.619	4	9.884
2.023	5	12.355
2.428	6	14.826
2.833	7	17.297
3.237	8	19.769
3.642	9	22.240
4.047	10	24.711
8.094	20	49.421
12.140	30	74.132
16.187	40	98.842
20.234	50	123.553
24.281	60	148.263
28.328	70	172.974
32.375	80	197.684
36.422	90	222.395
40.469	100	247.105

Capacity

litres	litres or UK gallons	UK gallons
4.546	1	0.220
9.092	2	0.440
13.638	3	0.660
18.184	4	0.880
22.730	5	1.100
27.276	6	1.320
31.822	7	1.540
36.368	8	1.760
40.914	9	1.980
45.460	10	2.200
90.919	20	4.399
136.379	30	6.599
181.839	40	8.799
227.298	50	10.998
272.758	60	13.198
318.217	70	15.398
363.677	80	17.598
409.137	90	19.797
454.596	100	21.997

Weight

kilograms (kg)	kg or lb	pounds (lb)
0.454	1	2.205
0.907	2	4.409
1.361	3	6.614
1.814	4	8.819
2.268	5	11.023
2.722	6	13.228
3.175	7	15.432
3.629	8	17.637
4.082	9	19.842
4.536	10	22.046
9.072	20	44.092
13.608	30	66.139
18.144	40	88.185
22.680	50	110.231
27.216	60	132.277
31.752	70	154.324
36.287	80	176.370
40.823	90	198.416
45.359	100	220.462